Encyclopedia of KISS

ALSO BY BRETT WEISS
AND FROM MCFARLAND

*Classic Home Video Games, 1989–1990:
A Complete Guide to Sega Genesis, Neo Geo
and TurboGrafx-16 Games* (2011)

*Classic Home Video Games, 1985–1988:
A Complete Reference Guide* (2009; paperback 2012)

*Classic Home Video Games, 1972–1984:
A Complete Reference Guide* (2007; paperback 2012)

Encyclopedia of KISS

Music, Personnel, Events and Related Subjects

BRETT WEISS

McFarland & Company, Inc., Publishers
Jefferson, North Carolina

Names: Weiss, Brett, 1967– author.
Title: Encyclopedia of Kiss : music, personnel, events
and related subjects / Brett Weiss.
Description: Jefferson, North Carolina : McFarland & Company, Inc.,
Publishers, 2016. | Includes bibliographical references and index.
Identifiers: LCCN 2016018018 | ISBN 9780786498024
(softcover : acid free paper) ∞
Subjects: LCSH: Kiss (Musical group)—Encyclopedias.
Classification: LCC ML421.K57 W45 2016 | DDC 782.42166092/2—dc23
LC record available at https://lccn.loc.gov/2016018018

BRITISH LIBRARY CATALOGUING DATA ARE AVAILABLE

ISBN (print) 978-0-7864-9802-4
ISBN (ebook) 978-1-4766-2540-9

© 2016 Brett Weiss. All rights reserved

No part of this book may be reproduced or transmitted in any form
or by any means, electronic or mechanical, including photocopying
or recording, or by any information storage and retrieval system,
without permission in writing from the publisher.

Front cover images © 2016 iStock

Printed in the United States of America

McFarland & Company, Inc., Publishers
Box 611, Jefferson, North Carolina 28640
www.mcfarlandpub.com

To the fantastic four:
Ace, Gene, Paul, and Peter

Acknowledgments

Special thanks to Bill Aucoin, Neil Bogart, Michael Brandvold, Eric Carr, Cher, Mark Cicchini, Fin Costello, Lydia Criss, Peter Criss, Sean Delaney, Paul Elliott, Jay Evans, Ace Frehley, Gordon G. G. Gebert, Julian Gill, Bob Gruen, Jim Johnson, Ken Kelly, Eddie Kramer, Bob Kulick, Bruce Kulick, David Leaf, Barry Levine, Ken Mills, Greg Prato, Mark St. John, Ken Sharp, Dale Sherman, Gene Simmons, Eric Singer, Tommy Sommers, Paul Stanley, Bill Starkey, Tommy Thayer, Eddie Trunk, Shannon Tweed, Vinnie Vincent, and Charis Weiss.

Special thanks also to my parents, who were cool with me liking KISS, and to every official and unofficial member of the KISS Army, the greatest, most devoted fans of any rock band in the world.

Table of Contents

Acknowledgments
vi

Preface
1

A Brief History
5

THE ENCYCLOPEDIA
7

Bibliography
211

Index
213

Preface

As a kid growing up in Fort Worth, Texas, during the 1970s, I had a blast shooting hoops, digging in the dirt, and riding my bike with friends. I also enjoyed reading comic books, watching TV, playing video games, and listening to rock music. However, other than the social aspect of it, I never really liked going to school.

Despite the fact that I now write for a living, and despite the fact that I've always been an avid reader, I was a terrible student. My teachers would tell me that I was "bright, but that I didn't apply myself." I'm sure I had undiagnosed ADHD (Attention Deficit Hyperactivity Disorder) as it was hard for me to sit still, follow instructions, and concentrate on what the teachers were saying. It didn't help that I had a miserable self-esteem and that I was often hopped up on allergy and bronchitis medicine.

I was painfully shy during the early years of elementary school and would try to obey the rules, but by the time I reached fifth and sixth grade, instead of listening to the teachers, I was much more interested in flirting with the cute girls, making the other kids laugh, and decorating my folders and book covers with drawings and magazine photos of my favorite rock band, KISS. Along with Captain Kirk, The Flash (the Barry Allen version, of course), and Julius "Dr. J" Erving, my boyhood heroes were Ace "The Spaceman" Frehley, Gene "The Demon" Simmons, Paul "The Starchild" Stanley, and Peter "The Catman" Criss.

I don't recall the exact moment I discovered KISS (probably around 1975, when I was eight years old and the classic double LP *Alive!* was new in stores), but during the late 1970s, when I was absolutely obsessed with the band and was wearing out the grooves on the second Holy Trinity of KISS albums—*Destroyer*, *Rock and Roll Over*, and *Love Gun* (*KISS*, *Hotter Than Hell*, and *Dressed to Kill* are the first Holy Trinity)—the aptly nicknamed "Hottest Band in the World" was everywhere, and it seemed to me like they were simply meant to exist by some divine decree, the way one thinks of such iconic figures of popular culture as Humphrey Bogart, John Wayne, Marilyn Monroe, Elvis Presley, and, of course, the Beatles, one of the two or three biggest influences on KISS.

Unlike school, KISS made perfect sense as they combined many of the things that I loved—movie monsters, science fiction, superheroes, cartoons, and rock and roll—into one loud, colorful, over-the-top extravaganza. I never questioned why grown men would don scary-cool makeup, giant platform boots, and outlandish costumes before getting up onstage to play music, and it never seemed odd to me that Gene spit blood and fire, or that Ace played a smoking, rocket-shooting guitar. I simply thought it was the most amazing thing I had ever seen (or heard).

Preface

During this more innocent, more naïve time (without access to the Internet or cable television, we kids relied on playground rumors for much of our information), I had no idea KISS's lyrics were inundated with sexual innuendo. And, like most fans, I didn't know anything about Ace and Peter's alcohol and drug abuse, or about all the arguing and discontentment that went on in the band. I just figured Ace, Gene, Paul, and Peter were four of the happiest people on the planet, as I was when I listened to their music.

As an enthusiastic KISS fan on a limited budget, I desperately wanted, but couldn't afford, most of the avalanche of merchandise that was produced at the peak of the band's popularity during the late 1970s. When my family would go to Kmart on Friday nights, I would drool over the tantalizing treasures on display in the toy aisle, such as the van model kit, the toy guitar, and the Mego dolls, but it would have taken me months to save up enough money to buy even one of these things on my meager dollar-per-week allowance. And, on those rare times when I did have extra money, such as birthdays and Christmas, I would buy what were by far the most important KISS items: the records. Despite the coolness of the costumes, makeup, pyrotechnics, and toy line, the music is what I've always liked best about KISS.

To compensate for my lack of funds when it came to KISS collectibles, I had to be creative. Instead of buying the KISS van model kit, which was about $10, I purchased an ordinary car model, which was only $2 and some change, and I decorated it with the temporary tattoos that were included with the band's second live album, *Alive II*. I also spent my allowance on rock music magazines, including copies of *Creem*, *Circus*, and *Hit Parader*, as long as KISS was featured on the cover. I even bought copies of such teen heartthrob magazines as *16* and *Teen Beat*, just to get a few more KISS pics.

After reading the magazines until they were in tatters (It fascinated me to no end that Ace claimed to be from the planet "Jendel," no matter how many times I read it), I would cut out the smaller KISS pictures and place them in a scrapbook, and I would get my dad to take the larger photos—the pinups, as they were called—to work and make multiple photocopies of them (thanks, Dad). I would tack the original pinups to the walls in my room (thanks, Mom) and hand out the black-and-white copies to kids at school, as though I were some kind of KISS evangelist.

My parents wouldn't take me to an actual KISS concert, not because they disapproved of the band, but because it would have meant driving downtown and spending money, and because they surely didn't want to see the show themselves. As such, watching KISS on television was about as good as it got in my little universe.

Long before YouTube, I would eagerly try to catch every televised KISS appearance that I could, including on such shows as *PM Magazine* and *The Midnight Special*. One of the best nights of my young life—I was 11 at the time—was the October 28, 1978, airing of the made-for-TV movie, *KISS Meets the Phantom of the Park*, which was about the greatest thing I had ever seen: my super-powered heroes foiling bad-guy schemes, battling robots and creatures, and performing onstage at an amusement park. Viewed through adult eyes, the film is hopelessly cheesy (though I still enjoy it), but back then it was my *Hard Day's Night*, my *Wizard of Oz*, my rock and roll fantasy, and my monster movie-of-the-week, all rolled into one.

I had a good friend with super-religious parents who wouldn't let him watch *KISS Meets the Phantom of the Park* (after all, KISS did stand for Knights in Satan's Service, or so some people thought), so, naturally, he came over to my house that evening after lying to his parents about what we were going to do. In the minutes leading up to the start of the movie, I was so excited that I kept leaving the living room as though I weren't going to watch it, and then I would run back in, diving on the carpet in front of the TV set, much to the amusement and bemusement of my friend and my parents. About the fifth or sixth time I performed this odd gymnastic maneuver, the movie began, and I sat transfixed before the television for the next two hours, blocking out the world and basking in the ethereal glow of what I thought was pure greatness.

By the time junior high school rolled around, most of the "cool" kids didn't like KISS anymore and would make fun of anyone who did, saying "KISS sucks." Since the band wore makeup and costumes, and since their cartoonish images were on everything from lunch boxes to puzzles to bubblegum cards, many people refused to take them seriously, even though the music they made was fantastic (if simplistic) rock and roll. This frustrated me to no end, as did the fact that KISS was rarely played on the radio because most disc jockeys and station managers, like most music critics, snubbed their noses at the band. One rare exception was the power ballad "Beth," which even grown-ups liked.

I knew KISS was great and that they didn't suck—I just wish they would have gotten more respect at the time. But that's all water under the proverbial bridge now as the four original members of KISS entered the hallowed halls of the Rock and Roll Hall of Fame on April 10, 2014, a ridiculous 15 years after they became eligible. Further, KISS has sold more than 100 million albums worldwide, and they've influenced the careers of countless entertainers, everyone from Garth Brooks to Lenny Kravitz to the late, great "Dimebag" Darrell.

To this day, I'm still a huge KISS fan. Otherwise, I wouldn't have written this book, which has been a massive (and massively fun) undertaking. A couple of years ago, while going through my collection of KISS books and magazines, it occurred to me that, other than an obscure Japanese book published during the late 1970s, no one had ever written an honest-to-goodness KISS encyclopedia. The Beatles, Elvis, the Rolling Stones, the Grateful Dead—each of these iconic bands has had at least one encyclopedia, but not KISS, so I took it upon myself to fill a gap in the rock and roll publishing industry.

The result is the titanic tome you are holding in your hands, a labor of love that catalogues, describes, and often critiques all of KISS's albums, songs, and tours, along with most of their important movie, TV, and comic book appearances. The book lists and describes hundreds of other things related to the band as well, including prominent friends, girlfriends, family members, influences, action figures, memorabilia, crew members, session musicians, songwriters, books, magazines, and much, much more.

The primary focus of the encyclopedia is on the original fab four—Ace Frehley, Gene Simmons, Paul Stanley, and Peter Criss—but replacement members Eric Carr, Vinnie Vincent, Mark St. John, Bruce Kulick, Eric Singer (the current drummer), and Tommy Thayer (the current lead guitarist) are given their due as well: their contributions to the KISS legacy certainly deserve documentation.

Whether you're a lifelong member of the KISS Army, someone who hopped aboard during the non-makeup era or the Reunion Tour, or you simply dig the current KISS lineup, I hope you have as much fun reading this book as much as I had writing it. After all, the main philosophy of KISS is that you should enjoy life.

And now, without further ado: "You wanted the best, you got the best, the hottest band in the world, KISS!"

A Brief History

The self-proclaimed "Hottest Band in the World," KISS is indeed one of the most popular rock groups in the history of the industry, having sold more than 100 million albums during its more than 40-year reign. KISS has 30 gold-certified albums (sales of 500,000 copies), more than any other American band. And, along with that other fabulous foursome, the Beatles, KISS is one of few musical acts in which each member has a distinct image and is readily identifiable by the general public. In fact, co-founder Gene Simmons has often called his beloved band "the heavy metal Beatles."

The original KISS lineup consisted of Gene "The Demon" Simmons (bass, vocals), Paul "The Starchild" Stanley (rhythm guitar, vocals), Ace "The Spaceman" Frehley (lead guitar, vocals), and Peter "The Catman" Criss (drums, vocals), each of whom lived up to his nickname by wearing kabuki-style makeup, and by donning such costume accouterments as chains, platform heels, shiny armor, spiked collars, black leather, and silver studs.

The black-and-white face paint not only gave KISS a cool, distinctive look, it enshrouded the band members in mystery as few fans ever saw them without their makeup (this was decades before nearly everyone had a cellphone camera in his pocket), at least until MTV's 1983 television special, *KISS Unmasking*. This low-key, but pivotal affair featured a naked-faced Gene and Paul, and, less interestingly, replacement members Vinnie Vincent and Eric Carr. (If KISS had unmasked while Ace and Peter were still in the band, it would have been a bigger deal.)

Along with the makeup and costumes, KISS, under the guidance of such key figures as Bill Aucoin and Sean Delaney, distinguished itself with its loud, bombastic, prop-filled live performances, which included explosions, flame throwers, confetti storms, hydraulic lifts, huge staircases, flashing lights, and a giant KISS logo backing the band. Ace wailed away on a smoke-spewing, rocket-shooting guitar, and Peter Criss pounded the skins with sparkling drumsticks while boosted by an elevating drum riser. Paul would prance, preen, banter, and boast, and then smash his guitar (a la Pete Townshend), while Gene reveled in his demonic persona by spitting blood, breathing fire, and wagging his preternaturally long tongue.

KISS was founded by Simmons, who was born Chaim Witz in Haifa, Israel, and Stanley, who was born Stanley Eisen in Queens, New York. They belonged to a New York band called Wicked Lester, which recorded an unreleased album for Epic Records. Late in 1972, Stanley and Simmons welcomed into the band street-tough drummer Peter Criss (born Peter Criscuola in Brooklyn, New York), who had placed an ad in *Rolling Stone*. Early in 1973, Ace Frehley (born Paul Frehley in the Bronx, New York) answered an ad in *The Village Voice*, showing up for his audition wearing one red and one orange sneaker. Despite his wardrobe malfunction (among other quirks), Ace was brought onboard (over Bob Kulick and others), and the band renamed themselves KISS shortly thereafter.

KISS released their self-titled debut album February 18, 1974. They cranked out two more albums (*Hotter than Hell* and *Dressed to Kill*) over the next 13 months, but toiled in relative obscurity until the debut of *Alive!* (September 10, 1975), a two-record epic that captured the band's explosive sound in all its live glory. KISS was certainly competent in the studio, recording such tight, memorable tunes as "Strutter," "Cold Gin," and "Rock and Roll All Nite," the latter of which would become the band's signature song, but the real appeal of KISS was seeing (and hearing) them live, and the *Alive!* album, which went quadruple platinum, let the listener experience the thrills of a KISS concert as well as mere audio possibly could.

Bolstered by the success of *Alive!*, KISS enjoyed tremendous success over the next few years, releasing a string of hit records (*Destroyer*, *Rock and Roll Over*, *Love Gun*, and *Alive II*), appearing on such shows as *The Paul Lynde Halloween Special* (1976) and *Tomorrow with Tom Snyder* (1979), basking in the popularity of the famed KISS Army, filming a popular if critically drubbed made-for-TV-movie (1978's *KISS Meets the Phantom of the Park*), and selling tons of merchandise, including dolls, bubblegum cards, model kits, jigsaw puzzles, board games, and toy musical instruments.

One misstep during this era was the unprecedented simultaneous release of four solo albums (one by each original band member) on September 18, 1978. Each record reached the top 50 on *Billboard*'s album chart, but they were massively overproduced, leaving many copies languishing in bargain bins. Plus, the solo records fueled rumors that the band was going to split up.

The next few years saw more misses (the concept album *Music from "The Elder"*) than hits (the disco single "I Was Made for Lovin' You," which reached #11 on the charts, but alienated many longtime fans), and strife within the band resulted in the exodus of Peter Criss, who left in 1980, and Ace Frehley, who departed for greener pastures in 1982. Numerous highs and lows followed, with Paul and Gene remaining together through good times and bad, accompanied by replacement members Eric Carr (1980–1991), Vinnie Vincent (1982–1984), Mark St. John (1984), Bruce Kulick (1984–1996), Eric Singer (1991–1996, 2001 to the present), and Tommy Thayer (2002 to the present).

One especially memorable highlight was the 1996 Reunion Tour, in which Ace and Peter rejoined Gene and Paul, donned their old-style stage makeup and costumes, and hit the road for a string of sold-out concerts. Another was the 2014 induction of the original members into the Rock and Roll Hall of Fame.

Despite their popularity and considerably large catalogue of catchy pop tunes and fist-pumping rock anthems, KISS is often disparaged by critics (this was especially true during the height of their popularity in the late 1970s), many of whom can't see past the band's image to appreciate the fine music. In addition, KISS has been vilified over the years for their sexually charged lyrics, salacious imagery, merchandising mentality, hedonistic philosophy, and occasional *Spinal Tap*–like moments.

KISS handles the criticism in stride, constantly praising their fans and laughing off their critics all the way to the bank. Accompanied by drummer Eric Singer (in Catman makeup) and guitarist Tommy Thayer (in Spaceman makeup), Paul and Gene, now well into their 60s, continue recording, touring, and merchandising. Once the dynamic duo retires, they plan on continuing KISS with other musicians/singers in their roles. As Paul and Gene have said numerous times, the KISS entity and concept is bigger than any individual band member.

But these are just the basics. Within the following pages, you'll find, as the late, great Paul Harvey would have said, the rest of the story.

THE ENCYCLOPEDIA

Abbott, Waring: Famed music photographer Waring Abbott, who has worked with such acts as Led Zeppelin and the Rolling Stones, took numerous photos of KISS during the 1970s. You can view his work in the 2002 book, *KISS: The Early Years*.

Academy of Music: KISS played some of their earliest shows at the Academy of Music in New York City. At the December 31, 1973, New Year's Eve show, where they opened for Iggy & the Stooges, Gene Simmons' hair caught fire during his fire-breathing stunt. Naturally, the band was playing "Firehouse." This historic concert was photographer Bob Gruen's first time to see KISS.

***Ace Frehley* (album):** Released in conjunction with the other three KISS solo albums on September 18, 1978, *Ace Frehley* was recorded at Plaza Sound Studios in New York and the Mansion in Sharon, Connecticut. Certified platinum on October 2, 1978, *Ace Frehley*, like the other band members' solo records, shipped over one million copies. The hard rocking, guitar-heavy album is generally considered to be the best of the four by fans and critics alike (though *Paul Stanley* sounds more like an actual KISS record).

Tracks on *Ace Frehley*, which was co-produced by Frehley and Eddie Kramer, include: "Rip It Out," "Speedin' Back to My Baby," "Snow Blind," "Ozone," "What's on Your Mind?," "New York Groove," "I'm in Need of Love," "Wiped-Out," and "Fractured Mirror," the latter of which is an instrumental that inspired several sequels. The album had one hit, "New York Groove," which reached #13 on the *Billboard* charts (the album itself hit #26). First recorded in 1975 by Hello (a British glam band), "New York Groove" was the most successful KISS single since "Beth," which charted at #7 in 1976.

In *Rolling Stone* #279 (Nov., 1978), Ace Frehley revealed that he loved working on the self-titled record, which increased his confidence in his abilities as a singer and songwriter, to the point of considering a solo career. "I've never had more fun doing an album," he said. "It was more exciting than KISS because I had more freedom. I didn't have to listen to three other guys telling me what to do."

***Ace Frehley—The Ultimate Fan Scrapbook*:** This book, written by Bill Baker, features many rare and candid photos of Ace Frehley, with and without makeup. Published by Tunis Media LLC on January 1, 2008.

***Ace Vision Volume 1*:** Released on VHS in 1994 exclusively for Ace Frehley's fan club, Rock Soldiers, *Ace Vision Volume 1*. features songs filmed during Ace's "Just 4 Fun Tour," specifically the March 13, 1993, show in Orlando, Florida at Station Fern Park. Tracks include: "Shock Me," "Rip It Out," "Rocket Ride," "Breakout," "Cold Gin," "New York Groove," "Parasite," "Shot Full of Rock," and "Rock Soldiers." Includes an interview with Frehley. A DVD version followed in 2004.

"Acrobat": According to KISS expert Paul Elliott (*KISS: Hotter Than Hell*), "Acrobat," the 11th track on disc one of *The Box Set*, is a previously unreleased song that was "reworked as a shortened instrumental for the first KISS album under the new title of 'Love Theme from KISS.' This version was recorded live at the Daisy in Long Island, New York, on August 25, 1973." Written by Ace Frehley and Gene Simmons.

Action Figures: The first and most collectible KISS action figures were the 1978 Mego "dolls," which have their own entry in this book. After a gap of almost two decades, in which no KISS figures were produced, the band signed a deal with McFarlane Toys (owned by comics artist Todd McFarlane), which created several high quality, highly detailed series of figures.

In the first McFarlane set from 1997, each of the band members' instruments doubled as a weapon, and there were three variations of each figure: one with a gold solo LP record, one with a black solo LP record, and one with a letter from the word "KISS." The 1998 Psycho Circus set, based on the comic book series, featured feral versions of the band members, each packaged with a sidekick. In 1999, McFarlane released a Psycho Circus: Tour Edition of each band member, based on KISS's world tour at the time.

McFarlane followed with: a 1999 Gene Simmons figure sold exclusively through Spencer's Gifts; a 2000 KISS Alive figure set (costumes circa 1976) sold separately and as a boxed set; a 12-inch Gene Simmons Alive figure from 2001; a 2002 Creatures set based on the *Unmasked* tour costumes, sold separately and as a boxed set, with Eric Carr taking the place of Peter Criss; a 12-inch Gene Simmons Creatures figure from 2002; a 12-inch Gene Simmons Destroyer figure from 2004; and a Love Gun Deluxe Boxed Set from 2004, featuring all four band members from the album cover, plus three scantily clad KISS ladies. In 2005, McFarlane released Starchild and Demon three-figure boxed sets, featuring the Paul and Gene figures from the Alive, Creatures, and Love Gun lines.

In 2009, Super Stars released figures featuring the *Alive!*-era costumes, packaged separately and in a boxed set. In 2010, Medicom released 12-inch, *Destroyer*-era figures of the Demon and the

Left: This dynamic Gene Simmons action figure was produced by McFarlane Toys in 1997. It includes an ax bass and a winged snake battle staff. *Right:* In 1997, McFarlane Toys released their first series of KISS action figures, including this one of Ace Frehley. Note that you could transform the Spaceman's guitar into a "space sled."

Starchild. In 2012, Figure Toy Company produced an 8-inch set (packaged with a mini replica *Love Gun* album cover) and a 12-inch set (packaged with a mini KISS concert T-shirt) of Love Gun Retro Action Figures, which are similar to the Mego dolls. Each figure has rooted hair, cloth clothing, and 16 points of articulation.

Numerous KISS mini-figures, bobble heads, bendables, plush toys, bears, busts, beanbags, Celebriducks, puppets, statues, and other such figures have been released over the years, including Mr. Potato Head toys.

Adams, Bryan: Born November 5, 1959, Bryan Adams is a Canadian singer, songwriter, producer, actor, and pop star. The year before he broke out in 1983 with the hit record, *Cuts Like a Knife*, which contains such hits as "This Time" and "Straight from the Heart," along with the title track, Adams had a hand in writing three KISS songs: "War Machine," "Rock and Roll Hell," and "Down on Your Knees." Like KISS, Bryan Adams has sold more than 100 million albums worldwide.

Aerosmith: Formed in Boston, Massachusetts in 1970, hard rock act Aerosmith is led by front man Steven Tyler and guitarist Joe Perry. KISS opened for Aerosmith several times in 1974.

In 2003, Aerosmith and KISS co-headlined a tour called the Rocksimus Maximus Tour by Aerosmith and the World Domination Tour by KISS. During a 2012 interview on Florida radio station The Bone, Perry dissed KISS while talking about the tour: "KISS is a comic book rock band and they got a couple hits, but they're more of a comic book. You see them in their spackled faces…. It's two different animals. They went the theatrical way and used rock and roll kind of as their soundtrack, and for Aerosmith, the music is our show. From that point of view, it's apples and oranges." Tyler chimed in with: "We were always a band that had something to prove. We always wanted to blow off whatever band it was, and I remember when we went out with KISS in '76 or something, one of our roadies got into a knife fight with their guys. So I hated them ever since."

"Ain't Quite Right": The Starchild slows things down for "Ain't Quite Right," the third track on his 1978 KISS solo album, *Paul Stanley*. He soulfully (and regretfully) sings of a girl who gave him good love, but something was amiss with their relationship. Co-written by Mikel Japp, "Ain't Quite Right" is a major departure from the average KISS song about mindless sexual conquest.

"Ain't That Peculiar": A demo recorded in the spring of 1989, "Ain't That Peculiar" was retooled to become "Little Caesar," the Eric Carr-sung track from *Hot in the Shade*. The tune was featured in its original form in 2001's *The Box Set* as song 14 on disc four.

***Alive!*:** Released September 10, 1975, *Alive!* is the album that "transformed KISS from cult heroes to all-American superstars … one of the great live recordings," wrote *KISS: Hotter Than Hell* author Paul Elliott. The double record, which was recorded at Detroit's Cobo Hall (along with venues in Wildwood, New Jersey, Davenport, Iowa, and Cleveland, Ohio), features loud, raucous versions of all the big songs from the band's first three albums, including: "Deuce," "Strutter," "Got to Choose," "Hotter Than Hell," "Firehouse," "Nothin' to Lose," "C'mon and Love Me," "Parasite," "She," "Watchin' You," "100,000 Years," "Black Diamond," "Rock Bottom," "Cold Gin," "Rock and Roll All Nite" (which trumped the studio version by reaching #12 on the charts), and "Let Me Go, Rock 'n' Roll." The album includes banter by Paul Stanley as well.

Produced by Eddie Kramer for Casablanca Records, *Alive!* peaked at #9 on the *Billboard* 200 chart and stayed on the list for 110 weeks. It was certified Gold in 1975 and went on to become Quadruple Platinum. Prior to release, *Alive!* was heavily remixed at Electric Lady Studios to correct mistakes, overdub vocals, and make the crowd noise more audible.

The gatefold cover of the original two-record vinyl release, which was photographed by Fin Costello, opened to reveal a handwritten note from each member of the band. The back cover shows a concert crowd shot with two fans—Bruce Redoute and Lee Neaves—holding up a handmade KISS sign.

In *Rolling Stone*'s special *500 Greatest Albums of All Time* issue from 2003, *Alive!* was ranked #159. Amusingly, in the magazine's original review in issue #203 (January 1976), Alan Niester skewered the double LP, saying: "KISS onstage could possibly be mildly entertaining for about 10 minutes, but on record, minus the impact of gaudy painted faces and stage theatrics, the band must be judged solely for its music. It's awful. Criminally repetitive, thuddingly monotonous…. They came up with the idea of dragging rock further into the pits of theatrical overkill, managing, in the process, to pick up a legion of young fans who hadn't heard these riffs in their previous incarnations (Grand Funk Railroad comes to mind)."

Noted KISS collector Mark Cicchini, one of the hosts of *Three Sides of the Coin*, has cited *Alive!* as his favorite album of all time.

In *KISS: Behind the Mask—The Official Authorized Biography*, Paul Stanley said *Alive!* "put us in a position to headline ... it was a recording that paid tribute to the audience as much as the band ... it was a real important album." Peter Criss and Ace Frehley are especially proud of the record. The Catman called his drumming on "100,000 Years" one the best solos he's ever done while Space Ace said, "A lot of guitar players come up to me and say *Alive!* is their rock 'n' roll bible. That's how they learned to play guitar, which I find flattering. If that album had bombed we would have been dropped from the label."

According to Bill Aucoin, *Alive!* was recorded live not only to capture the essence of the band's concerts on vinyl, but also because KISS was struggling financially after soft sales on their first three albums. "We decided to do a live album because it was less expensive than recording a studio record," he said in *KISS: Behind the Mask*. "We had never gotten a royalty statement from Casablanca."

Alive: The Millennium Concert: Originally intended to be *Alive IV*, *Alive: The Millennium Concert* was shelved because Mercury Records was absorbed by the Universal/Vivendi merger. Fortunately for fans, it was eventually released as disc four of the *KISS Alive! 1975–2000* set. It is also available separately on vinyl, and as an MP3.

Featuring a reunited Paul, Gene, Ace and Peter, *Alive: The Millennium Concert* was recorded at BC Place Stadium in Vancouver, Canada on New Year's Eve of 1999. Tracks include: "Psycho Circus," "Shout It Out Loud," "Deuce," "Heaven's on Fire," "Into the Void," "Firehouse," "Do You Love Me?," "Let Me Go, Rock 'n' Roll," "I Love It Loud," "Lick It Up," "100,000 Years," "Love Gun," "Black Diamond," "Beth," "Rock and Roll All Nite," "2,000 Man" (Best Buy edition only), "God of Thunder" (Best Buy edition only), and "Detroit Rock City" (iTunes edition only). The MP3 version available on Amazon includes all of these songs except for "God of Thunder." The vinyl edition contains all 18 songs.

Alive 35 World Tour *see* **KISS Alive 35 World Tour**

***Alive III*:** Produced by Eddie Kramer for Mercury Records, *Alive III* hit stores May 18, 1993. Although it reached #9 on the *Billboard* 200 chart, reviews were mixed, meaning the two-CD set isn't as critically acclaimed as the widely lauded *Alive!* and *Alive II*. Eduardo Rivadavia of allmusic.com said *Alive III* "in no way measures up to its legendary live predecessors" while Matthew Wilkening of ultimateclassicrock.com said "the record's got good energy and spirit" despite "a greater emphasis on technical ability." *KISS FAQ* author Dale Sherman wrote, "Strangely enough, for an album that is probably closest to being a true live album, it is usually considered the weakest of the *Alive* albums."

Recorded in Cleveland (Richfield Coliseum), Auburn Hills, Michigan (The Palace), and Indianapolis (Market Square Arena) in 1992 during the band's *Revenge* tour, *Alive III* features the following tracks: "Creatures of the Night," "Deuce," "I Just Wanna," "Unholy," "Heaven's on Fire," "Watchin' You," "Domino," "I Was Made for Lovin' You" (a hard rocking version of the disco hit), "I Still Love You," "Rock and Roll All Nite," "Lick It Up," "Forever," "I Love It Loud," "Detroit Rock City," "God Gave Rock N' Roll to You II," and "Star Spangled Banner." A bonus track, "Take It Off," was featured on the Japanese, European, and South American CD releases, as well as the U.S. vinyl release. The song was also included in the *Alive III* CD that came with the *KISS Alive! 1975–2000* CD box set.

Alive III was the first live recording released by the unmasked version of KISS, which at the time comprised Paul Stanley, Gene Simmons, Bruce Kulick, and Eric Singer. Derek Sherinian played keyboards and sang backing vocals. The liner notes of the album include a family tree designed by the band's Japanese fan club. It shows the various KISS lineups from 1973 to 1993, along with bands that the then-current and former KISS members were a part of.

Alive! Tour: To support *Alive!*, KISS toured North America from September 10, 1975, to April 28, 1976, and Europe from May 13 to June 6, 1976, for a total of 117 shows. Since *Destroyer* was released March 15, 1976, the latter part of the tour also featured songs from that album. Stage props included fire engine lights, a drum riser, Gene's blood-spitting and fire-breathing, Paul's fire helmet, Ace's smoking guitar, flamethrowers, bombs, Paul smashing his guitar, a confetti storm, and a lighted KISS logo.

Band lineup: Paul Stanley, Gene Simmons, Ace Frehley, and Peter Criss. Headlining act: Black Sabbath. Opening acts: 38 Special, Albatross, Artful Dodger, Atlanta Rhythm Section, Back Street Crawler, Black Sheep, Blue Öyster Cult, Bob Seger & the Silver Bullet Band, Booga Booga, Boz Scaggs, Brownsville Station, Diamond Reo, the Dixie Dregs, Double Yellow Line, Electromagnets, Fallen Angels, Gary Wright, Hammerhead, Harvest, Hot Lucy, Hydra, James Montgomery Band, Lakeland String Quartet, the Leslie West Band, Little Feat, Montrose, Mott, Mountain Smoke, Point Blank, REO Speedwagon, Rockets, Rory Gallagher, Rush, Savoy Brown, Slade, Styx, Target, and Thee Image.

Followed by: Destroyer Tour.

Alive II: For *Alive II*, which was released October 14, 1977, by Casablanca Records, producer Eddie Kramer recorded four shows at the Los Angeles Forum in August of 1977, during the *Love Gun* tour. According to *KISS FAQ* author Dale Sherman, "Beth" and "I Want You" were taken from recordings at Budokan Hall in Tokyo, April 2, 1977. As with *Alive!*, the recordings were remixed in studio, but this is not a bad thing—the double LP is about as dynamic and as exciting as *Alive!*.

The original vinyl release featured a gatefold cover that opened to reveal a photo of KISS in all their concert glory: a fiery, explosive image that sent the imagination soaring for anyone who had never seen the band perform live. It was packaged with a set of temporary KISS tattoos and a full-color booklet called "The Evolution of KISS."

Tracks, culled from *Rock and Roll Over*, *Destroyer*, and *Love Gun*, include: "Detroit Rock City," "King of the Night Time World," "Ladies Room," "Makin' Love," "Love Gun," "Calling Dr. Love," "Christine Sixteen," "Shock Me," "Hard Luck Woman," "Tomorrow and Tonight," "I Stole Your Love," "Beth," "God of Thunder," "I Want You," and "Shout It Out Loud." Paul Stanley provides engaging banter while Eddie Balandas kicks things off with, "You wanted the best, and you got the best, the hottest band in the world, KISS!"

Since KISS didn't think they had enough good material to fill two LPs, there are five new studio songs comprising side four, recorded at the Capitol Theatre in Passaic, New Jersey and Electric Lady Studios in New York City: "All American Man," "Rockin' in the USA," "Larger than Life," "Rocket Ride," and "Any Way You Want It." Gene Simmons got the idea for putting new studio songs on an otherwise live release from *Fandango!* (1975), ZZ Top's fourth album.

In the November 19, 1977, issue of *Sounds* magazine, Geoff Barton called *Alive II*, which reached #7 on the *Billboard* 200 chart, "the greatest live album of this year.... Conceivably of the decade. Possibly of the century. Perhaps of the millennium. Maybe even of all time. Or at least since KISS *Alive!* volume one."

Rolling Stone recently ranked *Alive II* KISS's ninth best album. In the magazine's original review in issue #256 (Jan., 1978), John Swenson said that "KISS has improved dramatically in its recording career" and that "*Alive II* captures the essence of live rock and roll very well." However, he also accused KISS of swiping guitar solos and screams from Pete Townshend and Roger Daltrey respectively.

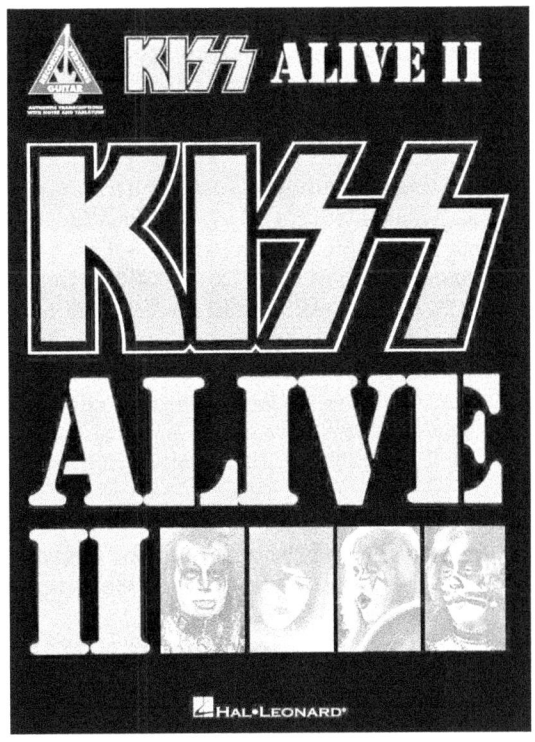

This songbook contains lyrics and musical notes for all 20 songs from KISS's 1977 double live album, *Alive II*.

Despite its excellence, there were some problems during the recording of *Alive II*, namely Ace Frehley's alcohol abuse, which would cause him to miss recording sessions. As such, Bob Kulick played guitar on "All American Man," "Larger than Life," and "Rockin' in the USA." For his part, Frehley (and Peter Criss) have complained in recent years that Gene Simmons and Paul Stanley were too controlling.

Alive II Tour: To support their second live album, KISS toured from November 15, 1977, to February 3, 1978, in the U.S., and from March 28 to May 19, 1978, in Tokyo, Japan, where they sold out the Budokan all five nights. Another landmark event on this tour, which consisted of 52 shows, was selling out Madison Square Garden three nights in a row.

Stage props included fire engine lights, a drum riser, Gene's blood-spitting and fire-breathing, Paul's fire helmet and smashed guitar, Ace's smoking guitar, hydraulic lifts, lighted staircases, Sam the Serpent (a giant coiled, fanged snake), flamethrowers, bombs, a confetti storm, and a lighted KISS logo.

Band lineup: Paul Stanley, Gene Simmons, Ace Frehley, and Peter Criss. Opening acts: AC/DC, Bow Wow, Detective, Nantucket, Piper, and Rockets. Average attendance: 13,550.

Followed by: Dynasty Tour.

Alive/Worldwide Tour: Better known as the Reunion Tour, the Alive/Worldwide Tour was hugely successful, grossing $143.7 million. It was the first tour since 1979's Dynasty Tour to feature all four original band members, each appearing in full costumes and makeup.

Backed by their vintage stunts (along with video screens and other modern flourishes), such as Simmons spitting blood and breathing fire, Stanley and Simmons flying, Frehley playing a smoking and shooting guitar, and all manner of platform risers and pyrotechnics, KISS played mostly 1970s era material. Since 1980's "Shandi" was a big hit in foreign markets, the band played it during many overseas shows.

Lasting from June 15, 1996, to July 5, 1997, for a total of 192 shows, the tour went through the U.S., Canada, Europe, Asia, Oceana, and South America. The first concert, occurring in Laguna Hills, CA, was a warm-up show at the KROQ 4th Annual Weenie Roast.

Prior to the tour, to get the world talking about the classic KISS lineup, the band, introduced by Tupac Shakur, made a surprise appearance at the *Grammy Awards* show on February 28, 1996. On April 16, 1996, KISS held a press conference (hosted by Conan O'Brien) for the tour aboard the U.S.S. *Intrepid* (a circa 1940s flight deck carrier-turned-tourist-attraction) located on the west side of Manhattan. At the event, Stanley said: "We had a great time doing *Unplugged*. That was the seed that got this whole thing going. We're so gassed to be here. This means so much to us. It's funny, because after 17 years of not being together, you kind of forget why you stopped being together anyway, so give us another 17 years, and we'll be able to figure it out."

Opening acts during the Alive/Worldwide Tour: the 4th Floor, 311, Alice in Chains, Alkbottle, Biohazard, the Bogmen, Caroline's Spine, Channel Zero, CIV, Core22, Coyote Shivers, Custard, D Generation, Deftones, Die Artze, Dog Eat Dog, Econoline Crush, El Fantastico Hombre Bala, Everclear, the Exponents, the Fauves, Fear Factory, the Fireballs, Johnny Bravo, Korn, L7, Live, Lush, Malon, the Melvins, Moonspell, the Mutton Birds, Naked Lunch, Neneh Cherry, the Nixons, No Doubt, Non-Intentional Lifeform, Otto, Outhouse, Pantera, Paradise Lost, Passion Orange, Poe, Powerman 5000, Pushmonkey, Rage Against the Machine, Red 5, the Red Hot Chili Peppers, Reef, Reel Big Fish, Royal Crown Revue, Satisfucktion, Sepultura, Sex Tiger, Sideburn, Silver Chair, Skunk Anansie, Snout, Sponge, Stabbing Westward, Stage, the Straws, Sugar Ray, Thunder, Uncle Meat, V8, the Verve Pipe, Waltari, Warpigs, and Zluty Pes. Average Attendance: 13,737.

Followed by: Psycho Circus World Tour.

"All American Man": The first song on side four of *Alive II*, "All American Man" was written by Paul Stanley and Sean Delaney (in Stanley's dining room). As with the other four songs on that side of the album, it was a new studio track for the double LP. Stanley, who brags that he's a tall, hot, "All American Man," provides vocals while Bob Kulick steps in for Ace Frehley on lead guitar. Despite Frehley's absence, and the fact that the song was rarely (if ever) played in concert, "All American Man" is a hard rocking, quintessential KISS tune.

"All for the Glory": Paul Stanley and Gene Simmons wrote "All for the Glory," the seventh track on *Sonic Boom*, but that's Eric Singer on lead vocals. It's a good song by a band that sounds united in its desire to rock your socks off. The chorus will sound hokey to some, but the anthemic nature of the tune should please most KISS fans.

"All for the Love of Rock & Roll": Eric Singer gets more time at the mic in "All for the Love of Rock & Roll," the 10th track on *Monster*. It's a fun, party-time anthem that would make Kid Rock proud. Like certain other songs on *Monster*, there's more cowbell. Written by Paul Stanley.

"All Hell's Breakin' Loose": The sixth track on *Lick It Up*, "All Hell's Breakin' Loose" is a fun, but unintentionally amusing rocker in which Paul Stanley raps so-bad-they're-good lyrics. Ill-advised rapping notwithstanding, "All Hell's Breakin' Loose," which was written by Stanley, Simmons, Carr, and Vincent, was the second (and final) single from the record. Unfortunately, it failed to chart in the U.S.

In *KISS: Behind the Mask—The Official Authorized Biography*, Stanley said Carr "came in" with the song and "was very proud of it," but was "a very sensitive guy and was completely destroyed at hearing what he believed was the ruination of the song" after the other band members altered it. "Eric was always more frustrated by what he wasn't than thrilled with what he was.... I just remember his jaw hitting the floor when he heard what had been done."

***All I Need to Know I Learned from KISS: Life Lessons from the Hottest Band in the Land*:** Written by Chris Epting, this eBook was published by Miniver Press on October 28, 2012. According to the publisher's description, Epting was interviewing members of the band when it "suddenly flashed before his eyes that ... the band he had loved since childhood actually played a huge part in shaping how he looks at the world. In that instant, he decided to write about his life-long journey with the band, starting out in the early 1970s when he joined the KISS Army and continuing until today. Epting takes us through the history of KISS, weaving in historic tidbits and trivia with his personal observations, while laying out the rules for living that he absorbed from "the hottest band in the land." Includes exclusive photos and an introduction by Robert DeLeo of the Stone Temple Pilots.

"All The Way": This obscure song, written and sung by Gene Simmons (who has admitted he got the lick from a song by Detroit, a Mitch Ryder band), is the sixth track on *Hotter Than Hell*. In Paul Elliott's *KISS: Hotter Than Hell*, the author said, "The song is built on a heavy staccato riff featuring Peter Criss bashing a cowbell and bringing some much-needed levity to one of Simmons's more forgettable numbers."

"Almost Human": A song that could only be written and sung by Gene Simmons, who got the idea from reading a book about lycanthropes, "Almost Human" has the Demon, in full menace mode, essentially playing the role of an amorous werewolf, growling that he's hungry for a woman's love and that he's going to change when the moon comes out. A funk-infused rock tune with a bit of an Oriental vibe (listen to the gong sound at the beginning), "Almost Human" is one of the stranger songs in the KISS oeuvre. It's the eighth track on *Love Gun*. Simmons played guitar on the song while Jimmy Maelen pounded the congas.

Altyn, John: John Altyn was an early KISS fan who dated Peter Criss's sister, Donna, and who watched the band rehearse in the Loft (1973), where he gave beers to Ace Frehley.

"Always Near You/Nowhere to Hide": A song that would feel right at home on KISS' controversial concept album, *Music from "The Elder,"* "Always Near You/Nowhere to Hide" is the seventh track on Gene Simmons' 1978 KISS solo album. The Demon sounds decidedly un-demonic, singing softly (if passive aggressively) that he is always near a girl and that she shouldn't run and hide. As on "True Confessions," the Citrus College Singers lend their voices to the song, as do Mitch Weissman and Joe Pecorino of the Broadway musical, *Beatlemania*.

***American Bandstand*:** *American Bandstand*, the popular music program produced by Dick Clark, was a huge influence on Paul Stanley, who has said many times that the show made him want to be a rock star.

See also: "Dick Clark's American Bandstand 50th Anniversary."

***American Idol*:** On the May 20, 2009, season finale episode of *American Idol*, Adam Lambert sang "Beth." Later in the show, KISS joined Lambert onstage for a medley of "Detroit Rock City" and "Rock and Roll All Nite." On the May 21, 2014, season finale of *American Idol*, winner and KISS fan Caleb Johnson joined the band onstage for a medley of "Love Gun" and "Shout It Out Loud." Gene Simmons was a guest judge on the January 25, 2005, episode.

American Music Awards: The *American Music Awards* show was created in 1973 by Dick Clark. KISS has never won an AMA, even though the awards are determined by a poll of the public and music buyers instead of a governing body (such as the National Academy of Recording Arts and Sciences, which determines Grammy winners). However, Paul Stanley and Gene Simmons did appear onstage at the 2002 show, presenting the "Favorite Pop Rock Male Artist" award to Lenny Kravitz, who said: "This is pretty amazing, because when I was 12-years-old, these guys turned me on to some serious rock and roll, and I wouldn't even be standing here today if I hadn't heard some KISS records, so this is really beautiful."

"And on the 8th Day": A tune that can be scoffed at by both secularists and theists, "And on the 8th Day" finds Gene "the Demon" Simmons, who wrote the song with Vinnie Vincent, claiming that the almighty created good ole rock music after he rested up from creating everything else. It's obviously a tongue-in-cheek extension of the Biblical myth, but the agnostic Simmons sings the song with an oddly devout seriousness that belies the goofy lyric. A curious, boneheaded anthem, it is the 10th and final track on *Lick It Up*.

And Party Every Day: The Inside Story of Casablanca Records: Written by Larry Harris (with Curt Gooch and Jeff Suhs), this book was published by Backbeat on November 30, 2009. According to the dust jacket, Harris "tells the tale with startling candor and humor. From Bogart's daring first signing, the insanely pyrotechnic KISS, through the discovery and superstardom of the Village People—not to mention extraterrestrial funk master George Clinton and his circus freaks, Parliament Funkadelic—and the descent into the manic world of disco and its attendant vices, this book charts Bogart's meteoric rise and eventual collapse. Beyond the decadence of the dance floor and the spectacle of fire-breathing rock stars, Harris reveals the down and dirty of the record business from how he controlled the charts to the nasty payola scandals that still infected the industry."

And Party Every Day: The Inside Story of Casablanca Records chronicles the record company that first took a chance on KISS.

According to a KISS-centric review of the book published on www.metal-rules.com, "There is not enough stuff about KISS," but there is "good KISS trivia about the early days and relationship between KISS' management, lawyers, agents, and record label and who was sleeping with who, who owed money (or favors) to who and so on. It was all about leveraging (or exploiting) relationships (on both sides) to reach a mutual goal. As it stands it was a very enjoyable read chronicling the excesses of the 1970s music industry and the story behind the people in the label that helped take KISS to the top."

Anderson, Ken: Ken Anderson, who died in 2014, organized KISS touring productions during the band's heyday. His obituary published on thecelebritycafe.com said: "Anderson was responsible for the blood spitting, pyrotechnic spectacles that made KISS concerts some of the most popular shows around. Anderson had worked on *Jesus*

Christ Superstar before teaming with KISS manager Bill Aucoin to produce the awe-inspiring events that made KISS a favorite among music fans."

"Animal": The fourth track on the Vinnie Vincent Invasion's 1986 self-titled album, "Animal" was released as single, and it was featured in the 1987 movie, *Summer School*.

***Animalize*:** The follow-up to *Lick It Up*, *Animalize* is a solid (if uneven), hard-rocking record with several great songs (such as "Heaven's on Fire" and "Thrills in the Night"), despite limited input from Gene Simmons, who contributed some of the album's weaker tracks.

Prior to leaving for Vancouver to film *Runaway* (1984) with Tom Selleck, Simmons recorded bass and vocals for a number of songs, leaving Paul Stanley to produce most of *Animalize* by himself. Stanley has said the experience was freeing, but somewhat overwhelming because he had to do so much on the album, including redoing some of Simmons' songs. In various interviews, Simmons has admitted that he was still searching for his post-makeup identity in the band, and that he was more invested in Hollywood.

Mark St. John, who has admitted he wasn't a KISS fan before joining the band (and who has said Stanley and Simmons were difficult to work with), played lead guitar on most of *Animalize*, replacing Vinnie Vincent. Unfortunately, St. John developed Reiter's Syndrome, a rare illness that made his hands sore, so he had to bow out of the *Animalize* tour early on. Bruce Kulick, who played lead on "Lonely Is the Hunter" and "Murder in High Heels," took St. John's place.

Released September 13, 1984, by Mercury Records, *Animalize*, which reached #19 on the *Billboard* 200 chart, includes the following tracks: "I've Had Enough (Into the Fire)," "Heaven's on Fire," "Burn Bitch Burn," "Get All You Can Take," "Lonely Is the Hunter," "Under the Gun," "Thrills in the Night," "While the City Sleeps," and "Murder in High Heels."

Animalize Live Uncensored *see* **KISS: Animalize Live Uncensored**

Animalize World Tour: From September 30, 1984, to March 29, 1985, KISS played 119 shows across the U.S., Canada, and Europe in support of their 12th studio album. The European leg of the tour was essentially the Unmasked Tour stage embellished with animal prints to resemble the *Animalize* album cover. However, in North America, where the record was a surprise hit, a much bigger set with large metal ramps and staircases was used. In addition, the tour featured Paul Stanley's flying trapeze act.

New guitarist Mark St. John, who had replaced Vinnie Vincent, was to play on the tour, but he developed an arthritic syndrome called Reiter's Syndrome, meaning he could only play three shows. Bruce Kulick, who was first hired for the tour as a temporary replacement for St. John, ended up replacing him—it became official December 7, 1984.

The December 8 show at Cobo Hall in Detroit, the first with Bruce Kulick as a full member of the band, was filmed for an episode of MTV's *Saturday Night Concerts* series, and for the VHS/laserdisc release, *KISS: Animalize Live Uncensored*.

Band lineup: Paul Stanley, Gene Simmons, Mark St. John, Bruce Kulick, and Eric Carr. Opening acts: Bon Jovi, Dokken, Krokus, Queensryche, Sentinel, Steelover, and W.A.S.P. Average attendance: 6,209.

Followed by: Asylum Tour.

***Animaniacs* #16:** KISS appeared in DC Comics' *Animaniacs* #16 (June 1996), in which Yakko, Wakko, and Dot mistakenly go to a wrestling match instead of a KISS concert. Wakko is on the cover in Gene Simmons makeup.

Ankh Warrior: When Vinnie Vincent joined KISS, he wore Ankh Warrior makeup (the Egyptian hieroglyphic symbol represents eternal life). Paul Stanley has admitted that it was a mistake to try to create new characters for the band, which is why Eric Singer currently wears Catman garb and Tommy Thayer portrays the Spaceman.

***Anomaly*:** Released by Bronx Born Records on September 15, 2009, *Anomaly* was the first full album of new solo material by Ace Frehley since *Trouble Walkin'*, released a decade earlier. The CD, dedicated to Eric Carr and Pantera guitarist Dimebag Darrell, includes the following tracks: "Foxy & Free," "Outer Space," "Pain in the Neck," "Fox on the Run," "Genghis Khan," "Too Many Faces," "Change the World," "Space Bear," "A Little Below the Angels," "Sister," "It's a Great Life," and "Fractured Quantum," the latter of which is an instrumental sequel to "Fractured Mirror."

Longtime Ace associate Anton Fig, famous for his work in David Letterman's house band, the

CBS Orchestra, plays drums on *Anomaly*. The CD cover folds into a pyramid. Other versions of the CD include a temporary tattoo.

Eddie Trunk gave a favorable review of *Anomaly* on www.kissopolis.com, saying: "This album is very dynamic in direction.... Throughout his voice sounds better than ever and his playing is solid, all due to the fact that he is sober without a doubt ... this is the first [solo album] he has done sober and it shows. If you are an Ace fan you will love this album."

Anthrax: On *Kiss My Ass: Classic KISS Regrooved*, thrash metal band Anthrax, who formed in 1981, covered "She." On their 1991 album, *Attack of the Killer B's*, the band covered "Parasite." On their 1993 EP, *Black Lodge*, they covered "Love Her All I Can." On the 2001 remastering of *Stomp 442*, they covered "Watchin' You." Anthrax cofounder Scott Ian is an outspoken KISS fan and has said that the first album he bought as a kid with his own money was *Alive!*

"Any Way You Slice It": The second track on *Asylum*, "Any Way You Slice It" was written by Gene Simmons and Howard Rice, who penned "New Attitude" for Patti LaBelle. It's one of many Simmons songs about how a girl—in this case a newly-come-of-age girl—wants to go to bed with him. Of the song, *KISS: Hotter Than Hell* author Paul Elliott wrote: "Simmons is in a playful mood on this freewheeling rocker" while drummer "Eric Carr is in bullish mood on a thumping mid song break.... Simmons finishes on a lighthearted note with a staggered barroom blues ending." Bruce Kulick is up to the task as well, jamming on lead guitar.

"Any Way You Want It": A respectful cover of the Dave Clark Five's 1964 British pop tune, which was written by Dave Clark and bandmate Lenny Davidson, "Anyway You Want It" is the fifth track on side four of *Alive II*. Like the other four songs on that side of the album, it was a new studio track for the double LP. Paul Stanley provides vocals and subs for Ace Frehley on lead guitar. Lyrically simplistic, the song tells of a woman who doesn't want money or a diamond ring, just the man's love. Dave Clark himself has said he is a fan of the KISS version of the song.

"Anything for My Baby": The seventh track on *Dressed to Kill*, "Anything for My Baby" is a light pop number with an upbeat chorus. Paul Stanley, who wrote the song, sings of his love for a girl, saying he would even rob and steal for her. Peter Criss's distinctive drum style shines on this song. The use of acoustic guitars, which supplement the electric guitars, was inspired by Bachman Turner Overdrive.

Anything KISS: An elaborate website, Anything KISS (anythingkiss.com) features news about the band, plus history, a discography, a videography, tributes, links, and much more.

Appice, Carmine: Rock legend Carmine Appice, who has worked with such performers as Ozzy Osbourne, Ted Nugent, and Rod Stewart, plays drums on Paul Stanley's "Take Me Away (Together as One)."

Archie Meets KISS: The Hottest Band in the World crossed over with Betty, Veronica, and the gang in *Archie* #s 627–630 (2012), written by Alex Segura with cover and interior art by Dan Parent.

Part four of *Archie Meets KISS*, a crossover of two iconic American brands.

Francesco Francavilla did alternate covers for each issue. When Archie and his pals find Riverdale overrun with monsters because of a bad magical spell, KISS steps in to save the day. This four-part comic book series was collected as a trade paperback and a hardcover. Both collections feature bonus material, such as a brief foreword by Gene Simmons and all four variant covers reprinted. The hardcover version includes 48 pages not found elsewhere, including a KISS photo gallery and the original pitch and script.

Are You Smarter Than a Fifth Grader?: In 2008, during a celebrity edition of the Jeff Foxworthy–hosted game show, *Are You Smarter Than a Fifth Grader?* (Fox, 2007–2009), Gene Simmons won $500,000 for the Elizabeth Glaser Pediatric AIDS Foundation. When given "science" as the subject of the million dollar question, Gene passed, saying: "In my life, I only gamble with myself ... no fear, because there are no repercussions ... but I know that $500,000 is going to do an enormous amount of good for some disadvantaged kids."

As Shannon Tweed and Nick Simmons looked on, Foxworthy revealed the million dollar question: "What element is represented by the letter 'K' on the periodic table?" To which Gene replied, "krypton." The correct answer was potassium, which Shannon answered from her front-row seat. Several audience members wore Gene's Demon makeup.

Art School: Several KISS members studied art in school, helping give them the ability and imagination to create their onstage personas. Paul Stanley and Eric Carr went to the High School of Art and Design. Peter Criss went to three years of art school as a teen while Ace Frehley, heeding the advice of a high school counselor, studied graphic art.

Ashley, Phil: Phil Ashley played keyboards on the keyboard-heavy *Crazy Nights*. He also tickled the ivories on "Hide Your Heart" and "Forever" from *Hot in the Shade*.

Asshole: Released in 2004 by Sanctuary, *Asshole* was Gene Simmons' second solo album (after *Gene Simmons*, which came out in 1978). Tracks on this widely panned CD include: "Sweet & Dirty Love," "Firestarter" (cover of the Prodigy song, featuring Jane's Addiction guitarist Dave Navarro), "Weapons of Mass Destruction," "Waiting for the Morning Light" (co-written by Bob Dylan), "Beautiful," "Asshole" (released as an edited single), "Now That You're Gone" (co-written by Bob Kulick), "Whatever Turns You On" (featuring vocals by Shannon Tweed and her mother, Louise), "Dog," "Black Tongue" (co-written and with spoken words and rhythm and solo guitars by Frank Zappa), "Carnival of Souls," "If I Had a Gun," and "1,000 Dreams."

Bruce Kulick plays guitar and Eric Singer drums on tracks one and three. The album title, due to its crudeness, does not appear on the front cover. The Japanese release contains two bonus tracks: "Everybody Knows" and "You're My Reason For Living." A DualDisc reissue, released in 2005, features 5.1 surround sound, stereo album mixes, lyrics, photos, the "Firestarter" music video, and web-links.

Asylum: Recorded at the legendary Electric Lady Studios, *Asylum*, which was released September 16 by Mercury Records, was hardly a return to the glory days of 1970s KISS. Rather, it has a "sound that was too similar to other pop-metal bands at the time, as well as unimaginative, predictable songs ... several tracks could have benefited greatly from a heavier sound" (Greg Prato, www.allmusic.com).

Bruce Kulick, who had replaced an ailing Mark St. John on the *Animalize* tour, plays lead guitar on the record, while Eric Carr pounds the drums. Paul Stanley was the guiding force on *Asylum* as Gene Simmons' interests were divided by Hollywood and his record label, Simmons Records.

Tracks include: "King of the Mountain," "Any Way You Slice It," "Who Wants to Be Lonely," "Trial By Fire," "I'm Alive," "Love's a Deadly Weapon," "Tears Are Falling," "Secretly Cruel," "Radar for Love," and "Uh! All Night."

"Tears are Falling," the only single from the record, is easily the best song on *Asylum*. Longtime MTV devotees will remember video for the song, directed by the prolific David Mallet. It features the band clad in pastel colors, performing on a cheap looking set with a volcano in the background.

Asylum Tour: To promote their 13th studio album, KISS toured North America, playing 91 shows from November 29, 1985, to April 12, 1986. In addition to their standard catalogue of songs, KISS covered the Who's "Won't Get Fooled Again," usually as part of the encore. During the

April 8 performance, King Kobra joined KISS in performing "Lick It Up," the first time a band had ever shared the stage with KISS. The March 30 show at the Hammond Civic Center in Hammond, Indiana was protested by locals because it was Easter Sunday, and only 1,900 tickets sold.

Shows on the Asylum Tour were colorful as the giant KISS logo backing the band turned different shades, and Gene, Paul, Bruce, and Eric Carr wore splashy, glam-metal outfits. Stage props included an inflamed drum kit, a confetti storm, bombs, Gene breathing fire, and Paul smashing his guitar and performing his trapeze stunt. Opening acts: Black 'N Blue, Blue Öyster Cult, King Kobra, Kix, and W.A.S.P. Average Attendance: 6,181.

Followed by: Crazy Nights World Tour.

At Any Cost: Gene Simmons has a cameo appearance in *At Any Cost*, a made-for-TV movie that originally aired in 2000 on VH1. A rock band called Beyond Gravity struggles to get a recording contract. Eddie Mills, Glenn Quinn, Maureen Flannigan, James Franco, and Cyia Batten star in the film, which features music by Mills, the Barenaked Ladies, Eagle Eye Cherry, former Candlebox member Kevin Martin, Scottish band Deckard, and Andreas Johnson.

Athens High School Choir Original Cast Recording of The Elder: This is an audio CD of *The Elder: A New Musical*, an Athens High School musical stage production in Athens, Wisconsin. Released in 1996, it is a tribute to the concept album, *Music from "The Elder,"* and includes the following tracks: "Prologue (Odyssey)," "Ceredigon," "Today," "Only You," "Just A Boy," "Dark Light," "Mr. Blackwell," "Children," "Just Once," "The One You Run To," "The Abduction of Kyra (Carr Jam)," "Under the Rose," "Walking in Your Sleep," "The Oath," "The One You Run To" (reprise), "Martya's Prayer," "Who Hears the Listener?," "Miles Away, Worlds Apart," "A World Without Heroes," "Take Me Home," "Escape from the Island," "The Vows," and "I."

Atlanta's Best KISSers: An Atlanta Tribute To The Hottest Band In The World: Released by Richenroll Studios in July of 2009, this CD features KISS cover tunes by a variety of Atlanta-based bands: "Detroit Rock City" (No Longer Mica), "Strutter" (Blizzard Of Mullet), "All The Way" (Tuesday Jammers), "Cold Gin" (Citizen Jayne), "Nothin' to Lose" (She Said No), "100,000 Years" (Richie Torrance Project), "Beth" (Rich Grillo and Andrew Black), "Strange Ways" (Aquatic), "Parasite" (The Andrew Black Band), and "Shout It Out Loud" (RATL).

Attack of the Phantoms *see* **KISS in Attack of the Phantoms**

Aucoin, Bill: KISS's manager from 1973 to 1982, Bill Aucoin is credited with discovering KISS and helping them on their way to fame and fortune. Peter Criss has called him the "fifth KISS."

Aucoin first saw KISS at their second performance at the Hotel Diplomat, which was August 10, 1973. In *Nothin' to Lose: The Making of KISS (1972–1975)*, Gene Simmons said, "When we came off the stage after our Diplomat performance, Bill cornered me. I still had my makeup on. As soon as I saw him, he invited me over to talk to him. He wasn't a manager, he was a director and producer of a TV show called *Flipside*."

"People thought I was an idiot for wanting to manage KISS," Aucoin said. "What I liked about them in the first place was that wonderful determination. They wanted to do something different and they wanted it very badly. That kind of devotion is worth more than anything. Aside from being fantastically exciting musicians, they were super showmen."

Aucoin got KISS a record deal with Neil Bogart in September of 1973 and signed with the band as their official manager the next month. Among many other accomplishments, Aucoin came up with the idea for a band member to breathe fire, though he had Paul in mind instead of Gene. According to *KISS FAQ* by Dale Sherman, "Aucoin would push the band to be distinctive and yet united in much the same that the Beatles were—with a uniform look that also spoke of the individual personas each member displayed onstage."

Aucoin, oftentimes the public face of the band during their heyday, funded KISS's first tour with his own personal credit card, putting his neck on the line until they got successful.

In addition to KISS, Aucoin managed a number of other musical acts, including Billy Idol and Billy Squier.

In the wake of Aucoin's passing on June 28, 2010, Paul Stanley and Gene Simmons released the following statement: "Bill Aucoin, our irreplaceable original manager, mentor and dear friend has died of complications arising from his ongoing battle with prostate cancer. He was instrumental in guiding us from the beginning, and without his vision, leadership and unending dedication, we could never have scaled the heights we have reached. Bill loved life and lived it to the fullest. Words can never convey his impact on us or those close to him. Over all the years, he never missed an opportunity to be with us at our shows near his home or fly in for special concerts, including our most recent Madison Square Garden show. He had hoped to attend our London show earlier this month but his illness prevented it. He still planned to visit us upon the start of our upcoming U.S. tour. We loved him, told him and have peace that he knew it. We will grieve and celebrate all he was and did. We have lost a part of us."

Audio Dog: In 2001, Bruce Kulick released his first solo album, *Audio Dog*. It features the following tracks: "Pair of Dice," "Strange to Me," "Change Is Coming," "Need Me," "I Don't Mind," "Monster Island," "Please Don't Wait," "Liar," "I Can't Take," "Dogs of Morrison," and "Skydome."

According to allmusic.com's Greg Prato, the former KISS guitarist "presents an album that—rather expectedly—doesn't stray far from the renowned KISS sound. Although his songwriting contributions while a member of KISS were never as pronounced as those by founding members Paul Stanley and Gene Simmons, he has certainly absorbed their songwriting styles, as most of the tracks on *Audio Dog* would've sounded right at home on a late '80s or early '90s KISS release."

Avantasia: The German rock band Avantasia formed in 1999. Eric Singer played on five of their albums: *Lost in Space Part I* (2007 EP), *Lost in Space Part II* (2007 EP), *The Scarecrow* (2008), *The Wicked Symphony* (2010), and *Angel of Babylon* (2010).

Babies Go KISS: The promo for this CD, which was released by RGS Music in Argentina October 27, 2009, reads as follows: "Rock On, Get Down and Chill Out with Babies Go! 'Babies Go' titles are instrumental melodies of your favorite artists. Our music maintains the tune of each song while updating the tone with a full orchestra of baby-friendly instruments so that you still recognize your favorites while allowing your babies to listen and enjoy too."

Tracks include: "Hard Luck Woman," "Lick It Up," "I Was Made for Lovin' You," "Forever," "Beth," "Rock and Roll All Nite," "New York Groove," "Detroit Rock City," "Christine Sixteen," "C'mon and Love Me," "Strutter," "Crazy Crazy Nights," "Hotter Than Hell," and "Shout It Out Loud."

***Baby Driver* (album):** Released April 18, 2013, by Blow Till Midnight Records, *Baby Driver* is a soft tribute to KISS by Berlin folk artist Marceese. The CD includes the following tracks: "Strutter," "Tomorrow," "Dony You Let Me Down," "Baby Driver," "Sure Know Something," "Hooked On Rock 'n' Roll," "Room Service," "What's On Your Mind," "Mr. Make Believe," "Baby Driver" (reprise), and "Cold Gin."

"Baby Driver" (song): Written by Peter Criss and Stan Penridge while they were in the band Lips, "Baby Driver" has throwaway lyrics, but a steady, hard-driving beat. The fifth track on *Rock and Roll Over*, it's a solid rock tune that Criss sings with enthusiasm. "Baby Driver" seems to be about a female driving a long distance, but, knowing KISS, it's probably code speak for a sexual dalliance. Criss has expressed dissatisfaction with the recording of the song, saying the original version had more soul and a riff done with voices (as opposed to guitars).

Bachman–Turner Overdrive: Formed in Canada in 1973, BTO, famous for such classic rock radio staples as "You Ain't Seen Nothing Yet" and "Takin' Care of Business," opened for KISS during the Alive! Tour.

"Back to the Stone Age": The whole band—Paul, Gene, Tommy, and Eric Singer—gets writing credits on "Back to the Stone Age," the fourth track on *Monster*. The Demon, sounding smooth (some fans will miss his more gruff approach), sings about returning to a simpler time since the world is driving him insane. Hard-driving drums and guitars complement the vocals.

"Bad, Bad Lovin'": Written and sung by Gene Simmons in 1976, "Bad, Bad Lovin'" is a previously unreleased demo that was included as track 11 on disc two of *The Box Set*. Originally, Simmons tinkered with the song until it became "Calling Dr. Love," the third track on *Rock and Roll Over*.

Bad Boys of KISS Tour: In June of 1995, Ace Frehley and Peter Criss hit the road with some of their solo band members on the Bad Boys of KISS Tour. In the November 4, 1995, edition of *The Morning Call*, Stephen Parish reviewed their Allentown, Pennsylvania, show: "Let's face it—it was no accident 'The Bad Boys' became the more demure half of KISS. Average composers and lyricists (although Criss deserves kudos for the timeless 'Beth') and mediocre vocalists (boy, can Ace Frehley play guitar!), 'The Bad Boys' quietly kept the pace with their respective instrumentation as KISS rocketed to mega-superstardom.... No one left disappointed; they saw (part of) where it all began."

Balandas, Eddie: Early KISS crew member Eddie Balandas is best known for getting *Alive II* off with a bang by shouting, "You wanted the best, and you got the best, the hottest band in the world, KISS!"

After Balandas died from congestive heart failure in October of 2010, Ace Frehley released the following statement: "I was very saddened to hear of the passing of my old bodyguard and dear friend, Eddie Balandas.... We had recently spent some time together in Indianapolis, Indiana this past August, and enjoyed reminiscing about our funny experiences together on tour with KISS in the '70s ... he had a heart of gold and was one of a kind!"

Badlands: In 1998, Ray Gillen formed Badlands and asked Eric Singer to be the drummer. Singer, who played on the band's self-titled debut album, left in 1989, when he joined Paul Stanley on the Starchild's solo tour. Disbanding in 1993, Badlands also featured former Ozzy Osbourne guitarist Jake E. Lee.

Ballard, Russ: Among KISS fans, Russ Ballard is best known as the writer of "New York Groove," which Ace Frehley covered masterfully on his 1978 solo album. "God Gave Rock 'N' Roll to You II" from *Revenge* is a cover of Ballard's "God Gave Rock and Roll to You." For his 1982 solo album, *Let Me Rock You*, Peter Criss recorded Ballard's "Let Me Rock You" and "Some Kinda Hurricane." Frehley covered Ballard's "Into the Night" on his 1987 album, *Frehley's Comet*.

***Bananas*:** KISS is on the cover of *Bananas* #18, the children's magazine. The issue, released in 1978, features an article about the band with color pictures from the 1977–78 tour. The 1977 *Bananas* yearbook, which has John Travolta and Farrah Fawcett on the cover, also has a KISS article. In issue #44 (1980), there's a one-page piece about Peter Criss leaving the band, accompanied by a photo of the Catman unmasked.

Issue #18 of *Bananas* magazine, which was similar to the more popular *Dynamite* magazine, featured KISS on the cover.

"Bang Bang You": Written by Paul Stanley and frequent collaborator Desmond Child, "Bang Bang You" is the third track on *Crazy Nights*. With the count-from-one-to-eight lyrics and obvious chorus, it's clear they were trying to write a hit, but the song was never released as a single. Despite a couple of flourishes by lead guitarist Bruce Kulick, "Bang Bang You" is a piece of pop fluff. It was probably influenced by the Sonny Bono-written Cher song, "Bang Bang (My Baby Shot Me Down)," which Child has said he likes.

Batman: Created by writer Bob Kane and artist Bill Finger, Batman first appeared in 1939 in *Detective Comics* #27. Gene Simmons, an avowed comic book fan, has often cited Batman as an inspiration for his makeup design.

Baxter, Jeff: Jeff "Skunk" Baxter played guitar on Gene Simmons' "Burning Up with Fever," "See You Tonite," "Tunnel of Love," and "Mr. Make Believe."

Beacon Theatre: When KISS did a show in March of 1975 at the Beacon Theatre in New York

City, the crowd began chanting "KISS! KISS! KISS!" before the band took the stage. It was at that moment that Peter Criss realized that KISS had made it as a popular act.

The Beatles: KISS has frequently cited the Fab Four as a huge influence. Ace, Gene, and Paul have each said they saw the band's 1964 breakout performance on *The Ed Sullivan Show*. On more than one occasion, Gene has called KISS "the heavy metal Beatles."

Like the Beatles, the original lineup of KISS was one of the few musical groups in which every member was readily identifiable by the general public and had a huge fan following. Also like the Beatles, KISS is heavily merchandised, and each member of KISS has a distinct look while at the same time fitting in with the band's overall image.

Several songs from Gene's 1978 solo record exhibit Beatles influence, most obviously "Mr. Make Believe." The Demon tried to get one or more Beatles to appear on the album, but he had to settle for Mitch Weissman and Joe Pecorino of the *Beatlemania* Broadway musical instead. Weissman performed on *Animalize* as well, playing bass and guitar on three songs.

Of course, the Beatles influenced countless other bands and the society at large. In *KISS*, the classic book by Robert Duncan, the author said the Beatles defined the generation: "When they grew their hair, we grew our hair. When they dropped acid, we dropped acid. When they knocked organized religion, we knocked it too. And, ultimately, when they broke up [in 1970], so did our generation fragmenting individual pursuits—some cutting their hair, some leaving it long, some continuing the drug world, some retreating, some taking up with jazz, some with folk, some with classical music, some staying with rock."

Beatles Meets KISS: Fronted by a cover that pays homage to *Abbey Road*, *Beatles Meets KISS* is a CD featuring KISS tunes with arrangements done in the style of the Beatles, with the vocal melodies staying similar to the original songs. Tracks include: "Love Gun," "Lick It Up," "Detroit Rock City," "Rock and Roll All Nite," "Hard Luck Woman," "Beth," "I Was Made for Lovin' You," "Shout It Out Loud," "Black Diamond," "Strutter," and "Deuce." Released in Japan on November 11, 2012, by Octave/Ultra-Vibe Inc. Other albums in the series include *Beatles Meets Queen* and *Beatles Meets Michael* [Jackson].

Beauvoir, Jean: Singer, guitarist, producer, and entertainment executive Jean Beauvoir is perhaps best known for sporting a blond Mohawk as bassist for the Plasmatics (circa 1980–81). During KISS' non-makeup era, he contributed bass and background vocals for and co-wrote various songs on *Animalize* and *Asylum*.

In an interview published on kissmonster.com, Beauvoir spoke about meeting Paul Stanley for the first time: "Probably around 1983, Paul and I met in a club … called Heartbreak…. And he actually came over to me—he didn't have any makeup on and I didn't recognize him. And he said, 'Hey, you're Jean Beauvoir and you play in the Plasmatics. I'm Paul Stanley from KISS.' I said, 'Woah, okay' [laughs]. And we started talking and hanging out a little bit…. We hung out probably for a year before we wrote anything. Then one day, we were just at his house and he had his little four-track on the table and we pulled out a guitar and we said, 'Let's try something.' And that's where it started."

Behind the Player: Released January 19, 2010, *Behind the Player* is a direct-to-DVD documentary in which Ace Frehley discusses his life's work as a guitarist. In addition, he gives guitar lessons on "Cold Gin" and "Shock Me." The DVD also includes rare photos, rare live footage, and info on Ace's guitar, gear, technique, and style. Rounding out the release is an all-star jam session featuring Ace playing with George Lynch, John 5, Matt Sorum, Chris Wyse, and Tommy Clufetos. Directed by Leon Melas.

Berg, Shelly: Shelly Berg played acoustic piano on "I Finally Found My Way" and "Journey of 1,000 Years" from *Psycho Circus*. The jazz pianist also worked with such performers as Gloria Estefan, Bobby McFerrin, Aretha Franklin, Queen Latifa, Ricky Martin, and Dionne Warwick.

Best of KISS 40: Released February 10, 2015, *Best of KISS 40* is a Japanese compilation CD. Tracks include: "Samurai Son," "Rock and Roll All Nite," "Shout It Out Loud," "Beth," "Hard Luck Woman," "Detroit Rock City," "Calling Dr. Love," "Christine Sixteen," "Love Gun," "I Was Made for Lovin' You," "Shandi," "I'm a Legend Tonight," "Lick It Up," "Heaven's On Fire," "Tears are Falling," "Crazy Crazy Nights," "God Gave Rock 'N' Roll to You II," "Psycho Circus," "Modern Day Delilah," and "Hell or Hallelujah." The release also includes an exclusive DVD with three live performances:

"Psycho Circus," "Shout It Out Loud," and "Hell or Hallelujah."

Best of Solo Albums: Many fans have said that if you took a few songs off each of Ace, Paul, Peter, and Gene's 1978 solo albums and made one record, you would have one heck of a KISS LP. For foreign markets, where KISS was still very popular as the 1970s gave way to the '80s, *Best of Solo Albums*, released between 1979 and 1981 by Casablanca, is basically that.

Tracks on the original German version, which frequently appeared in many American record stores as an import during the early 1980s, include: "New York Groove," "Living in Sin," "See You Tonite," "Rip It Out," "Fractured Mirror," "Don't You Let Me Down," "Radioactive," "Tonight You Belong to Me," "Take Me Away (Together As One)," "Rock Me, Baby," "I Can't Stop the Rain," and "Hold Me, Touch Me."

Tracks on the European release include: "New York Groove," "Rip It Out," "Speedin' Back to My Baby," "You Matter To Me," "Tossin' and Turnin'," "Hooked on Rock 'n' Roll," "Radioactive," "Mr. Make Believe," "See You in Your Dreams," "Tonight You Belong to Me," "Move On," and "Hold Me, Touch Me."

Tracks on the Australian edition include: "Hold Me, Touch Me," "Tonight You Belong to Me," "Move On," "Don't You Let Me Down," "Hooked on Rock 'n' Roll," "I Can't Stop the Rain," "New York Groove," "Speedin' Back to My Baby," "Rip It Out," "Radioactive," "Mr. Make Believe," and "Living in Sin."

Tracks on the Argentine version include: "Wouldn't You Like to Know Me," "It's Alright," "Hold Me, Touch Me," "You Matter to Me," "That's the Kind of Sugar Papa Likes," "I Can't Stop the Rain," "New York Groove," "Rip It Out," "What's on Your Mind?," "See You Tonite," "See You in Your Dreams," and "Radioactive."

Tracks on the African release include: "New York Groove," "See You in Your Dreams," "Tonight You Belong to Me," "You Matter to Me," "Rip It Out," "Hooked on Rock 'n' Roll," "Radioactive," "Move On," "Hold Me, Touch Me," "Mr. Make Believe," "Tossin' and Turnin'," and "Speedin' Back to My Baby."

"Beth": One of the most important songs KISS ever recorded, "Beth" is the eighth track on *Destroyer* and the B-side of the "Detroit Rock City" single. Written by Peter Criss, Stan Penridge, and Bob Ezrin, the song became a breakout (not to mention surprise) hit when DJs began flipping "Detroit Rock City" over and playing "Beth," a song that many kids used to try and convince their parents that KISS weren't actually "Knights in Satan's Service."

Regarded by some as the world's first power ballad (It's not—Black Sabbath's "Changes" was released in 1972, Alice Cooper's "Only Women Bleed" hit stores in 1975), "Beth" was subsequently released as a single and became KISS' first and highest ranking top-10 hit in the U.S., reaching #7 on the *Billboard* charts ("Forever" reached #8). The song, which uses orchestration (by the New York Philharmonic) and Criss's raspy voice to nice effect, also helped move copies of *Destroyer*, which had until that point been a retail disappointment. During the production of the song, it was originally titled "Beck," but Gene Simmons insisted on a name change because he felt that people would equate it with popular English guitarist Jeff Beck.

In *Rolling Stone* #279 (Nov., 1978), Criss revealed that his bandmates had reservations about "Beth." "KISS is a strange group, a lot of voting," he said. "They didn't want to do the thing, the kids aren't going to accept it, they said. Gene was against it because he said it didn't fit the concept. But our public is gonna dig it. KISS never made good albums, our shows always outsold our albums, but it's time that changed."

In *KISS: Behind the Mask—The Official Authorized Biography*, Simmons said he loved the song, but Bill Aucoin said, "Paul and Gene wanted to take 'Beth' off the album. I said, 'Look, I think it's a hit. I know it's not necessarily a KISS song but it does have a rock 'n' roll lyric to it. It's gonna stay on the album.'"

"Betrayed": Gene Simmons portrays the tough guy in KISS, and in "Betrayed," the second track on *Hot in the Shade*, he shows his mettle, and his metal (as in heavy metal). Written by Simmons, who based the song on a guy he read about who was always down on his luck, and Tommy Thayer, who worked with Simmons on the riffs, "Betrayed" has the Demon identifying with an unnamed everyman and screaming about being broke, alone, far from home, and, of course, betrayed. Eric Carr pounding the skins provides a formidable backdrop. Thayer subs for Bruce Kulick on lead guitar.

Biawitz, Joyce *see* **Joyce Bogart**

Billboard: Founded in Cincinnati on November 1, 1894, by William H. Donaldson and James Hennegan, *Billboard*, originally called *Billboard Advertising*, was a monthly magazine for billposters (hence the name), sign-printers, poster-printers, and the like. It went through a number of incarnations over the years, covering outdoor amusements, movies, radio, television, and the like, but began focusing almost exclusively on music in 1961 with the name change to *Billboard Music Week*, which was shortened to *Billboard* in 1963.

A respected trade publication, *Billboard* maintains a number of record charts tracking the most popular albums and songs in a variety of categories. The two charts that garner the most attention are the *Billboard* Hot 100 and the *Billboard* 200, which rank the top songs and albums (respectively) regardless of genre. KISS's highest charting song of all time in the U.S. was "Beth," reaching #7, followed by "Forever" at #8 and "I Was Made for Lovin' You" at #11. Regarding albums, *Sonic Boom* reached #2 while *Psycho Circus* and *Monster* peaked at #3.

In *KISS: Behind the Mask—The Official Authorized Biography*, Larry Harris admitted that he manipulated the system. "With my association with *Billboard*, I was able to get five KISS albums on the charts at one time," he said. This was around '77, '78. I walked in and gave them inflated sales figures, which they could have easily checked.... I helped manipulate the charts for all of our acts at Casablanca … if you go top one hundred in *Billboard* with your product, the rack jobbers, the people who sell records in Wal-Mart and Kmart, those huge mass merchandisers, will take your record."

BK3: On February 2, 2010, Bruce Kulick released his third solo album, *BK3*. Tracks include: "Fate," "Ain't Gonna Die" (written by Kulick, Jeremy Rubolino, and Gene Simmons), "No Friend of Mine," "Hand of the King" (written by Kulick, Rubolino, and Nick Simmons), "I'll Survive," "Dirty Girl," "Final Mile," "I'm the Animal," "And I Know," "Between the Lines," and "Life."

"Black Diamond": "Black Diamond," the 10th and final track on *KISS*, was written and introduced (vocally) by Paul Stanley and features lead vocals by Peter Criss, whose "streetwise nuances" are perfectly suited for the "tale of hard day-to-day struggle. And there is a surprise ending: a series of Who-inspired power chords slowing to a breathtaking, head-spinning climax; an emphatic conclusion to a classic first album" (*KISS: Hotter Than Hell*). During the early days of the band, KISS closed out many shows with "Black Diamond," which Stanley has said is about New York. In later years, subsequent KISS drummers Eric Carr and Eric Singer sang the song live.

Black Diamond: The Unauthorized Biography of KISS: Published in 1997 by Collector's Guide Publishing, this book was written by Dale Sherman. According to one Amazon reviewer, it has "countless instances of run-on sentences, dangling particles, awkward syntax and sentence structure, and grammatical errors," but it's nevertheless "an engaging biography chock-full of fascinating, little-known trivia, which succeeds in answering many questions fans such as myself may have had about the band." In *The Rock Report*, Ken Sharp called it "remarkable … the bible for the KISS army."

Black Diamond: The Unauthorized Biography of KISS—10th Anniversary Edition: An updating of Dale Sherman's *Black Diamond: The Unauthorized Biography of KISS*, this book was published in 2009 by Collector's Guide Publishing. The official publisher description of the book is as follows: "Updated to include new information about the band from the last 10 years, this candid biography tells the story of KISS from its formation in New York City in the early 1970s to today. Examining the individual careers of each band member and telling the story of the band as a whole, the book chronicles the struggle to make it, their missteps along the route to stardom, their battle to stay on top, and the problems that led to changes in the lineup over the years. Finally, the circumstances leading to KISS' 1996 reunion—with makeup—are discussed, and the state of the band today is revealed."

Black Diamond 2: An Illustrated Collector's Guide to KISS: This guide to KISS memorabilia, written by Dale Sherman, was published in 1997 by Collector's Guide Publishing. It features black-and-white photos and lots of history, but, as one Amazon reviewer states, it has "a disturbing amount of errors in facts, not to mention bad editing and spell checking."

Black 'n Blue: Tommy Thayer formed the hard rock/heavy metal band Black 'n Blue in 1981 with singer and high-school classmate/friend

Jaime St. James. They released such albums as *Black 'n Blue* (1984) and *Without Love* (1985). Gene Simmons produced two of their albums: *Nasty Nasty* (1986) and *In Heat* (1988), both of which feature writing credits for Simmons and Thayer. In October of 2010, when Black 'n Blue was inducted into the Oregon Music Hall of Fame in Portland, Thayer appeared with the other members of the band to accept the award.

Black Oak Arkansas: Late in 1974, KISS opened a number of shows for southern rock band Black Oak Arkansas, which formed in 1963.

Black Sabbath: When Bill Ward left Black Sabbath in 1985 after the reunion at the Live Aid benefit concert, Eric Singer took his place, playing drums on *Seventh Star* (1986) and *The Eternal Idol* (1987). Various KISS members have called Black Sabbath, which formed in Birmingham, England in 1968, an influence.

Blackjack: Active from 1979 to 1980, hard rock act Blackjack, featuring Bruce Kulick on guitar and Michael Bolton on lead vocals, recorded two albums: *Blackjack* (1979) and *Worlds Apart* (1980). Other band members included Jimmy Haslip (bass, backing vocals) and Sandy Gennaro (drums, percussion). Jay Z sampled a Blackjack song called "Stay," co-written by Kulick and Bolton, for the song "A Dream," which is on his #1 album, *The Blueprint 2: The Gift & the Curse*.

Bleecker Street Loft Party: On June 1, 1973, KISS opened for Wayne County and the Brats at a party on 54 Bleecker Street. It was their first gig in New York City.

Blood Spitting: Gene Simmons is known for spitting fake blood onstage. In *KISS: Behind the Mask—The Official Authorized Biography*, he spoke about the inspiration for this theatrical stunt: "I remember seeing Christopher Lee as Dracula in one of the Hammer films, *Blood of Dracula* or *Horror of Dracula*. I'll never forget when he bit into something and his mouth was covered with blood. I thought, that's cool, I should do that onstage. Why? Why do little boys stick frogs up girls' skirts? Because they squeal and that's fun."

Bloom County: In Berkley Breathed's comic strip *Bloom County*, which ran from 1980 to 1989, and was revived in 2015, Opus the penguin sometimes portrays a Gene Simmons parody character in a band called Deathtongue. One strip has the following caption: "The short and sexy boss tuba rocker of Deathtongue wants all his fans to know that despite the lipstick, hair, eye makeup, and panty hose, he isn't a sissy."

In 1985, Breathed drew a panel that directly parodies Simmons and Apple computers. It advises parents to purchase a "Banana Junior 6000" for their children because "Gene Simmons never had a computer when he was a kid." If your child doesn't have a computer, he or she will "very probably grow up to be a bass player in a heavy-metal rock band who wears women's fishnet pantyhose and sticks his tongue down to his kneecaps."

Blue Öyster Cult: Formed in 1967 (when they were known as Soft White Underbelly—the name change came in 1971), Blue Öyster Cult was the headlining act at the New Year's Eve show at the Academy of Music in 1973, which is widely viewed as KISS's first big concert. In 1975, the tables were turned and BÖC started opening for KISS.

In an interview published on www.antimusic.com, former BÖC bassist Joe Bouchard spoke about opening for KISS a couple of years after

Christopher Lee's portrayal of Count Dracula in the Hammer films influenced Gene Simmons to spit blood onstage.

headlining over them: "[KISS] opened for Nazareth in the middle and BÖC was the headliner. And then they had their big breakthrough with KISS *Alive!*, and after that they became headliners and we would have to open shows for them. And when we were nice to them, they completely turned it around and weren't nice to us. And that got to be a drag because I thought we were better and shouldn't be opening for them, but that's business and those things happen."

Bodine, Bill: Bill Bodine played bass on several tracks on Gene Simmons' 1978 KISS solo album. Bodine also worked with such acts as Cher, Van Morrison, Joan Armatrading, Leo Sayer, Olivia Newton-John, Melissa Manchester, and Laura Branigan.

Bogart, Joyce: Joyce Biawitz, now Joyce Bogart-Trabulus, co-managed KISS from 1973 to 1975 with Bill Aucoin. In 1976, Biawitz, who handled many of the marketing duties for KISS, married Neil Bogart. In the May 26, 1980, issue of *People*, Joyce Bogart claimed that she and Aucoin were instrumental in forming what became the KISS juggernaut: "We created the look, the logo, the props and even went to a magic shop to learn the gimmicks."

Along with Carole Daly, Joyce Bogart-Trabulus is co-founder of the Bogart Pediatric Cancer Research Program, where today she is a member of the Board of Trustees.

Bogart, Neil: One of the most instrumental figures in the history of KISS, Neil Bogart founded Casablanca Records and signed KISS to its first record contract in 1973. In addition, the label signed such acts as Donna Summer, the Village People, Cher, and Parliament (featuring George Clinton).

During the 1960s, Bogart, as Neil Scott, was a singer. "I recorded my first record, 'Bobby,' on the Portrait label," Bogart said in *Nothin' to Lose: The Making of KISS (1972–1975)*. "The song was about a girl dying in the hospital. It sold something like 200,000 copies and went top 40 in *Cashbox* and *Billboard*. After that, I released about five bombs in a row and my career went immediately downward. I really wanted to be an entertainer at the time but realized that in order to make a living, I'd have to get into the other end of the business."

Prior to starting Casablanca Records, Bogart was Cameo-Parkway Records' head of A&R (arts and repertoire), and then an executive at Buddah Records, which was home to such bubblegum acts as the Lemon Pipers, the 1910 Fruitgum Company, and the Ohio Express. In a 1968 *Time* magazine article called "Tunes for Teeny-Weenies," Bogart was dubbed "The bubblegum king of America."

In *Nothin' to Lose*, former KISS manager Bill Aucoin said, "Warner Brothers gave Neil $750,000 to start his own label. They were the money and distributor behind Casablanca. They saw Neil as the up-and-coming wonder kid of the recording industry."

Despite backing by Warner, "Neil never had the big money to sign a band like the Stones," said Buck Reingold, who was Vice President of National Promotion for Casablanca. "He had to take things from scratch and make them happen because he didn't have the bucks that Columbia, Atlantic, or RCA had to give big advances." As such, KISS was a good fit.

Bogart first saw KISS perform in September of 1973 at a private showcase at Henry LeTang School of Dance on 54th street in Manhattan. It was arranged by Aucoin, who had recently sent Bogart a demo tape of the band. "When I first saw them, their music hit me like a bolt of lightning," Bogart said. "Their sound, their image was something I had waited seven years to find. Here was a group whose music and visuals came together in perfect harmony."

After the show, Bogart told KISS he wanted them to be the first act signed to Casablanca Records. In *Nothin' to Lose*, he said, "I can honestly say that KISS is the first band I've devoted myself 100 percent to … they're probably one of the best rock and roll bands I've ever heard in my life…. When we started with KISS, people thought we were crazy."

According to Bogart's wife, Joyce, Neil was involved in every aspect of KISS's career, from marketing to photography to album cover art to advancing the band money to help get them off the ground.

In *Nothin' to Lose*, KISS expressed their appreciation for Bogart:

"Neil was really one of KISS's true early believers to the extent of whatever it cost, he reached, he went for it."—Gene Simmons

"Neil was very into salesmanship. When he believed in something, he sold it."—Paul Stanley

"I thought he was a genius. Neil wasn't afraid to take chances. He rolled the dice with us when a lot of other companies didn't want to touch us."—Ace Frehley

"I loved him. I wish he was still here. There was nobody like him. He was the last breed of those kinds of men. He was a visionary who thought outside of the box."—Peter Criss

In 1980, after PolyGram acquired Casablanca Records, Bogart founded Boardwalk Records, which signed Joan Jett. Shortly thereafter, Bogart died of cancer and lymphoma at the age of 39. *Creatures of the Night* is dedicated to Bogart, as is Donna Summer's 1982 self-titled album.

Bogart was born February 3, 1943, in New York City. He died May 8, 1982. Incredibly, KISS wasn't mentioned in his Associated Press obituary, which ran in such newspapers as *The New York Times*.

Bolton, Michael: During the height of his popularity, Michael Bolton, who is famous for his dramatic cover of "When a Man Loves a Woman," wrote "Forever" with Paul Stanley. His other KISS connection is by way of Bruce Kulick—the two were bandmates in Blackjack, and Kulick played on several Michael Bolton solo albums.

"Boomerang": One of the lesser songs in the KISS oeuvre (Paul Stanley in particular can't stand it), "Boomerang" is a fast, hard-driving number, but it lacks melody. It was written by Gene Simmons, who sings the song, and Bruce Kulick, who tears it up on lead guitar. Eric Carr's drums are vicious as well. The 15th and final track on *Hot in the Shade*, "Boomerang" ends the album with a noisy, up-tempo flourish, telling of a girl who keeps coming back like a boomerang.

Boutwell, Ron: Former head of KISS merchandising Ron Boutwell was instrumental in helping establish the KISS Army, along with greenlighting such merchandise as the Donruss bubblegum cards and the Bally pinball machine.

Bowen, Pamela: Paul Stanley married his first wife, actress Pamel Bowen, on July 26, 1992. They had one son together, Evan Shane Stanley, who was born June 6, 1994. They divorced in 2001, citing irreconcilable differences. A gorgeous blonde, Bowen appeared in the TV series *Loving* (1983), and in such films as *The Player* (1992) and *Shoot the Moon* (2012).

Bowie, David: With his androgynous look and flashy on-stage alter-ego, Ziggy Stardust, glam rocker David Bowie was a big influence on KISS. Bowie is best-known for such songs as "Space Oddity" and "Let's Dance," the latter of which was an MTV staple. Bowie died January 10, 2016.

***The Box Set*:** A five-disc collection of remastered demos, hits, outtakes, live recordings, and other songs, *The Box Set* was released November 20, 2001. It was packaged with a 120-page color booklet that features photos, essays, a bio by Jeff Kitts, and track-by-track commentary by the original lineup, mostly from Gene Simmons and Paul Stanley (though Ace Frehley and Peter Criss are included). The set features 94 songs and was released in three different versions: a standard edition; a replica guitar case rendition; and a pricey Premium Gold Edition, which features an official RIAA certified KISS *Alive!* gold record award fitted in a full size 46" × 16" × 4" custom guitar case, a special reissue *Alive!* hand-written liner-notes from the band individually printed in gold ink on parchment paper, and a gold hardcover edition of the book.

Disc 1 includes: "Strutter" (demo); "Deuce" (demo); "Keep Me Waiting" (Wicked Lester); "She" (Wicked Lester); "Love Her All I Can" (Wicked Lester); "Let Me Know" (demo); "100,000 Years" (demo); "Stop, Look to Listen" (Paul Stanley demo); "Leeta" (Gene Simmons demo); "Let Me Go, Rock 'n' Roll" (demo); "Acrobat" (live); "Firehouse" (demo); "Nothin' to Lose"; "Black Diamond"; "Hotter Than Hell"; "Strange Ways"; "Parasite"; "Goin' Blind"; "Anything for My Baby"; "Ladies in Waiting"; and "Rock and Roll All Nite."

Disc 2 includes: "C'mon and Love Me" (from *Alive!*); "Rock Bottom" (from *Alive!*); "Cold Gin" (from *Alive!*); "Watchin' You" (from *Alive!*); "Doncha Hesitate" (demo); "Mad Dog" (demo); "God of Thunder" (demo); "Great Expectations"; "Beth"; "Do You Love Me?"; "Bad, Bad Lovin'" (demo); "Calling Dr. Love"; "Mr. Speed" (demo); "Christine Sixteen"; "Hard Luck Woman"; "Shock Me"; "I Stole Your Love"; "I Want You" (sound check); "Love Gun" (demo); and "Love Is Blind" (demo).

Disc 3 includes: "Detroit Rock City" (edit); "King of the Night Time World" (from *Alive II*); "Larger Than Life" (from *Alive II*); "Rocket Ride" (from *Alive II*); "Tonight You Belong to Me"; "New York Groove"; "Radioactive" (demo); "Don't You Let Me Down"; "I Was Made for Lovin' You"; "Sure Know Something"; "Shandi"; "You're All That I Want, You're All That I Need" (demo);

"Talk to Me" (recorded live on Nov. 22, 1980, at Sydney's Parreta Stadium); "A World Without Heroes"; "The Oath"; "Nowhere to Run"; "Creatures of the Night"; "War Machine"; and "I Love It Loud."

Disc 4 includes: "Lick It Up"; "All Hell's Breakin' Loose"; "Heaven's on Fire"; "Get All You Can Take"; "Thrills in the Night"; "Tears Are Falling"; "Uh! All Night"; "Time Traveller" (demo); "Hell or High Water"; "Crazy Crazy Nights"; "Reason to Live"; "Let's Put the X in Sex"; "Hide Your Heart" (from *Hot in the Shade*); "Ain't That Peculiar" (demo); "Silver Spoon"; and "Forever" (single remix).

Disc 5 includes: "God Gave Rock 'n' Roll to You II"; "Unholy" (edit); "Domino" (demo); "Every Time I Look at You"; "Comin' Home" (from *MTV Unplugged*); "Got to Choose" (edit, from *MTV Unplugged*); "I Still Love You" (from *MTV Unplugged*); "Nothin' to Lose" (from *MTV Unplugged*); "Childhood's End" (with coda); "I Will Be There"; "Psycho Circus" (edit)"; "Into the Void"; "Within" (edit); "I Pledge Allegiance to the State of Rock & Roll"; "Nothing Can Keep Me from You" (from *Detroit Rock City: Music from the Motion Picture* soundtrack); "It's My Life"; "Shout It Out Loud" (from *Greatest KISS*); and "Rock and Roll All Nite" (from *Alive: The Millennium Concert*).

The Box Set reached #128 on the *Billboard* 200 and was certified gold by the RIAA on Dec. 18, 2001.

"Boyz Are Gonna Rock": The first track on the Vinnie Vincent Invasion's 1986 self-titled album, "Boyz Are Gonna Rock" was released as a single and spawned an infamously ridiculous music video, as described by Ernest Hilbert on ryeberg.com: "For teenaged boys/boyz stewed to their eyeballs with boiling loads of testosterone, Vinnie's screeching staccato performance was breathtaking. He was wild, literally; he looks feral … he's completely out of control.… He wields his guitar like a flamethrower. He spurts out thousands of notes, like burning sparks, sometimes hammering the strings with a microphone while on his knees.… He jabs his guitar into the camera. He seems to do everything with the instrument but play it."

Robert Fleischman sang "Boyz Are Gonna Rock," but the video shows Mark Slaughter, who replaced Fleischman in the band, lipsynching over Fleischman's vocal track.

The Brats: Formed by Rick Rivets, the Brats were a New York Dolls–influenced band that also consisted of Sparky Donovan, Keith West, and Andy Doback. On June 1, 1973, KISS opened for the Brats at the Bleecker Street Loft Party in New York. Wayne County also played the show. On July 13, 1973, the Brats headlined a concert at the Hotel Diplomat in New York City, where the Planets opened and KISS played between the two acts. KISS produced the show—it cost the band $650 to rent the Crystal Room at the Diplomat.

"Breakout": "Breakout" was composed by Ace Frehley and Eric Carr during the *Music from "The Elder"* era. It wasn't used on the album, but was later included on *Revenge* as a tribute to Eric Carr entitled "Carr Jam 1981." For Frehley's 1987 solo record, *Frehley's Comet*, Space Ace featured "Breakout" as the second song on the album, with lyrics added by Richie Scarlet. A demo of the song was recorded with Scarlet on vocals, and with Scarlet and Frehley both playing lead guitar, but the album track features Tod Howarth singing lead and Frehley playing the guitar solo parts by himself. When Frehley performs "Breakout" live, he dedicates it to Carr.

Breathing Fire: At the behest of manager Bill Aucoin, KISS worked the circus feat of fire breathing into their shows. Aucoin originally had Paul Stanley in mind, but Gene Simmons was the one who took up the torch (so to speak). Aucoin had asked the band who *didn't* want to breathe fire, and Simmons, misunderstanding the question, failed to raise his hand.

Brodsky, Joel: In addition to shooting album covers for such bands as the Doors, the Stooges, and Van Morrison, Joel Brodsky took the photo for the cover to KISS's self-titled debut album.

Brooklyn Boys Choir: The Brooklyn Boys Choir sung the choral part of "Great Expectations."

Brooks, Garth: For the album *Kiss My Ass: Classic KISS Regrooved*, country music legend Garth Brooks did a rousing cover of "Hard Luck Woman." During a 1994 appearance on *The Tonight Show*, Brooks, an avowed KISS fan, performed the song with the band. Brooks, who began his career in 1984, covered another rock classic, Billy Joel's "Shameless."

Bruce, Jack: In 1972, Gene Simmons bought an SVT bass cabinet that once belonged to Jack Bruce, the bassist for Cream. In *Nothin' to Lose: The Making of KISS (1972–1975)*, Simmons said, "For me it was a kind of connection with greatness and that there was actually a road to Mount Olympus, it wasn't just in the clouds." Bruce's name was stenciled on the cabinet.

Bruce Kulick & Bob Kulick: KISS Forever: A DVD that lets you learn "3 Decades of KISS Classics," *Bruce Kulick & Bob Kulick: KISS Forever* features instruction for playing the following songs: "All American Man," "Unholy," "Tonight You Belong to Me," "Crazy Crazy Nights," "Nowhere to Run," "Domino," "Larger Than Life," "Jungle," "Goodbye," and "Forever."

Budokan Hall: Officially called Nippon Budokan, Budokan Hall, which opened in Tokyo, Japan in 1964, is used primarily for martial arts. However, it's also a famous concert venue, hosting numerous bands that have recorded landmark live performances there, including Cheap Trick (*Cheap Trick at Budokan*), Bob Dylan (*Bob Dylan at Budokan*), and Eric Clapton (*Just One Night*). KISS has played the Budokan on a number of occasions, including a series of five sold-out shows during the Alive II Tour.

Buffet, Jimmy: In "Mañana," which is the eighth track on Jimmy Buffet's 1978 album, *Son of a Son of a Sailor*, the singer/songwriter best known for "Margaritaville" says, "Don't try to describe a KISS concert if you've never seen it."

Bumping Into Geniuses: My Life Inside the Rock and Roll Business: Written by Danny Goldberg, who did public relations for KISS during the late 1970s and was hired as a management-consultant in 1983, this book devotes several pages to the band. A former president of Atlantic Records and Mercury Records, Goldberg has a great deal of admiration for KISS, as he wrote in the book: "I soon developed a real respect for their two-dimensional but genuinely well-crafted version of rock and roll and was charmed by both the warmth and diabolical cleverness of Gene Simmons."

The book also reveals that when Goldberg became president of Mercury records, one of his first jobs was to "talk MTV into allowing us to release the *KISS Unplugged* as an album. Although I succeeded, it was obvious to me that MTV viewed this as a 'favor' and that the band had lost all relevance to the people who actually ran the network. So I prevailed upon Gene and Paul to put the makeup back on. Of course, they had been thinking about it anyway."

"Burn Bitch Burn": This dreadful Gene Simmons song, in which he laughably sings about putting his log in a girl's fireplace, is a good representation of how KISS was essentially Paul Stanley's band during most of the 1980s, while a distracted Simmons focused on his movie career and other interests. Doing what he can to salvage the tune, Stanley lends his vocals to the chorus.

"Burning Up with Fever": Jeff "Skunk" Baxter, formerly of the Doobie Brothers and Steely Dan, plays lead guitar on "Burning Up with Fever," the second track on the Demon's 1978 KISS solo album, *Gene Simmons*. Baxter's solo evokes Ace Frehley, and the song itself is a funk-infused pop rocker with a hint of Beatles, Stones, and early Doobie Brothers. Things begin bizarrely with Simmons counting 1–2–3–4, followed by a few purposely off-key acoustic guitar licks, and then the song kicks into gear. Disco diva Donna Summer sings backup vocals. Simmons has said that the song was inspired by Jeff Beck's "Rock Me Baby," complemented by the guitar scale that Leslie West used in "Mississippi Queen."

Bush, George W.: In a 2004 interview published on www.deangoodman.com, Gene Simmons, who is frequently outspoken about politics, said he believes President Bush isn't too bright, but that he's tough on terror. "I don't actually agree with almost any of his points of views," he said. "I don't agree with his point of view on stem cell research, separation of church and state. I think there should be women's rights, environmental issues. However, I can hug a tree next year. Right now, there's a war going on. I think he's the right guy for the job. He's a no-nonsense guy who's not terribly educated … in time of war, if you go through a bad neighborhood, I don't want a little French poodle, I want a Rottweiler on my hands. Rottweilers are not very popular, they even turn on your children. They will kill your children. But a Rottweiler is the correct dog to have when you get attacked."

Simmons voted for Al Gore in 2000, but, because of the terrorist attacks of 9/11, he voted for Bush in 2004.

Buslowe, Steve: Steve Buslowe played bass guitar on tracks 1–5 of Paul Stanley's 1978 KISS solo album. Buslowe also worked with such acts as Celine Dion, Meat Loaf, Bonnie Tyler, Ted Nugent, Bonnie Tyler, and Barbara Streisand.

"Cadillac Dreams": In "Cadillac Dreams," the ninth track on *Hot in the Shade*, Gene Simmons sings that money is all he needs (in stark contrast to the Beatles' "All You Need Is Love"). Written by Simmons and Vini Poncia, the song moves at a rapid clip, but is another mediocre (at best) Simmons song from the 1980s. Simmons has said that his demo for the tune, which is about growing up to live the America Dream of prosperity, is better than the actual finished version. Simmons plays rhythm guitar on the song.

Cadillac High School: During the fall of 1974, the Cadillac High School football team in Cadillac, Michigan, lost their first two games of the season. To provide inspiration and lighten the mood in the Vikings' locker room, the coaches played KISS music. The team immediately started winning games, thanks in part to their newly dubbed "KISS defense."

On www.neffzone.com/kiss, Jim Neff, who was an assistant coach for the Cadillac Vikings, and who had seen the band live in Flint, Michigan, explained his decision to use KISS music to motivate the players: "I chose a new and outrageous band—KISS. They were wild, bold, and loud. Plus, their name invoked an old football credo: Keep It Simple Stupid. It was a match that was meant to be. The 1974 team won its final seven games with KISS as an inspiration. The band heard about what we were doing and instantly adopted the Vikings as their team."

The following season, the Cadillac High student body made KISS the theme of their homecoming, prompting Neff to contact KISS management. This resulted in KISS visiting Cadillac on October 9, performing a homecoming concert in the school gymnasium (complete with firebreathing and smoke, but no blood spitting), playing around on the football field, getting a key to the city, and appearing in the homecoming parade, among other festivities, as Neff explained in the Cadillac High documentary on *KISSology—The Ultimate KISS Collection, Vol. 1: 1974–1977*: "From the minute they set foot in Cadillac, they were more than gracious. They were accommodating, posing with pictures…. They came into the school and were walking down the halls. They took pictures with the football team and the cheerleaders, the band, the policemen, the firemen … so everyone got in the mood to have a great time."

The next morning after the concert, at a celebratory breakfast, school and city officials wore KISS makeup. In fact, the band themselves applied makeup to some of the more important attendees, such as Gene Simmons putting makeup on school principal John Laurent.

When it was time for KISS to leave, a helicopter landed on the football field, and the band members jogged to the chopper and got on board, much to the excitement of the spectators. "Everyone was open-mouthed," Neff said. "We didn't have any idea this was going to happen. On to the helicopter they get, and they wave goodbye. As they leave, they toss flyers out that say, 'Cadillac, KISS loves you.'"

KISS also presented a plaque to Cadillac High School. Unfortunately, it was stolen and never recovered. On August 11, 2011, the Class of 1976 presented Cadillac High with a new plaque, "thereby righting the wrong that had occurred 36 years ago," Neff said. "The new plaque contains pictures, an original ticket to the homecoming concert, and one of the flyers KISS tossed from the helicopter as they left town. This wonderful new plaque now hangs next to the Cadillac Viking Sports Hall of Fame in the same hall that Gene Simmons led the football team down on the way to the concert."

In the decades since the Cadillac High event, Neff has been asked many times if KISS will return to the school, but expense, logistics, and the popularity of the band will likely keep that from ever happening. However, KISS tribute band Mr. Speed has played Cadillac several times, including on September 26, 2009, for a special event in the high school auditorium called "A Homecoming KISS."

"Calling Dr. Love": A tongue-in-cheek tribute to Gene Simmons' lovemaking prowess, "Calling Dr. Love" is the third track on *Rock and Roll Over* and is featured in the 2009 Dr Pepper Cherry commercial with Gene Simmons and his son, Nick. On *Alive II*, Paul Stanley famously introduces the song for everyone who's got "rock and roll pneumonia." The title, which was originally to be "Bad Bad Lovin'," was inspired by the Three Stooges short "Men in Black," in which an announcement over a hospital intercom states, "Calling Doctor Howard, Doctor Fine, Doctor Howard."

Reaching #16 on the *Billboard* charts, "Calling Dr. Love," which was written and sung by Simmons, "marries pop hooks to rock energy with a fast-paced melody that builds from verses full of rhythmically ascending phrases into a sing-along chorus fashioned around a call-and-response hook … a full-throttle hard rock arrangement that layers surging guitar riffs and a thumping bass line over a tight, fast-paced drum groove from Peter Criss. Ace Frehley contributes a searing solo that keeps the song in the hard rock arena, and Simmons tops the song off with a tongue-in-cheek growl of a vocal that brings out the sly humor in his smutty narrative" (www.allmusic.com).

Campise, Mick: The late Mick Campise was an original KISS road crew member during the mid–1970s, acting as production manager. You can read of his experiences in *Out On the Streets—The True Tales of Life On the Road With the Hottest Band In the Land—KISS!*

Caravello, Paul Charles: Eric Carr's birth name was Paul Charles Caravello. He changed it to Eric Carr after joining KISS.

Carnahan, Michael: Michael Carnahan played saxophone on Peter Criss's "Tossin' and Turnin'" and "Hooked on Rock 'n' Roll." He also worked with such acts as Cheryl Ladd, Dusty Springfield, Leo Sayer, and Melissa Manchester.

Carnival of Souls: A French Tribute to KISS: This independently produced tribute album, released in 1997, contains the following songs by various France-based bands: "God of Thunder" (Savitar), "You Confess" (Sand & Stromme), "Deuce" (Rip And Destroy), "She" (Krazy Lizzy), "Tell Me" (Blackstar), and "Deuce" (Blackstar).

Carnival of Souls: The Final Sessions: Inspired by Nirvana and Alice in Chains, KISS made the unfortunate decision to go grunge with *Carnival of Souls* (1997), the band's 17th studio album. There are a couple of good songs on the record—namely "Childhood's End" and "Seduction of the Innocent"—but *Carnival of Souls* is widely regarded as the band's worst full-length release. It's also the most obscure.

Tracks include: "Hate," "Rain," "Master & Slave," "Childhood's End," "I Will Be There," "Jungle," "In My Head," "It Never Goes Away," "Seduction of the Innocent," "I Confess," "In the Mirror," and "I Walk Alone." "Jungle" was released as a single, winning the 1997 Metal Edge Readers' Choice Award for Song of the Year.

In *KISS: Behind the Mask—The Official Authorized Biography*, Paul Stanley said: "I was dead set against doing that kind of an album, but there are times in the band where somebody acquiesces or gives in based upon somebody else feeling strongly about something. That album was Gene believing that's what we should do. I never believed that the world needs a second-rate Soundgarden, Metallica, or Alice in Chains. It was a very labored attempt at doing something that I think was a big misstep." For his part, Simmons, wanting to try something new and "make a home for Eric [Singer] and Bruce [Kulick]," called it a "very brave record.... I have no regrets."

Carr, Eric: Born Paul Charles Caravello on July 12, 1950, in Brooklyn, New York, Eric Carr adopted his stage name because there was already a Paul (Stanley, of course) in KISS, and because the band members were still hiding their identities under makeup.

According to *KISS FAQ* author Dale Sherman, Carr chose that specific name in part because "all the other band members' names had a rhythm of 1–2 when spoken (Gene Sim-mons, Paul Stan-ley, Ace Freh-ley) and the drummer's was the only one the opposite with 2–1 (Pe-ter Criss)."

Carr's original makeup/costume design was going to resemble a hawk, "but it came out looking too much like Big Bird from *Sesame Street*" said Greg Prato, author of *The Eric Carr Story*. "The Fox makeup/costume design was a last minute creation by Eric and Bill [Aucoin], supposedly the night before the Ace-Eric-Gene-Paul line-up was going to play its debut show at the Palladium in NYC.... After the show, Bill suggested Eric refine the make-up design a bit, and by the time the group launched their European tour shortly thereafter, Eric's official 'Fox design' was in place."

Inspired by the Beatles in 1964 to begin playing the drums, Carr was introduced to the world as a member of KISS on a June 1980 episode of ABC's *Kids Are People Too*. With the other three band members already seated onstage, the host welcomed Carr, who walked out, shook hands with the guys, and took his seat. Paul said, "What a cute guy." Ace said, "What do you think girls, is he a fox or what?" When the host asked Carr what it was like being in KISS, Carr said, "It's great … it's like a dream come true for me.... I wish everybody sometime in their life could have an experience like this."

Although he replaced Peter Criss in time for the *Unmasked* tour, Carr's first album to record with KISS was *Music from "The Elder,"* an artsy concept LP that was a radical departure for the band and an awkward fit for the hard rock drummer. In a November 8, 1989, interview with Jon Rubin, Carr said working on *"The Elder"* was "very hard. The material that I was asked to play was just so different from what I was used to, which was mainly the influence behind KISS' sound."

The next KISS record, the metalesque *Creatures of the Night*, fit Carr's John Bonham–influenced style perfectly, and he played on the next five KISS albums.

Sadly, Carr began complaining of fatigue and flu-like symptoms during the *Hot in the Shade* tour. It worsened to the point that he began bailing on meet-and-greets, which was unusual for Carr because he enjoyed spending time with fans. In early 1991, Carr was still feeling ill, so he went to the doctor and discovered something terrible: a cancerous growth on his heart. After having it removed, he began feeling better, even appearing on the 1991 *MTV Video Music Awards*, but in May of that year further tests showed that the cancer had spread to his lungs.

While the rest of the band, including replacement drummer Eric Singer, recorded *Revenge*, Carr was receiving chemotherapy treatments. Unfortunately for the Fox's family, friends, and many fans, Carr had a brain hemorrhage in September and a second one in November. On November 24, 1991, he passed away.

During one of his lecture tours in Australia in 2002, Gene Simmons spoke about the need to replace Carr.

"This is still a very emotional subject," the Demon said. "At first, when Eric was coughing up blood, he was referred to the KISS medics, and at first it did not seem to be serious. It wasn't until Eric had open-heart surgery that the tumors were found. Myself and Paul were the only people with Eric at the time, and we allowed Eric all the time in the world to recover and rejoin the band. Unfortunately, the cancer spread and we then knew he only had a matter of months to live. We sat down with Eric and told him that the band still had to move forward, which is when we then recruited Eric Singer and told Eric Carr he had been replaced. Eric was definitely upset with the decision, and when Eric was then released from hospital and we were doing the 'God Gave Rock and Roll to You' video, Eric asked if he could be a part of the video which we obliged to. Eric struggled to meet the video demands and did end up completing it, and unfortunately, a few months later Eric died."

On January 8, 1992, Stanley, Simmons, and Kulick sent a letter to *Rolling Stone*, criticizing the industry's most well-known magazine for not mentioning Carr's death. According to the *Los Angeles Daily News*, *Rolling Stone* music editor Jim Henke called the omission of an obituary for Carr "an unfortunate oversight" but denied it had anything to do with personal bias on behalf of the magazine or its editors.

To its credit, *Rolling Stone* ran an abridged version of the letter, but Simmons said they omitted the most important part of the missive, which read: "If your editorial policy is not to cover KISS, fine. But don't mix up editorial and human kindness. Eric Carr was a terrific drummer. More importantly he was a nice guy. To ignore his passing when MTV, CNN, and Rock Press have (covered it) shows what *Rolling Stone* really is—a vehicle for (publisher) Jann Wenner's opinions about music."

Just prior to joining KISS, Carr was in a group called Flasher, which was little more than a cover band. It was Flasher keyboardist Paul Turino who told Carr that KISS was auditioning for a drummer. In an interview conducted by Thomas Valentino in October of 1989, Carr said: "The very next day I went out and bought *Unmasked*. I got the telephone number of Aucoin Management and told them I was a drummer and I want to audition for KISS. They said send a tape of your playing, a picture, and a resume. I sent it in a bright orange folder because I figured that that there would be so many of these on the secretary's desk that maybe, just maybe it'll attract her attention. Sure enough, that's what happened. She saw my folder and grabbed it first. They called me and I went in the next day to meet Bill Aucoin. He gave me a list of songs to learn for the audition, in the event I was called for the audition. He told me I should shave my mustache off because they wouldn't want to see me in my mustache. I spent the rest of that day learning the five songs."

Needless to say, Carr was called in for the audition, impressed the band, and got the job. During the audition, he had Ace, Gene, and Paul sign his copy of *Unmasked* in case he never saw them again.

Prior to playing with Flasher, Carr had fairly lengthy stints with two other bands: The Cellarmen, which he formed with friends in 1965, and which dissolved in 1969; and the mixed-race outfit Salt 'N Pepper, which performed under various names (including Creation, Mother Nature/Father Time, Bionic Boogie, and Lightning) from 1970 to 1979. While calling themselves Lightning, the band recorded a self-titled album for Casablanca in 1979.

According to *KISS FAQ* author Dale Sherman, tragedy struck a Salt 'N Pepper performance in 1974: "Salt 'N Pepper was playing at a place called Gulliver's in Port Chester, New York when a fire—staged to cover up a robbery—broke out at a bowling alley next door. The fire spread quickly to the club, which had a dance floor built into the lower level of the building, and with electricity soon out and one exit locked shut, panic spread throughout the crowd. Carr had managed to pull the female lead singer along with him and battle his way out of the place, but many others were not so lucky. Twenty-four people died from smoke inhalation, including two members of the band. The incident made international news, and both Carr and another member of the band appeared on *CBS News* the following Sunday to discuss what had happened."

In 1999, Carr's family, working with Bruce Kulick and the label Spitfire, released *Rockology*, Carr's first solo album. The posthumous record hit stores October 19, eight years after Carr's death. Auto Rock Records released *Unfinished Business*, a second Carr solo album, on November 8, 2011.

"Carr Jam 1981": The 12th and final track on 1992's *Revenge*, "Carr Jam 1981" was recorded in May of 1981, when Eric Carr, who composed the drum-heavy instrumental with Ace Frehley, was new to KISS. The band included the song on the record as a tribute to Carr, who died November 24, 1991. The song featured the only drum solo Carr ever officially recorded with KISS. *See also*: "Breakout."

Casablanca Launch Party: Held February 18, 1974, in the Los Angeles Room of the Century Plaza Hotel to celebrate the release of the first KISS album, the Casablanca Launch Party was "simply amazing," wrote Larry Harris, author of *And Party Every Day: The Inside Story of Casablanca*. "The caterers had turned the ballroom into the Casablanca set. There were palm trees, camels (both live and stuffed), rattan furniture, and actors dressed in period costume playing the parts of Rick, Ilsa, and other characters…[There were] original set decorations and props from the movie…. In attendance were rock stars like Alice Cooper and Iggy Pop, and famous television personalities, including David Janssen and Ted Knight…. At the evening's midpoint, KISS took the stage … the retail people, who tended to skew older, walked out en masse and congregated in the lobby, taking cover from the painfully loud performance…. The younger attendees remained."

Casablanca Records: Founded June 13, 1973, by owner Neil Bogart with fellow former Buddah Records associates Larry Harris (artist relations, national album promotion), Cecil Holmes (national R&B promotion), and Buck Reingold (top-40 promotion), Casablanca Records, a subsidiary of Warner Bros. Records, signed KISS to a record deal on November 1, 1973. It was the first band the label signed (though its first single was Bill Amesbury's "Virginia (Touch Me Like You Do)").

In *Nothin' to Lose: The Making of KISS (1972–1975)*, Gene Simmons said, "Casablanca bet the store on a new act who didn't write singles, didn't sing about heartbreak or love, and didn't look like the Partridge Family. And all of that had to do with Neil Bogart, a man with a vision. Casablanca was unlike other labels. We could walk in, sit down, and have a heart-to-heart with Neil Bogart. Casablanca was the last of its kind."

Describing his time with the label, Bogart said, "I promote. I call radio stations. I go on the road to visit radio stations…. KISS was the first group we signed. When we signed them we affirmed that KISS *was* Casablanca…. I can honestly say KISS is the first band I've devoted 100 percent of myself to."

Other bands Casablanca signed during the era included Donna Summer, the Village People, Cher, and Parliament (featuring George Clinton).

Casablanca, which Bogart named after the classic film, was KISS's record label from 1973 to 1982. After *Creatures of the Night*, PolyGram, which had bought 50 percent of Casablanca in 1977 and the rest of the company in 1980 (forcing Neil Bogart out in the process), switched KISS to the Mercury label.

The last album released by the original incarnation of Casablanca was Animotion's *Strange Behavior* in 1986. The label was re-launched in 2000. For a complete history of the company, read *And Party Every Day: The Inside Story of Casablanca Records* by Larry Harris (with Curt Gooch and Jeff Suhs).

The Casablanca Singles 1974–1982: A boxed set aimed at hardcore KISS fans, *The Casablanca Singles 1974–1982* celebrates the 40th anniversary of the band's signing with Casablanca Records, where they recorded their first album and many classics to follow. During the Casablanca era, KISS released 29 singles, each on a seven-inch 45 RPM record. This set collects all of these singles, with B-sides (for a total of 58 songs), for the first time. This was significant because many of the songs had different edits, mixes, and material that wasn't on the standard album releases.

Tracks include: "Nothin' To Lose"/"Love Theme from KISS"; "Kissin' Time"/"Nothin' to Lose"; "Strutter"/"100,000 Years"; "Let Me Go, Rock 'N' Roll"/"Hotter Than Hell"; "Rock and Roll All Nite"/"Getaway"; "C'mon and Love Me"/"Getaway," "Rock and Roll All Nite" (live)/"Rock and Roll All Nite"; "Shout It Out Loud"/"Sweet Pain"; "Flaming Youth"/"God of Thunder"; "Detroit Rock City"/"Beth"; "Beth"/"Detroit Rock City"; "Hard Luck Woman"/"Mr. Speed"; "Calling Dr. Love"/"Take Me"; "Christine Sixteen"/"Shock Me"; "Love Gun"/"Hooligan"; "Shout It Out Loud" (live)/"Nothin' to Lose" (live); "Rocket Ride"/"Tomorrow and Tonight" (live); "Strutter '78"/"Shock Me"; "Hold Me, Touch Me"/"Goodbye"; "New York Groove"/"Snow Blind"; "Radioactive"/"See You in Your Dreams"; "Don't You Let Me Down"/"Hooked On Rock 'N' Roll"; "You Matter to Me"/"Hooked on Rock 'N' Roll"; "I Was Made for Lovin' You"/"Hard Times"; "Sure Know Something"/"Dirty Livin'"; "Shandi"/"She's So European"; "Tomorrow"/"Naked City"; "A World Without Heroes"/"Dark Light"; and "I Love It Loud"/"Danger."

Each of the 29 CD singles in this set is housed in a collectible picture sleeve from original single releases around the world, including Japan, Germany, Holland, Spain, the U.S., and Britain. The set also includes a booklet that tracks the genesis and chart history of each single, along with four KISS masks that you can wear. A vinyl edition of the set was released as well.

In a promo for *The Casablanca Singles 1974–1982*, Gene Simmons said: "Even I haven't heard some of this stuff, but this is all part of our master plan to celebrate KISS at this milestone in our careers. This box set represents us at the very beginning of our career, and documents the band's early success and subsequent growth." Paul Stanley added, "This collection is meant for the true KISS aficionado. The packaging really captures the development of both our music and image at a very crucial period in the band's history."

Caskets: Of the thousands of products licensed by the band, the KISS Kasket, released in 2001 with a retail price of $4,500 ($5,000 signed), is one of the strangest. Produced by White Light, the casket, according to the company, is "completely covered with a specially laminated photomural that features the KISS logo and the images of the band members [Ace, Paul, Gene, and Peter]. The words 'KISS Forever' are imprinted on the side of the casket. In addition, the KISS Kasket

The KISS Kasket, one of the strangest pieces of rock and roll merchandise ever produced, doubles as a beer cooler.

"can also be used as a Giant KISS Cooler, enabling fans and their friends to enjoy ice-cold sodas and beer served directly from the ice-filled, completely waterproof KISS Kasket."

"This is the ultimate KISS collectible," Gene Simmons said when promoting the KISS Kasket. "I love livin', but this makes the alternative look pretty damn good."

Dimebag Darrell, the late, great Pantera guitarist and huge KISS fan, was reportedly buried in a KISS Kasket.

In 2011, Eternal Image manufactured two more KISS Kaskets, each costing nearly $4,000: a standard version with 1978 solo album art and a premium version featuring a large photo of Gene, Paul, Tommy, and Eric Singer on top. Eternal Image also released a couple of different urns and a cremation casket.

Castle: In the ABC TV crime drama/comedy *Castle*, Gene Simmons played himself in "To Love and Die in L.A.," the 22nd episode of the third season. Featuring Nathan Fillion in the lead role, *Castle* debuted on ABC in 2009.

Castro, Peppy: A founding member of the psychedelic rock band the Blues Magoos, Peppy Castro (a.k.a. Emil Thielhelm) lived in Ace Frehley's boyhood neighborhood and claims to have taught the young Spaceman how to play electric guitar.

Cat #1: *Cat #1* was the first (and only) album by Criss, a band formed by Peter Criss more than a decade after he left KISS. Released August 16, 1994, it includes the following tracks: "Bad Attitude," "Walk the Line," "The Truth," "Bad People Burn in Hell," "Show Me," "Good Times," "Strike," "Blue Moon Over Brooklyn," "Down with the Sun," "We Want You," and an acoustic version of "Beth." Ace Frehley plays guitar on "Bad Attitude," "Walk the Line," and "Blue Moon Over Brooklyn."

Cat #1 rocks harder than Peter Criss's previous post–KISS records, such as *Out of Control* and *Let Me Rock You*. On the cover, half of Peter's face is painted with the patented Catman makeup.

In 1993, the band released a preview EP of this record called *Criss* that contained five songs, two of which that didn't actually appear on the album.

Catman: The stage alter-ego of Peter Criss. In *Makeup to Breakup*, Criss explained how the idea for the character came to him one night early in 1973: "I was designing one of my stage costumes at home. I was sketching it out and smoking a joint and then I just kind of zoned out and started staring at my wife's black cat, who was named Mateus. I realized that we both shared a lot of personality traits. We were both wild, independent, aggressive, powerful—yet also soft, gentle, warm, and comforting at the same time. I loved cats. I found them to be the most mystical, mysterious animals on the planet. They either loved you or scratched your eyes out. And, like me, they had nine lives."

When Criss donned his Cat makeup, it was a true transformation, as he wrote in *Makeup to Breakup*: "Forget about Peter Criscuola, the kid from Brooklyn. He didn't exist. I believed I was a superhero, the most iconic of cats, sitting up there overlooking my prey. I was a nasty little alley cat, ready to grab whatever I wanted. Don't get too close to me, I might attack. It was insane power tripping. I felt taller. My arms felt stronger. I was really transformed into this powerhouse of energy. I couldn't hit my drums hard enough."

Celebrity Apprentice: In January of 2008, Gene Simmons appeared on the Donald Trump reality show *Celebrity Apprentice*, which was spun off from *The Apprentice*. It was season one (season seven overall, if you count *The Apprentice*), and Simmons pitted his marketing wits against such celebs as Trace Adkins, Stephen Baldwin, Marilu Henner, and Piers Morgan, the latter of whom won. Simmons was the third person fired, and he said he respected Trump's decision.

The Cellarmen: Eric Carr's first band, the Cellarmen formed in 1965 and disbanded in 1969. The group recorded a number of demos, including "I Cry at Night," "Your Turn to Cry," "I Found You (the One I Adore)," "Then I Made a Wish," and "Stranger." For the Prolific label, they released a single called "I'm So Lonely," with "Something Tellin' Me" on the B side. In 1969, they backed singer Crystal Collins for her single, "No Matter How You Try," which featured "When You Grow Tired" as the B side.

Chaney, Lon: Gene Simmons is a huge fan of legendary silent screen star Lon Chaney (1883–1930), who contorted his body for *The Hunchback of Notre Dame* (1923) and scared audiences in *The Phantom of the Opera* (1925). Both films helped inspire Simmons to become a freakish character onstage. The Demon wrote "Man of 1,000 Faces" as a tribute to the great actor.

Chapin, Jim: Jazz drummer Jim Chapin (Harry's son) was a major influence on Peter Criss. During the early 1980s, after he left KISS, Criss studied with Chapin.

"Charisma": One of the more underrated Gene Simmons songs, "Charisma," the fifth track on *Dynasty*, has a steady beat, nice backup vocals, and the type of menace and bravado the Demon is famous for. Written by Simmons and Howard Marks, who was making fun of the way Simmons seemed comfortable talking about himself around girls, the song poses the question everyone has been asking for years (or maybe not): just what is it that's so appealing about Gene Simmons to the opposite sex? Fame? Fortune? Body? Brain? Fire? Flame? Name? Probably a combination of all of the above.

Charlie LoBue Guitars: During the early years of KISS, Gene Simmons frequently played a Charlie LoBue bass guitar. Paul Stanley used the brand as well. In a 1978 issue of *Guitar World*, Stanley said: "When we first got together, Charlie LoBue had a shop in New York called Guitar Lab, and he used to make some wonderful Instruments."

Chavarria, Paul: Heavily quoted in *KISS: Behind the Mask—The Official Authorized Biography*, Paul Chavarria was a KISS roadie from 1974–1979.

Cheap Trick: Formed in 1973, Cheap Trick is known for such classic rock hits as "Dream Police," "She's Tight," "The Flame," and "Surrender," the latter of which contains a reference to KISS albums. The band opened for KISS throughout the summer of 1977.

***Chelsea* (album):** Released in 1971, *Chelsea*, featuring Peter Criss on drums, was the first and only album released by the band of the same name. Tracks include: "Rollin' Along," "Let's Call it a Day," "Silver Lining," "All American Boy," "Hard Rock Music," "Ophelia," "Long River," "Grace," "Polly Von," and "Good Company."

Chelsea (band): Formed in 1970, Chelsea was a New York City pop rock band featuring a pre–KISS Peter Criss on drums. Other members of the band, which sounded a little like the British psychedelic group Procol Harum, included Michael Benvenga, Chris Aridas, Mike Brand, Peter Shepley, and Stan Penridge. Chelsea only recorded one album, the self-titled *Chelsea*, before disbanding in 1971. Criss, Benvenga, and Penridge remained together to form the pop rock trio Lips.

Cher: Born Cherilyn Sarkisian in El Centro, California, in 1946, Cher, who is sometimes referred to as "The Goddess of Pop," was half of the folk rock husband-and-wife duo, Sonny and Cher, who made it big in 1965 with the #1 single, "I Got You, Babe." Cher had solo success as well, performing such hits as "Dark Lady" (1974), "If I Could Turn Back Time" (1989), and "Believe" (1999).

A multi-talented star of the small screen (*The Sonny & Cher Comedy Hour*, *Cher*) and the silver screen (*Mask*, *Moonstruck*, *Mermaids*, *The Witches of Eastwick*), Cher dated Gene Simmons, who had Hollywood aspirations of his own, from 1979 to 1980. The relationship was covered heavily in the tabloids and supermarket magazines.

In the October 22, 1979, issue of *People*, writer Lois Armstrong dismissed KISS as a kiddie act, but said Gene and Cher's relationship was strong,

In 1970, Peter Criss was in the band Chelsea, which released a self-titled album. That's Criss top left.

despite admitted infidelities: "Oddest and most curious of all is that the liaison that may have brought the greatest solidity to her life is with, of all people, Gene Simmons, the four-years-younger, fire-breathing and blood-spitting bass guitarist for the kinky kindergarten rock group KISS."

In that same article, Cher said: "We had a wonderful suite at Chicago's Ritz-Carlton overlooking the lake, and Gene said at breakfast that it never ceases to amaze him how comfortable he is with me. He has never had a steady girlfriend, never had a relationship with anybody. That's pretty heavy stuff. He's a very strange, complicated and honest person ... the best relationship I've ever had with a human being."

Regarding Gene's lack of monogamy, Cher said: "I'm going through a very liberated phase right now. I think I have a very masculine attitude to dating. Gene might spend time with another woman and stay the night, but he wants her to leave in the morning so he can get on with his day."

Gene told *People* magazine: "I've always been afraid to talk about the relationship before. I thought it would be the death knell of KISS. From a publicity angle, this is not the most popular thing we could do. The fans who buy records think it's horrible. They're very jealous and possessive, but that's tough. I'm crazy about Cher, nuts about her. She's my first love. Cher's an untainted soul who has never done anything bad to anybody."

Gene and Cher amicably split up after Simmons fell for her friend Diana Ross, and they remain friends to this day.

***Chikara*:** Released only in Japan, *Chikara* was issued in 1988 in support of the band's Japanese tour. Only 100,000 copies were produced, and it came with a patch of the Chikara symbol. The CD, which is highly collectible, includes the following tracks: "Rock and Roll All Nite," "Detroit Rock City," "Love Gun," "I Was Made for Lovin' You" (extended 12" single version), "Creatures of the Night," "I Love It Loud" (1985 remaster), "War Machine" (1985 remaster), "Lick It Up," "All Hell's Breakin' Loose," "Heaven's on Fire," "Thrills in the Night," "Who Wants to Be Lonely," "Uh! All Night," and "Tears are Falling."

Child, Desmond: Songwriter and producer Desmond Child co-wrote a number of KISS songs, including "Heaven's on Fire," "I Was Made for Lovin' You," "Uh! All Night," "Let's Put the X in Sex," and "Hide Your Heart." He also worked with such acts as Aerosmith, Cher, Bon Jovi, and Alice Cooper.

ChildFund International: Gene Simmons works closely with the ChildFund International charity, sponsoring more than 1,400 impoverished children throughout Africa.

"Childhood's End": Track four on *Carnival of Souls*, "Childhood's End" was written by Gene Simmons, Tommy Thayer, and Bruce Kulick. Simmons sings the rather tuneful song, which has more melody and is less grungy than the previous three tracks on the record. With its sweeping sound and relatively sophisticated lyrical content, "Childhood's End" wouldn't sound out of place on *Music from "The Elder."*

In *KISS: Behind the Mask—The Official Authorized Biography*, Simmons said "Childhood's End" is based on the Arthur C. Clarke novel of the same name, which is "about the last stages of evolution when we become spirit entities. We leave the body and become energy sources and these elemental beings help us on our journey.... 'Childhood's End' was not about an actual person. It was just sort of rock 'n' roll nihilism. Rock 'n' roll guys killing themselves off was a very romantic notion."

"Christine Sixteen": In "Christine Sixteen," the second track on *Love Gun*, Gene Simmons sings (and talks) about an underage girl he's simply got to have. Simmons also wrote the song (on keyboards), which should come as no surprise given his penchant for penning perverted pop tunes. Controversial subject matter notwithstanding (certain radio stations refused to play it, others did so only after 7 p.m.), "Christine Sixteen" is a catchy number that the band released as a single, reaching #25 on the *Billboard* charts. Producer Eddie Kramer plays piano on the song while Simmons lays down a muscular bass line.

***Christine Sixteen: A High-School Tribute to KISS*:** Released in April of 2006, this indie CD features songs by students from Polyvalente La Frontalière Highschool, located in Coaticook, Québec, Canada. Includes 15 tracks, plus an interview with Bruce Kulick.

***Christine Sixteen 2: Another High-School Tribute to KISS*:** Released in May of 2007, this indie CD features songs by students from Polyvalente La Frontalière Highschool, located in Coaticook, Québec, Canada. Includes 16 tracks, plus an interview with Gene Simmons.

Christopher, Lyn: Paul Stanley and Gene Simmons sang backup vocals on three tracks on Lyn Christopher's 1973 self-titled album, which was recorded at Electric Lady Studios. "It was the first time Gene and Paul ever got paid to sing on a record," Christopher recalled in *Nothin' to Lose: The Making of KISS (1972–1975)*. "They shared my excitement to be singing on an album for a major label. I could tell it was a big deal for them." Simmons added, "It was an amazing experience to be on a record."

On episode 44 of *Three Sides of the Coin*, Christopher talked about working with Paul and Gene. "They were Wicked Lester at the time," she said. "Ron Johnsen who was producing them, he was producing me ... he just invited them in ... they came in and sang backgrounds.... I didn't audition them or anything.... Gene was very shy [but] he made me laugh all the time ... he did one-liners.... Paul was always staring at me ... they were very nice ... they've always been very nice ... gentlemen ... respectful."

By sheer coincidence, Peter Criss provided hand-claps on two of the songs on the album.

KISS was featured in *Circus* magazine numerous times over the years, including this 11th anniversary issue.

Circus: Published from 1966–2006, *Circus* magazine, which was called *Hullabaloo* until 1969, featured many KISS articles and cover appearances over the years, partly because KISS advertised in the mag. During their heyday, the band and its members were voted at or near the top many times in the *Circus* Readers' Poll that would run in each issue. Larry Harris, the Senior Vice President for Casablanca Records at the time, has admitted that he and his staff would buy several hundred issues of the magazine and fill out the polls in KISS-heavy fashion in order to stuff the ballot box.

Clark, Dick: Best known for hosting *American Bandstand*, Dick Clark was an early proponent of KISS, booking them on ABC's *In Concert* in 1974 for their first TV appearance, airing March 29. The band played "Nothin' to Lose," "Firehouse," and "Black Diamond."

After Clark died April 18, 2012, at the age of 82, Paul Stanley released the following statement: "As a little boy, I sat transfixed to our television every afternoon and Saturday night watching *American Bandstand*. Dick Clark was the face of rock and roll and its best ambassador. His decades of successes both in and outside of the music industry are unparalleled. He championed KISS when others turned away and was instrumental in breaking us through his show *In Concert*. Through the years, Dick was always available when I had a question or wanted guidance. Dick Clark was the rare exception who was a bigger person in real life than the public image or legend that was also to be his legacy. I will remember him with great respect and gratitude."

Clown White: The white makeup KISS wears is known as clown white. *Clown White* is also the name of a classic KISS fanzine.

Club Tour: Throughout 1973, beginning with the fabled January 30, 1973, show at the Popcorn Pub in Queens, KISS played 24 club dates (usually two sets), thus the informally named Club Tour. The band was experimenting with their makeup and costumes at this time, and they were still playing a few Wicked Lester songs, such as "Simple Mind" and "Keep Me Waiting." Props included fake Marshall amps (to give the illusion of bigger sound), fire engine lights, a chain link drum riser, and drumsticks filled with flash powder. Around this time, they hired Bill Aucoin as their manager, signed with Casablanca Records, and recorded their first album, 1974's *KISS*.

C'mon

Band lineup: Paul Stanley, Gene Simmons, Ace Frehley, and Peter Criss. Headlining acts: the Brats, Isis, Queen Elizabeth featuring Wayne County, and Wild Honey. Opening acts: Bloontz, City Slicker, the Detroit Dogs, Flaming Youth, Jackdaw, Luger, the Planets, the Rags, Rebillot Quartet, and Street Punk.

Followed by: KISS Tour.

"C'mon and Love Me": Inspired by the Moody Blues' "Question," Paul Stanley purportedly wrote "C'mon and Love Me" in under an hour. It is one of the band's better songs, featuring clever rhyming, solid musicianship, and an overall fun vibe. According to the lyric, Stanley, who loves the song and calls it autobiographical, meets a woman who saw his picture in a music magazine. Naturally, the turned-on twosome gets down and dirty. "C'mon and Love Me" is the sixth song on *Dressed to Kill*.

Cobo Hall: Named for Albert E. Cobo, who was mayor of Detroit from 1950 to 1957, the legendary Cobo Hall (now the Cobo Center) hosted a number of important KISS concerts at its arena, including three sold-out shows in 1976. The band recorded much of *Alive!* at Cobo, along with the *Animalize Live Uncensored* video. The arena is also featured in the video for "Modern Day Delilah."

Coins: In 1979, band members threw out special KISS coins to celebrate Mardi Gras in New Orleans. There were also Mardi Gras KISS coins in 1983, including Vinnie Vincent.

Bailey Mint released KISS coins in Australia in 1980 for the Unmasked Tour, including Eric Carr. Liberty Mint issued Alive/Worldwide coins—available in silver and gold—in 1997. The company released Psycho Circus World Tour Coins as well, also available in silver and gold. In 1999, Signatures Superstars produced a Psycho Circus World Tour Magnum Coin. A 2000 Farewell Tour Coin was released as well.

"Cold Gin": Gene Simmons is a teetotaler, and Paul Stanley reportedly only has the occasional glass of wine, so it's no surprise that the formerly hard-drinking Ace Frehley wrote "Cold Gin," a street-tough, hard-rocking song about alcoholism. Since Frehley, who wrote the tune on the subway, wasn't confident in his singing ability, Simmons sung lead vocals on the song, which is the fourth track on *KISS*, the band's debut album.

Colorforms: Housed in a flat box, Colorforms, which hold the distinction of being the first commercially released craft-type toy made of plastic, consist of thin die-cut vinyl sheet images and shapes that the user applies to a laminated (and usually illustrated) board. The sheets can be repositioned on the board again and again to create new designs and scenarios. Invented by Harry and Patricia Kislevitz, the toy first appeared in stores in 1951, and was one of the first toys advertised on television.

The box for the KISS Colorforms set, released in 1979, features an image of the band from the Barry Levine *Love Gun* photo session. By placing band members' body parts and musical instruments on the enclosed board, which depicts a guitar-shaped laser zapping a "KISS Tonight" sign positioned atop a city building, the player can sup-

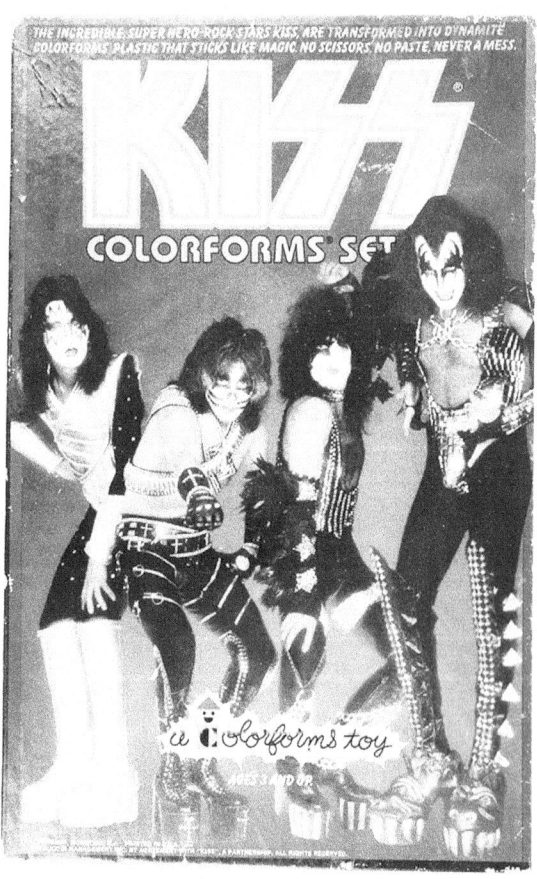

Released in 1979, the KISS Colorforms play set let kids design their own scenarios by placing band members' body parts and musical instruments on a board (courtesy KISSmuseum.com).

posedly "help KISS defeat their evil enemy, the Mad Rock promoter."

See also: "Rub n' Play Magic Transfer Set."

Comic Book Men: On the March 22, 2015, episode of *Comic Book Men*, entitled "KISS My Stash," Gene Simmons visits Jay and Silent Bob's Secret Stash comic store. Later in the episode, the Comic Book Men cast members don KISS makeup and join the band onstage at a concert in New Jersey's PNC Arts Center. *Comic Book Men*, developed by Kevin Smith, debuted on AMC in 2012.

***Comics Interview*:** Gene Simmons, an avowed comic book fan, is interviewed by Marty Herzog in *Comics Interview* #2, published by Fictioneer Books in April of 1983. Gene talks about how he wanted to be artist Jack Kirby and writer Stan Lee and how he was proud to be depicted as a super hero in comics. He also recalls the time writer Marv Wolfman came to his house to discuss comic book fanzines.

"Comin' Home": KISS is famous for enjoying extracurricular activities with females while on tour, but "Comin' Home," like "Beth" and Journey's "Faithfully," speaks of the difficulties and loneliness of life on the road, missing a girl back home in particular. Written by Paul Stanley (who sings the song) and Ace Frehley, it is the ninth track on *Hotter Than Hell*. The song enjoyed new life in 1995, thanks to the band playing it during MTV's *KISS Unplugged* concert.

Condoms: It's no secret that KISS is a sex-obsessed band, and they'll put their logo and images on just about anything to make a buck. Hence the KISS Kondoms, released by Global Protection Korp. in 2002. They were released in three-packs in three different styles: Love Gun Protection (featuring the "Spirit of '76" photo on the box), Studded Paul (Paul wearing studs on his sleeves), and Tongue Lubricated (Gene sticking his tongue out, of course).

In 2011, Condomania released a set with the following text on the box: "The second generation of KISS Kondoms, but the world's first approved condoms to feature a full color image right on the latex! KISS Kondoms are emblazoned with an illustration of Gene Simmons and his famous tongue stretching down the length of the condom!"

During the early 1990s, several promotional KISS condoms were released, promoting the band in general, the singles "Rise to It" and "Unholy," and the video *KISS Konfidential*.

Contessa, Maria: Maria Contessa designed the first true KISS costumes, along with later KISS outfits, as she explained in 1995 in issue one of *KISS Army Norway Magazine*: "It was back in 1973 when I had a costume store in New York City. One day these guys came into my store and they told me that they were going to be rock stars. They told me about the image and how they were going to look. They didn't have any money to pay for such costumes, but they told me that they would pay me back when they became rich. I said I couldn't take a chance like that but somehow it went their way. And strangely enough they became rich and famous and they paid me back as promised. So I made the first real KISS costumes. I still make costumes for them today but I don't spend that much time on rock costumes now as before. I have made most of the KISS costumes but there have been other designers involved as well. I have also done some stuff for Ace and his band. I helped Paul out when he did his solo tour."

Convention Tour: See "Worldwide KISS Conventions."

Cooley, Alex: Georgia-based Alex Cooley of Alex Cooley Presents promoted many KISS concerts during the 1970s.

Cooper, Alice: Known as "The Godfather of Shock Rock," Alice Cooper (a.k.a. Vincent Furnier) was a huge influence on KISS. Not only did he wear garish makeup, Cooper's concerts were Grand Guignol stage plays augmented by horror props, including fake blood. KISS's former manager, Bill Aucoin, essentially saw the band as four Alice Coopers onstage.

Prior to embarking on a solo career in 1975, Cooper was part of the Alice Cooper band, which released such hit albums as *School's Out* and *Billion Dollar Babies*. As a solo artist, he made a splash with *Welcome to My Nightmare* and *Alice Goes to Hell*, among other records.

In June of 1973, Ace, Paul, and Peter saw their first Alice Cooper concert at Madison Square Garden (Gene had to work). "Seeing that show was stunning," Paul said in *Nothin' to Lose: The Making of KISS (1972–1975)*. "I still remember him walking down the stairs when the show began with 'Hello Hooray' and it was godlike. The crowd was just going crazy…. What Alice was doing was perfect for him and I wanted to do my version of that." Peter added, "Paul and Ace literally ran all the way down the stairs to be right up in front of the stage. That's how impressed they were. I'll never forget."

On February 18, 1974, Cooper attended the Warner Bros. party welcoming KISS to the Casablanca record label and celebrating the release of their first album. It was held at the Century Plaza Hotel in Los Angeles.

Decades later, Eric Singer played drums for Alice Cooper on three albums: *Brutal Planet* (2000), *The Eyes of Alice Cooper* (2003), and *Along Came a Spider* (2008). He's toured with Cooper as well.

Cornyn, Stan: Stan Cornyn was Executive Vice President for Warner Bros. Records during the KISS era. He wrote of his experiences in *Exploding: The Highs, Hits, Hype, Heroes, and Hustlers of the Warner Music Group*, published by It Books in 2002.

Coronel, Stephen: Guitarist Stephen Coronel was in a pre–KISS band with Paul Stanley called Tree, and he was in several bands with his good buddy Gene Simmons, including the Long Island Sounds, Love Bag, and Cathedral." With Simmons, Coronel co-wrote "She" and "Goin' Blind."

In 1970, Coronel introduced Paul and Gene, and they started a band called Rainbow, which would become Wicked Lester. Unfortunately for Coronel, when Wicked Lester recorded a demo for Epic Records, the company said they'd offer the band a deal, but only if they got rid of Coronel. Gene gave Coronel the bad news, and studio musician Ron Leejack took his place.

Cort Guitars: In 2010, Gene Simmons partnered with Cort Guitars to create his own signature bass line called the GS-AXE-2, which includes the Axe Bass and the Punisher Bass, among others.

Costello, Fin: Noted rock photographer Fin Costello shot numerous memorable KISS photos, including pics for *Alive!*, *Creem* magazine, and the Cadillac High School event in Michigan.

In an interview with Costello published in the November 2005 issue of *KISS Kollector* magazine, he spoke about the first time he photographed the band on March 21, 1975, at the Beacon Theatre in New York: "I had only moved to the U.S. a few weeks before that show and was at AGI with Peter Corriston [who designed KISS' *Dressed to Kill* album sleeve] working on the design ideas for the first Rainbow cover when he asked me if I wanted to see KISS—who were virtually unknown then outside the New York area—at the Beacon just around the corner.... I have often described it as being akin to the Gates of Hell or Dante's Inferno. They were doing the first number when we came into the back of the theatre and I had never seen anything like it. Smoke, flames, etc. and the audience going ballistic. See the first tour program for the pictures from that gig. The costume and makeup were perfect for the scary theatrical show they had conceived."

Costumes: Second only to their iconic makeup, the costumes KISS wears are indelibly linked to the band, in both the minds of the critics, many of whom refuse to take KISS seriously because of their attire, and their fans, who enjoy seeing their heroes strut around in black leather, platform shoes, sequins, lightning bolts, metal studs, spikes, and the like.

In the beginning, before multi-platinum albums and sold-out stadiums, the band members wore black T-shirts, stockings, bandanas, and other cheap apparel, some of it designed by their mothers and girlfriends. During the band's first decade, Maria Contessa, Larry LeGaspi, and Pete Menefee designed many of the classic KISS costumes.

During the 1980s, KISS shed their makeup as well as their fancy costumes, beginning in 1983 with the *Lick it Up* album and the nationally televised event, *MTV Special: KISS Unmasking*. When KISS re-formed in 1996 for the Reunion Tour, the classic look of the band returned, heralded by a February 28, 1996, surprise appearance at the *Grammy Awards* in full makeup and costumes.

Countdown: Broadcast from 1974 to 1987, *Countdown* was a popular music show produced at ABC studios in Australia. In anticipation of KISS' forthcoming tour of the country, the program aired a special episode September 14, 1980, featuring music videos and an interview with the band. Ace, Gene, Paul, and Eric Carr appear relaxed and were obviously having a good time.

Carr, who admitted that he had never bought any KISS albums prior to learning of his audition, told the interviewer: "I was really quite positive about the whole thing, and I was really excited. I just went in there, I knew I was going to do my best, and I really relaxed. The guys were really great to me." To which a playful Paul joked, "We gave him milk and cookies." Ace, appearing buzzed, jumped in with, "Eric was so good. For the first week, though, he did have to wear diapers," cracking everyone up, except for Gene.

When the interviewer asked Gene about his makeup, Paul said, "He's a ballerina." Gene said, "It doesn't mean anything" and manically stuck his tongue out. About their new album at the time, *Unmasked*, Paul said: "We were going for a 'poppier' album … we wanted something a little bit lighter, but it's a rockier album than the last one. And the next album we do is going to be much heavier … things go full circle."

Coventry: On January 30, 1973, KISS played the Coventry (a.k.a. the Popcorn Pub—the facility's name changed from Popcorn Pub to Coventry around this time), a rundown club in Queens, New York that held approximately 700 people. This was the band's first real gig, and only a handful of people showed up to watch them play.

According to Curt Gooch and Jeff Suhs, authors of *KISS Alive Forever: The Complete Touring History*: "For a band that became renowned the world over for its garish, ridiculous appearance, KISS' attire for their first concert was, simply put, dull. Of the four, only Gene wore makeup that even hinted at what was to come, with pancake [makeup] covering his face and black greasepaint smudged formlessly around his eyes. Peter wore a small amount of rouge, and neither Paul nor Ace wore any makeup whatsoever. The band's clothing was very pedestrian as well."

In a 2008 issue of *Goldmine Magazine*, Lydia Criss said, "I remember it was a really cold winter night. The only people who showed up at that first Coventry show were me, Jan Walsh, who was Gene's girlfriend at the time, and her friend, plus the road crew—Eddie Solan; Joey Criscuola, Peter's brother; and Bobby McAdams—and the people who worked at the club."

In that same article, Paul said: "Coventry was important for us, because it was so difficult for a band like us to get any gigs because we didn't play Top 40, and we weren't part of the Mercer Arts crowd, which was the crowd that took in the New York Dolls and some of the Andy Warhol, Max's Kansas City bands. So, we needed a place that could be ours, and Coventry was a place in Queens that was just on the other side of the East River. It gave people in New York access to come see us, and it also set us a little apart from the New York glitter bands. Coventry was a place where we really cut our teeth, and it was the first place we ever played."

According to Gene Simmons, who wore velour bellbottoms, high heels with studs, and a white sailor shirt for that first gig, he booked the show. "On my way in to work in the city I used to pass by this club in Queens," he told *Goldmine*. "I called the club, got the manager on the phone, and started selling, which is what I've always done my entire life. I said to him, 'We've got a band called Wicked Lester, and I'm really excited about it. You should book us, because we're terrific.' So he agreed to put us on for three nights during the middle of the week when nobody went there. We had yet to name ourselves KISS. That first night we changed the name of the band from Wicked Lester to KISS."

After the first concert at the Coventry, word began to spread, and soon there were 100 to 150 at each Coventry show.

In *Nothin' to Lose: The Making of KISS (1972-1975)*, Ramones lead vocalist Joey Ramone recalled seeing KISS at the Coventry. "At the time I think they were the loudest band I ever heard," he said. "I liked a lot of their stuff. They were fun and had great songs. I saw them when they first started out and they just had dry ice; Gene had a skull and crossbones T-shirt. This was way before their image and show came together."

COVERED WITH KISSES: An Evansville Tribute to KISS: Released by an independent label in 2004, this tribute album features songs by bands based in Evansville, Indiana. Tracks include: "I Want You" (Vegas Radio), "Do You Love Me" (Static), "Rock Bottom" (the Huckleberrys), "100,000 Years" (Vegas Radio), "C'mon and Love Me" (Bosko), "Firehouse," (Hog Maw), "Parasite" (McWeisenheimer), "Detroit Rock City" (Six Hill's Giant), "War Machine" (Ken Rex), "Deuce" (Gonzo's Toybox), "I Was Made 4 Lovin' U" (B.O.T.), "Strange Ways" (Chowder Monkey), and "God of Thunder" (Ken Rex). In 2009, Dizzy Head Music released a remastered version of the CD.

"Crazy Crazy Nights": The first track on *Crazy Nights*, "Crazy Crazy Nights" was also the first single from the album. It only reached #65 on the U.S. *Billboard* charts, but did exceptionally well overseas, including the U.K. (#4), Norway (#7), the Netherlands (#28), and Australia (#34). It's a catchy, celebratory, fist-pumping pop anthem in which Paul Stanley ensures listeners that, despite setbacks, frustrations, and naysayers, everything's rockin.' The song, with its keyboards and party atmosphere chorus, has much more in common with hair metal of the day, such as Bon Jovi and Def Leppard, than it does early KISS. Written by Stanley and Adam Mitchell. The official video for the song shows an energized KISS performing live in concert.

Crazy Magazine: Appearing on newsstands from 1973 to 1983, *Crazy* was Marvel Comics' answer to *MAD*. KISS was featured on the cover of *Crazy* #41, dated August 1978. It is a parody of the *Alive!* cover. The cover of *Crazy* #62 (May 1980) depicts Irving Nebbish, the magazine's mascot, holding a Gene Simmons action figure.

KISS was featured on the cover of *Crazy* magazine twice, including the May 1980 issue, where it appears as though a Gene Simmons action figure has breathed fire on *Crazy* mascot Irving Nebbish.

Crazy Nights: KISS went full-on pop rock with *Asylum*, a trend that continued with the even more pop-ridden *Crazy Nights*, the band's 14th studio album. Released September 18, 1987 by Mercury Records, *Crazy Nights* was produced by Ron Nevison, who had worked with Ozzy Osbourne on *The Ultimate Sin* the year prior. Phil Ashley played keyboards, an instrument many of the band's longtime fans didn't think should feature so prominently on a KISS record. Even so, *Crazy Nights* is a fun party album that has more than its share of apologists.

Tracks include: "Crazy Crazy Nights," "I'll Fight Hell to Hold You," "Bang Bang You," "No, No, No," "Hell or High Water," "My Way," "When Your Walls Come Down," "Reason to Live," "Good Girl Gone Bad," "Turn on the Night," and "Thief in the Night." The cover photo, featuring KISS members reflected on broken glass, is by Walter Wick, who created the images for the popular *I Spy* and *Can You See What I See?* children's book series.

"Crazy Crazy Nights," the first single from the album, hit #4 in the UK, but only reached #65 on the *Billboard* Hot 100 in the U.S. "Reason to Live" and "Turn on the Night" were also released as singles.

Gene Simmons is no fan of the album. In *KISS: Behind the Mask—The Official Authorized Biography*, he said it was "one of my least favorite records of any of the ones that we've done. I thought it sounded thin … it's much too happy.… We just became what we looked like in the videos. Silly. Not as good as Bon Jovi, not as good as Poison. They were better versions of what we did. Better-looking guys, younger and thinner, who wrote better songs in that pop vein.… We couldn't really do the classic version of KISS without Ace and Peter. So we did the best we could with what we had."

Crazy Nights World Tour: Consisting of 130 shows played from November 13, 1987, to October 3, 1988, the Crazy Nights World Tour was in support of KISS's 14th studio album. In addition to Canada, Europe, and the U.S., the band played Japan, their first time there since the Alive II Tour in 1978.

Opening acts: Anthrax, Balaam & the Angel, Chastain, David Lee Roth, Dirty Looks, Edda, Forigjarnir, Great White, Guns N' Roses, Helix, Helloween, Kings of the Sun, Mantis, Megadeth, Royal Air Force, Ted Nugent, Testament, Treat, and White Lion. The August 20, 1988, show was the Monsters of Rock festival at Donington Park in North West Leicestershire, England, where Iron Maiden headlined.

Band lineup: Paul Stanley, Gene Simmons, Bruce Kulick, and Eric Carr. Since *Crazy Nights* was a keyboard-heavy record, KISS hired Gary Corbett to play keyboards behind the stage, making him an unofficial fifth member of the band. KISS didn't use many pyrotechnics during the tour, but Gene Simmons' bass shot rockets, and the band would end each concert with a fireworks display. Average Attendance: 5,691 (not including club, Japanese, or Monsters of Rock gigs).

Followed by: Hot in the Shade Tour.

***Creatures of the Night* (album):** In 1979, KISS released *Dynasty*, a commercially successful, but disappointing (to many fans, but not this author) record that bowed to the pressures of what was popular at the time: disco. The band followed with *Unmasked*, a bubblegum pop album, and *Music from "The Elder,"* an odd concept record. To get back to their hard rock basics, and to try and recover from the dreadful sales of the latter two albums, KISS released *Creatures of the Night* (Oct. 13, 1982), one of the band's heaviest records.

Beginning with the blistering title track, *Creatures of the Night*, which was produced by Michael James Jackson for Casablanca Records, grabs the listener by the throat and never lets go, not even during the requisite power ballad, the ultra-powerful "I Still Love You." KISS fans and music critics alike point to Eric Carr's loud, bombastic, John Bonham-style drums as one of the record's many strengths. Ace Frehley is pictured on the album cover (photographed by Bernard Vidal), but he had quit the band by this point. Vinnie Vincent, who wore Ankh Warrior makeup during the subsequent tour, played lead guitar on the album, as did Robben Ford ("Rock and Roll Hell" and "I Still Love You") and Steve Farris ("Creatures of the Night").

In 1985, KISS remixed and re-released *Creatures of the Night* with a new cover. The band wore no makeup on this cover, and Bruce Kulick replaced Ace in the photo, even though he didn't play on the album.

Tracks include: "Creatures of the Night," "Saint and Sinner," "Keep Me Comin'," "Rock and Roll Hell," "Danger," " I Love It Loud," "I Still Love You," "Killer," and "War Machine."

According to *KISS FAQ* author Dale Sherman, the LP was a "step in the right direction for proclaiming [the band's] roots," but "attracted little attention," helping lead to the decision for KISS to remove their makeup for their next album and tour, *Lick It Up*.

In *KISS: Behind the Mask—The Official Authorized Biography*, Paul Stanley said the album "was very much a recapturing of our desire and our focus as a band and reclaiming of what was important to us. We had become rich, fat, and lazy and became enamored with the idea of having our peers think we were smart and musical and really all the things that are poison to us. [*Creatures*] was that step of us declaring that we were back."

Despite the greatness of *Creatures of the Night*, it only reached #45 on the *Billboard* charts.

"Creatures of the Night" (song): The first track on the album of the same name, "Creatures of the Night" was a resounding return to hard rock for KISS, with sinister sounding vocals by Paul Stanley, loud, bombastic drums by Eric Carr, and forceful fretwork by session guitarist Steve Farris (later of Mr. Mr.). Mike Porcaro of Toto fame played bass on the song, subbing for Gene Simmons.

Penned by Stanley and Adam Mitchell, who wrote of darkness, madness, and howling in the shadows, "Creatures of the Night" reached #34 on the U.K. Pop Singles chart, but was not released as a single in the U.S. For the 1985 reissue of the *Creatures of the Night* album, producer Dave Wittman remixed "Creatures of the Night."

Creatures of the Night Tour: Also known as the 10th Anniversary Tour, the Creatures of the Night Tour, in support of the band's 10 studio album (not counting the 1978 solo records), began December 29, 1982, and ended June 25, 1983, for a total of 55 shows in the U.S., Canada, and South America. The concerts, employing a tank stage design, bombed in the U.S., despite KISS's return to its hard rock roots after a several-year foray into disco and pop. However, on June 18, 1983, they played for 137,000 screaming fans at Maracanã Stadium in Rio de Janeiro, Brazil. This was the biggest crowd of their career up until that point.

The Creatures of the Night Tour was the second tour with drummer Eric Carr and the first featuring lead guitarist Vinnie Vincent, who had recently replaced Ace Frehley. Since early press materials, ads, and the *Creatures of the Night* album cover depicted Frehley, as though he were still with the band, most fans were surprised by the appearance of Vincent, who sported makeup in the design of an Egyptian ankh, and whose screeching, high-speed playing style was much different than that of Space Ace.

Band lineup: Paul Stanley, Gene Simmons, Vinnie Vincent, and Eric Carr. Opening acts: Dareforce, Defectors, the Headpins, Herva Doce, Hotz, Molly Hatchet, Mötley Crüe, Night Ranger, the Plasmatics, the Shoes, Why On Earth, and Zebra. Average attendance: 5,350 (not including the Brazilian shows).

After the tour, KISS, sensing a change was needed to stay relevant, removed their makeup and elaborate costumes, beginning a new era for the band.

Followed by: Lick It Up World Tour.

Creem: Self-described as "America's Only Rock 'n' Roll Magazine," Creem was published from 1969 to 1989, followed by a brief resurrection during the early '90s as a glossy tabloid. The mag was an early proponent of KISS, giving them coverage when many publications ignored the band. A big reason for this was because KISS supported Creem, as former Casablanca Records Senior Vice President Larry Harris explained in KISS: Behind the Mask—The Official Authorized Biography: "I met Barry Kramer, the publisher and owner of Creem, and worked out a deal with them where we would purchase on a long-term bases the inside front cover for advertising KISS. We also supplied Creem with thousands of free KISS albums to give away to people who subscribed to the magazine."

During one photo shoot, Creem art director Charlie Auringer told KISS it was okay with their management if he could take their pictures sans makeup. They agreed, but it turns out Auringer had lied. "We got duped into doing that photo for Creem without makeup," Paul Stanley said in KISS: Behind the Mask. "It's a cool picture in terms of marking a certain period where most people never got a chance to see what we looked like."

Fortunately for classic KISS mystique, the photos weren't published back in the day, but you can easily find them online now.

The Creeps: Beth/Great Expectations: Released in 1997 by Quadrmedia/EMI Sweden, this CD single by the Swedish band, the Creeps, features covers of "Beth" and "Great Expectations."

Criscuola, Joey: The younger brother of Peter Criss, Joey Criscuola attended numerous early KISS concerts and was even there when Peter met Paul and Gene for the first time. He was also an early KISS roadie.

Criscuola, Peter: Born George Peter John Criscuola, Peter Criss went by the name of Peter Criscuola before shortening it to Peter Cris and then Peter Criss.

Criss (band): From 1991 to 1996, Peter Criss played in the aptly named Criss, which recorded a self-titled EP and one album: Cat #1.

Criss (EP): Released in 1993 as a preview of Cat #1, the first and only album by Peter Criss's post–KISS band, Criss, this mini CD contains five tracks: "The Cat," "Show Me," "Good Times," "What You're Doin,'" and an acoustic version of "Beth." Two of the tracks, "The Cat" and "What You're doing," didn't actually make it onto the Cat #1 album.

Criss, Gigi: Peter Criss married Gigi on May 3, 1998, and is still married to her. It was a small wedding, and Criss didn't invite his fellow KISS band members. In Makeup to Breakup, Criss said, "Gigi was the first woman I ever met that really loved God, like I do, so there was a spiritual connection there that I had never experienced.... No marriage will ever last on a foundation of sex alone."

Criss, Jenilee: Peter Criss's only child, Jenilee Criss was born in 1981. Her mother is Debra Jensen. In Makeup to Breakup, Criss recalled visitations with his daughter while separated from Jensen: "While we figured out the divorce, I got to see Jenilee every weekend and on holidays and birthdays. Saturday morning was like Christmas for me. I'd wake up elated and then pick her up like clockwork and take her to Disneyland or to the park. We'd eat Chinese food and rent spooky movies and then I'd bring her back Sunday night. Driving home alone after dropping Jenilee off was pure hell. I would play sad music and cry all the way home."

Criss, Lydia: The woman most associated with Peter Criss, Lydia Di Leonardo married the Catman in 1970. She was his first wife. Peter divorced her in 1979 after falling for 21-year-old Playboy centerfold and Coppertone model Debra Jensen (Peter was 33 at the time). Seeking legal-council from Hollywood divorce lawyer Marvin Mitchelson, Lydia received a $1 million-plus out-of-court settlement. After the divorce, she told *People* magazine, "Sure, I was jealous of the groupies, but I put up with it. If someone digs my old man, well, it is sort of a compliment."

Lydia photographed KISS in concert early in their career and supported Peter by working various jobs. Her book about the band, *Sealed with a KISS*, was published in 2006 by Lydia Criss Publishing. Buccaneer Books published a revised/expanded second edition in 2012.

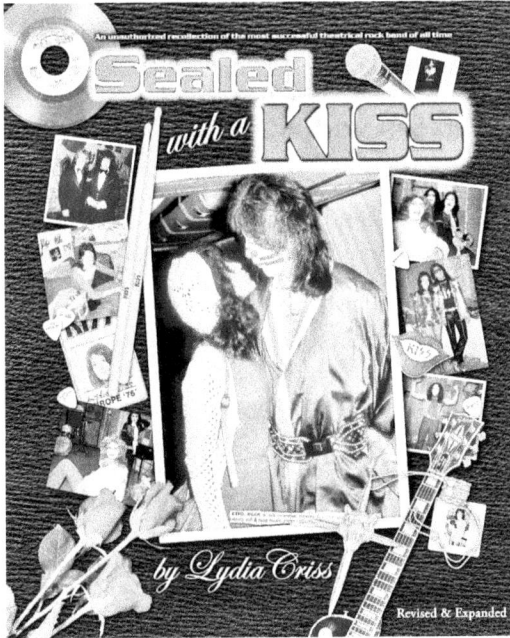

Written by Lydia Criss, Peter Criss's ex-wife, *Sealed with a KISS* is an "unauthorized recollection of the most successful theatrical rock band of all time."

Criss, Peter: Born George Peter John Criscuola on December 20, 1945, in Brooklyn, New York, Peter Criss is the oldest of any former or current KISS member. He was influenced at an early age by the jazz stylings of such drummers as Gene Krupa, whom he studied under during the late 1960s at the legendary Metropole club in New York City. Elvis Presley was a big influence as well.

In *KISS: Behind the Mask—The Official Authorized Biography*, Criss said, "Elvis was one of my first heroes.... I remember seeing Elvis on *The Jackie Gleason Show* ... and I was blown away. I went out and bought a little plastic guitar, and I'd stand in front of the mirror, put water in my hair, give it a little brush, and sing 'Hound Dog.'"

Before seeing Elvis on TV, Criss's first exposure to music was from the radio. "All day long, my folks [Joseph and Loretta Criscuola] played the radio," he said. "Nothing but swing music. I grew up on Benny Goodman, Tommy Dorsey, and Glenn Miller. And I loved it. I would play along with it and dream of someday being a drummer, a singer, and a songwriter."

As a child, Criss got a Rootie Kazootie drum set for Christmas, licensed from the 1950s kids' TV show, *The Rootie Kazootie Club*. Later, as a young teen, Criss played drums in a doo-wop group called Stars, performing in such public places as hallways and subways, drumming on a makeshift kit comprised of a snare drum (framed by a wooden box), two paint cans, and two trashcan lids.

When he was in high school, Criss worked weekends as a delivery boy in a butcher shop. "One of the butchers had a set of drums that were white mother-of-pearl, an exact duplicate of Gene Krupa's set," Criss recalled in *KISS: Behind the Mask*. "And he said, 'I'll sell them to you for $200.' It took me a lot of months of deliveries and tips, of working and saving, but one day, I had enough to buy them. I took them home, and I would play along with the records. And when guys would come by to say, 'Come on out and play baseball' or 'Let's go to a rumble,' I'd say, 'No, I gotta practice.' That's all I did. I'd go to school. I'd work. I'd practice."

All that practice paid off. One day, when Criss was 16, he was walking by a cellar, heard some guys playing electric guitars, and went inside to watch. As fate would have it, they had just fired their drummer, and Criss tried out successfully for the newly opened position.

"I joined them," he said. "They called themselves the Barracudas.... We played little clubs on the weekends and got paid about $10 or $15 a night doing six shows.... I had never been in a band with real instruments, so I never knew how to play with guys with amplifiers. But they liked me, 'cause I really wanted to play. And I sang, too."

Criss became a full-time professional musician in 1963, when he was an 18-year-old senior in high school. He and some friends were watching Joey Greco and the In Crowd at the Metropole Café, an historic club on Broadway near Times Square. During a break, Joey, who Criss knew, asked the future Catman to sit in on drums (the band's regular drummer had a broken leg, so they had been playing without one).

Although Criss knew his time with Joey Greco was going to be temporary, he quit everything to join them: his butcher job, the Barracadus, and school. When Joey Greco's drummer returned, Criss joined another band, and then another, and then another. In *KISS: Behind the Mask*, Criss claimed to have played with approximately 80 bands, including the Starliters and Brotherhood.

"From the time I was 18 until I was 24, I was really pushing hard to make it," he said. "That's when I changed my name [to Cris—later, in the band Infinity, Cris would be changed to Criss]... I wanted to make it, and I would do anything. In and out of groups all the time. Any chance with a name, I'd go with it, hoping I might make a connection."

During the late 1960s, Criss joined a band called Chelsea. "It was an excellent group, real musicians, who could play everything from jazz to hard rock to soul," he said. "Our problem was variety. You couldn't pin a sound on us; we had all kinds of sounds. We made an album that came out on Decca, but the guy who managed us was a real rich little bastard. This kid wanted to be the manager of a rock band, so his father got us. And when things got tough, he dropped us. Out of the whole deal, all I got was a free bass drum. And Decca dropped us."

Criss was stunned with disbelief that Chelsea's first and only album didn't sell well.

"It was so good," he said. "I was *so* up. I had my hopes so high on it. But it failed, and when it did, I had a nervous breakdown. I would just sit in the house and do nothing. Just kept listening to the album, saying, 'I don't believe this didn't make it.' I was shocked that the public wouldn't accept this music. It wasn't crap. Larry Fallon, who did Van Morrison's *Astral Weeks*, arranged the horns and strings. I was so happy to be playing with real musicians. It was the biggest shock of my life, and I felt that I had to make it. When I didn't, I was so shocked. I was like a baby."

In August of 1971, Chelsea became Lips, a band comprised of Criss and Chelsea bandmates Michael Benvenga and Stan Penridge. During the spring of 1972, Benvenga quit the band, and Criss and Penridge were all that was left of Lips. Shortly thereafter, Criss quit Lips and joined Infinity, a cover band consisting of middle aged men playing in a Mob bar called the King's Lounge. Criss joined Infinity at the behest of his old bandmate, Joey Lucenti.

At this point in his career, drumming for a cover band frustrated and depressed Criss, but his wife Lydia, who he had met in 1966 and married in 1970, had pressured him to take the job. But Criss felt he was talented and charismatic enough for bigger and better things, so he placed an ad in *Rolling Stone* that read: EXPD. ROCK & roll drummer looking for orig. grp. doing soft & hard music. Peter, Brooklyn.

During a party in April of 1972, Criss got a call from Gene Simmons, who responding to the ad, asked Criss if he was tall, thin, and good looking—getting a drummer with the right look was important to Simmons and Paul Stanley, who were needing a replacement for Tony Zarrella, the former drummer for their band, Wicked Lester. Simmons and Stanley arranged a meeting with Criss at Electric Lady Studios, and then they watched Criss play with Infinity at a club.

"Gene liked the savage way I'd beat those drums," Criss said in *KISS: Behind the Mask*. "He loved the aggressive vibe I gave off. They wanted a real animal on the drums, and I was their boy." A short time later, the band added Paul "Ace" Frehley to their lineup and changed their name to KISS.

To attract attention, KISS wore makeup and costumes and had elaborate stage props, including a drum riser for Criss. As the Catman, Criss played with KISS until he officially left the band on May 18, 1980. He was on the way out before then as he only played on one song on 1979's *Dynasty* (his own composition, "Dirty Livin'"), and he didn't play at all on 1980's *Unmasked*. Criss was replaced in the band by Eric Carr.

In *Makeup to Breakup*, Criss wrote about wanting to leave KISS, which was selling merchandise to kids and had abandoned its hard rock roots in favor of pop music and disco. "I was burnt out on KISS," he said. "I was sick of playing disco songs and selling Barbie dolls. Between the drugs and my marriage [to Lydia] dissolving, I was a wreck.... I didn't have any feelings then, I was so anesthetized with coke. But even if I hadn't been high, I still didn't want to be involved with them anymore and my playing would have suffered."

Another factor in Criss leaving KISS was the fact that "Beth," which he co-wrote with Stan Penridge when they were with Lips, was the band's biggest hit of all time, reaching #7 on the *Billboard* charts. That gave him the confidence to strike out on his own, which he did with his 1980 solo album,

Out of Control. He followed with 1982's *Let Me Rock You*, which, because of the poor sales of *Out of Control*, wasn't released in the U.S. until 1998.

In 1986, Criss played with a band called Jane, which featured a female lead singer, Jane Booke. They changed their name to Balls of Fire and disbanded the same year. After his brief stint with Jane/Balls of Fire, Criss stayed home for a couple of years to spend time with his daughter, Jenilee, who he had with his second wife, Debra Jensen.

From 1989 to 1991, Criss played in a band called the Keep with future KISS guitarist Mark St. John. St. John's brother Michael Norton played bass while former Black Sabbath vocalist David Donato sang lead. The band had evolved from St. John's prior band, White Tiger, but with Criss replacing drummer Brian James Fox. The Keep recorded demos, but they never found a record label. They played only one live gig: a May 1990 appearance during a drum clinic at a Guitar Center music store in Lawndale, California.

In 1991, the Catman formed a band called, appropriately enough, Criss, which featured future Queensrÿche member Mike Stone on lead guitar. Before disbanding in 1996, the band Criss recorded a self-titled EP in 1993 and an album called *Cat #1* in 1994.

In 1995, Peter Criss called Simmons and asked if he and Jenilee could come to one of the KISS conventions the Demon was putting together. At the con, Simmons and Stanley played a couple of songs with Criss. On October 31, 1995, MTV aired *KISS Unplugged*, in which Criss and Frehley joined in near the end of the set. This was a stepping stone to a full-blown KISS reunion, with Criss and Frehley reuniting with Simmons and Stanley. The original foursome toured and released a new album, 1998's *Psycho Circus*.

In *Makeup to Breakup*, Criss wrote about KISS's first full reunion show in 1996 at Detroit's Tiger Stadium: "I broke down and cried, I got so overwhelmed. It almost seemed like some sort of dream I was in. We were working so hard for that night, hours and hours of vigorous training. It was like boot camp. I had to look at thousands of hours of KISS on video. I had to go back to being the Catman … when I got behind the drums and started the show I was in shock."

In 2001, Criss left KISS over a contract dispute. Eric Singer, Criss's replacement, began wearing Catman makeup later that same year, causing some controversy among longtime KISS fans. Criss rejoined the band in 2002, but left again in 2004 as KISS didn't renew his contract after the World Domination Tour.

In 2008, Criss was working out and noticed a lump on his chest. He was diagnosed with breast cancer, but was successfully treated with a lumpectomy. In 2012, he released his autobiography, *Makeup to Breakup*.

Criss has been married to three different women: Lydia Criss (1970–1979), Debra Jensen (1979–1994), and Gigi Criss (1998 to the present). Jenilee, who was born in 1981, is his only child.

Criss-Penridge Alliance: In 1983, after having released a pair of unsuccessful post–KISS solo records, Peter Criss formed the Nashville-based Criss-Penridge Alliance (a.k.a. the Penridge-Criss Alliance) with Stan Penridge. The band recorded a series of demos and played some live shows, but Criss quit in 1984, before they could record an album.

Crown of Thorns: Paul Stanley co-wrote several songs for the rock band Crown of Thorns, which featured KISS songwriter Jean Beauvoir on vocals.

***CSI: Crime Scene Investigation*:** In "Long Road Home," which is the 17th episode of the 14th season of *CSI: Crime Scene Investigation*, a groupie is discovered dead in a stolen party limo. CSI investigates, leading them to a "fame experience" featuring a trio of rockers jamming with Gene Simmons, who plays himself. The script includes many rock puns, including song titles. Debuting October 6, 2000, *CSI: Crime Scene Investigation* ran for 15 seasons on CBS.

Cuomo, Bill: Bill Cuomo played keyboards on several songs on Peter Criss's 1978 KISS solo album. He also worked with such acts as Ry Cooder, the Little River Band, Smokey Robinson, Steve Perry, and Lynyrd Skynyrd.

Cuomo, Curtis: Writer/producer Curtis Cuomo co-wrote "Psycho Circus," along with several songs on *Carnival of Souls*. He also worked with such acts as Eddie Money and the Eric Singer Project.

Curly: For reasons that baffled other band members, Ace Frehley would frequently call people "Curly," especially when he was drunk.

Cusano, AnnMarie: Vinnie Vincent's first wife. Vincent was married to her during the early 1980s. They had twin girls, Elizabeth and Jessica.

Sadly, AnnMarie was reported missing in 1998, and it was discovered that she had been murdered. According to the *Hartford Courant*, a man named Gregory McArthur was sentenced for the crime in 2002. He received 60 years in prison for "felony murder, manslaughter, larceny and kidnapping in Cusano's death.... During the five-week trial, the jury found that McArthur had not intended to kill Cusano, but did so after the part-time prostitute refused to stay for a date in his Hartford apartment.... Officials never determined precisely how Cusano died, but McArthur told police that he had grabbed her in a choke-hold and she collapsed in his room."

Cusano, Diane: Vinnie Vincent's second wife. He met her at a KISS Convention in 1995 and married her in 1996. In January of 2014, at the age of 47, she died from conditions related to chronic alcoholism. While Cusano, who worked for a Nashville Realtor, supported Vincent during his post–KISS years, they apparently had a turbulent relationship.

According to www.rollingstone.com: "On the evening of May 22nd, 2011, Vinnie Vincent's wife, Diane Cusano, walked into the Rutherford County Sheriff's Department in Murfreesboro, Tennessee, 15 miles from her Smyrna home. She smelled of alcohol and was covered in blood. She told the on-duty deputy that her husband had slapped her face, grabbed her hair, dragged her through shattered glass and, as she tried to escape from their property, repeatedly hurled her to the ground. According to police, the two had been arguing over a conversation Vincent had had with another woman."

Vincent was charged with aggravated domestic assault, spent the night in jail, and was released on $10,000 bond the next morning.

Cusano, Vincent: Vincent Cusano was Vinnie Vincent's name before Gene Simmons suggested that he change it.

Custom Chevy Van: Released in 1977 by the AMT Corporation, the KISS Custom Chevy Van is a 1/25 scale hobby kit designed for the user to glue together. The pieces are white and can be painted as desired. To decorate the van, eight 4" × 6" decals featuring *Destroyer* and *Love Gun* art were included. The back of the box refers to Gene as "The Bat," Peter as "The Big Cat," Ace Frehley as "Space," and Paul Stanley as "Loveable." The kit was "recommended for modelers 10 years through adulthood." Features include: detailed chassis with V8 engine; bucket seats; custom steering wheel; CB radio; custom spoke wheels and wide Goodyear Rally GT tires; custom front end with lights, grille, and spoiler; woody rear bumpers; quad exhaust outlets; twin skylights; and louvered and bubble port holes.

Daily News: Manhattan's *Daily News*, founded in 1919, published one of the first reviews of a KISS show (1973 at the Coventry). It was written by Stan Mieses, who was impressed by the look of the band, but not their music.

The Daisy: When KISS played their first gig on January 30, 1973, at the Coventry, they wore little makeup. However, Ace, Gene, and Peter wore early versions of their now-iconic makeup designs a little later that year at a pair of shows March 9–10 at the Daisy in Amityville, Long Island. Paul wore eye makeup and rouge, but not the patented star.

To celebrate the 40th anniversary of those historical concerts, KISS granted an interview to Ethan Sacks of the *Daily News*. Paul Stanley recalled, "I remember playing the Daisy and locking ourselves in the owner's office because one of the bouncers said he was going to kill us because of the way we looked. The first night there really was a handful of people, but within a few times of playing there, they were literally breaking the windows to get into the place."

Sid Benjamin was the owner of the Daisy, which had a legal capacity of 144 people, but sometimes the club would cram in as many as 300 people or more.

The Daisy is where KISS first established a true fan base. "It's interesting that the crowds coming to see us at the Daisy connected with KISS faster than those in New York City," Gene Simmons said in *Nothin' to Lose: The Making of KISS (1972–1975)*. "KISS broke in the same town where *JAWS* and *The Amityville Horror* were filmed. We were embraced by people who weren't affected by style and don't care what's happening anywhere else."

According to Sid's son, Richard, the Daisy was a Rexall drugstore before it was converted into a nightclub. "The name of the club was a play on hippie flower power," he said in *Nothin' to Lose*.

"The Daisy first opened in the late sixties and closed about 10 years later. Everyone from KISS to Atilla [Billy Joel's early band] to the Stray Cats played there early in their career."

Damon, Jesse: Gene Simmons wrote two songs for Jesse Damon: "Everybody Needs Somebody" (with Damon) on *The Hand That Rocks* (2002) and "You're My Reason for Livin'" on *Nothin' Else Matters* (2004). More than a decade prior, Damon sang backing vocals on *Revenge*.

"Dance All Over Your Face": One of several mediocre songs on *Lick It Up* written and sung by Gene Simmons (actually, this one dips well below mediocre), "Dance All Over Your Face" is the ninth track on the album and is one of the weakest KISS songs of the 1980s. Simmons sings about a girl he saw with another man, so he's going to dance on her face, whatever that means.

Dancing with the Stars: On April 9, 2012, KISS played "Rock and Roll All Nite" on the competition program *Dancing with the Stars*, which debuted on ABC in 2005. The song helped usher in the program's "Rock Week" and featured dancers wearing KISS makeup.

"Danger": The fifth track on the hard rocking *Creatures of the Night*, "Danger" was written by Adam Mitchell (a racecar driver who was in a band called the Paupers) and Paul Stanley, whose vocal bravado tears through lyrics about fighting alone, walking the edge, and passing the point of no return. Drummer Eric Carr and lead guitarist Vinnie Vincent provide muscular instrumentation to match. Jimmy Haslip, a founding member of the Yellowjackets, plays bass.

"Danger Us": Written and sung by Paul Stanley, "Danger Us" is the eighth track on *Sonic Boom*. The lyrics are dopey, and the age and wear on Stanley's voice is evident (he sounds a little raspy), but fans of arena rockers will find plenty to like here.

"Dark Light": The sixth track on *Music from "The Elder,"* "Dark Light" works better as a stand-alone rock tune than any of the other songs on the record, but it still fits the overall concept, telling of a forthcoming evil. It was written by Gene Simmons, Anton Fig, Lou Reed, and Ace Frehley, who sings the song and provides a blistering guitar lead—one of his fastest. Frehley hated the idea of doing a concept album, but he really shines (so to speak) on "Dark Light." Bob Ezrin plays bass on the number, which was originally called "Don't Run."

Darrell, Dimebag: Born Darrell Lance Abbott on August 20, 1966, Dimebag Darrell was a guitarist for and founding member of Pantera and Damageplan. He was also a huge KISS fan, especially of Ace Frehley, covering "Snowblind" on *Return of the Comet: A Tribute to Ace Frehley* and "Fractured Mirror" on *Spacewalk: A Salute to Ace Frehley*. He also had an autographed tattoo of Frehley on his chest.

In a September 1995 interview published on guitarinternational.com, Dimebag said, "I'd have to say that Ace Frehley was probably my biggest influence. Just the whole image, and especially that vibrato he's got [mimics "wowwowwow" vibrato sound]. That was actually the reason I started playing guitar, by the way. I dressed up like him, got a fake Les Paul, skipped school to play in front of the mirror, then went from there."

Tragedy struck December 8, 2004, when a gunman named Nathan Gale shot and killed Dimebag Darrell while the guitarist was performing with Damageplan at the Alrosa Villa in Columbus, Ohio. A hardcore fan to the end, Darrell was buried in a KISS coffin.

Davidson, Joe: Joe Davidson was the original drummer for the pre–Wicked Lester band Rainbow, but he was quickly replaced by Tony Zarrella.

Dayton, Chip Rock: Longtime rock photographer Chip Rock Dayton is the author of *Outtakes*, a KISS book containing more than 200 photos. Dayton's work has also appeared on a variety of KISS merchandise, including albums, videos, and their first tour program. He first photographed the band in 1975 at a concert at the Beacon Theatre in New York City. "The KISS show at the Beacon blew me away," Dayton wrote in *Outtakes*. "I couldn't get enough of them. That was the first time I photographed KISS, and those images are very special to me."

The Decline of Western Civilization Part II: The Metal Years: The sequel to *The Decline of Western Civilization*, which was about punk rock, *The Metal Years* is a documentary covering heavy metal of the 1980s. Directed by Penelope Spheeris, it is famous for showing Chris Holmes of W.A.S.P. being interviewed in a swimming pool while thoroughly intoxicated, and for the scene in which Ozzy Osbourne tries to cook eggs. Less memorable, but still noteworthy is a segment in which Paul Stanley discusses heavy metal while lying in bed with gorgeous women. Stanley says, "Heavy metal is the true rock and roll of the '80s, and rock and roll was music made by people thinking with their crotches." Released June 17, 1988.

Delaney, Sean: Bill Aucoin's personal and professional partner, Sean Delaney, who worked with KISS from the early 1970s until the early 1980s, was a key figure in giving the band their image, convincing members to die their hair blue-black, wear taller platform boots, and don black and silver clothing. He helped run their rehearsals and would videotape their performances so they could learn from their mistakes and repeat the moves that were effective. He also acted as roadie, stage manager, and driver.

In an interview published in *KISSaholics* #16 (Sept., 1996), Delaney recalled seeing KISS in September of 1973 at a private showcase at the Henry LeTang School of Dance.

"I thought it was absolutely the worst thing that could possibly hit, I mean worst," he said. "It was so unlike anything that it had to be incredible. It was new, it was something that wasn't being done.... So try to imagine, in a small rehearsal studio, four guys are up there playing. In front of them are Bill Aucoin (KISS' future manager), Neil Bogart (future president of Casablanca Records), Joyce Biawitz (also KISS' future manager), and myself. They finished the first song and no applause. Gene walks down to Neil Bogart, grabs both of his hands, and makes him applaud ... and Neil started applauding because he was scared to death. And I said to myself at that moment, 'This I wanna be involved in'... because that's the kind of balls you have to have to do anything.'"

Delaney, who has claimed that it was he who convinced Aucoin to go see KISS at the Hotel Diplomat, co-wrote a number of songs on *Rock and Roll Over* and *Alive II*, remixed songs on *Double Platinum*, and helped produce *Double Platinum* and Gene Simmons' and Peter Criss's 1978 solo albums. He was also "involved with original concepts for the super-hero KISS characters and motifs used in the Marvel comics and *KISS Meets the Phantom of the Park* ... in fact, it is nearly impossible to find something done by the band in the 1970s where Delaney was not involved and his name somewhere in the credits, be it album, film, or books" (*KISS FAQ*).

And yet, some feel that Delaney is underappreciated, including Peter Criss. In *Makeup to Breakup*, he wrote: "Sean Delaney was, in my estimation, the fifth member of KISS. He was a tremendously talented creative force.... Sean never got the credit he deserved for making us into superstars...[He] had his hand in everything we created, from our personas to our wardrobe to our staging. He even contributed to the songs."

Delaney passed away from complications related to diabetes on April 13, 2003. He was 58. After he died, Gene Simmons released the following statement: "Sad to report that Sean Delaney, our first road manager, co-writer and much more ... has passed away. Bill Aucoin, the band's first manager, called to tell me the sad news. Our condolences to the Delaney family. Sean and I spoke only a few weeks ago. He told me he had just started working with a new English Country and Western band. Aucoin also told me about that venture. Sean seemed happy to be working on something he cared about again. He also asked if he could introduce us when we played in his home town, and I, of course said yes. We both made plans to see each other when we arrived in his city. Sadly, he will not be able to introduce us. But, in more ways than one, Sean was one of the pivotal people in all our lives. He believed, when the world did not. He was there for us in the beginning and helped shape the direction of the band. He will be missed."

See also: "Hellbox."

DeLeo, Robert: The bass player for the Stone Temple Pilots, Robert DeLeo is a huge KISS fan. In his foreword to *All I Need to Know I Learned from KISS: Life Lessons from the Hottest Band in the Land*, he wrote:

As a young boy growing up in the seventies, certain things came along that inspired, affected, or plain-out changed my life: skateboards, minibikes, surfboards, Puma Clydes, rock tumbling sets, Schwinn bikes, Duncan yo-yos, Vertibird, Yoohoo, Evel Knievel, making out, air guitaring and.... KISS.

Little did I know at the time I would grow up to entirely embrace music, get a record deal, dress up as KISS at one of my own shows (with Ace helping put on the band's make up!), be asked by KISS to go out on tour, serve jury duty with Paul!?!?!?, and have the opportunity to call and personally ask them for advice on this nutty profession we have chosen. KISS has created quite a legacy. Like all good characters in our lives through time, the Star Child, Space Man, Demon, and Cat have been lasting ones.

It's now thirty five years later that I completely understand what KISS means to me. They did to me exactly what they said they were going to do.... They robbed me of my virgin soul!

Delsener, Ron: A concert promoter for more than half a century, Ron Delsener promoted numerous KISS shows, beginning in 1975 at the Beacon Theatre in New York. He also booked gigs for the Beatles, Bob Dylan, David Bowie, and many others.

Demon: Thanks to his devilish makeup, demonic costumes, and fire-breathing, tongue-wagging antics, Gene Simmons' stage name is the Demon. In *Face the Music: A Life Exposed*, Paul Stanley wrote about his bandmate's persona: "Gene's makeup was arguably the strongest of all. It was symmetrical and symbolic. It was lascivious. It had the drama of kabuki. It was a striking image, and then when he stuck out his tongue—it just made sense. The Demon."

Derringer, Rick: Born Ricky Dean Zehringer on August 5, 1947, Rick Derringer played the guitar solo on "Exciter." Best known for recording "Hang on Sloopy" with the McCoys and "Rock and Roll, Hoochie Koo" with Johnny Winter, Derringer once expressed surprise that Paul Stanley is such a good guitar player.

Destroyer: In recent years, *Rolling Stone* ranked *Destroyer* KISS's third best album, saying it "shows KISS at the top of their game." However, when the record was originally released (March 15, 1976, by Casablanca Records), the magazine (issue #214, June 1976) trashed it for its "bloated ballads," "pedestrian drumming," and "lackluster performances."

Regardless, many fans consider *Destroyer* KISS's best, most polished album, thanks in no small part to its elaborate production by taskmaster Bob Ezrin (he would wear a whistle around his neck and bark orders at the band, much to their chagrin), who imbued the recording with such flourishes as sound effects, a children's choir, an orchestra, and a calliope. During Gene Simmons' menacing "God of Thunder," you can hear creepy-sounding children (Ezrin' sons David and Josh) screaming, an interesting effect to say the least.

The band's fourth studio album (and one of their proudest accomplishments), *Destroyer* is indeed a slick production with a variety of great songs, from the iconic "Detroit Rock City" to the anthemic "Shout It Out Loud" to the band's biggest hit, the power ballad "Beth," which reached #7 on the *Billboard* charts.

Destroyer, which features a great cover by fantasy artist Ken Kelly, was released in the aftermath of *Alive!*, the band's breakout live album. According to Paul Elliott (*KISS: Hotter Than Hell*), *Destroyer* was slow out of the starting gate in terms of sales, but ultimately achieved success, thanks in part to the popularity of "Beth." "Fans were shocked by KISS's new polished sound," Elliott wrote, "but once the band had returned to the road with the most extravagant stage show to date, *Destroyer* quickly reached platinum status."

Tracks include: "Detroit Rock City," "King of the Night Time World," "God of Thunder," "Great Expectations," "Flaming Youth," "Sweet Pain," "Shout It Out Loud," "Beth," and "Do You Love Me?." Certain vinyl releases include a 10th unlisted track, "Rock and Roll Party," which is listed and featured on the 1997 CD remastering of *Destroyer*, and on the 2012 remix, *Destroyer: Resurrected*.

Destroyer: Resurrected: Released August 21, 2012, by Mercury Records, *Destroyer: Resurrected* is a remix of *Destroyer*. It was remixed by Bob Ezrin, the producer on *Destroyer*. Although many fans derided *Destroyer: Resurrected* for its dearth of bonus material, William Clark of *Guitar International* praised the audio, saying, "Each track sounds crisper, clearer, and louder, which are always welcome qualities when you're listening to a classic album of the likes of *Destroyer*."

Ezrin included liner notes in the package, but, according to Dan Mistich of www.popmatters.com, "the only real bonus material is an additional recording of 'Sweet Pain' with Space Ace's original guitar solo included (on the original release, Dick Wagner, Alice Cooper's guitar player, was reportedly called in to lay down tracks in Frehley's absence)."

In an interview with Eddie Trunk, Peter Criss derided the CD, stating, "Why touch a masterpiece?"

Destroyer: Resurrected peaked at #11 on the *Billboard* charts. It features the original unused *Destroyer* cover art by Ken Kelly, which, with its burning buildings in the background, was deemed too violent by the record label. Said art shows KISS in their *Alive!* costumes.

Destroyer Tour: The Destroyer Tour was in support of the band's fourth studio album. Between April 11 and October 1, 1976, KISS played 67 shows in the U.S., Canada, and Europe. A highlight was the Anaheim, California gig in which they played to more than 42,000 people, their biggest U.S. crowd to that date. The American leg of the tour is sometimes referred to as the Spirit of '76 Tour. Stage props included fire engine lights, bombs, disco balls, flamethrowers, Ace's smoking guitar, Gene's blood-spitting and fire-breathing, staircases, Paul smashing his guitar, KISS Army banners, two cat statues on the drum riser, a large cat drum riser curtain, and a lighted KISS logo.

Band lineup: Paul Stanley, Gene Simmons, Ace Frehley, and Peter Criss. Opening acts: 38 Special, Artful Dodger, Blue Öyster Cult, Bob Seger & the Silver Bullet Band, Brownsville Station, Earth Quake, Ethos, Finch, Hammersmith, Hoa Bihn, the J. Geils Band, Johnny & Edgar Winter, Kansas, Montrose, Moon Pie, Point Blank, the Scorpions, Starz, Stray, Ted Nugent, and UFO. Average attendance: 11,073 (not including the 5/4/76 gig or the European leg of the tour).

Followed by: Rock and Roll Over Tour.

Detroit Metal City: *Detroit Metal City*, based on the comedy anime and manga series of the same name, is a live action film directed by Toshio Lee. Debuting in Japanese theaters August 23, 2008, it features a cameo appearance by Gene Simmons. The title was inspired by "Detroit Rock City."

Detroit Rock City **(movie):** Directed by Adam Rifkin and produced by Gene Simmons and noted KISS photographer Barry Levine, *Detroit Rock City* (1999) is set in 1978, chronicling the adventures of four teenage boys (played by Edward Furlong, Giuseppe Andrews, James DeBello, and Sam Huntington) trying to make it to a KISS concert in Detroit.

The film, which had a $15 million budget and grossed a disappointing $24,217,115 worldwide, features the music of Black Sabbath, AC/DC, Thin Lizzy, The Runaways, Van Halen, Blue Öyster Cult, Pantera, and Cheap Trick. At the end of the movie, KISS plays "Detroit Rock City" in concert. The New Line Platinum Series DVD release includes 15 minutes of deleted scenes, three feature-length commentaries (by KISS, Rifkin, and the cast and crew), and other special features.

"Detroit Rock City" (song): One of the better, more well-known songs in KISS's extensive library, "Detroit Rock City" is the first track on *Destroyer* and has been the opening song in many a KISS show (it originally replaced "Deuce"). KISS played the song on the first episode of *Gene Simmons Family Jewels*, and it's been a staple of pop culture in general for years, appearing in the video game *Rock Band* (2007) and in such films as *Role Models* (2008) and *The Dilemma* (2011). The Detroit Tigers and Detroit Red Wings sports teams have used the song as well.

"Detroit Rock City" was written by Paul Stanley (who sings lead) and producer Bob Ezrin, who's responsible for the creative intro, in which listeners hear a car revving up, a report of a fatal car crash and a snippet of "Rock and Roll All Nite" on the radio, and the skidding of tries followed by a jarring head-on-collision. Ezrin also came up with Ace Frehley's lead on the song. As suggested by the title, "Detroit Rock City" is a hard-rocking ode to the Motor City, which embraced KISS early in their career and is identified with the band as much as their native New York.

"Deuce": "Deuce," the thunderous, hard-driving show-opener during the early years of KISS, is the seventh track on *KISS*, the band's first album. In *KISS: Behind the Mask—The Official Authorized Biography*, Gene Simmons said the song was "written in my head on a bus. I heard the lick, the riff, the melody, the whole thing…. We arranged it right on the spot and knew that it would be a staple for years. Lyrically, I had no idea what I was talking about. Sometimes stuff means a lot, sometimes it means nothing."

A favorite of Ace Frehley's, "Deuce" was the first song the guitarist played with Simmons, Paul Stanley, and Peter Criss during his audition. "They played it as a three-piece and the song was in the key of A," Frehley said in *KISS: Behind the Mask*. "I thought, that's easy enough, so I got up and wailed for four minutes playing lead work over it."

Inspired by the Raspberries' top-five hit, "Go All the Way," Paul Stanley wrote the opening riff for "Deuce."

"The Devil Is Me": A heavy duty Gene Simmons song that would feel at home on *Revenge*, "The Devil Is Me" is the eighth track on *Monster*.

Simmons sings—smoothly instead of growly—about running from temptation, praying for salvation, screaming at God, fighting to be free, and ultimately hearing the Lord's decry that "The Devil Is Me." Written by Simmons, Paul Stanley, and Tommy Thayer.

Dick Clark's American Bandstand 50th Anniversary: In 2002, Dick Clark celebrated the 50th year of the seminal music show, *American Bandstand*, which started in 1952 as local program in Philadelphia called *Bandstand*. The anniversary special, which aired on ABC, celebrated acts that got their start on television through Dick Clark, including KISS, who performed a rousing rendition of "Detroit Rock City." Tommy Thayer and Eric Singer were with the band at this point.

Dickenson, Christopher see **Peter Criss Imposter**

Die Ärzte: On the German version of *Kiss My Ass: Classic KISS Regrooved*, punk rockers Die Ärzte cover "Unholy."

DiMarzio Pickups: During the late 1970s, Paul Stanley appeared in an ad for DiMarzio guitar pickups. The ad read: "Paul Stanley plays at high volume, but he has to be heard clearly. That's not easy, but for the Super II, it's no problem. That's what the Super II is made for, and who it's made for—anyone who has to be heard through any situation, and heard right." Another DiMarzio ad featured the entire band.

Dinosaur Jr.: On *Kiss My Ass: Classic KISS Regrooved*, alt rockers Dinosaur Jr., who formed in 1984, covered "Goin' Blind."

"Dirty Livin'": The fourth track on *Dynasty*, "Dirty Livin'" was written by Peter Criss, Stan Penridge, and Vini Poncia. In addition to putting pen to paper, Criss played drums and sang the song, his only contributions to *Dynasty*. Despite Criss's overall non-involvement with the album, "Dirty Livin'" is a fine tune—an intriguing mix of disco, drugs, living in New York, and the Catman's frustrated and burned out mindset at the time. It was the B side on the single release of "Sure Know Something."

Distroya!: Organized by Portland, Oregon's W.O.K. Records, *Distroya!* is a hard-to-find KISS tribute album devoted to *Destroyer*, featuring songs by Portland bands. Tracks include: "Detroit Rock City" (New Bad Things), "King Of The Night Time World" (Wallpaper), "God of Thunder" (Shine), "Great Expectations" (Last Pariah's), "Flaming Youth" (Born Wet), "Sweet Pain" (Pearl Scam), "Shout It Out Loud" (Frankie Machine & The Stiffs), "Beth" (Gashdig), and "Do You Love Me?" (Roger Nusic).

Dixon, Donna: During the *Creatures of the Night* era, Paul Stanley dated actress Donna Dixon, who played Sonny Lumet on *Bosom Buddies* (1980–1982), and who starred in such films as *Doctor Detroit* (1983), *Spies Like Us* (1985), and *Wayne's World* (1992).

In *Face the Music: A Life Exposed*, the Starchild, who met Dixon at a restaurant, wrote about her: "Donna was staggeringly attractive…. I loved having such a gorgeous girlfriend. As superficial as it may have been, she was beautiful in a way that made me happy. With hindsight, I can see that dating her was clearly another way of my trying to eradicate my own imperfections by being with someone seemingly perfect."

When Dixon broke up with Stanley, it left him depressed and despondent. Toward the end of their relationship, she had been evasive, disappearing for days at a time and showing up with curious, barely-explained items like a fur coat and a T-shirt from Martha's Vineyard. She even married *Doctor Detroit* co-star Dan Akroyd without telling Stanley during a time Stanley was under the impression they could get back together.

Many sources claim that Stanley wrote "I Still Love You" in response to Dixon breaking up with him, but Stanley has claimed he was happily involved in a romantic relationship with another woman at the time.

"Do You Love Me?": When *Destroyer* was in production, KISS was getting more and more popular. As such, they were questioning the intentions of the women they were with, or so "Do You Love Me?," the ninth track on *Destroyer*, would have the listener believe. Written by Paul Stanley (who has called it one of his favorite tracks), Kim Fowley, and Bob Ezrin, the song has a touch of sincerity that comes through in Stanley's vocals, and Peter Criss gets things underway in dramatic fashion with an emphatic drumbeat. At one point, Stanley talks some of the lyrics, leading certain music historians to claim that the Starchild invented rap music. Nirvana covered "Do You Love Me?" on the KISS tribute album *Hard to Believe*.

"Do You Remember Rock 'n' Roll Radio": This song is the first track and second single on the Ramones' 1980 album, *End of the Century*. KISS covered the tune for the 2003 tribute record, *We're a Happy Family: A Tribute to Ramones*. It is the sixth track on that CD and later appeared as a bonus song on the single-disc edition of *KISS Symphony: Alive IV*.

Dr Pepper Cherry: In 2009, Gene Simmons starred in a commercial for cherry-flavored Dr Pepper. As he sits on a rock and roll throne of sorts, fully outfitted in Demon regalia and surrounded by three beautiful women, he says the drink has a *"kiss of cherry,"* overemphasizing the word "kiss." Amusingly, Simmons' son, Nick, enters the scene and chastises him for his KISS-centric delivery. At the end of the commercial, after lauding the smoothness of the drink, Simmons says, "Trust me, I'm a doctor," with "Calling Dr. Love" playing in the background.

"Domino": The sixth track on *Revenge* and the album's third single (it failed to hit the *Billboard* Hot 100), "Domino," like "Unholy" off the same record, is a quality Gene Simmons tune. "The growled vocals and boogie thump on 'Domino' are vaguely reminiscent of ZZ Top's sleazier moments," wrote Paul Elliott in *KISS: Hotter Than Hell*. According to www.kissmonster.com, Simmons said the song "started out with a bass lick, much as 'Deuce' did. Once I had the meter down, I started writing rhyming words, but without a melody—so it was almost a rap. Then I talked the song through with the lick, and the melody just came naturally. The melody that came to me was the bass lick, so I just shadowed my melody with the lick on [rhythm] guitar." Clearly, the song, which is about a young girl who is a bad habit, borrows from Black 'N Blue's "Nasty Nasty," which was written by Simmons, Tommy Thayer, and Jaime St. James.

Don Kirshner's Rock Concert: Created by Don Kirshner, who had been executive producer and creative consultant on ABC's *In Concert* series, *Don Kirshner's Rock Concert* ran from Sept. 27, 1973, until early 1981. The show specialized in showing great musical acts, live and in person, including "everyone from '60s holdovers like the Byrds and Joan Baez to '70s hit makers like Abba and Fleetwood Mac. In and among the big names like the Rolling Stones were new bands such as the Ramones and New York Dolls, who gained entrance into Middle America through this program. Kirshner himself would often host the show despite his deadpan, lifeless style of delivery that Paul Shaffer parodied brilliantly on *Saturday Night Live* in the mid–70s" (Dave Swanson, ultimateclassicrock.com).

KISS appeared on *Don Kirshner's Rock Concert* on May 28, 1977, but it was a disappointment when compared to their awesome live performance on ABC's *In Concert* three years before. Instead of live footage, viewers saw staged promotional videos from *Rock And Roll Over*. Songs included: "I Want You" (which aired again on April 7 for the show's anniversary program), "Hard Luck Woman," and "Love 'Em and Leave 'Em."

Kirshner, as dry and as emotionless as ever, introduced the band thusly: "Breathing fire, sparks flying from the Frankenstein machine, fantastic costuming and makeup are the visually identifiable features of the phenomenal group, KISS. In a relatively short time, this group, on Neil Bogart's Casablanca and Filmworks label, is one of the hottest bands in the country. Managed by Bill Aucoin, tonight we have this exclusive presentation of this performance by KISS."

On September 27, 1979, Kirshner introduced two more promotional KISS videos on his program: "I Was Made For Lovin'" and "Sure Know Something" from *Dynasty*, saying: "KISS has been described as rock's most explosive incendiary device. Six years of success seem to be only the beginning, selling out in concerts throughout the world and record sales in the millions—attest to the continued popularity of this colorful group. Guided by manager Bill Aucoin, KISS is always full of surprises, and here's a startling example."

"Doncha Hesitate": Written and sung by Paul Stanley, "Doncha Hesitate" (1975) failed to make the cut on *Destroyer* since it had a more primitive sound evoking the band's first three albums. However, KISS did include the song as track five on disc two of *The Box Set*.

"Don't Touch My Ascot": Written by Tony Cervone, Greg Collins, and Jared Faber for the 2015 direct-to-DVD movie, *Scooby-Doo! and KISS: Rock and Roll Mystery*, "Don't Touch My Ascot" is a humorous song that was performed by KISS, Collins, and Faber. Noted KISS collector Mark Cicchini of *Three Sides of the Coin* compared it to Van Halen's "Could this be Magic."

"Don't You Let Me Down": The fourth track on Peter Criss' 1978 KISS solo album, "Don't You Let Me Down" has a "hint of Ben E. King's 'Stand by Me' and a cheesy synthesizer sound that wouldn't be out of place on a Barry Manilow song … it's a sweet little tune confirming Criss as the soppiest man ever to play drums in a heavy metal band" (Paul Elliott, *KISS: Hotter Than Hell*). "Don't You Let Me Down," one of two singles released from the record (the other was "You Matter to Me"), was written by Criss and Stan Penridge.

Doro: The second solo album by German female hard rock singer Doro Pesch, *Doro* (1990) was produced by Tommy Thayer and Gene Simmons (with Pat Regan). Thayer played guitar on the record, and Thayer and Simmons wrote and co-wrote some of the songs.

Double Platinum: The first "greatest hits" compilation by KISS, *Double Platinum* is a two-album release from Casablanca in 1978, packaged in a gatefold silver sleeve with two embossed KISS logos on the cover. It opens to reveal each band member's face in bas-relief (like the face on a silver coin). The record included a printed "Platinum Award" thanking the KISS Army for making the band a "Double Platinum Success." Later releases weren't as slickly packaged, replacing the embossed logos with red print and the bas-relief images with photos. The 1997 remastering on CD was patterned after the original vinyl release.

There are 20 songs on *Double Platinum*, including "Strutter '78," which is a disco-influenced version of "Strutter," and which was obviously included to entice collectors. A number of other songs were remixed for the album by Sean Delaney and Mike Stone.

According to Ron Albanese of www.kissasylum.com, "*Double Platinum* is the best KISS compilation ever. I like the album's vibe. It is great driving music in a classy package. While the changes administered to some of the album's songs committed audio murder.… Paul's vocals on 'Firehouse' took a beating … others fared well.… 'Do You Love Me' is crisper here than on *Destroyer*.… 'Hard Luck Woman' reveals more than its first studio treatment on *Rock and Roll Over*.… 'Calling Dr. Love' is more demonic than the 1976 model, it begins with a series of groans that sounds as though the song was recorded in Hell, and the guitars zoom in like a jet…

'C'mon and Love Me' was transformed into pure super pop from the mild-mannered ordinary pop it was on *Dressed to Kill*."

Tracks on *Double Platinum*, which reached #22 on the *Billboard* 200, include: "Strutter '78," "Do You Love Me?," "Hard Luck Woman" (remix), "Calling Dr. Love" (remix), "Let Me Go, Rock 'n' Roll," "Love Gun," "God of Thunder," "Firehouse" (remix), "Hotter Than Hell," "I Want You," "Deuce" (remix), "100,000 Years" (remix), "Detroit Rock City" (remix), "Rock Bottom (intro)/ She" (remix), "Rock and Roll All Nite," "Beth," "Makin' Love," "C'mon and Love Me" (remix), "Cold Gin," and "Black Diamond" (remix).

"Down on Your Knees": The closest thing KISS has to an AC/DC song, "Down on Your Knees" is the second track on *Killers*, the UK release that followed *Music from "The Elder."* It's a dirty, unapologetic, hard rock tune, the exact opposite of the portentous (some might say pretentious) songs on the record that preceded it. Written by Paul Stanley, Mikel Japp (who has said he played guitar on the song), and Bryan Adams, "Down on Your Knees" has Stanley settling for an eager-to-please girl who's all he's got. Yep, it's about casual sex.

Dracula: Christopher Lee's onscreen portrayal of Dracula, who debuted in Bram Stoker's 1897 gothic horror novel, influenced Gene Simmons to spit blood onstage.

"Dreamin'": Written by Paul Stanley and Bruce Kulick, "Dreamin'" is the ninth track on *Psycho Circus*. Stanley sings the song, which sounds a little like Alice Cooper's "I'm Eighteen." A pleasing rocker, it would fit right at home on Stanley's 1978 solo album.

Dressed to Kill: Released March 19, 1975, by Casablanca Records, *Dressed to Kill* is the third KISS album. Produced by Neil Bogart and recorded at Electric Lady Studios in New York City, the record includes the following tracks: "Room Service," "Two Timer," "Ladies in Waiting," "Getaway," "Rock Bottom," "C'mon and Love Me," "Anything for My Baby," "She," "Love Her All I Can," and "Rock and Roll All Nite," which would become the band's signature tune with the release of the *Alive!* version.

Dressed to Kill, which clocks in at just 30:07, peaked at #32 on the *Billboard* charts and was certified gold on February 28, 1977. The comical cover depicts the band wearing ill-fitting suits, posing in

New York on the southwest corner of 23rd Street and 8th Avenue. According to Bob Gruen, who took the photo, Criss and Stanley each owned the suit they were wearing, but Ace and Gene borrowed theirs from Gruen, and Gene wore Gruen's wife's clogs.

Recently, *Rolling Stone* ranked *Dressed to Kill* KISS's sixth best album, calling it focused and sonically strong. In the magazine's original review in issue #191 (July 1975), Gordon Fletcher wrote: "KISS does not play music—it makes very high-volume noise. If rock & roll intrigues you, though, you'd best be advised that for all the simplicity, overstatement and repetition within its records, KISS does make fantastically successful rock. Driven by Gene Simmons's remarkably inventive bass lines and the cacophonous poundings of drummer Peter Criss, KISS makes Chuck Berry chords and basic rock progressions come alive with energetic urgency. Simple? Yes. Repetitive? Yessir! But like the Stooges, KISS manages to avoid monotony."

Dressed to Kill: An Independent Tribute to KISS: Released in 1995 by Rock Dream Records, this tribute album includes the following tracks: "King of The Night Time World" (Razamanaz), "I Was Made For Lovin' You" (Good Girls Don't), "Sure Know Something" (Bobby Bandiera), "I Want You" (Adrian Dodz), "God of Thunder" (Fuel), "Breakout" (Glen Evans), "Love Gun" (Flipp), "Hotter Than Hell" (by Hotter Than Hell, a KISS tribute band), "Parasite" (Endangered Species), "Beth" (Fiendz), "Rocket Ride" (Relayer), and "Rip It Out" (Haphazard). The CD was reissued in 1997 with a bonus track: "Put It Back On" by Fractured Mirror, an Ace Frehley tribute band.

Dressed to Kill Tour: In support of their third album, KISS toured the U.S. from March 19 to August 28, 1975, playing a total of 71 shows. Bill Aucoin used his American Express Card to fund much of the tour as the band had little money at the time. The shows in Detroit (May 16), Cleveland (June 21), Davenport, Iowa (July 20), and Wildwood, New Jersey (July 23) were recorded for the *Alive!* album.

Band lineup: Paul Stanley, Gene Simmons, Ace Frehley, and Peter Criss. Headlining acts: Black Sabbath, Golden Earring, Hunter-Ranson, Johnny Winter, the Marshall Tucker Band, the Ozark Mountain Daredevils, Rare Earth, Uriah Heep, War, and ZZ Top. Opening acts: ASTIGAFA, the Atlanta Rhythm Section, Brian Auger's Oblivion Express, Diamond Reo, the Flock, Heavy Metal Kids, Hydra, the James Gang, Jo Jo Gunne, Journey, M-S Funk, Montrose, Mushroom, Nazareth, Passport, Point Blank, Pure Prairie League, REO Speedwagon, Rush, Salem Witchcraft, Skyscraper, Smokehouse, Status Quo, Stu Daye, Ted Nugent, Ted Nugent & the Amboy Dukes, Thin Lizzy, the Tubes, and Vitale's Madman. Average attendance: 5,973.

Ian Dove of the *New York Times* reviewed the March 21 performance at the Beacon Theatre in New York City, saying: "The whole audience was standing on the seats for the last 45 minutes, an event even in these days of rock emotionalism.... It may be overly simple and unpretentious rock, not so much sung as shouted, but KISS communicates a sense of fun and commitment to the music."

Followed by: Alive! Tour.

Dressed to Thrill: A Tribute to KISS with Female Vocalists: Released February 25, 2014, by Genterine Records, this CD features the following tracks: "Detroit Rock City" (Radio Cult), "Ladies Room" (Killer Kowalski), "See You Tonight" (Mantlepiece), "Parasite" (Viva La Venus), "A World Without Heroes" (October Layne), "C'mon and Love Me" (Hollywood Groupies),

Dozens of KISS tribute albums have been released over the years, including *Dressed to Kill: An Independent Tribute to KISS.*

"Forever" (Confession Box), "I Was Made for Lovin' You" (Karma Lingo), "Rock and Roll All Nite" (Radio Cult), "Hard Luck Woman" (Willem & Dakota), and "Love Her All I Can" (Killer Kowalski).

Duncan, Robert: The author of *KISS* (1978, Popular Library), the first book about the band, Robert Duncan was an early proponent of KISS. He was also managing editor of the KISS-friendly *Creem* magazine from 1975 to 1976.

Dylan, Bob: On Gene Simmons' 2004 solo album, *Asshole*, legendary folk singer Bob Dylan co-wrote "Waiting for the Morning Light" with Simmons. Dylan is famous for penning and singing such classic anthems of the hippie era as "Blowin' in the Wind" and "Like a Rolling Stone."

***Dynasty*:** Disco fever ran rampant during the late 1970s. KISS and their manager, Bill Aucoin, who wanted an album that would appeal to a broader audience, weren't immune, releasing the disco-influenced *Dynasty* March 23, 1979. The band's seventh studio album, *Dynasty*, which reached #9 on the *Billboard* album chart and was certified triple platinum, featured the following tracks: "I Was Made for Lovin' You" (which reached #11 on the singles chart), "2,000 Man" (a cover of the obscure Rolling Stones tune), "Sure Know Something," "Dirty Livin'" (the only song on the record written and sung by Peter Criss), "Charisma," "Magic Touch," "Hard Times," "X-Ray Eyes," and "Save Your Love."

Featuring a cover photo by Francesco Scavullo, whose work graced the covers of countless magazines, *Dynasty* originally came packaged with a poster of the band appearing to wear black turtlenecks. They were actually wearing white straitjackets, but they were blacked out because Casablanca felt the image would be inappropriate for kids. The album was produced by Vincent Poncia, who had also produced Peter Criss's 1978 solo LP. Criss has claimed that he demanded Poncia produce the record or he would quit, but Gene Simmons has said that it was a group decision. Ironically, Poncia, citing Criss's drug use, declining ability, and injuries suffered from an automobile accident, proclaimed that Criss no longer had sufficient skills to play on a KISS album, replacing him during pre-production of the record with session drummer Anton Fig.

In *Rolling Stone* #298 (Aug., 1979), reviewer David Fricke panned the LP, blaming its "sorry lack of spark" on Poncia, who "reduced the guitars, drums, and even Gene Simmons' bloody howl to a pseudo-sophisticated whimper that makes the group's ragged 1974 debut disc sound like apocalypse now." The band has disparaged the album as well, saying they lost their way and calling it a mistake to hire Poncia.

Personally, I love the album, though I typically prefer KISS's harder rocking records.

Dynasty Tour: Also known as The Return of Kiss, the Dynasty Tour was in support of the band's seventh studio album, beginning June 15 and ending December 16, 1979. KISS played 79 shows in the U.S. and three in Canada. It was their first tour since the Alive II Tour, which ended April 2, 1978, in Japan.

The Dynasty Tour was noteworthy for many things, including a decline in attendance by longtime fans as many were turned off by the disco-tinged *Dynasty* album and the more family-friendly nature of the band. KISS debuted flamboyant new costumes that matched the color of each band member's solo album, and they introduced several new production stunts, including Gene Simmons flying through the air, Paul Stanley's mirrored guitar, and Ace Frehley's lighted, rocket-shooting guitar. A plan for Paul Stanley to shoot lasers out of his left eye (à la *KISS Meets the Phantom of the Park*) was deemed too dangerous by Stanley and Bill Aucoin and was left on the cutting room floor.

The Dynasty Tour was the last with Peter Criss until the 1996 Alive/Worldwide Tour (a.k.a. the Reunion Tour), and it was the only tour to feature songs from all four solo albums: "Radioactive" (Simmons), "Tossin' and Turnin" (Criss), "New York Groove" (Frehley), and "Move On" (Stanley). Many fans felt that the Dynasty Tour was the beginning of the end of the classic KISS era. Average attendance: 10,523.

Followed by: Unmasked Tour.

"Easy as it Seems": The ninth track on *Unmasked*, "Easy as it Seems" is the "funkiest of all KISS songs, begun with a deft bass line ... and polished to perfection by Vini Poncia, who co-wrote the track with Paul Stanley. Over smooth harmonies and crisp guitar chords, Stanley proves himself not just a great rock 'n' roll singer, but a great singer, period" (Paul Elliott, *KISS: Hotter Than Hell*). Stanley, who had the Spinners in mind when he wrote the song, plays bass on the number, subbing for Gene Simmons.

"Easy Thing": The sixth track on Peter Criss's 1978 KISS solo album, "Easy Thing" is one of Criss's many post–*Destroyer* ballads that tries (and fails) to capture the greatness of "Beth," the most famous song Criss has ever written or sung. Criss sings sweetly and sincerely over acoustic guitar and orchestration (before and after electric guitar kicks in), but "Easy Thing" is ultimately forgettable. Written by Criss and Stan Penridge.

"Eat Your Heart Out": KISS tries something different from time to time, hence the Eagles- or Crosby Stills and Nash-like a cappella harmony that begins "Eat Your Heart Out," the seventh track on *Monster*. The opening isn't great (nor is it embarrassing), but it is a nice intro to a solid, old-school rocker about a sexual tryst. Cowbell helps keep the beat. Written and sung by Gene Simmons.

Eisen, Eva: Paul Stanley's mother. She died Sept. 29, 2012, in Los Angeles, CA, at the age of 88. According to her *Newsday* obituary, "Mrs. Eisen was born in Berlin, Germany on Nov. 16, 1923. Fleeing the Nazi uprising, she lived for a brief time in Amsterdam, Holland with her mother and stepfather before moving to New York City in 1939. She was later introduced to William Eisen, her husband of 63 years, with whom she lived in Manhattan, Mount Vernon, and Queens before settling in Port Washington."

In *Face the Music: A Life Exposed*, Stanley described his parents as neglectful, unhappy, and unsupportive, but he focused on Ms. Eisen's more positive traits after her death, as her obituary revealed: "My mother found so much pleasure and fulfillment in all the various types of music that she so loved. Through her that same passion was introduced and nurtured in us all. She lived long enough to see, enjoy and love a very grateful and fortunate extended family. She found numerous ways to contribute to her community [including volunteering at a soup kitchen] and was appreciated and loved by those who knew her. My mom was the matriarch of our family and words cannot express our loss."

Eisen, Stanley: Paul Stanley's birth name was Stanley Bert Eisen.

Eisen, William: Paul Stanley's father. In *Face the Music: A Life Exposed*, Stanley said his dad, who had a miserable childhood and hated his own dad, was neglectful, critical, and unsupportive. However, he also called him "very bright and well-read." In a 2014 interview with Chris Epting of ultimateclassicrock.com, Stanley said Mr. Eisen read Stanley's book, and that it was "very hard for him. But it was essential to tell the truth…. My parents didn't do what they did to be mean…. My dad is 94 now and that to me is a blessing."

Electric Hellfire Club: For their third studio album, which was released in 1996, industrial metal band the Electric Hellfire Club covered "Calling Dr. Love." Both the record and the song are spelled "Calling Dr. Luv."

Electric Lady Studios: Paul Stanley and Gene Simmons' first time to sing on a record was at Electric Lady Studios: background vocals for Lyn Cristopher's self-titled LP. Wicked Lester recorded their unreleased record at Electric Lady Studios, and Paul and Gene would hang out there for hours and hours, soaking up the atmosphere and the music, even when they weren't working on the album. KISS recorded *Dressed to Kill* and part of *Destroyer* and *Dynasty* there.

The origin of Electric Lady Studios dates back to 1968, when Jimi Hendrix and his manager Michael Jeffery bought a closed nightclub called The Generation, which was located at 52 W. 8th Street in New York's Greenwich Village.

According to electricladystudios.com: "Instead of renaming the club and continuing with the live venue business model (Jimi's original vision for the project), advisors Eddie Kramer and Jim Marron convinced Hendrix to convert the space into a professional recording studio. Architect John Storyk designed each structural detail, and from there the origins of New York's famed Electric Lady Studios were born. It would be the only artist-owned recording studio in existence at the time. On August 26, 1970, Hendrix hosted the grand opening of his psychedelic studio lair to fellow musicians and friends. Guests included Steve Winwood, Eric Clapton, Ron Wood, and Patti Smith."

Unfortunately, Hendrix died a month into recording at ELS, but the studio's legend grew as such performers as Bob Dylan, John Lennon, the Clash, AC/DC, Hall & Oates, the Rolling Stones, Led Zeppelin, Stevie Wonder, and David Bowie recorded there. Recent acts to record at ELS include Lana Del Rey, Arcade Fire, U2, Daft Punk, and Beck.

Ellis, Don: Don Ellis was the head of Epic Records when Wicked Lester recorded an unreleased album for the company. Later, in 1972, Ellis and business associate Tom Werman watched Gene, Paul, and Peter perform in the Loft, but the record executive was unimpressed. In *Makeup to Breakup*, Peter Criss said, "We cranked that volume up and Don's hair looked like it was waving in the breeze from the sheer magnitude of our sound ... it was so loud you couldn't even make out any chord changes.... Ellis couldn't wait to get out the door."

Elsas, Dennis: One of the first disc jockeys to play KISS on the radio, Dennis Elsas was the music director at New York's WNEW-FM from 1972 to 1976.

***Emerald Monkey: Heroes of the Night*:** Recorded by Emerald Monkey, this CD is a track-by-track tribute to *Creatures of the Night*, supplemented by four bonus songs: "Shout It Out Loud," "No One to Blame," "All We Need," and "Take the Time." Released in 2008 by TributeAlbums.com.

Empire State Building: After receiving their platinum album awards for *Alive!*, KISS wanted to do a special photo shoot, so Barry Levine took pics of them on top of the Empire State Building, resulting in one of the most iconic photos ever taken of the band. Ace and Peter have admitted they were drunk on champagne during the shoot.

***Entertainment Weekly*:** Featuring a recently reunited KISS on the cover, the August 16, 1996, issue of *Entertainment Weekly* contains an article called "On the Road with KISS."

The Envy: Gene Simmons produced the Envy's self-titled 2010 EP, which was only available at the band's live shows.

Epic Records: Early in the life of KISS, before Ace Frehley joined the band, and before they began calling themselves KISS, Tom Werman and Don Ellis of Epic Records went to the Loft to see them play, but Ellis didn't like their music, so the label took a pass. Previously, Epic Records was set to release the Wicked Lester album, but Paul and Gene, not happy with the record, walked away from the deal.

Erebus Pictures: In 2015, Gene Simmons partnered with WWE Studios to create Erebus Pictures, which is named after the Greek primordial deity representing the personification of darkness. The company was founded to "finance and produce elevated horror movies."

"The horror genre continues to fascinate me as it proves to be endlessly thrilling and engaging for audiences," Simmons said in a press release about the venture. "I am so thrilled to be working with the masterminds from WWE Studios in launching Erebus Pictures."

***The Eric Carr Story*:** Written and published by Greg Prato, this is a biography of the late, great KISS drummer. According to publicity released by the author, it is "Comprised of all-new interviews, the book also doubles as a study of 1980's era KISS. You'll find insight into all of KISS' albums that featured Carr (from producers Bob Ezrin, Michael James Jackson, and Ron Nevison), as well as those closest to him (sister Loretta Caravello, girlfriend Carrie Stevens, KISS guitarist

Greg Prato's *The Eric Carr Story* tells the tale of the Fox, who in 1980 replaced Peter Criss as the drummer for KISS. Carr passed away November 24, 1991, at the age of 41.

Bruce Kulick), and music-related friends (Eddie Trunk, Dream Theater's Mike Portnoy, Anthrax's Charlie Benante). Also included is one of the last-ever interviews conducted with KISS' original manager, Bill Aucoin, and for the first time ever, KISS fans will be able to learn what the real storyline to KISS' controversial release *Music From 'The Elder'* was all about (thanks to an explanation from Ezrin)." Released March 21, 2011.

Eric Singer Project: During the 1990s, Eric Singer began a sideline project (so to speak) called the Eric Singer Project. Current band members include Eric Singer (drums, vocals), Bruce Kulick (guitar), John Corabi (guitar, bass), and Chuck Garric, the latter of whom replaced original member Karl Cochran. The band has released three albums: *Lost and Spaced* (1998), *ESP* (1999), and *ESP Live in Japan* (2007), plus a DVD: *ESP Live at the Marquee* (2007).

"Escape from the Island": The ninth track on *Music from "The Elder,"* "Escape from the Island" is a hard rocking instrumental with crunching lead guitar from Ace Frehley and pounding, jungle beat drums by Eric Carr. It also has a screaming siren, a la "Firehouse." Frehley, Carr, and Bob Ezrin (on bass) recorded the song in Ezrin's basement at his home in Montreal. The trio wrote the song as well.

ESP: Released in 1999 by the Eric Singer Project, *ESP* features the following tracks, all covers: "Teenage Nervous Breakdown," "Four Day Creep," "Free Ride," "Still Alive & Well," "Never Before," Goin' Blind," "Set Me Free," "Changes," "S.O.S. (Too Bad)," "Foxy Lady," "Twenty Flight Rock," and "Won't Get Fooled Again."

***ESP: Live at the Marquee*:** This 2006 DVD features the Eric Singer Project performing the following cover tunes: "Do Your Own Thing," "Watchin' You," "Unholy," "Love (I Don't Need It Anymore)," "Four Day Creep," "Nothing to Lose," "War Machine," "Jump the Shark," "Born to Raise Hell," "Free Ride," "Power to the Music," "Black Diamond," "We're an American Band," "I Love It Loud," "Domino," "Smokin' in the Boys Room," and "Jungle."

***ESP Live in Japan*:** Released in 2007 by the Eric Singer Project, *ESP Live in Japan* features the following tracks, all covers: "Watchin' You," "Love (I Don't Need It Anymore)," "Unholy," "Do Your Own Thing," "Domino," "Black Diamond," "Oh! Darling," "War Machine," "School's Out," "I Love It Loud," and "Power To The Music."

Evans, Jay: Jay Evans co-founded the KISS Army with Bill Starkey. In an April 8, 2014, article published on www.indystar.com, Evans said they called it the KISS Army because "KISS Fan Club sounded too wimpy."

Evans recalled wearing KISS clothing to school. "We all showed up at school in our KISS T-shirts and got taunted," he said. "Still, it didn't really dampen our enthusiasm. Usually, in high school, anything you get taunted for, you want to shy away from. But we just didn't."

Today, when he walks through a mall and sees "some greasy-haired kid wearing a KISS Army T-shirt," Evans thinks, "Gosh, I conceived that, and this is what's happened to it since then. It's a really weird feeling."

"Every Time I Look at You": With songs like "Beth" and "Forever," KISS can do power ballads with the best of them, and "Every Time I Look at You," the ninth track on *Revenge*, is further proof. Paul Stanley, who has stated on more than one occasion of his love for ballads, "sings sweetly over acoustic guitars on a tune that echoes Cat Stevens's 'The First Cut is the Deepest,'" said Paul Elliott, author of *KISS: Hotter Than Hell*. Written by Stanley and Bob Ezrin, with a guitar solo by Dick Wagner.

Everything KISS: A website featuring thousands of product reviews and more than 100 KISS collections from various collectors around the globe, Everything KISS, which began in 2007, can be found at www.everythingkiss.com.

"Exciter": A song that rocks so hard it would have sounded right at home on *Creatures of the Night*, "Exciter," which was originally called "You," is the first track on *Lick It Up*, the debut of the makeup-less KISS. It was written by Vinnie Vincent and Paul Stanley, who, in typical KISS fashion, sings about knowing what a girl wants: passion and fire, lust and desire. He also sings of pleasure and pain, referring to sadomasochism. Rick Derringer of "Rock and Roll, Hoochie Koo" fame plays lead guitar, and he has said he was happy Gene and Paul asked him to contribute to the song.

***Expecting Mary*:** In the 2010 comedy-drama, *Expecting Mary*, which was directed by Dan Gordon, Gene Simmons plays Mary's biological father, Taylor, an older rocker getting ready to go on tour. During a pivotal scene in the film, Mary (Olesya Rulin) approaches Taylor to reveal that she is pregnant and wants his emotional support.

Exploding: The Highs, Hits, Hype, Heroes, and Hustlers of the Warner Music Group: Written by Stan Cornyn (with Paul Scanlon), who was Executive Vice President for Warner Bros. Records during the KISS era, this book is an insider, behind-the-scenes account of the music industry. The cover painting parodies such rock and pop music stars as Gene Simmons, Madonna, and Mick Jagger. Published July 29, 2003, by It Books.

Extract: In the 2009 comedy film, *Extract*, which was directed by Mike Judge (*Beavis and Butthead*), Gene Simmons plays a ruthless, power-hungry attorney named Joe Adler. Jason Bateman stars as Joel Reynolds, the owner of Reynold's Extract, a flavoring-extracts company. Amusingly, Simmons defends an employee of the company who lost one of his testicles during a workplace accident.

Extreme: On *Kiss My Ass: Classic KISS Regrooved*, Extreme, who formed in 1985, covered "Strutter." The band was fronted by Gary Cherone, who had a short and unpopular stint as lead singer for Van Halen, singing on 1998's *Van Halen III*.

Extreme Makeover: Home Edition: In February of 2012, KISS appeared on ABC's *Extreme Makeover: Home Edition*, helping the needy owners of a home-based, non-profit school acquire new musical instruments.

E-Z-O: Active from 1982 to 1990, E-Z-O is a Japanese heavy metal band. Gene Simmons produced their self-titled American album from 1987, which features tracks written by such KISS songwriters as Adam Mitchell and Jaime St. James.

Ezrin, Bob: Bob Ezrin, producer for such acts as Alice Cooper, Peter Gabriel, Lou Reed, and Pink Floyd, produced three KISS albums: *Destroyer*, which was a slick, experimental departure from the band's grungier studio efforts; *Music from "The Elder,"* a concept album that was derided by many KISS fans (and by the band members themselves); and *Revenge*, which was a triumphant return to KISS's hard rock roots. Ezrin also played keyboards on *Music from "The Elder."*

In an interview published on www.hit-channel.com in 2012, Ezrin spoke about working with KISS on *Destroyer*: "I'd heard the record they made before *Destroyer* (*Dressed to Kill*) and they sounded fairly competent, pretty good. I assumed that they were more sophisticated musically than they were and I found out that they were playing instinctually. They really didn't have any musical education or background, so we really had to start from scratch … to go back to the beginning and actually learn a little bit about music, about structure, about rhythm, about what keys go together."

Face the Music: A Life Exposed: Published by HarperOne on April 8, 2014, this is Paul Stanley's absorbing, entertaining, brutally honest autobiography. The back cover describes the book thusly: "Well known for his onstage persona, the 'Starchild,' Paul Stanley has written a memoir with a gripping blend of personal revelations and gritty war stories about the highs and lows both inside and outside of KISS. Born with a condition called microtia (an ear deformity rendering him deaf on the right side), Stanley's traumatic childhood experiences produced an inner drive to succeed in the most unlikely of places: music. Taking readers through the series of events that led to the founding of KISS, the personal relationships that helped shape his life, and the turbulent dynamics among his bandmates over the past forty years, this book leaves no one unscathed—including Stanley himself."

Fairbairn, Bruce: Canadian Bruce Fairbairn produced *Psycho Circus*. He also produced such popular records as Loverboy's *Get Lucky*, Bon Jovi's *Slippery When Wet*, and Aerosmith's *Permanent Vacation*. When Tommy Thayer was with Black 'n Blue, Fairbarn co-produced the band's *In Heat* (1988) LP with Gene Simmons.

Family Guy: KISS guest-stars on two episodes of the edgy, irreverent animated series, *Family Guy*: "A Very Special Family Guy Freakin' Christmas" (season 3, episode 16—Dec. 21, 2001), in which Peter watches *KISS Saves Santa* on television; and "Road to Europe" (season 3, episode 20—Feb. 7, 2002), in which Peter and Lois wear costumes and face paint and go to a KISS concert. The latter episode reveals that Lois dated Gene Simmons when he was Chaim Witz and she was nicknamed "Loose Lois." Both episodes feature the voices of Ace, Gene, Paul, and Peter.

Simmons appears without his bandmates in "Don't Make Me Over" (season 4, episode 4—June 5, 2005), where he is on the tour bus for the pop band Meg and the Griffins. In that same episode, he appears on *Saturday Night Live* (during the goodbyes) and sticks his tongue in George W. Bush's ear. Further, Gene provides the voice for prisoner number three.

Famous Monsters of Filmland: Established in 1958 by publisher James Warren and editor Forrest J Ackerman, *Famous Monsters of Filmland* is a monster movie magazine that is still being published. Gene Simmons, a huge fan of the genre, got the inspiration for his makeup design from a photo of Lon Chaney, Sr., as the Phantom of the Opera that he saw in an issue of *Famous Monsters*. Issue #226 (July 1999) features an exclusive interview with Simmons called "Why I love classic monster movies!"

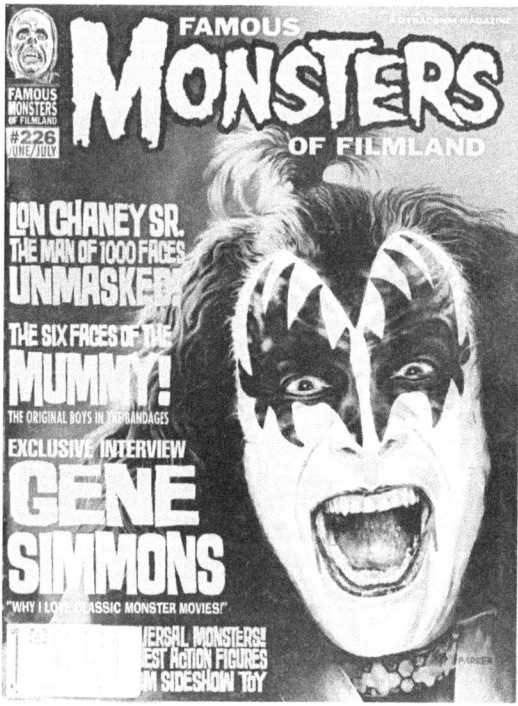

Issue #226 of *Famous Monsters of Filmland*, a magazine Gene Simmons grew up reading, features an exclusive interview with the Demon titled "Why I Love Classic Monster Movies!"

"Fanfare": Composed by Paul Stanley and Bob Ezrin, "Fanfare" is the atmospheric, neoclassical instrumental intro to *Music from "The Elder,"* the band's lofty, oft-criticized concept album. The brief piece, which incorporates such medieval instruments as the racket and the krummhorn, was performed by the American Symphony Orchestra, setting a rather pretentious (if not unappealing) tone for the rest of the record. It leads directly into the next track, "Just a Boy."

Fangoria: Established in 1979, *Fangoria* is a horror magazine that is still being published. Issue #298 (Nov., 2010) features interviews with known horror aficionado Gene Simmons and his bandmate Paul Stanley, who reveals that he's a monster movie fan as well. Simmons is featured on the cover and on a foldout poster bound into the magazine.

Fanzines: Short for "fan magazine," fanzines run the gamut from a few stapled pieces of paper featuring poorly written text and crude images, to slick publications that would look good on the newsstand at any bookstore.

In *The Ultimate KISS Fanzine Phenomenon: 1976-2009*, *KISSer*, published by Randy Paul from 1976 to 1978, is revealed to be the first KISS fanzine. *KISSer* was followed by Sam Ricardo's

The first issue of *KISSer*, the very first KISS fanzine, was published during the winter of 1976.

Flash (1977–78) and Joe Lewellen's *KISS Underground* (1977–1980, among many others. Along with concert reviews, record reviews, opinion pieces, and the like, some of the better fanzines actually feature interviews with band members.

In *The Ultimate KISS Fanzine Phenomenon*, Paul Stanley claimed KISS fanzines grew out of a need among fans. "At the end of the day the fanzines came about because we never garnered the respect or coverage from the press that other bands that were nowhere near our level of fame got," he said. "The fans wanted to write the articles that they never saw. They wanted to record the news that they thought was lacking in national publications."

Nowadays, most fanzines are published online via email, blogs, websites, and the like, such as KISSfanzine.com.

Farewell Tour *see* "**KISS Farewell Tour**

Farris, Steve: Steve Farris played lead guitar on "Creatures of the Night." Farris also worked with such acts as Eddie Money, Alice Cooper, and Mr. Mister.

Fig, Anton: Anton Fig played drums on Ace Frehley's 1978 KISS solo album. On *Dynasty*, he played drums on every track but "Dirty Livin.'" He also played drums on *Unmasked*. Fig is best-known for his work with David Letterman's house band, the CBS Orchestra.

Fillmore East Press Launch: On January 8, 1974, KISS did a special dress rehearsal at the Fillmore East for agents and certain press members. *Rolling Stone* magazine, which has a history of being critical of the band, mentioned the event thusly in its "Random Notes" section: "The four Kissers play very heavy, loud and ultimately monotonous rock in the Black Sabbath tradition; they wear sheet-white make-up and black leather and studs. Midway through their act, dry ice overtakes the stage and the bassist flashes a flaming torch in the air. And they finish in a rain of firecrackers. A sure crowd-pleaser. For crowds of kiddies, that is…"

FINAL EXIT: Tribute to KISS Split EP: Recorded by the Japanese band Final Exit, this EP features "Love Gun" and "Detroit Rock City," plus two tracks entitled "Some Songs," which are medleys of classic KISS hits. The B side features non–KISS tunes by the Spanish band Ironia. Released by Machismo Records in Australia in 1998.

"Firehouse": The third track on *KISS*, the band's first album, "Firehouse" was written by Paul Stanley during his time at the Manhattan High School of Music & Art in New York. The inspiration for the piece came from the Move's 1968 pop hit, "Fire Brigade."

Stanley sings lead vocals on the song while Warren Dewey, KISS's engineer at the time, provides the fire engine sound effects. During live performances, Stanley wears a fireman's hat while Gene Simmons breathes fire. A staple of KISS concerts, "Firehouse" is a rousing song with a "startlingly tense staccato solo [by Ace Frehley] in which he hangs on, striking every note repeatedly until the listener might think everybody will explode, only then releasing the note to travel on down the scale" (Robert Duncan writing in *KISS*, the first book about the band).

First KISS: Limited to 1,000 copies, *First KISS* was released by Mercury Records in 1990.

It is a repackaging (but *not* remastering) of four CDs—*KISS*, *Hotter Than Hell*, *Dressed to Kill*, and *Destroyer*—housed in a clear, LP-sized plastic case with a red sticker on the front that says "First KISS." According to *KISS FAQ* author Dale Sherman, some fans were disappointed with the release because they had "hoped for something like *The Originals*, possibly with better-quality mastering of the material than had appeared on the first CDs of the older albums released in the States."

First KISS…Last Licks: Released November 1989 by Mercury Records, *First KISS…Last Licks* is a vinyl LP limited to 800 copies, making it highly sought after by KISS collectors. Tracks include: "Love's A Slap In The Face," "Betrayed," "Prisoner of Love," "The Street Giveth and the Street Taketh Away," "Nowhere to Run" (remix), "Partners in Crime" (remix), "Deuce" (demo), and "Strutter" (demo).

First KISS: My 40-Year Obsession with the Hottest Band in the World: Written by Michael Buffalo Smith, this eBook was published by BookBaby on December 6, 2013. According to author publicity, it is a "memoir about my obsession with the hard rockin,' grease paint wearin,' fire breathin' band KISS. I discovered them right as they were beginning their careers some 40 years ago, and have remained a diehard fan since. This book is kind of a fan letter to Gene, Paul, Peter, and Ace as well. While I spent way too much money on KISS records and merch over the years, the boys always delivered the show. And it was the show that drew me in."

"Fits Like a Glove": "Fits Like a Glove" is the eighth track on *Lick It Up*. At this point in the album, the listener may sorely miss Ace Frehley, as this would have been a good time for one of his spacey tunes. Instead, we get another grungy, down-and-dirty rocker from Gene Simmons, who brags that his snake is ready to bite, and that he'll go through a girl like a hot knife through butter.

"Flaming Youth": Written by Gene Simmons, Paul Stanley, Ace Frehley, and Bob Ezrin, "Flaming Youth" is the fifth track on *Destroyer*. Paul Elliot, author of *KISS: Hotter Than Hell*, called it KISS's "own youthful rallying cry in the vein of the Who's 'My Generation,'" blazing with "positive energy" and celebrating rock music as "a life affirming force." Producer Bob Ezrin has said the arrangement of the tune owes a great deal to the Beatles.

Ezrin's idea to feature a calliope in this upbeat party song, in which Paul Stanley proclaims that "Flaming Youth" will metaphorically set the world on fire, is a nice creative touch, but the band has said they didn't care for it. Dick Wagner, who also worked with Lou Reed and Aerosmith, played lead guitar on the song, but was uncredited.

FLAMING YOUTH: *A Norwegian Tribute To KISS*: Released in 1994 by Rec 90/Voices of Wonder, this record, as the title suggests, is a Norwegian KISS tribute album. Tracks include: "Deuce" (Graceland), "Strutter" (Grunt People), "Love Gun" (Ramjam), "Mainline" (Mothers Love), "Parasite" (Hedge Hog), "Tomorrow" (the Stuck), "Shock Me" (Motorpsycho), "Calling Dr. Love" (Blant De Primitive), "Beth" (Gartnerlosjen), "She" (Paraplegic),"Coming Home" (Merry Go Round), "Strange Ways" (Spacemen Spiff), "Watchin' You" (Lost At Last), "Shout It Out Loud" (DumDum Boys), "Cold Gin" (Muck), "I Was Made for Lovin' You" (The Jungle Medics), "Rock and Roll All Nite" (Cosmic Dropouts), and "Paul Stanley" (a hidden reggae track).

Folgers Coffee: In 2000, Folgers made a commercial featuring Paul Stanley singing the famous "Folgers in Your Cup" song. It was never aired, but it did surface on YouTube in 2014. In an October 2000 interview to promote *The Last KISS* pay per view concert, Stanley said this about the commercial: "Life is strange. I got a call asking if I was interested in singing a Folgers commercial. And, like many other things, I thought, 'Why not?' I wasn't at all concerned with who thinks it is okay or not okay, cool, not cool, rock 'n' roll or not. I had a blast doing it, and, like I said, isn't that what this is all about?"

Fontana, Richie: Richie Fontana played drums on tracks 1–4 of Paul Stanley's 1978 KISS solo album. He also worked with such acts as Billy Squier and Laura Branigan.

Foo Fighters: Led by ex–Nirvana drummer Dave Grohl, the Foo Fighters covered Ace Frehley's "Ozone" for the "Special Tour Edition" of their self-titled debut album.

***Forbes*:** In 2011, Gene Simmons received the Lifetime Achievement Award from *Forbes* at the magazine's The Entrepreneur Behind the Icon event, which was in celebration of their 13th annual Celebrity 100 List in Hollywood. In an interview during the event, Simmons said: "Anybody in celebrity thinks they're in celebrity, but it's really a business. It was never called show. It still isn't. It's called show business. *Forbes* is doing the right thing by shining a spotlight on the nature of celebrity and how celebrities are finally waking up to the idea that they're a product." The September 23, 1996, issue of *Forbes* features KISS on the cover.

Ford, Lita: In 1984, Eric Singer was the touring drummer for Lita Ford. The blond female rocker was the lead guitarist for the Runaways in the late 1970s before finding fame during the 1980s as a solo artist.

Ford, Robben: Robben Ford played lead guitar on "Rock and Roll Hell" and "I Still Love You." He also collaborated with such performers as Miles Davis, Joni Mitchell, and George Harrison.

"Forever": KISS struck gold when they recorded "Forever," the seventh track on *Hot in the Shade* and the second single released from the record. The power ballad, written by Paul Stanley and Michael Bolton, reached #8 on the *Billboard* Hot 100 chart, the second highest charting song in the history of KISS (after "Beth," which hit #7). The song also spurred ticket sales for the *Hot in the Shade* tour.

Bruce Kulick's acoustic work on "Forever," which he had originally done on electric guitar, complements Stanley's impassioned performance on vocals perfectly. An inspired Stanley sings that he sees his future when he looks into a girl's eyes, and that her love makes his heart come alive. The music video for the song is an understated affair, with the band playing to an empty room as orange light shines through ornate windows. Simply beautiful.

Foster, Bruce: Noteworthy for being the first outside musician to perform on a KISS album, Bruce Foster played piano on "Nothin' to Lose," the second track on *KISS*. Of the experience, Foster told www.kissfaq.com: "I remember honing my piano part down to the measures of music that would make it count artistically. A creative pool of talent gathered in the studio that day helped me massage it into something that made a subtle statement of added excitement woven into the track."

4th and Loud: A 2014 reality TV show, *4th and Loud* chronicled the inaugural season of LA KISS (a.k.a. Los Angeles KISS), the arena football team owned by Paul Stanley and Gene Simmons. In his review of the show, Jon Dunmore, via www.poffysmoviemania.com, said it had "all the prescribed reality show beats ... the premise (rock entrepreneurs initiate a major league football team), the struggle (never been done before), the drama (the guy with the head injury, the two brothers trying to stay on the team, the guy who got time off work to tryout), the human interest (the player who was conceived at a KISS concert by his parents who had met just that night), the talking heads ('I've just been knocked down, but it's about getting back up again!' Where've I heard that before?), the action (tinted in Reality Show Stankvision), with the added bonus of Gene and Paul milling through the frame at regular intervals, and the KISS logo up in yo face absolutely freakin' everywhere."

Even those who don't care for football or KISS may enjoy the cheerleader tryouts in *4th and Loud*, featuring scantily clad, buxom young babes.

Fowley, Kim: A producer and songwriter, the late Kim Fowley co-wrote "King of the Night Time World" and "Do You Love Me?" Fowley also worked with such acts as Blue Cheer, Alice Cooper, Helen Reddy, and the Runaways.

Fox: When Eric Carr joined KISS, he wore Fox makeup. In episode #562 of the *Joe Rogan Experience*, Paul Stanley derided the design: "I think where we went astray is when we first replaced Peter and we decided we needed a new character. And the problem with that kind of stuff is that it started to become—interestingly, I think—disingenuous. It took an air of 'fake' in the sense that it became a menagerie. I mean, we had a Fox and an Egyptian Warrior. Next we would have the Turtle Boy and the Frog Man."

Fox, Rik: Rik Fox was an early KISS fan. In *Nothin' to Lose: The Making of KISS (1972–1975)*, he said: "I was one of a very small elite group who actually got to see KISS from the ground up. I used to date Peter Criss's sister Joanne. I'd watch the band rehearse as a three-piece in the loft. You could see the seeds of magic already starting to brew."

Fox, Samantha: During the *Crazy Nights* era, Paul Stanley dated British actress, model, and singer Samantha Fox, a beautiful blonde famous for the number one hit, "Touch Me (I Want Your Body)." On one of their dates, they went to see the musical *Phantom of the Opera*, which Stanley would later star in as the title character.

In an October 19, 2010, interview with Fox published on www.blabbermouth.net, Fox spoke about Stanley. "It was a wonderful time," she said. "I was a big KISS fan anyway.... I had a great time with Paul and learned a lot from him. He's a very talented guy. We had a great love affair.... I have great memories of Paul. He's a really nice guy. He's a bit older than me but what can I say? I'm sure he lied about his age then! KISS is still a fantastic band and in 1989 they'd done far more than I'd done."

In August of 2009, Fox announced that she was going to enter into a civil partnership with her female manager, Myra Stratton.

"Fractured Mirror": A repetitious, but hypnotic instrumental, "Fractured Mirror" is the ninth and final track on *Ace Frehley*. A fitting finish to a terrific solo album, it's a gorgeous song in which "church bells give way to a melancholy, chiming guitar figure and then soaring melodic passages" (Matthew Wilkening, ultimateclassicrock.com). "Fractured Mirror" inspired a number of sequels, including "Fractured Too" by Frehley's Comet.

Frame of Mind: Peter Criss had a small role as a detective in *Frame of Mind* (2009), a JFK assassination drama that went straight to DVD. On his website, Criss said he was friends with the film's co-producer and co-writer, Charles Kipps.

"Freak": In "Freak," the third track on *Monster*, Paul Stanley sings about being ridiculed for not fitting in, and being proud of it. A fairly catchy song, "Freak" is a battle cry, not a cry for sympathy (as though KISS would have it any other way). Tommy Thayer's wailing guitar punctuates the proceedings. Written by Stanley and Thayer.

Frehley, Ace: Born Paul Daniel Frehley on April 27, 1951, in The Bronx, New York, lead guitarist Ace Frehley is widely regarded as the best musician of the original four members of KISS, despite never having had a formal music lesson. His killer solos on such songs as "Deuce," "Parasite," and "100,000 Years" helped define the early KISS sound.

According to an interview with Blues Magoos co-founder Peppy Castro published on www.vanyaland.com, Castro taught Frehley to play guitar. "He got my phone number off of my mother, we lived in the same neighborhood, and he just called me up and he asked me if I would show him some stuff on guitar," Castro said. "We sat down and I showed him how to play a few bar chords, and I think it just touched him some way, and it changed his life."

In his autobiography, *No Regrets*, Frehley said everyone in his family played instruments and that, "From the beginning, I was drawn to rock 'n' roll and started figuring out songs by the Beatles and the Stones on my brother's acoustic guitars. One day, by chance, I picked up my friend's new electric guitar and checked it out. I plugged it in, turned the amp on to 10, and strummed a power chord. I immediately fell in love. It was a life-changing event! I was only 12, but I was totally hooked."

Although Frehley's dad (Carl Daniel Frehley) had told him on more than one occasion that he was wasting his life playing rock music, he did buy him his first electric guitar as a Christmas present. "Probably because it beat the alternative," Frehley wrote. "There were worse vices, worse behavior, as I'd already demonstrated. See, at the same time that I was teaching myself guitar and forming my first band, I was also running with a pretty tough crowd. So while it may be true that the rock 'n' roll lifestyle nearly killed me as an adult, it's also true that without music, I might never have made it to adulthood in the first place."

Now claiming sobriety for several years running, Frehley was an alcoholic and a troublemaker from an early age. "I started hanging out with the toughest guys in the neighborhood when I was still in grammar school, playing poker, drinking, cutting school," he wrote. "At first I was uncomfortable with some of the things I had to do, but I learned pretty quickly that alcohol made everything a lot easier. I didn't like to fight, but fearlessness came with a few beers. Talking to girls was sometimes awkward, but with a little buzz I could charm them right out of their pants."

During the mid–late 1960s, Frehley, sometimes going by the nickname of "Punky," played in a number of bands, including the Four Roses, the Exterminators, King Kong, Honey, the Magic People, and the Muff Divers. When a band he was in called Cathedral began getting paid to play gigs, Frehley dropped out of high school, but he later returned and graduated. Frehley was also in a band called Molimo, who, in 1971, recorded a three-song demo for RCA Records. However, in 1972, RCA backed out of any potential recording contract for an LP.

Late in 1972, Frehley's best friend, Bob McAdams, showed him an ad in *The Village Voice* that read:

LEAD GUITARIST WANTED
with Flash and Ability. Album Out
Shortly. No time wasters please.
Paul 268–3145

"The open audition was scheduled for January 3, 1973, which gave me a few weeks to consider the invitation," Frehley wrote in his autobiography. "Paul and his partner in this project, Gene Klein (whom I would come to know as Gene Simmons), had played together in a band called Wicked Lester, and while they had indeed been offered a contract from Epic Records, that deal had fallen through. So the ad, like so many others I'd come across, was not entirely true.... But that's okay. It's become part of the KISS mythology and I'm all cool with that, just as I'm all right with some people thinking the *Village Voice* advertisement sought a 'guitarist with flash and balls.'"

Frehley's mother (Esther Anna Frehley) drove him to the audition at the Loft since he couldn't afford cab fare, and since the 50-watt Marshal amp he wanted to bring wouldn't fit on the subway.

Clad in jeans, a T-shirt and mismatched shoes (one red sneaker, one orange sneaker—it was a mistake on Frehley's part, not a quirky fashion statement), Frehley chugged a beer to give him a little courage, entered the Loft, and proceeded to crumple up and throw on the floor an application that he was given. "Being a musician wasn't a job to me—it was a way of life," Frehley explained in his book. "If they wanted to know more about me, they could ask."

While Frehley was waiting his turn, Bob Kulick, who would later become a studio musician for KISS, was finishing up his audition. Instead of sitting quietly, Frehley recalled in his book that he pulled out his guitar and "started warming up with some scales in the far corner of the room; my actions were definitely a distraction. As they conducted a post-audition interview with Bob, I continued to play, trying to stay loose." (Kulick has denied this story, saying that Frehley waited his turn.)

After Simmons scolded Frehley for his rudeness, it was time for the future Spaceman's audition. Gene, Paul, and Peter played "Deuce," with Paul cueing Ace when it was time to play the solo.

"At the appointed time I ripped into a blistering solo, tried to impress them with every cool lick I had in my repertoire," Frehley wrote. "I wasn't even sure what they were looking for, but it felt right. I liked the energy in the room, I liked the fact that they were playing loud and hard. And I really liked the song itself—a lot.... I'd left the audition feeling confident that I would get the gig.... I was excited about it.... The songs we played were catchy, and Paul, Gene, and Peter were solid musicians."

Frehley, who was heavily influenced by the stage antics and brilliant playing of Jimi Hendrix and Pete Townshend, appreciated that Gene and the boys were creating a theatrical rock band, something for the eyes as well as the ears.

"I liked the *show*," he wrote. "And I understood how visual effects could supplement the music and make the concert experience more memorable."

A couple of weeks after the audition, Paul called Ace back in to hang out and jam some more, and he got the job. Since they didn't want two "Pauls" in the band, Frehley, who had already been performing as "Ace," simply went by his nickname, although to this day he still signs legal documents as "Paul Frehley."

According to *KISS FAQ* author Dale Sherman, Ace got his nickname in 1968 during his stint with King Kong: "Frehley had helped a bandmate hook up with a girl Frehley knew and was called a real 'Ace' for doing so. Although Frehley continued using Punky as a nickname for a couple of years after that, he liked the new nickname and began using it by 1970."

By January of 1973, Wicked Lester had become KISS, and Frehley designed the band's now-famous logo, which Stanley polished up a bit. KISS practiced in the Loft religiously, which took some getting used to for the laid-back Frehley, who, when it came time to pick a character for himself, chose the Spaceman because of his fascination with "space travel and science fiction and technology in general."

To supplement his Spaceman persona, Frehley played a smoking Les Paul Gibson guitar and one that fired rockets. Frehley's guitar playing and showmanship were fantastic, and his solos on *Alive!* inspired many future guitar heroes to pick up the instrument for the first time. In addition, he began singing lead on certain songs, beginning with "Shock Me" on *Love Gun*. However, his alcohol and drug use and erratic behavior (fights, car crashes, lateness, and the like) began causing problems within the band during the late 1970s.

In his autobiography, *KISS and Make-Up*, Simmons said, "Ace simply never showed up" during the recording of most of the studio songs on *Alive II* so "We had to use other guitar players, like Bob Kulick and Rick Derringer."

In May of 1976, the year before *Alive II* hit stores, Ace married his longtime girlfriend, Jeanette Trerotola. KISS played three songs at the reception sans makeup: "Rock and Roll All Nite," "Shout It Out Loud," and "Nothing to Lose." Despite such happy times as these, trouble was on the horizon.

With the release of the disco-flavored *Dynasty* (1979), the poppy *Unmasked* (1980), and the conceptual *Music from "The Elder"* (1981), Frehley grew increasingly disenchanted with musical direction of KISS. Adding to Frehley's misery was that ever since Criss had left in 1980, the Spaceman was outvoted 2–1 by the like-minded Simmons and Stanley on many band decisions as Criss replacement Eric Carr was a hired gun and not a full band member.

Frehley, emboldened by the fact that his 1978 KISS solo album was the most critically acclaimed of the four and the only one to produce a hit ("New York Groove"), left KISS for greener pastures in 1982, although it wasn't announced until 1983. While Frehley had no musical involvement with *Killers* or *Creatures of the Night*, he appeared on the covers of both albums. He also appears in the video for "I Love It Loud." When KISS began the *Creatures of the Night* tour in December of 1982, Vinnie Vincent had already replaced him.

In 1984, the Spaceman formed a band called Frehley's Comet. Their self-titled debut album sold nearly half a million copies, but subsequent releases *EP Live+1* and *Second Sighting* didn't fare as well. In 1989, Frehley, dropping the Frehley's Comet name, released *Trouble Walkin'*, a fine album that only reached #102 on the *Billboard* charts.

In 1995, Frehley teamed with Criss on The Bad Boys of KISS Tour, and in 1996, Ace, Paul, Peter, and Gene reunited for the much-ballyhooed Alive/Worldwide Tour, better known as the Reunion Tour. In 1998, the reformed lineup produced a new album, *Psycho Circus*, though Frehley and Criss had less involvement with the record than many fans were led to believe.

After the KISS Farewell Tour of 2000/2001, Frehley quit KISS to focus on his solo career. Tommy Thayer, wearing the Spaceman costume and makeup, took his place.

In 2009, Frehley released *Anomaly*, which debuted at #27 on the *Billboard* 200 albums chart, and in 2014, he released *Space Invader*, which hit #9. In 2011, he released his autobiography, *No Regrets*. As of this writing, Frehley is engaged to Rachael Gordon and has released *Origins Vol. 1*, an album of cover tunes.

Frehley, Charley: During the mid-1960s, Ace's older brother Charley played with the Spaceman in a band called the Micro Organism. They also played together in the Four Roses.

Frehley, Jeanette: Jeanette Trerotola became Jeanette Frehley on May 10, 1976. Prior to their divorce, Ace and Jeanette had one child: a daughter, Monique, born on July 9, 1980. Jeanette co-wrote "Speedin' Back to My Baby."

Frehley, Monique: Ace Frehley's daughter with Jeanette, Monique lent her speaking voice to "A Little Below the Angels," which appeared on Frehley's 2009 solo album, *Anomaly*. She also sang backup on "Dolls," which was on *Frehley's Comet*. She was supposed to appear in the film *Detroit Rock City*, but her part was cut, much to her disappointment.

Frehley, Paul: Ace Frehley's birth name was Paul Frehley. He changed it to Ace when he joined KISS because there was already a Paul in the band.

Frehley's Comet (album): Ace Frehley's first solo album after leaving KISS, *Frehley's Comet* was released July 7, 1987, by Frehley's band of the same name, which formed in 1984. Tracks include: "Rock Soldiers," "Breakout" (co-written by Eric Carr, sung by Tod Howarth), "Into The Night" (originally written and recorded by Russ Ballard for his 1984 eponymous album), "Something Moved," "We Got Your Rock," "Love Me Right," "Calling To You," "Dolls" (featuring background vocals by Monique Frehley, Lara Kramer and Chay Fig, daughters of Ace Frehley, Eddie Kramer, and Anton Fig respectively), "Stranger In A Strange Land," and "Fractured Too" (a sequel to "Fractured Mirror").

Anton Fig, famous for playing in David Letterman's house band, the CBS Orchestra, played drums on the record. Produced by Eddie Kramer and Ace Frehley and released by Megaforce, *Frehley's Comet* reached #43 on the *Billboard* 200.

Frehley's Comet (band): After leaving KISS, Ace Frehley formed Frehley's Comet, active from 1984 to 1988. Members included Frehley (lead guitar, lead vocals), John Regan (bass guitar, drums, backing vocals), Anton Fig (drums, percussion, 1984–1987), Tod Howarth (rhythm guitar, keyboards, piano, lead vocals, 1986–1988), Richie Scarlet (lead guitar, vocals, 1984–1985), Arthur Stead (keyboards, 1984–1985), Billy Ward (drums, percussion, 1987–1988), and Jamie Oldaker (drums, percussion, backing vocals, 1988). The band released an EP called *Live+1* (1988) and two albums: *Frehley's Comet* (1987) and *Second Sighting* (1988). They also released *Frehley's Comet: Live...+4* (1991), a concert film.

Frehley's Comet: Live...+4: Recorded live at the Hammersmith Odeon in London, England on March 19, 1988, *Frehley's Comet: Live...+4* is a direct-to-video concert movie featuring Ace on lead vocals and guitar, John Regan on bass and vocals, Tod Howarth on guitar, vocals, and keyboard, and Jamie Oldaker on drums, percussion, and vocals. It was released July 1, 1991, on VHS and later on DVD. Tracks include: "Rip It Out," "Something Moved," "Cold Gin," "Shock Me," "Breakout," and "Rocket Ride." The "+4" in the title refers to four music videos: "Into the Night," "Rock Soldiers," "Insane," and "It's Over Now," the latter sung by Howarth.

***French Kissin': Montreal Salutes the Hottest Band in the Land*:** This tribute album was released in 1995 by the Canadian label,

Mother House Records. It includes the following tracks: "Man of 1,000 Faces" (Talamasca), "Baby Driver" (Mange L'ours Mange), "Almost Human" (Corpusse), "Shock Me" (Matt Laurent), "Watchin' You" (Doctor Hadley), "Charisma" (Pushing Up Daisies), "Detroit Rock City" (Slaves On Dope), "Makin' Love" (Fractured II), "Deuce" (Anonymous), "Hard Times" (Scrubmuffin), "Sure Know Something" (Highlands), "I Was Made for Lovin' You" (Flavor Injectors), "Fanfare" (Aaron Cohen), "Rock Bottom" (Exil), "The Oath" (4-Ever), "Hotter Than Hell" (Scissorhead), and "Ville Solitaire (Naked City)" (Catharsis).

Fridays: To promote their new album, *Music from "The Elder,"* KISS appeared on the weekly ABC sketch comedy series *Fridays* on January 15, 1982. Ace, Gene, Paul, and Eric Carr did a rousing set, performing three songs from the record: "I," "A World Without Heroes," and "The Oath." For many Americans, since KISS had been touring out of the country, it was their first time to see Carr perform, and the first time to see the band in their new costumes and shorter haircuts.

Gallup Poll: A poll conducted by the Gallup Youth Survey in 1977 indicated that KISS was the most popular musical act in the country, just ahead of the Eagles, the Beatles, Led Zeppelin, and Boston (in that order). In the June 22, 1977, issue of *Newsday*, George Gallup, reporting on the poll, quoted an "enthusiastic supporter of KISS," who said: "They're a unique group; they do what they feel on the stage and show you a good time. They paint their bodies and shoot off rockets and things like that."

Gass, Craig: A noteworthy Gene Simmons impersonator, Craig Gass appeared with Gene on *The Howard Stern Show* in 2001, interviewing Simmons while talking like him. Gass often makes fun of Gene's cockiness and his penchant for making a buck at every opportunity.

Gene Simmons (album): Released in conjunction with the other three KISS solo albums on September 18, 1978, *Gene Simmons* reached #22 on the *Billboard* album chart. Tracks include: "Radioactive," "Burning Up with Fever," "See You Tonite," "Tunnel of Love," "True Confessions," "Living in Sin" (featuring the spoken-word voice of Cher), "Always Near You/Nowhere to Hide," "Man of 1,000 Faces" (inspired by actor Lon Chaney), "Mr. Make Believe," "See You in Your Dreams," and "When You Wish Upon a Star," the latter a sincere take on the Disney song.

The record, which is the most eclectic of the four KISS solo albums, is loaded with guest-stars, including Helen Reddy (backing vocals on "True Confessions"), Bob Seger (backing vocals on "Radioactive" and "Living in Sin"), Donna Summer (backing vocals on "Burning Up with Fever" and "Tunnel Of Love"), Aerosmith's Joe Perry (guitar on "Radioactive" and "Tunnel Of Love"), and Cheap Trick's Rick Nielsen (guitar on "See You in Your Dreams"). Even a pre–*Married with Children* Katey Sagal gets in on the act, lending background vocals on some tracks.

Gene Simmons played guitar on several songs, handing bass chores to Neil Jason. Simmons, wanting to separate from the hard rock KISS sound, invited the Beatles to appear on the album, but Ringo Starr declined. Simmons has claimed on several occasions that John and Paul wanted to be on the record, but didn't have time. The best he could do, then, was have *Beatlemania* (a Broadway musical) cast members Mitch Weissman and Joe Pecorino lend backup vocals.

Recorded primarily at The Manor in Oxfordshire, England, *Gene Simmons* is a fun record to listen to, but the Demon himself has downplayed the quality of the quirky LP.

Gene Simmons: A Rock 'N' Roll Journey in the Shadow of the Holocaust: Released in January of 2012 by Mill City Press, this book was written by Ross Berg. Amazon reviewer K. Kearse summed up the work nicely, saying it "provides a unique perspective and interesting insight into the life of one of the founding members of KISS: bass player and entertainment entrepreneur, Gene Simmons. In his tribute to the God of Thunder and his mother, Flora, this book explores the roots of the development of Gene Simmons as a person and as a larger than life character … in a very readable style, Berg blends together the horrors of the Holocaust, the evolution of comics and horror films, childhood experiences, and a mother's love for her son and examines their influences on the growth and transformation of Chaim Witz to Gene Klein to Gene Simmons. This book is a one-of-a-kind commentary on Jewish life in the shadow of the Holocaust and the evolution of a rock star. A very distinctive and very important volume in Kisstory, a must-have for anyone interested in the band."

Gene Simmons Dominatrix: Published by the Simmons Comics Group in 2007, this series ran six issues. The solicitation for the first issue reads as follows: "It's 'T&A meets CIA' in Dominatrix, when Dominique Stern, a professional dominatrix, becomes ensnared in a world of government cover-ups and international conspiracies. After a client loses his composure during an intense session and blurts out top-secret information, Dominique finds herself a reluctant superhero who must save herself, her friends, the government jerk who got her into this mess, and quite possibly her country." Written by Sean Taylor. Art by Flavio Hoffe and Esteve Polls. Covers by Alex Garner. Issue #2 featured a retailer incentive variant cover by Stephen Mooney. The series was collected as a trade paperback in 2008.

Gene Simmons Family Jewels: A reality show airing on A&E from 2006 to 2012, *Gene Simmons Family Jewels* follows the off-stage antics of Simmons, his girlfriend (and eventual wife) Shannon Tweed, and Nick and Sophie, their kids. Highlights of the show include the marriage of Simmons and Tweed and the family's trip to Israel, where Gene was born. The deluxe edition of the season one DVD boxed set features a 20-page hardcover family photo album and CD containing two songs: "Rain Keeps Fallin'" and "You're My Reason for Livin.'" In 2012, Gene pulled the plug on the show in order to focus more on KISS and various business interests.

Gene Simmons House of Horrors: This comic book series ran for three issues in 2007. The solicitation for the first issue reads as follows: "You knock at the door of the old mansion up on the hill, and who answers? Your host, none other than Gene Simmons, beckoning you inside. The door slams shut. You try to run, but it's too late … you've entered the home of SIMMONS COMICS GROUP and there's no turning back. *Gene Simmons House of Horrors* kicks off an all-new line of comics created by the rock legend. Up first, this quarterly anthology of tales of terror, all presided over by the man in black, Gene Simmons, who also scripts all his own dialogue for the comic." Written by Gene Simmons, Dwight MacPherson, Leah Moore & John Reppion, Chris Ryall, Sean Taylor, and Tom Waltz. Art by Jon Alderink, Grant Bond, Esteve, Zornow, and others. Issue #1 features cover art by Todd McFarlane. In 2008, the series was collected as a trade paperback, featuring a new introduction from Simmons, along with three prose short stories written by Simmons' son, Nick.

Gene Simmons Is a Powerful and Attractive Man: And Other Irrefutable Facts: Written by Christina Vitagliano and illustrated by Corey Marier and Craig Marier, this book, released March 31, 2015, by Plume, parodies the God of Thunder, poking fun at his legendary ego. According to Plume, the book is "peppered with words of wisdom straight from the Demon's tongue, hilarious reactions to Gene from kids, reimagined movie posters featuring Gene Simmons in the title role, and much, much more." Simmons himself wrote the foreword.

Gene Simmons "Meet and Greet" Bass Experience: For prices ranging from $4,000 to $10,000 (depending on the guitar), you can hang out with the Demon and get one of several autographed Axe or Punisher Bass guitars. In addition, you'll receive a certificate of authenticity signed by Simmons, an autographed hard shell Gene Simmons fitted bass case, a private backstage meet and greet with Simmons with up to four family members (five people total), photos and video with your own cameras, and up to four other items of your KISS memorabilia (no other instruments) autographed by Simmons.

Gene Simmons Rock Camp: An offshoot of Rock 'n' Roll Fantasy Camp, in which fans interact with and learn music from famous rock stars, Gene Simmons Rock Camp took place in Las Vegas March 27–30, 2014. In addition to Simmons, Tommy Thayer was featured as a guest performer. Other guests included Scott Ian (Anthrax), Sebastian Bach (Skid Row), Steve Stevens (Billy Idol), and Dave Ellefson (Megadeth).

Gene Simmons Tongue: The Demon launched *Gene Simmons Tongue* magazine in 2002, a time of struggle for print publications competing with the Internet. Unfortunately, it only lasted five issues. The first installment depicted Hugh Hefner on the cover and included features on Bill Maher, Tommy Lee, and Fred Durst, who supplied a photo of himself as a young boy dressed as KISS' Ace Frehley. In his inaugural column for the mag, Simmons wrote: "We will not try to reinvent the wheel. We may not in fact have very much profound content. We will certainly not pretend we do, in any case."

Gene Simmons Zipper: Published in 2007 by Simpsons Comics Group, this three-issue series features scripting by Tom Waltz and art by Casey Maloney. Adriano Loyola and Maloney provide cover art. The solicitation for the first issue reads as follows: "International superstar Gene Simmons creates his own version of the classic 'stranger in a strange land' with his latest comic book, *Zipper*! After a daring escape from his other-dimensional home, the Nether Ether, denizen Xeng Ral finds himself on planet Earth—lost, alone, curious and confused. Protected only by a specially equipped exo-suit, Xeng Ral sets out to explore his new world, finding both allies and enemies, all the while desperately evading those who would hunt him down from the Nether Ether." In 2008, the series was collected as a trade paperback.

Gerber, Steve: Marvel Comics writer Steve Gerber (1947–2008) introduced KISS to the Marvel Universe in *Howard the Duck* #12–13 (1977). He also wrote the first full KISS comic book, *Marvel Comics Super Special* #1 (1977). In *KISS: Behind the Mask—The Official Authorized Biography*, Gerber said: "The KISS comic was aimed at the real audience of the band. It was a leap for comic books at the time.... It had to be approached like we were publishing a rock 'n' roll magazine.... It had to be something spectacular.... It had to be something to just leap off the stands at you.... It was the first time I had written a comic book on living human beings."

Gerstein, Richard: Richard Gerstein played piano on Gene Simmons' "True Confessions" and "Always Near You/Nowhere to Hide." He also played keyboards on several songs on Peter Criss's 1978 KISS solo album.

"Get All You Can Take": Written by Paul Stanley and Mitch Weissman, "Get All You Can Take," the fourth track on *Animalize*, is not one of Stanley's finer moments. He sings at too high of a pitch, and it's difficult to understand what he's saying much of the time. The chorus, despite the use of an "F" bomb to try and shake things up, is bland, and the song is just plain noisy. Jean Beauvoir plays bass.

"Getaway": In *KISS: Hotter Than Hell*, author Paul Elliot called "Getaway" a "freewheeling, feel good rock 'n' roll number that sounds like it was composed and recorded in a matter of minutes and is all the better for it. The spontaneity of songs like this give *Dressed to Kill* a freshness lacking on *Hotter Than Hell*." The fourth track on *Dressed to Kill*, "Getaway" was written by Ace Frehley, who played a blistering guitar solo on the song, but was too shy to sing lead. As such, Peter Criss lends his typically raspy pipes.

Gibson Guitars: Ace Frehley prefers guitars created by Gibson, including his famous Cherry Sunburst, three-pickup Les Paul Custom. He nicknamed it the "Budokan" because it was the guitar he played when KISS broke the Beatles' sell-out record at Japan's Nippon Budokan arena in 1977. He played it during the 1996 Reunion Tour as well. In 2012, Gibson Custom recreated a limited number of the guitars for sale, calling it the Ace Frehley Budokan Les Paul Custom. Frehley has endorsed Gibson guitars and strings at various points in his career.

Tommy Thayer plays Gibson guitars as well, including his Spaceman Ephiphone Les Paul. During the 1970s, Gene Simmons played Gibson bass guitars, including the Gibson Grabber, the Gibson Ripper, and the Gibson Thunderbird.

The Gibson Guitar Corporation was founded in 1902 in Kalamazoo, Michigan by Orville Gibson.

Ace Frehley plays Gibson guitars and appears in various ads for the company, including this one for electric guitar strings.

Gill, Julian: Julian Gill is the author of numerous books published by KissFAQ.com Publishing, including: *The KISS & Related Recordings Focus: Music! The Songs, The Demos, The Lyrics, And Stories!*; *Kings of the Night Time World, 1972–1982*; *The Other Side Of The Coin*; *Rock And Roll All Nite: The Music Of KISS*; *Gene, Ace, Peter & Paul: A Detailed Exploration of the 1978 KISS Solo Albums*; *KISS Alive! 1998–2008*; *The KISS Album Focus, Vol. I: Kings of the Night Time World, 1972–1982*; *The KISS Album Focus, Vol. II: Hell or High Water, 1983–1996*; *The KISS Album Focus, Vol. III: Roar of Grease Paint, 1997–2006*; and *The KISS Album Focus, Vol. 4: Never Enough, 2006–2013*. Gill also co-hosts the KissFAQ podcast.

"Gimme More": The fifth track on *Lick It Up*, "Gimme More" is, according to *KISS: Hotter Than Hell* author Paul Elliott, a "huffing, puffing, run-of-the-mill heavy metal song badly sung by Paul Stanley, who shares writing credits with Vinnie Vincent … fast and loud but bereft of the style and melody that KISS fans have come to expect from Paul Stanley."

Gin Blossoms: On *Kiss My Ass: Classic KISS Regrooved*, the Gin Blossoms, who formed in 1987, covered "Christine Sixteen."

Glickman, Carl: With Howard Marks, Carl Glickman formed Glickman/Marks Management, helping such acts as KISS, the Isley Brothers, and Diana Ross handle their money. He passed away March 28, 2013.

Glickman/Marks Management: Former business management company for KISS, Diana Ross, and the Isley Brothers. You can read about the outfit in *KISS and Sell: The Making of a Supergroup*.

"Go Now": To close some of its early club shows, KISS played a cover of "Go Now," a Bessie Banks song from 1964 that the Moody Blues recorded and made popular later that year. In *Nothin' to Lose: The Making of KISS (1972–1975)*, Gene Simmons said, "Paul sang lead and we all jumped in on the harmonies. It sounded like the original Moody Blues version crossed with the Allman Brothers—the middle section of it breaks into dual guitar."

"God Gave Rock 'N' Roll to You II": A remake of Argent's anthemic "God Gave Rock 'N' Roll to You," which appeared on the British band's 1973 album, *In Deep*, "God Gave Rock 'N' Roll to You II" was recorded for the 1991 feature film, *Bill & Ted's Bogus Journey*. It is song #3 on the movie's soundtrack. It is also the fifth track on *Revenge*, the KISS comeback album from 1992. The original Argent song was written by Russ Ballard while tweaks for the remake were done by Paul Stanley, Gene Simmons, and Bob Ezrin. Stanley and Simmons share lead vocals while Eric Carr, who was sick with cancer at the time, joins in on backing vocals.

Some fans love and are inspired by "God Gave Rock 'N' Roll to You II" while others scoff at the notion of a hedonistic band like KISS giving a deity credit for their music. Some think it's funny and even a little embarrassing, but it was a top five hit in England. Surprisingly, Simmons has called it one of the best songs KISS has ever done.

The official video, which was directed by Mark Rezyka, shows the band playing music, interspersed with footage of Simmons and Stanley donning their old makeup designs.

"God of Thunder": KISS plays "God of Thunder," which is track three on *Destroyer*, at virtually every show they do. Although written by Paul Stanley (a demo version sung by Stanley is on 2001's *The Box Set*), it is Gene Simmons' trademark tune. Stanley has said he wanted to sing the song, but Ezrin wisely thought it was a better fit for Simmons. The Demon's guttural voice, a pair of boys who sound like they are having fun burning in hell (producer Bob Ezrin's kids, David and Josh), and crunching guitar work give the already dark lyrics a spooky sound. In addition to commanding you to kneel before the god of thunder, Simmons spits blood when the song is performed live, his super long, seemingly supernatural tongue wagging like a demon possessed.

Gods of Thunder: A Norwegian Tribute To KISS: Released September 5, 2005, by KISS Army Norway/Voices Music Entertainment, this album features 20 KISS covers by a variety of acts, including such KISS tribute bands as the KISSettes and Unmasked.

"Goin' Blind": Gene Simmons, who has cited the song as a favorite, wrote "Goin' Blind" with Stephen Coronel, a former bandmate of Simmons and Paul Stanley during the Wicked Lester era. In *KISS*, the book by Robert Duncan, the author said the song "is beautiful in a way, but too depressing in lyrics and mournful musical dronings to be fully accessible."

Originally called "Little Lady," "Goin' Blind," which tells the disturbing tale of a 93-year-old having an affair with a 16-year-old, is the third track on *Hotter Than Hell*. The song was covered by the Melvins for their 1993 album, *Houdini*, featuring Kurt Cobain on drums.

Going Platinum: KISS, Donna Summer, and How Neil Bogart Built Casablanca Records: Written by Brett Ermilio (Neil Bogart's nephew) and Josh Levine, *Going Platinum* was published by Lyons Press on November 4, 2014. The authors used family archives, photos, interviews, and anecdotes to tell the story of the founder of KISS's first record company.

Gold: Released January 11, 2005, by Mercury Records, *Gold* is a robust, two-disc greatest hits collection. Disc one includes: "Strutter," "Nothin' To Lose," "Firehouse," "Deuce," "Black Diamond," "Got to Choose," "Parasite," "Hotter Than Hell," "C'mon and Love Me," "She," "Anything for My Baby," "Rock Bottom" (live), "Cold Gin" (live), "Rock and Roll All Nite" (live), "Let Me Go, Rock 'n' Roll" (live), "Detroit Rock City," "King of the Night Time World," "Shout It Out Loud," "Beth," and "Do You Love Me?"

Disc two includes: "I Want You," "Calling Dr. Love," "Hard Luck Woman," "I Stole Your Love," "Love Gun," "Christine Sixteen," "Shock Me," "Makin' Love," "God of Thunder" (live), "Tonight You Belong To Me," "New York Groove," "Radioactive" (single version), "Don't You Let Me Down," "I Was Made for Lovin' You," "Sure Know Something," "Shandi," "Talk to Me," "A World Without Heroes," "Nowhere to Run," and "I'm A Legend Tonight."

Goldberg, Danny: Danny Goldberg was a publicist for KISS during the peak of their popularity in the late 1970s. In 1983, he was hired as a management-consultant for the band. He devoted several pages to KISS in his book, *Bumping Into Geniuses: My Life Inside the Rock and Roll Business*. Goldberg also did PR for Led Zeppelin and was the manager for Nirvana. Later he was president of Atlantic Records and Mercury Records, and chairman of Warner Bros. Records.

Goldmine KISS Collectibles Price Guide: Penned by Tom Shannon, who also wrote *Warman's KISS Collectibles Field Guide: Values and Identification*, *Goldmine KISS Collectibles Price Guide* was published in 2000 by Krause Publications. According to Krause, the book features "detailed listings of 2,000 items of the band's merchandise, every U.S. recording, and more than 250 licensed products produced from 1974 to 1998, including action figures, bean toys, costumes, posters, and videos. The photos and insert lists help novice collectors ensure they are purchasing complete copies of LPs. The licensed product section gives dates of manufacture and elaborate descriptions."

The *Goldmine KISS Collectibles Price Guide* was published in 2000 and featured pricing for more than 2,000 items.

"Good Girl Gone Bad": "With its chugging boogie riff and gruff vocals from Gene Simmons, 'Good Girl Gone Bad' is redolent of ZZ Top," wrote Paul Elliott, author of *KISS: Hotter Than Hell*. Elliott compares the song, which is the eighth track on *Crazy Nights*, to the adult sound of "Naked City." Simmons, who wrote the song with Davitt Sigerson and Peter Diggins, sings about a girl who's out of control, but he's having fun with her. The guitar solo is unmistakably Bruce Kulick.

Good Morning America: On August 1, 1996, ABC's *Good Morning America* ran a four-minute KISS reunion segment, focusing on the appeal and success of the band. Entertainment Editor Joel Siegel said: "The last time I saw these guys, my hair was darker; I didn't need bifocals. I have since put on a few chins, but they look exactly the same. It's not self-parody, it's heavy rock and roll, and surprised the heck out of me—I liked it, all over again." The narrator of the segment said KISS "either invented or influenced hard rock and grunge and heavy metal, and added fireworks and fiery effects that put the show in rock and roll show. And scared the hell out of parents around the world."

On October 11, 2012, KISS appeared on *Good Morning America* to promote their new album, *Monster*. They performed "Hell or Hallelujah" and "Rock and Roll All Nite."

"Goodbye": The ninth and final track on Paul Stanley's 1978 KISS solo album, "Goodbye" is a fitting finale, with the Starchild singing about time slipping away, leaving though he wishes he could stay, and saying goodbye, but only for now. A strong ending to a strong LP.

Gordon, Rachael: As of this writing, Rachael Gordon is Ace Frehley's fiancé. On September 8, 2014, she called *KISS & Tell* author Gordon G.G. Gebert and told him off, defending Frehley and cursing at Gebert. The incendiary phone call was recorded and showed up on YouTube.

"Got Love for Sale": Once again, Gene Simmons writes and sings about a woman who has *got* to have him. In fact, she can't live without his "love" (obviously a euphemism for sex—the word "love" rarely means love in pre–1980s KISS songs). "Got Love for Sale," the third track on *Love Gun*, rocks fast and hard and features excellent lead guitar licks by Ace Frehley. Simmons wrote the song at the Sunset Marquis Hotel in West Hollywood, California, when the band had gotten back from their legendary tour of Japan.

"Got to Choose": The first track on *Hotter Than Hell*, "Got to Choose" was written and sung by Paul Stanley, who has called it one of his favorite songs. A slow, but heavy tune, it's about a dude whose girlfriend cheats on him with another guy, with her being commanded to decide between the two. Stanley got the riff from a Wilson Pickett number called "Ninety-Nine and a Half (Won't Do)."

Got to Foo: A SAGAFOO.COM Tribute to KISS: This CD, released October 31, 2008, features the following tracks: "Reputation" (Sagafoo), "Baby Driver" (Chris Davis), "Strange Ways" (the Chandelears), "Secretly Cruel" (Double Virgo), "C'mon and Love Me" (Jayjerz), "Let Me Know" (Das Fark), "God of Thunder" (Bat Lizard Stew), "I Can't Stop the Rain" (Eucky Cheeze), "Sure Know Something" (Casaboontha), "Strange Ways" (Jim Tucker), "You're All That I Want" (Mixmaster Jason Herndon), "Dirty Livin'" (Das Fark), "Take Me" (Jayjerz), "Rock and Roll All Nite" (Casaboontha), "Reputation" dub remix (Sagafoo), and bonus versions of "Strange Ways" by Jim Tucker and Jayjerz. There was also a promo release limited to 50 hand-numbered copies, featuring an alternate track listing and an alternate cover.

Grammy Awards: Although KISS has never received a Grammy Award, and they've only been nominated for a Grammy once (in 1999 for "Best Hard Rock Performance" for "Psycho Circus"), the original lineup made headlines at the February 28, 1996, show—the *Thirty-Eighth Grammy Awards*—by making a surprise appearance onstage in full makeup and costumes. Rap star Tupac Shakur introduced the band, saying: "You know how the *Grammys* used to be, all straight-looking folks with suits. Everybody looking tired. No surprises. We tired of that. We need something different ... something new ... we need to shock the people ... so let's shock the people!"

After Ace, Gene, Paul, and Peter appear onstage, greeted by a nice round of applause, Shakur said: "These my homeboys, and I seen just about everything now." Gene yelled, "Alright Los Angeles!"; Peter yelled, "Great to be here!"; Ace said, "We're real happy to be here to present the next award"; and Paul read off the list of nominees for "Best Pop Performance by a Duo or Group with Vocal." Hootie and the Blowfish won for their hit single, "Let Her Cry."

The *Grammy Awards* stunt, which was the first time the boys had appeared in makeup and costumes since the "Shandi" music video released 16 years prior, was a prelude to the April 16 press conference announcing that the original version of KISS was getting back together.

Grand Funk Railroad: In 2001, Bruce Kulick joined the classic rock band Grand Funk Railroad, who formed in 1969. He remains their guitarist to this day.

"Great Expectations": Bob Ezrin produced *Destroyer*, which has many of his trademark flourishes, including orchestration and choir singing (by the Brooklyn Boys Choir) in the Gene Simmons–sung "Great Expectations," the fourth track on the album. Ezrin and Simmons wrote the song, which is quite lovely, if more than a little sexually suggestive and misogynistic. Some call the song "embarrassing melodrama" while others (including this author) love it. It's about a passionate female in the audience who is driven wild by the music and the lusty presence and playing of the singer, the guitar player, and the drummer, who seem to comprise one person.

The Great Kiss Off: Held June 8, 1974, at Woodfield Mall in Schaumburg, Illinois, The Great Kiss Off was a kissing contest to help promote *KISS*, the band's first album. It was also a fundraiser for St. Jude's Children Research Hospital, in Memphis, Tennessee. Vinnie Toro and Louise Heath were the winning couple, locking lips for more than 114 hours (with a five minute break every hour).

The second place couple received $500 while Toro and Heath got $1,000 for their efforts. The winning prize was originally going to be a trip to Toronto to see KISS in concert. Unfortunately, that show was cancelled. The prize was then to be an eight-day cruise to Acapulco, but the couple accepted the monetary equivalent of $1,000 instead. Eleven couples competed, each previous winners of a kissing contest near where they lived. During the event, Ace, Paul, Gene, and Peter walked around the mall in full costume and makeup, startling unsuspecting shoppers.

Greatest Hits Live: Tracks one through six on this Ace Frehley compilation disc, which was released in 2006 by Megaforce, were taken from the *12 Picks* album: "Rip It Out," "Breakout," "Cold Gin," "Shock Me," "Rocket Ride," and "Deuce." Tracks seven through 12 were taken from *Loaded Deck*: "Strangers in a Strange Land," "Separate," "New York Groove," "Rock Solders," "One Plus One," and "Give it to Me Anyway." A two–LP picture disc limited to 500 copies was released in 2009.

Greatest KISS: Released April 8, 1997, by Mercury Records, *Greatest KISS* is, as the title suggests, a greatest hits album. It includes the following tracks: "Detroit Rock City," "Hard Luck Woman," "Sure Know Something," "Deuce," "Do You Love Me?," "I Was Made for Lovin' You," "Calling Dr. Love," "Christine Sixteen," "Beth," "Strutter," "Cold Gin," "Plaster Caster," "Rock and Roll All Nite," "Flaming Youth," "Two Sides of the Coin," and "Shout It Out Loud," the latter of which is an exclusive live version recorded at Tiger Stadium in Detroit, Michigan on June 28, 1996. The album only reached #77 on the *Billboard* 200 chart. The Japanese, Mexican, and European/Australian versions each have 20 tracks.

Greektures of the Night: A Greek Tribute to KISS: Released in July of 2008 by Gerasimos Kavvadas, this tribute features two CDs. Most of the bands are Athens-based.

Disc one includes the following tracks: "Creatures of the Night" (Delivers), "I Am A Legend Tonight" (Luv Sux), "Black Diamond" (Crosswinds), "Calling Dr. Love" (Prejudice Reborn), "Love Gun" (The Ivory Tower), "I Love It Loud" (Roxy Bitch), "C'mon and Love Me" (Livestock), "God of Thunder" (WC), "Gimme More" (Marauder), "Who Wants to be Lonely" (Reverse Split), and "Beth" (Julian's Lullaby).

Disc two includes: "Detroit Rock City" (M/M & C.), "Hide Your Heart" (4Bitten), "Deuce" (Sinnis' Blues Band), "Strutter" (SSIK), "Nothin' to Lose" (Wild Machine), "I Was Made for Lovin' You" (Gallard featuring Lonely Jove), "The Oath" (Metalmorfosis), "Tears Are Falling" (Cain), "Psycho Circus" (Spiral Zeus), and "Forever" (Blind Shot).

Grítalo Fuerte: Tributo a KISS: Released by Sleaze Records in 1997, this tribute album features songs by various Argentinian bands. Tracks include: "Love Gun" (Nepal), "King of the Night Time World" (Elmer), "Rocket Ride" (Satelite 68), "Christine Sixteen" (Los Wincofones), "Let Me Know" (Guru), "Room Service" (Cruz Del Sur), "Save Your Love" (Nasty), "Sure Know Something" (Dreams), "Tears Are Falling" (A. Kokolio & G. Carbonell), "What's On Your Mind" (Flores Muertas), "C'mon and Love Me" (Krill), "Nothin' to Lose" (Nervios), "God Gave Rock 'N' Roll To You II" (Parte Del Asunto), "I Stole Your Love" (Brigada Anti Disturbious), "Makin' Love" (Secta Cactus), "She" (Tio Jack), "Naked City" (Kim), "Hotter Than Hell" (Besa Mi Culo), and "I Was Made for Lovin' You" (Gatos Sucios).

Gruen, Bob: Celebrated rock and roll photographer Bob Gruen, who got his career off to a good start taking pictures of Bob Dylan at the Newport Folk Festival in 1965, is best-known for his famous photo of John Lennon wearing a sleeveless New York City T-shirt (as seen in his 2005 book, *John Lennon: The New York Years*). Gruen, who took a lot of pics for *Creem* magazine, photographed KISS on numerous occasions during the 1970s, including some really nice shots live, backstage, and in Japan, and for the iconic *Dressed to Kill* album cover.

Guardian of the Gods: An Inside Look at the Dangerous Business of Music: Written by Mark Rodgers, *Guardian Of The Gods* was published by Monkey Boy Media June 20, 1999. The book chronicles the career of Andre Augustine, KISS' former security manager. Augustine, who was hired just before the Revenge Tour, also worked with such musical acts as Aerosmith, Prince, Bon Jovi, Run-D.M.C., and Public Enemy. Rodgers said he wrote the book, which includes some amusing Ace Frehley anecdotes and lots of photos from Augustine's private collection, so he could "get backstage at Aerosmith concerts."

Guitar Hero: Warriors of Rock: The sixth main game in the *Guitar Hero* series, *Warriors of Rock* was released September 28, 2010, by Activision for the Xbox 360, PlayStation 3, and Nintendo Wii. The game, in which players press color-coded buttons on a plastic guitar in unison with on-screen prompts, includes "Love Gun" on its list of playable songs. In addition, users could download "Calling Dr. Love," "Detroit Rock City," and "Rock and Roll All Nite."

Guitar World Presents KISS: Published August 1, 1997, by Hal Leonard Corporation for *Guitar World*, *Guitar World Presents KISS* is a softcover collection of interviews that appeared in the popular music magazine.

Gulliver's Travels: Directed by Rob Letterman, the modern retelling of *Gulliver's Travels* starring Jack Black in the title role hit theaters December 25, 2010. In his bachelor pad, Gulliver plays a *Guitar Hero*–like game featuring a Lilliputian KISS cover band. "Rock and Roll All Nite" is on the movie's soundtrack.

Halloween Costumes: Numerous KISS costumes and masks have been released over the years, but the first were produced by Collegeville in 1978. These early costumes came with a plastic mask with hair (synthetic strands or solid plastic) and plastic costume, the latter of which bore no resemblance to the actual costumes KISS wore. Rather, each was decorated with art depicting the respective band member. Retail-level KISS costumes would get much more elaborate in the following decades, such as the relatively convincing designs by Illusive Concepts in 1997 and Costumes Galore in 2008.

Ad for the 1978 KISS Halloween costumes, produced by Collegeville, the first commercially available costumes patterned after the band.

"Hard Luck Woman": A great acoustic number that Paul Stanley originally wrote with Rod Stewart in mind ("Rod the Bod" never did record the song), "Hard Luck Woman" is the ninth track on *Rock and Roll Over* and the first single off the record, reaching #15 on the *Billboard* charts. Sung to raspy perfection by Peter Criss (who was angered because Stanley didn't write it with him in mind), "Hard Luck Woman" works well as a crossover number, as evidenced by country legend Garth Brooks—an avowed KISS fan—covering the tune for *Kiss My Ass: Classic KISS Regrooved*. With its softer sound, "Hard Luck Woman" was never a concert staple, but an electric version is featured on *Alive II*.

Hard Rock Comics #5: A follow-up to the unauthorized *Rock 'N' Roll Comics* #9, Revolutionary's *Hard Rock Comics* #5 was published in July of 1992. The story, entitled either "Tales from the Tours" (on the cover) or "KISS—Gods of Thunder" (on the splash page), was written by Spike Steffenberger, who used information gleaned from an interview with Paul Stanley and Gene Simmons (the Demon and the Starchild approved of the project). Scott Pentzer drew the interior and the cover. Followed by *KISS Pre-History*, a three-issue series published in 1993.

"Hard Times": Sung with driving force by Ace Frehley, "Hard Times," the seventh track on *Dynasty*, isn't as famous as "Cold Gin," "Shock Me," or "New York Groove," but it is a solid Ace song, in which the street-tough Spaceman recalls a rough and tumble life in the city, fighting, hanging out, and getting high. And how, in 1979 when he wrote the autobiographical tune, he was on the right track and didn't want to look back, but believed he was nevertheless stronger for the experience. Strong lead guitar work is icing on the proverbial KISS cake. Frehley, who has cited the song as one of his favorites, played bass on the track.

Hard to Believe: KISS Covers Compilation: *Hard to Believe* is a KISS tribute album featuring contributions from an assortment of independent, punk, and underground groups of the late 1980s, including Nirvana, the key band of the grunge movement of the early 1990s. The original version of the record released overseas in 1990 (by Waterfront/Damp Records) includes the following tracks: "Detroit Rock City" (Bullet La Volta), "Is That You?" (Girl Monster), "I Want You" (King Snake Roost), "Christine Sixteen" (All), "Sure Know Something" (Whippers Snappers), "Lick It Up" (the Hard-Ons), "Do You Love Me?" (Nirvana), "Beth" (Coffin Break), "Deuce" (Hellmenn), "Parasite" (Smelly Tongues), "Love Gun" (Surfin Ceasars), "Snowblind" (Skinyard), "War Machine" (Instigators), "Makin' Love" (Thrust), "Rip It Out" (Chemical People), "Charisma" (Plunderers), and "Beth" (version 2/hidden track, Coffin Break). According to www.kiss-related-recordings.nl, the American version (1993) and reissue contains some different bands and tracks than the original: the Hellmen, the Whipper Snappers, the Surfin' Caesars, and the Plunderers are gone, replaced by Hullabaloo ("Calling Dr. Love"), Threepeople ("Deuce"), and the Melvins ("God of Thunder").

Harkin, Brendan: Brendan Harkin is credited with playing guitar on "Easy Thing," track #6 on *Peter Criss*. However, in an interview published on www.kissasylum.com, he claimed that he played on other songs on the album as well: "Sean [Delaney] said, 'I can only give you a small credit because Peter wants big names on there.' And I guess I wasn't a big name."

Harper, Tom: Tom Harper played bass on "Shandi." He was also Paul Stanley's guitar tech on the *Dynasty* tour.

Harris, Doyle: During his stint with Glam-Nation, Eric Singer went by the stage name of Doyle Harris.

Harris, Larry: With his cousin Neil Bogart, Larry Harris co-founded Casablanca Records, the label that released the first few KISS albums. Harris was managing director and senior vice president of Casablanca, and he was with Bogart on that fateful day when Bogart saw KISS perform for the first time in September of 1973 at a private showcase at Manhattan's Henry LeTang School of Dance.

In his book, *And Party Every Day: The Inside Story of Casablanca Records*, Harris described that mini-concert: "Four seven-foot monsters in eight-inch platform boots took the stage.... Paul Stanley's black star was in place, as were Ace Frehley's silver explosions, and Gene Simmons and Peter Criss had their respective batwings and cat whiskers under development. But the makeup looked cheap ... there were no costumes to speak of ... no production at all ... no blood, no fire, no explosions or drum risers, just pure energy and sound.... The volume level in that small room was indescribable.... I couldn't hear for two days afterwards ... but, despite the onslaught, I couldn't help but be impressed as I watched the performance.... KISS was an incredibly compelling band.... Neil and I both knew that anyone capable of provoking this type of visceral response was the stuff of future superstardom."

A few days after the show, Harris, as he wrote in *And Party Every Day*, met with KISS to "make them feel that Casablanca was the only label for them." Harris also suggested that they destroy some guitars like the Who and "put their logo on the drumhead and figure out a way to use more speakers and amplifiers in their production so it would look more massive," which they "did on the cheap by using fake speaker cabinets."

Hartman, Lisa: Paul Stanley dated actress and singer Lisa Hartman during the mid–1980s. She starred on the TV show *Knots Landing* (1979), and in such movies as *Where the Boys Are* (1984) and *Someone Else's Child* (1994). In 1991, she married country music star Clint Black.

Haslip, Jimmy: A founding ex-member of the fusion group, the Yellowjackets, Jimmy Haslip played bass on "Danger" from *Creatures of the Night*. He was also in the band Blackjack with Bruce Kulick.

"Hate": The first track on *Carnival of Souls: The Final Sessions*, which was KISS's concession to the grunge movement of the 1990s, "Hate" was written by Gene Simmons, Scott Van Zen, and Bruce Kulick. Simmons' gruff vocals accompany heavy guitars and noisy feedback.

Have Love, Will Travel: This second KISS tribute album by Berlin folk artist Marceese includes the following tracks: "Tomorrow and Tonight," "Man of 1000 Faces," "Plaster Caster," "I Want You," "Radioactive," "Got Love for Sale," "Easy Thing," "Move On," "Dirty Livin,'" "Rip It Out," "Rock and Roll All Nite," and "Charisma." Released in Germany January 23, 2015, by Timezone Records.

Hayseed Dixie—Kiss My Grass: A Hillbilly Tribute to KISS: Released in 2003 by Dualtone, this tribute album by the popular "rockgrass" band, Hayseed Dixie, features the following songs: "Calling Dr. Love," "Detroit Rock City," "Christine Sixteen," "Cold Gin," "Let's Put the X in Sex," "Love Gun," "Lick It Up," "I Love It Loud," "Rock and Roll All Nite," and "Heaven's On Fire."

Headliners: KISS: Published by Ace Books in 1978, *Headliners: KISS* is a mass market paperback written by John Swenson. It is one of the earliest books about the band, and like *KISS* by Robert Duncan, which was the first book about KISS, it lacks all the dirt that we know now, such as the excessive in-fighting among band members and the substantial drug and alcohol abuse by Ace Frehley and Peter Criss. Even so, it's a fun read that is filled with black-and-white photos. It also has a small poster attached to the inside of the front cover. The book begins with a description of a KISS concert and ends with info on the solo albums, the forth coming tour, vital statistics for the band, and a "Discography and Awards" chapter.

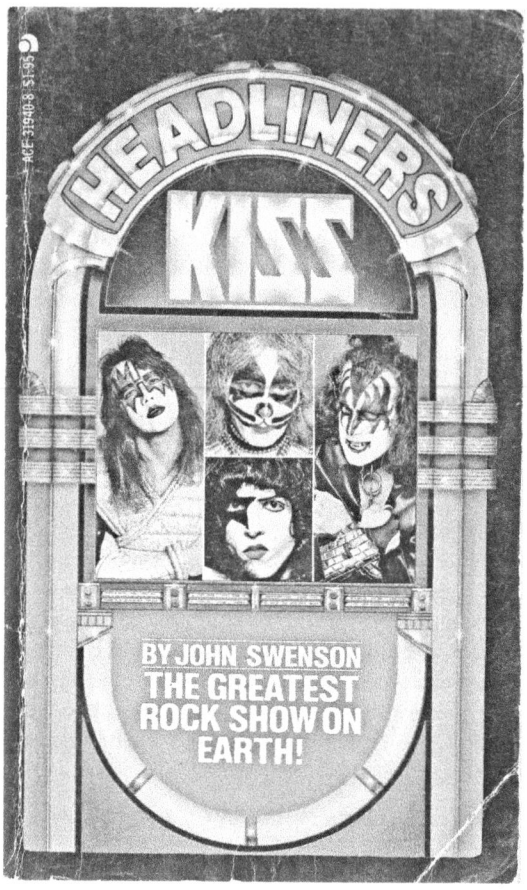

Written by John Swenson, *Headliners: KISS* was one of the first books published about Ace, Gene, Paul, and Peter.

"Heart of Chrome": The seventh track on *Revenge*, "Heart of Chrome" was written by Paul Stanley, Vinnie Vincent, and Bob Ezrin. It's a typical Paul Stanley rocker with an atypical lyric, in which the Starchild chastises an untrustworthy girl for selling their sexy conversations to the BBC. Stanley got the idea for the title from a Jim Steinman song called "Chrome Heart."

Heath, Louise: With her partner Vinnie Toro, Louise Heath was the co-winner of "The Great Kiss Off" kissing contest of 1974. The couple smooched for more than 114 hours, with a five-minute break every hour.

"Heaven's on Fire": A simple, but scintillating piece of pop metal, "Heaven's On Fire" is the second track on *Animalize* and the first single from the album, reaching #49 on the *Billboard* charts.

It was written by Desmond Child and Paul Stanley.

The Starchild begins the song with a Tarzan-like yodel (which was originally Stanley doing vocal exercises, but the band decided to leave in) and proceeds to sing about his blood boiling hot, his heart raging with fever, and how the girl he's with should eat a certain part of him like a piece of cake. In short, it's another hard rocking KISS sex song, but it's one of relatively few tunes by the band that you can really dance to. During the mid-late 1980s, it was a staple at various bars and dance clubs around the country.

In the video for "Heaven's On Fire," band members are shown jamming onstage and making out with scantily clad girls in a hotel room. A live version of the tune appears on the 1986 *Hear 'n Aid* album that raised money for famine relief in Africa.

Hefner, Hugh: Prior to dating Gene Simmons, Shannon Tweed lived with *Playboy* founder, free speech advocate, and notorious womanizer Hugh Hefner at the Playboy Mansion. In *KISS and Tell*, she wrote: "I certainly never thought he was going to marry me. That wasn't the deal, though for a time in the back of this girl's mind was the thought that it wouldn't be out of the question for me. But truly, it wasn't that kind of relationship. It was sexual attention and excitement and good times, though I can honestly say I loved him. Not in the same way I love Gene, not the way you love the father of your children, when you know that you want to be with him forever."

See also: "Hugh Hefner: Playboy, Activist and Rebel."

"Hell or Hallelujah": The first track on *Monster*, "Hell or Hallelujah" gets *Monster* off to a rousing, high energy, but not quite perfect start. The song begins with a "tantalizingly raw opening riff straight out of Paul Stanley's 'I Stole Your Love' playbook," said Matthew Wilkening of ultimateclassicrock.com. "From there, things lean a bit too heavily on the band's sleek, up-tempo, borderline-metal '80s sound, as opposed to the groove-oriented rock of their '70s glory days, but the song still packs a nice punch…. Eric Singer and Tommy Thayer are in great form throughout, and the latter teams up with Stanley for a nice, high-pitched Zeppelin style vocal-guitar duel during the solo section." The semi-autobiographical song, written and sung by Stanley, is about how the frontman paid his dues to achieve his status as a rich rock star.

"Hell or High Water": On "Hell or High Water," one of the better, catchier Gene Simmons songs of the 1980s, the Demon sings in convincing fashion about how he's going to love and hold onto a girl no matter what. His refrain in conjunction with the chanted chorus works particularly well. Written by Simmons, who penned the lyrics and the melody, and Bruce Kulick, who tears it up on lead guitar.

Hellbox: *Hellbox* is the autobiography of Sean Delaney, who died before the book was published, leaving Bryan Kinnaird to piece together the text. Published by Xlibris Corp August 13, 2004, the book chronicles Delaney's life and career and his time with KISS.

An Amazon review of the book by Tim Brough reads: "Delaney was a lynchpin in the creation of KISS, and has been slowly, quietly deleted from the band's history…. The result is a mess of a book with some tantalizing details…. It's nice to hear some of the KISStory from a perspective outside the band."

Henry LeTang School of Dance: In September of 1973, Casablanca Records co-founders Neil Bogart and Larry Harris saw KISS play for the first time. It was a private showcase at Henry LeTang School of Dance, located on 54th street in Manhattan. Kenny Kerner, Richie Wise, Bill Aucoin, Joyce Biawitz, Sean Delaney, Eddie Solan, and Lydia Criss were also there.

"Hide Your Heart": Sung with vigor by Paul Stanley, "Hide Your Heart" is the third track on *Hot in the Shade* and the first single from the album. It only reached #66 on the *Billboard* charts, but it's actually a catchy and infectious song that should have charted higher. Written by Stanley, Desmond Child, and Holly Knight, it was originally intended for the 1987 KISS album, *Crazy Nights*, but didn't make the cut. However, Bonnie Tyler recorded it for her 1988 album, *Hide Your Heart*.

Ace Frehley (*Trouble Walkin'*), Molly Hatchet (*Lightning Strikes Twice*), and Robin Beck (*Trouble or Nothin'*) also recorded the song. Stanley originally wanted to call it "Bite Down Hard," but Knight already had a song with that title, so they changed it to "Hide Your Heart."

Hilsen, Jesse: Former psychotherapist for Paul Stanley and former financial adviser for KISS, Jesse Hilsen gained dubious notoriety when his ex-wife appeared on CBS's *48 Hours* in December of 1993, claiming that he had never paid alimony or child support.

Hit 'N Run Mini Tour: This brief tour, which lasted from July 20 to October 26, 2007, for a total of five shows, took place in Michigan, Nevada, Wisconsin, and California. Paul Stanley was sick and couldn't play San Jacinto, California, but the show went on with Gene Simmons, Tommy Thayer, and Eric Carr. This was one of the rare times the band played without Stanley. The events were chronicled in an episode of *Gene Simmons Family Jewels*. A show scheduled for Whistler, British Columbia, Canada was cancelled.

Hit Parader: Published from 1942 to 2008, *Hit Parader* magazine has featured KISS on the cover many times. Like *Creem* and *Rock Scene*, *Hit Parader* was an early proponent of the band.

The June 1979 issue of *Hit Parader* magazine. Many fans of the era would clip out photos from issues of *Hit Parader*, *Creem*, and the like and make their own KISS scrapbooks (courtesy KISSmuseum.com).

The Hitchhiker: In 1986, Gene Simmons guest-starred as Mr. Big on an episode of the Canadian HBO anthology series *The Hitchhiker* called "O.D. Feelin'." At the end of the episode—SPOILER WARNING—he cuts open a bag of cocaine, the powder engulfs him, and he turns into a skeleton.

"Hold Me, Touch Me (Think of Me When We're Apart)": The seventh track on *Paul Stanley*, this song was the only single from the album, reaching #46 on the *Billboard* charts. It is a gentle, earnestly sung ballad in which a soft spoken Starchild tells his sleeping lover to hold him, touch him, and think of him when they're apart. Feathery guitars, keyboards, and background vocals add to the mellow, blatantly romantic vibe.

Hollywood RockWalk: The Sunset Boulevard/Los Angeles location of retail giant Guitar Center is home to the Hollywood RockWalk, a hall of fame that honors musicians. Said musicians make handprints in blocks of cement to be displayed at the store. The Paul/Gene/Tommy/Eric Singer version of KISS was inducted into the RockWalk on May 18, 1993. Peter Criss was inducted June 20, 1996, while Ace Frehley and Eric Carr were honored July 25, 1996.

Hollywood Walk of Fame: On August 11, 1999, 25 years after the release of their debut album, KISS became the 2,325th recipient of a star on the Hollywood Walk of Fame. The KISS star is located at 7092 Hollywood Blvd (on Marshfield Way as it merges into Hollywood Blvd). At the dedication ceremony, Paul Stanley thanked the cheering fans: "This is really more about you people than it is about us. We could never have done any of this. We always tried to make our mark by bucking the system and going against the rules. You've been with us since the beginning. We wouldn't be here without you, so this star is for you people. It's got our name on it, but every one of you is responsible for it. So we thank you, and this is a big day for all of us."

"Hooked on Rock 'n' Roll": The ninth track on *Peter Criss*, "Hooked on Rock 'n' Roll" is an old fashioned, good-time "rock and soul" song, written by Criss, Stan Penridge, and Vini Poncia. Criss sings of a music-induced fever that won't cool down. Includes a guitar solo by Toto's Steve Lukather.

"Hooligan": The seventh track on *Love Gun*, "Hooligan" is a street-tough number that is unmistakably the work of Peter Criss (with co-writer Stan

Penridge), whose grandmother used to call him a hooligan. The Catman sings about being a creep and an illiterate dropout whom the chicks dig.

"Hot and Cold": Written and sung by Gene Simmons, "Hot and Cold" is typical of the Demon as he brags about his tower of power and tells a girl that if it's too loud she's too old, if it's too hot she's too cold. The sixth track on *Sonic Boom*, the song has a good beat (more cowbell!), evoking such tracks as "Calling Dr. Love" and "Love 'Em and Leave 'Em."

***Hot in the Shade*:** Released October 17, 1989, by Mercury Records, *Hot in the Shade* is KISS's 15th studio album. The LP has a harder sound than the previous two records, *Asylum* and *Crazy Nights*, and keyboards are only used on two songs, the singles "Hide Your Heart" and "Forever," a power ballad written by Paul Stanley and Michael Bolton that reached #8 on the *Billboard* Hot 100 chart. The album's other single was "Rise to It." *Rolling Stone* ranked *Hot in the Shade* KISS's 10th best album, saying it "stands tall as a surprisingly solid slab of late-eighties hard rock."

Dale Sherman, author of *KISS FAQ*, wasn't so kind, calling it a "musical mess by most fans," though he does give it credit for its "experimentation" and "variety of musical approaches." He also called it Gene Simmons' "triumphant return to the fold" after devoting too much time to movies and producing and managing other acts.

In *KISS: Behind the Mask—The Official Authorized Biography*, Paul Stanley revealed that he is proud of *Hot in the Shade*. "That was a good first step toward getting back home, not recreating what we had done before, but reasserting ourselves, redefining ourselves," he said. "*Hot in the Shade* is an album that really goes back to what people think of as vintage KISS." Conversely, Bruce Kulick, citing the lack of a producer, called it his "least favorite KISS album … there was nobody cracking the whip and everything was compromised and ultimately the music suffered."

Tracks include: "Rise to It," "Betrayed," "Hide Your Heart," "Prisoner of Love," "Read My Body," "Love's a Slap in the Face," "Forever," "Silver Spoon," "Cadillac Dreams," "King of Hearts," "The Street Giveth and the Street Taketh Away," "You Love Me to Hate You," "Somewhere Between Heaven and Hell," "Little Caesar," and "Boomerang." At 15 songs, *Hot in the Shade* is one of the band's longest records.

Hot in the Shade Tour: From May 11, 1990, to November 9, 1990, KISS played 123 shows in the U.S. and Canada in support of their 15th studio album. To reflect the *Hot in the Shade* album cover, the stage featured a huge sphinx named Leon, which would open its mouth to emit fireworks and hundreds of laser lights. When the mouth was fully opened at the beginning of the show, KISS would appear in silhouette amongst the laser beams.

This was the only tour in which Gene Simmons didn't breathe fire. In addition, there was no "You wanted the best, you got the best" introduction. During the final verse of "God of Thunder," off-stage keyboardist Gary Corbett would sing the part through a synthesizer, making it appear as though the sphinx were singing. Sadly, this was the last tour with Eric Carr, who died November 24, 1991.

Band lineup: Paul Stanley, Gene Simmons, Bruce Kulick, and Eric Carr. Opening acts: Danger Danger, Downtown Bruno, Faster Pussycat, the Good Rats, Joe Lynn Turner, Little Caesar, The Red & The Black, Saraya, Shake City, Slaughter, Vixen, and Winger. For the June 15 concert in Toronto, Whitesnake was the headliner over KISS, Slaughter, and Faster Pussycat. Average Attendance: 6,589.

Followed by: Revenge Tour.

***HOT LICKS—Bruce Kulick of KISS: Rock Guitar Masterclass*:** Released on VHS in 1986, *HOT LICKS* features Bruce Kulick explaining various guitar techniques, including picking, tuning, finger tapping, and hand exercises. He does this in part through such songs as "King Of the Mountain," "Tears Are Falling," and "Uh! All Night." Clips of KISS in action are included. The DVD version, released in 2004, adds six audio tracks (taken from *Audio Dog* and *Transformer*) and a Kulick solo from the April 22, 1988, KISS show at Budokan Hall in Tokyo, Japan.

Hotel Diplomat: KISS played a couple of important shows at the dilapidated Hotel Diplomat in New York during their formative era, including a gig with the Brats (headliners) and the Planets (opening act) on July 13, 1973. To publicize that first Hotel Diplomat concert, which is when Eddie Kramer, Sean Delaney, and Bill Aucoin saw KISS for the first time, the band put up posters all over town. In addition, Gene Simmons, acquiring addresses from such trade publications as *Record World*, *Billboard*, and *Cashbox*, sent mailers to record executives. The ones who showed up saw fans (Peter's sisters and some family friends) dressed in homemade KISS T-shirts designed by Paul and Peter.

In *KISS: Behind the Mask—The Official Authorized Biography*, Aucoin said: "When I first saw KISS at the Hotel Diplomat in 1973 they didn't have much of a show. They had the red beacons, a couple of amps. They were wearing black jeans. No one could afford leather. The show was just a regular rock 'n' roll show except they had spontaneity. They wanted to do something different and they wanted it very badly. That kind of devotion is worth more than anything. It's so special and you start picking up on it. I saw that magic in them."

***Hotter Than Hell* (album):** Released October 22, 1974, by Casablanca Records, *Hotter Than Hell* was the second KISS album, recorded during and after extensive touring for the band's first album. Lacking a hit single, the album only reached #100 on the *Billboard* charts. Produced by Kenny Kerner and Richie Wise, and recorded at the Village Recorder Studios in Los Angeles, the LP includes the following tracks: "Got to Choose," "Parasite," "Goin' Blind," "Hotter Than Hell," "Let Me Go, Rock 'n' Roll," "Watchin' You," "Mainline," "Comin' Home," and "Strange Ways." On June 23, 1977, the album was certified gold.

The exotic album cover, inspired by Japanese kabuki theater, was designed by Norman Seeff, with help from John Van Hamersveld. Gene Simmons has said on more than one occasion that the photos session for the cover, which depicts a wild party scene on the back, were one of the few times he's seen Paul Stanley drunk, and that he had to carry his bandmate to the car afterward and lock him in the back seat.

Rolling Stone recently ranked *Hotter Than Hell*, which was remastered in 1997, KISS's fifth best album, citing its "first-rate riff-rockers" and "glammy grooviness." In the magazine's original review in issue #179 (Jan., 1975), Ed Naha said that the album "does not sound as bad as the band looks ... the boys in the band sound tighter and more lethal than in the past ... despite its flaws, KISS does succeed in churning out quite a bit of high-energy instrumentation and cheerful, nonsensical vocalizing."

"Hotter Than Hell" (song): Called one of the band's "best entries in the metal arena" and a "gutsy rocker full of pile-driving riffs" by Donald A. Guarisco of www.allmusic.com, "Hotter Than Hell" is the fourth track on the album of the same name. Written and sung by Paul Stanley (under the influence of Free, specifically of their hit song "All Right Now"), it is also the B-side to "Let Me Go, Rock 'n' Roll," the only single from *Hotter Than Hell*.

In *KISS Meets the Phantom of the Park*, the evil KISS robot duplicates perform an altered version of "Hotter Than Hell" called "Rip and Destroy."

Hotter Than Hell Tour: Beginning October 17, 1974, and ending February 22, 1975, KISS toured the U.S. and Canada in support of their second album, *Hotter Than Hell*. They played 53 shows in all. The costumes and stage effects were largely the same as the KISS Tour, but Ace added a shooting mechanism to his guitar.

Band lineup: Paul Stanley, Ace Frehley, Gene Simmons, and Peter Criss. Headlining acts: Black Oak Arkansas, Dr. John, Foghat, Golden Earring, Jo Jo Gunne, Quicksilver Messenger Service, REO Speedwagon, Rush, Wishbone Ash, and ZZ Top. Opening acts: Arosa, Ballin' Jack, Camel, Cannonball, the Clowns, Cockney Rebel, Easy Stream, Eddie Boy Band, Eli, Fancy, Fantasy, Heartsfield, Hickock, Hydra, If, the James Montgomery Band, Joe, John Hammond, Kenny Kramer, Man, Mercury, Mike Quatro, Neil Merryweather & Space Rangers, Pezband, Point Blank, the Raspberries, the Road Crew, Rockets, Rush, the Sam Hurrie Band, Scream, Skyhook, Smokehouse, Stampeders, Stone Wall, T. Rex, Third Rail, Tongue, Trapeze, UFO, and Yesterday & Today. Average attendance: 3,936.

Followed by: Dressed to Kill Tour.

***Hotter Than Hotter Than Hell: A Tribute to KISS*:** This indie release from July 29, 2014, recorded by the tribute band Hotter Than Hotter Than Hell, features the following tracks: "Got to Choose," "Parasite," "Goin' Blind," "Hotter Than Hell," "Let Me Go, Rock 'n' Roll," "All the Way," "Watchin' You," "Mainline," "Comin' Home," and "Strange Ways." Produced by Jeff Westlake.

The Hottest Show on Earth Tour: Serving North America, this tour lasted from July 23, 2010, to July 28, 2011, for a total of 58 shows. It was a follow-up to the Sonic Boom Over Europe Tour. KISS donated one dollar from each ticket sold to the United States Armed Forces to benefit the Wounded Warriors Project. Opening bands included The Academy Is…, Bad City, the Envy, and a local act for every city (winners of a contest held by Guitar Center).

On July 30, 2010, D. X. Ferris of *Rolling Stone* magazine, who had gone to the show in Pittsburgh at the First Niagara Pavilion the night before, had this to say: "KISS proved why they are the reigning kings of theater rock, delivering an electric two-hour, 21-song set of glam-rock smashes, newer tunes, over-the-top pyrotechnics and plenty of blood-spitting…. With three massive video screens and bright LED lights, KISS kicked the show off with fiery jams like 'Modern Day Delilah' and 'Cold Gin,' but the band hit their stride once they launched into 'Let Me Go, Rock 'N' Roll,' which found KISS saturated in blinding white light and sent the crowd into a frenzied clap-along…. Throughout the gig, guitarist Tommy Thayer and drummer Eric Singer filled in solidly for original members Ace Frehley and Peter Criss, especially when Thayer reprised Frehley's sparks-shooting guitar solo in 'Shock Me.'…While the band delivered fan favorites, [they] mined their catalog for deeper cuts like the faux-disco 1979 single 'I Was Made for Lovin' You,' during which Paul Stanley zoomed over the crowd suspended by wires."

Followed by: The Tour.

How to Rock Fans & Influence People: An Australian Tribute to KISS: This tribute album, released in 1997 by Drought Productions, features the following tracks: "Unholy" (Hyper), "Almost Human" (Street Trash Circus), "Shock Me" (Loudhailer), "Shandi" (Matt Bradshaw), "Cadillac Dreams" (Root Beer), "Beth" (Brad Drought), "Is That You?" (Pain), "A Kiss Medley" (Good Fellas), "Love Gun" (Big Tuna), "Detroit Rock City" (Empire), and "Cold Gin" (Bad Karma).

Howard the Duck: KISS made their comic book debut in Marvel's *Howard the Duck* #12 (June 1977), a cameo in a story called "Mind-Mush!" In the following issue, #13, KISS made their first full comic book appearance in a story called "Rock, Roll Over, and Writhe!" Both issues were written by Steve Gerber, with art by Gene Colan (pencils) and Steve Leialoha (inks).

Howell, John Shane: John Shane Howell played classical guitar on Gene Simmons' "Radioactive" and "Burning Up with Fever."

Hugh Hefner: Playboy, Activist and Rebel: Directed by Brigitte Berman, this 2009 documentary opens with Gene Simmons, sitting amongst his KISS collection, saying: "Show me any guy, of any age, anywhere in the world, at any time in history, today or tomorrow, that wouldn't give his left nut to be Hugh Hefner at 20, at 50, at 80."

Humble Pie: In *Nothin' to Lose: The Making of KISS (1972–1975)*, Paul Stanley cited English band Humble Pie, featuring Peter Frampton on guitar, as a huge influence. Formed in 1969, "Humble Pie was one of the inspirations behind KISS's sound," Stanley said. "Seeing them perform at the Fillmore and watching Steve Marriott command and preach to an audience was something that inspired me." Humble Pie is famous for such songs as "Black Coffee," "30 Days in the Hole," and "Natural Born Bugie."

"I": The 11th and final track on *Music from "The Elder,"* "I" is a celebratory, fist-pumping, foot-

The last page of Marvel's *Howard the Duck* #12 (May 1977), the first appearance of KISS in a comic book.

stomping rock anthem in which the hero of the story, despite initial misgivings, believes that he can emerge triumphant. It was written by Bob Ezrin and Gene Simmons, who sings the song, trading verses with Paul Stanley. Allan Schwartzberg recorded drum overdubs on the track because Eric Carr couldn't quite capture the feel of it.

"I Can't Stop the Rain": Written by Sean Delaney, "I Can't Stop the Rain" is the 10th and final track on Peter Criss's 1978 KISS solo album. The Catman sings with accompanying orchestration, bemoaning the fact that the only girl he's ever loved has slipped through his fingers. Not exactly "Beth," but not bad either.

"I Confess": The 10th track on *Carnival of Souls: The Final Sessions*, "I Confess" wouldn't sound too terribly out of place on *Music from "The Elder,"* thanks to its atmospheric instrumentation and Gene Simmons' soft (except during the chorus), but demonic voice. Bruce Kulick lays down a killer guitar solo in the song, which was written by Simmons and Ken Tamplin. Simmons got the idea for "I Confess" from the 1953 Alfred Hitchcock film of the same name, starring Montgomery Clift and Anne Baxter.

"I Finally Found My Way": The KISS reunion record, *Psycho Circus*, brought with it another Peter Criss ballad, "I Finally Found My Way," the eighth track on the album. Written by Paul Stanley and Bob Ezrin (with Peter Criss in mind), "I Finally Found My Way" was released as a promo single, but not as a standard album single. Ironically, session musician Kevin Valentine played drums on the song instead of Criss.

In *Makeup to Breakup*, Criss expressed his dissatisfaction with the tune. "It was just a blatant attempt at another 'Beth,' except it sucked," he wrote. "The lyrics were about this pitiful, pathetic loser who finally finds his way back to God or Bob Dylan or some chick, who knows?"

"I Got The Touch": This pop-oriented Ace Frehley demo from 1985 appeared on the bootleg album *Wicked Lester and Progeny Demo Sessions*.

"I Just Wanna": The 11th track on *Revenge*, "I Just Wanna," like "Heaven's On Fire," is one of those up-tempo Paul Stanley songs that would sound right at home in a gentleman's club. Stanley, singing that he's going to set the night on fire like a Roman candle, wrote the song with ex–KISS guitarist Vinnie Vincent. Stanley teasingly almost drops the "F" word several times, but is just saying the first syllable in "forget." Parts of the song evoke the Who's rendition of Eddie Cochran's 1958 hit, "Summertime Blues."

"I Know Who You Are": Unreleased until it appeared on disc two of *Love Gun: Deluxe Edition*, "I Know Who You Are" is a demo version of "Living in Sin" from Gene Simmons' 1978 KISS solo album, but with a different chorus.

"I Love It Loud": Lead guitarist Vinnie Vincent made one of his most important contributions to KISS when he co-wrote "I Love It Loud" with Gene Simmons, who provides lead vocals. The song, which is the sixth track on *Creatures of the Night*, begins with a tribal drumbeat from Eric Carr, followed by Simmons chanting. According to Donald A. Guarisco of allmusic.com, the song "plays like a pledge of allegiance to hard rock" with "an infectious chorus" and "a stomping, rhythmic style that pushes the verses and choruses along at a steady mid-tempo pace … a charming, well-crafted slice of party rock." Simmons has said that when he wrote the song, he wanted to come up with something that sounded like the Who's "My Generation."

In the music video, a camp classic, a teenage boy watches KISS perform in concert on TV as the song destroys his suburban home and possesses him, much to the horror of his parents. For the 1985 reissue of *Creatures of the Night*, producer Dave Wittman remixed the song.

"I Pledge Allegiance to the State of Rock & Roll": A good-time party anthem, "I Pledge Allegiance to the State of Rock & Roll" is no "Rock and Roll All Nite," but it does get the adrenaline going as Paul Stanley sings enthusiastically about giving his blood and soul to the music and lifestyle he loves. Stanley plays bass on the song, which is the third track on *Psycho Circus*. Written by Stanley, Curtis Cuomo, and Holly Knight.

"I Still Love You": A truly powerful power ballad, "I Still Love You" is the seventh track on *Creatures of the Night*, a truly powerful record. Paul Stanley, who wrote the song with Vinnie Vincent, sings the song with emotional conviction, making the listener feel the pain and desperation of a traumatic, one-sided breakup. Many sources claim

Stanley wrote the lyrics for actress Donna Dixon after she broke up with him, but the Starchild has said it was more of an homage to Led Zeppelin. The instrumentation in "I Still Love You" starts slowly and builds with the chorus, befitting a song that, in a just world, would've been a #1 hit. Featuring Robben Ford on lead guitar and Eric Carr on bass.

"I Stole Your Love": The first track on *Love Gun*, "I Stole Your Love" gets the album off to a good, hard-rocking start. During The Love Gun Tour, the song, which was written and sung by Paul Stanley, opened many shows. According to Donald A. Guarisco of www.allmusic.com, "Musically, Paul Stanley took his inspiration for 'I Stole Your Love' from the Deep Purple classic 'Burn' and fashioned a fast-paced rock track that matched twisty verses that sped through countless notes at a blinding pace to a slower, punchier chorus that delivered its hooks in a stomping style. KISS gives the song a tight arrangement ... after a stop-start intro where choppy guitar riffs are punctuated by quick bursts of drums, the song kicks into a taut arrangement where power chords are pushed along at a fast clip by steady drum work from Peter Criss."

"I Walk Alone": The 12th and final track on *Carnival of Souls: The Final Sessions*, "I Walk Alone" was written by Gene Simmons and Bruce Kulick, who also provides lead vocals. Oddly enough, Kulick's voice sounds a little like that of former KISS guitarist Ace Frehley, but overall the song, which is about someone who has only himself to lean on, doesn't sound much like anything else KISS has ever recorded.

"I Want You": After the experimental nature of *Destroyer* with producer Bob Ezrin, KISS got back to meat-and-potatoes rock with producer Eddie Kramer and *Rock and Roll Over*. The first track on the album, "I Want You," was sung by Paul Stanley, who wrote the song at a sound check onstage in England. It's a terrific vehicle for the KISS frontman, showing he's just as comfortable singing the slow, folksy beginning of the song as he is when it kicks into hard rock overdrive, and then slows down again. Stanley also plays acoustic guitar on the song, which tells the dramatic tale of a guy who really, *really* wants a girl. For years, "I Want You" was a KISS concert staple—a rousing rendition can be found on *Alive II*.

"I Was Made for Lovin' You": Certified Gold in the U.S. August 16, 1979, the disco-flavored "I Was Made for Lovin' You" was KISS' second Gold single, reaching #11 on the *Billboard* charts. It was the first single released from "Dynasty" and is the first track on the album. Written by Paul Stanley, Vini Poncia, and Desmond Child, the song is a fantastic dance number, but the band typically does a hard rock version of the song when they play it live (the disco sound of the track turned off many longtime KISS fans).

Although he's featured on the album cover and in the official music video, which was filmed at the Savannah Civic Center in Savannah, Georgia, Peter Criss doesn't play drums on the song—Anton Fig does. Interestingly, Stanley, who sings the song, also plays bass, subbing for Gene Simmons. Since the disco genre was popular at the time, Stanley wrote the track as a challenge to himself to create a disco hit.

An extended 12" rendition of the song was released, in addition to the standard 7" version.

"I Was There" Button: The most collectible of KISS buttons, the black metal "I Was There" button, emblazoned with a lightning bolt "S," was given to attendees of the series of concerts at the Los Angeles Forum Aug. 26, 27, and 28, 1977. The button commemorated the fact that the concerts were being recorded for the band's second live album, *Alive II*.

"I Will Be There": Written by Paul Stanley, Bruce Kulick, and Curtis Cuomo, "I Will Be There" is the fifth track on *Carnival of Souls*. The song channels the *MTV Unplugged* albums of grunge masters Nirvana and Alice in Chains, with Stanley sounding right at home singing along with acoustic guitars (unlike the heavier "Rain" and "Master & Slave," where Stanley is out of his element). The song is about the singer being there for someone, regardless of where their lives lead.

"I Will Be with You (Where the Lost Ones Go)": A duet sung by Paul Stanley and Sarah Brightman, "I Will Be With You (Where the Lost Ones Go)" is the sixth track on Brightman's 2008 album, *Symphony*.

Icon: KISS: Released August 31, 2010, this is a re-release of Universal Music's *20th Century Masters–The Millennium Collection: The Best of KISS*. Tracks include: "Strutter," "Deuce," "Hotter Than Hell," "C'mon and Love Me," "Rock and Roll All

Nite" (live), "Detroit Rock City" (remix), "Beth," "Hard Luck Woman," "Calling Dr. Love," "Love Gun," "Christine Sixteen," and "I Was Made for Lovin' You."

Icon 2: KISS: Released simultaneously with *Icon: KISS, Icon 2: KISS* includes all the songs from *Icon: KISS*, plus a second disc featuring hits from the 1980s: "I Was Made for Lovin' You," "Shandi," "A World Without Heroes," "I Love It Loud," "Lick It Up," "Heaven's On Fire," "Tears are Falling," "Crazy Crazy Nights," "Hide Your Heart," and "God Gave Rock 'N' Roll to You II."

Iggy and the Stooges: Established in 1967, garage/protopunk rockers Iggy and the Stooges played on the same bill as KISS during the Dec. 31, 1973, New Year's Eve show at the Academy of Music in New York City, where Gene Simmons' hair caught fire.

In an April 19, 2007, *Rolling Stone* interview, David Fricke asked Iggy Pop, the frontman for the band, "Was it hard later to see bands like Kiss and Alice Cooper score big with a cartoon version of the Stooges' shocks tactics? KISS opened for you in New York on New York's Eve, 1973." To which Pop replied: "Dude, it's etched in my mind. KISS were third on the bill that night, probably getting fifty bucks, but they had a giant KISS sign made of lights that must have weighed five hundred pounds. Obviously, someone poured money into this band. It was a business plan.... We had a cooler group."

IKONS: Released October 21, 2008, by Mercury Records and Universal Music Group, *IKONS* is a four-CD box set in which each color-coded disc spotlights and is named after an original KISS band member.

Disc 1 (Red): "The Demon" includes the following tracks: "God of Thunder," "Almost Human," "Calling Dr. Love," "Ladies Room," "Christine Sixteen," "Deuce," "Rock and Roll All Nite," "Cold Gin," "Parasite," "Larger Than Life," "Love 'Em and Leave 'Em," "Plaster Caster," "Radioactive," and "Charisma."

Disc 2 (Purple): "The Starchild" includes: "Detroit Rock City," "Love Gun," "Take Me," "Strutter," "C'mon and Love Me," "Hotter Than Hell," "100,000 Years," "Rock Bottom," "Do You Love Me?," "All American Man," "Mr. Speed," "I Stole Your Love," "Wouldn't You Like to Know Me," and "I Was Made for Lovin' You."

Disc 3 (Blue): "Space Ace" includes: "New York Groove," "Shock Me," "2,000 Man," "Rocket Ride," "Snow Blind," "Speedin' Back to My Baby," "Talk to Me," "What's on Your Mind," "Rip It Out," "Save Your Love," "Hard Times," "Two Sides of the Coin," "Dark Light," and "Into the Void."

Disc 4 (Green): "The Catman" includes: "Hard Luck Woman," "Baby Driver," "Hooligan," "Beth," "I Can't Stop the Rain," "Black Diamond," "Mainline," "Don't You Let Me Down," "Dirty Livin'," "Getaway," "Strange Ways," "That's the Kind of Sugar Papa Likes," "Easy Thing," and "I Finally Found My Way."

"I'll Fight Hell to Hold You": The second track on *Crazy Nights*, "I'll Fight Hell to Hold You" is an energetic pop rocker in which Paul Stanley, who wrote the song with Adam Mitchell and Bruce Kulick, pledges his allegiance to a girl, swearing he'll be there for her no matter what. Stanley obviously pours his heart and soul into the vocal.

"I'm a Legend Tonight": The first track on *Killers*, the UK release that bridged the gap between the obtuse *Music from "The Elder"* and the blistering *Creatures of the Night*, "I'm a Legend Tonight" is an anthemic tune with a catchy chorus. Written by Paul Stanley and Adam Mitchell, the song features Stanley singing about making a woman feel right once the work day is done. Stanley has referred to the song, which was recorded at Mitchell's house in Hollywood Hills, as "pap."

***I'm a Legend Tonight: An Italian Tribute to Eric Carr*:** Produced by Italy's Bologna Rock City Records in partnership with EricCarr.com, this tribute CD was released January 17, 2012. Tracks include: "Crazy Crazy Nights," (Danger Zone), "Lick It Up" (Crying Steel), "Who Wants to Be Lonely" (Markonee), "Under the Gun" (H.A.R.E.M), "War Machine" (Midnite Sun), "Forever" (Deadly Tide), "I Love It Loud" (Neurasthenia), "Creatures of the Night" (Sange Main Machine), "I'm a Legend Tonight" (Kissexy), "King of the Mountain" (Noise Pollution), "Heaven's On Fire" (Superhorrorfuck), "A World Without Heroes" remix (M. Luppi/R. Priori), "Rock and Roll Hell" (Gunsmoke), "Hide Your Heart" (Live 4 Win), and "Uh! All Night" (Kiss Web All Star).

"I'm Alive": The fifth track on *Asylum*, "I'm Alive" was written by Paul Stanley, Bruce Kulick, and Desmond Child. Like "Exciter," it's a fast-paced song that starts off quickly and doesn't let up. However, unlike that superior tune, "I'm Alive," in which Stanley sings about living for love (sex, actually), seems out of control—a breakneck speed song, created solely, it seems, for the sake of playing and singing fast.

"I'm an Animal": The ninth track on *Sonic Boom*, "I'm An Animal," which would feel right at home on the hard-driving *Creatures of the Night*, was written by Gene Simmons, Paul Stanley, and Tommy Thayer. Mark Eglinton of www.thequietus.com likes the song's "huge, lumbering riff of Zeppelin-esque proportions" and feels that it is a "beast of a track bristling with stalker menace." Eric Anderson of www.dailyiowan.com proclaims the Simmons-sung number as "one of the finest moments on the album."

"I'm Gonna Love You": The first track on Peter Criss's 1978 KISS solo album, "I'm Gonna Love You" is a "rollicking opener, a swinging rock 'n' roll number featuring soulful backing vocals and a brass arrangement inspired by the Memphis soul sound popularized by Al Green" (Paul Elliott, *KISS: Hotter Than Hell*). Written by Criss and Stan Penridge, the song has Criss opining that he'll love a girl, come rain or shine.

"I'm In Need of Love": A bluesy plea for love intersected with one of Ace Frehley's patented guitar solos, "I'm in Need of Love" is the seventh track on the Spaceman's 1978 KISS solo album. In addition to the solo, Frehley creates a trippy reverberating effect throughout much of the song as he sings about wanting to be turned on.

In Concert: KISS made their national TV debut on the March 29, 1974, episode of *In Concert*, a show created by Don Kirshner in 1972. After Paul Stanley introduced the band with, "Hey world, we're KISS! We want everybody here to come along with us; you've got nothin' to lose," they dazzled the audience with powerful versions of "Nothin' to Lose," "Firehouse," and "Black Diamond." KISS looked and sounded terrific, performing an exciting, exuberant, confident set, betraying the long hours they spent rehearsing night after night.

In Concert ran until 1975. It was revived in 1991 as *ABC's In Concert*, and in January of 1992 it was renamed *ABC in Concert*. The final broadcast of *ABC in Concert* was September 11, 1998.

"In My Head": Written by Gene Simmons, Scott Van Zen, and Jaime St. James, "In My Head" is a depressing, lyrically abstruse song about looking behind Simmons' mask and peering into his head, where you'll find termites (metaphorical, one presumes) and boxes of hate. Simmons' persona as a cocky, self-reliant kind of guy doesn't mesh well with "In My Head," which is the seventh track on the grungy *Carnival of Souls: The Final Sessions*. KISS just isn't cut out for this type of song, which evokes Alice in Chains on a bad day.

"In the Mirror": The 11th track on *Carnival of Souls*, "In the Mirror" was written by Paul Stanley, Bruce Kulick (who provides a Hendrix-type riff), and Curtis Cuomo. It's about taking a good, honest look at oneself, but Stanley's vocals don't fit the grungy vibe of the song.

The Inner Sanctum: This Australian documentary from 1980 gives an historical overview of KISS, laced with humor. It features *Unmasked*-era concert footage, merchandising, pyrotechnics expert Gary Heston, fans in KISS makeup, backstage footage, band members visiting children in a hospital, a parody song by comedian Norman Gunston, and interviews with manager Bill Aucoin, road manager George Sewitt, and publicist Patti Mostyn. Gunston quips that Patti "gives great headlines."

Inside the Casbah: A History of Casablanca Records And Filmworks: This hard-to-find VHS video was released in 1996. It chronicles the record label that was home to such acts as KISS, Cher, T. Rex, Donna Summer, Parliament, and the Village People. It includes videos of "C'mon And Love Me" and "Sure Know Something," promos for *Alive II* and the Dynasty Tour, the Casablanca newsreel for the KISS solo albums release, and commercials for *Rock and Roll Over*, *Love Gun*, *Alive II*, *Double Platinum*, the solo albums, and *Dynasty*.

Inside the Tale of the Fox: The Eric Carr Story: This unofficial DVD, directed by Jack Edward Sawyers and released in April of 2000, is a documentary of the late Eric Carr, who replaced Peter Criss in 1980. It is a must-own for fans of the drummer, featuring commentary from Bill Aucoin, Bruce Kulick, Bob Kulick, and Carr's parents. There's home movies, outtakes, and private video as well, plus lots of interview footage with Carr, who says he psyched himself up for the KISS audition by telling himself: "Look, Eric, you're going to do the best you can, you know you're going to play, you know the songs, and that's all you can do…. I never even expected to be called for an audition, but when it happened I just had a feeling deep down inside that I was going to get it."

"Into the Night": The third track on *Frehley's Comet*, "Into the Night" hit #27 on *Billboard*'s Mainstream Rock Tracks (as opposed to their more noteworthy Hot 100). It was written by Russ Ballard ("New York Groove"), who originally recorded it for his self-titled 1984 album.

"Into the Void": Not to be confused with the Black Sabbath tune of the same name, "Into the Void" is full-on Ace Frehley, who sounds great here on lead vocals and lead guitar. Space Ace co-wrote the song, which is the fourth track on *Psycho Circus*, with Karl Cochran. A spacey, but energetic rocker, "Into the Void" will definitely appeal to fans of Frehley's 1978 solo album. During live performances, Frehley was in the spotlight (literally and figuratively) when KISS played "Into the Void."

Into the Void…with Ace Frehley: Written by Ace Frehley's former girlfriend and personal assistant, Wendy Moore, this book was published in 2004 by Pitbull Publishing. According to a review published on www.metal-rules.com, it is a "warts-and-all, behind-the-scenes documentation of what life is like within Frehley's personal circle. When Moore first met Frehley, she was a Valley Girl in her mid–20s who had never touched drugs, barely drank alcohol, and led a normal life as a struggling musician with her band." Followed in 2009 by a sequel, *Out of the Void*.

"Is That You?": The first track on *Unmasked*, the trashy, kitschy "Is That You?" is about a girl with a bad reputation who attracts the boys she likes then metaphorically sticks them with her knife. It was written by Gerard McMahon, who penned "Cry Little Sister" from the 1987 horror comedy, *The Lost Boys*. McMahon wrote "Is That You?" based on an encounter he had with a dominatrix in a hotel bar late one night after a gig.

"It Never Goes Away": The guitars in "It Never Goes Away," the eighth track on the grunge-heavy *Carnival of Souls: The Final Sessions*, sound something like vintage Black Sabbath, but, of course, not as good. Paul Stanley sings the heavy, plodding number, which he wrote with Bruce Kulick and Curtis Cuomo.

Italians Kiss Better: An Italian Tribute to KISS: This album, released in December of 2003, features songs by a variety of acts, including several KISS tribute bands. Tracks include: "I Was Made for Lovin' You" (Juliet KISS), "Tomorrow and Tonight" (Spit), "Deuce" (KISS Konfusion), "Detroit Rock City" (Kissexy, a female tribute band), "Firehouse" (Strange Ways), "Strutter" (Landslide Ladies), "Lick It Up" (KISS Unmasked), "100,000 Years" (Markonee), "I Still Love You" (War Machine), "Shout It Out Loud" (Destroyer, a female tribute band), "Shock Me" (Strip KISS), "C'mon and Love Me" (Magic Touch), "Let Me Go Rock 'n' Roll" (Demon 'n' Kisses), "Cold Gin" (Z-A-P), "A World Without Heroes" (Priori/Luppi), a live version of "I Love It Loud" (ELECTRIC CIRCUS), "Rock and Roll All Nite" (Italian Jam), and "Love Gun" (Arthemis), the latter of which is a bonus track on the second pressing.

"It's Alright": The Starchild's 1978 KISS solo album, *Paul Stanley*, is filled with splashy pop rockers, and "It's Alright," the sixth track on the record, is no exception, practically inviting the listener to sing (or at least clap) along. Stanley sings that "It's Alright" if a girl wants him to stay the night.

"I've Had Enough (Into the Fire)": Written by Paul Stanley and Desmond Child, who collaborated with Stanley on the disco hit "I Was Made for Lovin' You," "I've Had Enough (Into the Fire)" is the first track on *Animalize*. It sounds a lot like "Exciter," the first song on the previous album, *Lick It Up*. It's an energetic, hard-rocking, quickly paced tune that shows off Stanley's wailing vocals and introduced fans to the band's new lead guitarist, Mark St. John, who had replaced Vinnie Vincent. Most casual KISS fans likely didn't notice the difference as both could lay down a blistering solo.

Jackets: Like the 1977 KISS Radio, the original KISS jacket from 1978 was available through mail-order only, making it a scarce collector's item today. Produced by Atex USA and fashioned from Tyvek, a material created by DuPont, the multi-colored jacket was garish and plastic-looking, featuring the KISS logo and flames on the front and the KISS logo, flames, and a drawing of the band on the back.

In 1979, Atex released a black KISS jacket with

flames around the cuffs, red lightning bolts on one shoulder, and a drawing of the band on the back. An Australian version released in 1980 features Eric Carr on the back instead of Peter Criss.

Jackson, Michael James: Michael James Jackson co-produced (with Gene Simmons and Paul Stanley) *Creatures of the Night* and *Lick It Up*. He also produced the four original songs on *Killers*.

James Gang: Formed in Cleveland in 1966, the James Gang played on the same bill as KISS several times in 1975. This was after Joe Walsh had left the band.

Japp, Mikel: On Paul Stanley's 1978 KISS solo album, Mikel Japp co-wrote "Move On," "Ain't Quite Right," and "Take Me Away (Together as One)." He also co-wrote "Saint and Sinner" from *Creatures of the Night* and "Down on Your Knees" from *Killers*.

Jason, Neil: Neil Jason played bass on both Gene Simmons' and Peter Criss's 1978 KISS solo albums. In a 35-year retrospective interview with KissFAQ.com's Tim McPhate, Jason talked about contributing to Simmons' record: "I actually was honored and thrilled that a bass player of his stature [asked me to play]—because in his band, this guy rules. He plays the right stuff, sings the right stuff. If [you] see them in concert, what they do is pretty amazing. Try putting on the gear and doing songs like that and playing for three hours and making people have a party—this is not easy. He played great on all the things he ever played on. So for him to want another bass player, because he wanted to concentrate on the songs and on singing and production and guitar playing, I appreciated that. I thought it was unbelievable. So I got an amazing chance to work with him. And on some tunes, yeah I tried to play like I was Gene Simmons. And on the other tunes I did stuff that Gene would not think to do, but it matched his song. It was cool. It was a lot of fun."

Jendel: In various interviews over the decades, Ace "The Spaceman" Frehley has claimed he is from the planet Jendel. This is but one of his many quirky personality traits.

Jensen, Debra: Peter Criss married *Playboy* centerfold (January 1978 issue) and Coppertone model Debra Jensen (born Debra Svensk on March 12, 1958) on December 22, 1979. He met her at a party thrown by Rod Stewart and dated her several months before leaving his first wife, Lydia.

In *Makeup to Breakup*, Criss revealed that he saw her dancing "sensuously" with another girl at the party and was immediately attracted to her. "I went right onto the dance floor, grabbed her hand, and pulled her away," he wrote. "Of course, I told her I was the drummer for KISS." Jensen was not impressed with Criss's resume, but liked him anyway. "I hate that band," she told Criss. "They wear makeup and look like maniacs … but I think you're cute."

During the filming of *KISS Meets the Phantom of the Park*, Jensen would visit the set, which Criss admitted "spelled doom for the film. I had to be on the set at six in the morning, and we would stay up all night and fuck and do blow until five when I got the call that the car was outside waiting for me … the later we stayed up … the more I forgot my lines and started slurring my words."

Criss and Jensen had one child, a daughter named Jenilee, who was born in 1981. They divorced in 1994.

The Jewish Mother's Hall of Fame: While not explicitly a KISS book, *The Jewish Mother's Hall Of Fame*, published by Doubleday on April 2, 1986, features an entire chapter on Gene Simmons' mother, Florence Klein. The book also includes chapters on the mothers of such celebrities as Bob Dylan, Abbie Hoffman, Dr. Joyce Brothers, and Steven Spielberg. Written by Fred A. Bernstein.

Jigoku No Shosan: KISS Tribute in Japan: This Japanese tribute album, released in 1998 by Mercury/PolyGram-Nippon, includes the following tracks: "Shout It Out Loud" (the Yellow Monkey), "Deuce" (Diamond Yukai), "Parasite" (King Show), "I Was Made for Lovin' You" (Nomiya, Maki with Dimitri), "Beth" (Scudelia Electro), "Nothin' to Lose" (Rolly the Rockrolly) "Hard Luck Woman" (K. Nakayama with Red Kross), "Cold Gin" (Onda's Boozer Brothers), "Detroit Rock City" (the Pugs), and "C'mon and Love Me" (Psychodelicious).

Jigoku-Retsuden: Released only in Japan, *Jigoku-Retsuden*, which translates to *Intense Transmission from Hell*, features a CD containing 15 classic KISS tunes re-recorded in 2008 by Paul, Gene, Tommy, and Eric Singer. It also includes a DVD of a 1977 performance at Budokan Hall in Tokyo.

In 2009, KISS re-released the CD as part of the digipack deluxe edition of *Sonic Boom*.

Jigsaw Puzzles: In 1977, American Publishing Corp. produced puzzles based on the *Destroyer* and *Love Gun* album covers. The next year, Milton Bradley came out with four KISS puzzles, one for each band member.

Johnsen, Ron: The head engineer at Electric Lady Studios during the early 1970s, Ron Johnsen gave Wicked Lester access to the facility. He provided Gene and Paul with session work (for Lyn Christopher, Tommy James, Mr. Gee Whiz, and others) and produced the unreleased Wicked Lester album, which was supposed to come out on Epic Records. Coincidentally, he also worked with Peter Criss's old band, Chelsea.

Journey: Formed in San Francisco in 1973, Journey opened for KISS during the *Dressed to Kill* era. The band's current drummer, Deen Castronovo, decided he wanted to be a musician after hearing KISS for the first time.

In an interview published on the Lehigh Valley Music blog in 2011, Castronovo spoke about discovering the band: "I wanted to be in KISS 'cause they were my Beatles. When I was seven-years-old, my older brother brought over *Dressed to Kill*. He brought it from a friend of his and said, 'Let me check this out.' And I was like, 'OK.' And then I looked at it and I was like, 'Yeah! That's what I want to do when I get older.' That was it. I mean, that was it. I became a drummer right after that. They were the superheroes of rock and roll, no question. Every year I was Peter Criss for Halloween. I'm still a huge KISS fan. Huge."

"Journey of 1,000 Years": Gene Simmons was clearly channeling *Music from "The Elder"* when he wrote and sung the terrific "Journey of 1,000 Years," the 10th and final track on *Psycho Circus*. A fitting finale to an underrated record, the song has an appealing grandiosity and large-scale sound.

"Jungle": As Paul Elliott wrote in *KISS: Hotter Than Hell*, "Jungle," the sixth track on *Carnival of Souls*, has a "semi-funky grunge-lite riff" that "recalls Collective Soul's U.S. hit 'Shine.'" Paul Stanley wrote the song with Bruce Kulick and Curtis Cuomo, but, as with a couple of earlier songs on the record, he "again sounds unconvincing." The lyrics feature the typical city-as-dangerous-jungle metaphor.

"Just a Boy": Written by Paul Stanley and Bob Ezrin, "Just a Boy" is the second track on *Music from "The Elder,"* and the first with lyrics ("Fanfare" is an instrumental intro that leads directly into "Just a Boy"). The song, which features Stanley singing falsetto over softly strummed acoustic guitars, gets the epic story underway in fine fashion, telling of a boy who, piloting a ship at sea, feels he's too young to be a hero. Stanley plays lead instead of Ace Frehley, contributing a gentle guitar solo. Stanley and Ezrin have dismissed "Just a Boy" over the years, saying that it has some merit as a quasi-Broadway show tune, perhaps, but not as a KISS song.

Kabuki: When you hear someone say KISS wears kabuki-style makeup, they're referring to the makeup worn by the performers in classical Japanese dance-drama, an art form that dates back to the 17th century. Kabuki theater was created by Izumo no Okuni.

***KAOL: A World Without Heroes*:** A companion recording to Dale Sherman's KISS novel, *A World Without Heroes*, this KISS Army OnLine CD includes the following tracks: "A World Without Heroes" (Nile Carter & Kathy LaBonte), "A Million to One" (Saccharine Jesus), "Mr. Blackwell" (Sand), "Black Diamond" (Bone Daddy), "I'm a Legend Tonight" (Roy Coffin, Jr.), "I Want You" (Scott Kenerson & Tommy Rifai), "Nothin' to Lose" (Bone Daddy), "Dark Light" (Robero Boschian), "Master & Slave" edited (Black Star), "The Jungle" edited (Kathy LaBonte), "Parasite" edited (The Thrill Cycle), "I Can't Stop the Rain" edited (Bone Daddy), "What's On Your Mind?" (Aced Out), "Just a Boy" (Benny Bruce), "Watchin' You" (Kathy LaBonte), "Into the Void" (Scott Kenerson), "Getaway" (Kathy LaBonte), "War Machine" edited (Loungelizardboots), "Only You" (Wade Sampson), "Odyssey" (Tommy Rifai & Kathy LaBonte), "Shout It Out Loud" edited (Sound Magazine, a Partridge Family tribute band), "Dreamin'" (the Elm Street Ensemble), "Rock and Roll Hell" (Tongue), "I" (Creatures of the Night), "The Oath" (the Steve Sizemore Group), and "A World Without Heroes" reprise (Kathy LaBonte). Released in 2000 by MusiCare Online. Fifteen of the tracks are new while 10 are short versions of previously released songs.

***KAOL: Music from the Folder '99: A Tribute to KISS*:** Released in 1997 by MusiCare

OnLine, this album by KISS Army OnLine features KISS covers by a variety of fan bands. Tracks include: "Got Love for Sale" (the Mass), "Strange Ways" (Bone Daddy), "Mr. Speed" (Shirk Smile), "Naked City" (Kathy Labonte), "X-ray Eyes" (Jheni Clason), "Creatures of the Night" (Destroyer), "War Machine" (Loungelizardboots), "Got to Choose" (Ace Steele's Fabulous Disaster), "A World Without Heroes" (Janiece Teichmann), "See You Tonight" (Nile Carter), "Sweet Pain" (Mistress Julie), "Domino" (Where's Izzy), "C'mon and Love Me" (Black Krystol), "Hard Times" (Roberto Boschian & Bubba Felix), "Almost Human" (Assgoblins), "Let Me Know" (Backlash), "Firehouse" (Hooligans), "God of Thunder" (Jurassic Army), "All American Man" (Cronic Disorder), and "Love Theme from KAOL" (Kathy Labonte). The front cover is a tribute to *Music from "The Elder"* while the back cover pays homage to the Beatles' *Sgt. Pepper's Lonely Hearts Club Band*. Includes a collector's guitar pick.

KAOL: Music from the Folder '99: A Tribute to KISS **(Remaster):** Released in 1999, this remastered version of *KAOL: Music from the Folder '99* features a different mix of songs (though some are the same). Tracks include: "Got Love for Sale" (the Mass), "Strange Ways" (Bone Daddy), "Mr. Speed" remix (Shirk Smile), "Naked City" remix (Kathy Labonte), "X-ray Eyes" new version (the KAOL All Stars), "Creatures of the Night" remix (Destroyer), "War Machine" (Loungelizardboots), "Comin' Home" (Superstar 16), "World Without Heroes" (Nile Carter & Kathy Labonte), "Beth" (Mark Gray), "She" (Sand), "Love Her All I Can" (Lithium), "Strutter" (Benny and the Jet City Band), "See You Tonight" (Nile Carter), "God of Thunder" (Jurassic Army), "All American Man" (Chronic Disorder), "You Turn to Cry" (the Cellarman, featuring Eric Carr), "Remembering Eric" (a 1990 audio clip/bonus track), and "Love Theme From KAOL" remix (Kathy Labonte).

KAOL 2: Creatures of the Net: Released in 1998 by MusiCare OnLine, this Kiss Army OnLine album features KISS covers by a variety of fan bands. Tracks include: "Kissin' Time" (the KAOL All Stars), "100,000 Years" (Bone Daddy), "Deuce" (Rip & Destroy), "Shout It Out Loud" (Sound Magazine, a Partridge Family tribute band), "Jungle" (Kathy LaBonte), "Love Gun" (Psycho Cafe), "Goin' Blind" (the Mass), "Parasite" (the Thrill Cycle), "Rockin' in the U.S.A." (Destroyer), "Hard Luck Woman" (Nile Carter and the Two Timers), "Two Timer" (the Palace Guard), "Detroit Rock City" (Jurassik Army), "Plaster Caster" (Mark Perillo & Robert Cosentino), "Larger Than Life" (LoungeLizardBoots), "Christine Sixteen" (Rolando D'Lugo), "Master & Slave" (Black Star), "Rip and Destroy" (the Phantoms of the Park), "I Cry At Night" (the Cellarmen, featuring Eric Carr), and "Epilogue."

Katsaros, Doug: Prolific keyboardist Doug Katsaros played piano on Paul Stanley's "Hold Me, Touch Me (Think of Me When We're Apart)." He also worked with such acts as Cher, Rod Stewart, Judy Collins, Elton John, Aerosmith, Liza Minnelli, Todd Rundgren, Peter Frampton, Christina Aguilera, and Peter, Paul and Mary, among many others. Interestingly, he played keyboards on a CD called *Sin-Atra*, a 2011 heavy metal tribute to Frank Sinatra co-produced by former KISS studio guitarist Bob Kulick.

Kaye, Carol: Carol Kaye was a publicist for KISS during their heyday, working on such projects as *Love Gun*, the solo albums, the comic books, and *KISS Meets the Phantom of the Park*. Around the time *Alive II* was released, she was on the cover of the *Wall Street Journal* in an article that began: "Carol Kaye is a publicist with a problem, she can't seem to squelch the rumors that KISS does not stand for Knights in Satan's Service."

Keel: Gene Simmons produced Keel's 1985 album, *The Right to Rock*. He also co-wrote three tracks on the record: "Easier Said Than Done," "So Many Girls, So Little Time," and "Get Down." In addition, Simmons produced Keel's 1986 LP, *The Final Frontier*.

"Keep Me Comin'": Even for a band as transparent and as sex obsessed as KISS usually is, this song, the third track on *Creatures of the Night*, is an especially obvious metaphor. As Paul Stanley works himself into a frenzy, he sings of a girl who, now that she let him in, must "Keep Me Comin'." Stanley, inspired by Led Zeppelin's "Whole Lotta Love," wrote the song with Adam Mitchell.

"Keep Me Waiting": The third track on disc one of *The Box Set*, "Keep Me Waiting," which sounds a little like the Doobie Brothers, is originally from the unreleased Wicked Lester album. Recorded in 1971, it was written by Paul Stanley and features Gene Simmons on bass, Steve Coronel on lead guitar, Brooke Ostrander on keyboards, Tony Zarella on drums, and Ron Leejack on guitar.

Kelly, Ken: Artist Ken Kelly, famous for his *Conan* paperback book covers, painted the iconic covers for *Destroyer* and *Love Gun*, defining images of the band as larger-than-life heroes. Gene Simmons originally wanted renowned fantasy artist Frank Frazetta to paint the *Destroyer* cover, but his asking price of $15,000 was too high, plus he wanted to keep the original art. Therefore, the band commissioned Frazetta's cousin, Ken Kelly, who was happy to receive $5,000 for the job.

In a 2011 interview published on www.kissfanzine.com, Kelly spoke about working with KISS: "I had some input into the *Love Gun* cover but not the *Destroyer* cover. Dennis Woloch, the art director for KISS, knew just what he wanted for that one. I was the mechanic who put his thoughts to paper." Of his KISS legacy, Kelly said: "I am continuously reminded by fans ... about the hours of enjoyment they got out of staring at the KISS covers while listening to the record. Reminds us of how different it was back then, no computers, large albums. It was a different world. I am delighted to have played the small role I did in the KISS world."

Kelly also painted the cover for Ace Frehley's 2014 solo album, *Space Invader*. In an article published on www.blabbermouth.net, Kelly said: "It was very exciting when I was approached with the idea of doing an album cover for Ace. I had spoken to Ace on a few occasions about the possibility, so I was delighted when it actually happened. I am very pleased with the results and proud to play a part of Ace's continuing successful career!"

In that same article, Frehley himself added, "I've been talking with Ken Kelly since 2007 about painting a CD cover for me and it has finally happened! I couldn't be more excited about the new *Space Invader* cover, and the music behind it is also going to rock your world!"

Kelly, Larry: Larry Kelly sang lead in some of Ace Frehley's pre–KISS bands. In addition, he and Sue Kelly share writing credits with Frehley on "Rip It Out."

Kerner, Kenny: Kenny Kerner co-produced *KISS* and *Hotter Than Hell* with Richie Wise. An important figure in the history of the band, Kerner suggested to Neil Bogart that he sign KISS to Casablanca Records. In an interview published on kissmonster.com, Kerner said: "Neil would leave demo tapes for me outside of his office. And I would come by once a week, pick them up, take them home, listen to them and bring them back. One trip found me taking the KISS demo tape out of the box—from Electric Lady, I knew Eddie Kramer because I had worked with him before. And I listened to it and it just blew me away."

Kerrang!: Established in 1981, *Kerrang!* magazine, based in the UK, has featured KISS on its covers and within its pages many times over the years, giving them crucial exposure during the non-makeup era.

Keychains: In the insert sheet packaged with the *Dynasty* LP, fans could order keychains produced by Funky Enterprises. There were 24 different designs. A year earlier, each KISS solo album contained order forms for keychains, one for each member of the band. The earliest KISS keychains date back to 1975, with two releases: one featuring the KISS logo, one featuring the KISS Army logo. Countless other KISS keychains have been released over the years, including *Animalize*, *Psycho Circus*, Farewell Tour, Alive in Japan, World Domination Tour, KISS Coffeehouse, puzzle cube, *Alive II*, bottle opener, KISS Kruise, and, most notoriously, Unholy Condom (1992), which contained one condom inside.

This early piece of KISS memorabilia, the KISS Army keychain, was produced in 1975.

Kids Are People Too: On a July 1980 episode of *Kids Are People Too*, which ran on Sunday mornings from 1978 to 1982 on ABC, Ace, Gene, and Paul introduced Eric Carr, their replacement for Peter Criss. Prior to KISS appearing onstage, the host asked a boy in the audience who his favorite band member was. The boy responded with "Peter Criss," but quickly changed his answer to "Ace Frehley."

When a girl from the audience asked, "How do you feel about Peter Criss leaving the group?," Paul responded with: "We felt bad to lose Peter because he was a member of the family, but we really haven't lost him. We spend a lot of time with him, and he really is like family. When you have a brother or a sister, you don't lose them just because they move out of the house."

"Killer": A song about a ruthless femme fatale, "Killer" is the eighth track on *Creatures of the Night*. It was written by Vinnie Vincent and Gene Simmons. The Demon's growling vocals tell of the titular temptress, and chugging guitars and bass provide a fitting backdrop. On the 1985 re-release of *Creatures of the Night*, "Killer" is track number two, switching places with "Saint and Sinner."

Killers: This album is a foreign issue released on the Phonogram label in 1982. In addition to a variety of re-released classic KISS tunes, *Killers*, which found the band trying to get back on track after the experimental, commercially disastrous *Music from "The Elder,"* features four new songs produced by Michael James Jackson: "Nowhere to Run" (produced for a prospective sequel to *Music from "The Elder"*), "Partners in Crime," "Down on Your Knees" (co-written by Bryan Adams), and "I'm a Legend Tonight." Although Ace Frehley is pictured on the album cover (photographed by Barry Levine from *"The Elder"* sessions), Bob Kulick plays lead guitar on the four new songs, employing his own style instead of aping Ace.

Tracks on the European version include: "I'm a Legend Tonight," "Down on Your Knees," "Cold Gin," "Love Gun," "Shout It Out Loud," "Sure Know Something," "Nowhere to Run," "Partners in Crime," "Detroit Rock City," "God of Thunder," "I Was Made for Lovin' You," and "Rock and Roll All Nite." The Australian version adds "Talk to Me" while the Japanese version adds "Escape from the Island" and "Shandi." The album was most successful in Norway, reaching #6 on the charts, and it was a commonly seen import in many American stores.

King Kobra: On King Kobra's 1988 album, *King Kobra III*, Gene Simmons co-wrote "Legends Never Die" while Simmons and Paul Stanley co-wrote "It's My Life." Tommy Thayer co-wrote "Number One" while Peter Criss provided backing vocals for "Take it Off."

"King of Hearts": The 10th track on *Hot in the Shade*, "King of Hearts" was written by Paul Stanley and Vini Poncia, who were clearly trying to keep up with Bon Jovi, one of the hottest bands in the country at the time. It's an energetic, but generic rocker in which Stanley sings about love, fantasy, and making a getaway with a 19-year-old girl who takes his heart away.

King of the Hill: Gene Simmons voiced the role of a character named Jessie in "Reborn to Be Wild," the second episode of the eighth season of the Fox animated series, *King of the Hill* (1997–2010). In the cartoon, Hank Hill makes his son, Bobby, join a local church youth group. Much to his horror, Hank discovers that the group—including tattooed Pastor K—worships God through skateboarding and rock music. The members of Sum 41, a Canadian rock band, appear briefly as skateboarding punks/worshippers.

"King of the Mountain": The first track on *Asylum*, this song begins with a powerful Eric Carr drum volley—an explosion of sound Peter Criss would be hard pressed to pull off. Then Paul Stanley chimes in, singing with typical braggadocio about hitting the top, shooting through the night, taking it all, and, of course, being "King of the Mountain." Written by Stanley, Desmond Child, and Bruce Kulick, who had recently taken the place of Mark St. John, "King of the Mountain" isn't a great song, but it is a guitar-shredding good one.

"King of the Night Time World": Immediately following the dramatic conclusion to the first track on *Destroyer*, "Detroit Rock City," "King of the Night Time World" kicks into gear with Ace Frehley's reverberating guitar and Peter Criss's steady drum beat. As such, the two songs were often played back to back in concert. Paul Stanley sings the song, which was originally recorded by Mark Anthony's band, Hollywood Stars. Stanley rearranged the song and rewrote some of the lyrics.

Telling a dark and glamorous tale of a teenager who escapes his problems through rock and roll dreams, "King of the Night Time World" is a strong, atmospheric rocker that benefits from *Destroyer*'s high production values.

King's Lounge: When Peter Criss first met Paul Stanley and Gene Simmons, he asked them to come see him play with his band at the King's Lounge. In *Nothin' to Lose: The Making of KISS (1972–1975)*, Stanley said, "[Peter] certainly had a vibe about him and he really had the sense that he was playing Madison Square Garden rather than a small dive in Brooklyn."

KISS (album): Released February 18, 1974, by Casablanca Records, *KISS* is the band's self-titled debut album. Produced by Kenny Kerner and Richie Wise and recorded at Bell Sound Studios in New York City, the record includes the following tracks: "Strutter," "Nothin' to Lose" (which was released as single, but failed to chart), "Firehouse," "Cold Gin," "Let Me Know," "Kissin' Time" (a cover of the Bobby Rydell tune that didn't appear on the album until the July 1974 re-release), "Deuce," "Love Theme from Kiss" (an instrumental composed by all four members), "100,000 Years," and "Black Diamond."

Some of the songs were written by Paul Stanley and Gene Simmons during the Wicked Lester era. During the late 1980s, a repressing of the album by Mercury Records featured a live version of "Nothin' to Lose" in place of the studio version.

On June 8, 1977, *KISS*, which features a *Meet the Beatles*-like cover photo of the band by Joel Brodsky, was certified Gold. Peter Criss's makeup on the cover looks different than the design he had already established, owing to the fact that Brodsky hired a makeup artist for the shoot. Ace Frehley looks different as well as he had died his hair silver.

Rolling Stone ranked *KISS* the band's best album, saying it "crackles with an energy and exuberance that even the much-lauded *Alive!* doesn't match … song-wise, there ain't a stinker in the bunch." In the magazine's original review in issue #158 (April 1974), Gordon Fletcher called it "an exceptional album" that "could have been better had the group incorporated more of their concert sound into the recording studio…. Onstage they rain a Black Sabbath–like fury, but here they sound more like a cross between Deep Purple and the Doobie Brothers."

In *KISS: Behind the Mask—The Official Authorized Biography*, Stanley admitted that *KISS* "doesn't in any way capture what the band was about live and sonically," but called it their "*Declaration of Independence* … everything that came after that is based on that album." Simmons said the record was "an extension of the first demos we did" while Frehley called it "one of our best records because it had that spontaneity and that tough kind of sound." Criss said he put his "whole heart and soul into it" and that "we made our dream come true."

KISS (book): Written by Robert Duncan and published by Popular Library in 1978, *KISS* was the first book about the band. Published as *The Savoy KISS of Death* in the UK, the mass market paperback covers the history of the group, their impact on society, their music, their makeup, their stage shows, and much more, including humor,

Written by Robert Duncan, this mass market paperback, released in 1978, was the first book published about KISS.

handwriting analysis, quotes from the band, and 16 pages of black-and-white photos. Like other writings in the 1970s about KISS, what the book doesn't cover is all the dirt that we know now, such as the excessive in-fighting among band members and the substantial drug and alcohol abuse by Ace Frehley and Peter Criss. The original release is now a hard-to-find collectible, but, thanks to the miracle of self-publishing (Lulu.com in this case), *KISS* was re-published with a new introduction by the author in April of 2014.

KISS (Dark Horse comic book): This comic book series ran from 2002 to 2003 for a total of 13 issues. It featured writing by Joe Casey, Scott Lobdell, and Mike Baron and art by Mel Rubi, Peter Vale, and Derek Rudolphs. Covers were drawn by J. Scott Campbell, Leinil Francis Yu, and Mel Rubi, though each issue had a corresponding photo cover release featuring the original band members.

The solicitation for the first issue is as follows: "The most ass-kicking rock band returns to comics, written by the most rockin' of young comics writers. Joe Casey (*Superman*, *Wildcats*, *X-Men*) presents a bold new direction for KISS—years after the split-up of these four super-powered warriors, they've followed very separate paths. The Demon is a bounty hunter; the Starchild lives with a race of women warriors in South America; the Spaceman is cruising the solar system with no human contact; and the Catman's getting in touch with his bestial side.

When Catman finally goes too far, the others know they have to band together to save the Catman's humanity. But there's another hand at work, pushing the Four Who Are One into a corner. This new comic, overseen by Gene Simmons, turns the ultimate rock-and-roll icons into the ultimate superhero team."

The Slings & Arrows Comic Guide (2003, Slings & Arrows Ltd.) describes the first four issues thusly: "After the pretentious tedium of *Psycho Circus*, any *KISS* comic that actually focused on the band members was guaranteed success, and so it's proved. Here the glam-metal granddads are cast as the superheroes their make-up aspired to, once legendary, now retired and separated, as writer Joe Casey draws literally from the group's history."

The series was reprinted in four trade paperbacks: *Rediscovery!* (1–3), *Return of the Phantom!* (4–6), *Men and Monsters!* (7–10), and *Unholy War!* (11–13).

KISS (IDW comic book): Published in 2012 and 2013, this comic book series lasted eight issues. Each issue featured a number of variant covers, including photos of Gene Simmons, Paul Stanley, Tommy Thayer, and Eric Singer. Chris Ryall and Tom Waltz wrote the series while Jamal Igle, Casey Maloney, Wagner Reis, and Kenneth Loh handled the interior art. Jamal Igle, Nick Runge, Michael Gaydos, Casey Maloney, Xermanico, Sam Shearon, Tom Jerman, and Kenneth Loh drew the covers.

In the "Dressed to Kill" storyline, four ordinary humans in 1920s Chicago find themselves caught up in a battle of epic proportions that will reverberate across time and space. The solicitation for the "A World Without Heroes" arc reads as follows: "In a forgotten time of swords and sorcery, dragons and wizards, warriors and maidens, a once-united kingdom has become irreversibly divided. Ruled separately now by four very different overlords, the Destroyer finds a land—and its estranged inhabitants—ripe for the taking. He unleashes his Chaos forces against the planet, led by the ruthless General, Black Diamond. In retaliation, the Elder sends the enigmatic She to deliver the four cosmic talismans, gifting the overlords with the powers of the Demon, Starchild, Catman, and Celestial!"

The series has classic KISS references throughout, including Abner Devereaux (from *KISS Meets the Phantom of the Park*), his "daughter" Christine Sixteen, and villains called the Destroyer God and the Elder.

KISS (pinball machine): Released by Bally in June of 1979, the *KISS* pinball machine was designed by Jim Patla (*Playboy*, *Rolling Stones*), with art by Kevin O'Connor (*Flash Gordon*, *Star Trek*). The backglass painting depicts the band in concert, columns of fire exploding in the background, the letters K-I-S-S flashing above. The table has two flippers, four pop bumpers (each depicting a member of the band), two slingshots, eight standup targets, one four-bank drop target, two roll-under spinners (each bearing Gene's face), and a right out-lane detour gate. A brief, blip-bleep-bloop version of "Rock and Roll All Nite" plays at the beginning of the game while "Shout It Out Loud" plays when the user loses a ball.

A total of 17,000 machines were produced, plus an unreleased prototype with voice effects ("Shoot

KISS (pinball machine)

the K," "Kiss!," "Too much Rock and Roll!"). The machine made a brief appearance in the 2008 comedy film, *Role Models*. For the German release, the lightning bolt double "S" in the band's name was altered to avoid similarities to the Nazi SS symbol.

In 2015, Stern released a new *KISS* pinball machine. Here's the promotional info from Stern's website:

> Stern Pinball's KISS pinball machines reflect the energy, excitement, and experience of a live KISS concert. Players will experience 10 famous KISS hits in the concert arena playfield and embark on an exhilarating experience ultimately becoming elite members of the KISS Army. Players score points and finish game objectives to fuel the audience's energy and excitement. Higher scores amp the experience— the higher the energy level, the bigger and louder the show—resulting in a KISS concert experience like none other. Players are awarded for completing game goals with a variety of in-game front row seats, backstage VIP access and fun multi-ball modes that thrill players of all skill levels. The game is built on Stern's new SPIKE pinball platform, which includes an upgraded high-fidelity 3-channel audio system over 3 times more powerful than previous generation pinball audio systems. KISS Pinball includes an amazing array of modern and retro features to appeal to players of all skill levels:
>
> - 10 famous KISS hit songs: "Deuce," "Hotter than Hell," "Lick It Up," "Shout It Out Loud," "Detroit Rock City," "Calling Dr. Love," "Rock and Roll All Nite," "Love Gun," and "Black Diamond"
> - Custom speech from Paul Stanley and Gene Simmons
> - Full-color high-intensity animated LED music lights
> - High-fidelity stereo sound effects and music
> - Original Gene Simmons/Demon head molded toy
> - K-I-S-S spell-out Drop Targets
> - Blood-Spitting Demon Bass Solo player experience
> - Fire-Breathing Demon "God of Thunder" Multiball Event
> - Flying Starchild "Love Gun" Multiball Event

Backglass for Stern's 2015 KISS pinball machine. "Partnering with rock royalty like KISS is a natural for us," said Gary Stern, chairman and CEO of Stern Pinball.

KISS Alive Forever: The Complete Touring History: Written by Curt Gooch and Jeff Suhs, this remarkably detailed book was published by Billboard Books on September 1, 2002. It chronicles more than 1,900 KISS concerts, categorized by tour. Includes start dates, end dates, set lists, opening acts, show locations, promoters, road crew interviews, 200-plus photos, descriptions of the shows, and more.

In episode 114 of *Three Sides of the Coin*, Suhs revealed that he came up with the idea for *KISS Alive Forever* after being disappointed that KISS's own massive tome, *KISStory*, didn't have extensive tour information.

KISS Alive! 1975–2000: This boxed set, released by Universal Music Group on November 21, 2006, includes four discs: *Alive!*, *Alive II* (with a bonus track—the radio edit version of "Rock and Roll All Nite"), *Alive III* (with a bonus track—the live version of Take It Off"), and the previously unreleased *Alive! The Millennium Concert*, which was recorded on December 31, 1999, in Vancouver Canada.

Tracks on *Alive! The Millennium Concert* include: "Psycho Circus," "Shout It Out Loud," "Deuce," "Heaven's on Fire," "Into the Void," "Firehouse," "Do You Love Me?," "Let Me Go, Rock 'n' Roll," "I Love It Loud," "Lick It Up," "100,000 Years," "Love Gun," "Black Diamond," "Beth," "Rock and Roll All Nite," "2,000 Man" (Best Buy edition only), "God of Thunder" (Best Buy edition only), and "Detroit Rock City" (iTunes edition only).

Alive! The Millennium Concert was originally going to be released by itself as *Alive IV*, but the band and/or the label was unhappy with the recording, so KISS released *KISS Symphony Alive IV* instead. According to *KISS FAQ* author Dale Sherman, *KISS Alive! 1975–2000* was ignored by many fans because "its release came after there had been two previous issues of *Alive!* and *Alive II* on CD, the still-quite-available 1993 *Alive III* album, the 1996 live compilation album *You Wanted the Best*, and live material collected on the five-disc KISS box set of 2000." Moreover, "some fans may have mistaken the *Symphony* disc" as being the fourth one in the set.

KISS Alive 35 World Tour: From March 16, 2008, to December 13, 2009, KISS performed 103 shows on the KISS Alive 35 World Tour, playing the classics and, at certain venues, "Modern Day Delilah" and "Say Yeah" from *Sonic Boom*. Buckcherry was the opening act. The band, wearing *Destroyer*-themed costumes, visited a number of locales they had never been to before, including Bulgaria, Greece, Latvia, Russia, Luxembourg, Colombia, Peru and Venezuela. The tour spawned some double–CD sets as well.

William Simpson of *StageShottz Magazine* (stageshottz.com) caught the October 24, 2009, show in Birmingham, Alabama, and wrote: "With the crowd chanting 'KISS … KISS … KISS,' the curtain dropped to a stage filled with enough smoke to eclipse the first six rows; then Simmons, Stanley, and Thayer emerged. The set was heavy with classics from the *Alive!* era…. One thing fans have come to expect from KISS is great pyrotechnics, and the band did not disappoint…. Unlike some new bands that like to mix their political beliefs in with their songs, KISS is the original party band as Stanley told the crowd. 'If you came to solve global warming, or end all wars, or get all of your questions answered, you came to the wrong damn place.'"

Followed by: Sonic Boom Over Europe Tour.

KISS and Make-Up: Authored by Gene Simmons (with no ghost writer or co-author), this autobiography was devoted to Simmons' mother, holocaust survivor Flora Klein, "who gave me life and taught me to reach for the sky," and Shannon, Nicholas, and Sophie, who "taught me how to love someone other than myself."

The book, published by Crown Publishers on Dec. 4, 2001, does indeed spend a lot of time on Simmons' family, but it also covers his "adolescent years attending a Jewish theological center for rabbinical studies in Brooklyn; his love of all things American, including comic books, super-heroes, and cowboys; and his early fascination with girls and sex, which prompted him to start a rock band in school after he saw the Beatles on *The Ed Sullivan Show*."

While maintaining that he's never been drunk or taken drugs, Simmons readily acknowledges in the book that he's slept with approximately 4,600 women. In addition, he discusses the formative years of KISS, his brother-like relationship with Paul Stanley, he and Paul's difficulties with Ace Frehley and Peter Criss (he calls Ace lazy and Peter a whiner), his celebrity girlfriends Cher and Diana Ross, and much more.

The *Library Journal* review of the book, written by Caroline Dadas, said Simmons "clearly takes pride in his rise from an underprivileged kid to a stinking-rich cult figure, disclosing the number of women he has slept with and including early comic-book sketches drawn as an adolescent. These divulgences will entertain only the most loyal KISS followers, many of whom are probably not that interested in the man behind the greasepaint. This is the first authorized biography of the band (and a self-aggrandizing one at that), so there may be some demand. Fans, however, are better off with Dale Sherman's more objective portrait, *Black Diamond: The Unauthorized Biography of KISS*."

Clearly, given the sales of *KISS and Make-Up* (the softcover edition boasts that it was a *New York Times* Best Seller), Dadas underestimated how much the "most loyal KISS followers" want to know about "the man behind the greasepaint," but she makes a good point about Sherman's book. What Dadas should have pointed out is that Simmons doesn't spend near enough time talking about his beloved band's music. Simmons could have also written more about the positives Ace and Peter brought to the band.

KISS and Motley Crue: The Tour see **The Tour**

KISS and Sell: The Making of a Supergroup: Published by Billboard Books on April 1, 1997, *KISS and Sell* was written by C. K. Lendt, who was the band's tour business manager. According to a review written by *Entertainment Weekly*'s David Browne, who gave the book a B+, it is lacking in "gory financial details" but "makes up for it in gory details of other sorts. Stanley and Gene Simmons spend fortunes renovating apartments to impress fleeting girlfriends Donna Dixon and Cher, respectively. Women of all shapes and sizes pass through Simmons' hotel rooms, although Lendt claims the blood spewer was so afraid of real blood that he once dismissed a groupie because it was that time of her month.... Beneath the backstage tales lies Lendt's sobering thesis that KISS were 'a case of reaching too far too soon.' He relates the crash-and-burn sagas of Frehley (who partied himself to oblivion) and drummer Peter Criss, particularly Criss' decline into an unstable, gun-toting drug user.... According to Lendt, KISS sold $100 million worth of merchandise between 1977 and 1979, and they were only too eager to spend it. Lendt recalls watching perpetually bored guitarist Ace Frehley blow $30,000 in a casino and seeing a $60,000 recording-studio deposit go down the drain when singer-guitarist Paul Stanley decided he didn't feel comfortable there. Lendt's recollections of the makeup-free KISS of the '80s are fascinatingly bleak. Oblivious to plummeting record and ticket sales, KISS kept spending, with dire results. After one tour, Stanley returned home to find his apartment dark, because his office had forgotten to pay the electric bill. (Meanwhile, Simmons bought wigs to compensate for a receding hairline.) By the time KISS dismissed Lendt's company in 1988, the multiplatinum band was almost broke—which puts its top-grossing reunion tour into very real, dollars-and-sense perspective."

KISS and Tell: Written by Shannon Tweed (with Julie McCarron), *KISS and Tell* is the autobiography of the gorgeous blonde who is now married to Gene Simmons. In the foreword to the book, Simmons calls Tweed, his then-longtime girlfriend, "everything I never knew I wanted. She makes me a better man. She gives me more freedom than I want. I love her more today than I did when we first met."

In the book, which was published by Simmons Books/New Millennium Press in 2003, Tweed discusses, among other things, her and Gene's life together, including how they first met at a party at Hugh Hefner's Playboy Mansion. Tweed also discusses, with candor, her wild, uninhibited younger days as a Playboy Playmate, her obsession with Tom Jones, and her life as a soccer mom who drives her kids to school. Black-and-white photos are peppered throughout, plus there's a color section in the middle. Includes nude photos of Tweed.

KISS & Tell: Written by Bob McAdams, who was best man at Ace Frehley's wedding in 1976, and Gordon G.G. Gebert, who was close friends with Space Ace during the Frehley's Comet era, *KISS & Tell* was published by Pitbull Publishing in 1997. It is an exposé that angered many KISS fans when it came out because it dug up a lot of dirt on the band, primarily about Frehley, who is described as being lazy, selfish, irresponsible, dishonest, immoral, perverted, and bad at business. Gebert's primary problem with Frehley was in regard to a falling out over the guitarist's Rock Soldiers fan club.

An expanded special edition of the book was released in 2010. In a June 2, 2011, interview published on www.legendaryrockinterviews.com,

Gebert said the new edition is "266 pages long—42 pages more than the original book. The stories are expanded and new stories and photos were added. I was able to finally write the untold final chapters about my court appearances at Ace Frehley's bankruptcy hearings and the startling truth of what went down. Bob McAdams and I both agree the book is finally in a version we are both happy with. More unreleased photos are in the new version, too."

In that same interview, Gebert explained that he wrote the book "because Ace publicly betrayed me. If he didn't publicly accuse me of embezzlement, no book would've been written. I have no respect for authors that write tell-all books to make money, and I understand some people's misconstrued anger, but fans have to understand that *KISS & Tell* was written in self-defense."

KISS & Tell More!: Written by Gordon G.G. Gebert and published by Pitbull Publishing in 1998, *KISS & Tell More!* is the sequel to Gebert and Bob McAdams' *KISS & Tell*. Along with a few more stories about Ace, Gene, Paul, and Peter, the book includes rare photos and "hilarious anecdotes about the repercussions and KISS fan feedback to *KISS & Tell*," along with descriptions of radio interviews Gebert gave. Documentation on Ace filing bankruptcy is included as well.

According to Amazon reviewer "Darth Marc," the book is "75% full of Internet posts/threads that were at one point (and still may be) posted online. The author then copied and edited these postings and reprinted them … there are also reprints of court papers and legal documents which I also found boring and not worth the price I paid for the book. There are a few stories and anecdotes made by the author and by some other writers but these are short interludes between the predominant Internet threads/posts."

KISS: Animalize Live Uncensored: Shot at Cobo Hall Arena in Detroit December 8, 1984, and first aired in edited form on MTV January 26, 1985, *KISS Animalize Live Uncensored* was released on VHS and laser disc April 19, 1985. It features R-rated banter from Paul Stanley (which gets old in a hurry), along with the following songs: "Detroit Rock City," "Cold Gin," "Creatures of the Night," "Fits Like a Glove," "Heaven's on Fire," "Thrills in the Night," "Under the Gun," "War Machine," "Young and Wasted," "I Love It Loud," "I Still Love You," "Love Gun," "Lick It Up," "Black Diamond," and "Rock and Roll All Nite." Bruce Kulick had replaced an ailing Mark St. John on lead guitar at this point, and Eric Carr belts out an impressive drum solo.

Some fans have criticized the recording for being embellished in the studio, a technique used for KISS's live albums, and when you can actually see onscreen movements that don't quite match the sound, it's a little distracting. Even so, the band, appearing comfortable sans makeup, put on an energetic performance, and they sound great.

On January 14, 2003, *KISS Animalize Live Uncensored* was released on DVD in Brazil, and it showed up in certain U.S. stores as an import.

A raucous DVD, *KISS: Animalize Live Uncensored* features songs performed at Detroit's Cobo Hall.

KISS Army: Other bands have fans, KISS has an army. The KISS Army was founded in 1975 by Bill Starkey and his pal, Jay Evans, a pair of teenagers from Terre Haute, Indiana.

In the foreword to Dale Sherman's *KISS FAQ*, Starkey revealed that he first saw KISS in concert, at Evansville's Roberts Stadium. "It was a Sunday Night, and it was cold outside, so what else was there to do in Evansville, Indiana?," Starkey wrote. "[It was] a visual and audible assault on the senses. The concert volume was so loud that you could feel it thumping against your chest and through the wooden bleachers."

Starkey loved the excitement and unpredictability of the show. "You had this sense of fear, or at least fear of the unknown, because you did not know what to expect," he wrote. "I enjoyed the songs on the first and only KISS album I owned, but they sounded much, much different ... almost like they were being played way too quickly. I did not have time to catch my breath before something else happened. Sirens, flash pots, fire breathing, and blood puking—my first rock concert had it all."

Shortly thereafter, Starkey went to another KISS concert and told Evans, who was already a fan, about the shows. Evans' interest in the band prompted him to pick up the phone while the pair were hanging out in Starkey's basement.

"Jay bravely called the radio station WVTS-FM ... to request some KISS music," Starkey wrote. "He was told that they were not allowed to play new acts and especially not KISS."

Undaunted, the duo "continued to spread the good news about KISS. Jay would make copies of their albums with an 8-track recorder and give them out to anyone who believed us." They also wrote angry letters to Rich Dickerson, the program director of WVTS-FM.

"We decided to start a writing campaign calling ourselves the KISS Army," Starkey recalled in *KISS FAQ*. "Headquarters? My basement. I was the president, he was Field Marshall Evans ... we wrote insults to Rich Dickerson telling him how great KISS was and how the music and bands he played sucked ... we were rock 'n' roll terrorists with a pen and a phone line."

Further, Jay and Bill "convinced the younger kids in the neighborhood to paint up like the four members. We would parade them around the mall and at drive-thru restaurants. We called them 'The Unknown Soldiers of the KISS Army.' We were having a blast and recruiting new people to our cause.... I took Jay and two carloads of our classmates to their first, my third KISS show. That was the beginning of the real KISS Army."

One classmate who went to that KISS show was Rob Smith, who "used the school's printing press to mass produce KISS T-shirts. We'd pick days when we'd all wear T-shirts to school."

While many classmates saw this as uncool, saying things like "Kiss my ass," certain kids joined in on the fun. "Now others were calling the radio station on behalf of the KISS Army," Starkey wrote in *KISS FAQ*.

By July of 1975, WVTS had begun playing KISS records. In the weeks leading up to a KISS concert at the new Hulman Civic-University Center in Terre Haute that fall, Dickerson worked with Starkey and Evans to help promote the show.

One evening, the fledgling KISS Army visited WVTS-FM, where Rich's wife, Tricia told them that the KISS show had sold out and that KISS's management had heard about it. They wanted to meet Starkey and discuss the formation of a national KISS Army.

"You cannot imagine how stone-cold silent we were—stunned," Starkey wrote. "I was going to meet KISS!!!?? That was not on our agenda. What was I going to do next? What was I going to say? Here I was without a job, let alone a car, and I was going to meet my rock 'n' roll heroes."

Starkey continued: "KISS came to Terre Haute to a sellout crowd that placed them only with Elvis in terms of sold-out concerts in Terre Haute at the time. I was called backstage unexpectedly right before Rush took the stage. I would watch the show from the side of the stage while sitting on an anvil case with Mr. Bill Aucoin, who I would meet for the very first time. I would come onstage to receive a plaque from the band with my name on it. But the real satisfaction came from seeing the faces of my high school classmates. The ones who loved to bully all of us about KISS and their lack of radio play. Now they were at the altar of KISS ready to enlist in the KISS Army themselves."

Soon after the sold-out Terre Haute show, the KISS Army became the official fan club of the group. In 1976, Aucoin commissioned Howard Marks Inc. graphic designer Vincent DiGerlando to create an official KISS Army logo. Order forms for the KISS Army first appeared with the logo in 1976 in copies of *Destroyer*, the band's fourth studio album. For five dollars, fans would get a quarterly newsletter, a KISS Army membership card, a KISS discography, biographies on each band member, a membership charter certificate, an iron-on patch, a 22" × 35" poster, five 8" × 10" concert photos, and five wallet-size photos.

Former head of KISS merchandising Ron

Boutwell estimated that the fan club, at its peak, had nearly 100,000 members and earned around $5,000 per day. After a period of dormancy, KISS re-launched the KISS Army as the group's official fan club on August 23, 2007.

One important thing Starkey did in the introduction to *KISS FAQ* is clear up an urban legend that had been surrounding the KISS Army for decades.

While Starkey and company did indeed visit WVTS-FM, they didn't, as many people believed, demand that the DJ play KISS by five o'clock or else the KISS Army would surround the station and not allow him to leave. This is a story even KISS themselves bought into, as chronicled in *KISStory*, a massive book covering the history of the band.

"Wow! Incredible!," Starkey exclaimed upon reading of the account in *KISStory*. "How I wished it would have happened that way. I was made out to be a real badass who practically risked jail time for my favorite rock group."

Today, you can go to www.kissonline.com to join the KISS Army. There's a free version and a $50 version, the latter of which offers such perks as a KISS concert tour T-shirt and five limited edition 8 × 10 photos.

KISS Army Brasil: An MP3 Tribute to KISS Vol. 1: This free download was released in 2006. It features 15 tracks, including three by Killers, a KISS cover band.

KISS Army Brasil: An MP3 Tribute to KISS Vol. 2: This free download was released in 2009. It features 12 tracks, including songs by such bands as Killers, Rock Bottom, Parasite, and Virtual KISS.

KISS Army Brasil: An MP3 Tribute to KISS Vol. 3: This free download was released in 2009. It features 11 tracks, including songs by such bands as Killers, Rock Bottom, Parasite, and Virtual KISS.

KISS ARMY SWEDEN: MP3 Tribute to KISS: Released in 2005, this free download features 72 tracks by a variety of Swedish artists, including such KISS tribute acts as KYSS, Ace in the Pole, and Peck.

KISS Army Worldwide!: The Ultimate Fanzine Phenomenon: Featuring an introduction by Gene Simmons, *KISS Army Worldwide!* covers fan-made magazines (i.e., fanzines) about KISS created between the years 1976 and 2009. It's a slick, 240-page coffee table book filled with photos, including amateur performance photos, concert and publicity posters, pictures of fans wearing KISS makeup, and fanzine covers. Includes commentary from Simmons, Paul Stanley, and various fanzine publishers, along with a KISS Army article by Bill Starkey.

In "The Final Word" at the back of the book, Stanley wrote, "I think that in the best sense, these fanzines are a reflection or validation of the passion that we had when they started them and that we have tried to maintain. That's what those fanzines were born out of."

KISS Asylum: Self-described as "The Longest Running KISS Website & The Online Home for KISS Fans Everywhere," KISS Asylum began in 1995. Check it out at www.kissasylum.com.

KISS: Asylum of Death—Interviews: Released by Petal Productions in 2006, this unauthorized DVD contains the following: *Dynasty*-era interviews in which the band defends their disco-era sound (Paul Stanley says "I Was Made for Lovin' You" was "number one or number two all around the world"); the infamous and amusing 1974 clip of Gene Simmons appearing with Totie Fields on *The Mike Douglas Show*; an "unmasked" interview in which the band has their backs to the camera; an interview conducted by Billy Crystal; an early '90s interview with a British KISS collector and seller; and a *Revenge*-era interview with Gene, Paul, Eric Singer, and Bruce Kulick.

KISS: Behind the Mask—The Official Authorized Biography: Written by Ken Sharp and David Leaf, this is an excellent, highly entertaining book about the band. In addition to insider history, the book quotes liberally from numerous luminaries, including such rock icons as Alice Cooper, Brian Wilson, Bob Seger, Joe Perry, Lenny Kravitz, Ted Nugent, Ozzy Osbourne, Nancy Wilson, Billy Squier, Roger Daltrey, Nikki Sixx, and Angus Young. Band members contribute as well, along with producers, comic book creators (Stan Lee and Steve Gerber), and various others associated with KISS throughout their history. It also features dozens of rare photos (including a color section in the center), along with album-by-album, song-by-song commentary.

The *Publishers Weekly* review notes: "The authorized bio presents more than enough new material to make it essential for hardcore fans. Much of the book's first half presents a previously unpublished work based on the only in-depth interviews the band gave in 1980.... The book's second half, however, is the true highlight for KISS fans: a comprehensive look at all of the KISS albums ever made."

KISS by Monster Mini Golf: Located in Las Vegas across from the Hard Rock Hotel & Casino, KISS by Monster Mini Golf is an 18-hole indoor mini-golf course and arcade. It also features a V.I.P. room, KISS decorations and music, the first KISS wedding chapel, and the world's largest KISS gift shop. In the promo video for the fun spot, Paul Stanley says: "Someone came to us with this idea of KISS mini-golf, and we thought, 'another way to weave our way into the fabric of Americana.'" Or, as a cynic might say, "another way to make more money."

KISS: Cat Tales: Released by GIG Visual Media in 2007, this unauthorized DVD finds Peter Criss at a Q&A session at a KISS convention in Philadelphia in 2003, fielding questions from fans. Criss, who had recently rejoined KISS (again) for the forthcoming World Domination Tour, says he can't wait get back on the road with KISS, expresses displeasure over Tommy Thayer taking over for Ace Frehley, and discusses Paul Stanley's sexuality. For some questions, he told fans they'd have to read this answers in his forthcoming book, which, unfortunately, didn't come out until nearly a decade later. Criss apologizes for his coarse language because of the kids in the room. The DVD also shows KISS in the dressing room preparing for a show and "ultra-rare 'beneath the stage' footage shot during 'Beth' and encores."

KISS Checkers Set: The Rock and Roll Over Checkers Game!: In 2009, Brian Heiler of www.toplessrobot.com ranked this checkers set #8 on his list of "The 9 Least Rocking Items of KISS Merchandise." He wrote, "Many times, rock bands can often attach their name to something and make it a little cooler—musical instruments, items of clothing, and so on. But Jimi Hendrix would probably have trouble making a board game cool, and Satan himself could not make the game of checkers rock. Checkers might be the least rocking activity on Earth, and yet here KISS is, with a checkers set. Hell, *Chutes and Ladders* would be less shameful." The package includes a thin game board, an instruction booklet, and 24 game pieces.

KISS Chronicles: 3 Classic Albums: Essentially the CD version of *The Originals*, *KISS Chronicles: 3 Classic Albums* is a repackaging of *KISS*, *Hotter Than Hell*, and *Dressed to Kill*. Released June 21, 2005, by Mercury/Universal.

KISS Classics: Published by Marvel Music (an imprint of Marvel Comics) in 1995, *KISS Classics* reprints *Marvel Comics Super Special* #s 1 and 5. The issue also includes an article called "The Marvel/KISS Connection," which features a preview of *KISSNation*, a comic book that only lasted one issue.

KISS Coffeehouse: The KISS Coffeehouse opened in 2006 in Myrtle Beach, South Carolina. Paul Stanley and Gene Simmons attended the grand opening celebration. Unfortunately, it closed down in 2013, with the general manager citing a "steady decline" in business. Menu items included such drinks as Room Service, Demon Dark Roast, Pyro Pistachio, KISS Army Blend, French KISS Vanilla, and KISS Frozen Rockuccino, along with a variety of sweet treats. Decorated on the inside with KISS memorabilia, the facility was fronted by 20' tall KISS boots, the store logo, *Rock and Roll Over* art, and large photos of the band members.

KISS Collectibles: Identification and Price Guide: The first official price guide for KISS memorabilia, *KISS Collectibles* was released by Avon Books June 1, 1993. Authored by Karen Lesniewski and John Lesniewski, the book features listings of toys, T-shirts, records, 8-track tapes, bootleg merchandise, tour books, jewelry, pins, and much more. Includes 58 pages of photos, eight of which are in color.

KISS Conventions *see* **World Wide KISS Conventions**

KISS Cover to Cover: Released April 5, 2005, by Lunar Moth Entertainment, this tribute album features songs that KISS themselves covered. Tracks, performed by an assortment of bands, include: "Kissin' Time" (Nightmare), "Then She Kissed Me" (Jon Rubin), "Any Way You Want It" (Picture 21), "Tossin' and Turnin'" (Marc Zouhar), "New York Groove" (Great Jones), "When You Wish Upon a Star" (Syntax Error), "2000 Man" (Captain T & Ostronomy), "God Gave Rock n' Roll to You III" (V.O.G.), and "Do You Remember Rock n' Roll Radio" (SLACK).

KISS Covered in Scandinavia: A wide variety of Scandinavian bands, ranging from rock to pop to jazz to barbershop, lend their talents to this double CD, which was limited to 15,000 copies.

Tracks include: "Detroit Rock City" (Moon Flower), "Cold Gin" (Hakan Hemlin & Mike Nilsson), "Escape from the Island" (Lindgren 5 Steps), "God of Thunder" (Entombed), "Rock Bottom" (Leila K), "Beth" (The Creeps), "Goin' Blind" (Borgvall Chamber Ensemble), "All American Man" (Hellacopters), "Black Diamond" (Infinite Mass), "C'mon and Love Me" (Sator), "Love Gun" (Dia Psalma), "Do You Love Me" (Livin' Sacrifice), "Parasite" (Gone), and "Rock and Roll All Nite" (Happy Nite Quartet).

The second CD includes interviews with Ace (1987), Peter (1988), Gene (1992–1993), and Paul (1992–1993). A three-CD version, limited to 5,000 copies, includes an interview with KISS before and after the reunion of the original band members. Released in 1997 by Pink Honey Records. In 1998, the two interview CDs were released together as *KISS Uncovered*.

KISS: Crazy Nights: Released on VHS in 1988, *KISS: Crazy Nights* features the three music videos released from the *Crazy Nights* album: "Crazy Crazy Nights," "Reason to Live," and "Turn on the Night."

KISS Deutschland: A Tribute to KISS: Released in Germany in 1999 by Weser Label/Indigo, this tribute album features the following tracks: "I Want You" (The Traceelords), "Rip It Out" (Florian Hedwig), "I'll Fight Hell to Hold You" (Rod Gonzales), "Any Way You Want It" (Jean $immons), "I Stole Your Love" (Stier), "Not for the Innocent" (Free Key Bit-Chess), "Shandi" (The New Wave Hookers), "Love Gun" (The Romp), "Flaming Youth" (Shameless), "I'm A Legend Tonight" (Mark Lawson), "Coming Home" (Piledriver), "Calling Dr. Love" (Larger Than Life), "I Was Made for Lovin' You" (Marijka), "Talk to Me" (Silly Encores), "Firehouse" (King's Crowd), "God of Thunder" (Frankiss), "Wouldn't You Like to Know Me" (Blackwell), "Do You Love Me?" (S.U.M.P.), "Deuce" (Tony Gorilla), "Domino" (Big Tiger), "Shout It Out Loud" (KISS Forever Band), and "Zucho Zirkuss" (D.J. S. & Falk N. Horst).

KISS Documented Volume One: Great Expectations 1970–1977: Written by Scott Parker, this book was self-published through Amazon's CreateSpace Independent Publishing Platform on June 12, 2011. Parker reviews concerts, recordings, and radio and TV appearances from the band's early years.

KISS Dolls *see* **Mego Dolls**

KISS DVD Board Game: Published in 2008 by GDC-GameDevCo Ltd., the *KISS DVD Board Game* is for 2 to 4 players. From the back of the box: "Follow KISS on tour and travel the world collecting merchandise, albums and programs. You'll even start your own KISS tribute band! Do you have what it takes to become the leader of the KISS® Army?! Players travel to the different zones on the game board (each zone represents one particular aspect of being a KISS Army member). Collect KISS cards by landing on the "DEMON," "STARCHILD," "CATMAN," and "SPACEMAN" spaces. Once you have collected the required KISS cards for a zone, you redeem them for a KISS Army card. Once you collect all 4 KISS Army cards (1 in each zone) you have become the leader of the KISS Army and win the game!"

The *KISS DVD Board Game*, released in 2008, lets you "follow KISS on tour."

KISS Encyclopedia: The only known KISS encyclopedia other than the one you are holding in your hands, this book, published in 1977 by Shinko Music Publishing Co., was released exclusively in Japan. It is long out of print, far from comprehensive, and very hard to find.

KISS: Exposed: Released on VHS in 1986 and DVD in 2002, *KISS: Exposed* includes the following tracks: "Who Wants to Be Lonely" (music video); "Uh! All Night" (music video); "I Love It Loud" (live, 1983, Rio de Janeiro); "Deuce" (live, 1974, San Francisco), "Strutter" (live, 1976, Detroit), "Beth" (live, 1977, Houston), "Detroit Rock City" (live, 1980, Australia), "Tears are Falling" (music video), "Lick It Up" (music video), "All Hell's Breakin' Loose" (music video), "I Love It Loud" (music video), "I Stole Your Love" (live, 1977, Houston), "Heaven's On Fire" (music video), "Ladies Room" (live, 1977, Houston), and "Rock and Roll All Nite" (live, 1980, Australia). There's also plenty of tongue-in-cheek footage, such as the interviewer walking around Paul Stanley's rented mansion (which, according to the video, contains a dungeon-like bedroom for Gene Simmons), talking to band members and looking at memorabilia while bikini-clad women mill about.

KISS FAQ: All That's Left to Know About the Hottest Band in the Land: Written by Dale Sherman, who has been chronicling the adventures of KISS since the 1980s, *KISS FAQ* was published by Backbeat Books on July 1, 2012. It features a foreword by KISS Army founder Bill Starkey and covers all manner of KISS minutia, including fun facts and history on record labels, comic books, the band's logo, the real locations of live albums, drug references in songs, opening bands, *KISS Meets the Phantom of the Park*, TV appearances, and much more.

KISS Farewell Tour: Despite its title, this was not the last KISS tour, but it was the last featuring the original lineup of Paul Stanley, Gene Simmons, Ace Frehley, and Peter Criss. It lasted from March 11, 2000, to April 13, 2001, for a total of 142 shows in the U.S., Canada, Japan, and Australia.

When KISS reunited in 1996, Ace and Peter were essentially hired hands. Near the end of the Farewell Tour, Peter was unhappy with a new contract he was supposed to sign, so he and KISS parted ways. Peter's last concert during this tour was October 7, 2000, at the North Charleston Coliseum in North Charleston, South Carolina, where he destroyed his drum kit in frustration at the end of the show. Gene and Paul hired Eric Singer to take his place, a controversial move since they had Singer wear the Catman makeup created by Peter, who would return to KISS (temporarily) for the 2003 World Domination Tour.

Ace Frehley's last show with the band was the final concert of the Farewell Tour, occurring at Carrara Stadium in Australia. Frehley has stated that he took the "farewell" in the title seriously and that he quit to focus on his solo career. Tommy Thayer, wearing the Spaceman makeup, replaced Ace.

During the Farewell Tour, the band wore replicas of their *Destroyer*-era costumes, and the stage featured two KISS logos on each side of a giant video screen (a la Psycho Circus World Tour) and staircases similar to what they used from 1976 to 1978, but with brighter lights and a futuristic chrome design. Props and stunts included burning drumsticks, a confetti storm, smoke bombs, Paul and Gene flying, Paul shooting T-shirts into the audience with a T-gun, rising platforms, Paul smashing his guitar, Gene spitting blood and fire, and Ace's smoking, flying, and rocket-shooting guitars.

In *Face the Music: A Life Exposed*, Paul revealed his dissatisfaction with the tour, in which they had to play the same songs night after night. "The Farewell Tour was us wanting to put KISS out of its misery," he wrote. "And for a while, honestly, we lost sight that we didn't have to stop; we had to get rid of them [Ace and Peter]. So the Farewell Tour was really because it was unbearable to be with those guys—not just on a personal level. The playing was ... 'erratic' is a nice way of putting it. You just never knew what was gonna happen day to day on stage, and it was a challenge getting somebody to leave their room to come to the lobby. Forget about the show.... I thought we were disappointing people. People may have loved the excitement and the novelty of seeing us again, but many nights we weren't very good."

One noteworthy aspect of the Farewell Tour is that the band played two non-makeup-era songs: "Lick It Up" and "Heaven's On Fire." In addition, they played the late-makeup-era single, "I Love It Loud," the recording of which did not involve all four members of the original lineup. The June 27, 2000, show in East Rutherford, New Jersey was filmed for a pay-per-view event called *The Last KISS*, which was released later on home video and is part of *KISSology—The Ultimate KISS Collection, Vol. 3: 1992–2000*.

Followed by: World Domination Tour.

KISS 4K: Published by Platinum Studios beginning in 2007, *KISS 4K* is a comic book series that ran 11 issues: six regular installments, a "Merry Kissmas" Christmas special, three online editions, and limited edition preview issue #0. The creative team included writers Ricky Sprague and Fred Van Lente, along with artists Rodolfo Migliari, Daniel Campos, Kevin Crossley, and Bob Hall. The online issues were by Adam Black. A mysterious figure reveals to each KISS member that they carry the warrior spirits of the 4K: the Demon, the Starchild, the King of All Beasts (Catman), and the Celestial (Spaceman).

The first issue of *KISS 4K*, a comic book series from 2007. It features the Demon, the Starchild, the King of All Beasts (Catman), and the Celestial (Spaceman).

KISS 40: Released May 27, 2014, to celebrate the band's 40th anniversary, *KISS 40* is a two-disc CD anthology spanning 1973 to 2013, featuring one song off every album, including live records and the band's 1978 solo releases. Tracks include: "Nothin to Lose," "Let Me Go, Rock 'n' Roll," "C'mon and Love Me," "Rock and Roll All Nite" (from *Alive!*), "God of Thunder" (demo from *KISS: The Box Set*), "Beth," "Hard Luck Woman," "Reputation" (previously unreleased demo), "Christine Sixteen," "Shout It Out Loud" (from *Alive II*), "Strutter '78," "You Matter to Me," "Radioactive," "New York Groove," "Hold Me, Touch Me," "I Was Made for Lovin' You" (single edit), "Shandi," "A World Without Heroes," "I Love It Loud," "Down on Your Knees," "Lick It Up," "Heaven's on Fire," "Tears are Falling," "Reason to Live," "Let's Put the X in Sex," "Forever" (remix), "God Gave Rock 'N' Roll to You II," "Unholy" (from *Alive III*), "Do You Love Me?" (from *KISS Unplugged*), "Room Service" (from *You Wanted The Best, You Got The Best!!*), "Jungle" (radio edit), "Psycho Circus," "Nothing Can Keep Me from You" (from *Detroit Rock City: Music from the Motion Picture*), "Detroit Rock City" (from *KISS Symphony: Alive IV*, "Deuce" (from *KISS Instant Live*), "Firehouse" (from *Alive: The Millennium Concert*), "Modern Day Delilah," "Cold Gin" (from *Alive 35*), "Crazy Crazy Nights" (from *Sonic Boom Over Europe*), and "Hell or Hallelujah." The package also includes a 20-page booklet.

The KISS 40th Anniversary World Tour: When KISS hit the big 4–0 in 2014, the band not only entered the Rock and Roll Hall of Fame and landed on the cover of *Rolling Stone* magazine, they hit the road on an extensive world tour, beginning June 23 at the USANA Amphitheatre in West Valley City, Utah. Def Leppard co-headlined the first 42 shows.

Raymond Johnston of the *Prague Post* had this to say about the June 8, 2015, show at the 02 Arena in Prague, the capital and largest city of the Czech Republic:

> The 40th anniversary tour is now winding down, but there was little sign that the band members were bored with the act…. The capacity crowd, with many people in KISS makeup and platform shoes, made it hard to see from the stage floor, but oversized video screens helped to compensate…. The band's current lineup now includes original members Gene Simmons on vocals and bass and Paul Stanley on

KISS Friends

vocals and rhythm guitar, plus Tommy Thayer on lead guitar and Eric Singer on drums. With this lineup they have been exploring more of the back catalog live, even delving into the "without makeup" era.... Highlights of the show included Simmons elevating on wires to a platform high above the stage for a bass solo. Not to be outdone, Stanley rode a wire out to a small platform in the middle of the crowd for "Love Gun" from the album of the same name. This was accompanied by an illuminated mirrored disco ball. Thayer shot fireworks out of his guitar, and Singer's drum station elevated into the air.

KISS Friends Project: This amateur CD, released independently in Spain, features the following tracks: "Deuce," "C'mon and Love Me," "Mr. Speed," "I Stole Your Love," "I Was Made For Lovin' You," "I Love It Loud," "Thrills in the Night," "Domino," "Legends of Rock & Roll" (a KISS-inspired song), and "God Gave Rock & Roll to You II."

KISS: Greatest Hits, Volume 1: This trade paperback collects *Marvel Comics Super Special* #1 and #5. New cover art by Nick Runge. Published by IDW Publishing.

KISS: Greatest Hits, Volume 2: This trade paperback collects *Psycho Circus* comics 1–6. New cover art by Nick Runge. Published by IDW Publishing.

KISS: Greatest Hits, Volume 3: This trade paperback collects *Psycho Circus* comics 7–13. New cover art by Mister Sam. Published by IDW Publishing.

KISS: Greatest Hits, Volume 4: This trade paperback collects *Psycho Circus* comics 14–19. New cover art by Sam Shearon. Published by IDW Publishing.

KISS: Greatest Hits, Volume 5: This trade paperback collects *Psycho Circus* comics 20–25. New cover art by Sam Shearon. Published by IDW Publishing.

KISS: Hell's Guardians—Interviews: This unauthorized DVD, released in 2007 by Petal Productions, features various interviews and news stories, including reports on the group from ABC's *20/20* and the Australian version of *60 Minutes*, both from the 1970s. There are also two European MTV interviews from the non-makeup era, along with a pre-recorded Muscular Dystrophy Association fundraiser appearance on the annual Jerry Lewis telethon.

KISS: Hotter Than Hell: Subtitled "The Stories Behind Every Song," *KISS: Hotter Than Hell* was written by Paul Elliott. The book features an interview with Paul Stanley and Gene Simmons, along with examinations of each KISS album and song from *KISS* through *Psycho Circus* and *The Box Set*. It also features commentary from noteworthy KISS fans. Published by Thunder's Mouth Press October 25, 2002.

Along with Paul Stanley and Gene Simmons interviews, *KISS: Hotter than Hell* includes examinations of each KISS album and song from *KISS* through *Psycho Circus* and *The Box Set*.

KISS: Immortals: A 29-webisode series that began February 29, 2000, *KISS: Immortals* was the result of a partnership between VH1.com and Brilliant Digital Entertainment. The computer-animated cartoon, which features the real voices of Ace, Gene, Paul, and Peter, was released on DVD May 29, 2001, by Slingshot Entertainment, but it only features nine episodes, angering many who bought it.

From the official product description: "Using your DVD player, DVD-ROM drive, or DVD-compatible game station (Playstation 2, etc.), you can become legendary rock group KISS as they journey through a strange world where their music is illegal! Controlling this animated adventure with your remote control, game controller, or mouse and keypad, you can help KISS stop the evil Domino as she attempts to rule this surreal universe with her iron fist and ruthless weaponry. Bring KISS back home from the surreal side of things!"

KISS in Attack of the Phantoms: Released in Europe on October 26, 1979, *KISS in Attack of the Phantoms* is the theatrical version of the made-for-TV movie, *KISS Meets the Phantom of the Park*. In Australia, the film was released on a double bill with Alice Cooper's *Welcome to My Nightmare*.

In addition to the title alteration, there are a number of edits, such as having Paul shoot Sam's remote control with his eye laser instead of simply removing it with his hand. There are other, more substantive edits as well, such as having the band weaken after Sam grabs the talismans (instead of before), and streamlining Melissa's search for Sam in the park, helping tighten the plot and make it more coherent. The changes were made in part because the test audiences found the original version to be unintentionally funny.

Musically, instead of ending with "God of Thunder," the film closes with "Mr. Make Believe" from Gene's solo album. Other solo album songs are used as well, including Ace's "New York Groove" during the robot werewolf battle. The film score was heavily edited, and much of it was cut.

KISS in Attack of the Phantoms is included on the DVD boxed set, *KISSology—The Ultimate KISS Collection, Vol. 2: 1978–1991*.

KISS: Interviews: Released in 2011 by Blue Media Marc, this unauthorized DVD contains promotional footage, rare interviews and exclusive uncut interviews, and former band members' personal film footage, along with video taken on the road by crew members.

KISS—Invasion (A Look at the Lost Egyptian God, Vinnie Vincent): Despite the title, this unauthorized DVD is a group interview, not a bio of Vinnie Vincent. It is the full, uncut *Night Flight* interview from 1982, during the *Creatures of the Night* era. Released in 2011.

KISS Kasket *see* **Caskets**

KISS Kids: Written by Chris Ryall for IDW Publishing, *KISS Kids* is a four-issue comic book series published in 2013. The art by Jose Holder is cartoonish, as are the stories featuring Li'l Demon, Starchild, Catkid, and Spacey, a.k.a. the KISS Kids gang. In-jokes for longtime KISS fans abound, but the content is clearly aimed at readers of all ages. As the publisher said in the solicitation, "No blood or fire here, just laughs and fun tales of the little costumed maniacs and the crazy town in which they live." *Batman: The Animated Series* co-creator Bruce Timm drew a variant cover for issue #2. A trade paperback, released in 2014, collects all four issues and features an introduction by Gene Simmons.

KISS Kompendium: Published in 2009 by HarperCollins, *KISS Kompendium* is a slick, full-color, oversized hardcover book. It includes: *Marvel Comics Super Special* #1 and #5; Todd McFarlane's *KISS: Psycho Circus* for Image Comics; Joe Casey's *KISS* comics for Dark Horse Comics; and Ricky Sprague's *KISS 4K* comics for the KISS Comics Group. Gene Simmons provides the foreword.

KISS Konfidential: Released on VHS August 16, 1993, *KISS Konfidential* features the following songs, live in concert: "Creatures of the Night," "Deuce," "I Just Wanna," "Unholy," "Heaven's on Fire," "100,000 Years" (filmed in Detroit, 1976), "Nothin' to Lose" (filmed in San Francisco, 1975), "Hotter Than Hell" (filmed in Detroit, 1976), "Let Me Go, Rock 'n' Roll" (filmed in Japan, 1977), "Domino," "Lick It Up," "Forever," "Take It Off," "I Love It Loud," "God Gave Rock 'N' Roll to You II," and "Star Spangled Banner." Most of the footage is from the *Revenge* tour. There's documentary material as well, including Eric Singer and Bruce Kulick talking about one another and their time in the band. Re-released in 2005 on DVD as part of *KISS—Konfidential & Xtreme Close Up*.

KISS—Konfidential & Xtreme Close Up: A DVD collecting two previously released videos on one disc: *KISS Konfidential* and *KISS: X-treme Close-Up*. Released January 25, 2005.

KISS: Krazy Killer: According to the back of the packaging, this unauthorized DVD contains "Exclusive home footage of Gene and Paul with their lawyers and the police," storming the "much talked about Detroit KISS Konvention," which occurred July 17, 1994. The duo "takes back their old KISS Kostumes and boots which they claim were stolen from their New York warehouse. Then they have an unexpected question and answer session, followed by Peter Criss, which makes the whole place go wild!" This is followed by "an unedited and very entertaining interview with the whole band in a TV studio." Published in 2006 by Petal Productions.

KISS Live!: Written by Mick St.Michael, *KISS Live!* was published in the UK by Omnibus Press in August of 1996. As of this writing, there's one review of the book on amazon.com, written by Nelwin Aldriansyah: "KISS' successful reunion in 1996 has triggered a sudden wave of the so-called 'KISS experts.' These 'experts' tried their best to cash-in from the rejuvenated KISS mania that soared the demand for KISS memorabilia. This book is a perfect example of those who want to milk KISS fans for the money. There's no new story inside, no shocking truth, no new facts, even no new pictures. This book is more like a photo book, with giant pictures and little stories in between. Most of the photos came from the *Creatures* promo tour in the U.K."

There's one review on www.amazon.co.uk as well, written by Veille: "I admit I would buy Gene Simmons shopping list if he decided to sell it— but I'm very pleased with this book. Good quality photos along with a free poster, and although most of the facts are already known by older fans, for any just beginning to love their music (and they have many newcomers already), it's a good start and a must."

KISS: Live on Letterman: The 50th edition of CBS's popular webcast, *Live on Letterman*, featured KISS performing at the Ed Sullivan Theater in New York City. The 48-minute concert was webcast live October 10, 2012, and was made available on demand on CBS.com. Songs include: "Hell or Hallelujah," "Shout It Out Loud," "Calling Dr. Love," "I Love It Loud," "Detroit Rock City," "Got to Choose," "Christine Sixteen," "Strutter," "Lick It Up," and "Deuce."

KISS Live: The Ultimate Halloween Party: On October 31, 1998, Fox aired *KISS Live: The Ultimate Halloween Party*, part of which consisted of three songs screened live from Dodger Stadium in Los Angeles, California during the Psycho Circus World Tour: "Psycho Circus" and "Let Me Go, Rock 'n' Roll" on the East Coast and "Psycho Circus" and "Shout It Out Loud" on the West Coast. The special included a Smashing Pumpkins song as well, "Cash Car Star," with the band dressed up like the Beatles.

KISS Logo: Designed by Ace Frehley and refined by Paul Stanley, the KISS logo, featuring the patented lightning bolt SS, is an iconic branding, emblazoning album covers, merchandise, and, most prominently, used as a huge lighted backdrop to live KISS shows. For albums and items released in Germany, the logo has been altered to avoid similarities to the double S Nazi symbol.

KISS Loves You: Released November 11, 2007, *KISS Loves You* is a documentary. According to IMDB, it is a "film that began back in 1994 when the band KISS was at a career low and KISS fans around the world were starting tribute bands, uniting at unofficial KISS Conventions and growing increasingly more nostalgic for the 70's era classic KISS line-up. The zeitgeist exhibited at these conventions was not lost on the band, and in 1996 they responded, rising up like a grease-painted phoenix into a new era of success. On the surface, KISS fans got exactly what they longed for, but for some the return of their idols brought unexpected consequences. *KISS Loves You* follows a few KISS fans along the way." Directed by Jim Heneghan, the film includes appearances by Sebastian Bach and Dee Snider. Ace, Paul, Gene, and Peter are shown via archival footage.

KISS Meets the Phantom: The official magazine tie-in to *KISS Meets the Phantom of the Park*, *KISS Meets the Phantom* was published by Big Shot Publications in 1978. In addition to numerous photos from the film, the mag contains interviews with Ace, Gene, Paul, and Peter. Of working on the film, Gene called it a "dream come true" while Ace said it was "very educational." Paul called it a "new challenge" while Peter said he "learned a lot from doing the movie." The interviews indicate that there would be more KISS movies in the future, but, thanks in large part to *KISS Meets the Phantom of the Park* being such an embarrassment, that never happened.

KISS Meets the Phantom of the Park: Debuting on NBC October 28, 1978, *KISS Meets the Phantom of the Park* is a made-for-TV movie beloved by many KISS apologists who were kids when it first aired. However, it is reviled by critics and film fans in general, thanks to wooden acting, cheap special effects, and a cartoonish plot. It was produced by Hanna-Barbera (*Scooby-Doo, The*

Flintstones) and directed by Gordon Hessler (*Murders in the Rue Morgue, The Golden Voyage of Sinbad*).

The back of the 1988 GoodTimes VHS box describes the plot thusly: "KISS are scheduled for a sell-out concert at California's Magic Mountain amusement park when park-goers begin to vanish without a trace. Behind it all is Abner Devereaux (Anthony Zerbe), the eccentric creator of the park's life-like cybernetic creatures. When Melissa (Deborah Ryan) turns to KISS to help her find her missing boyfriend, Devereaux feels threatened and creates cybernetic KISS look-alikes."

The problems with the film, in which each band member has Marvel Comics–like super powers, are the stuff of legend, from Ace Frehley's squawking dialogue ("Awk!") and African-American stunt-double to the unconvincing fight scenes to the fact that Peter Criss's voice was dubbed over by Michael Bell (except for the poolside performance of "Beth").

In *Makeup to Breakup*, Criss called the film "the lamest thing I could have imagined.... When I was told that we had to fight the Wolfman one day and Frankenstein the next, my brain started to hurt. Why should I have powers to levitate things with my hands? What did any of this have to do with rock 'n' roll? Our fans were going to think that we were pansies. I became a rock 'n' roll drummer because I was a rebel, I was fighting the system, fighting the Vietnam War. Now we were just buffoons."

Despite all of this, *Phantom of the Park* did well in the ratings and was released theatrically outside of the United States, where it was re-edited and renamed *KISS in Attack of the Phantoms*. Although *Phantom of the Park* is unavailable on DVD or Blu-ray, *Attack of the Phantoms*, which adds various songs from KISS's 1978 solo records, is part of the *KISSology—The Ultimate KISS Collection, Vol. 2: 1978–1991* DVD boxed set.

KISS "Meets the Press": Released by MDV Visual in 2011, this unauthorized DVD includes the following: KISS talking about religious groups at the Sioux Falls Arena in South Dakota, February 19, 1983; an interview with Wendy O. Williams of the Plasmatics; KISS getting a star on The Hollywood Walk of Fame August 11, 1999; a USA TV interview with Gene Simmons about the Rock Against Drugs campaign (1987); Eric Carr co-hosting the *Radio 1990* TV show; Peter Criss putting his handprints in cement at The Guitar Center/Hollywood RockWalk; and Gene Simmons promoting *Runaway* and an episode of *The Hitchhiker* that he was in.

KISS MY ANKH: A Tribute to Vinnie Vincent: Released August 27, 2008, by Split-Screen Entertainment, *KISS MY ANKH* features

The official magazine tie-in to the made-for-TV movie, *KISS Meets the Phantom of the Park*. In addition to numerous photographs from the film, the mag contains interviews with Ace, Gene, Paul, and Peter.

Kiss My ANKH pays tribute to Vinnie Vincent, who replaced Ace Frehley as lead guitarist in KISS.

Kiss My Ass

a variety of bands performing songs written or co-written by Vinnie Vincent. Tracks include: "Killer" (DoubleVirgo), "I Still Love You" (Gods of Fire), "Lick It Up" (Future 86), "A Million to One" (Steve Brown), "Boyz Are Gonna Rock" (Mike Weeks), "Back on the Streets" (Jazan Wild), "That Time of Year" (Adler's Appetite), "Love Kills" (Vic Rivera and Kelli McCloud), "Unholy" (Curse God and Die), "I Just Wanna" (The Dead Zookeepers), and "Shout It Out Loud" (C.C. Banana with Chris Caffery), the latter of which has nothing to do with Vincent.

Kiss My Ass: Classic KISS Regrooved: Released in 1994 to coincide with the 20th anniversary of KISS's self-titled debut album, *Kiss My Ass* is a tribute record authorized by the band. Tracks include: "Deuce" by Lenny Kravitz, "Hard Luck Woman" by Garth Brooks (the only song in which KISS performs as the backing band), "She" by Anthrax (produced by Paul Stanley and Gene Simmons), "Christine Sixteen" by the Gin Blossoms, "Rock and Roll All Nite" by Toad the Wet Sprocket, "Calling Dr. Love" by Shandi's Addiction, "Goin' Blind" by Dinosaur Jr., "Strutter" by Extreme, "Plaster Caster" by the Lemonheads, "Detroit Rock City" by the Mighty Mighty Bosstones, and "Black Diamond" by Yoshiki. The album was certified Gold by the Recording Industry Association of America and spent 13 weeks on the charts. U.S. vinyl issues and non–U.S. versions included a 13th track: "Unholy" by Die Arzte.

KISS My Ass: The Video: *KISS My Ass: The Video* has the same cover photo as the *Kiss My Ass: Classic KISS Regrooved* tribute album, and it has footage of the band watching Anthrax and the Gin Blossoms in the studio recording their tribute tracks. The rest of the video deviates from the album, however, featuring interviews with the band, photos from the 1970s of KISS without makeup, the making of *KISStory* (the massive 1995 book), and the following live-in-concert songs: "Parasite," "Do You Love Me," "Radioactive," "Move On," "Love Gun," "New York Groove," "Makin' Love," "I Love It Loud," "C'mon and Love Me," "Hooligan," "Shock Me," "I," "She," and "Black Diamond." Also includes a 1976 rehearsal of "Take Me."

KISS My Ass Tour: From April 2, 1994, to February 13, 1995, KISS played 23 shows in North America, South America (where they were headliners on the Monsters of Rock Festival), Asia, and Australia. Around the same time (June 21, 1994, to be exact), the *Kiss My Ass: Classic KISS Regrooved* tribute album hit stores. On the tour, Paul Stanley did something he hadn't done before. During his guitar-smashing routine, he would first soak the instrument with lighter fluid and then set it on fire, à la Jimi Hendrix. Other stage props included bombs, fireworks, lasers, Leon the Sphinx, strippers, a giant KISS logo curtain, and Gene Simmons breathing fire.

Band lineup: Paul Stanley, Bruce Kulick, Gene Simmons, and Eric Singer. Opening acts: Angra, Black Sabbath, Dr. Sin, Fleetwood Mac, Gatos Sucios, Hermetica, I Mother Earth, Lita Ford, Logos, Mother Station, Open Skyz, the Pat Travers Band, the Poor, Raimundos, Screamin' Cheetah Wheelies, Slayer, Snake Dance, Stick, Suicidal Tendencies, Tumulto, Victimas del Dr. Cerebro, and Viper. Average attendance unknown.

Followed by: Alive/Worldwide Tour, a.k.a. the Reunion Tour.

KISS of Death: Released in 1995 by Eat Me Records, this Polish death metal tribute album includes the following tracks: "Parasite" (Nokturnel), "Deuce" (Chaotic), "God of Thunder" (Meorpheaus Descends), "Makin' Love" (Demented Tom & Co.), "The Oath" (Equinox), "War Machine" (Crucifix), "Got to Choose" (Weapon Of Death), and "Tears are Falling" (Killer Addiction).

KISS of Death: A SSIK Tribute to KISS: Released in 1999 by Dwell Records, this tribute CD features death metal versions of the following tracks: "Rocket Ride" (From The Depths), "Deuce" (Hostile Intent), "God of Thunder" (Blood Coven), "Strutter" (Shallows Of The Mundane), "Goin' Blind" (Hate Theory), "War Machine" (Acheron), "The Oath" (Equinox), "Cold Gin" (Crematorium), "Strange Ways" (Vile), "I Love It Loud" (Tchort), "Detroit Rock City" (Debauchery), and "Shout It Out Loud" (Scary German Guy).

KISS of Death—A Tribute to KISS: This tribute CD by Pretty Boy Floyd, released October 26, 2010, includes the following tracks: "King of the Night Time World," "Room Service," "I Stole Your Love," "I Love It Loud," "Goin' Blind," "Deuce," "Creatures of the Night," "Detroit Rock City," "Firehouse," "Love Gun," "Shout It Out

Loud," "Christine Sixteen," "Strutter," "Let Me Go, Rock 'n' Roll," and "Black Diamond." Re-released by Cleopatra March 31, 2015.

KISS on Tour Game: Produced by American Publishing Corp. in 1978, this hard-to-find board game came packaged with the following items: 1 game board, 10 City Cards, 15 KISS Cards, 5 Record Cards, 5 Fan Cards, 2 dice, and 4 generic player pieces. The board, which features a band member in concert in each corner, is laid out as a large star, and the Ken Kelly box art is from the *Love Gun* album cover. Players move their game piece from the Record Shop space and go on tour. City spaces include: Dallas, Memphis, Los Angeles, Atlanta, Miami, London, Toronto, New York, Chicago, and Tokyo. Designed for up to four players.

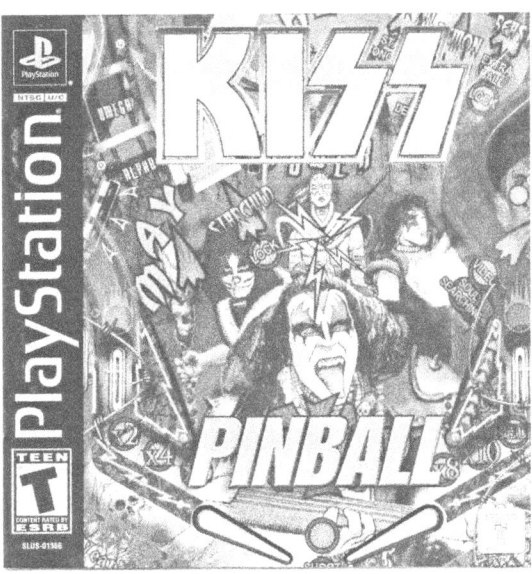

KISS Pinball for Sony's PlayStation video game console features two scrolling tables.

KISS fans can "go on tour" with the band by playing this vintage board game, released by American Publishing Corp. in 1978.

KISS Online: The name of the official KISS website, which is at www.kissonline.com.

KISS Phono *see* **Record Player**

KISS Pinball: Not to be confused with either the Bally or the Stern *KISS* pinball machine, *KISS Pinball* is a PlayStation video game published by Take 2 Interactive April 25, 2001. The game has two scrolling tables—Last Stop Oblivion and Netherworld—and four game modes: novice, regular, arcade, and tournament.

Objectives include collecting weapons and lost souls, getting past security to snag an autograph, lighting PASS to access backstage, shooting a spinner to upgrade record sales, hitting the Statue of Liberty repeatedly to reveal the Destroyer Skull to start 3-ball, spelling MAYHEM to light video mode, discovering hidden power-ups, and locking balls with Gene's tongue (that's not nearly as gross as it sounds).

The player's perspective is directly above each table. As the screen scrolls to follow the ball, you can see approximately one third of the table. Both tables have the standard two-flipper layout, with the ability for players to nudge the table up, left, and right to influence ball movement. Care should be taken not to tilt the machine, so nudge sparingly.

Unfortunately, the game is less fun than it sounds. Load times are long, flipper action is clumsy, scrolling makes aiming the ball difficult, ball physics are out of whack, and the music and sound effects are terrible. Instead of actual KISS tunes, you hear generic guitar, repetitious sounds, and lame voice effects, including the clichéd, unimaginative "Let's get ready to rumble." In short, *KISS Pinball* is a cheaply produced disappointment.

KISS Pre-History: A three-issue biographical series based on interviews with Paul Stanley

KISS Psycho Circus

and Gene Simmons, *KISS Pre-History* was the follow-up to *Hard Rock Comics* #5. Published by Revolutionary, each issue was written by Spike Steffenhagen and drawn by Scott Pentzer, with painted cover art by Scott Jackson. Story titles are as follows: "Picture's Only Begun" (#1), "Set the World On Fire" (#2), and "Hard Times" (#3).

KISS Psycho Circus: Published by Image Comics from August 1997 to June 2000, *KISS Psycho Circus*, written by Brian Holguin, ran 31 issues. According to *The Slings and Arrows Comic Guide* (2003, Slings and Arrows Ltd.), "Godlike versions of the band inhabit the scarred bodies of sad clowns and other performers in the traveling circus [that visits small towns], taking under their wings hurt confused kids.... While they look kind of demonic, they are actually interested in punishing the truly wicked." References to KISS song titles abound. The Gene character is referred to by his actual nickname, the Demon, but Ace is Celestial, Paul is Starbearer, and Peter is King of Beasts. Art is by Angel Medina, Clayton Crain, Kevin Conrad, and Brian Haberlin. Michael Golden drew the first few covers. The issues were compiled into four trade paperbacks: *Psycho Circus, Destroyer, Whispered Scream,* and *Leg & Nigh.*

KISS: Psycho Circus Comic Magazine: Published in 1999 by McFarlane/Medina/Image, this magazine ran for five issues. In addition to reprinting stories from the *KISS Psycho Circus* comic books, it includes such extras as articles about and interviews with the band.

KISS Psycho Circus: The Nightmare Child: Based on characters from Image Comics' *KISS Psycho Circus*, a series that ran from 1997 to 2000, *The Nightmare Child* is a *Doom*-like first-person-shooter for the PC and Sega Dreamcast. Released October 30, 2000, the game puts the four members of a band called Wicked Jester (a reference to Wicked Lester) in a hellish world of hideous creatures, demons, and circus mutants, including bosses. Beginning as a mere mortal, the player must battle said baddies to progressively acquire the powers of the Elder, the supernatural alter-egos of KISS: Demon, Starbearer, Beast King, and Celestial.

According to Michael L. House, former writer for the All Game Guide, there are three types of weapons you can wield: "melee (beast claws, thornblade, twister and punisher), common (zero cannon, magma cannon, windblade and scourge), and ultimate (stargaze, galaxion, spirit lance and draco). In addition to the weaponry, temporary power-ups and instant items such as health, attack, and defense powers are available."

Along with battling enemies, players should assemble Elder armor comprised of gauntlets, boots, a belt, a vest, a plate, and a mask. There are four realms to explore: Water, Fire, Air, and Earth.

According to Jon Thompson, also of the All Game Guide, "None of the levels play differently from the other, and no interesting twists or tricks are brought into play. It's simply 'kill, collect item, kill some more,' and it is a game we've played a number of times before." Further, there's not much KISS in the game. "The music is dismal, rarely even allowing you to hear a KISS song," Thompson said. "Instead, it shoves sub-standard ambient and techno sounds in your ears."

A special Collector's Edition was released for the PC in a lenticular box, with cover art from the four 1978 KISS solo albums. The package also included an official VIP backstage pass and neck chain from the Psycho Circus Tour, a KISS poster signed by all four band members, a limited version of the game's official strategy guide, and a game disc that is signed by each member of the development team.

KISS: Psycho Circus Tour Magazine: Published by Metal Edge in 1999, this one-shot publication features two pull-out posters, vintage and reunion concert photos, an article called "Bruce Fairbairn: The Producer's View," a *Music from "The Elder"* comic strip, interviews with Ace, Gene, Paul, and Peter, fan art, temporary tattoos, and much more.

KISS Records: In 2009, KISS released their 19th studio album, *Sonic Boom*, under their own label, KISS records. Their next album, 2012's *Monster*, was released under the Universal Music Group label.

KISS: Revenge Is Sweet: Written by Joe Stevens, this book was published September 1, 1997, by Omnibus Press. According to the publisher, it "focuses on how four men in black and white paint changed the world of rock and roll," telling of the "triumphs and tragedies, the fights, the personal changes, and the reconciliations." Includes info on the 1996 Reunion Tour, a KISS discography, and more than 100 photos.

KISS: Still on Fire

KISS: Revenge Is Sweet is loaded down with text on and photographs of America's favorite rock band, focusing on their beginnings all the way up to their reunion tour.

KISS: Rock the Nation Live!: Released December 13, 2005, by Image Entertainment, this two-disc DVD set was reviewed by Greg Prato of www.allmusic.com: "This double-DVD set reconstructs the complete set of a KISS 'rock' concert (2003's *KISS Symphony* saw the band collaborate with—a symphony). And in this case, the group's 2004 summer tour is showcased—by combining highlights from shows in Washington, D.C., and Virginia Beach.... From a sound and visual point of view, *Rock the Nation Live* is arguably the finest live KISS DVD to hit the marketplace."

KISS: Satanik Kreatures—Interviews: This unauthorized DVD contains the famous Tom Snyder interview from October 31, 1979, in which Ace Frehley keeps cracking Snyder up with his quips. Ace appears to make Gene and Paul uncomfortable while discussing alcohol and drugs, likewise Peter mentioning his gun collection. "They're toy guns," Gene said. The disc contains several other interviews as well, including some with Gene and Paul from the *Crazy Nights* era. Released in 2006 by Petal Productions.

KISS Satan's Music: Published by Celebrity Comics, a subdivision of Personality Comics, the unauthorized *KISS Satan's Music* ran for two issues in 1992. The biographical text by Richie Prosch (#1) and Mark Stanislowski (#2) is accompanied with illustrations by Nora Tapp and Kenneth Becker.

KISS School of Marketing: 11 Lessons I Learned While Working With KISS: Written by Michael Brandvold, a freelance music industry consultant, *KISS School of Marketing* is an eBook expanded from an article Brandvold wrote that was re-posted by Gene Simmons on his website. "This expanded book includes one additional lesson and a special encore chapter," Brandvold said on his blog. "In addition, I have added some of my favorite photos that I have taken of KISS over the years." Released in 2012. A 2.0 edition with even more content was released as well.

KISS 7" Vinyl Guide: Limited to 400 copies, *KISS 7" Vinyl Guide* by Henk Vant Zand is essentially a checklist in book form of all the seven-inch (45 rpm) KISS singles released from 38 different countries, supplemented by more than 1,700 photos. Includes info on misprints, promos, test prints, acetates, picture discs, colored discs, and the like. Published privately in 2013, this is a valuable resource for hardcore KISS collectors.

KISS Solo: Published by IDW in 2013, *KISS Solo* is a four-issue comic book series in which each band member goes it alone. Issue #1 spotlights the Demon (written by Chris Ryall, art by Angel Medina), #2 the Starchild (written by Tom Waltz, art by Tone Rodriguez), #3 the Celestial (a.k.a. the Spaceman, written by Chris Ryall, art by Alan Robinson), and #4 the Catman (written by Tom Waltz, art by Roberto Castro). Angel Medina provides cover art, but there's also a photo variant cover for each issue. The series was collected into a trade paperback in August of 2013.

KISS Special Wizard Edition: A 16-page promo comic released by Wizard in 1998.

KISS: Still on Fire: Published in the U.K. by Caroline Publishing, *KISS: Still on Fire* (Aug. 31, 1988) was written by Dave Thomas and Anders

Holm. It is a biography of the band with black and white and color photos. Includes discography.

KISS Symphony: Alive IV: Released under the Sanctuary Records label, *KISS Symphony: Alive IV* is the fourth in the series of "Alive" albums, following *Alive!*, *Alive II*, and *Alive III*. It features KISS performing by themselves and with the Melbourne Symphony Orchestra (who wore tuxedos and KISS makeup), as conducted by David Campbell.

There were two editions. The two-disc version was released July 22, 2003. Disc one includes act one and two while disc two includes act three. Act one features KISS by themselves performing "Deuce," "Strutter," "Let Me Go, Rock 'n' Roll," "Lick It Up," "Calling Dr. Love," and "Psycho Circus." Act two features KISS doing an acoustic set with the Melbourne Symphony Ensemble, performing "Beth," "Forever," "Goin' Blind," "Sure Know Something," and "Shandi."

Disc two features KISS with the entire 60-piece Melbourne Symphony Orchestra, performing "Detroit Rock City," "King of the Night Time World," "Do You Love Me?," "Shout It Out Loud," "God of Thunder," "Love Gun," "Black Diamond," "Great Expectations" (featuring the Australian Children's Choir), "I Was Made for Lovin' You," and "Rock and Roll All Nite."

The single-disc edition was released October 7, 2003, and includes: "Deuce," "Lick It Up," and "Calling Dr. Love" from act one; "Beth," "Goin' Blind," and "Shandi" from act two; and "Detroit Rock City," "King of the Night Time World," "Do You Love Me?," "Shout It Out Loud," "God of Thunder," "Love Gun," "Black Diamond," "Great Expectations," and "Rock and Roll All Nite" from act three. Plus, there's a bonus track: "Do You Remember Rock 'n' Roll Radio?"

The songs were recorded at the Etihad Stadium (known at the time as Telstra Dome) in Melbourne, Australia, on February 28, 2003. This was Peter Criss's last album with KISS, and it featured new member Tommy Thayer, dressed as the Spaceman.

KISS Symphony: The DVD: Released September 9, 2003, this is the two-disc home video release of *KISS Symphony: Alive IV*, supplemented by such features as: KISS landing in Melbourne; KISS meeting members of the Melbourne Symphony Orchestra; fans getting ready for the show; an interview with KISS; the MSO putting on KISS makeup; production rehearsal; and a performance of "Sure Know Something" with the MSO on the Australian TV show, *Rove Live*.

KISS, the Auction: On June 25 and 26, 2000, Butterfields, an auction house then owned by eBay, hosted an auction of KISS memorabilia. The sale brought in more than $1.6 million and featured such items as Gene Simmons' axe guitar used on the Creatures of The Night Tour ($40,250) and a set of four original KISS costumes on life-size mannequins from the 1996–97 Alive/Worldwide Tour ($189,500). A 200-page catalogue of the items accompanied the sale, which included more than 800 lots.

KISS: The Early Years: Published November 26, 2002, by Three Rivers Press, *KISS: The Early Years* is a book featuring 250 photos shot by famed rock photographer Waring Abbott between 1974 and 1981, including rare, behind-the-scenes pics of Gene, Paul, Ace, Peter, and Eric Carr. Gene and Paul provide commentary about life on the road, applying makeup, and much more.

"Kiss the Girl Goodbye": Softly sung by Peter Criss with acoustic guitar accompaniment by Stan Penridge, who wrote the song with Criss, "Kiss the Girl Goodbye" is the eighth track on Criss's 1978 KISS solo album. It's the closest thing to "Beth" on the record, with Criss mourning the fact that he and his girl will have to be apart. The lyric is hopeful, however, as he promises he'll love her even more when he gets back.

KISS—The Hottest Band in the Land: Written by Michael Heatley, this obscure book was published by UFO Music in November of 1996. It features 80 pages of facts, history, stories, and color photos.

KISS—The Medley: A Dance Orgasm: Released in Japan in 1998 by DeDance Records/AvexTrax, this tribute album features dance versions of the following KISS songs: "Shout It Out Loud," "Lick It Up," "Heaven's On Fire," "Shock Me," "Love Gun," "Christine Sixteen," "God of Thunder," "Strutter," "Coming Home," "Rock Bottom," "Love Her All I Can," "Then She Kissed Me," "Let Me Go, Rock 'n' Roll" "Parasite," "Deuce," "Black Diamond," "New York Groove," "She," "Watchin' You," "Got to Choose," "Nothin' to Lose," "Tomorrow," "2000 Man," "Tonight You Belong To Me," "I Was Made for Lovin' You," "Rock and Roll All Nite," and "I Was Made for Lovin'

You," the latter of which is a house-mix, hidden bonus track. The Canadian version was released as *Then They Kissed Me—A Dance Orgasm* and does not include the bonus song.

KISS: The Official Story: Written by official KISS biographer Peggy Tomarkin, who also wrote KISS tour books and fan club newsletters under the pseudonym of Bob Steele, this book is a chronology of the band from 1972 to 1980. It was published in 1981.

KISS: The Real Story, Authorized: Written by Peggy Tomarkin, *KISS: The Real Story, Authorized* was distributed by Dell Publishing in March of 1980. It begins with several pages of color photos, followed by a listing of important dates in the band's history accompanied by text and monochromatic and black-and-white photos. Here's an example of one of the shorter entries:

March 28, 1974

The Tour is underway. Exhausting. Exhilarating. (Can it be both?) "Nothin' to Lose" was released. The 1st KISS single. Come on deejays—play it!

In addition, the book contains reprints of concert posters and vintage articles, such as a *New York Times Magazine* feature by Colette Dowling called "An Outrage Called KISS."

KISS—The Second Coming: This DVD documentary, released in 1998, chronicles the reunion of the four original KISS members. It begins with a brief overview of the band before the reunion, followed by Peter Criss reuniting with KISS for a song at a fan convention, Peter and Ace Frehley joining the band for the *MTV Unplugged* concert, behind-the-scenes footage of the reunion tour (with some concert footage), and a promotion for the *Psycho Circus* CD. Written, produced, and directed by Tommy Thayer.

Kiss This: A Main Man Records Tribute to KISS: Released in 2003 by Main Man Records, this tribute album features music by a variety of acts. Tracks include: "Speedin' Back to My Baby" (the Donnas), "Beth" (The Youth Ahead), "Rip It Out" (Frankenstein 3000), "Do You Love Me?" (Shawn Mars), "Plaster Caster" (Ze Malibu Kids), "Love Her All I Can" (Flat Morrison), "I Want You" (All Boro Kings), "Getaway" (George Is Dead), "C'Mon and Love Me" (Digger Phelps), "Parasite" (Hat Trick of Misery), "Cold Gin" (Billy Rubin), "Detroit Rock City" (Gene Walk Group), "Got to Choose" (the Electric Magic Sideshow), "She" (Stag), "I Stole Your Love," (Spank Daddy), "Heaven's On Fire" (Project C9), "Hard Luck Woman" (Luzer), "Makin' Love" (Tick Non Stop), "Coming Home" (Cryptkeeper Five), "Let Me Go, Rock 'n' Roll" (Blister), "God of Thunder" (Slack), "Hotter Than Hell" (Vulgar Sandwich), "Nothin' to Lose" (Mutant Monster Beach Party), and "All the Way" (Frankenstein 3000).

KISS Tour: Sometimes called the First Tour, the KISS Tour was the band's first tour in support of an album—their 1974 self-titled debut. From December 31, 1973, to October 4, 1974, KISS played 84 shows throughout the U.S. and Canada. After the first couple of nights, Paul abandoned his bandit mask makeup in favor of the now-iconic star. Stage props included fire engine lights, a drum riser, sparkling drumsticks, Gene spitting blood and breathing fire, a lighted KISS logo, Ace's smoking guitar, and flamethrowers.

Band lineup: Paul Stanley, Ace Frehley, Gene Simmons, and Peter Criss. Headlining acts: 10cc, Aerosmith, Argent, Billy Preston, Blue Öyster Cult, the "All New" Fleetwood Mac, Iggy & The Stooges, the James Gang, Kathi McDonald, Manfred Mann's Earth Band, Nazareth, the New York Dolls, the Quicksilver Messenger Service, Redbone, Renaissance, Rory Gallagher, Rush, Savoy Brown, Silverhead, Suzi Quatro, Teenage Lust, and Uriah Heep. Opening acts: 13th Floor, Barbarossa, Chris Jagger, Conqueror Worm, Fat Chance, Flight, Fludd, Flying Saucer, Isis, Island, Les Variations, Max Onion, Michael Fennely, Mike Quatro, Mojo Boogie Band, Mood Jga Jga, Outlaws, Redbone, Ritual, Ronny Legg, Ross, Rush, Silverhead, Smack Dab, Sweetwater, Thunderhead, and Wizzard. Average Attendance: 2,645.

Followed by: Hotter Than Hell Tour.

KISS Trivia Challenge: This PC game was released in 1999 by WizardWorks. In a May 1999 press release, Paul Rinde, senior vice president of Product Acquisition and Development for WizardWorks, said, "KISS is one of the greatest rock 'n' roll bands of all time, and they have a huge worldwide following of dedicated fans who want to learn everything possible about the band. Our upcoming KISS title will give those fans the information they've been looking for with more than 8,000 trivia questions that will challenge even the most seasoned KISS follower." The game includes video clips, full-length videos, and exclusive voice-over narration by Ace, Gene, Paul, and Peter.

KISS Unplugged: *MTV Unplugged*, showcasing musicians and bands doing live acoustic performances, began in 1989. KISS appeared on the series October 31, 1995, sounding surprisingly good—at least it was a surprise to some of their critics, who often claim KISS is all flash and no substance.

Gene, Paul, Bruce Kulick, and Eric Singer played the majority of the set, but Ace and Peter joined in near the end for the final quartet of songs, marking the first time in 15 years that the original four members had played together onstage. The excitement exhibited by the crowd helped convince Paul and Gene that a full-blown reunion tour would be a good, marketable idea, something they were probably already thinking of anyway (see "Alive/Worldwide Tour").

MTV aired just 11 songs, but the home video release featured 15: "Comin' Home" (with "a feverish and electric opening that gets the crowd on its feet in a hurry," said Shawn M. Haney of allmusic.com), "Plaster Caster," "Goin' Blind," "Do You Love Me?," "Domino," "Sure Know Something," "A World Without Heroes," "Rock Bottom," "See You Tonight," "I Still Love You," "Every Time I Look at You," "2,000 Man," "Beth," "Nothin' to Lose," and a rousing and unique version of "Rock and Roll All Nite" featuring all four original members taking turns singing verses of the iconic anthem. Both the VHS and DVD versions included a behind-the-scenes documentary as well.

The requisite *KISS Unplugged* CD, released March 12, 1996, reached #15 on the *Billboard* 200 chart. A bonus track, "Got to Choose," only appeared on the vinyl and CD releases in Japan.

KISS (Virgin Modern Icons): Introduced by Sylvie Simmons (a music journalist unrelated to Gene), *KISS (Virgin Modern Icons)* was published by St. Martin's Press in February of 1998. According to the publisher, "The career of 70s band KISS is the focus of this book. It looks at their success from 1972, when the band was formed, the release of their album *Alive!*, and the moral outrage and critical hostility they attracted."

KISS World: A prospective traveling amusement park and museum conceived by Gene Simmons years ago. Unfortunately, it never came to pass.

KISS Xtreme Close Up: Released on VHS August 18, 1992, *KISS Xtreme Close Up* is a documentary featuring interviews with Paul, Gene, Eric Singer, and Bruce Kulick. It also includes excerpts from numerous videos and concerts spanning 1975 to 1992, along with full versions of the following videos: "Unholy" (1992), "Love 'Em & Leave 'Em" (1976), "Hard Luck Woman" (1976), "Rise to It" (1989), "Hide Your Heart" (1989), "Forever" (1989), and "I Just Wanna" (1992). It was re-released in 2005 on DVD as part of *KISS—Konfidential & Xtreme Close Up*.

The KISS Years: Written by Barry Levine, *The KISS Years*, published by Studio Chikara in April of 1997, is a slick, full-color photo book featuring more than 200 images of classic KISS shot by Levine. The book features many familiar and unfamiliar highlights from the *Destroyer*, *Love Gun*, *Music from "The Elder,"* and Alive/Worldwide Tour 1996–1997 eras, including pics from the famous Empire State Building and starry background shoots.

In the afterword to the book, Levine wrote: "Throughout my years photographing celebrities in the entertainment industry, shooting KISS was the most fun, satisfying experience of them all.

The KISS Years is loaded down with more than 20 years of photographs taken by definitive KISS photographer Barry Levine.

The group's unique persona and identifiable image helped me transcend all photographic barriers established in the medium. I gained the ability to design lighting, props, and sets which, eventually, influenced other photographers and inspired me to produce motion pictures."

KISS Your Face Makeup Kit: Packaged with a 16-page instruction booklet, this product mistakenly says on the front of the box that it "contains all you need to make yourself up like Gene, Paul, Criss, Ace, or your own design." A correctly stated version was released as well, containing the word "Peter" instead of "Criss." Both versions featured oil-based makeups. A third version with water-soluble makeup was released after some consumers complained of allergic reactions. Released by Remco in 1978, the KISS Your Face Makeup Kit was the first official KISS makeup set, but others by different companies followed, including a reunion-era Techni-Face/Paper Magic Group kit from 1997 and a *Sonic Boom* set released by Rubies.

KISSED BY KISS: Written by Andrea Ciccomartino, this Italian book comes with a KISS tribute CD that features 22 tracks, including songs by such acts as Shockproof, Wicked Starrr, and Virus. Published in June of 2014.

KISSES: Published in 1992 by Spoof Comics, which is a subdivision of Personality Comics, *KISSES* is an unauthorized one-shot comic book featuring the members of KISS as females. Written and drawn by Allan Jacobsen, with inks by Mike Halbleib, Kenneth Becker, and Keith Quinn.

KISSFAQ.com: This in-depth website features news, message boards, a discography, and more.

"Kissin' Time": In 1974, KISS released *KISS*, their eponymous debut album for Casablanca Records. Unfortunately, the record wasn't selling well. To help give it a boost, Casablanca founder Neil Bogart had KISS, much to their chagrin, record a lyrically modified (by producer Kenny Kerner and others) version of "Kissin' Time," the 1959 hit single sung by Bobby Rydell and written by Bernie Lowe and Kal Mann. Gene, Paul, and Peter each sing lead on the song, which is catchy and gimmicky in its naming of various U.S. cities.

"Kissin' Time" was released as a single on May 10, 1974, and added to *KISS* (as the sixth track) in July of that year. While it only reached #83 on the *Billboard* charts, it helped publicize the band, leading to a KISS-sponsored kissing contest (see "The Great Kiss Off") and appearances on *The Mike Douglas Show* and ABC's *In Concert*.

Kissin' Time: A Tribute to KISS: Released in 1996 by Tribute Records, this tribute album features KISS songs recorded primarily by Scandinavian bands. Tracks include: "War Machine" (Transport League), "Calling Dr. Love" (Blakk Totem), "Deuce" (Million), "Flaming Youth" (Kisses From The Past), "I Want You" (Mrs. Hippie), "I Stole Your Love" (Breakfast Conspiracy), "The Oath" (Snowy Shaw), "Larger Than Life" (Rock Soldiers), "New York Groove" (Mummy Dearest), "C'mon and Love Me" (Dressed To Kill, the only non–Scandinavian band on the disc), "Makin' Love" (Zodiac's Fate), "Let Me Go, Rock 'n' Roll" (Kiss Of Thunder), and "Almost Human" (Clean Cut Clan & Mobile Whorehouse).

KISSIN' TIME: Canada's Tribute to KISS: This CD, released October 31, 2012, by Keep It Live Records, features the following tracks by a variety of Canadian bands: "King of the Night Time World" (Gord Prior), "War Machine" (West Memphis Suicide), "C'mon and Love Me" (Bobnoxious), "Goin' Blind" (The Buffalo Brothers), "Lick It Up" (The Salads), "I Was Made for Lovin' You" (R.E.D), "Deuce" (Before The Damned), "Love Gun" (Curtis), "100,000 Years" (Grim-Skunk), "Hard Luck Woman" (Sarah Smith), "Detroit Rock City" (Tracenine), "God Gave Rock 'N' Roll to You" (Zealots Desire), and "Rock and Roll All Nite" (Spiro Papadatos).

KISSMONSTER: Found at www.kissmonster.com, this detailed website features history, touring info, a discography, multimedia, and more.

KISSNation: Published by Marvel Comics in 1996, *KISSNation* is a one-shot comic book featuring a story by Gene Simmons, Mort Todd, and Stan Lee, with interior art by Nathaniel Palant and cover art by Dave Chlystek. The real-life KISS find themselves face to face with their super-powered counterparts. Dr. Strange and the X-Men guest-star. The issue also includes KISS articles, rare photos, and a poster by KISS album artist Ken Kelly.

KISSology—The Ultimate KISS Collection, Vol. 1: 1974–1977: This two-disc DVD boxed was released October 31, 2006.

Disc one includes the following appearances and performances: "Acrobat"—Lone Beach Auditorium (Previously Unreleased Track), February 17, 1974; ABC's *In Concert*, March 29, 1974; *The Mike Douglas Show*, April 29, 1974; Winterland, January 31, 1975; *The Midnight Special*, April 1, 1975; KISS Alive! Promo Clips, 1975; *Documentary: Cadillac, Michigan*, October 9 and 10, 1975; and Cobo Hall, January 26, 1976.

Disc two includes: *So It Goes*, August 1976; *The Paul Lynde Halloween Special*, October 29, 1976; Budokan Hall, April 2, 1977; *Don Kirshner's Rock Concert*, May 28, 1977; and The Summit, September 2, 1977. Includes a 20-page booklet and an iron-on that is a replica of KISS's "Spring Tour '75" backstage pass.

First pressings also contain one of three different bonus discs: one released through Walmart (Capitol Centre, Dec. 20, 1977), one through Best Buy (Cobo Arena, Jan. 25, 1976), and one through Amazon and other major retailers (Madison Square Garden, Feb. 18, 1977).

KISSology—The Ultimate KISS Collection, Vol. 2: 1978–1991: This three-disc DVD boxed was released August 14, 2007.

Disc one includes: *Land of Hype and Glory* excerpt, January 10, 1978; *KISS in Attack of the Phantoms* movie, 1979; and *The Tomorrow Show with Tom Snyder* excerpt, October 31, 1979.

Disc two includes: "Shandi" music video, 1980; CNN interview with Peter Criss, September 24, 1980; *Countdown* excerpt, September 21, 1980; *Rockpop*, September 13, 1980, featuring "She's so European" and "Talk to Me"; *KISS Invades Australia* documentary, November 1980; Sydney Showground concert, November 22, 1980; *Fridays*, January 15, 1982, featuring "The Oath," "A World Without Heroes," and "I"; and *Top Pop*, November 1982, featuring "I Love it Loud."

Disc three includes: Maracana Stadium concert, June 18, 1983; *MTV Special: KISS Unmasking* interview, September 18, 1983; Cascais Hall concert, October 11, 1983; The Spectrum concert, December 18, 1987; The Palace of Auburn Hills concert, October 14, 1990; *Day in Rock*, November 25, 1991; and "God Gave Rock 'N' Roll to You II" music video, 1991.

First pressings also contain one of three different bonus discs: Nippon Budokan concert, April 21, 1988 (various retailers); Capital Centre concert, Largo, MD, July 8, 1979 (Walmart, Sam's Club, Amazon); and The Ritz concert, August 13, 1988 (Best Buy).

KISSology—The Ultimate KISS Collection, Vol. 3: 1992–2000: This four-disc DVD boxed set, featuring various appearances and performances, hit stores December 18, 2007.

Disc one includes: The Palace of Auburn Hills, November 27, 1992; *MTV Unplugged: Behind the Scenes*, 1995; and *MTV Unplugged*, 1995.

Disc two includes: Tiger Stadium, June 28, 1996; *MTV VMA Performance*, Brooklyn Bridge, September 4, 1996; and Dodger Stadium, October 31, 1998, part one.

Disc three includes: Dodger Stadium, October 31, 1998, part two; *Detroit Rock City* Premiere Party, August 9, 1999; and *The Last KISS*, Continental Airlines Arena, June, 27, 2000.

Disc four includes: Coventry, December 12, 1973.

First pressings also contain one of three different bonus discs: KROQ Weenie Roast, Irvine Meadows, California, June 15, 1996 (various retailers); Pacaembú Stadium, August 27, 1994 (Best Buy); and Madison Square Garden, July 27, 1996 (Walmart). Fans who pre-ordered the DVD set during VH1 Classic's *24 Hours of KISSmas* marathon, which aired December 7 and 8, 2007, got a bonus disc featuring the 1999 feature film, *Detroit Rock City*.

KISSopolis: Billing itself as "The Center of All Things KISS," KISSopolis, founded in 2009, is a website featuring news, photos, tour information, and more: www.kissopolis.com.

KISS-OPOLY: Released in 2003, *KISS-OPOLY* is a KISS version of *Monopoly*, the famous board game that dates back to 1903. Game tokens include Paul and Gene's guitars, Gene's boot, Paul's fire hat, a bag of money, and the KISS Army logo. Board spaces have been altered as well, featuring such things as the solo albums, the original KISS pinball machine, and "Detroit Rock City." Card examples include: "You broke a string on the Starchild's guitar. Pay $50," "You took 2nd Place in the Girls of KISS Beauty Contest. Collect $100," and "You're in the Army now! All tokens advance to All Access Pass," among others.

KISSteria: A one-hour A&E special, *KISSteria* aired on July 20, 2010. Advertising for the program was as follows: "For the first time in their 35-year career, rock icons KISS give you an all access pass to the Alive 35 Australian tour. When Paul and Gene decide to launch a spontaneous mini-tour with only one week's notice, the entire KISS family must scramble to make it a reality. Malfunctioning pyrotechnics, faulty flying rigs, and missing drummers are the least of their challenges."

Paul and Gene guide much of the program, as does KISS manager Doc McGhee. Eric Singer and Tommy Thayer are featured as well. Stanley talks more about his painting than probably anyone cares to hear about, and the show seems more like reality television than a documentary film, which is not surprising since it was produced by the Greif Company, co-producer of *Gene Simmons: Family Jewels*. Regardless, it is kind of fun, and most diehard KISS fans will "lick it up."

KISStory: The first printing of *KISStory*, a massive 440-page hardcover weighing nine pounds, was published in 1994. It was signed by Gene, Paul, Bruce Kulick, and Eric Singer. The second printing, published to cash in on the 1996 Reunion Tour, was signed by the original band (rumor has it that some copies of this version were signed by autopen). Unsigned versions were produced as well. Each book is numbered and comes in a black slipcase.

The book, authored by Jeff Kitts, features historical text on the band and is lavishly illustrated with rare photos, newspaper articles, reviews, magazine covers, sketches of costumes and stage shows that were never produced, and much more. There are a few errors in the book (such as stating *KISS Killers* has five new songs instead of four), and the binding on the first printing is fragile, but this is a coffee table book that all hardcore KISS fans should own.

KISStory II: Toys, Games and Girls: Like *KISStory*, *KISStory II* is a massive hardcover book housed in a black slipcase. However, instead of focusing on history and rare photos of the band, it's almost exclusively devoted to merchandising, which essentially makes it a super expensive, out-of-date catalogue. Even so, if you're into KISS collecting, but don't have access to the thousands of items produced over the years, it's neat to see many of them in one book. *KISStory II: Toys, Games and Girls*, published by Warner in 2000, includes a foldout poster, and some copies were signed by Gene Simmons.

Kisstory Science Theatre: You can access this rather informal KISS podcast via kisstory.podomatic.com.

Klein, Gene: Before changing his last name, Gene Simmons was Gene Klein (before that he was Chaim Witz). When he was writing, publishing, and doing art for comic book and science fiction fanzines during the 1960s, he was working under the name of Gene Klein.

Knight, Holly: Songwriter Hall of Fame inductee Holly Knight co-wrote a number of KISS songs, including "Hide Your Heart" and "I Pledge Allegiance to the State of Rock & Roll." She also played keyboards on *Unmasked*.

Knights in Satan's Service: As KISS got more and more popular during the mid-to-late 1970s, many religious fundamentalists—especially in the southern Bible belt states—became convinced that the members of KISS were Satanic, especially Gene Simmons, with his demonic makeup and fire-breathing and blood-spitting stage antics. Around 1976, rumors spread that KISS was an acronym for Knights in Satan's Service. Variations included Knights in Service of Satan, Kings in Satan's Service, and Kids in Satan's Service. The truth behind the band's name is far less colorful. One day in 1973, while Gene, Paul, and Peter were driving around, trying to come up with a new name for their band (they went by Wicked Lester at the time), Paul suggested KISS, and it was quickly agreed upon. KISS has always been unapologetically hedonistic, but rumors of Satanism were greatly exaggerated.

***Knights in Satan's Service* (2003):** Released on the Jam Factory label in August of 2003, this unusual tribute album, set to an electro beat, mixes KISS commercials, quotes by band members, and samplings of KISS songs, resulting in a cacophony of KISS sounds. Tracks include: "This Kiss Planet," "Satan's Service," "Numbing Themselves," "Kiss Radio," "Kill the Power," "Drooling Blood," "Like a Tree," "Goontown," "Phantom 2000," "Heavy Metal Beatles," "Sure Know Something," "Million Albums," and "Take the Cake."

***Knights in Satan's Service* (2014):** Produced by Walter Carlos and Stephen Finley for

Artificial Head Records, this tribute CD was released September 6, 2014. Tracks include: "Black Diamond" (Jody Seabody and the Whirls), "She" (Linus Pauling Quartet), "Parasite" (Clockpole), "Strutter" (the Freakouts), "Almost Human" (Funeral Horse), "I Stole Your Love" (the Hangouts), "Lick It Up"/"Tears Are Falling" (Hell City Kings), "Deuce" (The Swamps), "Goin' Blind" (Jealous Creatures), "All Hell's Breakin' Loose" (Stout City Luchadores), "Rip It Out" (Cornish Game Hen), and "Save Your Love" (the Ex-Optimists). Also released in four different colors of vinyl: red, blue, purple, and green.

Kramer, Barry: Barry Kramer was publisher and owner of the late, lamented *Creem* magazine, an early supporter of KISS. Kramer died in 1981.

Kramer, Eddie: A recording producer and engineer, Eddie Kramer has worked with the likes of the Beatles, Led Zeppelin, the Rolling Stones, Jimi Hendrix, David Bowie, and Eric Clapton. For KISS, he produced the band's five-song demo that won them their first recording contract. He also produced *Alive!*, *Rock and Roll Over*, *Love Gun*, *Alive II*, *Double Platinum*, *Alive III*, and Ace Frehley's 1978 solo LP. Further, Kramer played piano on "Christine Sixteen."

Krampf, Craig: Craig Krampf played drums on tracks 6–9 of Paul Stanley's 1978 KISS solo album. He also worked with such acts as Steve Perry, Alice Cooper, Alabama, and Melissa Etheridge.

Kravitz, Lenny: On *Kiss My Ass: Classic KISS Regrooved*, Lenny Kravitz (with Stevie Wonder) covered "Deuce." Kravitz, who has said he grew up listening to KISS, is famous for such songs as "Fly Away" and "Are You Gonna Go My Way."

KROQ 4th Annual Weenie Roast: The first show of the Alive/Worldwide Tour, in which the original four KISS members reunited, was a June 15, 1996, warmup for the KROQ 4th Annual Weenie Roast at the Irvine Meadows Amphitheater in Irvine, California. The warmup was sorely needed as the band experienced numerous technical issues.

Krupa, Gene: Peter Criss grew up idolizing jazz and big band drummer Gene Krupa, a legend in the field. On his website, Criss said: "He was my idol. I got to talk to him and he really liked me. He gave me lessons for about six months. He was great to take the time out to teach me. He once said to me, 'You got it kid, You really got it. I've never seen anyone who wants it so bad, so I'll take the time out to teach you.' Today when I do a drum solo I have that Drum Boogie Sound and nobody uses it. The kids go wild but it's not original. I'm doing something that was done in 1935."

Kulick, Bob: Born Robert J. Kulick in Brooklyn, New York on January 16, 1950, Bob Kulick auditioned for KISS as lead guitarist in January of 1973, right before Ace Frehley. Paul, Gene, and Peter were impressed with Kulick, but found Frehley to be a better fit for their eccentric act.

In *KISS: Behind the Mask—The Official Authorized Biography*, Gene said Kulick "didn't have the look; he had a beard, and he was a little chubbier back then." According to some sources, Kulick didn't like the idea of wearing makeup.

Kulick kept in touch with KISS, and years later, when the band was having trouble with a drinking, drugging Ace during the recording of *Alive II*, he was brought in to play guitar (uncredited) on three of the album's five new studio tracks: "All American Man," "Larger Than Life," and "Rockin' in the USA." Kulick also played on *Unmasked*, *Killers*, and *Paul Stanley*. In 1989, he played on Stanley's solo tour.

Some sources say Kulick played on *Creatures of the Night*, but none of his work went on the album—it only appeared in outtakes. Gene wanted him to play on his 1978 solo album, but Kulick was busy working with Paul on his. In *KISS: Behind the Mask*, Kulick said, "Gene and Paul looked at me like I was their savior—whenever they needed anyone to plop some lead guitar on a record, it was 'Let's call Bob.'"

For the recording of *Alive II*, Kulick said: "Ace was in the lounge on the floor while I was doing solos. They ascertained that Ace was incapable of giving them what they needed in the timeframe that they needed it. They had a deadline. So they brought in the guy who they knew could play, who they knew all along was the better player but they picked the guy who fit the band better imagewise."

Kulick has played for a number of other acts over the years, including Meat Loaf, Michael Bolton, Lou Reed, Alice Cooper, W.A.S.P., and Diana Ross. In a 2011 interview published on www.metal-rules.com, Kulick said: "The Diana Ross thing, that was Gene. Gene calling me, 'You want to play on Diana Ross's record? Come to the studio in an hour. I've got this setup for you.' I went down there and played. And then came back tomorrow for the next song. Is she happy, she totally is, she's stoked and over the moon about it."

When KISS was looking for a new guitarist in 1984 because Mark St. John got sick, Kulick recommended his brother, Bruce, who played for the band until 1996.

Kulick, Bruce: Born Bruce Howard Kulick on December 12, 1953, in Brooklyn, New York, Bruce Kulick was the first KISS member to not use a stage name. While subbing for Mark St. John during the *Animalize* tour, he officially replaced the ailing guitarist on December 8, 1984, remaining with the band until 1996. He played lead guitar on five KISS studio albums: *Asylum*, *Crazy Nights*, *Hot in the Shade*, *Revenge*, and *Carnival of Souls: The Final Sessions*. He also played on *Alive III* and *KISS Unplugged*.

The younger brother of Bob Kulick, who had tried out for KISS in 1973, Bruce spent 1975 to 1978 touring with such acts as George McCrae, Andrea True, and Meat Loaf. Late in 1978, he formed Blackjack with vocalist Michael Bolton (then Michael Bolotin), releasing two albums—1979's *Blackjack* and 1980's *Worlds Apart*—before breaking up. Kulick played on three Michael Bolton solo albums as well: *Michael Bolton* (1983), *Everybody's Crazy* (1985), and *The Hunger* (1987). Kulick also played guitar on Billy Squier's 1980 album, *The Tale of the Tape*, and on the Good Rats' 1981 album, *Great American Music*.

Kulick joined KISS as a matter of convenience for the band, as well as for his guitar playing expertise. When St. John fell ill, KISS didn't want to go through the laborious process of finding another guitarist—a stranger—so they hired Bruce, who they had met through Bob, and who had already played lead on "Lonely Is the Hunter" and "Murder in High Heels" from *Animalize*.

In *Face the Music: A Life Exposed*, Paul Stanley wrote about Mr. Kulick: "Bruce was a real mensch, and very funny. If you asked him how he was, he would give you a 10-minute dissertation about how his fuzz box wasn't working right, or describe his upset stomach in details better left unspoken, or complain about how he had gas before. But he was a terrific guitar player and a great team player."

In *KISS: Behind the Mask—The Official Authorized Biography*, Kulick spoke about collaborating with Paul and Gene: "As a guitar player Paul's got great feel, especially for KISS music. I liked working with Paul more so than Gene on solos. Gene would sometimes come up with something out of left field, but Paul was very clear about his ideas.... Writing with Paul and Gene is interesting. They're both very different and very difficult in their own way.... Paul and Gene always compete. I think it's healthy ... they compete and it makes them strive to do better."

On episode 14 of *Three Sides of the Coin*, Kulick revealed that he was allowed to be himself in KISS. "Much as we did the classic songs, I was never told to really be Ace or play exactly like Ace," he said. "In my 12 years [with the band] even my style changed, but there's a certain identifiable sound that is different from Ace, different from what Tommy does now in the band.... I like to say I waved the flag for the non-makeup era."

Kulick has released three solo albums: 2001's *Audio Dog*, 2003's *Transformer*, and 2010's *BK3*. As of this writing, he plays guitar for classic rock act Grand Funk Railroad, a gig he's had since 2001. He's married to Lisa Kulick, whom he wed January 4, 2014.

Lacey, Steve: Steve Lacey played guitar on Gene Simmons' "Radioactive" and Paul Stanley's "Love in Chains."

"Ladies in Waiting": "Ladies in Waiting," in which Gene Simmons compares picking up girls to making selections at a meat market, is the third track on *Dressed to Kill*. It's in stark contrast to the previous song on the record, "Two Timer," where Simmons complains about an unfaithful girlfriend. Perhaps shopping in the "meat market" is in response to getting cheating on. Or it's just another raunchy (if catchy, particularly the chorus) song early in the life of KISS.

Ladies of the Night: A Historical and Personal Perspective on the Oldest Profession in the World: Written by Gene Simmons (with Julie McCarron), this book was published December 9, 2008, by Phoenix Books. The *Publishers Weekly* called it an "entertaining if sometimes simplistic short overview of prostitution.... The book doesn't cover what Simmons admits is the dark side of prostitution, focusing primarily on one of his favorite issues: money."

"Ladies Room": "Ladies Room" is a fitting follow-up to Gene Simmons' "Calling Dr. Love." Both feature naughty lyrics by KISS' resident demonic bassist, who implores a jewel in the rough to meet him in the women's restroom for a sexual encounter. Paul Elliott, author of *KISS: Hotter Than Hell*, wrote that the song is "livelier than 'Calling Dr. Love,' with Simmons' bass upfront on a heavy riff and more rattling of the cowbell from [Peter] Criss." Written in a rehearsal studio, "Ladies Room" is the fourth track on *Rock and Roll Over*.

Land of Hype and Glory: Hosted by Edwin Newman, *Land of Hype and Glory*, an NBC special that aired January 19, 1978, was the first news program to view KISS in a serious light. Newman gives an overview of the history of KISS, backed by footage of the band posing for photos, applying makeup, appearing at a radio station, and performing in concert. Merchandising and KISS giving blood for *Marvel Comics Super Special* #1 are shown as well.

Newman, who discusses the business of rock music in general, also interviews the band. Paul says, "I think KISS is more exciting than four slobs walking onstage who need a shave … we're putting glamor back into rock and roll … we try to make it as colorful as possible." Gene says, "Our music is intentionally easily accessible. We don't try to make the music too complex and too self-indulgent … so that our fans can understand it … that's the kind of music we like to play."

LaPiere, Georganne: Actress Georganne LaPiere, who played Heather Webber on *General Hospital*, is Cher's sister. Paul Stanley dated her for more than a year during the 1980s.

"Larger Than Life": Peter Criss really pounds the skins on "Larger Than Life," one of many KISS songs in which Gene Simmons brags about his sexual prowess with women. Bob Kulick, subbing for Ace Frehley, turns in a blistering solo while Paul Stanley's distinctive backup vocals help carry the song. The third track on side four of *Alive II*, "Larger Than Life," like the other four songs on that side of the album, was a new studio track for the double LP.

Las Vegas Residency: In the fall of 2014, beginning November 5 and ending on the 23rd, KISS played nine dates at The Joint, one of the music venues inside the Las Vegas Hard Rock Hotel & Casino. Speaking about the engagement to *Forbes*, Paul Stanley said: "What was exciting with the residency is that we didn't have to create a stage that had to be taken down nightly. This is one of the smaller venues we've played in decades. The challenge was to create a bigger show in a smaller venue, and I think we've done a great job."

Josh Bell of *Las Vegas Weekly* wrote this about the November 5 show: "The KISS performing a mini-residency at The Joint is the best KISS of 2014, even if it's not close to the best KISS of the band's career … the stage show was every bit the over-the-top KISS extravaganza, barely downsized for the smaller venue … there was music, too, although not as much of it as you might expect from a band whose catalog spans four decades.… Stanley and Simmons may no longer be the best (Stanley mumbled his way through most of his vocals, although Simmons' voice sounded strong), but no one can say that they aren't still trying their best."

"Last Chance": The 12th and final track on *Monster*, "Last Chance," which is about living life to the fullest before you die (a common theme with KISS), was written by Paul, Gene, and Tommy Thayer. It's not a particularly memorable song to finish an album, but it's no turkey either. It's loud and tightly produced like most of the rest of *Monster*.

The Last KISS: On October 7, 2000, Showtime aired *The Last KISS*, a pay-per-view special. It was filmed live at the Continental Airlines Arena in East Rutherford, New Jersey on June 27, 2000. The concert, featuring one of the last performances by the original lineup of Ace, Paul, Gene, and Peter, is available on *KISSology—The Ultimate KISS Collection, Vol. 3: 1992–2000*.

Late Show with David Letterman: KISS performed "Modern Day Delilah" on the *Late Show with David Letterman* on October 6, 2009. After the show, Letterman went onstage to greet the band, and Gene Simmons licked his ear. On October 10, 2012, KISS performed "Shout It Out Loud" on the program. *See also*: "KISS: Live on Letterman."

Led Zeppelin: The original KISS lineup has cited Led Zeppelin as an influence many times, often playing covers of the band's songs during sound checks. Comprised of Robert Plant (vocals), Jimmy Page (guitar), John Paul Jones (bass, keyboards), and John Bonham (drums), Led Zeppelin was formed in London, England in 1968. They broke up in 1980, the year after Bonham died. Some of their signature songs include "Stairway to Heaven," "Black Dog," "Whole Lotta Love," and "Rock and Roll."

Paul Stanley, who has played various Led Zeppelin songs during his solo concerts, spoke about the band during a brief interview in October of 2012 at the New York City premiere of *Celebration Day*, the Led Zeppelin concert film. "They wrote the book," he said. "They are the reason most bands are here today. Their DNA is in everything that everybody does. They were so innovative and were such visionaries."

Lee, Stan: Former President and Chairman of Marvel Comics, Stan Lee co-created and wrote the original stories for such legendary super-heroes as Spider-Man, Thor, the Hulk, Iron Man, and the X-Men. During Lee's reign, Marvel published the first KISS comic books, including appearances in *Howard the Duck* and issues 1 and 5 of *Marvel Comics Super Special*. Lee still works with Marvel and appears in cameos for many of their live action films.

In 2012, longtime comic book junkie Gene Simmons spoke to noisecreep.com about his admiration for Stan "The Man" Lee. "I started reading Marvel Comics in my youth, like many millions of young boys," he said. "For me, Stan Lee's stories had a profound, empowering quality that continues to this day. I witnessed superheroes with flaws. With self-esteem issues. With doubts about themselves. And I connected. I was so awed by the stories and the mythology of Stan's superheroes, that I wrote him a long letter, comparing Marvel's heroes to Greek Mythology and their gods. And Stan Lee wrote back a postcard. I remember it, as if it happened yesterday. 'You will do great things,' he said. And he signed it Stan Lee. I felt as if I was touched by the very Gods of Olympus at that moment. And that feeling as never left me."

Lee, Will: Will Lee played bass on three songs on *Ace Frehley*: "Ozone," "I'm in Need of Love," and "Wiped-Out." In an August 20, 2013, interview published on www.kissasylum.com, Lee spoke about the record: "It seems Ace took people by surprise because everyone—from the band to the label—wasn't sure what he was going to bring to the table with his solo album. And Ace ended up turning in this great, guitar-heavy album with lots of attitude and some slamming tracks…. And on top of that, he scored the lone hit from the solo albums with "New York Groove."

Leejak, Ron: When Gene Simmons had to fire Steve Coronel from Wicked Lester because the brass at Epic didn't like his guitar playing, studio musician Ron Leejak took his place. Leejak played lead guitar and banjo for the band.

"Leeta": In 1969, when Gene Simmons was in a band called Bullfrog Bheer, he wrote and sung "Leeta," a slow, sad number about a girl he used to love. It's a sweet song that fans of the Demon should find highly interesting from an historical perspective. KISS included this Bobby Vinton–esque ditty as the ninth track on disc one of the five–CD collection, *The Box Set*.

The Lemonheads: On *Kiss My Ass: Classic KISS Regrooved*, the Lemmonheads, who formed in 1986, covered "Plaster Caster."

Lendt, C. K.: In July of 1976, C. K. Lendt was hired as on-the-road liaison for KISS's business managers, the Glickman/Marks Management Company. He was the company's first employee. Lendt eventually became KISS's tour business manager, but was released by the band in 1988. He recounted his experiences in *KISS and Sell: The Making of a Supergroup*.

Les Paul Guitars *see* **Gibson Guitars**

"Let Me Go, Rock 'n' Roll": The only single released from *Hotter Than Hell*, "Let Me Go, Rock 'n' Roll" is the fifth song on the album (it was originally supposed to appear on *KISS*). Gene Simmons wrote the disposable, party-rock lyrics during his lunch break while still working his day job at the Puerto Rican Interagency Council. In *KISS: Behind the Mask—The Official Authorized Biography*, Simmons said he "wrote the lyrics from top to bottom and then Paul added the chordal pattern. And I took that riff from an old Paul thing that he wrote called, 'Where There's Smoke There's Fire.'" Simmons sings lead on the song as well. Certain music critics call "Let Me Go, Rock 'n' Roll," which weighs in at just 2:15 in length, a warm-up of sorts to the band's breakout hit, "Rock and Roll All Nite."

"Let Me Know": Gene and Paul share lead vocals on "Let Me Know," the fifth track on *KISS*, the band's first album. Despite Ace Frehley's hard-rocking guitar lead, the tune and lyrics are boy-meets-girl, bubblegum pop all the way. When Stanley first met Simmons, "Let Me Know" (previously titled "Sunday Driver") was the song Stanley played for him, and it was subsequently recorded by Wicked Lester.

Let Me Rock You: Peter Criss's third solo album, *Let Me Rock You* was released in May of 1982 in Europe, Japan, and Mexico. Because the former KISS drummer's second solo record, *Out of Control*, sold so poorly, *Let Me Rock You* didn't make it to the U.S. until 1998. The LP features Criss on the cover with no makeup (a first) and includes the following tracks: "Let It Go," "Tears" (a single co-written by Vinnie Cusano, who would become Vinnie Vincent), "Move on Over," "Jealous Guy" (a cover of the 1971 John Lennon tune), "Destiny," "Some Kinda' Hurricane," "Let Me Rock You," "First Day in the Rain," "Feels Like Heaven" (written by Gene Simmons), and "Bad Boys." Produced by Vini Poncia, who also helmed *Dynasty*, *Peter Criss*, and *Unmasked*.

"Let's Put the 'X' in Sex": One of two original songs on the greatest hits album, *Smashes, Thrashes & Hits* (the other is "(You Make Me) Rock Hard"), "Let's Put the "X" in Sex" begins the record on a party-hearty note, with a typically fine, typically flamboyant performance by Paul Stanley, who wrote the tune with frequent collaborator Desmond Child. The tongue-in-cheek lyrics are sung to a semi-catchy beat. Some compare the song to Robert Palmer's "Addicted to Love."

Levine, Barry: Arguably KISS's most well-known photographer, Barry Levine took many famous photos of the band, including the colorful Mylar background shots, the starry background pics, and the iconic Empire State Building photos. His book, *The KISS Years*, has one of his patented KISS "Spirit of '76" images on the cover. Levine's photos were used on countless classic KISS merchandise, including posters, the Colorforms Set, the Custom Chevy Van model kit, Donruss trading cards, the record player, the toy guitar, the transistor radio, and the *KISS On Tour Game*. Levine began photographing KISS in 1976.

Lick It Up (album): The first KISS album to hit platinum sales in the U.S. since 1979's *Dynasty*, *Lick It Up* is an exciting LP. The record gets off to an energetic start with "Exciter," and, of course, the album also features the title track, a terrific, radio-friendly song that many '80s-era KISS fans readily associate with the band.

More importantly, *Lick It Up* was a reboot of sorts for KISS. Not only were Ace Frehley and Peter Criss, who were replaced by Vinnie Vincent and Eric Carr respectively, increasingly a thing of the past, *Lick It Up* was the debut album of makeup-less KISS, who had removed their face paint at the suggestion of Paul Stanley. As such, longtime fans and casual observers alike couldn't help but ogle the cover of the record, which shows the band standing sans face paint in front of a white background, wearing normal rock and roll clothing (black jackets and the like) of the era.

Greg Prato of allmusic.com called *Lick It Up* "undoubtedly KISS' best non-makeup album." Conversely, Simmons has dismissed the record over the years, saying he was too occupied with Diana Ross and the cult of celebrity at the time to commit fully. Stanley believes it's a good album, however, but not quite up to *Creatures of the Night* standards.

Tracks include: "Exciter," "Not for the Innocent," "Lick It Up," "Young and Wasted," "Gimme More," "All Hell's Breakin' Loose," "A Million to One," "Fits Like a Glove," "Dance All Over Your Face," and "And on the 8th Day."

"Lick It Up" (song): Although it received a fair amount of radio airplay and plenty of hype, "Lick It Up," the first single and the third track on the album of the same name, only hit #66 on the *Billboard* charts in the U.S. However, it did reach the top 40 in Canada (32), Switzerland (24), and the UK (31). Written by Paul Stanley, who sings lead on the song, and Vinnie Vincent, it is a catchy party tune with a simple, instantly recognizable riff and a dopey, but fun-loving chorus.

Matthew Wilkening of ultimateclassicrock.com ranked "Lick It Up" #1 on a list of the "Top 10 KISS Without Makeup Songs," saying it "keeps picking up steam and energy until it feels like the whole world is singing the chorus along with you in your car."

A cornerstone of the non-makeup era of KISS, "Lick It Up" is a perennial favorite that has made its way onto the set list of many live shows. In the music video, the band walks around a burned out town ridden with post-apocalyptic hotties, culminating in a faux live performance.

Lick It Up—A Millennium Tribute to KISS: Released in 2008 by Versailles Records, this tribute CD features the following tracks: "Lick It Up" (Ron Keel, Richard Kendrick), "Detroit Rock City" (the Slashtones featuring Joe Lynn Turner), "Forever" (Richard Kendrick), "I Love

It Loud" (Richard Kendrick, AJ Caruso, Fran Gilbert, Gerald Kloos, Chris Heaven), "Beth" (Rose Reiter), "Shout It Out Loud" (Kerri Kelli), "Heaven's On Fire" (Chris Catena, Teenage Rampage) "The Oath" (Mind's Eye), "Shock Me" (KISS Alive!, Reckless Fortune), "Tears are Falling" (Johnny Dee, Richard Kendrick), "She" (Snowblynd), "I Stole Your Love" (Jason McMaster, SSIK), "Let's Put the X in Sex" (Chuck Bonnett), "Black Diamond" (Ryan Roxie), "New York Groove" (Dead End Kidz), "C'mon and Love Me" (Andrew Santagata), "Deuce" (Supermodel Autopsy), and "Parasite" (Katet).

Lick It Up World Tour: Featuring the same tank stage design that the band used for the Creatures of the Night Tour, the Lick It Up World Tour was the first official KISS concert series sans makeup. Gene Simmons, no longer a monstrous demon onstage, dropped the blood-spitting routine, but kept the fire-breathing act.

The tour began October 11, 1983, and ended March 17, 1984, for a total of 93 shows in the U.S., Europe, and Canada. The January 9, 1984, show at the Mississippi Coast Coliseum in Biloxi, Mississippi drew just 1,507 fans, making it the smallest crowd at a major venue that KISS had ever played for.

After the European leg of the tour, KISS fired Vinnie Vincent for "unethical behavior," but re-hired him for the American part of the tour because they didn't have time to audition another guitarist. Vincent was fired again after the tour ended, making the March 17, 1984, show at Roberts Stadium in Evansville, Indiana his last with the band.

Band lineup: Paul Stanley, Gene Simmons, Vinnie Vincent, and Eric Carr. Opening acts: Accept, Axe, Great White, Heaven, Heavy Pettin', Helix, Highfever, the Pat Travers Band, Riot, Tigres de Oro, and Vandenberg. Average attendance: 5,052.

Followed by: Animalize World Tour.

"Life in the Woods": When KISS played clubs during their formative period, they often performed a song called "Life in the Woods," but they never recorded it.

***Lightning*:** Recorded and Mixed at The Sound Place in New York for Casablanca Records, *Lightning* was released by Eric Carr's pre–KISS band, Lightning. The band began as Salt 'N Pepper and went by a number of other names as well, including Creation, Mother Nature/Father Time, and Bionic Boogie. Because the band broke up in 1979, the same year the record hit stores, *Lightning* was released in limited quantities. Tracks include: "Disco Symphony," "In And Out Of Love," "Baby Without Your Love," "I Love The Way You Love Me," and "One Step At A Time."

Linet, Lew: Lew Linet was Wicked Lester's manager and KISS's first manager. KISS fired Linet before they recorded their first album because he thought they were too loud and didn't want them wearing makeup.

Lips: From 1971 to 1973, Peter Criss was the drummer in Lips, a pop rock trio comprised of Criss and two of his former Chelsea bandmates: Michael Benvenga and Stan Penridge. Although they failed to get a record contract, Lips produced a demo that featured the following tracks, some of which would later develop into KISS songs: "Beck" (which would become "Beth"), "Baby Driver," "Don't You Let Me Down" (short version), "Don't You Let Me Down" (original version), "Dirty Livin,'" "You're My Woman," "Don't You Let Me Down," "Don't Let The Blues Surround You," "Hooked On Rock and Roll," "I'm Gonna Love You," and "The Kind Of Sugar Papa Likes."

"Little Caesar": Eric Carr sings lead and plays bass on "Little Caesar," the 14th track on *Hot in the Shade*. It's one of only two times Carr sang lead vocals on a KISS album, and the song is a favorite among many fans of the late, great drummer, who sings about fighting to be a man. Gene Simmons and Paul Stanley provide the chorus. Carr originally titled the song "Ain't That Peculiar," but Simmons made him change it because that was already the title of a Marvin Gaye song. When Carr was a young boy, the other kids nicknamed him Little Caesar, thus the song title.

***Live to Win*:** Paul Stanley's second solo album (following 1978's *Paul Stanley*), *Live to Win* was released October 24, 2006. It contains the following tracks: "Live to Win," "Lift," "Wake Up Screaming," "Everytime I See You Around," "Bulletproof," "All About You," "Second to None," "It's Not Me," "Loving You Without You Now," and "Where Angels Dare." Former KISS lead guitarist Bruce Kulick plays bass on "Everytime I See You Around," "Second to None," and "Loving You Without You Now." Recorded in Hensen Recording Studios and released by New Door, the record reached #53 on the *Billboard* 200.

In a review published on www.popmatters.com, Marc A. Price called *Live to Win* "a fun but not very satisfying chunk of slick, over-chewed bubble gum." Conversely, Greg Maki of www.live-metal.net called it "an outstanding rock album ... as a songwriter and singer, [Paul Stanley] is as good as there is in the rock world today, with or without Gene Simmons and whoever else is in KISS at the time."

Live to Win—A Casual Guide to the Music of KISS Frontman Paul Stanley: Written by Neil Daniels, this book was published August 19, 2015, through Amazon's CreateSpace Independent Publishing Platform. According to the author, the book "celebrates Stanley's musical legacy and gives nuggets of information and trivia about his career as well as a biography, discographies, a timeline, reviews and tributes from leading musicians and respected music writers. There are also previously unseen live photographs of the American rock icon."

Live+1: Produced by Ace Frehley, John Regan, Tod Howarth, and Scott Mabuchi for Megaforce records, *Live+1* is a five-song EP released by Frehley's solo group, Frehley's Comet, on February 2, 1988. "Rip It Out," "Breakout," "Something Moved," and "Rocket Ride" were recorded at the Aragon Ballroom in Chicago, Illinois on September 4, 1987, while "Words Are Not Enough" is an abbreviated version of a demo recording the band made in 1985. Anton Fig, famous for playing in David Letterman's house band, the CBS Orchestra, played drums on the record, which reached #84 on the *Billboard* 200.

Live+4: In 1988, Frehley's Comet released *Live+4*, a concert video on VHS. An Amazon review written by Johny Bottom reads as follows: "This is without a doubt Ace's finest hour without KISS and the Spaceman makeup. The live show in England is great. Ace belts out his own KISS tunes 'Cold Gin,' 'Shock Me,' and 'Rocket Ride,' along with solo material from Frehley's Comet, 'Something Moved' and 'Breakout.' After the show (which is way too short to satisfy Ace fans) you get four MTV videos: 'Into the Night,' 'Rock Soldiers,' 'Insane,' and 'It's over now.'"

"Living in Sin": Sean Delaney and Howard Marks assisted Gene Simmons in writing "Living in Sin," the sixth track on the Demon's 1978 KISS solo LP. If the record had spawned a second single, "Living in Sin," a catchy tune with a memorable chorus about living in sin at the Holiday Inn (an idea from Marks), probably would have been it. As with "Radioactive," the album's only single, Bob Seger sings backup vocals. A little over halfway through the song, Cher, who was Simmons' girlfriend at the time, provides a spoken word phone call in which she excitedly asks the rock star if he shows his face personally (presumably during sex). Cher's daughter Chastity speaks on the song as well.

Loaded Deck: Released January 20, 1998, by Megaforce Records to cash in on the KISS Reunion Tour, *Loaded Deck* is an Ace Frehley greatest hits album containing the following tracks: the previously unreleased "One Plus One" and "Give It to Me Anyway"; "Do Ya"; "It's Over Now"; "Shot Full of Rock"; "Stranger in a Strange Land"; live versions of "Separate," "New York Groove," "Rock Soldiers," and "Remember Me"; and the instrumentals "Fractured Too" and "Fractured III." The Japanese release contains a live bonus song, "Shock Me." Produced by John Regan and Ace Frehley.

The Loft: Located at E. 23rd Street in New York City, the Loft was the birthplace of KISS. In addition to spending countless hours rehearsing at the Loft, this is where Paul, Gene, and Peter first auditioned Ace Frehley.

In *Nothin' to Lose: The Making of KISS (1972–1975)*, Gene said the Loft was a "roach-infested fire trap with no windows. It cost $200 a month to rent the Loft, which was a lot of money at the time." Paul said, "Our Loft was a little room on the fourth floor. We put egg crates on the walls to absorb the sound but that didn't work ... we rehearsed constantly ... before Ace joined the band I remember spending Thanksgiving in the Loft eating turkey sandwiches and drinking sherry with Peter to stay warm.... It was a romanticized vision of the struggling artist."

"Lonely Is the Hunter": Written and sung by Gene Simmons, "Lonely Is the Hunter" is the fifth track on *Animalize* and one of the weaker KISS songs of the 1980s It's tired (and tiring), slow-chug of a song that you'll probably find yourself skipping past more often than not. Bruce Kulick plays lead guitar on the track, subbing for Mark St. John.

"Long, Long Road": This Paul Stanley-sung song was recorded for the unreleased Wicked Lester album. It's a soft, reverent, peaceful tune of reflection and remembrance—very nice. According to *KISS FAQ* author Dale Sherman, it was "written by an English team of writers, although no one seems to remember who."

"Long Way Down": One of several solid, but ultimately forgettable songs on *Monster*, the pop rocker "Long Way Down" is the sixth track on the record and one of many KISS songs in which the band (Paul Stanley in this case) mentions a girl (a gypsy in this case) bringing a guy to his knees. Written by Stanley and Tommy Thayer.

***Lost and Spaced*:** Released in October of 1998 by the Eric Singer Project, *Lost and Spaced* features the following tracks, all covers: "Set Me Free," "Four Day Creep," "Free Ride," "Still Alive & Well," "Never Before," "Goin' Blind," "Teenage Nervous Breakdown," "Changes," "S.O.S. (Too Bad)," "Foxy Lady," "Twenty Flight Rock," "Won't Get Fooled Again," "Snortin' Whiskey," and "We're an American Band."

"Love 'Em and Leave 'Em": Not surprisingly, "Love 'Em and Leave 'Em," which is the sixth track on *Rock and Roll Over*, was written and sung by Gene Simmons, who has famously slept with thousands of women, the vast majority of which were one-night stands. A girl approaches Simmons, hikes up her dress, and makes plans to see him later that night, but he warns her that he loves them and leaves them. As with "Sweet Pain," the song was derived from the unreleased "Rock and Rolls Royce," which Simmons wrote as an ode to America's obsession with cars.

***Love Gun* (album):** KISS's sixth studio album, *Love Gun* was recorded at Record Plant in New York City and released June 30, 1977, by Casablanca Records, at the pinnacle of the band's popularity. The album, one of the band's best, was certified platinum upon release and shipped the same day as the first all–KISS comic book, *Marvel Comics Super Special* #1.

As with *Destroyer*, the cover for *Love Gun* was painted by Ken Kelly, who again depicted the band members as larger-than-life fantasy figures, this time in an otherworldly temple with a gathering of face paint-wearing buxom brunettes at their feet. Like *Rock and Roll Over*, *Love Gun* was produced by Eddie Kramer, who helped give the recording a good, hard rock sound.

For the first time on a record, every member of KISS sings lead, including Ace Frehley, who makes his lead vocal debut with "Shock Me," a terrific concert staple ("Love Gun" and "I Stole Your Love" are live favorites on the album as well). Speaking of concerts, KISS embarked upon a massive tour to support *Love Gun*, their most expensive stage production up until that point.

Despite the increasing popularity and accompanying merchandising of KISS at the time, *Love Gun*, which originally came with a cardboard pop gun, is a raunchy record as Paul Stanley sings about his penis on the title track and Gene Simmons sounds like a dirty old man on "Christine Sixteen," a tale of under-age "romance." The album ends on a sweeter note with "Then She Kissed Me," a sincere, surprisingly good cover of the Crystals' 1963 hit, "Then He Kissed Me."

Rolling Stone recently ranked *Love Gun* KISS's fourth greatest album, calling "many of the songs top notch" and saying it "ranks as a true group effort." In the magazine's original review in issue #246 (Aug., 1977), Charles M. Young said the album loses "much of the energy in the overdubs" and doesn't take "enough advantage of Peter Criss' excellent voice." However, Young did admit that the record has "some nice riffs" and that "Then She Kissed Me" is "funny for all the right reasons."

In *KISS: Behind the Mask—The Official Authorized Biography*, Stanley took a lot of the credit for *Love Gun*, saying "I was going into Electric Lady Studios on my own and cutting tracks that we would ultimately go in and copy. By then I had a very clear vision of what I wanted to do and in some ways what KISS was going to do…. It was a great time for me. I really had free reign to book studio time and work out my songs. For better or for worse, I worked out all the parts. If I didn't play them I told someone else what to play."

Tracks include: "I Stole Your Love," "Christine Sixteen," "Got Love for Sale," "Shock Me," "Tomorrow and Tonight," "Love Gun," "Hooligan," "Almost Human," "Plaster Caster," and "Then She Kissed Me."

The spring, 1977 issue of the *KISS Army Newsletter* lists three songs for *Love Gun* that failed to make the final cut: "Have Love Will Travel," "Sincerely," and "Tunnel of Love," the latter of which Simmons ended up recording for his 1978 solo album.

***Love Gun: Deluxe Edition*:** Disc one of this release, which hit stores October 27, 2014, is a remastered version of *Love Gun*. Disc two contains the following demos: "Much Too Soon" (previously unreleased), "Plaster Caster," "Reputation" (also available on *KISS 40*), "Love Gun," "Tomorrow and Tonight," and "I Know Who You Are" (previously unreleased). In addition, there are three previously unreleased live tracks recorded at the December 20, 1977, show at the Capitol Centre in Landover, Maryland: "Love Gun," "Christine Sixteen," and "Shock Me."

Rounding out the package are a seven-minute interview with Gene Simmons, a "Love Gun" teaching demonstration by Paul Stanley, and liner notes written by Def Leppard's Joe Elliott, a huge KISS fan.

"Love Gun" (song): The sixth track on *Love Gun*, "Love Gun" failed to become a hit single (it stalled out at #55 on the *Billboard* charts), despite the popularity of the band at the time, and despite the song's catchy, hook-laden nature. Paul Stanley, who wrote the song while traveling to Japan on an airplane, played bass (as well as rhythm guitar) on the tune, which is essentially an ode to his penis—this is one of many KISS songs in which the singer brags on his sexual prowess.

Stanley has stated in various interviews that "Love Gun" is one of his favorite songs to perform live. Memorable for its machine gun guitar riff, "Love Gun" plays during the opening credits of the movie *Detroit Rock City* (1999) and is mentioned in *Role Models* (2008), in which Wheeler (Seann William Scott) humorously explains what the song is about.

Love Gun Tour: From July 8 to September 5, 1977, KISS played 32 shows in Canada and the U.S., in support of their sixth studio album. Ace Frehley sang lead vocals in concert for the first time on this tour, belting out "Shock Me" to the delight of his many fans. The band had a new stage show and new costumes as well.

Props included fire engine lights, Peter Criss' drum riser, Gene Simmons' blood-spitting and fire-breathing, Paul Stanley's fire helmet, Ace's smoking guitar, hydraulic lifts, lighted staircases, Sam the Serpent (a giant coiled, fanged snake), flamethrowers, bombs, Stanley smashing his guitar, a confetti storm, and a lighted KISS logo.

This was KISS at the peak of their power, delivering night after night of mind-blowing, ear-shattering, eye-popping shows. Opening acts included Cheap Trick and Styx. Average Attendance: 9,476.

Followed by: Alive II Tour.

"Love Her All I Can": Written and sung by Paul Stanley, "Love Her All I Can" is the ninth track on *Dressed to Kill*. Inspired by a NAZZ (Todd Rungren's old band) song called "Open My Eyes," the song has simplistic, puppy love lyrics that somehow provide a solid spine for the hard driving musicianship. Donald A. Guarisco of allmusic.com called the number a "lightning-fast blast of pop-metal that works both as a great example of KISS' tightness as a musical unit and a good sample of its economical songwriting skills." Guarisco was especially complimentary of the songs instrumentation, referencing Ace Frehley's "nimble-fingered guitar soloing" and comparing Peter Criss's solo to "Ginger Baker's work with Cream." The 1972 version of "Love Her All I Can," recorded for the unreleased Wicked Lester album, is the fifth track on disc one of *The Box Set*. It has a lighter, more pop-oriented sound than the KISS rendition.

"Love in Chains": The eighth track on Paul Stanley's 1978 KISS solo album, "Love in Chains" eschews the gentle nature of the previous song, "Hold Me, Touch Me (Think of Me When We're Apart)," in favor of "a melodramatic and near-hysterical rocker with a punchy chorus and plenty of flashy lead guitar. Lyrically, it's a first for Paul Stanley … 'Love in Chains' is not the S&M anthem that might be expected, but a metaphor for Paul's sexual frustration" (Paul Elliott, *KISS: Hotter than Hell*). Steve Lacey plays guitar on the song as Bob Kulick wasn't available.

"Love Is Blind": This acoustic demo was written, sung, and recorded by Gene Simmons early in 1977, but it didn't appear on an official KISS album until 2001's *The Box Set*, a five-disc collection. It is track 20 on disc two.

"Love Kills": Featured in *A Nightmare on Elm Street 4: The Dream Master* (1988), "Love Kills" is the third track on the Vinnie Vincent Invasion's 1988 album, *All Systems Go*. The song was one of the band's few claims to fame.

"Love Theme from KISS": One of the quirkier, more unusual songs in the KISS catalogue, "Love Theme from KISS" is a slow, low-key instrumental. The eighth track on the band's self-titled debut album, it is the only KISS song in which all four original band members get songwriting credits. When the tune was first recorded, it was seven minutes long, but the band pared it down before release to 2:24.

"Love's a Deadly Weapon": Written by Paul Stanley, Gene Simmons, Rod Swenson, and Wes Beech, "Love's a Deadly Weapon" is the sixth track on *Asylum*. Like "I'm Alive" before it, "Love's a Deadly Weapon" is a rapid rocker, blazing along at a blistering pace. Unfortunately, as with "I'm Alive," it's too fast for its own good, resulting in a hot mess. Lyrically forgettable, the song finds Simmons singing about the hot thunder flowing through his blood, and about a hot and willing girl dressed in red.

"Love's a Slap in the Face": This is a cliché-ridden song in which Gene Simmons sings about love being a ball in chain, hurting so good, screaming and shouting, and having been up, down, and all around. Simmons, less a Demon here than a pop rocker, sounds silly during the teenybopper chorus. When Simmons wrote the song (with Vini Poncia), which is the sixth track on *Hot in the Shade*, he was shooting for the "imagery" of the Phil Spector–produced "He Hit Me (It Felt Like a Kiss)," which was recorded by the Crystals in 1962.

Ludwig Drums: In 1974, KISS got new instruments, including a Ludwig Silver Sparkle Drum Kit set for Peter Criss. Years later, Eric Carr endorsed Ludwig Drums.

Lukather, Steve: Toto's Steve Lukather played lead guitar on Peter Criss's "That's the Kind of Sugar Papa Likes" and "Hooked on Rock and Roll."

Lunch Box: Produced by the King-Seeley Thermos Company, the original KISS lunch box hit store shelves in 1977 and is now highly collectible. The front is decorated with a Barry Levine photo from the *Love Gun* shoot while the back features the band in concert on the *Love Gun* tour. Each of the four sides depicts a band member. The box includes a red thermos with a drawing of the band members' faces surrounding the KISS logo.

Years later, various other KISS lunch boxes were produced, including at least seven different designs from the National Entertainment Collectibles Association (circa early 2000s).

Lyn Christopher: In 1972, during the Wicked Lester era, Paul Stanley and Gene Simmons sang background vocals on three tracks—"Celebrate I," "Celebrate II" and "Wedding"—on *Lyn Christopher*, the 1973 self-titled album by the relatively obscure pop/soul singer. It was the first time Simmons and Stanley were paid to sing on a record.

Peter Criss, who did *not* meet Paul and Gene during the recording of the LP, did uncredited handclaps on "Celebrate I" and "Celebrate II." The record, which was recorded at Electric Lady Studios, was re-released on CD by the Universal Music Group in 2014.

Macy's Thanksgiving Day Parade: On November 27, 2014, KISS lip-synched "Rock and Roll All Nite" at Macy's Thanksgiving Day Parade. After the cold and rainy event, which was shot at odd camera angles, Paul Stanley tweeted: "Bluntly, We were screwed over & misled by the exec in charge of #MacysThanksgivingDayParade. We ALL deserved better."

MAD: Amazingly enough, KISS was never featured properly on the cover of an issue of *MAD* magazine, at least in the U.S. (though they were on the cover of an edition released in Mexico). However, Alfred E. Neuman is dressed up like Gene Simmons on the cover of a June 1982 *MAD* paperback book called the *Mad Weirdo Watcher's Guide*.

"Mad Dog": Written and sung by Gene Simmons, "Mad Dog" is a demo that was included as track 6 on disc 2 of *The Box Set*. It was originally intended for *Destroyer*, but was "reworked as the core riff to that album's 'Flaming Youth' track" (Paul Elliott, *KISS: Hotter Than Hell*).

Madison Square Garden: The current incarnation of Madison Square Garden, the famed sports and concert facility in New York City, dates back to 1968. Ace, Gene, Paul, and Peter, while they were playing clubs and other small venues, dreamed of playing at the Garden. Their dream came true February 18, 1977.

You could be the coolest kid in school by carrying this KISS lunch box with thermos, released in 1977 by the King-Seeley Thermos Company.

In *Makeup to Breakup*, Peter Criss recalled the emotions he felt playing "the mecca of our dreams.... As soon as I got the tour schedule, I called my mother to tell her that we were going to be at MSG. The day of the show, all four of us were scared.... It hit us when we walked backstage and saw all those photos of Sinatra and Ali. This was the world's greatest arena. I think I threw up twice before the show. Paul was climbing the walls.... When I got up behind the drums, I scanned the audience and I found my folks.... I started bawling and my makeup started to run down the sides of my face."

In the April 8, 1977, issue of *Performance*, a weekly newspaper, Tom Ray reviewed the KISS concert at the Garden, saying, "This reviewer cannot recall having seen musicians work harder at pleasing their fans ... each number is tightly rehearsed and geared to maintain hysteria.... KISS knows how to rock as hard and as fast as any ... in the nearly two-hour show, there was never a lapse in action or intensity."

From December 14 to 16 of 1977, during the Alive II Tour, KISS sold out three consecutive shows at the Garden, proving that they had truly made it as one of the most popular bands in the world.

MADtv: On the October 31, 1998, episode of *MADtv*, the original KISS members appear in a number of sketches. They go on a date with a man's daughter, wife, and mother, and they appear as full-size action figures.

Magazines: During their more than four-decade run, KISS has been cover-featured on countless teen idol and rock music magazines, including *Creem*, *Hit Parader*, and *Rock Scene*, and such late 1970s specials as: *Award Winning KISS*, *Creem KISS Special*, *Super Teen Special #1*, *Super Rock Awards*, *Teen Machine Presents KISS*, *Teenstar Poster*, *Grooves #1*, *Teen Throbs KISS Collection*, *The Best of KISS*, and *TV Superstar KISS Mania*.

Magic Bullet Theory: In 2003, Mark St. John released *Magic Bullet Theory*, a solo instrumental CD. This was his last published work before his tragic death in 2007.

MAGIC—KISS Kronicles 1973 to 1983: In 2015, Ros Radley did a Kickstarter campaign for his prospective book, *MAGIC—KISS Kronicles 1973 to 1983*, which he described as a "day by day chronicle of KISS's first 10 years and a detailed study of the evolution of their image from 1973 to 1983."

"Magic Touch": A terrific song on a terrific (if underrated) album, "Magic Touch" is the sixth track on *Dynasty*, KISS's nod to the disco era. An earnest and impassioned Paul Stanley sings about a girl whose "Magic Touch" is tantalizing, yet ethereal and allusive. The song, written by Stanley, has a dramatic and robust sound, both vocally and in terms of instrumentation. Stanley plays bass, subbing for Gene Simmons. As with all the songs on *Dynasty* except for "Dirty Livin'," Anton Fig plays drums instead of Peter Criss.

"Mainline": A song about a man desiring a woman sexually (a common theme with KISS), "Mainline" was written by Paul Stanley, but sung by Peter Criss (who absolutely insisted that he sing the song) in his typical pop-oriented, boogie-beat style. It is the eighth track on *Hotter Than Hell*.

Makeup: To set themselves apart from the pack, KISS began wearing makeup early on, first rouge, eyeliner, eyebrow pencil, and lipstick, similar to the New York Dolls. In short order, they adopted the more familiar, more elaborate designs—Catman (Peter Criss), Demon (Gene Simmons), Spaceman (Ace Frehley), and Starchild (Paul Stanley)—which were settled upon in time for the band's first album (Paul toyed with mask makeup and a couple of other designs, but ultimately decided on the star).

When Eric Carr replaced Peter Criss, he took on the persona of a Fox (after designing and then rejecting Hawk makeup). When Vinnie Vincent replaced Ace Frehley, he wore golden Ankh Warrior makeup.

On September 18, 1983, wanting to shake things up and leave the 1970s behind, Gene Simmons and Paul Stanley, along with hired guns Vinnie Vincent and Eric Carr, appeared on MTV (via *MTV Special: KISS Unmasking*) without their makeup. *Lick It Up* was their first album cover sans makeup. In 1996, when the original band members reformed, they wore their classic makeup.

Today, Eric Singer wears the Catman makeup while Tommy Thayer wears the Spaceman design, which is a sore point with purists and certain Peter and Ace fans. They can wear the classic makeup because Simmons and Stanley bought the designs from Criss and Frehley years ago, transactions which Criss and Frehley probably regret.

Because of the makeup (and costumes), many critics didn't take KISS seriously during their heyday, but the band has gotten more respect in recent years, culminating in their belated 2014 induction into the Rock and Roll Hall of Fame.

Makeup to Breakup: My Life In and Out of KISS: The autobiography of Peter Criss, this book was published by Scribner on October 23, 2012. Shortly after publication, Nathan Rabin reviewed the book for www.avclub.com: "*Makeup to Breakup* positively vibrates with rage toward Criss' former bandmates, KISS' management, and everything KISS represents.... But before Criss despised the other members of KISS, he embraced them as a band of brothers on a single-minded mission to conquer the world. *Makeup to Breakup* affectionately chronicles the group's oft-told tale of glory won, lost, then regained, from its humble origins as a band that combined the theatricality of Alice Cooper with the androgynous role-playing of glam rock, to its late-'70s peak as one of the biggest bands in the world, a money-making machine that left a trail of devastation in its wake. Criss' book is wonderfully sleazy and graphic even for a rock-star memoir.... Criss is a quintessential survivor. As he notes more than once, he really should have died at least a half-dozen times by now, a casualty of car accidents, drugs, suicidal depression, or Herculean self-abuse; yet he survived to tell a tale that may not qualify as art, but is a hell of a nastily fun read."

In a 2013 interview with www.metalsludge.tv, Peter's ex-wife, Lydia Criss, disparaged *Makeup to Breakup*, saying: "Peter is very dramatic, he's an exaggerator, he's a complainer, he's a liar ... when we were married there was a point where I was actually uncomfortable with him putting me on such a pedestal and then his book comes out and he basically says he didn't care for me that much.... I suppose with Peter's comments in his book, he's trying to get even with me for what I wrote, which was the truth, in my book [*Sealed with a KISS*]. Peter's book is not the truth."

"Makin' Love": The 10th and final track on *Rock and Roll Over*, "Makin' Love" was written by Paul Stanley and Sean Delaney. It's a hard rocking number in which Stanley, who envisioned it as an homage to Led Zeppelin's "Whole Lotta Love," implores a girl not to say no. The blistering lead by Ace Frehley is pure heavy metal, as is the riff, which has been copied by many guitarists over the years.

"Man of 1,000 Faces": A tribute to the great silent film star Lon Chaney, "Man of 1,000 Faces" is the eighth track on Gene Simmons' 1978 KISS solo album. The 1960s-influenced pop number, which features more mature lyrics than most of Simmons' output, is a grand listening experience that has orchestration to spare. Not only does Simmons tribute Chaney in the song, he is writing about himself, a Jewish immigrant living in America and acting like a Demon onstage.

Manfred Mann's Earth Band: In 1974, KISS opened several shows for Manfred Mann's Earth Band, an English prog rock act established in 1971.

Mark St. John Project: After the demise of White Tiger, Mark St. John formed a band called the Mark St. John Project with Phil Naro. Their only release was this self-titled, limited edition EP.

Marks, Howard: The late Howard Marks was KISS's business manager from 1976 to 1988. He was part of Glickman/Marks Management (with Carl Glickman), which you can read about in *KISS and Sell: The Making of a Supergroup*. Marks also co-wrote "Charisma" and played the role of the father in the "I Love It Loud" video.

Mars Attacks KISS: *Mars Attacks KISS* is a one-shot comic book published by IDW in Jan-

Published by IDW in 2013, *Mars Attacks KISS* takes place in 1970s New York, where "four teens are handed the power to become godlike figures ... unless some attacking Martians find a way to steal that power for themselves!"

uary of 2013. Written by Chris Ryall with art by Alan Robinson, the story ties into the Mars Attacks trading cards of the 1950s and the Marvel KISS comic books of the late 1970s. The original solicitation for the issue read, "In 1970s New York, four teens are handed the power to become godlike figures … unless some attacking Martians find a way to steal that power for themselves!" Cover art by Ray Dillon.

Marsh, Dave: Noted music critic Dave Marsh has authored several books, including *Born to Run* (1979) and *Glory Days* (1987), both about Bruce Springsteen. He was an editor for *Creem* during the magazine's early years, and he's a longtime contributor to *Rolling Stone*.

Marsh, a committee member of the Rock and Roll Hall of Fame, is known for hating certain hugely popular bands, including Air Supply, Journey, Queen, the Grateful Dead, and, most notably, KISS, whom he tried unsuccessfully to keep out of the Rock and Roll Hall of Fame. "KISS is not a great band," he said about the band's prospective induction. "KISS was never a great band, KISS never will be a great band, and I have done my share to keep them off the ballot."

"Musically, I was done with [KISS] before I ever turned the first album over to the second side," Marsh wrote in the March 11, 2014, issue of *Rock & Rap Confidential*, a monthly publication he edits. "KISS had an extraordinary aptitude for adopting every cliché in hard rock history, and a complete absence of any ability to create so much as a hint of a new one."

Paul Stanley responded publicly to the comments, calling Marsh an "ugly little troll" and the Rock Hall "tainted, corrupted, and distorted."

Marshall Amps: In the early days of KISS, to give their shows more of an imposing presence, the band stacked fake Marshall amplifiers onstage, including hollow cabinets to make the music seem even louder than it was. As KISS became more popular and got better funded, real Marshall amps replaced the fakes. Marshall Amplification, the makers of Marshall amplifiers, was founded in London, England in 1962.

Marvel Comics Super Special #1: One of the most famous of all KISS collectibles is *Marvel Comics Super Special* #1 (Sept., 1977), which is better known as the first all–KISS comic book. Produced in magazine-sized format, the issue was written by Steve Gerber and drawn by Alan Weiss, John Buscema, Rich Buckler, and Sal Buscema. In addition to the story, which features KISS as superheroes battling Mephisto and Doctor Doom, the issue includes photos of Ace, Gene, Paul, and Peter giving blood. The blood was not for the Red Cross. Rather, it was mixed in with the ink used in producing the comic book—a stunt that helped it sell more than 400,000 copies.

For Jim Johnson, a former reviewer for the late, lamented *Comics Buyer's Guide*, *Marvel Comics Super Special* #1 has special significance. "After I joined the KISS Army fan club, one of the newsletters touted that KISS was going to be featured in an upcoming comic book from Marvel," he told me in an interview. "I had not been a comic book collector at that point, but that comic, actually a magazine, turned me into a fan of something other than KISS: the comic book industry, whose products I have been reading for over 35 years and writing about for more than 15. This hobby has spawned working relationships and lasting friendships. It's a good bet that had I not been exposed to KISS, my life would be nothing like it is today."

Marvel Comics Super Special #1 was the first all–KISS comic book. It was hugely popular, thanks in part to a media stunt in which band members mixed their blood in with the ink used to print the issue.

Marvel Comics Super Special #5: The second full appearance of KISS in a comic book, this magazine-sized issue was written by Ralph Macchio (with co-plotting by Alan Weiss), drawn by John Romita, Jr., and inked by Tony Dezuniga. In his introduction to the issue, editor Rich Marschall wrote: "The members of KISS are superheroes … who transcend music … and boldly create their own universe … these are the guys who take elements of emotion and cause them to be writ large … who project a personality into a character, forming an ontology around each figure … the 42-page, full color chronicles of the comics avengers herein … tells of KISS's essence better than prose could do."

In the story, which is called "The Land of Khyscz," an evil sorcerer in an otherwise idyllic world goes back in time to a rock concert to feed off the crowd's emotion in order to gain enough force to subjugate Earth. KISS, exhibiting super powers, steps in to stop the sorcerer, battling various bad guys in the process, including a motorcycle gang.

The issue also includes bios of the creators and an article by Toby Goldstein called "KISS Talk About Their First Movie," referring to *KISS Meets the Phantom of the Park*. The band members have disavowed and disparaged the film many times over the years, but the article puts a positive slant on things, such as this quote attributed to Paul and Gene: "It's a great first effort. From what we've heard back from the people at the studio, it stands as a film, regardless of the fact that we're a band."

Marzullo, Tom: Production manager for KISS during the 1980s.

"Master & Slave": Like several songs on the grunge-influenced *Carnival of Souls*, "Master & Slave," the third track on the album, sounds like a bad version of Alice in Chains, one of the two or three best bands of the grunge era. As with the previous track on the record, "Rain," Paul Stanley, Bruce Kulick, and Curtis Cuomo wrote "Master & Slave," which was sung by Stanley. Also like "Rain," Stanley sounds out of his element here.

May, Brian: Prior to re-joining KISS in 2001, Eric Singer toured with acclaimed Queen guitarist Brian May.

Mazer, Larry: Former KISS manager Larry Mazer was instrumental in getting the band back to their hard rock roots with *Revenge* and convincing them to record *Alive III*. On episode 54 of *Three Sides of the Coin*, Mazer claimed that a condition of him managing KISS was for Gene Simmons to drop some of his outside interests and get back to being more involved with the band. "For this to work, this is what has to happen," Mazer said. "Simmons Records has got to go away. Liza Minnelli [who Simmons was managing] has got to go away. The B-movies have got to go away. The Demon has got to come back into the band. And they bought into it. Paul didn't resist at all."

McAdams, Bob: Co-author of the Ace Frehley bio *KISS & Tell*, Bob McAdams was the Spaceman's best friend for many years and was the best man at his wedding in 1976. More importantly, McAdams showed Frehley the ad in *The Village Voice* in which Paul, Gene, and Peter were looking for a lead guitarist for their band.

McCartney, Paul: KISS has long cited Paul McCartney (and the Beatles in general) as a big influence. On the 2014 tribute album, *The Art of McCartney: The Songs of Paul McCartney Sung by the World's Greatest Artists*, KISS covered Wings' two-song medley, "Venus and Mars/Rock Show."

McFarlane Toys see **Action Figures**

McGhee, Doc: Doc McGhee became KISS's manager in 1996, during the reunion era. In an interview published on celebrityaccess.com, he spoke of the state of the band at the time. "They weren't doing really well," he said. "They had just gone through that whole grunge thing that had killed almost every (hard rock) band that had any kind of following. We went from 'rock and roll all night and party every day' and 'have a great life' to 'kill your mom' and 'piss off, everybody.' I don't know why but it happened. There were no production values; there was no nothing (in the music); and people were leaving rock to go to hip hop because there were no rock stars out there. Everybody was the same. So I said, 'Let's put this back up.'"

In *Face the Music: A Life Exposed*, Paul Stanley wrote about hiring McGhee: "Based on what booking agencies told us, it was clear that a reunion tour was going to be way bigger than we could handle on our own. We needed a new manager. We immediately thought of Doc McGhee. When Bon Jovi when to Europe with us in 1984, Doc was managing them. He took them to super-stardom. He had also taken Mötley Crüe to the top…. He immediately started riffing—we could do the 'Seven Wonders of the World Tour' and kick it off by playing in front of the sphinx and the pyramids in Egypt. He thought big. Ridiculously big, just like we had."

McGhee remains KISS's manager to this day. He is also a co-owner of the arena football team, LA KISS. Amusingly, he voiced Chip McGhoo in *Scooby-Doo! And KISS: Rock and Roll Mystery*.

McGurl, Mike: Working with the band from 1973 to 1976, Mike McGurl was KISS's first tour manager.

McMahon, Gerard: Producer, singer-songwriter, and multi-instrumentalist Gerard McMahon wrote "Is That You?" from the *Unmasked* album, but he's perhaps best-known for "Cry Little Sister," which he recorded for the soundtrack to the 1987 vampire film *The Lost Boys*.

***Me, Inc.: Build an Army of One, Unleash Your Inner Rock God, Win in Life and Business*:** Published October 21, 2014, by HarperCollins, *Me, Inc.* is a business book written by Gene Simmons, whom many people consider to be an extraordinary businessman. According to the publisher, the book was inspired by Sun Tzu's military strategy classic, *The Art Of War*, and "is organized around 13 specific, easy-to-understand principles for success—'The Art of More'—drawn from Simmons's own triumphs and failures. From finding the confidence necessary to get started, to surrounding yourself with the right people, to knowing when to pull the plug and when to double-down, these principles can help you attain the freedom and wealth of your dreams."

Meat Loaf: In the wake of the release of Meat Loaf's epic, best-selling *Bat Out of Hell* (1977), former KISS guitarist Bruce Kulick toured with the singer (born Marvin Lee Aday) and his band.

Megadeth: For *Kiss My Ass: Classic KISS Regrooved*, the thrash metal band Megadeth, which was formed in Los Angeles in 1983, covered "Strange Ways," but the song didn't make the cut, so it went unreleased. Fortunately, you can check it out on YouTube.

Mego Dolls: In 1978, Mego, the company that made the "World's Greatest Superheroes" line of Marvel and DC figures, produced four KISS action figures, one for each member of the band. Constructed of vinyl, the jointed figures are 12½" tall and have rooted hair, prompting many collectors to call them dolls. The figures wear *Love Gun*-era costumes, and the cardboard boxes they came in have cut-out instruments.

Early in the production run, the figures had skinny bodies (which are harder to find today), but, as per request from KISS, Mego changed to a more muscular design. Paul's head was recycled from the Captain's head from Mego's Captain and Tennille release, but the other three heads were original. During the production phase, KISS nixed Mego's original cost-saving measure of using the same head for all four figures. The faces were molded in flesh tone and painted black and white, and the Gene figure's tongue is sticking out. According to megomuseum.com, one doll is rarer than the other four: "Mego had shorter runs of Peter Criss because of unofficial rumors that he was leaving the band. In fact, Peter did not leave the band until the KISS figures were well out of production in 1980."

Mego Peter Criss doll—ahem, action figure—from 1978.

The Melvins: The Melvins, an American metal band that has been rocking since 1983, covered "Goin' Blind" for their 1993 LP, *Houdini*. They also recorded the song for their *A Live History of Gluttony and Lust* album, which came out in 2006. In addition, The Melvins recorded "Love Thing," which is a cover of "Love Theme from KISS," for their 1989 album, *Ozma*. A song called "Creepy Smell" on *Ozma* features the intro from "Living in Sin."

Mending Kids International: On November 9, 2013, Mel Gibson presented the Mending Kids International Humanitarian Award to Gene Simmons and his family. On August 16, 2015, during a Mending Kids fundraiser, Johnny Depp and guitarist Gilby Clarke (Guns N' Roses) joined Simmons onstage as he sang and played bass on "Rock and Roll All Nite." One of several charities Simmons supports, Mending Kids International provides crucial surgeries for needy children.

Mensinger, Eric: Before changing his name, current KISS drummer Eric Singer was Eric Mensinger.

Mercury Records: Founded in 1942 primarily as a classical and jazz label, Mercury Records was bought out in 1963 by the Grammophon-Philips Group, the company that would become PolyGram. After the *Creatures of the Night* album, PolyGram transferred KISS to Mercury, meaning *Lick It Up* was the first KISS album produced under the Mercury Records label. *Psycho Circus* was the last.

Merlis, Bob: As publicity manager for Warner Bros. Records, Bob Merlis helped publicize KISS's first album. He was also responsible for co-ordinating the band's January 8, 1974, Fillmore East press launch.

Metal Edge: *Metal Edge* was a hard rock/heavy metal magazine published from 1985 to 2009. KISS received a number of "Readers' Choice Awards" from the mag, including "Band of the Year" (1996), "Album of the Year" (1998, *Psycho Circus*), and "Stage Show of the Year" (2000).

Metal Hammer Golden Gods: During the June 15, 2015, *Metal Hammer Golden Gods* award show in the U.K., Gene Simmons won the Legend award while Tommy Thayer was crowned Defender of the Faith.

Metalhead to Head: Ace Frehley appeared in episode #12 (June 2014) of Fuse TV's web-only interview show, *Metalhead to Head*. The Spaceman and Chris Caffrey demonstrate guitar soloing.

Meyrowitz, Wally: KISS's booking agent from their club days through the late 1970s. According to Bill Aucoin, Meyrowitz was "an intricate part of getting the tours done, trying to get as much money as we could to sustain ourselves on the road because even at the beginning, we had a bigger show than anyone else had" (www.classicbands.com).

Miami Vice: In the first episode of season two of *Miami Vice* (1984–1989), Gene Simmons plays Newton Windsor Blade, an untouchable drug dealer aboard a boat, surrounded by bikini-clad babes. The episode is called "Prodigal Son." Thanks to a tip from Blade, James "Sonny" Crockett (Don Johnson) and Ricardo "Rico" Tubbs (Philip Michael Thomas) head to New York to go after Jimmy Borges, played by illusionist Penn Jillette.

The Midnight Special: On April 1, 1975, KISS played an energized set on *The Midnight Special*, an excellent musical variety show that ran on NBC from 1972 to 1981. The set consisted of "Deuce," "She" (with a killer Ace Frehley solo), and "Black Diamond." According to www.anythingkiss.com, "C'mon and Love Me" was performed, but never broadcast. Flip Wilson, wearing a sparkly cowboy outfit, introduced the band thusly: "Y'all, my next guests are pretty outrageous in their appearance, so I figure this outfit should make me feel right at home. Let's have a very warm *Midnight Special* welcome for KISS."

Mieses, Stan: Working for the *Daily News* in 1973, Stan Mieses wrote one of the first reviews of a KISS show (at the Coventry). Five years later, thanks to an invitation from the band's publicist, Mieses accompanied KISS on their first tour of Japan.

Mighty Mighty Bosstones: On *Kiss My Ass: Classic KISS Regrooved*, the Mighty Mighty Bosstones, a ska band that formed in 1983, covered "Detroit Rock City."

The Mike Douglas Show: In 1974, *The Mike Douglas Show*, a daytime talk program that ran from 1961 to 1982, featured KISS promoting their first album, *KISS*. Before a live audience, the band performed "Firehouse," complete with flashing red lights, billowing smoke, and Gene Simmons breathing fire.

More famously, prior to the band's performance, Simmons appeared alongside Douglas as a featured guest. Douglas asked the demonic, makeup wearing, skull-clad rocker, "What are you?" To which Simmons replied, "I'm really just a member of KISS." But then Simmons told Douglas that his "audience looks appetizing" and that he is "evil incarnate," just prior to flashing his impossibly long tongue.

Douglas was bemused by Simmons, but the real star of the show was comedienne Totie Fields, who rolled her eyes, asked if Simmons' mother was watching, and said he was up for adoption. Best of all, she said, "Wouldn't it be funny if under this he was just a nice Jewish boy … you can't hide the hook." (Regarding "the hook," Fields was referring to the stereotype that Jews have large, hook noses, a remark that wouldn't go over so well in today's more politically correct environment.)

In addition to KISS and Totie Fields, Vinnie Toro and Louise Heath, winners of "The Great Kiss Off," appeared on the episode. Toro told Douglas, "We felt we were the greatest kissers in the world; we just wanted to prove it to everyone else."

Millennium: In season 3, episode 5 of the Fox TV series *Millennium* (1996–1999), Ace, Gene, Paul, and Peter appear briefly as themselves, in concert. They also appear as Lew Carroll (Paul), Hector Leachman (Gene), Sick Cop (Ace), and Nice Cop (Peter). The episode, in which "a killer stalks members of a production crew as they film a movie based upon Frank's cases" (IMBD.com), is entitled "…Thirteen Years Later." On the set of the show, *Millennium* star Lance Henriksen said of KISS: "It's like a circus … a wonderful circus … it's a little bit like being on Broadway, their tours, because they play every night for a couple of hours … there's a lot of energy … they are wonderful performers … these guys are very funny." Of the episode, he said: "It's gonna be a great Halloween show."

Miller, Alan: A publicist for the band during the 1970s, Alan Miller was the first member of the KISS camp to reach out to KISS Army co-founder Bill Starkey.

"A Million to One": The seventh track on *Lick It Up*, "A Million to One" is the most mature, most believably dramatic song on the record. Paul Stanley, recreating the "emotive power of his solo album, warns a departing lover that she'll never find another like him…. Here, KISS manage to ease off the gas for the only time on the album and the effect is stunning" (Paul Elliott, *KISS: Hotter Than Hell*). Written by Stanley and Vinnie Vincent.

Minnelli, Liza: The daughter of Judy Garland and movie director Vincente Minnelli, actress and singer Liza Minnelli, who won an Oscar for her performance as Sally Bowles in *Cabaret* (1972), is known to modern audiences as Lucille Austero in the hit sitcom, *Arrested Development*. During the mid–1980s, when Gene Simmons had more irons in the fire than was good for KISS, he briefly managed Minnelli's music career.

Simmons was rumored to have dated Ms. Minnelli, but in his autobiography, *KISS and Make-Up*, he denied it. "Liza and I had a totally professional relationship," he said. "We talked endlessly about movies, music, and her aspirations to break into the pop field. I enjoyed her company. I enjoyed going to events with her, like the grand opening of the first Hard Rock Café. I respected her as an artist, and I wanted to help her with her career. But that was all I wanted."

"Mr. Blackwell": A song of foreboding doom, growled by the inimitable Gene Simmons, "Mr. Blackwell" is the ninth track on the concept album, *Music from "The Elder,"* focusing on the villain in the epic story. Written by Simmons and Lou Reed, it is a choppy (in a good way), oddly arranged, highly inventive tune that fans of "God of Thunder" should enjoy.

"Mr. Make Believe": Instead of bragging like he does in so many of his songs, Gene Simmons tries hard to please and asks for one more chance in "Mr. Make Believe," a pretty pop number that is the ninth song on the Demon's 1978 KISS solo album. Tinged with a touch of melancholy, "Mr. Make Believe" shows Simmons' tender side and features some very nice acoustic guitar. Mitch Weissman and Joe Pecorino of *Beatlemania* (the Broadway musical) fame provide backup vocals.

"Mr. Speed": Gene Simmons may be "Dr. Love," but Paul Stanley is "Mr. Speed," a smooth talker who brags that he has the kind of love that women need. Written by Stanley and Sean Delaney, "Mr. Speed" is a "great little rocker buzzing with spontaneity … a routine tale of Stanley's sexual prowess freshened by an infection melody, hooky riff and loose, off-the-cuff performance" (Paul Elliott, *KISS: Hotter Than Hell*). It is the seventh track on *Rock and Roll Over*.

Mitchell, Adam: Adam Mitchell introduced Vinnie Vincent to Gene Simmons. In addition, Mitchell co-wrote (mostly with Paul Stanley) a number of KISS songs, including "Creatures of the Night," "Crazy Crazy Nights," and "I'll Fight Hell to Hold You." He also played rhythm guitar on "Creatures of the Night."

"Modern Day Delilah": The first track on and the first single released from *Sonic Boom*, "Modern Day Delilah" is a crowd pleaser that let everyone know KISS could still crank out a big, gaudy, old-school rocker. Ryan Ogle of www.blabbermouth.net said the song "kicks things off with a driving groove and huge chorus…. Toss in a smokin' solo from Thayer and you've got a song worth getting excited over." The "Delilah" of the title is in reference to the Biblical temptress from the *Book of Judges*, who betrayed Samson by having his hair cut off, thereby removing his strength.

Written and sung by Paul Stanley, "Modern Day Delilah" was listed by *Classic Rock Magazine* as the 11th best song of 2009, but it peaked at #50 on the *Billboard* charts. The music video begins and ends with giant-sized KISS walking through Detroit.

Molimo: Prior to joining KISS, Ace Frehley played lead guitar in a band called Molimo, a Jefferson Airplane wannabe that recorded a demo for RCA Records in 1971. For years, that demo was lost to time. During the spring of 2014, however, a collector named Chris Reisman found an acetate of the recording in a barn in upstate New York filled with thousands of records.

"I went up there every Tuesday for a month straight," Reisman told *The Village Voice*. "I was able to get through everything, and in the last wall unit's last shelf of records was a corner full of test presses and acetates, and it was in there. At the time, I had no clue what it was, but I just bought them all. The owner had no idea where or when he acquired the disc."

After Frehley left Molimo, they changed their name to Tomorrow Morning and, coincidentally enough, signed to Casablanca, releasing one single in 1974.

"Molly": Written by Paul Stanley and sung by Gene Simmons, the Paul McCartney–esque "Molly" was recorded for the unreleased Wicked Lester album. On various Wicked Lester bootlegs, the track was often listed as "Some Other Guy" or "Going 'Round the Bend."

***Monster* (album):** Released October 9, 2012, under the Universal Music Group label, *Monster* is the 20th studio album by KISS, following on the heels of 2009's *Sonic Boom*. As with *Sonic Boom*, Tommy Thayer (guitar) and Eric Singer (drums), under the employ of Paul Stanley and Gene Simmons, are in Spaceman and Catman makeup respectively. According to Fred Thomas of allmusic.com, the record is "a tremendous throwback to the superhuman partying and heavy metal Ragnarök of KISS albums like *Destroyer* and *Love Gun*, with meaty riffs, ham-fisted drumming, and a combination of Simmons' patented demonic growls and Stanley's interstellar party-starting, not to mention amounts of cowbell that would have been above average even in 1977."

The comparison is valid, but *Monster* never quite reaches the heights of vintage KISS. Even so, it's a fun record to listen to, especially given the fact that Paul and Gene were in their early 60s during the recording of the album and still rockin' it. As Johnny Price of *Rock Revolt Magazine* stated, "I don't think that this will go down as one of their all-time classics, but it actually is a very strong album."

Tracks include: "Hell or Hallelujah" (the first single off the album), "Wall of Sound," "Freak," "Back to the Stone Age," "Shout Mercy," "Long Way Down" (the album's second and final single), "Eat Your Heart Out," "The Devil Is Me," "Outta This World," "All for the Love of Rock & Roll," "Take Me Down Below," and "Last Chance."

***Monster* (book):** Limited to just 1,000 copies, *Monster*, released August 21, 2012, is a massive tome measuring 3' tall, 2.5' wide, and 2" thick. Equally massive was the sticker price of $4,250. The book, chronicling the 40-year history of the band, features 127 photos, including never-before-seen images from the KISS archives. Each copy is dated, numbered, and signed by Paul, Gene, Tommy, and Eric Singer. The book was printed in high-definition inks and hand-stitched and bound in Italy by the same binder that The Vatican uses.

During the publicity phase of *Monster*, Paul Stanley said, "This book is way beyond my expectations.

The photos are incredible at this size. It's not a coffee table book, it's a coffee table!" In a noisecreep.com interview, Tommy weighed in on the weighty book: "About 90 percent of the photos are previously unseen. Real special archive stuff. We've got vast archives and pulled some just unbelievably rare stuff. The most ardent fans will say, 'I've never seen most of these shots.' It's amazing … you see a different dynamic and emotion when it's blown up that big. You look into the eyes of those shots and you see more depth than you've ever imagined."

Monster: The Gene Simmons Boxed Set: Originally set to be released in 2007, this boxed set will purportedly contain upwards of 100–200 Gene Simmons songs, including demos and other rare recordings. Unfortunately, as of this writing, it has yet to surface, with no release date in sight.

Monster World Tour: In support of their album *Monster*, KISS toured Austria, Europe, Japan, North America, and South America from November 7, 2012, to November 8, 2013, for a total of 56 concerts. Along with the typical pyrotechnics, the new stage show featured a giant robotic spider with glowing eyes. The monstrosity walked across the stage, lifted the band in the air, and shot fire from its legs.

Band lineup: Paul Stanley, Gene Simmons, Tommy Thayer, and Eric Singer. Opening acts: Rosa Tattooada, Diva Demolition, Thin Lizzy, Mötley Crüe, Satan Takes a Holiday, Hardcore Superstar, Reckless Love, Kvelertak, Ingenting, Five Finger Death Punch, Bitch & Chips, Rival Sons, Shinedown, and Leogun. The tour spawned a June 20, 2013, TV special: *The KISS Monster World Tour: Live from Europe*.

Olivier with www.sleazeroxx.com saw the July 26, 2013, show in Toronto and wrote: "KISS pulled out all the stops in terms of delivering an over-the-top spectacle that no other band can deliver. There were more pyros, explosions, risers, and lights than I had ever seen at any concert—including any prior KISS show.… Sonically, the band sounded great and the songs were well-played … song selection was eerily similar to some of their most recent shows.… I think that KISS should take a page out of Iron Maiden's playbook and vary their set list.… How about 'Fits Like A Glove' rather than 'Lick It Up'? And how about 'Makin' Love' rather than 'Calling Dr. Love'?… At the end of the night, I still felt like I had seen a great show and would most likely go see KISS again."

Followed by: The KISS 40th Anniversary World Tour.

Montrose: Formed in San Francisco in 1974, hard rockers Montrose, featuring Sammy Hagar on lead vocals, opened several shows for KISS during the *Alive!* tour.

Moore, Gary: In 1987, Eric Singer toured with Gary Moore on Moore's Wild Frontier Tour.

Morello, Tom: Rage Against the Machine guitarist Tom Morello, a huge KISS fan, gave a rousing induction speech for the band when they entered the Rock and Roll Hall of Fame in 2014. He also praised the band's fans during his speech: "Tonight proves beyond any shadow of a doubt that the high school bullies and the critics were mistaken. We KISS fans were right, so let's celebrate."

Motorpsycho: Norwegian band Motorpsycho covered "Watchin' You" for their 1994 release, *Another Ugly EP*.

Mott the Hoople: Founded in England in 1969, Mott the Hoople opened various shows for KISS in 1975. Their most well-known song is probably "All the Young Dudes," which was written by David Bowie.

The Move: Formed in Birmingham, England in 1966, the Move was a popular British band that never really took off in the United States. Regardless, they were one of Paul Stanley's favorite groups. The Move's 1968 hit, "Fire Brigade," influenced Stanley to write "Firehouse."

"Move On": Co-written by Mikel Japp, "Move On" is the second track on *Paul Stanley*. The Starchild drew inspiration from Bad Company when working on the song. It's doubtful that Stanley's mother actually told him when he was a young boy not to get tied down to one woman when he got older—that he should "Move On"—but this is nevertheless a catchy and robust pop tune with Stanley's tongue planted firmly in cheek. Includes female backup singers from Desmond Child & Rouge and some rocking lead guitar by Bob Kulick.

Mike Wilkening of ultimateclassicrock.com called "Move On" a "mini-epic that demonstrates the full range of [Paul Stanley's] creative tastes and vocal abilities."

MTV Saturday Night Concerts: KISS Animalize Live: Aired January 26, 1985, this was an edited version of the commercially sold video, *KISS: Animalize Live Uncensored*, which hit stores April 1, 1985. The 90-minute concert was paired down to 55 minutes for broadcast, thanks in part to much of Paul Stanley's R-rated banter being cut.

MTV Special: KISS Unmasking: On September 18, 1983, Gene, Paul, Vinnie Vincent, and Eric Carr appeared on MTV, sans makeup, revealing their true faces to the world. The band felt it needed a new direction, especially after the disappointing sales of the hard rocking *Creatures of the Night*. Since Peter and Ace were gone, and KISS was nowhere near at the height of their popularity, this event lacked the publicity and shock factor it would have received four or five years prior, though it was still an historical event. The telecast itself was rather understated, with "video jockey" J. J. Jackson announcing each band member—one by one—as they sat at a table, looking serious amidst a quiet, non-descript setting.

When asked by Jackson what it felt like, Gene said, "It feels good ... we've always been close to our fans.... I think it's time for them to get to know us a little bit more.... It feels very comfortable." Paul, whose idea it was to unmask for the release of *Lick It Up*, said, "It feels great. To me it doesn't feel all that different."

In his 2001 autobiography, *KISS and Make-Up*, Gene said he was "scared stiff" about the move, but that it was the right thing to do. "*Lick it Up* was released and immediately tripled the sales of *Creatures of the Night*. It went platinum and we were soon filling up concert halls again. This was clearly a new lease on life."

MTV Unplugged *see* **KISS Unplugged**

MTV Video Music Awards: Although the *MTV Video Music Awards* (the VMAs for short) began way back in 1984, KISS has never won an award and has only received one nomination: "Best Cinematography" for "All Hell's Breakin' Loose" (1984). However, the program did feature KISS in 1991, a performance that would turn out to be Eric Carr's last public appearance with the band.

KISS, newly reformed with the original lineup, also performed for the closing of the 1996 show, playing "Rock and Roll All Nite." Comedian Dennis Miller introduced the band thusly: "Alright what do ya say we seal the show with a great, big, sloppy, tongue-in-the-throat, fireworks-exploding-blood-spurting lip-lock, live from under the Brooklyn Bridge. You wanted the best, you got the best! It's KISS!"

MTV's Most Wanted: Hosted by Ray Cokes, *MTV's Most Wanted* was broadcast from London, England from 1992 until 1995. On March 17, 1994, Paul and Gene appeared on the show to promote the tribute album, *Kiss My Ass: Classic KISS Regrooved*. In addition to responding to phone calls from fans, the duo played an acoustic version of "Goin' Blind."

"Much Too Soon": An early (1974) demo sung by Gene Simmons, "Much Too Soon" was unreleased until it appeared on *Love Gun: Deluxe Edition*. It's a soulful tune with a pleasant, late-'60s sound and a nicely sung chorus that will get stuck in your head.

Munroe, Rick: An original member of the KISS road crew, Rick Munroe was the band's lighting director from 1974 to 1977. You can read of his experiences in the book he co-authored, *Out On the Streets—The True Tales of Life On the Road With the Hottest Band In the Land—KISS!*

Munson, Art: Art Munson played guitar on more than half of Peter Criss's 1978 KISS solo album. Munson began his career with Dick Dale and the Del-Tones, and he toured with the Righteous Brothers and Paul Williams. In addition, he had minor acting roles in *Phantom of the Paradise* (1974) and *A Star Is Born* (1976).

"Murder in High Heels": "Murder in High Heels" is the ninth and final track on *Animalize*. Like the song before it, "While the City Sleeps," it was sung and co-written by Gene Simmons (with Mitch Weissman). Unfortunately, it's just as forgettable as its predecessor, ending the album on a sour note (so to speak). Bruce Kulick plays lead guitar, subbing for Mark St. John. Simmons got the idea for the title of "Murder in High Heels" from a 1950s pulp fiction novel of the same name.

Muscular Dystrophy Association: In 1979, KISS recorded a public service announcement to help raise funds for the Muscular Dystrophy Association. Appearing in their *Dynasty*-era costumes: the band said: "We're here to fight a super menace" (Gene); "It takes a lot of power to fight a problem that's larger than life, so we're calling on you" (Peter); "When this disease strikes, it's good to know help is there, but the Muscular Dystrophy Association can't give help unless it gets help; research and medical services cost a lot of money" (Paul); "It takes a determined army to win a fight this big; please stand with us, call and make a pledge right now" (Ace).

Music from "The Elder": Hailed as a masterpiece by some and a colossal embarrassment by others, *Music from "The Elder,"* released November 10, 1981, by Casablanca Records, was a major departure for KISS. The band, lambasted by longtime fans for the disco-influenced *Dynasty* and the sugary pop *Unmasked*, had hired Bob Ezrin to help them create a back-to-the-basics hard rock record. However, he instead suggested a concept album along the lines of the Who's *Tommy* or Pink Floyd's *The Wall*. (Some sources say Paul Stanley and Gene Simmons, wanting critical acclaim, brought the idea to Ezrin.)

Ace Frehley hated the idea, but was outvoted two-to-one by Stanley and Simmons, who were intrigued by Ezrin's challenge (as the replacement for Peter Criss, new member Eric Carr was an employee of KISS, so he had no say in the matter). The frustrated Frehley, distancing himself from the project, recorded his guitar parts at his home studio in Connecticut and shipped the tapes to Ezrin via Federal Express.

Although it was lambasted by critics and fans alike, *Music from "The Elder,"* which features woodwinds and a string section, is a fine record that has aged well. It's an epic, grandiose spectacle that fans of theater rock should enjoy, from the falsetto-voiced "Just a Boy" and "The Oath" to the oxymoronic "Dark Light" to the impassioned "World Without Heroes" to the celebratory "I." Simmons wrote the rock opera-style storyboard for the album, which tells a rather murky tale of a medieval young boy chosen by an ancient order of guardian gods, The Elder, to become a noble warrior and overcome an ancient evil.

Tracks include: "Fanfare" (instrumental), "Just a Boy," "Odyssey," "Only You," "Under the Rose," "Dark Light," A World Without Heroes" (the only single from the record), "The Oath," "Mr. Blackwell," "Escape from the Island," and "I."

Unfortunately, the album sold poorly, and KISS decided not to tour in support of it. They did, however, perform three of the songs in a rousing set on the January 15, 1982, episode of ABC's *Fridays*. KISS also appeared on the syndicated TV program, *Solid Gold*, where they pantomime their way through "I." That same episode also featured the music video for "World Without Heroes."

Frehley, who has said that around half of his solos and overdubs for *Music from "The Elder"* didn't make it on the record, left KISS after the release of the album, though he does appear on the cover of the hard-rocking follow-up, *Creatures of the Night*. Speaking of covers, *Music from "The Elder"* was the first KISS record in which an image of the band doesn't appear on the album. The front depicts a hand (Stanley's hand, actually) reaching for a door knocker while the interior of the original gatefold cover shows a long wooden table, a candle, and four ornate chairs. Clearly, KISS was experimenting with something different, and the public just didn't buy it (so to speak).

In *KISS: Behind the Mask—The Official Authorized Biography*, Stanley called *Music from "The Elder,"* which only reached #75 on the *Billboard* 200 chart, the "biggest misstep of our whole musical career. It was everything that was wrong with us. It was pompous, contrived, self-important, and fat. It was mediocre. We were living in fancy houses. I think the band was losing focus of what made us what we are and how good and special that was."

Simmons said, "The record was interesting, but I don't think it had the soul of the band.... As a KISS record, I'd give it a zero. As a bad Genesis record, I'd give it a two.... I blame me. I really believed in the vision.... I wrote this short story and I wanted to make it into a film. Ezrin said it was a great idea for a concept record.... I wanted credibility, which is very stupid really when you think about it. When you've got everything else, who cares?"

Music from The FAQ: MP3 Tribute to KISS: This free download, produced by members of KISSFAQ (www.kissfaq.com), was released May 5, 2008. It features 23 tracks, including songs by 2000 Man and Dressed to KISS.

Music from The FAQ II: MP3 Tribute to KISS: This free download, produced by members of KISSFAQ, was released August 11, 2008. It features 19 tracks, including songs by LoveGun07 and Revenge.

Music from The FAQ III: MP3 Tribute to KISS: This free download, produced by members of KISSFAQ, was released February 1, 2009. It features 19 tracks, including songs by Les Paul (cover band) and Warmachine731.

Music from The FAQ IV: MP3 Tribute to KISS: This free download, produced by members of KISSFAQ, was released in September of 2009. It features 11 tracks, including three songs by Les Paul (cover band).

Music from The FAQ V: MP3 Tribute to KISS: This free download, produced by members of KISSFAQ, was released in April of 2012. It features 11 tracks, including songs by Shandi777 and Eric Carr91.

Music from The FAQ VI: MP3 Tribute to KISS: This free download, produced by members of KISSFAQ, was released in March of 2013. It features 20 tracks, including songs by Shandi777 and Alive 2000.

Music from The FAQ VII: MP3 Tribute to KISS: This free download, produced by members of KISSFAQ, was released in September of 2014. It features 14 tracks, including songs by the Funnel and Barfer at the Moon.

My Dad the Rock Star: Gene Simmons created and executive-produced *My Dad the Rock Star* (2003–2004, Nelvana production company), a Canadian animated series that ran on Teletoon for two seasons. The show revolves around William "Willy" Zilla, a 14-year old boy trying to maintain a normal life despite being the son of Rock Zilla, a Hot-Blooded Rock Star with green hair and a long tongue.

My First Mister: In *My First Mister* (2001), which was directed by Christine Lahti, Gene Simmons plays Mrs. Wilson Benson's Fantasy Head in an uncredited role. The film is about an alienated teenager (Leelee Sobieski) who befriends a lonely clothing store manager (Albert Brooks). Carol Kane, Michael McKean, John Goodman, and Desmond Harrington also appear.

"My Way": "My Way" is not a cover of the timeless Frank Sinatra number. Rather, it is a synthesizer-heavy song sung by Paul Stanley that evokes (but is not as good as) Van Halen's "Dreams." The high-pitched tune, which is track six on *Crazy Nights*, was written by Stanley (who came up with the song on the keyboards), Desmond Child, and Bruce Turgon, a bassist, guitarist, and songwriter who played with Foreigner and the Lou Gramm Band.

"Naked City": The fourth track on *Unmasked*, "Naked City" was written by Gene Simmons, Vini Poncia, Bob Kulick, and Pepe Castro, who spin a *noir*-influenced yarn of lonely people looking for other lonely people. Despite the fact that Simmons, who sings the tune, has dismissed *Unmasked* as one of the lesser KISS albums, "Naked City" is one of his better songs from the 1980s. It's got a killer bass line and some nice riffing, but Kulick has complained that the band turned what began as a hard rock song into a relatively light pop number.

Nathan, Marc: As the regional promotion director for Casablanca Records from 1975 to 1976, Marc Nathan helped songs from *Alive!* receive radio airplay, most notably "Rock and Roll All Night."

Navarro, Dave: On Gene Simmons' 2004 solo album *Asshole*, Dave Navarro played guitar on "Firestarter," which is a cover of the 1996 song by the Prodigy. Navarro was a founding member of Jane's Addiction and is a former member of the Red Hot Chili Peppers.

Nazareth: Founded in 1968, Scottish hard rockers Nazareth opened for KISS during tours supporting *KISS* and *Dressed to Kill*. They're probably best known for their hits, "Love Hurts" and "Hair of the Dog."

Neaves, Lee: Detroit teenager Lee Neaves is one of the two boys featured on the back cover of *Alive!* He's on the right, holding the homemade KISS sign. Bruce Redoute is on the left.

Nelson, Eric: Eric Nelson, bassist for Nick Gilder, played bass on tracks 6–9 of Paul Stanley's 1978 KISS solo album.

"Never Enough": Written by Paul Stanley and Tommy Thayer, "Never Enough" is the third track on *Sonic Boom* and the third and final single from the album. Sung by Stanley, it has a classic KISS sound that covers several of the band's trademark philosophies, such as living life to the fullest and giving all you've got. During one brief moment, at around two-and-a-half minutes in, the drums and guitar sound like "Plaster Caster." This is a fine KISS song that will please longtime fans of the band.

Never Too Young to Die: In perhaps his most infamous film role, Gene Simmons plays the wicked hermaphrodite, Velvet Von Ragner, in the 1986 B-movie, *Never Too Young to Die* (directed by Gil Bettman). Simmons' character murders a secret agent (played by *Bond* actor George Lazenby), spurring the agent's son—a high school gymnast played by John "Full House" Stamos—to avenge his death (with the help of another agent). Robert "Freddy Krueger" England is also in the film, which noted critic Leonard Maltin called "pretty awful, though Simmons scores a few points for outrageousness in his portrayal of a power-crazed hermaphrodite."

New England: An American rock band that was active primarily from 1978 to 1982, New England's self-titled debut album released in 1979 was co-produced by Paul Stanley. The record had a top-40 single, "Don't Ever Wanna Lose Ya," featuring background vocals by Stanley.

The New Guy: Gene Simmons makes a cameo as a reverend in *The New Guy* (2002), a teen comedy in which terminally uncool band geek Dizzy Gillespie Harrison (DJ Qualls) gets expelled from school, learns how to be cool in prison, and becomes a popular football star at the high school across town. The film also features Eliza Dushku, Zooey Deschanel, pro skater Tony Hawk, and country/folk singer Lyle Lovett. No word on whether Lovett and Simmons had a jam session offstage.

New York Dolls: Other than the Beatles, no band is credited more with influencing KISS than the glitzy, cross-dressing, make-up-wearing New York Dolls. Formed in 1971, the band's classic lineup consisted of vocalist David Johansen, guitarist Johnny Thunders, bassist Arthur Kane (the subject of the 2005 film, *New York Doll*), guitarist and pianist Sylvain Sylvain, and drummer Jerry Nolan, who Peter Criss has referred to as his best friend. Not only did the Dolls influence KISS, they were early pioneers of both punk and glam rock, paving the way for such acts as Blondie, the Ramones, the Sex Pistols, and the Smiths.

"New York Groove": If any song is more identified with Ace Frehley than "Rocket Ride" or "Shock Me," it's "New York Groove," the sixth track on *Ace Frehley*. A hit single that KISS played in concert during their 1979 and 1980 tours, and during the 1996 reunion tour, "New York Groove" made it to #13 on the *Billboard* charts, the highest-charting KISS-related song since "Forever" reached #8 in 1990.

"New York Groove," a funky, quirky song with inspired instrumentation, was written by Russ Ballard and first recording by the glam band Hello in 1975. Frehley's version has been used in various media, including as the opening intro theme to *NY Ink*, a reality television series, and in a TV ad for the Marriott Hotel Chain.

"New York Groove" was ranked #1 on a listing of "Top 10 KISS Solo Album Songs" by Mike Wilkening of ultimateclassicrock.com, who wrote: "The syncopated disco-rock beat was perfect for the times, and native New Yorker Frehley's somewhat weary, detached vocals give the song extra layers of depth."

On November 18, 2014, *The Village Voice* ranked "New York Groove" the 32nd best song about New York: "The Spaceman's most-beloved solo song … it's a great, uplifting song, and perfect for Frehley. The impossible-to-resist stomp-along underpinnings driving the tune are topped with fittingly triumphant and Ace-like sentiments…. When the song takes a half-step up at a minute in, the irresistible factor rises commensurately."

New York Philharmonic: Founded in 1842, the famed New York Philharmonic orchestra played on the original *Destroyer* recording of "Beth."

Newman, Randy: On the cover of Randy Newman's 1979 album, *Born Again*, which satirizes commercialism, the singer/songwriter/pianist is shown sitting at an executive desk, wearing a suit and KISS-style makeup with green dollar signs around his eyes.

According to Kevin Courrier, writing for www.criticsatlarge.ca, Newman originally "planned to close out *Born Again* with a cover of KISS's 'Great Expectations,' but he opted for his own original, 'Pants,' which was unfortunate because it was a one-note retread of the sexual perversities better expressed on 'You Can Leave Your Hat On.' On the other hand, 'Great Expectations,' which [is on] KISS's 1976 album, *Destroyer*, would not only have matched up perfectly with the theme of *Born Again*, it would have also been a fascinating song for Newman to cover."

Nielsen, Rick: Lead guitarist, backing vocalist, and chief songwriter for Cheap Trick, Rick

Nielsen played guitar on Gene Simmons' "See You in Your Dreams."

Night of the Fox: The ERIC CARR Tribute Concert: This concert commemorating the late, great KISS drummer took place on July 13, 2013, at the Elks Lodge Event Hall in Tucker, Georgia. It included live performances from Nostalgica (acoustic KISS tribute), Vintage Boogie Band (classic rock), and Little Caesar (Eric Carr tribute). School of Rock ('70s–'90s covers) was going to play, but had to cancel.

A No Balls Records Tribute to KISS: Released in Germany in May of 2008 by No Balls Records, this small boxed set features four singles on vinyl, each with a silkscreened reverse side. Discs include: a live version of "Deuce" (Adam West); "C'mon And Love Me" (the Strap-Ons); "Rip It Out" (Electric Eel Shock); and "Black Diamond" (Chuck Norris Experiment).

"No, No, No": Written by Gene Simmons, Bruce Kulick, and Eric Carr, "No, No, No" is the fourth track on *Crazy Nights*. The hard-rocking song begins with a bang by Kulick and Carr, doing their best take on Van Halen's "Eruption." Then Simmons begins growling in boogie-woogie style. At the end, it's all sound and fury, signifying nothing (to quote Shakespeare), other than some serious abuse of Gene's vocal cords.

No Regrets: A Rock 'n' Roll Memoir: Ace Frehley's autobiography, written with Joe Layden and John Ostrosky, *No Regrets* was published by Simon & Schuster April 1, 2011. Nathan Rabin of the A.V. Club (www.avclub.com) called it a "curiously underwhelming" memoir by "Sober Ace, a sane, reflective chap in a tweed jacket who is nowhere near as interesting as Space Ace. *No Regrets* consequently has the curious quality of trying to make its author's life seem less unusual and compelling than it actually is."

Conversely, William Pinfold of Record Collector (recordcollectormag.com) said the book is "surprisingly even-handed," "extremely likeable," and "an engaging read for fans," covering Frehley's "formative years in Brooklyn, his brushes with gangs, rock stars, and the police, the KISS years and beyond," including his struggles with drugs and alcohol.

NOH8 Campaign: According to their website, the NOH8 Campaign is a "charitable organization whose mission is to promote marriage, gender, and human equality through education, advocacy, social media, and visual protest." Created by celebrity photographer Adam Bouska and partner Jeff Parshley as a response to California's Proposition 8, which banned same-sex marriage, the group "stands against discrimination and bullying of all kinds."

Gene Simmons and Paul Stanley have appeared in NOH8 promo spots, with Stanley tearing duct tape off his mouth (the tape symbolizes voices being silenced by discriminatory legislation), speaking about our differences and what we have in common, and urging people to make the world a better place by "taking a photo, writing your congressman, talking to kids about bullying … just doing something."

Norton, Mark: Before changing his name to Mark St. John, the late KISS guitarist was Mark Norton.

"Not for the Innocent": The second track on *Lick It Up*, "Not for the Innocent" is a heavy, but fairly standard Gene Simmons number in which he advises everyone to lock up their daughters because KISS is coming to town. The song was written by Simmons and lead guitarist Vinnie Vincent, who kicks in with a fiery solo around three minutes in. Simmons has said the genesis of the song came from the title of *No Rest for the Wicked*, a record by a band called Hydra.

"Nothin' to Lose": The first single from KISS's self-titled debut album, "Nothin' to Lose" tackles the taboo topic of anal sex, specifically a man convincing his girlfriend to have it and her enjoying it. The song was written by Gene Simmons, with Simmons and Paul Stanley singing the verses and the R&B-influenced Peter Criss belting out his raspy voice on the chorus, where he improvises with laughs, claps, and the like. Bruce Foster, doing his best Jerry Lee Lewis, plays the piano on the track, which is one of the band's trademark tunes. "Love Theme from KISS" was on the B-side of the single, which failed to chart.

Nothin' to Lose: The Making of KISS (1972–1975): A collaboration between Ken Sharp, Gene Simmons, and Paul Stanley, this excellent book chronicling the early days of the band features interviews with Simmons and Stanley, along with Ace Frehley and Peter Criss. Plus, it contains quotes from many other people crucial to the origin of KISS (or were at least there at or near the beginning), such as Neil Bogart, Bill Aucoin, Lyn Christopher, and Steve Coronel.

One of those interviewees was Binky Philips, a high school friend of Paul Stanley's who played lead guitar for the Planets, a band that opened for KISS in July of 1973 at the Hotel Diplomat. In his *Huffington Post* review of the book Philips wrote: "Ken Sharp has a gift, it would seem. I know firsthand how skillful and relentless he is in wringing out as many details from you as he can … but, here, much, much more importantly than minutia/trivia, Ken has gotten four guys, drenched in decades' worth of animosity and ill will, to go back and relive 'The Hungry All For One, One For All days.' In almost every quote from Paul, Gene, Ace, and Peter, the air of wistful and still-dazzled-by-it-all reminiscence is palpable.… *Nothin' To Lose* offers a richly detailed day-to-day accounting of all the myths in their legend, and the mundanity of a band's early life, as they really happened."

"Nothing Can Keep Me from You": A fairly typical power ballad about how not even mountains, oceans, and rivers can keep two lovers apart, "Nothing Can Keep Me from You" was written by Diane Warren and sung by Paul Stanley for the KISS-inspired feature film, *Detroit Rock City*. It is the 15th and final track on the movie's soundtrack album. It also appears as track #15 on disc 5 (of 5) of *The Box Set*, a 2001 collection of demos, hits, and other songs.

"Nowhere to Run": The seventh track on *Killers*, "Nowhere to Run" was written and sung by Paul Stanley. It's about a girl Stanley had an affair with, but who left and went back to a guy she was already seeing. Things get off to a bang with a "resonating power chord that recalls the Who's classic 'Won't Get Fooled Again,'" wrote Paul Elliott in *KISS: Hotter Than Hell*. "This Paul Stanley track is the best of the four new songs on this collection. A gentle mid-section, sung falsetto, echoes *Dynasty*'s 'Sure Know Something.'"

Nugent, Ted: Outspoken rocker Ted Nugent, who hails from Detroit, opened shows for KISS during the Dressed to Kill Tour. In an August 28, 2014, interview with radio.com, the Motor City Madman spoke about his appreciation for KISS: "A lot of real purist types think that KISS's kabuki, vaudeville, burlesque stuff is counterproductive to the music. *No! It's what it is.* It's great music and if you don't like the rest of the stuff, go see ZZ Top. Which, in its own way, is the same thing! Or, Bruce Springsteen! His whole 'working class' thing is as real as the kabuki makeup … some of my die-hard rhythm and blues fans dismiss KISS, or anything that isn't gung-ho rhythm and blues, grinding rock and roll. But I've never subscribed to that. I'm much more open-minded than that."

"The Oath": The eighth track on *Music from "The Elder,"* "The Oath," with the possible exception of "I," rocks harder than any other song on the record. The lyrics, written by Stanley, Bob Ezrin, and Tony Powers, continue the epic story of a boy hero, who, through a dream, becomes a man after entering an ancient door.

Obama, Barack: In 2012, the politically-minded Gene Simmons told noisecreep.com that he voted for Obama in 2008, but regretted the decision. "The country is so divided. I voted for President Obama last time but I have to say I'm very disappointed in his job. He's been a piss-poor president as far as I'm concerned."

In 2011, Simmons, who was born in Israel, told CNBC's Jane Wells what he thought about Obama's recommendation that Israel's borders be redrawn to pre–1967 levels: "President Obama, I voted for an idea. What I didn't realize what I was getting was an idealist. If you've never been to the moon, you can't issue policy about the moon. You have no fucking idea what it's like on the moon. For a president to be sitting in Washington, D.C., and saying, 'Go back to your '67 borders in Israel,' how about you live there and try to defend an indefensible border nine miles wide? On one side you've got hundreds of millions of people who hate your guts, on the other side you've got the Mediterranean. Unless you control, in Israel, unless you control those Golan Heights, it's an indefensible position."

"Odyssey": Sung by Paul Stanley and written by Tony Powers, who, interestingly enough, also wrote "We're The Banana Splits" theme song from *The Banana Splits Adventure Hour*, the big, ambitious, operatic, show tune-like "Odyssey" is the third track on *Music from "The Elder."* Powers played keyboards on the song as well, while Allan Schwartzberg contributed drum overdubs. If you don't like "Odyssey," in which the boy hero of the story traverses time and space, you probably won't like *Music from "The Elder."*

The Official® Price Guide to KISS Collectibles: Released July 20, 2004, by Random House, this book sold out within a few months and was never reprinted, making it a collectible in its own right. Fortunately, it is available as a digital download in Apple's iBook format. Written by Ingo Floren, the volume lists more than 10,000 items (dolls, posters, promos, shirts, jewelry, buttons, records, record awards, press kits, and the like), supplemented by more than 500 photos. The book also includes an introduction, tips on how to identify first pressings and official memorabilia, and interviews with Dennis Woloch and Michael Doret, who designed some of the classic KISS album covers of the 1970s.

Olympic Winter Games: On February 24, 2002, Ace, Gene, Paul, and Eric Singer played "Rock and Roll All Nite" on a rotating stage at the Closing Ceremony of the *XIX Olympic Winter Games*. KISS lip-synced the song, as required by the venue, but it exposed the band to a huge worldwide audience. After the song, figure skaters Katarina Witt and Kristi Yamaguchi appeared onstage with the band. Of the performance, the announcer said: "Gene Simmons and the boys in their mid–50s, still bringin' it." Sadly, it was one of Ace Frehley's last performances with KISS.

One for All: Released July 24, 2007, by MRI, *One for All* is a Peter Criss solo album chock-full of ballads. It includes the following tracks: "One for All" (inspired by the 9/11 terrorist attacks), "Doesn't Get Better (Than This)," "Last Night," "What a Difference a Day Makes" (a cover of the 1959 Dinah Washington song, "What a Diff'rence a Day Makes," which dates back to 1934 when it was originally composed in Spanish by Maria Grever as "Cuando Vuelva A Tu Lado"—Stanley Adams wrote the English language lyrics), "Hope," "Faces in the Crowd," "Send in the Clowns" (a cover of the song Stephen Sondheim wrote for the 1973 musical, *A Little Night Music*), "Falling All Over Again," "Whisper," "Heart Behind these Hands," "Memories," and "Space Ace," which Criss said in *Makeup to Breakup* is about how he was betrayed by his former bandmate, Ace Frehley.

One Life Music—A Tribute to Paul Stanley: This German EP from Seven Hell singer Chris Preisser, released by Rock Werk Records on December 10, 2010, includes the following tracks: "Live to Win," "Hide Your Heart," "Bulletproof," "Tonight You Belong to Me," and "Million to One."

One Live KISS see **Paul Stanley: One Live KISS**

"100,000 Years": Written by Paul Stanley and Gene Simmons, "100,000 Years" is the ninth track on *KISS*, the band's first album. Simmons got the idea for the song from reading a book of the same name. *KISS: Hotter Than Hell* author Paul Elliott wrote that "100,000 Years" is "one of the most dynamic of early KISS songs, more complex than, say, 'Deuce' or 'Strutter,' yet no less anthemic. Ace Frehley contributes fiery solos and Paul Stanley sings as if he's already performing before a sold-out stadium."

"Only You": Written by Gene Simmons, who also plays rhythm guitar on the song, "Only You" is the fourth track on *Music from "The Elder."* It cements the protagonist of the album as a messiah-like hero: only he has the answers, knows the secrets, and is the light and the way. Unlike the previous three tracks on the record, which are very soft, "Only You" is a pop rocker, featuring some relatively aggressive guitar work. However, as sung by Simmons and Paul Stanley, it fits in nicely with the theme of the record, going so far as to include the refrain from "Just a Boy."

The Oprah Winfrey Show: In 1987, during the *Crazy Nights* era, Paul Stanley and Gene Simmons appeared on *The Oprah Winfrey Show*, which ran from 1986 to 2011. They appeared with authors Jackie Collins and Pamela Des Barres (a former groupie famous for sleeping with numerous rock stars during the 1970s). Winfrey asked them about one-night stands, casual sex, groupies, and the like. Early in the show, Simmons said: "The reason we started strumming guitars is because we wanted women, and lots of them ... and their daughters." Stanley responded with: "It's really great. It's kind of like being at a buffet where everything's laid out, and you don't have to take this or this or this, but it's all there to be eaten if you want it."

Oreckinto, Peter "Moose": Co-author of *Out On the Streets—The True Tales of Life On the Road With the Hottest Band In the Land—KISS!*, Peter "Moose" Oreckinto was a member of the original KISS road crew, acting as a roadie and sound mixer. He also handled pyrotechnics and almost lost his hand in an accident related to that position in late 1974.

The Original Wicked Lester Sessions: This is a bootleg of the unreleased Wicked Lester album, which was recorded in 1972 for Epic Records. Different versions of the unreleased Wicked Lester album exist, but a complete one includes all 11 Wicked Lester recordings that were intended for the LP: "Love Her All I Can," "Sweet Ophelia," "Keep Me Waiting," "Simple Type," "She," "Too Many Mondays," "What Happens in the Darkness," "When the Bell Rings," "Molly," "We Want to Shout It Out Loud," and "Long, Long Road." Tracks 1, 3, and 5 were included in 2001's *The Box Set*.

The Originals: With the rising popularity of KISS in the wake of *Alive!* and *Destroyer*, Casablanca saw fit to release *The Originals* (July 21, 1976), a boxed, limited-edition, specially priced repackaging of the first three KISS albums: *KISS*, *Hotter Than Hell*, and *Dressed to Kill*. Included in the package were a 14-page booklet on the history of the band (photos and text by Richard Robinson), six biographical trading cards, and a KISS Army sticker. The first pressing of 250,000 copies sold out, prompting a second printing in May of 1977. The re-issue says "Second Pressing" on the top/right corner of the front cover. The Japanese version was packaged with a second booklet containing lyrics. Complete copies of *The Originals* are highly collectable.

The Originals II: Released only in Japan, *The Originals II* is a repackaging of the three KISS studio albums that followed *Alive!*: *Destroyer*, *Rock and Roll Over*, and *Love Gun*. Included in the package are a gatefold picture sleeve, an eight-page lyric booklet, an eight-page photo booklet, four KISS masks, and an obi strip (a strip of text-heavy paper looped around the left side of the cover). As with *The Originals*, *The Originals II* is sought after by collectors. Neither *The Originals* nor *The Originals II* has ever been released on CD.

Ostrander, Brooke: When Stephen Coronel introduced Gene Simmons to Paul Stanley, it was at the apartment of Brooke Ostrander, a keyboardist Simmons knew. Ostrander played horns and piano for Rainbow/Wicked Lester. Ostrander brought in his pal, Joe Davidson, to drum for the band, but Davidson was quickly replaced by Tony Zarrella.

The Other Side of the Coin: One of many books written by Julian Gill and published by KissFAQ Publishing, *The Other Side of the Coin* was released October 11, 2007. It is a compilation of previously published articles and interviews from kissfaq.com. Interview subjects include Sean Delaney, Charles Frehley (Ace's brother), and members of Criss (Peter's old band), among others. The book was dedicated to Mark St. John. *See also:* "Gill, Julian."

The Other Side of the Coin **is one of many KISS books written by Julian Gill and published by KissFAQ Publishing.**

Out of Control: Recorded while Peter Criss was still officially a member of KISS, *Out of Control* is the Catman's second solo album (after 1978's *Peter Criss*), hitting stores in September of 1980. Sporting an erupting jukebox on the cover painted by American pop artist Todd Schorr, the LP, published by Casablanca Records, contains the following tracks: "By Myself," "In Trouble Again," "Where Will They Run?," "I Found Love" (the only single from the album), "There's Nothing Better," "Out of Control," "Words, "You Better Run" (a cover of the 1966 Young Rascals tune), "My Life," "Feel Like Letting Go," and a brief opening snippet of "As Time Goes By." "Out of Control" and "There's Nothing Better" were originally recorded as demos for *Dynasty*, but they were rejected.

In a 1980 appearance on *The Tomorrow Show*, Criss told Tom Snyder that the name for the album came from the fact that people were always telling him he was out of control. *Out of Control* sold poorly, failing to reach the *Billboard* 200 album chart, but it was finally released on CD in 1997.

Out of the Void: The sequel to *Into the Void… with Ace Frehley*, *Out of the Void*, written by Frehley's former girlfriend and personal assistant Wendy Moore, was released at the 2009 KISS Expo in Los Angeles. According to Moore, she wrote the book to answer questions fans had after reading *Into the Void*.

Out on the Streets—The True Tales of Life on the Road with the Hottest Band in the Land—KISS!: Released by TOKK Publishing in 2014, *Out On the Streets* "comes directly from the collective efforts of J. R. Smalling, Peter Oreckinto, Rick Munroe and the late Mick Campise, who comprised the core of the band's original road crew from 1974 to 1976." The book gives readers insight into what it was like on the road with KISS, sleeping with groupies, battling with such headline acts as Aerosmith, logging over 90,000 miles on the road in 1974 alone, and much more. Includes rare photos, original itineraries, detailed production schematics, and more.

Unfortunately, the guys who host *Three Sides of the Coin* were heavily disappointed with the book. In their review in episode 197, they said it seemed like a vendetta against the band, that it was "all over the place," that it spent too much time on tough driving conditions and a lawsuit against Universal, and that it could've used an editor to help pull out and spotlight the good stuff and "get rid of the crap."

"Outta This World": Written and sung by Tommy Thayer, "Outta This World," the ninth track on *Monster*, is essentially Thayer's Ace Frehley song on the record, right down to the spacey title. It sounds a lot different than the other songs on *Monster*, making for a nice change of pace. Cowbell helps keep the beat.

Outtakes: Prior to writing the KISS photo book *Outtakes*, which was published by Studio Chikara on October 15, 1999, super KISS fan Chip Rock Dayton had been photographing rock stars for 30 years. *Outtakes* features more than 200 of his black-and-white and color photos—mostly of KISS live in concert—but some backstage. The majority of the pictures depict the original lineup, but there is a chapter entitled "The Debut of Eric Carr."

According to publisher ad copy, "KISS was so impressed with Chip's imagery they selected him to shoot the cover of their first tour program. Over the years, Chip's photos have appeared in KISS albums, videos, and their mammoth self-published book, *KISStory*."

Longtime KISS photographer Chip Rock Dayton wrote *Outtakes* in 1999. It was published by Studio Chikara and is lavishly illustrated with rare photographs.

Oz: In the HBO prison drama, *Oz* (1997–2003), Peter Criss played inmate Martin Montgomery in two episodes: "Visitation" (season 5, episode 1) and "Laws of Gravity" (season 5, episode 2). Montgomery, a minor league baseball player and alcoholic, was serving time for beating an umpire to death with a baseball bat.

"Ozone": Like "Snow Blind" before it, "Ozone," the fourth track on *Ace Frehley*, is about drugs. However, instead of being a downer, it's an upbeat (if spacey) song, one of the more interesting, more creative recordings on a great album. Amidst excellent acoustic and electric guitar accompaniment, Frehley sings that he's the kind of guy who enjoys getting high. In 1995, the Foo Fighters covered "Ozone" for the "Special Tour Edition" of their self-titled debut album.

Pacific University Legends Golf Classic, hosted by Tommy Thayer: Inspired by the KISS lead guitarist in 2007, this now-annual event, which includes "music by Tommy Thayer and friends," raises funds for Pacific University's Athletics Program in Oregon. Numerous celebrities have participated, including Gene Simmons, Clint Black, George Lopez, Clint Howard, and Darius Rucker.

***PACO STANLEY: A Tribute to Starchild*:** Released October 31, 2014, in Spain by Earth Records, this tribute album featuring lead vocals and guitar by Paco Stanley includes the following tracks: "Live to Win," "Strutter," "I Stole Your Love," "A Million to One," "I Was Made for Lovin' You," "Hold Me, Touch Me," "Detroit Rock City," "The Oath," "Love Gun," "Tonight You Belong to Me," "Heaven's On Fire," "C'mon and Love Me," "Goodbye," and "Shandi."

Palisades Free Library: On May 26, 1973, KISS played one of their strangest gigs ever: a benefit concert art at the Palisades Free Library in Palisades, New York. Approximately 300 people were in attendance, including CBS News correspondent Morely Safer. KISS played the small concert at the behest of their manager. The event raised more than $3,000.

"Paralyzed": Despite penning downbeat lyrics that express hopelessness, Gene Simmons, who wrote the song with Bob Ezrin, sounds like he's having fun singing this, the 10th track on *Revenge*. "Paralyzed" doesn't always flow smoothly, but it's hardly the worst post-makeup Simmons song. The Demon has stated that he prefers the more down and dirty demo version.

"Parasite": The second track on the second KISS album, *Hotter Than Hell*, "Parasite" was written by Ace Frehley, but sung (with menace) by Gene Simmons, since Frehley had yet to gain the confidence in his vocal abilities to sing lead. It's a meat-and-potatoes, hard-rocking tune about a parasitic woman who won't go away, even though her man wants her to. Anthrax covered the song for their 1994 album, *The Island Years*.

Parenteau, Mark: An early supporter of getting KISS played on the radio, Mark Parenteau was the music director and afternoon DJ for Detroit's WABX-FM.

"Partners in Crime": There were four new songs on *Killers*, which was a UK release comprised mostly of greatest hits tracks. Three are excellent, but one, "Partners in Crime," is a turkey. For a rocker, it's slow and sleepy sounding, and the chorus is even duller than the rest of the song. It was written by Adam Mitchell and Paul Stanley, who sings about an illicit hookup with a girl who has a lover at home. Stanley has said that he hates the song.

***The Paul Lynde Halloween Special*:** Forty-one minutes into *The Paul Lynde Halloween Special*, which aired October 29, 1976, on ABC, Lynde introduces KISS, saying "Beth" is a "monster of a hit." Criss is shown at a piano in a fancy room, lip-syncing the song. After "Beth," Margaret Hamilton, wearing her witch makeup and costume, introduces Lynde to KISS. After a few corny jokes by Lynde, KISS lip-syncs "King of the Night Time World," and Gene does his fire breathing trick. The band "performs" "Detroit Rock City" as well. Other celebrities who appeared on the special, which is where many kids of the day saw KISS for the first time, include Billie Hayes, Billy Barty, Tim Conway, Roz "Pinky Tuscadero" Kelly, Florence Henderson, Betty White, Donny Osmond, and Marie Osmond.

***Paul Stanley* (album):** Paul Stanley's first solo album, released September 18, 1978, alongside the other three band members' solo records, is widely known as the most KISS-like of the four, which only makes sense since he's the frontman.

Reaching #40 on the *Billboard* 200, the LP, which Stanley has called autobiographical in nature, includes the following tracks: "Tonight You Belong to Me," "Move On," "Ain't Quite Right," "Wouldn't You Like to Know Me," "Take Me Away (Together as One)," "It's Alright," "Hold Me,

Touch Me (Think of Me When We're Apart)," "Love in Chains," and "Goodbye."

"Hold Me, Touch Me (Think of Me When We're Apart)" was the only single from the LP, reaching #46 on the *Billboard* charts. Bob Kulick, the older brother of former KISS lead guitarist Bruce Kulick, played lead and acoustic guitar on the album. Carmine Appice, who played drums for such acts as Rod Stewart, Vanilla Fudge, and King Cobra, pounded the skins on "Take Me Away (Together as One)."

Paul Stanley: One Live KISS: Released October 1, 2008, this concert DVD features Paul Stanley backed by the house band from the CBS television shows *Rock Star: INXS* and *Rock Star: Supernova*. Tracks include: "Live to Win," "Hide Your Heart," "A Million to One," "Got to Choose," "Move On," "Bulletproof," "Tonight You Belong to Me," "Lick It Up," "Wouldn't You Like to Know Me," "Magic Touch," "I Still Love You," "Strutter," "Everytime I See You Around," "Do You Love Me," "I Want You," "Love Gun," "Lift," "Detroit Rock City," and "Goodbye."

Pearl Drums: During the mid–1970s, Peter Criss began playing Pearl drums. In fact, he endorsed Pearl drums. According to www.petercrissdrums.com, "Peter would frequently visit a drum store in New York called Professional Percussion Centre, and the owner at the time, Frank Ippolito, introduced him to Pearl Drums, who were willing to give Peter an endorsement to use their drums. Later on when KISS became big, other drum companies, including Ludwig, would approach Peter to use their drums, but out of appreciation and loyalty for Pearl, he declined all their offers." Years later, Eric Singer endorsed Pearl Drums.

Pedulla Guitars: During the 1980s and '90s, Gene Simmons frequently played Pedulla bass guitars. The company celebrated its 40th anniversary in 2015.

Peek, Amber: Tommy Thayer's wife. He met the jewelry designer at a party in Dallas in 2003 and married her June 4, 2006. In an article about their wedding published on www.weddingstyle magazine.com, Peek said: "My husband can wear makeup and spandex and somehow it's really cool.... It's fun to watch him play.... He definitely is the rocker guy," but he is also a "solid guy" with a "soft heart."

Penridge, Stan: During the early 1970s, Stan Penridge played guitar in Chelsea and Lips, featuring Peter Criss on drums. In addition, he co-wrote a number of KISS/Peter Criss songs: "Beth," "Baby Driver," "Dirty Livin'," "Hooligan," "Don't You Let Me Down," "Hooked on Rock 'n' Roll," "That's the Kind of Sugar Papa Likes," "Easy Thing," and "I'm Gonna Love You." He also played guitar on several tracks on the Catman's 1978 KISS solo album, and he worked with Criss on *Out of Control*.

In 1984, Criss and Penridge went their separate ways. In 2000, Penridge filed a lawsuit against KISS, claiming unpaid songwriting royalties. Sadly, he died of a heart attack May 11, 2001, which was before the case was settled. He was 50 years old.

See also: "Criss-Penridge Alliance."

People: The August 18, 1980, issue of *People* magazine features KISS on the cover, including new member Eric Carr, decked out in his Fox costume. In the article, which profiles all four band members, Carr said, "I become the Fox because I'm wily." The piece also touches on how long it took for Carr to design the makeup (60 hours), Peter Criss leaving the band, the "recession-racked music industry," and slow sales for *Unmasked*.

The April 10, 1978, issue of *People* depicts Cher and Gene Simmons on the cover while the January 21, 1991, issue has an article on the Peter Criss imposter.

People's Choice Awards: Originating in 1975, the *People's Choice Awards* is a CBS TV show that awards pop culture performers and their works based on popularity. KISS won but a single "People's Choice Award": "Favorite New Song" for "Beth" in 1977. The tune tied for the award with "Disco Duck," the novelty song by Rick Dees and His Cast of Idiots. Peter Criss, who co-wrote and sang "Beth," has cited the award as giving him the confidence to leave KISS and form a career as a solo artist.

Perry, Joe: Aerosmith founding member and lead guitarist Joe Perry holds the distinction of being the first rock star to jam with KISS onstage in concert during a tour, doing so at shows in Houston, Los Angeles, and Oklahoma in 2003. Perry also played guitar on two songs on Gene Simmons' 1978 KISS solo album: "Radioactive" and "Tunnel of Love."

Personality Comics Presents KISS: Published by Personality Comics, this unauthorized biographical comic book series ran three issues in 1992. Each issue had a limited trading card edition.

Peter Criss (album): Released in conjunction with the other three KISS solo albums on September 18, 1978, *Peter Criss*, which is more rhythm and blues than rock and roll, contains the following tracks: "I'm Gonna Love You," "You Matter to Me," "Tossin' and Turnin'" (a cover of the 1961 Bobby Lewis tune), "Don't You Let Me Down," "That's the Kind of Sugar Papa Likes," "Easy Thing," "Rock Me, Baby," "Kiss the Girl Goodbye," "Hooked on Rock 'n' Roll," and "I Can't Stop the Rain."

Like the other band members' solo records, *Peter Criss* shipped over 1,000,000 copies, but many were relegated to bargain bins a few months after release; in fact, all four KISS solo records were bargain bin fodder. Despite being the only one to have two singles, "Don't You Let Me Down" and "You Matter to Me," the ballad-heavy *Peter Criss* was the lowest charting of the four, reaching #43 on the *Billboard* album chart. It is widely regarded as the weakest release musically as well. The record was produced by Vini Poncia, who would go on to produce *Dynasty* and *Unmasked*.

In *Rolling Stone* #279 (Nov., 1978), Peter Criss implied that his self-titled album was his first step toward a potential solo career. "I see myself eventually on my own without the makeup and the bombs, without theatrics," he said. "I could dig getting up there with a white suit and three chick-singers. I don't know if this is it for the band—nothing lasts forever. I've made it. At least now it's a stepping stone for each of us. If the band split up I really wouldn't mind."

Peter Criss Imposter: In 1990, the popular tabloid *Star* ran a story about a homeless man—allegedly ex-drummer Peter Criss—living under the bridge of the Santa Monica Pier in California, begging for money and suffering from an alcohol-related illness. The headline read, KISS STAR HITS THE SKIDS. In response, comedian Tom Arnold and former Crosby, Stills & Nash drummer Dallas Taylor rushed to his aid. In addition, 28-year-old actress/model Cheryl Anne Thompson, who claims she dated Criss during the early 1980s, sent him a first class ticket to Boston so she could help him out.

In reality, the homeless "Peter Criss" was 39-year-old Evanston, Illinois, native Christopher Dickinson, who had been "passing himself off as the KISS drummer for years," said an article in the January 21, 1991, issue of *People*. After being found out, Dickinson told the magazine, "It just got to be well-known around Santa Monica that that's who I was. I had gotten my real ID stolen. Why I said it, I don't really know. I was just very confused, very mixed up from alcohol."

When Thompson met Dickinson, who had long hair and resembled Criss only vaguely, at the airport, she immediately knew he was a fake. "I really almost threw up," she told *People*. "I wanted to run out of there as fast as I could." Despite the deception, Thompson helped Dickinson anyway and was touched by the fact that "anyone who'd come that far knowing that I was going to find out had to be desperate."

As for Criss, the ruse hit him at a bad time. Although he was living comfortably (if somewhat anonymously) in Redondo Beach, California, with Debra Jensen, his wife of 11 years, and their 8-year-old daughter, Jenilee, his mother was dying. At her funeral, he was bombarded with questions about the *Star* article, to which he could barely respond since he was grieving for his mom.

On an episode of *The Phil Donahue Show* that aired shortly after the imposter incident, Peter Criss appeared, along with Jensen, Dickinson, and Thompson. Criss told Dickinson the article was more the *Star*'s fault than his, but he bitterly denied having an affair with Thompson. Lydia Criss called into the show, offering her former husband her support and calling Thompson a liar. Arnold appeared on the show via satellite.

The Phantom of the Opera: Horror buff Gene Simmons has often cited the Lon Chaney, Sr., version of *The Phantom of the Opera* (1925) as an inspiration for his makeup design.

In 1999, Paul Stanley played the title role in the Toronto production of Andrew Lloyd Weber's musical, *The Phantom of the Opera*. He portrayed the Phantom from May 25 to August 1, and again from September 30 to October 31. "It was incredible," Stanley said of the experience in *Fangoria* #298. "A lot of intense work, but an incredible point in my life."

Philips, Binky: A school friend of Paul Stanley, Binky Philips was a guitarist and songwriter for the Planets, a New York band that opened for

KISS July 13, 1973, at the Hotel Diplomat in New York City (the Brats were the headlining act). Philips watched KISS at the Loft early in 1973, when Ace Frehley had just joined the band.

Piano Tribute to KISS: Released by CC Entertainment on October 16, 2012, this CD featuring music by the Piano Tribute Players features the following tracks: "Rock and Roll All Nite," "Beth," "I Was Made for Lovin' You," "New York Groove," "Lick It Up," "Hell or Hallelujah," "Detroit Rock City," "Calling Dr. Love," "Shout It Out Loud," and "Love Gun."

Pinball Machine *see* *KISS* **(pinball machine)**

Pinball Magazine: *Pinball Magazine* #3, published in 2015, features art from Stern's *KISS* pinball machine on the cover. The issue includes "interviews with former pinball designer Jim Patla, former Bally Marketing and Licensing Director Tom Nieman, graphic artist Kevin O'Connor (responsible for the artwork on both Bally's and Stern's *KISS* pinball machines), pinball designer John Borg (Stern's *KISS*), and Stern's Marketing and Licensing Director Jody Dankberg."

Plant, Robert: In *Nothin' to Lose: The Making of KISS (1972–1975)*, Gene Simmons compared a young, pre–KISS Paul Stanley to Robert Plant, Led Zeppelin's legendary frontman: "He had the right stance onstage, looked good, and sang with a high voice like Robert Plant." In *Face the Music: A Life Exposed*, Stanley, who first saw Led Zeppelin live during the summer of 1969, wrote, "Robert Plant sang like a banshee … commanding … magnetic … he created a style that didn't exist before … he was more than just a singer … the physical embodiment of a rock god … an archetype in the making. Everybody wanted to look and sound like Plant."

"Plaster Caster": Kicking off with a nifty bass line and ending with a hot lead guitar flourish, "Plaster Caster" is Gene Simmons' ode to the Plaster Casters, Chicago groupies who would make plaster casts of the erect private parts of their various rock star lovers. For a dirty, punk-influenced song, "Plaster Caster," the ninth track on *Love Gun*, is surprisingly melodic, "a model of songwriting economy that constantly ascends as it builds from moody verses into its snarling, triumphant chorus" (Donald A. Guarisco, www.allmusic.com).

Playboy: Gene Simmons was featured in the March 1999 "Sex and Music" issue of *Playboy*, depicted on the cover in full makeup and costume with three "Girls of KISS." The entire band (Ace, Gene, Paul, and Eric Singer) appears inside, posing with gorgeous women who are wearing KISS makeup and little else. During the photo shoot, Paul joked: "They're not really naked, and we're not really enjoying ourselves."

Simmons' wife, Shannon Tweed, was Playboy Playmate of the Month in the November 1981 issue of *Playboy*, which was founded by Hugh Hefner in 1953.

Playboy Mansion: In her autobiography, *KISS and Tell*, Shannon Tweed wrote about meeting Gene Simmons at the Playboy Mansion: "Gene had short hair for his movie role [*Runaway*] and was wearing white silk pajamas—only pajamas. He looked a little shiny, a little shady, with slicked-back hair and a cocky grin…. I can't say it was love at first sight, at least not for me. He immediately went into his whole Gene routine. I was not impressed."

Of living with Hugh Hefner at the Playboy Mansion prior to meeting Simmons, Tweed said: "I could see the day when sitting around, partying, drinking, and doing whatever nonsense we felt like doing was not going to be all that I needed. The relationship didn't have that permanent feeling. It was intense in a different way. It was all so shiny and new and thrilling."

PM Magazine: A syndicated news entertainment program that ran from September 1978 to August 1991, *PM Magazine* featured KISS several times. In 1978, Paul Stanley appeared on the program, talking about the fans, the music, the makeup, and the band's live shows.

In 1979, a segment showed behind-the-scenes and onstage footage of a KISS show at the Hemis-Fair Arena in San Antonio, Texas. When the host asked Paul and Gene, "You guys are truly one-of-a-kind, but how do you feel when people try to imitate what you do?," the Starchild responded: "I think when fans do it, it's great; bands can't really do it, because when the try to do it, they look so silly. There's only room for one KISS, and that's us."

In February of 1983, *PM Magazine* had a seven-minute KISS comeback segment of sorts, mentioning replacement members Eric Carr and Vinnie Vincent, the new album *Creatures of the*

Night, and the band embarking on a new 100-city tour. There's also some nice concert footage (including Ace), a playful scene in which a *PM Magazine* photographer tries to film the band without their makeup, and interview excerpts with Gene and Paul. When Paul is asked if KISS stands for "Knights in Service to Satan," he said: "It could just as easily stand for 'Knights in Your Sister's Skirt'… it's amazing that there are people around who are so warped that they spend their time trying to … make KISS mean something … those people are sick."

Earlier in the episode, Gene admitted that KISS has gimmickry, but no more than anyone else. "It's as much of a gimmick as Sinatra coming out dressed in tails," he said. "You get up on stage and you have an obligation to the audience, to give them the best show they've ever seen, and we do it like this. Some people like to come out in jeans and a tie-dyed sweat shirt … that's not my idea of what a star is supposed to be like."

Podcast Rock City: This KISS podcast can be found at podcastrockcity.podomatic.com.

PodKISSt: The Fanzine for Your Ears: Founded in January of 2007, *PodKISSt* is, as its name suggests, a KISS podcast. You can find the show at podkisst.com.

PolyGram: Formed in 1962 as the Grammophon-Philips Group (GPG), the result of a merger between PPI and DGG, PolyGram officially became PolyGram in 1972. PolyGram bought 50 percent of Casablanca in 1977 and the rest of the company in 1980. After the *Creatures of the Night* album, PolyGram transferred KISS to their Mercury label.

In 1998, the distillery company Seagram bought PolyGram. Seagram proceeded to merge PolyGram with MCA, forming the Universal Music Group.

Poncia, Vini: In addition to producing Peter Criss's second post–KISS solo album, *Let Me Rock You*, Vini Poncia produced *Dynasty* and *Unmasked*, along with co-writing several songs and singing backup vocals on those two records. He also co-wrote five tracks on *Hot in the Shade*.

Popcorn Pub see **Coventry**

Popeye: In a July 15, 2012, article about KISS in London's *Sunday Express*, Gene Simmons said: "I've learned some important life lessons over the years, principally: be the best you can be but be yourself. I espouse Popeye's philosophy of life: 'I am what I am and that's all that I am, I'm Popeye the sailor man.'"

During the late 1970s, in a Canadian magazine called *Vibrations*, Simmons cited Popeye as a key inspiration in his life: "'I yam what I yam, and that's all that I yam!' That's Popeye's classic line. Here's a guy who doesn't care that he looks strange, with his big arms and no hair. But he's proud of what he is. He's a prophet."

Created by E. C. Segar, *Popeye* first appeared in 1929 in Segar's comic strip, *Thimble Theatre*.

Porcaro, Mike: Mike Porcaro, a longtime bassist for Toto, played bass on "Creatures of the Night." Sadly, he passed away March 15, 2015, at the age of 59.

Postlethwaite, Fritz: During KISS's formative years and through their heyday, Fritz Postlethwaite worked his way from monitor mixer to tour manager. In a 2011 interview published on www.kissfanzine.com, he said: "I worked with them for a long time and I spent a great deal of time with the members individually and socially, even when we weren't working. They were all good friends and very different personalities."

Powers, Tony: Tony Powers wrote "Odyssey" from *Music from "The Elder."* Amusingly enough, he also wrote "We're The Banana Splits," the catchy theme from the classic kids' show, *The Banana Splits*.

Presley, Elvis: Along with KISS and the Beatles, Elvis Presley, a huge influence on all four original members of KISS, is one of the most heavily merchandised rock acts of all time, spawning bubblegum cards, figurines, toys, and thousands of other items. Often called "The King of Rock and Roll," Presley, who died August 16, 1977, at the age of 42, has sold more than one billion records worldwide (including singles, albums, downloads, and every other format).

"Prisoner of Love": One of many throwaway Gene Simmons songs from the 1980s, "Prisoner of Love" is the fourth track on *Hot in the Shade*. Simmons wrote the largely tuneless song with Bruce Kulick, who does provide some pretty nifty guitar licks. That's Eric Carr on cowbell.

Prophecy: A Tribute to Eric Carr: Produced and performed (primarily) by Ralph E.

Carle, *Prophecy* was released in April of 2000 by Lunar Moth Records. Tracks include: "Intro" (Eric Carr radio station ID); "Not Dead Yet" (featuring Karl Cochran); "Imaginary Friends"; "Your Turn To Cry"; "Prophecy"; "Never Say I Love You Again"; "Green Monster '91"; "She Loves Me"; "So Much More"; and "Your Turn to Cry" (original Eric Carr/Cellarmen version).

***Psycho Circus* (album):** Released September 22, 1998, by Mercury, *Psycho Circus* was the first KISS album to feature the original band lineup in almost two decades. It followed in the wake of the 1996 reunion tour, which excited longtime fans.

Unfortunately, despite the presence of a typically fine Ace Frehley song ("Into the Void") and a Peter Criss-sung ballad ("I Finally Found My Way"), the Spaceman and the Catman are underutilized on the album. Bruce Kulick plays the solo on "Within" while Tommy Thayer plays lead on every song but "Into the Void," "You Wanted the Best," and "In Your Face." Session musician Kevin Valentine plays drums on every song but "Into the Void."

Despite this, *Psycho Circus*, which hit #3 on the *Billboard* 200 chart, remains a solid and even classic KISS album. Produced by Bruce Fairbairn, who had worked with the likes of Aerosmith and Bon Jovi, and who is alleged to have minimized Frehley's and Criss's contributions, the record contains the following tracks: "Psycho Circus," "Within," "I Pledge Allegiance to the State of Rock & Roll," "Into the Void," "We Are One," "You Wanted the Best," "Raise Your Glasses," "I Finally Found My Way," "Dreamin'," and "Journey of 1,000 Years." All four band members sing lead on the anthemic "You Wanted the Best."

The limited edition version of *Psycho Circus* includes a bonus song, "In Your Face," written by Gene Simmons and sung by Ace Frehley, along with six live bonus tracks: "Psycho Circus," "Let Me Go, Rock 'n' Roll," "Into the Void," "Within," "100,000 Years," and "Black Diamond."

Entertainment Weekly's Matt Diehl reviewed *Psycho Circus* and wrote that it "sounds like it was recorded two decades ago—thank God.... This new effort proves that in the circus of hard-rock dinosaurs, KISS remain its Barnum & Bailey. A-"

"Psycho Circus" (song): The first track on the album of the same name, "Psycho Circus" begins, fittingly enough, with circus music, leading into classic-style KISS. Ringmaster and singer Paul Stanley, who wrote the tune with Curtis Cuomo, does a good job making fans glad makeup-wearing KISS was back in the recording business.

"Psycho Circus" was released as a single (with "In Your Face" on the B side), becoming KISS's first #1 hit on the *Billboard* Hot Mainstream Rock Tracks chart (as opposed to the more commonly referenced *Billboard* Hot 100), which ranks the most-played songs on mainstream rock radio stations. It was also nominated for a Grammy for Best Hard Rock Performance, losing to Jimmy Page and Robert Plant's "Most High." Tommy Thayer plays lead guitar on the song while Kevin Valentine pounds the skins.

***Psycho Circus* (video):** This "Limited Edition" VHS package includes an animated 3D version of the "Psycho Circus" video, a pair of 3D glasses, a standard version of the "Psycho Circus" video, and a bonus CD containing the songs "Psycho Circus" and "In Your Face." The CD also contains a screensaver and a way to connect to KISS Online. The front of the box says "Collect all Four!," referring to the fact that there were four different CD designs printed, each with the face of a different band member.

Psycho Circus World Tour: From October 31, 1998, to January 3, 2000, KISS played 62 shows in North America, South America, and Europe, in support of their 18th studio album (not counting the 1978 KISS solo albums). It was a follow-up to the Reunion Tour and featured the original lineup of Ace Frehley, Gene Simmons, Paul Stanley, and Peter Criss.

KISS wore replicas of their *Destroyer*-era costumes, and the stage featured a massive Imax 3D video screen and two huge KISS logos. By donning 3D glasses that were provided at the door, fans could watch 3D images onscreen, making it the first concert tour in history to boast 3D visual effects. Frehley played a new Gibson Les Paul guitar dubbed "UFO Light Guitar" (designed by Steve Carr) because of its unique lighting effects.

Three songs from the opening show at Dodger Stadium on October 31 were screened live for *KISS Live: The Ultimate Halloween Party*, a Fox television special: "Psycho Circus" and "Let Me Go, Rock 'n' Roll" were shown on the East Coast while "Psycho Circus" and "Shout It Out Loud" aired on the West Coast. The special included a Smashing Pumpkins song as well, "Cash Car Star," featuring

Pucker

Billy Corgan and the gang dressed up like the Beatles.

Opening acts: Big Wreck, Bionic, Buck Cherry, Caroline's Spine, Econoline Crush, Everclear, the John Hayes Project, Junkbox, Lit, Los Villanos, Natural Born Hippies, Nickelback, Ozone Monday, PUYA, Rammstein, and the Smashing Pumpkins (only at the Dodger Stadium show). Average attendance: 12,826.

Followed by: KISS Farewell Tour.

PUCKER UP: A Canadian MotorCity Tribute to the Hottest Band in the Land: Released in 1996 by Persuasion Records, *PUCKER UP* features the following tracks: "Rip It Out" (Starter), "King of the Night Time World" (Guitar Army), "Charisma" (Sister Kaos), "Strutter" (the Philbins), "Love Her All I Can" (Xntrik), "I Love It Loud" (Kryptonics), "Almost Human" (Riddle Me This...), "Got to Choose" (the Howells), "God of Thunder" (Cryogenics), "I Stole Your Love" (Grind), "Beth" (Lame), "Let Me Go, Rock 'n' Roll" (Barely Breathing), "Parasite" (Shadwell's Jacket), and "Getaway" (Lee Mc Cormack's Superstar Revue). The CD had a limited print run of 500 copies.

Punky: Ace Frehley's band nickname during the mid-late 1960s was "Punky." Luckily, "Ace" is the nickname that stuck in the long run.

Queen 4 A Day: On Queen 4 A Day's 2000 album, *Shameless*, Gene Simmons and Tommy Thayer co-wrote "American Man." Bruce Kulick played guitar on "I Don't Think I Love You" while Eric Singer played drums on "What U Want Is What You Get." Singer sang backup vocals on the record as well.

"Radar for Love": As soon as Paul Stanley begins singing "Radar for Love," the ninth track on *Asylum*, anyone with the slightest knowledge of rock and roll will recognize the similarities between it and Led Zeppelin's "Black Dog." In fact, Stanley himself has called it a "tip of the hat" to Plant, Page, Jones, and Bonham. Derivative or not, it is one of the better songs on *Asylum*, which admittedly isn't saying a whole lot. Written by Stanley and Desmond Child.

Radio: The KISS Radio was released in 1977 by Aucoin Mgt. It was available via mail order only, making it highly collectible today. The super six transistor portable came with a battery and carrying strap and featured a photo of the band standing on clear pedestals on one side (from the Barry Levine *Love Gun* photo session) and separate shots of each band member on the other side. One control adjusted volume while the other changed stations. During their prime, KISS was rarely played on the radio, at least relative to their popularity, giving the item a certain sense of irony. Snippets of "Love Gun" and "Detroit Rock City" played during TV commercial for the radio.

In 1998, Signatures Series released a small KISS FM Auto-Scan Radio with retractable earphone.

The original KISS transistor radio was available only through mail order, making it a true rarity today, especially complete in the box.

Radio Control Van: Considered a Holy Grail of KISS collectibles, the KISS Radio Control Van, released by Azrak Hamway in 1977, was packaged in three different types of boxes: one with a flap, one with no flap, and a Canadian variant with French and English text. The van can go forward and backward, and it can turn. It is red, with a *Destroyer* album cover decal on both sides and an orange stripe with the KISS logo across the top.

In the April 10, 2013, episode of the Travel Channel's *Toy Hunter*, host Jordan Hembrough takes a number of KISS collectibles to Gene Simmons' house, including this van (no box flap). Despite his vast collection, Simmons doesn't own the hard-to-find van and is eagerly checking it out. Hembrough says, "Is this something you're interested in?" To which Simmons replies, "No, I'm just drooling because you're here." Hembrough offers the van for $1,600, but the Demon pays him with a signed gold *Rock and Roll Over* record instead.

"Radioactive": The first track on the Demon's 1978 KISS solo album, "Radioactive" sounds satanic and spooky (a la "God of Thunder") for the first minute or so, but when Simmons starts singing, the tempo picks up, and the song turns into a catchy pop single. In fact, it's the only single released from the record, reaching #47 on the *Billboard* charts.

Aerosmith's Joe Perry plays lead guitar on the song while Bob Seger sings backup vocals. The song is 3:50 in length, but the single version, which features "See You In Your Dreams" on the B side, omits the ethereal intro, making it just 2:54. When the single was released in the UK, a limited red edition was produced that featured "When You Wish Upon a Star" on the reverse side. The red 45 was also packaged with a Gene Simmons mask.

"Rain": Paul Stanley, Bruce Kulick, and Curtis Cuomo wrote "Rain," the second track on *Carnival of Souls*. If there was any doubt that Stanley wasn't cut out to join the grunge movement of the 1990s, "Rain," a clunky, meandering song sung by the Starchild, quashed those doubts.

Rainbow: Formed in the summer of 1970, Rainbow, not to be confused with the Ritchie Blackmore band of the same name, featured Paul Stanley, Gene Simmons, Stephen Coronel (lead guitar), Brooke Ostrander (keyboards), and Joe Davidson (drums). Shortly thereafter, Tony Zarella replaced Davidson. The band changed its name to Wicked Lester sometime in 1971 or 1972 (accounts vary).

"Raise Your Glasses": Written by Paul Stanley and Holly Knight, "Raise Your Glasses" is the seventh track on *Psycho Circus*. Although many dismiss it as an overly cheerful novelty tune, it's actually a fun and catchy song, if a little corny. Sung by Stanley, it's one of many KISS songs that celebrate achievement through not giving up.

The Ramones: On the 2003 tribute album *We're a Happy Family: A Tribute to the Ramones*, KISS covered the influential punk band's "Do You Remember Rock & Roll Radio?" Three decades earlier, in 1973, lead singer Joey Ramone saw KISS play at the Coventry, as did drummer Tommy Ramone. The Ramones formed in 1974 and disbanded in 1996.

Randall, Elliot: Elliot Randall played guitar on Peter Criss's "Easy Thing" and "I Can't Stop the Rain," and he played guitar on Gene Simmons' 1978 solo album. An industry veteran, Elliot also worked with such acts as Carly Simon, Richie Havens, John Lennon, Steely Dan, and Yoko Ono.

Ranno, Ritchie: Ritchie Ranno, best known as the guitarist for Starz, played guitar on Gene Simmons' "Tunnel of Love."

Ravitz, Mark: An artist and designer who currently has a studio in Brooklyn, New York, Mark Ravitz created the first KISS logo stage sign, based on Ace Frehley's lettering. He was also lead stage designer on the *Destroyer* and *Rock and Roll Over* tours.

"Read My Body": A funk-metal song that evokes Def Leppard's "Pour Some Sugar on Me," "Read My Body" is the fifth track on *Hot in the Shade*. It was written by Bob Halligan, Jr., and a singing and rapping Paul Stanley, who implores a girl to read his body if she wants to know what's on his mind.

"Reason to Live": With its pop stylings, *Crazy Nights* was built for radio. "Reason to Live," the eight track on the album and the second single, is a fantastic power ballad that should have hit big. Unfortunately, the song only reached #64 on the *Billboard* charts (33 in the UK). Sung with conviction by Paul Stanley, who wrote the song with Desmond Child, "Reason to Live" is a song that everyone can like, even those who don't care for most of the KISS catalogue. It's not quite as strong as "I Still Love You" (few power ballads are), but it's right up there with "Forever."

Record Player: Manufactured in 1978 by the newly formed Tiger Electronics, the KISS Phono, like many children's record players, is designed to play 45s, but is wide enough to play LPs. It is housed in a red and white, suitcase-shaped plastic box that opens to reveal the KISS logo, with photos of each band member from the cover of the *Alive II* album. The outside is adorned with a photo of the band onstage, the same image used for the back of the King-Seeley lunch box. The KISS Phono is now a highly prized collectible among fans, especially in good working condition.

Recording

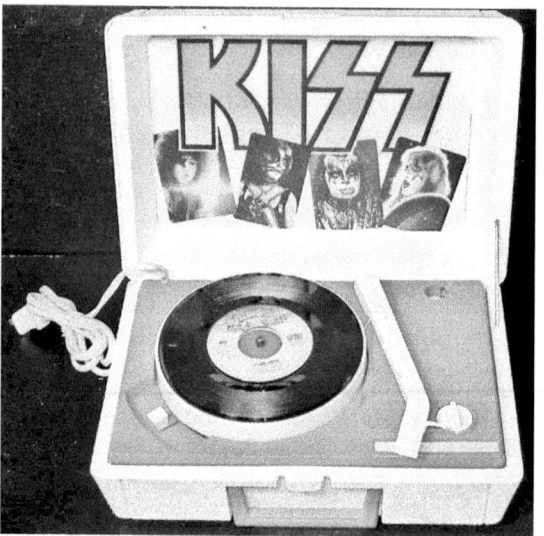

Tiger released this record player, the KISS Phono, in 1978. Now worth around $3,000 in near mint condition, it originally sold for $16.

Recording Industry Association of America: According to the music trade organization, the RIAA, KISS has 30 gold-certified albums (500,000 copies sold), more than any other American band. KISS also has 14 platinum albums (1,000,000 copies sold) and three multi-platinum albums.

Red Surf: Released before George Clooney was famous, *Red Surf* (1989) is a low-budget action flick starring Clooney and Doug Savant as drug-dealing surfers. Gene Simmons, as "Doc," plays an aging, ponytail-wearing surfer who helps the bad guys with their illegal enterprise. Directed by H. Gordon Boos, *Red Surf* also stars Dedee Pfeiffer (Michelle's younger sister). No word if Simmons hooked up with her during the filming of the movie.

Reddy, Helen: Famous for her signature hit, "I Am Woman," pop star Helen Reddy provided backup vocals on Gene Simmons' "True Confessions."

Redoute, Bruce: Detroit teenager Bruce Redoute is one of the two boys featured on the back cover of *Alive!*, holding the homemade KISS sign. He's on the left while Lee Neaves is on the right.

Reed, Lou: Lou Reed was the guitarist, vocalist, and principal songwriter for the Velvet Underground, a highly influential rock band. In 1972, Reed went solo—he's best known for the 1972 hit, "Walk on the Wild Side." On *Music from "The Elder,"* Reed helped write "Dark Light," "Mr. Blackwell," and "A World Without Heroes."

Regan, Pat: Pat Regan played brass horns on "Cadillac Dreams." He also worked as an engineer on *Hot in the Shade*.

Reingold, Buck: A key figure in helping promote "Rock and Roll All Nite" as a single and the *"Alive!"* album in general, Buck Reingold was the vice president of national promotion for Casablanca Records from 1974 to 1976.

Remedy: Ace Frehley had a small role as a character named Johnny in *Remedy*, a 2005 indie crime drama directed by Christian Maelen. Frehley also contributed to the film's soundtrack.

Reo Speedwagon: Formed in 1967, Reo Speedwagon, now a staple of classic rock radio, played on various bills with KISS in 1974 and 1975.

The Replacements: On their 1984 album, *Let It Be*, the Replacements, a post-punk, indie rock band, covered "Black Diamond" in straightforward fashion.

"Reputation": Available on *Love Gun: Deluxe Edition* and on *KISS 40*, "Reputation" is a Gene Simmons demo. On mikeladano.com, the website for LeBrain's Record Store Tales & Reviews, the reviewer called "Reputation" "another decent tune from the *Love Gun* sessions…. You can hear that aspects of this song later made it into other Gene Simmons compositions such as 'Radioactive.' While the song is definitely a demo, and not quite as good as most finished KISS songs, it does boast a cool dual guitar solo and rocking piano a-la 'Christine Sixteen.'"

Return of the Comet: A Tribute to Ace Frehley: Released in 1997 by Shock Records, this tribute to Space Ace includes the following tracks: "Rock Bottom" intro (Bruiz), "Rip It Out" (Brian Tichy), "Cold Gin" (L.A. Guns), "Strange Ways" (Eric Singer and Karl Cochran), "Getaway" (Tubetop), "Shout It Out Loud" (The Presidents Of The United States of America), "Snowblind" (Dimedag Darrell), "Dancing with Danger" (Tod Howarth), "Love Her All I Can" (Eric Singer and Karl Cochran), "Speedin' Back to My Baby" (Lee McCormack and Dallas Remple), "Rocket Ride"

(Gilby Clarke, with drums by Eric Singer under the stage name of Doyle Harris), "Remember Me" (Mitch Weissman and Richie Scarlett), "New York Groove" (the Impostors 6), "Back On The Streets" (a previously unreleased Frehley's Comet song, re-recorded by the Comet Band), "Animal" (a previously unreleased Frehley's Comet song, re-recorded by the Comet Band), "California Burns" (Tod Howarth), and "Liar" (Bruce Kulick).

Reunion Tour see **"Alive/Worldwide Tour**

***Revenge*:** Released May 19, 1992, by Mercury Records, *Revenge* is KISS's 16th studio album, reaching #6 on the *Billboard* 200 chart. Produced by Bob Ezrin, who has said it was like stepping back in time, the record was a return to form for KISS: a loud, raunchy, hard rock/metal album, counterbalanced by a remake of a classic ("God Gave Rock 'N' Roll to You II") and a power ballad ("Every Time I Look at You").

After a decade of distraction, the 1980s, Gene Simmons was back in full force, wearing black leather, donning a sinister looking beard and a snarl, and contributing such kickass songs as "Unholy" and "Domino." He was complemented by equally committed Paul Stanley, Bruce Kulick, and new drummer Eric Singer, who had replaced an ailing Eric Carr.

On the 21st anniversary of the record, Matthew Wilkening of ultimateclassicrock.com wrote a retrospective, calling it "the most consistent, hard-hitting, and critically acclaimed album ever released by the non-makeup version of KISS," filled with "tightly-focused, riff-heavy, and borderline metallic songs."

Tracks include: "Unholy," "Take It Off," "Tough Love," "Spit," "God Gave Rock 'N' Roll to You II," "Domino," "Heart of Chrome," "Thou Shalt Not," "Every Time I Look at You," "Paralyzed," "I Just Wanna," and "Carr Jam 1981." Tommy Thayer sang backup vocals on several songs.

Sadly, *Revenge* was released in the wake of the death of Eric Carr from complications related to heart cancer, hence the commemorative "Carr Jam 1981" to end the album.

Revenge Tour: This was the first KISS tour with Eric Singer, who had replaced the late, great Eric Carr, who died of cancer on November 24, 1991. The band played 77 shows in the U.S. (including club dates to get Singer ready), Canada, and Europe, from April 23 to December 20, 1992. During the UK leg of the tour, KISS used the Hot in the Shade Tour stage set, but for U.S. and Canada, the band employed a giant Statue of Liberty replica.

During "War Machine," explosions would disintegrate the statue to expose a chrome-colored skull and skeletal bones. At the end of each show, the statue's hand would stick out its middle index finger, something certain audience members took personally, as though KISS were flipping off the fans. The shows included strippers during "Take It Off."

Despite the back-to-basics hard rock of the *Revenge* album, a change welcomed by many longtime fans, the tour was cut short due to poor ticket sales, but the shows in Cleveland, Detroit, and Indianapolis lived on because they were recorded by Eddie Kramer for the *Alive III* album.

Band lineup: Paul Stanley, Gene Simmons, Bruce Kulick, and Eric Singer. Opening acts: Danger, Faster Pussycat, Fortress, Great White, Jackyl, Shooting Gallery, Trixter, and Vesuvius. Average attendance: 5,029 (not including club dates).

Followed by: KISS My Ass Tour.

"Rip and Destroy": Near the end of *KISS Meets the Phantom of the Park*, in order to get the fans to riot, the evil robot version of KISS performs "Rip and Destroy," a reworking of "Hotter Than Hell." Paul Stanley wrote the new lyrics.

"Rip It Out": Written by Ace Frehley, Larry Kelly, and Sue Kelly, "Rip It Out" is the first track on Ace Frehley's 1978 KISS solo album. It gets the guitar-heavy album off to a great start, featuring Frehley's authoritative vocals (you get the sense he's glad to be on his own) and blistering fretwork. Anton Fig, famous for his work in David Letterman's house band, the CBS Orchestra, drums his heart out on the song, which is about a girl who's been lying and cheating. This is a fantastic rocker that ranked #2 on a listing of "Top 10 KISS Solo Album Songs" on ultimateclassicrock.com.

"Rise to It": The first track on *Hot in the Shade*, "Rise to It" was written by Paul Stanley and Bob Halligan, Jr. The song begins with blues-based guitar from Bruce Kulick, who also contributes a scorching solo. A solid tune, in which Stanley brags that he is ready, willing, and able to rise to the occasion (yes, it's another obvious sexual double entendre from KISS), "Rise to It" was released as a single, but only reached #81 on the *Billboard* charts.

In the official music video for "Rise to It," Stanley and Simmons are shown in a pseudo-flashback, putting on their old makeup, with Paul saying they could take off their makeup and play rock music while Gene tells him again and again that he's nuts. The video ends with the pair in full makeup and costume. Simmons' outfit is from *Unmasked* while Stanley's is from *Love Gun*.

Rising Sun Tour: From July 18 to July 28, 2006, KISS played seven shows comprising the Rising Sun Tour: one concert in Las Vegas, Nevada, one in Santa Ynez, California, and five in Japan. Band lineup: Paul Stanley, Gene Simmons, Tommy Thayer, and Eric Singer, each in full makeup and costumes.

Followed by: Hit 'N Run Mini Tour.

Rock Against Drugs: In a Rock Against Drugs ad campaign commercial (1987), Gene Simmons appears in a monster mask and growls: "Drugs are great. Drugs make me strong. Drugs make me smart. Drugs make me feel good. Drugs make me cool!" Then he yanks off the mask and says: "You believe that crap? Huh? You believe all that stuff they're handing you about drugs? You want to believe in something? How about yourself? Don't do drugs."

Rock & Brews: Founded by Paul Stanley, Gene Simmons, concert tour manager Dave Furano, concert merchandising industry pioneer Dell Furano (Dave's brother), and restaurateur/hotelier Michael Zislis, Rock & Brews is, according to their website, a "family dining and entertainment destination, featuring reasonably priced casual American cuisine, as well as dishes that reflect local tastes, and an extensive craft beer selection. Guests are at the center of an energized rock experience, with the atmosphere reminiscent of your favorite rock concert featuring concert lighting, your favorite rock music with multiple screens sharing some of rock's greatest moments, rock art, and a larger-than-life 'Wall of Rock' mural. And, appealing to rockers of all ages, most Rock & Brews have a play area for children, and many are dog-friendly."

The idea for the restaurant chain was born after a KISS concert, when the five founders were talking and having a beverage backstage. Dave said, "What's better than Rock & Brews?" The first Rock & Brews opened in El Segundo, California, in April of 2012. Regarding the business venture, Stanley told *The Hollywood Reporter*: "We are spreading our tentacles. It's a family-friendly place where you don't have to compromise your palate. Most of the time when you bring your kids to a restaurant, you are eating cardboard pizza or dried-out macaroni and cheese. This is really your place where you can hang out, choose from one of our 80 craft beers, hear quality rock music, and have a great night with your friends. "

"Rock and Roll All Nite": The 10th and final track on *Dressed to Kill*, "Rock and Roll All Nite" is typically the final song played at a KISS concert. Written by Paul Stanley (chorus) and Gene Simmons (verses) from a suggestion by Neil Bogart, who felt the band needed a definitive, fist-pumping anthem, it is one of the most famous party tunes in the history of rock music. The song, which is in regular rotation on classic rock radio and is frequently heard in various sports arenas around the country, exemplifies the rock and roll spirit, essentially encouraging listeners to "have a good time all the time" (to quote one of the drummers in *This is Spinal Tap*).

KISS's most recognizable song among the general public, "Rock and Roll All Nite" suggests a symbiotic relationship between KISS and the audience, which is a primary (not to mention primal) aspect of the band and one of the reasons for its longevity. Sung by Simmons (with Lydia Criss, studio musicians, roadies, and others singing on the chorus), "Rock and Roll All Nite" sputtered out at #57 on the *Billboard* charts, but the more robust live version from *Alive!* reached #12.

According to Robert Duncan, writing in his 1978 book, *KISS*, the song "was, and *is*, the anthem of the '70s. It has the kind of rousing Universal Rebel lyrics that people are moved to paint on signs and scrawl on bathroom walls."

Rock & Roll All Nite: A Tribute to KISS—1974-2014: Released by Versailles Records January 13, 2015, this double album features songs by current/former members of such acts as the Alice Cooper Band, Dio, Guns N' Roses, the Vinnie Vincent Invasion, Foreigner, Ratt, Slash's Snakepit, Heart, Keel, L.A. Guns, Dangerous Toys, Britny Fox, Lillian Axe, White Lion, and Slaughter.

Tracks on disc one include: "Rock and Roll All Nite" (Leaving Eden), "Flaming Youth" (Sinful Lilly), "Let's Put the X in Sex" (Charlie Bonnett

III), "Love Gun" (Mystic Force), "Save Your Love" (Erling Solem), "Beth" (Rose Reiter), "Deuce" (Kissed Alive!), "I Stole Your Love" (Sikk featuring Jason McMaster), "God of Thunder" (Fallen Martyr), "Calling Dr. Love" (Street Light Suzie), "Shout It Out Loud" (Keri Kelli/Chuck Bonnett), "Come On And Love Me" (Loaded Dice), and "Strange Ways" (Blacksmith).

Disc two includes: "Lick It Up" (Ron Keel/Richard Kendrick), "I Love It Loud" (Chris Heaven/A.J. Caruso), "I Was Made for Lovin' You" (Supercharger), "War Machine" (the Furnace), "Black Diamond" (D. Lefevre/Ryan Roxie), "Domino" (the Eden Project), "Detroit Rock City" (Hachiman), "Forever" (Richard Kendrick), "Unholy" (Mpg), "Charisma" (Dogbane), "Creatures of the Night" (Willow Wisp), and "I Want You" (Groove Studio All Stars).

Rock and Roll All Nite: The Music of KISS: Written by Julian Gill, *Rock And Roll All Nite: The Music Of KISS* is, according to KISSFAQ.COM Publishing, a revamped 2012 printing of *KISS & Related Recordings Focus*: "Originally debuting as a feature on the KISSFAQ website, this unofficial and unsanctioned work is a companion book to the 'KISS Album Focus' trilogy. It delves specifically into the recording history of KISS, and the associated past members, on a song-by-song basis." Released June 14, 2012. *See also:* "Gill, Julian."

Rock and Roll Hall of Fame: Finally, after 15 years of eligibility, KISS was inducted into the Rock and Roll Hall of Fame April 10, 2014, alongside Peter Gabriel, Daryl Hall and John Oates, Nirvana, Linda Ronstadt, and Cat Stevens. Special awards were given to The E Street Band (The Award for Musical Excellence), and to late Beatles manager Brian Epstein and former Rolling Stones manager Andrew Loog Oldham (Ahmet Ertegun Award for Lifetime Achievement).

KISS was shunned by the Rock Hall for years, thanks in part to music critic and board member Dave Marsh, who famously said: "KISS is not a great band, KISS was never a great band, KISS never will be a great band, and I have done my share to keep them off the ballot."

When KISS was inducted, things weren't all hugs and kisses. Paul Stanley and Gene Simmons were upset that only the original members were inducted, so they refused to perform for the event, much to the chagrin of Ace Frehley and Peter Criss. They did take the stage to accept their awards, though, as did Frehley and Criss.

Their acceptance speeches were amicable enough, with Simmons saying

To Ace Frehley: his iconic guitar playing has been imitated, but never duplicated, by generations of guitar players around the world. To Peter Criss, whose drumming and singing.... Well, there's not a guy out there who beats the sticks who sounds just like Peter. Nobody's got that swing and that style. Something happened, 40 years ago: I met the partner and the brother I never knew I had—Paul Stanley. You couldn't ask for someone more awesome to be on the same team. I am humbled. I was going to say a few kind words about Eric Carr, Rest in Peace. Mark St. John, Rest in Peace. Vinnie Vincent, the great Bruce Kulick, and of course, here we are 40 years later with the great Eric Singer and Tommy Thayer, and we continue on. However, we wouldn't be here today without the initial Fantastic Four. God bless you all.

All in all, Stanley and Simmons have been highly critical of the Rock and Roll Hall of Fame, with Simmons saying disco acts and hip-hop artists shouldn't be included and Stanley criticizing the credentials of the board members and questioning the biased nature of the induction process. Of the Grateful Dead (who were inducted in 1994), Stanley told radio.com's Brian Ives: "The Rock and Roll Hall of Fame went to the Grateful Dead and other bands and asked them [which members] they wanted to have inducted. They didn't ask us! Hence, you get, what is it, 14 members of the Grateful Dead, including their lyricist [Robert Hunter], inducted? Because the Grateful Dead's people said, 'It's all or nothing.' Well, that's a courtesy that wasn't extended to us."

"Rock and Roll Hell": Gene Simmons dismisses his talents as a musician, but he delivers some pretty tasty bass licks in "Rock and Roll Hell," the fourth track on *Creatures of the Night*. Robben Ford, named one of the "100 Greatest Guitarists of the 20th Century" by Musician magazine, played lead guitar on the song, which was written by Simmons, Bryan Adams (yes, *that* Bryan Adams), and Jim Vallance. "Rock and Roll Hell" is an anthemic battle cry of teenage rebellion, but some KISS fans claim it is about Ace Frehley and his departure from the band.

Rock and Roll Legends: A Conversation with KISS: Released on VHS in 2001 and on DVD in 2005, this video features conversations with Paul Stanley and Gene Simmons from 1990, while KISS was promoting *Hot in the Shade*. The duo discusses their influence on other bands, how they would do anything for their fans, rumors of a reunion tour, and more. Eric Singer and Bruce Kulick speak for a few minutes as well. There's also footage of Paul talking about the death of Eric Carr (among other topics), taken from an interview during the recording of the music video for *Revenge* in 1992. The DVD version includes a photo gallery.

***Rock and Roll Over*:** The first KISS album to ship platinum, *Rock and Roll Over* is, as the title suggests, a return to basic rock and roll, following on the heels of the far more experimental *Destroyer*. Produced by Eddie Kramer for Casablanca Records and released on November 11, 1976, *Rock and Roll Over* was recorded in Nanuet Star Theater in upstate New York (near Ace Frehley's house) instead of a traditional recording studio. The band treated it as a live concert of sorts, and Kramer executed a number of production stunts to get what he was looking for sonically, such as having Peter Criss play the drums in the bathroom and placing microphones all over the theater.

The result is a terrific, vitality-infused record that fans of the first three KISS albums will love, from the anthemic "I Want You" to the concert staple "Calling Dr. Love" to the Rod Stewart–esque "Hard Luck Woman." The album, which was originally packaged with a sticker of the front cover and a photo press release pamphlet, reached #11 on the *Billboard* 200. "Hard Luck Woman" hit #15 on the *Billboard* singles charts while "Calling Dr. Love" reached #16. *Rolling Stone* recently ranked *Rock and Roll Over* KISS's eighth best album, calling it lean and hard-edged. The cartoonish cover, drawn by Michael Doret, is nifty as well.

Tracks include: "I Want You," "Take Me," "Calling Dr. Love," "Ladies Room," "Baby Driver," "Love 'Em and Leave 'Em," "Mr. Speed," "See You in Your Dreams," "Hard Luck Woman," and "Makin' Love."

***Rock and Roll Over Tour*:** Lasting from November 24, 1976, to April 3, 1977, this tour was in support of KISS's fifth studio album. The band, playing 70 shows, hit several milestones, including performing at Madison Square Garden for the first time—a dream come true for the band. In addition, they performed in Japan for the first time, playing Budokan Hall four nights in a row and breaking that venue's concert attendance record held by the Beatles.

On December 12, 1976, at the Lakeland Civic Center in Lakeland, Florida, Ace Frehley suffered a near-fatal electrical shock onstage, delaying the show for a quarter of an hour, and later inspiring the Spaceman to write "Shock Me."

Band lineup: Paul Stanley, Gene Simmons, Ace Frehley, and Peter Criss. Opening acts: Blackfoot, Bob Seger & The Silver Bullet Band, Bow Wow, the Climax Blues Band, the Dictators, Dr. Hook & the Medicine Show, Graham Parker & The Rumour, Head East, Jesse Bolt, Legs Diamond, Natural Gas, the Raisin Band, Sammy Hagar, Tom Petty and the Heartbreakers, and Uriah Heep. Average Attendance: 10,868.

Followed by: Love Gun Tour.

"Rock and Roll Party": A "hidden" final track on certain vinyl releases of *Destroyer*, "Rock and Roll Party" is unlisted on the album jacket. According to www.kissmonster.com, "This piece was the work of Bob Ezrin who spliced one of Paul's raps from the *Alive!* album and looped it. He'd overlay aural effects from the choir on 'Great Expectations.'"

In an interview with Bob Ezrin on kissonline.com, Ezrin said the brief, spooky sounding instrumental "was necessary to round off the experience if you were listening to the album from top to bottom and that you really needed something to close the book." In issue #58 of the *Firehouse* fanzine, Paul Stanley said, "Bob was trying to think of a way to extend the album, because as good as it was, it was short … we needed to fill up the record."

On the 1997 CD remastering of *Destroyer*, "Rock and Roll Party" is listed as the 10th song.

"Rock Bottom": The fifth track on *Dressed to Kill*, "Rock Bottom" was written by Ace Frehley and Paul Stanley, who sings the song. The down-on-your luck ditty, in which Stanley complains that a woman never treats him like she should, begins with a minute-and-a-half or so of beautifully played acoustic guitar (if it were strummed by Jimmy Page, critics would hail it as pure genius) and shifts gears to typical hard rocking KISS, with some killer licks by Frehley.

***Rock Fantasy*:** Published from 1989 to 1992 by Rock Fantasy publishers, *Rock Fantasy*, featuring rock stars as super-heroes or wizards, ran 21 issues. KISS was featured in #10 and #18, the latter under the title of *KISS II: R.F. 18*.

Rock Fantasy #10 includes two stories: "KISS Fights the Shadow of Death," written by Michael Valentine Smith with art by Smith, Don Rinehart, Dave Deffner, Ron Hall, Bob Kerr, and Sante White; and "KISS This," written and drawn by Peter C. Knight.

KISS II: R.F. 18 also features two stories: "KISS II," written by Michael Valentine Smith with art by Jerry Minor; and "KISS In: Stoned," written and drawn by James Harmon. The latter was a continuation of "KISS This."

"Rock Me Baby": The seventh track on Peter Criss's 1978 KISS solo album, "Rock Me Baby" was written by Sean Delaney. The song sounds a whole lot like "I'm Gonna Love You," the first track on the record. The Catman implores a woman to rock him till he drops, and he also asks her who she's been loving since her man has been gone.

Rock 'N' Roll Comics #9, an unauthorized biography/overview of KISS told as a graphic narrative, was published by Revolutionary Comics in 1990.

***Rock 'N' Roll Comics* #9:** Published in March of 1990 by Revolutionary Comics, a latecomer to the black-and-white comic book explosion of the 1980s, *Rock 'N' Roll Comics* #9 is an unauthorized biography/overview of KISS told in words and pictures over 32 pages. The story, written by Robert V. Conte, is called "KISS Their Rise to Greatness— and Beyond!!!" It features pencils by Greg Fox and inks by Fox, Mark Mazz, and Mitch Waxman. The cover art by Scott Jackson is based on the *Alive!* album cover. The issue sold well and was reprinted twice. In addition, the story was reprinted in the larger-sized *Rock 'N' Roll Comics Magazine* #1, published in June of 1990. Followed by the authorized *Hard Rock Comics* #5.

Rock 'n' Roll Fantasy Camp: Located in Las Vegas, Nevada, Rock 'n' Roll Fantasy Camp lets fans interact with and learn music from famous rock stars. Paul Stanley, Gene Simmons, and Tommy Thayer have each participated as featured performers. Of the camp, Simmons once said: "Mentoring adult and young rockers at the fantasy camp has always been an amazingly rewarding experience for me. I enjoy teaching and handing over lessons I've learned from the business to young and upcoming talent."

***Rock 'N' Roll Sinners—Volume II: Rock Scribes on the Rock Press, Rock Music & Rock Stars*:** This book is the second in a trilogy self-published by Neil Daniels through Amazon's CreateSpace Independent Publishing Platform. It features interviews with rock and heavy metal journalists, including such writers as Phil Alexander, Mick Wall, Dave Thompson, Jaan Uhelszki, and Bernard Doe. Released September 5, 2013, the book is noteworthy because it features Gene Simmons on the cover.

"Rock or Be Rocked": This Ace Frehley demo from 1985 appeared on the bootleg album *Wicked Lester and Progeny Demo Sessions*. It sounds a little like Frehley's "Rock Soldiers."

***Rock Scene*:** A magazine that covered KISS early in the band's career, *Rock Scene* ran from 1973 to 1982 for a total of 54 issues. KISS was the dominant cover image six times.

"Rock Soldiers": The first track on *Frehley's Comet*, "Rock Soldiers" is one of Ace Frehley's signature solo songs. It's partly autobiographical, it spawned a semi-popular music video, and it became the name of the official Ace Frehley fan club. Written by Frehley and Chip Taylor.

Rock the Nation World Tour: This tour ran from May 8 to August 17, 2004, for a total of 59 shows in the U.S., Mexico, Australia, and Japan. It marked the return of Eric Singer (in Catman makeup) because Gene Simmons and Paul Stanley chose not to renew Peter Criss's contract. The band, featuring Tommy Thayer (in Spaceman makeup) on lead guitar, played songs spanning their entire career, including some from the non-makeup era. Poison was the opening act. The tour spawned a series of *KISS Instant Live* two–CD albums, along with a DVD set called *KISS: Rock the Nation Live!*

Followed by: Rising Sun Tour.

Rockabye Baby! Lullaby Renditions of KISS: This CD was released August 28, 2012, by Rockabyebaby Music. It includes the following tracks: "Shout It Out Loud," "Rock and Roll All Nite," "C'mon and Love Me," "Calling Dr. Love," "Deuce," "Strutter," "Love Gun," "Detroit Rock City," "I Was Made for Lovin' You," "Sure Know Something," "Hard Luck Woman," and "Beth." The promo for the disc reads as follows: "Rockabye Baby transforms timeless rock songs into beautiful instrumental lullabies. Guitars and drums are traded for soothing mellotrons, vibraphones and bells, and the volume is turned down from an eleven to a two. Rockabye Baby is the perfect way to share the music you love with the littlest rocker in your life."

"Rocket Ride": A definitive Ace Frehley song, "Rocket Ride" is at once fast and ethereal. Unlike the other four studio tracks on side four of *Alive II*, in which Frehley failed to show up for the recording sessions, Space Ace plays lead (and sings) on this song. He also wrote it (with Sean Delaney) and plays bass. Given that this is a KISS track (#19 on *Alive II*), the rocket ride in question is a sexual metaphor, but it exudes space travel nevertheless, thanks to Frehley's soaring fretwork and unusual voice. KISS rarely (if ever) played "Rocket Ride" in concert, but Frehley himself has played it live many times during his solo career.

"Rockin' in the USA": Whether supporting the troops or touting the greatness of America, KISS has always been a patriotic band, a theme that drives "Rockin' in the USA," in which Gene Simmons, who wrote the song, sings that France was okay, but that he'd rather be "Rockin' in the U.S.A." The second track on side four of *Alive II*, "Rockin' in the USA," like the other four songs on that side of the album, was a new studio track for the double LP. Bob Kulick subs for Ace Frehley on lead guitar in this upbeat tune.

Rockin' the Corps: On April 1, 2005, KISS played three songs at the Rockin' the Corps concert: "Detroit Rock City," "Love Gun," and "Rock and Roll All Nite." Organized by Support The Corps, the free event, which was held at the Marine Corps Air Station Camp Pendleton in Oceanside, California and shown to troops all over the world, also featured such acts as Destiny's Child, Ted Nugent, Godsmack, and Hootie & The Blowfish, along with such celebrities as Cindy Crawford, Alyssa Milano, Sharon Stone, Karl Malone, and Louie Anderson.

The performers pledged their support for the troops and thanked them for their service. Among other things, Paul Stanley said: "Do y'all feel important tonight, because y'all are very important. We want y'all to know we love ya, we celebrate ya, we are proud to celebrate this great country with ya, and no matter how tough times may get, y'all gotta take a little time to rock and roll all night and party every day."

On September 6, 2005, Image Entertainment released a heavily edited DVD of *Rockin' the Corps*, as well as a 14-song CD featuring all three KISS tunes.

Rockology: This posthumous Eric Carr solo album hit stores October 19, 1999, eight years after the drummer's death. It includes four songs that Carr had written for an animated series he was planning, plus some tunes that were intended to be KISS songs. Carr played drums, keyboard, bass, and acoustic guitar on the record, along with singing lead and backing vocals. Adam Mitchell played keyboards and sang backing vocals. Bruce Kulick, who produced the album for Spitfire Records, played lead and rhythm guitar.

Tracks include: "Eyes of Love," "Somebody's Waiting," "Heavy Metal Baby," "Just Can't Wait," "Mad Dog," "You Make Me Crazy," "Nightmare," "Nightmare" (live demo), "Too Cool for School," "Tiara," "Can You Feel It," and "Nasty Boys."

Role Models: Directed by David Wain, *Role Models* is a 2008 film that features a number of hilarious references to KISS. It also includes KISS songs, the *KISS* pinball machine, and characters in KISS makeup and costumes.

Rolling Stone: The April 10, 2014, issue of *Rolling Stone* magazine celebrated the 40th anniversary of KISS with an in-depth cover feature by Brian Hiatt called "KISS Forever," which includes quotes from each original member, including a now-sober Ace Frehley, who talks about his alcohol and drug abuse. The article also discusses Gene Simmons' KISS memorabilia collection, Paul Stanley's house, Peter Criss getting fired, and the Roll and Roll Hall of Fame induction, among other topics.

Despite the longevity and popularity of both the magazine and the band, this was the first time KISS was depicted on the cover of *Rolling Stone*, which was founded by Jann Wenner in San Francisco November 9, 1967. KISS fans have long lamented the anti–KISS bias shown by *Rolling Stone* (despite some positive album reviews), exhibited colorfully by an April 7, 1977, article, "KISS: The Pagan Beasties of Teenage Rock" by Charles M. Young, which compared their music to buffalo farts.

Rolling Stone #209, cover dated March 25, 1976, includes an article called "Success—It's Just a KISS Away," written by David McGee. Instead of featuring KISS on the cover, the editors in their infinite wisdom elected to showcase actress Mary Hartman.

The Rolling Stones: As with many other bands, KISS was heavily influenced by the Rolling Stones. KISS covered "2000 Man" on *Dynasty*. The song was from *Their Satanic Majesties Request* (1967), an experimental psychedelic LP that Gene Simmons has called one of his favorite albums of all time.

In a March 3, 2015, interview with thequietus.com, Simmons said: "The Stones decided to go outside of their comfort zone. That's what I find interesting, whether *Satanic Majesties* is the Stones trying to do *Sgt. Pepper's* and ripping off the Beatles or not, it has production value and songwriting that isn't found on any other Stones records … the strings and backwards stuff, there is some very good material on that record. They happen not to like the record. I think it's a unique record that shows that the Stones have some depth."

Romney, Mitt: Gene Simmons voted for Barack Obama in 2008, but switched his allegiance to Mitt Romney in 2012. "I will tell you that he's much more qualified," Simmons told *The Hollywood Reporter*. "He's a businessman, he ran the Olympics…. He knows how to create jobs. President Obama is a wonderful family man. And that's about where the résumé stops." Tommy Thayer has posted photos on Facebook of himself golfing in a party with Romney.

"Room Service": The first track on *Dressed to Kill*, "Room Service" is an upbeat, '50s-sounding rocker in which Paul Stanley, who authored the song, sings about life on the road, namely getting laid by an assortment of groupies (KISS toured heavily during their first few years, but they rarely complained), including a stewardess. As though foreshadowing "Christine Sixteen," Stanley mentions a lovely 16-year-old. Luckily, the underage child's father intervenes before anything can happen. In his 1978 book, *KISS*, Robert Duncan called "Room Service" "sleazy in the finest KISS tradition … their first blatant and complete road song."

Ross, Carol: A publicist for KISS from 1974 to 1980 (and then again when they took their makeup off, and again for a brief stint during the 1990s), Carol Ross is a former MCA Records employee who helped the band with many of its early promotional stunts, including Cadillac High, the Empire State Building photo shoot, and mixing the band members' blood with the ink for *Marvel Comics Super Special* #1.

On episode #90 of *Three Sides of the Coin*, Ross said Cadillac was hugely successful from a publicity standpoint: "After Cadillac, everything fell into place…. Cadillac was the catalyst … everybody starting turning their heads, because now they were being accepted more in the mainstream … it was the turning point for the media."

Ross, Diana: Born March 26, 1944, pop/R&B diva Diana Ross was the lead singer for the Supremes, one of the most celebrated musical groups of all time, charting 12 #1 singles on *Billboard*'s Hot 100 during the 1960s. After leaving the all-female Motown act in 1970, Ross found success as a solo artist, scoring such #1 hits as "Ain't No Mountain High Enough," "Touch Me in the Morning," and "Love Hangover."

In 1980, Cher, who was Gene Simmons' girlfriend at the time, introduced the Demon to Diana Ross. Shortly thereafter, Simmons left Cher for Ross. In a June 1, 2015, article published on www.azcentral.com, Simmons explained the situation:

"Initially, Cher and I had a relationship and we lived together in Malibu. One Christmas I asked her what I should buy her and she said, 'Call my friend Diana Ross, she will tell you exactly what I like as she is my best friend.' So I called Diana up and we went shopping. Then our feelings for each other developed very fast and we started a relationship together…. Diana Ross kept me on my toes and I ended up having a relationship with her for two years. I loved that she was such a strong woman who was confident in her own skin. That's the most seductive thing…. I guess thereafter, Cher and Diana never spoke."

In addition to singing, Ross is an actress, starring in such films as *Lady Sings the Blues* (1972), where she played Billie Holiday, *The Wiz* (1978), in which she took on the role of Dorothy Gale, and, amusingly enough, *Double Platinum* (1999), a made-for-TV musical that has nothing to do with the KISS album of the same name.

Rothberg, Gerald: The publisher of *Circus* magazine from 1969 to 2004, Gerald Rothberg was important to KISS' early success, covering the band in depth when such publications as *Rolling Stone* short-changed them.

Unused transfers from the KISS Rub n' Play Magic Transfer Set.

Rub n' Play Magic Transfer Set: Like the KISS Colorforms set, the unfortunately titled Rub n' Play set hit stores in 1979. Both were produced by Colorforms Corporation, but the Rub n' Play set, which has a drawing of the band members holding figures of themselves on the box, is less versatile than the Colorforms toy. The set contains two sheets of Magic Transfers, three sheets of punch-out figures, and a rubbing tool. The text on the box instructs users to "Rub down the Magic Transfers to Create Stand-Up Play Figures."

Runaway: Written and directed by Michael Crichton (*Jurassic Park*, *The Andromeda Strain*), *Runaway* (1984) takes place in a near future in which robots serve humankind by performing menial tasks. Unfortunately, they malfunction on occasion and become dangerous. Enter Tom Selleck (as single father Sergeant Jack Ramsey) and Cynthia Rhodes (as love interest and partner Karen Thompson), members of the Runaway Squad, a team that takes down runaway robots. They go up against Gene Simmons (as Dr. Charles Luther), a maniacal genius plotting to create an army of mechanical menaces.

The film, which "combined the influences of *Blade Runner*, comic books, and Crichton's ongoing fascination with the dangers of high technology" (www.allmovie.com), was overshadowed by three other sci-fi thrillers released the same year: *Star Trek III: The Search for Spock*, *The Terminator*, and *2010: The Year We Make Contact*. However, it does have its fair share of fans, including *Creature Features Movie Guide Strikes Again* author John Stanley, who called it "exciting" and "imaginative" with a "rousing, outrageous climax."

Runaway features one of Simmons' more prominent acting roles. Of his performance, a writer for www.cyberpunkreview.com said: "Gene Simmons is the really fun one to watch. All he really does well is 'look evil,' but he does this so well … we're not talking high quality here, but it is fun."

Rush: Formed in Canada in 1968, Rush is comprised of bassist/lead singer Geddy Lee, lead guitarist Alex Lifeson, and drummer Neal Peart. Rush opened more than 50 KISS shows in 1974 and 1975, developing a mutual friendship with the band.

Rush: Beyond the Lighted Stage: This 2010 documentary about the famous prog rock band features early footage of KISS, live in concert, along with KISS-related interviews. In the film, Gene Simmons says, "As soon as we heard that first Rush record, were just like, 'What is this?' This is like Canadian Zeppelin…. We literally said, 'We want that band to open Canada.' We then took them across America." Rush guitarist Alex Lifeson adds, "With KISS, we probably played 50 [or] 60 shows the first couple of tours, where they were just this weird band from New York…. We got very, very close." The documentary also shows early photos of KISS (sans makeup in some cases) hanging out with Rush backstage.

"**Russian Roulette**": A Gene Simmons song filled with the type of sexual innuendo KISS is known for, "Russian Roulette," written by Simmons and Paul Stanley, is the second track on *Sonic Boom*. Mark Eglinton of thequietus.com praised the tune, saying it is "raw, punchy … done with a freshness of attitude that's been absent for a long, long time." He also said that the Demon's voice has "actually developed more than a semblance of melody."

Sagal, Katey: Singer, songwriter, and actress Katey Sagal (*Married…with Children*, *Sons of Anarchy*) sang harmony on the demo for "Calling Dr. Love." Unfortunately, her vocals didn't make the cut as Paul Stanley and Gene Simmons sang falsetto on the final recording instead. Later on, however, she did contribute backing vocals to Simmons' 1978 solo album. Around this time, she also dated Simmons.

"**Saint and Sinner**": Written by Gene Simmons and Mikel Japp (who has said he and Gene had a lot of fun working on the song), "Saint and Sinner" is the second track on *Creatures of the Night*, stretching Simmons' vocal range a bit as he sings of breaking up with a girl (the saint) who he (the sinner) says can kiss his heart goodbye. It is a solid, melodic number, but a bit of a letdown from the excellence of the first song on the album (the title track). Like many of the songs on *Creatures of the Night*, "Saint and Sinner" features Eric Carr loudly pounding the drums. However, Vinnie Vincent's lead guitar work is fairly restrained. On the 1985 re-release *of Creatures of the Night*, "Saint and Sinner" is track number eight, switching places with "Killer."

St. John, Mark: Born Mark Leslie Norton February 7, 1956, in Hollywood, California, Mark St. John changed his name—at least his stage name—when he joined KISS in 1984. St. John played lead guitar on one KISS album: 1984's *Animalize*.

Prior to joining KISS, St. John was a guitar instructor in California. He was also in a respected cover band called the Front Page. When KISS was shopping around for a replacement for Vinnie Vincent, Grover Jackson of Jackson Guitars recommended St. John for the job.

St. John's fast, Eddie Van Halen–like fretwork helped define *Animalize*, giving it a distinct, hard rock sound. However, he didn't write any of the songs, as he related in a 1999 interview published on www.kissasylum.com: "I was a hired hand," he said. "My work is all over that album, but I don't get credit or paid for it. No type of royalties at all. That was the agreement when I got in the band. They didn't want me to get any publishing, meaning I couldn't contribute any songs to the band … they wanted someone that they could control so they could make all the money."

St. John claimed he was a "dog on a leash" during the recording of *Animalize* while Paul Stanley said St. John was difficult to work with and "not the sharpest pencil in the pack." *In Face the Music: A Life Exposed*, Stanley said: "One afternoon, I told him, 'Come in tomorrow with a solo for this song.' He came in and played it the next day. It was pretty good. 'Cool,' I said. 'Now play it again.' He played a completely different thing. 'What?' he said. 'I can't play the same thing twice.'"

In the fall of 1984, *Animalize* was selling well and KISS was touring, but St. John developed arthritis in is hands—a condition called Reiter's Syndrome—so he was only able to play a few concerts during the *Animalize* tour (though Stanley has claimed he didn't play any shows). Bruce Kulick was his "temporary" substitute.

St. John, who appeared in one KISS video— "Heaven's On Fire"—has blamed the swelling in his hands on the stress and unhappiness related to working with Paul and Gene, and although his condition began to improve, KISS named friend-of-the-band Bruce Kulick his official replacement on Dec. 8, 1984. In the www.kissasylum.com interview, St. Johns called his brief stint with KISS "the worst time of my life," filled with "lies and deceit."

In 1985, St. John formed White Tiger with one-time Black Sabbath vocalist David Donato. White Tiger was a glam metal act that released a self-titled record in 1986. In 1990, St. John worked with Peter

Criss in a band called the Keep (which was essentially White Tiger with Criss replacing Brian Fox on drums), but their demo failed to generate any interested among record company executives.

St. John resurfaced a few years later, appearing as a guest at several KISS conventions. In 1999, he and Phil Naro formed the Mark St. John Project, which released a limited edition EP in 1999. In 2003, St. John released an instrumental CD called *Magic Bullet Theory*.

Sadly, Mark St. John died of a brain hemorrhage on April 5, 2007. After his death, Stanley released the following statement: "Mark tried his best to become the guitar player that KISS and our fans needed, so that we could continue moving forward. I enjoyed and am proud of our work together on *Animalize* and know how much he wanted to take that leap to the stage to play with us live. He was gracious in his acceptance that it wouldn't happen and was supportive of Bruce and a gentleman when it was clear that his ailment would end his time with us."

Sample This: The Incredible Story of the Incredible Bongo Band: This 2012 documentary, directed by Dan Forrer and narrated by Gene Simmons, tells of the Incredible Bongo Band, a group of session players led by MGM Records executive Michael Viner and consisting of Perry Botkin, Jr., Mike Deasy, King Erisson, and Jim Gordon. They produced two instrumental albums: *Bongo Rock* (1973) and *Return of the Incredible Bongo Band* (1974), each of which has been sampled extensively by various hip hop artists.

"Samurai Son": The first track on the Japanese release *Best of KISS 40*, "Samurai Son" is a collaborative effort between KISS and the female Japanese pop group, Momoiro Clover Z. *See also:* "Yume No Ukiyo Ni Saitemina."

Sanctuary Records: During the 1990s and into the 2000s, various hard rock and heavy metal acts that were popular during the 1980s released albums under the Sanctuary Records label. This includes the 2003 live album recorded in Australia with the Melbourne Symphony Orchestra, *KISS Symphony: Alive IV*.

SATIN: A Million to One: This free downloadable KISS tribute, released in 2005, features 20 songs by the Norwegian band Satin.

"Save Your Love": The ninth and final track on *Dynasty*, "Save Your Love" is the weakest song on the album and certainly one of the lesser Ace Frehley songs during his time with KISS. Instead of evoking any particular emotion out of the listener, the rhythm and beat of the song just sort of sit there, seemingly indifferent (though the lyrics aren't indifferent as Frehley sings about wanting a controlling girl out of his life). The chorus, sung by Paul Stanley, is downright terrible, but it's not necessarily the Starchild's fault as he didn't have much to work with. Anton Fig subs for Peter Criss on drums.

Savoy Brown: During their first national tour, KISS opened a number of shows for Savoy Brown, an English group that began in 1965 as the Savoy Brown Blues Band.

"Say Yeah": A hook-laden pop rocker that would sound right at home on *Asylum* or *Crazy Nights*, "Say Yeah" is the 11th and final track on *Sonic Boom*. Tommy Thayer delivers a powerful, fret-bending solo, and you can't help but get in a good mood while singing along with the fist-pumping chorus. Written and sung by Paul Stanley.

Scher, John: Longtime concert promoter John Scher has been with the Metropolitan Talent agency since 1971, promoting shows for such bands as the Grateful Dead, the Rolling Stones, the Who, and, more recently, Paul Simon and ZZ Top. He promoted plenty of KISS shows as well.

Schwartzberg, Allan: In addition to playing drums on Gene Simmons' and Peter Criss' 1978 solo albums, Allan Schwartzberg did drum overdubs on "I" and "Odyssey" and on *Animalize* and *Asylum*.

Scooby-Doo: Paul Stanley lends his voice to "A Scooby-Doo Halloween" (Oct. 25, 2003), which is episode 6 of season 2 of *What's New Scooby-Doo?* The Scooby Gang goes to a Halloween festival in Banning Junction, home to Velma's aunt and uncle. The festivities, which are headlined by KISS, get interrupted by the ghost of the town's founder and a bunch of living scarecrows. Fortunately, the good guys win, and cartoon KISS proceeds to play "Shout It Out Loud."

Produced by Warner Bros. Home Entertainment, *Scooby-Doo! and KISS: Rock and Roll Mystery* is a 2015 animated movie that hit digital HD platforms July 10 and Blu-ray/DVD July 21. According to www.usatoday.com, "KISS members

Gene Simmons, Paul Stanley, Eric Singer, and Tommy Thayer voice their own characters in the movie, which centers on a Halloween concert at the group's amusement park KISS World. Scooby, Shaggy, and the rest of the Mystery Inc. gang drop by to hear some tunes but wind up partnering with the musicians to take on the Crimson Witch, a spooky lady with a nefarious plan to summon the evil and powerful Destroyer from the alternate dimension of Kissteria. The cartoon mystery features six classic KISS numbers plus a new song ["Don't Touch My Ascot"] by the band just for the film, which features guest voice stars Kevin Smith, Jason Mewes, Darius Rucker, Garry Marshall, Penny Marshall, Jennifer Carpenter, and Pauley Perrette."

Special features include two 1978 episodes from *The Scooby Doo Show*: "To Switch a Witch" and "The Diabolical Disc Demon," the latter of which features a villain with Gene Simmons–like makeup.

Sea Tales: In the 2007 animated children's DVD collection, *Sea Tales*, Gene Simmons voices The Selfish Sea Giant. The DVD, which boasts fairy tales from Robert Lewis Stevenson, Mark Twain, Oscar Wilde, Hans Christian Anderson, and other legendary wordsmiths, also features the voice talents of Larry King and Betty White.

Sealed with a KISS: Written by Peter Criss's first wife, Lydia, *Sealed with a KISS* features more than 1,500 rare and previously unpublished photos taken by Lydia, plus memorabilia and memories from the early days of KISS. As expected, the book focuses primarily on Peter and Lydia, featuring a personal as well as professional account of their relationship. Published by Buccaneer Books in 2006, *Sealed with a KISS* was updated, expanded, and re-released in 2012.

Second Sighting: The second and last Ace Frehley solo album released under the Frehley's Comet band name, *Second Sighting* hit stores May 24, 1988. Produced by Frehley's Comet and Scott Mabuchi for Megaforce Records, the disc includes the following tracks: "Insane," "Time Ain't Runnin' Out," "Dancin' With Danger" (a cover of the Streetheart tune), "It's Over Now," "Loser in a Fight," "Juvenile Delinquent," "Fallen Angel," "Separate," "New Kind of Lover," and "The Acorn Is Spinning," an instrumental. Jamie Oldaker, who had previously worked with Bob Seger and Eric Clapton, was the drummer on the record, replacing Anton Fig. *Second Sighting*, which only reached #81 on the *Billboard* 200, spawned two non-charting singles: "Insane" and "It's Over Now."

"Secretly Cruel": The eighth track on *Asylum*, "Secretly Cruel" is one of many forgettable songs written and sung by Gene Simmons during the 1980s, when he was distracted by Hollywood. In issue #155 of *Kerrang!*, which features KISS on the cover, the Demon said it was inspired by a "girl who used to write in and describe all the great things she would do with my pictures. She had this giant poster of me standing sideways, then she would position herself in a certain way and that was her thrill."

"Seduction of the Innocent": Named after Fredric Wertham's infamous 1954 book, which warned that comic books cause juvenile delinquency, "Seduction of the Innocent" is the ninth track on *Carnival of Souls: The Final Sessions*. Once again on the grunge-influenced album, KISS channels Alice in Chains, but the song clearly hails from the fiendish mind and gruff voice of Gene Simmons, who wrote the lyrics and melody with Scott Van Zen. This is one of the better tracks on *Carnival of Souls*, thanks in part to a guitar riff that could charm a snake.

***Seduction of the Internet: A Detention Hall Tribute to KISS*:** Released in November of 2006, this free download was put together by members of The KISS Army Detention Hall message board. It features 20 tracks by a variety of acts.

"See You In Your Dreams": In "See You In Your Dreams," Gene Simmons, who wrote and sung the song, doesn't bed the babe, which is unusual for a KISS number. Rather, she'll meet him in her dreams, which is a different kind of testament to Simmons' massive ego. Katey Sagal and Michael Des Barres sang on the original demo, but they're not featured on the final album cut, which is track #8 on *Rock and Roll Over*. Simmons liked the brief, popish tune, but thought it could be better, so he reworked it for his 1978 solo album as track #10.

"See You Tonite": From the opening guitar strums by Jeff "Skunk" Baxter, which evoke the Beatles' "Do You Want to Know a Secret," to the snappy chorus, the acoustic "See You Tonite" is pure Fab Four from beginning to end. It is the third track on the Demon's 1978 KISS solo album, *Gene*

Simmons. Simmons has claimed the song dates back to around 1969, when he was in Bullfrog Bheer with Steve Coronel. Fans of "Hard Luck Woman" should enjoy it.

Seef, Norman: Longtime photographer Norman Seef, who has taken photos of such iconic rockers as the Eagles, Fleetwood Mac, and the Rolling Stones, did the infamous *Hotter Than Hell* album cover shoot.

Seger, Bob: Singer-songwriter Bob Seger, famous for such hits as "Turn the Page" and "We've Got Tonight," sang backing vocals on two songs on Gene Simmons' 1978 solo album: "Radioactive" and "Living in Sin." His group, Bob Seger & the Silver Bullet Band, performed on the same bill as KISS several times during the 1970s.

Sewitt, George: Former KISS road manager George Sewitt also managed Peter Criss and Ace Frehley at various points during their solo careers. In *Makeup to Breakup*, Criss claimed that Sewitt convinced him and Frehley to reunite with KISS for *MTV Unplugged*.

***Sex Money KISS*:** Written by Gene Simmons, *Sex Money KISS* was published by New Millennium Press in June of 2003. It's a self-help book of sorts, in which Simmons says you should pinch your pennies, work hard like he does, and avoid drinking, smoking, taking drugs, and using credit cards. He also advises against getting married, calling it "The worst thing a man can do, financially and biologically speaking," which is ironic considering his 2011 marriage to longtime girlfriend Shannon Tweed. In addition, Simmons, who espouses puritanical values in all aspects of life other than the bedroom, praises his hard-working partner in crime Paul Stanley while disparaging the self-destructive habits of former bandmates Ace Frehley and Peter Criss. Includes 24 pages of color and black-and-white photos.

Shaffer, Paul: Paul Shaffer, best known as David Letterman's longtime musical director, played keyboards on Peter Criss's 2007 solo album, *Out of Control*.

"Shandi": The second track on *Unmasked*, "Shandi" was the only single from the album in the U.S., reaching #47 on the *Billboard* charts. The song was a huge hit overseas, where it peaked at #4 in Norway, #5 in Australia, and #6 in New Zealand. It is unabashedly light-as-a-feather pop, with Paul Stanley, who wrote the song with Vini Poncia, singing softly and sweetly about being unable to break up with a girl, that their goodnight should be goodbye.

If there was any doubt at this point that KISS had turned from a hard rock band into a pop group (at least temporarily), "Shandi" put those doubts to rest. Stanley plays lead guitar on the song, subbing for Ace Frehley, while Tom Harper (Paul's guitar tech) takes Gene Simmons' place on bass. Anton Fig plays the drums while Holly Knight handles keyboards. Stanley got the idea for the song from Bruce Springsteen's "Sandy" while Vini Poncia cribbed the title "Shandi" from an obscure singer named Shandi Cinnamon.

Shandi's Addiction: On *Kiss My Ass: Classic KISS Regrooved*, Shandi's Addiction, featuring Rage Against the Machine's Tom Morello on lead guitar, covered "Calling Dr. Love."

Shannon, Scott: Longtime industry professional Scott Shannon, who was the program director and deejay at WMAK-AM in Nashville from 1969 to 1974, suggested that KISS cover Bobby Rydell's "Kissin' Time," which the band recorded for a second printing of their self-titled debut album.

According to Peter Criss, Shannon also helped "Beth," which was on the B-side of "Detroit Rock City," become a hit single. In *Makeup to Breakup*, the Catman wrote: "Scott Shannon, who was working in the promotion department of Casablanca, loved the song and urged a deejay in Atlanta to flip the single over and play 'Beth.' The reaction was immediate and overwhelming."

"She": Co-written by Gene Simmons and Stephen Coronel, "She" is the eighth track on *Dressed to Kill*. A heavy, plodding number with chunky, head-banging guitars, it is the longest song on the record, clocking in at 4:08. Donald A. Guarisco of www.allmusic.com called "She," which was sung by Simmons and Paul Stanley, a "scorching midtempo riff-fest that became an enduring part of the group's live set … the lyrics are sexy and mystical all at once as they portray a woman who is as powerful as she is desirable."

The original 1971 version of "She," recorded for the unreleased Wicked Lester album, is the fourth track on disc one of *The Box Set*. It has a lighter sound and even includes a flute, played by Brooke Ostrander.

Sherinian, Derek: *Derek Sherinian*, who has worked with such acts as Alice Cooper and Billy Idol, played keyboards and sang backup vocals on *Alive III*.

"She's So European": Written by Gene Simmons and Vini Poncia, "She's So European" is a perfectly serviceable pop tune. The eighth track on *Unmasked*, the song finds Simmons singing about a girl who is European (she talks with an accent and walks like a lady), but only in her mind.

"Shock Me": Finally, after studio six albums, Ace Frehley worked up the nerve to sing lead, and the result was excellent. According to Matthew Wilkening of ultimateclassicrock.com, "Shock Me" remains Frehley's best KISS song: "Ace's loopy, out-of-sync vocal style has rarely been showcased better than on top of the lazy, grinding guitar riff of 'Shock Me,' and the song served for years as his showcase piece during the band's concerts."

Frehley got the idea for "Shock Me," which is the fourth track on *Love Gun*, from when he got electrocuted during a concert on December 12, 1976, at the Lakeland Civic Center in Florida. According to ultimateclassicrock.com, "The near-fatal production snafu occurred early in the group's set, after 'Detroit Rock City.' KISS performed that song atop their set before descending to the stage for the next song. As Frehley came down from the top of the set, he grabbed onto a metal rail to steady himself—inadvertently completing an electrical circuit with his guitar. He was seized by the electrical current and unable to move, but finally broke free and fell several feet to the stage below." After a 10-minute break backstage, Frehley finished the set.

On the *Alive II* version, Stanley famously introduced the song thusly: "We got a little surprise for you tonight. We're gonna turn the microphone over to Ace Frehley. 'Shock Me!'" At the conclusion of the song when played live, Frehley would go into his solo, smoke would billow from the guitar, and he would then walk off and leave it reverberating on a guitar stand.

Shock Rockers: The Story of KISS: Written by Robert V. Conte, who served as consultant on Mercury Records' "KISS Remasters" compact disc series, and who wrote the text for Cornerstone's KISS trading card sets, *Shock Rockers: The Story of KISS* was published by Studio Chikara in 2001. The book tells of how "Gene Simmons, Peter Criss, Ace Frehley, and Paul Stanley created a worldwide phenomenon that has made generations 'rock and roll all night and party every day!'"

"Shocker": The title track to horror maestro Wes Craven's 1989 film of the same name, "Shocker" was recorded by the Dudes of Wrath and composed and sung by Paul Stanley and Desmond Child. The song also features Vivian Campbell and Guy Mann-Dude on guitars, Rudy Sarzo on bass, and Tommy Lee on drums. Michael Anthony and Kane Roberts provide backing vocals. In the movie, Eric Singer has a cameo as a member of a fictional rock band.

"Shout It Out Loud": One of the band's best songs, "Shout It Out Loud" is a fist-pumping rock anthem on par with "Rock and Roll All Nite" and "Tomorrow and Tonight." These are fun, simple songs that celebrate the joys of rocking, rolling, and in general having a great time all the time. The seventh track on *Destroyer*, "Shout It Out Loud" was influenced by the Hollies' "We Wanna Shout It Out Loud," which Stanley and Simmons covered during their Wicked Lester days. Simmons and Stanley wrote "Shout It Out Loud" with Bob Ezrin one morning before going into the studio.

Shout It Out Loud: The Story of KISS's Destroyer and the Making of an American Icon: Written by James Champion, this book was published October 13, 2015, by Backbeat Books. According to the author, it is a "complete history of KISS's *Destroyer*, featuring new as well as archived interviews, bringing to life the band's seminal record and its meteoric rise."

"Shout Mercy": A song about casual, crazy, no-strings-attached sex, "Shout Mercy" is the fifth track on *Monster*. Paul Stanley's voice, still distinctive and strong, is nevertheless raspier than in earlier albums, but he's in his 60s here, so this is understandable. Written by Stanley and Tommy Thayer, "Shout Mercy" is a solid (if formulaic) rocker.

Silent Rage: Silent Rage's *Don't Touch Me There* album from 1989 was co-produced by Gene Simmons. Bruce Kulick and Adam Mitchell wrote the 10th track on the record, "All Night Long."

"Silver Spoon": Written by Paul Stanley and Vini Poncia, "Silver Spoon," the eighth track on *Hot in the Shade*, features a rocking riff by Bruce Kulick and some nifty backup vocals by a trio of females: Charlotte Crossley, Valerie Pinkston, and Kim Edwards-Brown. It's a cool rock tune that is partially autobiographical, as a confident Stanley sings that he always knew he would be somebody. Bon Jovi fans should enjoy it.

Silverhead: Founded in the UK in 1972, Silverhead toured with KISS early in 1974.

Simmons Abramson Marketing: A marketing partnership between Gene Simmons and Rich Abramson. Among other interests, the company represents the Indy Racing League, which includes the Indianapolis 500.

Simmons Comics Anthology: Volume 1: Published in 2013 by Arcana Comics and Simmons Comics Group, this book collects the first chapters of *Gene Simmons Zipper*, *Gene Simmons Dominatrix*, and *Gene Simmons House of Horrors*. It also includes the first chapter of the first crossover between Zipper and Dominatrix, *The Slave Trade*.

Simmons Comics Anthology: Volume 2: Published in 2013 by Arcana Comics and Simmons Comics Group, this book collects the second chapters of *Gene Simmons Zipper*, *Gene Simmons Dominatrix*, and *Gene Simmons House of Horrors*. It also includes the second chapter of the first crossover between Zipper and Dominatrix, *The Slave Trade*.

Simmons Comics Anthology: Volume 3: Published in 2013 by Arcana Comics and Simmons Comics Group, this book collects the third chapters of *Gene Simmons Zipper*, *Gene Simmons Dominatrix*, and *Gene Simmons House of Horrors*. It also includes the third and final chapter of the first crossover between Zipper and Dominatrix, *The Slave Trade*.

Simmons Comics Anthology: Volume 4: Published by Arcana Comics and Simmons Comics Group in 2015, this book collects the fourth chapters of *Gene Simmons Zipper*, *Gene Simmons Dominatrix*, and *Gene Simmons House of Horrors*. It also includes new *Gene Simmons House of Horrors* stories.

Simmons Comics Group: Working with IDW, Gene Simmons established the Simmons Comics Group in 2007. The company published *Gene Simmons Dominatrix* (six issues), *Gene Simmons Zipper* (six issues), and *Gene Simmons House of Horrors* (three issues). The issues were reprinted in *Simmons Comics Group Omnibus*, published in 2009 by IDW. The issues were also published over four volumes in the *Simmons Comics Anthology*. Writers include: Gene Simmons, Chris Ryall, Leah Moore, John Reppion, Joshua Hale Fialkov, Tom Waltz, Sean Taylor, Dwight L. MacPherson, and Jason Henderson. Artists include Todd McFarlane, Esteve Polls, Flavio Hoffe, Casey Maloney, Matt Busch, and Jeff Zornow.

According to *KISS FAQ* author Dale Sherman, a fourth title called *Skullduggery* by Gene's son, Nick, was supposed to be released. "IDW held off on publishing *Skullduggery* after seeing the artwork that Nick would later admit was not up to the level it needed to be," Sherman wrote. "Two years later, Nick would redo the artwork for release as a three-issue mini-series known as *Incarnate* through Radical Comics, a comic book studio co-founded by Barry Levine. That series would later face charges of plagiarism in early 2010 from fans of manga (Japanese comics), with Nick saying the series were 'homages' to said comics and not to be taken as merely copying what had been done before. Nevertheless, Radical canceled a planned paperback reprint of the issues after the accusations went public."

Simmons Comics Group Omnibus: The solicitation for this book, which collects *Gene Simmons Dominatrix* (six issues), *Gene Simmons Zipper* (six issues), and *Gene Simmons House of Horrors* (three issues), reads as follows: "What do an alien, a professional dominatrix, and a collection of pulp horror stories have in common? The warped and twisted mind of Gene Simmons … you'll get more tales of the sexy, bizarre, and horrifying than you ever dreamed. *Gene Simmons Zipper* follows Denizen Xeng Ral from the cross-dimensional galaxy known as the Nether Ether as he flees a dystopic planet called Etheria. *Dominatrix* introduces professional dominatrix Dominique Stern as she fights to save herself, her friends, and even the country, after a client accidentally blurts out top secret information. And finally, *House of Horrors* takes you on a ride through tales so weird we can only say they'll leave you breathless!" Published in 2009 by the Simmons Comics Group.

Simmons, Gene: KISS bassist and co-lead singer Gene "the Demon" Simmons was born Chaim Witz August 25, 1949, in Haifa, Israel to Feri Witz, a struggling carpenter, and Flora Klein, a Hungarian Jew and Holocaust survivor. The poverty-stricken couple separated when Simmons was around six or so, and Simmons migrated to America with his mother when he was eight.

In the June 28, 2011, episode of his reality series, *Gene Simmons Family Jewels*, Simmons is shown returning to Israel for the first time since he left, meeting his step-siblings and getting choked up while visiting his father's grave. Later in the episode, Simmons expressed regret that he didn't go back to Israel sooner.

"I've been arrogant about lots of things, especially my father," he said. "I wanted to prove to myself and to everyone else and to my father that I didn't need him. So once I proved it and became successful, I wanted to stand stubbornly on my pride.... Unfortunately, I never saw my father again until I stood over his grave, and that was not easy."

Simmons has praised his mother many times over the years, citing her bravery in the face of the horrors of the Holocaust, which she endured at the age of 14. Simmons is famously anti-drug and anti-alcohol, which he credits to his mother as he didn't want to break her heart. His only vice, as he as admitted many times over the years, is sex. In his autobiography, *KISS and Make-Up*, Simmons said he's slept with more than 4,600 women, though nowadays he claims to live a life of monogamy with his wife, Shannon Tweed, whom he married October 1, 2011. The couple has lived together since 1983, and they have two children: Nick and Sophie. Simmons resisted getting married for decades because he enjoyed his freedom and didn't want to be like his father.

When Simmons and his mother came to America, they assumed Flora's maiden name of Klein, and, to better fit in in their adoptive country, little Chaim took the name of Eugene and then simply Gene.

As an impoverished native of Israel, Simmons was astounded by America and the riches it offered. In a September 30, 2014, interview with Dan Rather, Simmons recalled his first impressions of the U.S. "I never saw anything so big," he said. "The people were big, the cars were big, the sandwiches were enormous. People had refrigerators full of their own food.... I remember ... going to [my] first supermarket.... I walk in, and it's like city streets with people going down one street and up the other, carrying tons of food.... I just couldn't fathom it.... America, the land of plenty ... it's a wonderland."

Simmons told Rather that coming to America was the best thing that ever happened to him: "The magic and the blessing that is America is that, yes, even if you're the sons and daughters of Nazis, you can come here and nobody will try to kill you, and you can have all the rights and freedoms that native-born children in America have. This is the promised land."

Once in America, Simmons quickly became a huge comic book, TV, and monster movie fan. Comics helped him learn to read while watching television and movies helped him learn to speak English. In *KISS and Make-Up*, Simmons wrote, "Kids who grew up during the fifties say that they were raised by television, and sometimes they say it in this self-pitying tone, like they missed out on something. For me, it was the best experience I ever had. That first summer, out in Queens, was all about television. All the other kids wanted to go out and play baseball. I didn't care about baseball. Once I discovered television, why would I ever want to leave home?"

When he was in middle school, Simmons began writing, drawing, and producing amateur publications about comics and science fiction called fanzines (i.e., fan-made magazines), including his first, *Cosmos*, which merged with *Stiletto* to become *Cosmos-Stiletto*. He contributed to other peoples' fanzines as well. In short, the future fire-breather was a nerd.

As much as Simmons enjoyed these geeky pursuits, he liked the idea of getting girls to notice him even more. "So I put together a band with two friends from school, Danny Haber and Seth Dogramajian," the Demon wrote in *KISS and Make-Up*. "We went to school together at Joseph Pulitzer Middle School in Queens, New York, and we were all friends, because we were all obsessed with comic books and science fiction.... But after the Beatles, it became clear to us that ... it wasn't going to get us where we wanted to go with the girls. So we formed a band called Lynx. I didn't even think about how to spell it, but I had the animal in mind. At school, when we performed [and won] the talent show, we were introduced as the Missing Links, which of course changed the spelling."

Simmons suddenly found himself more popular with girls (in *KISS and Make-Up*, he describes his first sexual encounters), and more popular at school in general. Simmons remained an avid comics, science fiction, and television buff, but he also played in various small-time bands, including the

Long Island Sounds, the Love Bag, Rising Sun, Cathedral, Coffee, and Bullfrog Bheer, the latter of which recorded a number of demos, including "Leeta," which is on KISS's 2001 CD collection, *The Box Set.*

In 1970, guitarist and longtime friend and bandmate Stephen Coronel introduced Simmons to Paul Stanley, who was then known as Stanley Eisen. They didn't hit it off right away as Stanley thought Simmons was abrasive and arrogant, but they did find common ground musically. They formed a band called Rainbow with Coronel, keyboardist Brooke Ostrander, and drummer Joe Davidson, who was quickly replaced by Tony Zarrella. In 1971 or 1972 (accounts vary), Rainbow changed its name to Wicked Lester.

Wicked Lester recorded a demo album for Epic Records (sans Coronel, who was replaced by Ron Leejack), but Simmons and Stanley weren't happy with the direction of the band (Simmons wrote that they "sounded like the Doobie Brothers, and there wasn't nearly enough guitar"), so they walked away from the contract, and the album was never produced.

Shortly thereafter, the twosome recruited Peter Criss and Ace Frehley, and in 1973 they recorded a five-track demo at the famed Electric Lady Studios with Eddie Kramer producing, culminating in the birth of KISS. Prior to this, Simmons and Stanley hung out at Electric Lady every chance they got, singing backup vocals for such performers as Lyn Christopher.

Prior to working with Christopher, Gene had dropped the name Klein in favor of Simmons. According to *KISS FAQ* author Dale Sherman, Gene has "told variations of how he came up with the name and actually dismisses it as simply one he thought would look good for rock 'n' roll in his autobiography." However, "there is more evidence that he based the name on that of early rockabilly singer 'Jumpin' Gene Simmons."

Simmons is, for many, the face of and spokesman for KISS. While Paul Stanley is the band's prototypical frontman, Simmons is the "God of the Thunder," the "Doctor of Love," and the singer of their trademark concert closer, "Rock and Roll All Nite." In addition, Simmons' outrageous onstage exploits, such as breathing fire, spitting blood, and sticking out his gargantuan tongue (during the late 1970s, there was a rumor going around that Gene had grafted a cow tongue onto his own tongue), seem to garner the most media attention. Further, he has voiced his strong political opinions—liberal on social issues and conservative on fiscal and foreign policy issues—on TV and in the press many times.

If the KISS Army had a general, it would be Paul Stanley, who steered the ship during the non-makeup era of the 1980s, when Simmons, who appeared uncomfortable onstage without his demon visage, was distracted by a budding acting career and dating such celebrities as Cher and Diana Ross. However, Simmons is probably the band's #1 fan and promoter. During the early years, he sent press kits to record executives and would make fliers that he and his bandmates would post all over town to promote forthcoming shows. If you go into Simmons' house today, you'll find one of the world's largest KISS memorabilia collections on full display.

Given the thousands of items bearing the KISS insignia, Simmons, who has recorded two solo albums (1978's *Gene Simmons* and 2004's *Asshole*), is often accused of being a sellout, a label he wears proudly. In a 2001 interview published on www.johnglassie.com, Simmons joked, "Every time we play a concert we sell out! I want to sell out every day." In that same interview, however, Simmons revealed that there are certain things he won't label with the KISS brand. "I wouldn't promote booze," he said. "A major cigarette company came to us and offered us millions to put their name next to ours, and there is not enough money in the world to get me to help people get hooked on that crap."

Simmons is proud of KISS and the influence they've had on other bands, but he frequently downplays his skills as a musician, and the musical abilities of KISS in general. In a 1977 interview with *Rolling Stone*, he said something that has fueled critics for years: "We're not a great band. The musicianship is average, maybe even below." Further, Simmons frequently says that rock as art is overrated and that KISS songs are the musical equivalent of fast food.

Simmons, who writes books and gives lectures about business and success, loves the current KISS lineup of himself, Stanley, Tommy Thayer, and Eric Singer, in part because he doesn't have to put up with Ace Frehley and Peter Criss, who he criticized heavily in *KISS and Make-Up*, citing their drug and alcohol abuse.

Thanks to his Jewish heritage, religion has played a role in Simmons' life, but he's an agnostic. In a 2001 interview conducted by John Glassie of *The*

New York Times, Simmons said: "In America, my mother put me into Yeshiva, a Jewish theological seminary, to get me off the streets. And I started heavily studying the Old Testament. I made peace with my Jewishness, which is to say that it has less to do with God and more to do with a religion that doesn't knock on your neighbor's door and try to sell you a bill of goods. I do think there are lots of good things about all religions. But a lot of things I find faulty as practiced by man. I think God shouldn't care whether we believe in God or not. Unless there's a self-esteem problem."

Simmons is an intelligent, articulate man, especially for a demonic bass player who breathes fire. Thanks to prodding from his mother, he got an associate's degree in education at the Sullivan County Community College in Sheldrake, New York, followed by a bachelor's degree at Richmond College in New York City. Prior to becoming a rock star, Simmons held a brief stint as a sixth grade teacher in Spanish Harlem, using *Spider-Man* comics as a teaching tool, much to the disdain of his superiors. He worked a number of odd jobs as well, including deli cashier, assistant at the Puerto Rican Interagency Council, temp at the Kelly Agency, and assistant editor at *Vogue*.

A wealthy entrepreneur who shares his riches with the needy, Simmons is heavily involved in charity organizations, including ChildFund International, through which he sponsors more than 1,400 impoverished children throughout Africa. His charitable outlook comes from his meager upbringing in war-torn Israel, as he told Dan Rather.

"We had nothing," Simmons said. "There was a rocket-hole in the one bedroom my mother and I shared.... There was no electricity. We had an outhouse. I had never seen toilet paper or Kleenex, never heard of it, never saw it. Didn't start brushing my teeth until I was 11-years-old. Never heard of toothpaste or a tooth brush. And one day, a cardboard box came through the mail ... there was a can of peaches.... I had never seen food inside of a metal container ... my mother let me have the nectar.... I had never tasted anything so sweet ... all of a sudden I had the sense that the world cared because I didn't know who [the care package] came from ... all of a sudden we were not alone.... I promised myself that if I ever did well in life, I'd make sure that other little boys and girls around the world would feel that hope."

Simmons, Nick: Born January 22, 1989, Nick Simmons is the son of Gene Simmons and Shannon Tweed. He starred alongside his parents and sister Sophie in the reality TV show, *Gene Simmons Family Jewels*. Nick is also a musician, writer, voice actor (for Cartoon Network's *Robot Chicken*), and comic book creator. In 2010, he was accused of plagiarism for his comic book, *Incarnate*, to which he responded: "Like most artists I am inspired by work I admire. There are certain similarities between some of my work and the work of others. This was simply meant as an homage to artists I respect, and I definitely want to apologize to any manga fans or fellow manga artists who feel I went too far. My inspirations reflect the fact that certain fundamental imagery is common to all manga. This is the nature of the medium. I am a big fan of *Bleach*, as well as other manga titles. And I am certainly sorry if anyone was offended or upset by what they perceive to be the similarity between my work and the work of artists that I admire and who inspire me."

Simmons Records: In the 1980s, Gene Simmons' record label, Simmons Records, released albums by such hard rock acts as House of Lords,

The October 1999 issue of *Guitar World* magazine features Gene "the Demon" Simmons on the cover.

Silent Rage, and Gypsy Rose. More recently, the resurrected label released records by the Canadian act, Kobra and the Lotus.

Simmons, Sophie: Born July 7, 1992, Sophie Simmons is the daughter of Gene Simmons and Shannon Tweed. An actress, singer, and fashionista, she starred alongside her parents and her brother Nick in the reality TV show, *Gene Simmons Family Jewels*.

Simon Simonazo: *Simon Simonazo* was a weekly humor comic book published in Mexico from 1979 to 1986. Several issues featured a parody superhero version of KISS called Chiss. One issue had a color-coded cover parody of the 1978 KISS solo albums featuring Galacto Sanchez (Paul), Demon Perez (Gene), Gato Ramirez (Peter), and Kosmico Camacho (Ace).

"Simple Type": Written by Gene Simmons, "Simple Type" was recorded for the unreleased Wicked Lester album. It's a good (if unpolished) tune sung by Simmons and Paul Stanley. Simmons reworked the opening riff, which evokes "Bang a Gong (Get It On)" by T. Rex, for the beginning of "Charisma."

Sinatra, Frank: Peter Criss has called the great crooner Frank Sinatra, who is famous for such songs as "My Way," "Fly Me to the Moon," and "New York, New York," a huge influence many times over the years.

Singer, Eric: Born Eric Doyle Mensinger on May 12, 1958, in Cleveland, Ohio, Eric Singer is the current drummer in KISS. Much to the disdain of certain purists and longtime KISS fans, he wears Peter Criss's makeup design and a similar Catman costume. During a December 14, 2014, interview on *The Cassius Morris Show* podcast, Singer addressed the fans who have a problem with him portraying the Catman. He respects their passion, but doesn't understand why they keep complaining.

"It's always been a non-issue for me, emotionally or otherwise," Singer said. "I don't get ... those fans, either fans or former fans that continually complain ... they continue to talk about it non-stop ... because me, myself, when I'm done with something, whether it's a former friend, ex-girlfriend ... anything ... a band ... or product.... If they change the way the product tastes or the way it looks, if I don't like it anymore, guess what? I go, 'Oh, okay. I don't really care for it anymore.' I stop buying it, I stop supporting it, or I don't listen to it, I don't eat it.... Whatever it is, I move on from it."

In a May 31, 2014, interview with *Rolling Stone*, Singer spoke about the hypocrisy of Ace and Peter complaining about replacement band members wearing their makeup.

"When I came in to play with the makeup, Ace was in the band, and had no problem with me playing with Peter's makeup while he went onstage and made that KISS money," Singer said. "In fact, he loved it, and he didn't want Peter back in the band. And then go forward the next year, when Ace decided to leave. When we fast forward, all of a sudden they bring Peter back, and you got Tommy Thayer playing guitar wearing the Ace makeup, and all of a sudden, no one minded it was Ace's makeup design. Peter had no problem, did he?"

According to *KISS FAQ* author Dale Sherman, Singer began playing drums when he was just 11-years-old, "typically helping with performances by his father, a jazz musician who had worked with Perry Como, among others. In 1983, Singer moved from Ohio to Los Angeles in hopes of getting work as a professional drummer. After working with a band called Icebreaker and doing some video work as a drummer for a *Playboy* special, he signed up to tour with Lita Ford."

Lita Ford was dating Tony Iommi at the time, connecting Singer to the Black Sabbath founder and guitarist. Singer replaced Black Sabbath drummer Bill Ward and played with the band for two-and-a-half years, appearing on two albums: *Seventh Star* (1986), featuring Glenn Hughes on vocals, and *The Eternal Idol* (1987), featuring Tony Martin on vocals. Thanks to Lita Ford, Singer appeared on Olivia Newton-John's music video for "Culture Shock."

Singer toured with Gary Moore in 1987 and did session work for Drive and the Cult. In 1988, he formed Badlands with former Ozzy Osbourne guitarist Jake E. Lee and former Black Sabbath singer Ray Gillen. Singer played on Badlands' self-titled debut album (1989) before leaving the band over personal differences. During his brief stint with Badlands, Singer, a longtime KISS fan, made his first KISS connection.

"While with Badlands, [Singer] ran into Dennis St. James, who was about to go on a short solo tour with Paul Stanley in 1989," Sherman wrote in *KISS FAQ*. "As Stanley was looking for a drummer on the tour, Singer was brought in following the suggestion of St. James."

In 1990, Singer played on Bill Ward's first solo album, *Ward One: Along the Way*. He then joined Alice Cooper's band on an on-again, off-again basis, playing with them on the tour for *Hey Stoopid* in 1991, and later pounding the skins on three albums: *Brutal Planet* (2000), *The Eyes of Alice Cooper* (2003), and *Along Came a Spider* (2008).

Nineteen-ninety also saw the debut of the Eric Singer Project, which Singer formed with Bruce Kulick, John Corabi (Mötley Crüe, Ratt), and Karl Cochran. The band recorded three albums: *Lost and Spaced* (1998), *ESP* (1999), and *ESP Live in Japan* (2007), the latter of which featured Chuck Garric (Alice Cooper's band), who had replaced Karl Cochran.

In 1991, when KISS began recording *Revenge*, Eric Carr was battling cancer, so Paul brought in Singer to replace him on what was supposed to be a temporary basis. Sadly, Carr's illness worsened, making it impossible for him to perform. Singer played drums on most of *Revenge* and officially became a member of KISS in December of 1991, the month after Carr died.

Singer recorded *Carnival of Souls: The Final Sessions* with KISS late in 1995 and early in 1996, and toured with the band until later in 1996, when the original lineup reunited for the Alive/Worldwide Tour (a.k.a. the Reunion Tour). Singer rejoined KISS in 2001, debuting his Catman makeup and costume for the Farewell Tour. During his time away from KISS, Singer toured with Queen guitarist Brian May.

Peter Criss rejoined KISS late in 2002, replacing Singer, but was let go in March of 2004. Singer was brought in once again, touring with the band and playing drums on *Sonic Boom* (2009) and *Monster* (2012). A prolific, critically acclaimed drummer, Singer also played for the German metal band Avantasia in 2002, and from 2007 to 2010.

Although he remains a steady member of KISS, Singer has said he will probably quit the band if Paul Stanley or Gene Simmons retires. On the aforementioned episode of *The Cassius Morris Show*, Singer said: "Me personally, if Gene and Paul aren't in KISS, I don't think I have much interest in being in KISS…. What I'm saying is, if Paul Stanley decides, 'Okay, I don't wanna do this anymore. Let's just get somebody to replace Paul.' That doesn't sound inviting to me. Same thing if Gene left. I mean, if it was just gonna be Paul, Tommy, and I with a different guy, it doesn't sound inviting to me; it just doesn't…. Maybe it's because I've been around them so long and I realize the importance of what they do. I mean, they are the pillars of KISS, if you will."

The Singles: Released by Concept Records only in Australia through a mail order TV commercial, *The Singles* (1985) is a greatest hits compilation. Tracks include: "I Was Made for Lovin' You," "Rock and Roll All Nite," "Sure Know Something," "Shout It Out Loud," "Hard Luck Woman," "Shandi," "I," "I Love It Loud," "Strutter '78," "Talk to Me," "Beth," "Detroit Rock City," "Calling Dr. Love," "Then She Kissed Me," "Lick It Up," and "Heaven's On Fire."

16 Magazine: The first issue of *16 Magazine*, featuring Elvis Presley on the cover, hit newsstands in May of 1957. The last issue was printed in 2001. The publication featured KISS on its covers and within its pages numerous times, including the July 1980 issue, which features Paul Stanley's "Life Story" and a Gene Simmons pull-out poster, and the September 1980 issue, which has a cover feature called "KISS Krack-Up! Are They Really Breaking Up?"

60 Minutes: In 1979, during the *Dynasty* era, the Australian version of *60 Minutes* had a feature on KISS, with the reporter describing the band thusly: "This is *Star Wars* with a beat. Heavy metal meets Captain Marvel. It's a calculated assault on the senses." Not surprisingly, the episode focused on the revenue the band generated (manager Bill Aucoin stated that KISS grossed approximately $117 million per year) and their costumes and makeup. One fan in Paul garb said, "I'm just coming here because of their show, not 'cause of their music."

Talking about the makeup and their hidden identities, Gene equated KISS with Santa Clause while Ace compared them to Batman and Frankenstein, saying they wear the clown white to maintain their mystique. At one point Paul said, "There's still a tremendous amount of apathy in rock and roll, a lot of bands going out on stage looking like they rolled out of bed. We're in here doing a spectacle."

When the narrator mentioned that parents had organized a "pray-in" outside of a concert hall in Lubbock, Texas, where KISS was set to perform, Ace had a relatively rare moment of seriousness and said, "There's no credence to this devil worship…. We're all normal people … fun loving guys

... all American ... we're just doing this for fun. This is our livelihood." Gene compared the band to the Beatles: "The same thing happened to four guys from Liverpool, England ... devil's music ... their records were banned in the south and torn up."

Near the end of the show, Gene summed up the band's basic approach: "We're going on the line as saying that we're trying not to do anything too deep. We're trying to provide people with an escape. We're trying to provide people with the best show of their life."

Skid Row: Skid Row, fronted by Sebastian Bach, covered "C'mon and Love Me" on their 1992 EP, *B-Side Ourselves*. The EP features five cover tunes, each originally recorded by a band that influenced Skid Row.

Slade: Most casual KISS fans probably don't realize that the English rock group Slade was a big influence on the band. Their popular, arena-rocking anthems, "Mama Weer All Crazee Now" and "Cum on Feel the Noize," helped inspire KISS to write a few anthems of their own, including their iconic hit, "Rock and Roll All Nite."

In the book *Headliners: KISS*, Gene Simmons said: "Seeing Slade finally made all the pieces fit together. Their set was really simple, all running around the stage. And singing songs that never meant anything. Their song structure was 'Mama we're all crazy now,' and our song structure is 'We'll drive you wild, we'll drive you crazy.'"

Slingerland Drums: Early in his career, Peter Criss played Slingerland drums, including the Radio King kit, the Black Beauty Pearl kit, and the Silver Mylar kit. Currently owned by Gibson, the Slingerland Drum Company was founded in 1913 in Kalamazoo, Michigan, by Henry Heanon Slingerland.

Smalling, J. R.: In addition to being KISS's stage manager from 1974 to 1976, J. R. Smalling shouted the band's trademark opening on the *Alive!* album: "You wanted the best and you got it, the hottest band in the land.... KISS!" You can read of his experiences in *Out On the Streets—The True Tales of Life On the Road With the Hottest Band In the Land—KISS!*, which he co-authored.

Smashes, Thrashes & Hits: This greatest hits album, released November 15, 1988, by Mercury Records, features two new songs, "Let's Put the X in Sex" and "(You Make Me) Rock Hard," plus a re-recorded version of "Beth" with Eric Carr on the mic. Carr's voice is smooth, but Peter Criss's raspier vocals work better on a song like "Beth."

Tracks, most of which were remixed, include: "Let's Put the X in Sex," "(You Make Me) Rock Hard," "Love Gun" (remix), "Detroit Rock City" (remix), "I Love It Loud" (remix), "Deuce" (remix), "Lick It Up," "Heaven's On Fire," "Calling Dr. Love" (remix), "Strutter" (remix), "Beth," "Tears Are Falling," "I Was Made for Lovin' You," "Rock and Roll All Nite" (remix), and "Shout It Out Loud" (remix). The UK edition adds "Crazy Crazy Nights" as the second track.

Smith, Joe: Joe Smith was president of Warner Bros. Records from 1972 to 1975, helping guide the label launch of *KISS*, the band's first album.

Smoking Guitar: The smoking guitar is one of Ace Frehley's trademark special effects. In *KISS: Behind the Mask—The Official Authorized Biography*, the Spaceman recalled that he originally bought some smoke bombs at a magic shop in Canada and "put the smoke bomb inside the compartment where the volume and tone controls are on the Les Paul, and I just left a little hole with the fuse coming out that I could light with a cigarette lighter. And the smoke would go through the canals where the wires are and would come out through the pickups."

The smoke bombs gummed up the works of Frehley's guitar so he "revamped a guitar with a special pickup with a movie light built in and a whole electronic system that would trigger a smoke bomb and trigger movie lights ... then I came up with the rocket idea and most recently the pinwheel."

Snider, Dee: Twisted Sister frontman Dee Snider is a huge fan of the original KISS lineup. Unfortunately, in September of 2015, he and Paul Stanley had a public dispute, which Snider discussed on episode 144 of *Three Sides of the Coin*.

"Snow Blind": Following the rousing "Rip It Out" and "Speedin' Back to My Baby," "Snow Blind," the third track on *Ace Frehley*, is a bit of a downer (though it's still a good song). A confounded Frehley sings of being lost in space and that he doesn't want to sing, conditions no doubt brought on by drug abuse (like the Black Sabbath tune, "Snowblind," "Snow Blind" refers to being high on cocaine). The nimble-fingered guitar solo midway through seems at odds with the sleepy, stuttering nature of the rest of the song.

Solan, Eddie: A good friend of Ace Frehley, Eddie Solan, who would drive Ace to the Loft during the early days of the band because he didn't have a car, was the first KISS soundman, serving as a roadie from 1973 to 1974. During the recording of *KISS* at Bell Studios, he took some landmark photos of the band.

Solid Gold: KISS chose not to tour in support of *Music from "The Elder,"* but they did appear on an episode of *Solid Gold* (1980–1988), pantomiming their way through "I." Andy Gibb introduces KISS thusly: "One of the most exciting performances you can ever go to is a concert by our next guests. Their hard-driving music and spectacular theatrics make them one of rock's most exciting bands." Later on in the episode, comedian Marty Cohen and Madame the puppet, wearing KISS-inspired makeup and costumes, joke around as they introduce the "World Without Heroes" music video.

A Solo Guitar Tribute to Paul Stanley— The Songwriter: This German CD features 11 acoustic instrumental songs by Oliver Schneiss: "Turn On The Night," "Shandi," "Anything for My Baby," "I Was Made for Lovin' You," "Second to None," "Wouldn't You Like to Know Me," "Sure Know Something," "Psycho Circus," "Fanfare," "Just A Boy," and "Hide Your Heart." Released December 2014.

"Somewhere Between Heaven and Hell": Written by Gene Simmons and Vini Poncia, "Somewhere Between Heaven and Hell" is the 13th track on *Hot in the Shade*. It's an above average rocker in which Simmons sings about a girl who can't seem to make up her mind whether she wants him or not. Hardcore riff courtesy of Bruce Kulick. Simmons has said he prefers the demo to the actual song because it's much heavier.

Songbooks: There have been many KISS songbooks released over the years featuring lyrics, music, and sometimes photos. Along with songbooks for such albums as *Alive II*, *Destroyer*, *Love Gun*, and *Rock and Roll Over*, there are a number of greatest hits compilations, including *The Best of KISS* (1994) and *KISS for Easy Guitar* (1995). Some, such as the Hal Leonard Play-Along books, contain sound-alike audio CDs.

This songbook, published by Hal Leonard, includes sheet music and a sound-alike CD.

Sonic Boom: Released October 6, 2009, *Sonic Boom* is KISS's 19th studio album and was the band's first studio album in 11 years. Released on the KISS Records label, it is a nice throwback to 1970s KISS, down to the circular cover art by Michael Doret, who also did the cover for *Rock and Roll Over*.

In a review published on www.ultimate-guitar.com, the writer said: "You'll get your standard KISS fare on *Sonic Boom*, with both the sleazy rockers and arena anthems coming out in full force.... Stanley's enthusiasm and vocal delivery has not been affected in the slightest by age. He's still a dynamo at what he does, and that's jaw-dropping at 57 years of age. Simmons' up-to-no-good vocals are always a hoot, particularly when paired with some of the cheesy lyrics heard on *Sonic Boom*. Singer and Thayer make a good showing, with Thayer actually bringing the record up to a different level. There are some incredibly juicy riffs.... Thayer deserves credit for keeping the album fresh at many points along the way."

In the U.S. and Canada, *Sonic Boom*, which included three discs, was released exclusively through Walmart, but owners of certain independent stores would purchase the CD at Walmart and then sell it at their location for a higher price. Most Walmart stores displayed *Sonic Boom* alongside other new KISS merchandise in a special "KISS Corner" section.

Disc one features the new *Sonic Boom* tracks: "Modern Day Delilah" (the album's first single), "Russian Roulette," "Never Enough" (second single), "Yes I Know (Nobody's Perfect)," "Stand," "Hot and Cold," "All for the Glory," "Danger Us," "I'm an Animal," "When Lightning Strikes," and "Say Yeah" (third single).

Disc two is a compilation of "KISS Klassics": "Deuce," "Detroit Rock City," "Shout It Out Loud," "Hotter Than Hell," "Calling Dr. Love," "Love Gun," "I Was Made for Lovin' You," "Heaven's On Fire," "Lick It Up," "I Love It Loud," "Forever," "Christine Sixteen," "Do You Love Me?," "Black Diamond," and "Rock and Roll All Nite."

Disc three features the following songs recorded live in Buenos Aires on April 5, 2009, at River Plate Stadium: "Deuce," "Hotter Than Hell," "C'mon and Love Me," "Watchin' You," "100,000 Years," and "Rock and Roll All Nite."

Sonic Boom Over Europe Tour: To support *Sonic Boom*, KISS hit the road from May 1, 2010, to June 27, 2010, for a total of 36 shows. Paul Finn of www.kissinuk.com caught two of the performances and wrote: "Paul's vocal cords have been a point of discussion ever since the 2008 tour, this tour will hopefully put those discussions to rest.... At Birmingham he sounded great, a little strained at times but no real problems.... Tommy fires rockets from his guitar, and goes up on one of the risers. Not to be outdone, Eric's drums rise up with a jet of CO2 while he crosses his arms, shakes his head at Tommy and fires a bazooka! Brilliant stuff, cheesy but very entertaining.... The lighting was amazing.... Gene flying to the lighting rig is back again, this time to 'I Love It Loud'... no real surprises in the setlist, but the band are sounding so tight this time round you can definitely forgive them."

Followed by: The Hottest Show on Earth Tour.

The Soul Lives in Berlin: French Kisses Issue I, Vol. I: This 1996 French EP, produced and performed by Cyril Laurent (formerly of the heavy metal band Moon Revolution), consists of three tracks: "God of Thunder," "Charisma," and "She."

Soul Station: An 11-piece musical group featuring Paul Stanley on lead vocals and Eric Singer on drums, Soul Station played their first gig on September 11, 2015, at the Roxy Theatre in Los Angeles. Of this side project, Stanley said: "We're living in a time of being fed canned pre-programmed backing tracks and lip-syncing in place of the electricity and passion of real live R&B. When I was a boy, before I ever saw the Who or Led Zeppelin, I saw Solomon Burke and Otis Redding. I saw the Temptations and all that music is part of the foundation of the music I've made. Soul Station is my chance to celebrate it for a night that's real, live, and faithfully recreates the sound with the respect it deserves. Whether it's the Stylistics, the Dramatics, the Temptations, Smokey [Robinson] and the Miracles, Blue Magic and on, these songs, arrangements, and sound just blow you away.... I don't play guitar in the band and we don't do a single KISS song. That's not what this is about. It's magical to hear those songs played right and we're making magic."

Sound Magazine: A Partridge Family tribute band, Sound Magazine covered "Shout It Out Loud" Partridge-style and has performed the song in concert.

South Park: The season 10, episode 8 installment of *South Park*, the irreverent animated series Trey Parker and Matt Stone created in 1997, features Paul Stanley's solo song, "Live to Win." The episode is called "Make Love, Not Warcraft."

Space Invader: Released by E1 Music on August 19, 2014, *Space Invader* is Ace Frehley's self-produced solo follow-up to 2009's *Anomaly*. Cover art is by Ken Kelly, who painted the covers for *Destroyer* and *Love Gun*. The album debuted at #9 on the *Billboard* 200 albums chart, the only time a solo album from a past or current KISS member has hit the top 10 in the U.S.

Tracks include: "Space Invader," "Gimme a Feelin'" (radio edit), "I Wanna Hold You," "Change," "Toys," "Immortal Pleasures," "Inside the Vortex," "What Every Girl Wants," "Past the Milky Way," "Reckless," "The Joker" (a cover of the Steve Miller Band song), and "Starship." The deluxe edition features two extra tracks: the radio edit of "Space Invader" and the explicit version of "Gimme a Feelin'." Recorded at The Creation Lab in Turlock, California.

Spaceman: During the early days, when KISS was deciding on their stage personas, Ace Frehley became the Spaceman. In his autobiography, *No Regrets*, he said he chose the character because "I was fascinated with space travel and science fiction and technology in general." Frehley also goes by the name of Space Ace.

In 2002, Tommy Thayer adopted the Spaceman persona when he took over as lead guitarist for KISS. Although Thayer is a fine musician, his wearing the Spaceman makeup and costume has caused controversy among KISS purists and Frehley himself. In a September 10, 2014, interview with *The Village Voice*, Frehley said: "I could sense he always wanted to be me. He used to be in a KISS cover band ... he was hired by Paul and Gene to put on my makeup and costume and play my guitar solos—a business deal.... What they really should have done is, if they wanted to dress up a guy to play lead guitar, they should have come up with different makeup like they did with Eric Carr and Vinnie Vincent."

Spacewalk: A Tribute to Ace Frehley: Ace Frehley was a huge influence on a generation of aspiring guitarists, as evidenced (at least in part) by this tribute record, which includes the following tracks: "Deuce" (Marty Friedman), "Shock Me" (Gilby Clarke), "Rip It Out" (Scott Ian), "Hard Luck Woman" (Ron Young & Jeff Watson), "Snowblind" (Snake Sabo), "Rock Bottom" (Sebastian Bach), "Parasite" (Tracii Guns), "Cold Gin" (John Norum), "New York Groove" (Bruce Bouillet), "Fractured Mirror" (Dimebag Darrell), and "Take Me to the City" (Ace Frehley). The Japanese version includes a 12th track, "Save Your Love" (Sabastian Bach). Released in 1996 by Triage Records.

Speaking in Tongues: Released as both an audio CD and a DVD in 2004 by Sanctuary Records, *Speaking in Tongues* features Gene Simmons on the lecture circuit, speaking in Australia. The Demon discusses fame, fortune, girls, success, KISS, his sometimes-difficult childhood (and how it helped make him the man he is today), and more, including what led him to become a musician. He even offers advice on dating, marriage, career goals, and life in general, all with a sense of humor.

"Speedin' Back to My Baby": Written by Ace Frehley and his wife at the time, Jeanette, "Speedin' Back to My Baby" is the second track on Ace Frehley's 1978 KISS solo album. The song, which has a nice beat, gets out of the starting gate with a screaming guitar solo and continues at a fast pace as Frehley sings about whether or not he should return to a cheating girl.

Spin the Bottle: An All-Star Tribute to KISS: This tribute album, released April 27, 2004, by Koch Records, features the following tracks: "Detroit Rock City" (Dee Snider), "Love Gun" (Tommy Shaw), "Cold Gin" (Mark Slaughter), "King of the Night Time World" (Fozzy), "I Want You" (Kip Winger), "God of Thunder" (Buzz Osborne), "Calling Dr. Love" (Page Hamilton), "Shout It Out Loud" (Motörhead), "Parasite" (Doug Pinnick), "Strutter" (Phil Lewis), and "I Stole Your Love" (Robin McAuley). The Japanese release includes two bonus tracks, each by a local Japanese act: "Deuce" and "Parasite." Produced by Bob Kulick and Bruce Bouilett.

"Spinning Wheel": For the 2014 Engelbert Humperdinck album *Engelbert Calling*, the crooner sang a duet with Gene Simmons called "Spinning Wheel." It's a cover of the popular Blood, Sweat and Tears song from 1969 and has been performed by Humperdinck before.

Spirit of '76 Poster: In 1976, to promote the band's forthcoming summer tour, the KISS merchandising machine released the iconic "Spirit of '76 Poster," which was photographed by Barry Levine and patterned after Archibald MacNeal Willard's famous *The Spirit of '76* painting (previously known as *Yankee Doodle*). The poster can be seen in the first episode of *WKRP in Cincinnati* (Sept. 18, 1978), where new program director Andy Travis is shown unrolling and pinning it up, signifying that things were going to change at the station.

"Spit": One of the most ridiculous songs in the KISS library, "Spit" is the fourth track on *Revenge*. A sexual ode to fat women everywhere, the song manages to steal from both *This is Spinal Tap* ("Big Bottom") and Led Zeppelin ("Whole Lotta Love"), and even includes a brief guitar take on "The Star-Spangled Banner" (shades of Jimi Hendrix). Written by Gene Simmons, Scott Van Zen, and Paul Stanley. Simmons and Stanley sing lead. Simmons drew inspiration for the song from the term "swapping spit," and from the 1970 Fleetwood Mac song, "The Green Manalishi (With the Two Prong Crown)."

SpongeBob SquarePants: In the November 23, 2007, *SpongeBob SquarePants* episode, "20,000 Patties Under the Sea," Gene Simmons voiced the Sea Monster, a creature who buys 640 Krabby Patties. Shannon Tweed voiced the mom fish.

"Stand": Written and sung by Paul Stanley and Gene Simmons, "Stand" is the fifth track on *Sonic Boom*. It begins like a standard KISS rocker, but has a "cheesy, cheesy chorus which no other band on the planet would get away with. Not content with that, it even dives into a multi-vocal layered mid-section" (Mark Eglinton of thequietus.com). The latter is an embarrassment that evokes Spinal Tap's "(Listen to the) Flower People."

Stanley, Paul: One of the greatest, most charismatic frontmen in the history of rock and roll, singer and rhythm guitarist Paul Stanley, a.k.a., the Starchild, has always been the heart and soul of KISS, naming the group, writing and singing many of their hit songs, leading the band onstage (his banter is kitschy good fun), and holding fast to the idea and philosophy behind KISS during good times and bad.

When each band member produced a solo album in 1978, Paul's sounded the most like a KISS record. When Gene Simmons was distracted during the 1980s by the promise of a film career, Paul held the KISS ship steady, devoting his life to keeping the band together and putting his indelible, overarching stamp on such albums as *Asylum* and *Crazy Nights*.

Born Stanley Bert Eisen on Jan. 20, 1952, in New York City, Paul Stanley grew up to become the quintessential rock star, adored and lusted after by millions of fans around the world. However, he certainly wasn't born with a silver spoon in his mouth (or a black star on his face), as he recalled in his 2014 autobiography, *Face the Music: A Life Exposed*: "I was born with an ear deformity called microtia, in which the outer ear cartilage fails to form properly and, to varying degrees of severity, leaves you with just a crumpled mass of cartilage. I had nothing more than a stump on the right side of my head. And my ear canal was also closed, so I was deaf."

Predictably, kids made fun of Stanley's gnarled nub of an ear, gawking, staring, and calling him "Stanley the one-eared monster." The confusion and pain caused by feeling different and being made fun of made Stanley an introvert who felt insecure, incomplete, and plagued by self-doubt and internal conflicts.

Stanley's birth defect had a tremendous impact on his life, as did his father and mother (William and Eva Eisen), who introduced him to classical music (for which he remains "forever grateful"), but were less than ideal parents, oftentimes leaving he and his sister Julia at home for hours at a time when they were only six and eight years old (respectively). Stanley wrote that his parents "were not happy people. I don't know what the basis for their marriage was beyond what later became known as codependency. They didn't provide anything positive for each other. There was no warmth or affection in the house."

According to Stanley's bio, his sister "got into a lot of trouble and eventually spent many years in and out of mental institutions ... by the time I was in junior high, Julia was getting more and more self-destructive.... Julia would hang out in the East Village and crash at people's apartments and take drugs."

Stanley was deathly afraid of his sister (he relates

The July 1980 issue of *16 Magazine* features the unlikely duo of Bo Duke and Paul Stanley on the cover.

a story of the time she came after him with a hammer), and he wrote that his parents were so consumed with her that they had little time for him. Stanley often had to fend for himself when the nurturing love of a father or mother would have served him well.

"I was alone a lot," Stanley wrote. "I approached every day with a sense of foreboding, as I faced the unknown without any safety net. Every new day was uncertain, every new day was unprotected, every new day meant dealing with a world I wasn't equipped to deal with."

Stanley found refuge from a confusing, painful world in music. "I'll never forget hearing Beethoven's Piano Concerto no. 5 in E-flat major—the *Emperor Concerto*—for the first time," he wrote. "I was five, and I was completely blown away."

When he got older, Stanley discovered rock and roll on the radio, including such acts as Eddie Cochran, Little Richard, and Dion & the Belmonts. "It was pure magic," he wrote. "They sang about a glorified life of teenagers that I quickly came to dream of. All that singing about an idyllic concept of youth touched me emotionally. It filled me with the wonder of being a teen and transported me to a wonderful place, a place where life's angst concerned relationships and *love*. Man, what perfect lives these young people lived!"

The first record Stanley owned was a 78 RPM shellac single of "All I Have to Do Is Dream" by the Everly Brothers, which his mother bought for him at a record shop in the Bronx. He was also influenced by such stars as Jerry Lee Lewis, who he saw on Dick Clark's *American Bandstand*, and the Beatles, whose shaggy appearance convinced Stanley to grow his hair long, which was a good way to cover his deformed ear.

When he was 13, Stanley, inspired by such acts as the Who, the Rolling Stones, the Kinks, and the Dave Clark Five, asked for an electric guitar for his birthday. However, his parents got him an acoustic instead. He began playing music with neighborhood kids, and when he turned 14 he bought an electric guitar, a three-quarter-size, two pick-up Stratocaster knockoff built by Vox. The future Starchild spent a lot of time in his room, playing the guitar, listening to the radio, and reading music magazines.

A budding artist and an avowed misfit, Stanley began attending Manhattan's High School of Music & Art during the fall of 1967. "I had been one of the best visual artists in my junior high—drawing was my thing," he wrote. "But equally important, I hoped this specialized school would be a more comfortable environment than the meat grinders I had attended up to that point. I had gone from being stared at for something beyond my control—my ear—to being stared at for something of my own making—my outlandish clothes."

Stanley graduated high school in June of 1970. He enrolled at Bronx Community College, but dropped out after a week because of his hearing problems, and because it took time away from his true goal: to play music for a living.

Prior to joining Gene Simmons' band, Rainbow (later Wicked Lester), in 1970, Stanley belonged to smalltime act Uncle Joe (a.k.a. Incubus) and then the Post War Baby Boom.

"Outside of my band, the Post War Baby Boom, I didn't have anything else in my life," Stanley wrote. "Just my guitar, my stereo, and, more and more often, concerts [Jimi Hendrix, the Yardbirds, Traffic, the Grateful Dead, Jefferson Airplane, and the like]. I envied kids who had social circles and weekend get-togethers, but I didn't have any of that. I had not figured out how to be a part of things. So I often went to shows by myself. It was something fulfilling.... I found myself bathing in music every weekend."

During the early years of KISS, interpersonal problems were few, and Stanley enjoyed spending time with his bandmates. "I thought of us as the four musketeers and figured we'd be together forever," he wrote. "We were the Vikings, the Huns, the Mongols, wreaking havoc in every town we invaded. We were the Beatles skiing downhill in *Help!* We were KISS. There was a genuine sense of camaraderie as we ate together, traveled together, got dressed for a show together, and played together—and onstage we were a unified force ... it was fun to be KISS."

Unfortunately, things began to unravel as KISS got more and more popular. Ace and Peter's addiction to alcohol and drugs began affecting the way they played onstage and in the studio. "Between their sycophantic friends and all the press, Peter and Ace began to believe they were world-class virtuosos, despite mounting evidence to the contrary," Stanley wrote. "Both ... were fucked up all the time.... Ace was a shadow of his former self.... Peter spent all his emotional energy worrying about his place in the hierarchy without the ability to be honest with himself about the quality of what he brought to the table."

Worse, Paul accused two of his three bandmates of anti–Semitism, a painful admission since he and Gene are both Jewish (Paul's mother and her family fled to Amsterdam from Nazi Germany). "Ace and particularly Peter felt powerless and impotent when faced with the tireless focus, drive and ambition of me and Gene," Paul wrote. "As a result, the two of them tried to sabotage the band—which, as they saw it, was unfairly manipulated by [us] money-grubbing Jews."

Thing weren't rosy between Paul and Gene either as the former felt the latter saw the band "as a vehicle for himself as an individual. Gene was in it for Gene. Whatever the reasons, he didn't share the collective mentality I had. I found security in the band—it provided something lacking in my life. I wanted to belong ... for me it was all about the team, and I coveted the band above all else."

Despite the popularity of KISS during the late 1970s, Stanley struggled with insecurities and self-doubt. "Performing provided pure escapism and joy and elation," he wrote. "In my everyday life, I could never free myself of my insecurities, and the increasing rancor inside the band left me feeling more isolated than ever.... I needed the crowd to love me. Nobody else did. Not even me. It can be very lonely walking offstage when you feel like that."

To help bolster his self-esteem, Stanley sought counseling, had reconstructive surgery on his ear (in 1982), and, most publicly (and futilely), slept around. "As far as the women I hooked up with, I knew it wasn't about deep conversation," he wrote. "I chose them because of what I *hoped* could convince myself: *I must be worthwhile because this beautiful woman wants to be with me.*"

Although his romantic relationships didn't garner the media attention of Gene Simmons and Cher, Stanley dated a number of celebrities, including Lita Ford, Leslie Ann Warren, Samantha Fox, Donna Dixon, and Lisa Hartman.

During the 1980s, after Ace and Peter had left the band, after the makeup came off, and when Gene was preoccupied with Hollywood, Paul thought the Demon's contributions were significantly less than that of an equal partner: "Gene would stagger into the studio after not sleeping all night—he was too busy once again making movies or working with other bands. Or he spent the whole time on the phone, working this or that angle. The few songs Gene brought in seemed to have been written by other people, with Gene pasting his name on after the fact ... the songs were not impressive.... KISS albums were in essence solo albums for me ... a situation I did not want."

After Paul confronted Gene, the Demon made amends by giving the Starchild a black Porsche 928, a remedy only marginally better than a Band-Aid on cancer. Fortunately, Gene made amends with a strong, dedicated performance on 1992's *Revenge*, and with an all-in attitude on the Reunion Tour.

Stanley's primary focus has always been KISS, but he has indulged in several side projects, including a 1989 club solo tour (featuring Bob Kulick and Eric Singer), a 2006 solo album (*Live to Win*), and a stint in 1999 as the Phantom in a Toronto production of Andrew Lloyd Webber's popular musical, *The Phantom of the Opera*. The latter was a role that Stanley has called a highlight of his life.

In 2001, Paul divorced Pamela Bowen, his wife of nine years. They had one child together, a son named Evan Shane Stanley, born June 6, 1994. To help deal with the anguish and stress of the divorce, Paul took up painting, a hobby that he remains active in today. In 2009, he told *INsite Magazine*, "A friend of mine, my best friend, said that I needed to paint.... I went out and bought canvasses and paints and brushes and all kinds of other supplies and just decided to throw caution to the wind.... I was using colors and textures to put my emotions, or what was going on inside me, on canvas. It was purely a relief and, I guess, cathartic therapy for me that once other people started seeing clearly connected with them."

On November 19, 2005, Paul married longtime girlfriend Erin Sutton. They have three children together: Colin (Sept. 6, 2006), Sarah (Jan. 28, 2009), and Emily (Aug. 9, 2011).

Today, Paul, despite having had throat surgery and a pair of hip replacement surgeries, seems like a happy, well-adjusted family man, and he's still a formidable frontman for KISS, despite some loss of vocal range (which is understandable given his age). He's also involved in a variety of charities, most notably AboutFace, an organization that provides support for people with facial differences.

"Stanley the Parrot": When Gene Simmons met Paul Stanley for the first time in 1970, the future Demon played the Beach Boys–influenced "Stanley the Parrot" for the future Starchild. Stanley wasn't impressed with the song, but he was struck by Gene's "soft, melodic voice" (*Nothin' to Lose: The Making of KISS (1972–1975)*). The chord structure for "Strutter" was loosely based on "Stanley the Parrot."

Starchild: With his leading man good looks and flashy rock star persona, Paul Stanley's stage moniker the Starchild is a nice fit for the KISS frontman. In *Face the Music: A Life Exposed*, Stanley wrote about selecting the star-over-one-eye makeup design: "First I tried out red makeup. Then I tried a ring around my eye like Petey the dog in the *Little Rascals*. But stars had always fascinated me, and now, of course, I also intended to be the frontman of the band, the focal point. No longer would I be the awkward kid, the outcast. I would be *the Starchild*. I painted a star around my right eye. It was hard work trying to draw a two-dimensional symbol on a three-dimensional object—my face. It looked one way from the front and another from the side. I was tired by the time I finally created one good star. I didn't want to struggle through painting another one on the left side."

Paul "the Starchild" Stanley, featured on the cover of *Power Play* (2015), a British magazine.

Starkey, Bill: In addition to founding the KISS Army with his buddy Jay Evans, Bill Starkey wrote the foreword to Dale Sherman's 2012 book, *KISS FAQ*, in which Starkey said he first saw the band on a Friday night during the mid–1970s on an episode of *Don Kirshner's Rock Concert*. A resident of Terre Haute, Indiana, Starkey was alerted to the show by an ad in the newspaper depicting "an unusual thing" [Gene Simmons] playing bass. Starkey's first KISS album was *KISS*, which his dad brought home from his job at a local record pressing plant. Starkey's father also took him to see his first KISS concert: KISS opening for ZZ Top on December 8, 1974, at Roberts Stadium in Evansville. "Sirens, flash pots, fire breathing, blood puking—my first concert had it all," Starkey said.

"The Star-Spangled Banner": On September 29, 2013, Gene Simmons sang "The Star-Spangled Banner" at London's Wembley Stadium for the NFL International Series game between the Pittsburgh Steelers and Minnesota Vikings. Prior to the event, he said in a press release: "I'm excited to be touching down in London to sing our U.S. National Anthem at the Vikings-Steelers game. I always love playing a role in these types of high-action, fast-paced games, not to mention returning to the UK and performing in front of some the best fans in the world!"

The previous year, on September 10, 2012, Simmons sang the song at an Oakland Raiders/San Diego Chargers game at Oakland-Alameda County Coliseum. On August 25, 2013, Paul Stanley sang "The Star-Spangled Banner" at Dodger Stadium for a Dodgers game against the Boston Red Sox. Stanley also threw out the first pitch and promoted the L.A. KISS Arena Football League team. On June 16, 2014, Simmons, accompanied by four members of the USO, sang the song before a Dodgers game.

Steele, Bob: Bob Steele was the pseudonym of Peggy Tomarkin, who wrote KISS tour books and fan club newsletters during the band's glory days.

Stevens, Carrie: Eric Carr dated actress and Playboy Playmate of the Month (June 1997) Carrie Stevens from 1987 to 1991. In an interview published on www.legendaryrockinterviews.com in 2013, Stevens spoke about her relationship with Carr in light of his illness: "While Eric was sick, he and I did a lot of spiritual work. We read Louise

Hay books. We learned that the point of power is in the present moment, and said positive affirmations and focused on relaxation. Stress is a killer. It's a daily struggle not to dwell on the past and not to worry about the future. It's especially hard because I miss Eric to this day and I am sad that he is gone. But in this moment, I feel loved and respected by him, Loretta [Carr's sister] and his friends and fans and that is what I must be grateful for, in this moment."

"Stop, Look to Listen": The eighth track on disc one of *The Box Set*, "Stop, Look to Listen" was recorded in 1966 by Paul Stanley (vocals), Matt Rael (guitar) and Neil Teeman (drums) when they were in a band called Uncle Joe (there was no bass guitarist). The boys were only 14 at the time, but the song, which betrays influence by the Kinks and the Who, actually sounds pretty decent.

"Strange Ways": One of KISS's heavier tunes, "Strange Ways" is the 10th and final track on *Hotter Than Hell*. It was written by Ace Frehley, but sung by Peter Criss since the Spaceman was too intimated by Paul Stanley and Gene Simmons to handle the vocals himself. Many call "Strange Ways," which is a favorite among hardcore KISS fans, a forerunner to grunge. Various bands have covered the song over the years, including Megadeth, Hyposrisy, Ulver, and Vicious Rumors.

Strange Ways Podcast: You can access this KISS podcast, which, according to the website, beams to you "all the way from planet Jendel," via strangewayskisspodcast.podomatic.com.

"The Street Giveth and the Street Taketh Away": Gene Simmons' vocals notwithstanding, KISS sounds like '80s hair metal band Cinderella in this, the 11th track on *Hot in the Shade*. A decent song with a silly title, it was written by Simmons and Tommy Thayer, who provides both acoustic and lead guitar.

Street Punk: Fronted by Jon Montgomery, Street Punk shared the bill with KISS the second time KISS played the Crystal Room at the Hotel Diplomat. "KISS brought the house down," said Street Punk bassist Donnie Nossov in *Nothin' to Lose: The Making of KISS (1972–1975)*. "No one had seen anything like that before. As it turns out, after they were done, 80 percent of the audience left and we did our show to an almost empty Crystal Room."

The String Quartet Tribute to KISS: This CD, performed by the Ya Baby! String Quartet, was released by Vitamin Records April 20, 2004. In his review of the album, Johnny Loftus of www.allmusic.com wrote: "This string tribute to KISS actually has pretty cool cover art for a budget release, incorporating violins into a graphic reminiscent of the band's famous face paint. That said, the chamber quartet versions of KISS faves like 'Detroit Rock City,' 'Strutter,' 'Love Gun,' and 'Rock and Roll All Nite' have little connection to the originals. They're the chuckle-worthy equivalent of standing in an elevator and hearing a Muzak remake of a metal classic."

Tracks include: "Detroit Rock City," "Calling Dr. Love," "Strutter," "Hard Luck Woman," "Beth," "Rock and Roll All Nite," "Goin Blind," "Love Gun," "Shout It Out Loud," "I Was Made for Lovin' You," and "New York Groove."

"Strutter": The first song on the first KISS album and the third (and final) single off that record, "Strutter" was written by Gene Simmons (music) and Paul Stanley (lyrics), the latter of whom handles the vocals and has called it an homage of sorts to Bob Dylan's "Just Like a Woman." "Strutter," which is about a satin-clad tease, established the band's melodic, but hard-rocking sound right from the beginning. It's a great starting point for a band that would become legendary. In his 1978 book, *KISS*, Robert Duncan called "Strutter," which has opened numerous KISS shows, "a masterpiece of the heavy metal genre ... that it is a first cut of a first album by a new group is incredible."

"Strutter '78": The first track on *Double Platinum*, "Strutter '78" is a disco-flavored update/recut of the great KISS song, "Strutter," but it doesn't sound all that different from the original, other than extended solos and some additional vocals by Stanley at the end. In the September 1996 issue of *Guitar World*, Gene Simmons said of the remade song, "I look back at that and think, 'Why?' The original version is the classic and the best."

Stuart, Rick: Rick Stuart was the director of security and a bodyguard for KISS from 1975 to 1976. He was interviewed extensively on episode 129 of *Three Sides of the Coin*.

Styx: Founded in 1972, Styx, now a staple of classic rock radio, opened for KISS during the *Alive!* tour. The band is famous for such songs as "Come Sail Away" and "Lady."

Sub, Paul: Paul Sub owned the Popcorn Pub (a.k.a. the Coventry), the famed Queens, New York, club where KISS played their first concert on January 30, 1973. He paid the band $50 for two sets that evening.

***Succession: A 30th Anniversary Tribute to Dynasty*:** Commemorating KISS's 1979 disco LP, *Dynasty*, this downloadable album features all nine tracks from the record in the correct order, each covered by a different musical artist or group: "I Was Made for Lovin' You" (the Wildflowers), "2,000 Man" (Andy Samford), "Sure Know Something" (Tim McPhate), "Dirty Livin'" (the Coal Bin Bros.), "Charisma" (Shawn Fox), "Magic Touch" (Anthony Tyler), "Hard Times" (Roxy Swain), "X-Ray Eyes" (Das Fark), and "Save Your Love" (Beeblesaurus). Produced by Mikel Black. Released July 9, 2009.

Summer, Donna: Disco diva Donna Summer, who, like KISS, was on the Casablanca Records label, sang background vocals on two songs on Gene Simmons' 1978 solo album: "Burning Up with Fever" and "Tunnel of Love." As with KISS, Summer has sold more than 100 million albums.

"Sunday Driver": When Paul Stanley met Gene Simmons for the first time in 1970, Stanley played "Sunday Driver" for Simmons. "I liked 'Sunday Driver' and was struck by how good the construction and melody was," Simmons said in *Nothin' to Lose: The Making of KISS (1972–1975)*. "The lyrical point of view of 'Sunday Driver' sounded English, like 'Eight Days a Week' or 'A Hard Day's Night' by the Beatles. I also really liked his voice." After a bit of retooling, "Sunday Driver" became "Let Me Know," the fifth track on *KISS*.

Sunshine Promotions: Sunshine Promotions promoted numerous KISS shows during the 1970s.

Super Bowl: On January 31, 1999, during the pre-game ceremonies of Super Bowl XXXIII, the original KISS lineup played "Rock and Roll All Nite," complete with makeup, costumes, and pyrotechnics. KISS dancers covered the field. Regarding the game itself, the Denver Broncos beat the Atlanta Falcons 34 to 19.

"Sure Know Something": The third track on *Dynasty* and the second single from the record, "Sure Know Something" is a great pop tune, but it only reached #47 on the *Billboard* charts (though it made the top 10 in several other countries, such as Australia, where it hit #5). The throwaway lyrics belie the excellence of the slickly produced song, which has a terrific up-tempo beat and features some of Gene Simmons' best work on bass guitar, though he reportedly hated playing it. Paul Stanley co-wrote the song with Vini Poncia, and it's a great showcase for the Starchild's distinctive and confident voice. During the verses, Stanley sings falsetto, as he's wont to do at times, and he even plays lead guitar on the track. Anton Fig subs for Peter Criss on drums. A stripped-down version showcased the tune nicely on KISS's *MTV Unplugged* performance.

Sutton, Erin: On November 19, 2005, Paul Stanley married longtime girlfriend Erin Sutton at the Ritz-Carlton, Huntington in Pasadena, California. It was Stanley's second marriage (his first wife was to actress Pamela Bowen). In an April 7, 2014, article published on celebrity.yahoo.com, Stanley revealed why he didn't invite Gene Simmons to the wedding: "Gene had been very, very vocal about not only dismissing the idea of marriage, but really has a very disrespectful and demeaning attitude towards people who did. So for me, it really came down to you don't belong at my wedding. It would taint it. It would do something, it would be contradictory, and for me, that would be offensive. He understood. Lo and behold, he got married, too."

By all accounts still happily married, Stanley and Sutton have three children together: Colin, Sarah, and Emily.

"Sweet Ophelia": Written by Barry Mann and Gerry Goffin, "Sweet Ophelia" is the ninth track on Barry Mann's 1971 album, *Lay It All Out*. Wicked Lester covered the song on their unreleased album, featuring Paul Stanley on vocals. It's a terrific tune that, with some lyrical tweaking, would fit in nicely on *Music from "The Elder."*

"Sweet Pain": The sixth track on *Destroyer*, "Sweet Pain," which speaks to the joys of sado-masochism, is another naughty song written and sung by Gene Simmons, who croons that he has a whip and that his love will drive his lover insane. The female backup singers are a nice touch, and Ace Frehley is replaced on guitar by Dick Wagner, who does a solid job mimicking everyone's favorite Spaceman. As with "Love 'Em and Leave 'Em," the song was derived from the unreleased "Rock and

Rolls Royce," which Simmons wrote as an ode to America's obsession with cars.

Sybesma, Steve: From 1974 to 1997, Steve Sybesma was co-owner and concert promoter for Sunshine Promotions, promoting many KISS shows during the 1970s.

"Take It Off": Written by Paul Stanley, Bob Ezrin, and Kane Roberts, "Take It Off" is a ribald rocker featuring Stanley at a gentlemen's club imploring a girl to wave her panties in the air, lick her lips, and shake her hair. It's essentially an ode to stripper bars, with a typically swaggering Stanley singing about girls onstage instead of his usual arena: the bedroom. Many liken the song, which is the second track on *Revenge*, to Def Leppard's "Pour Some Sugar On Me," an apt comparison.

"Take Me": The second track on *Rock and Roll Over*, "Take Me" was written by Paul Stanley and Sean Delaney as a celebration of oral sex, namely in the back seat of a car with the radio playing and moonlight shining on the girl's hair. KISS is rarely subtle, so when Paul Stanley implores the girl to put her hand in his pocket, grab onto his rocket and "Take Me," it's obviously not to the movies or outer space. A punchy, energetic song with lots of "ahs" and "yeahs."

"Take Me Away (Together as One)": The fifth track on *Paul Stanley*, "Take Me Away (Together as One)" is a "starry-eyed love song given a dreamlike quality by its gentle verses and Stanley's whispered, love-struck lyrics. Of course, being Paul Stanley from KISS, he can't resist rocking out on chorus, but this remains one of his most sensitive songs" (Paul Elliott, *KISS: Hotter Than Hell*). Co-written by Mikel Japp, "Take Me Away (Together as One)" is the longest track on *Paul Stanley*, weighing in at 5:26.

"Take Me Down Below": Gene Simmons and Paul Stanley each take a turn singing lead on "Take Me Down Below," which uses a submarine and an elevator as sexual metaphors. The 11th track on *Monster*, the song manages to keep a cohesive structure, despite each section matching the style of its respective singer.

"Talk to Me": Although Ace Frehley was disillusioned with and tired of being in an increasingly popish KISS during the recording of *Unmasked*, he turned in a terrific tune in "Talk to Me," the third track on the album. While it wasn't released as a single in the U.S., it was a hit overseas, reaching its peak in Switzerland at #10 on the Swiss Singles Chart. It was a top-40 song in Australia, Germany, and the Netherlands as well. The song is tightly structured, and the Spaceman's voice sounds strong, making for one of the better KISS songs from the early 1980s. Interestingly, Frehley played bass on the song.

Tallarico, Carl: Carl Tallarico pounded the skins on the ethereal instrumental, "Fractured Mirror," the only song on Ace Frehley's 1978 solo album not to feature Anton Fig on drums.

"Tears Are Falling": Easily the best and most memorable song on *Asylum*, "Tears are Falling" is the seventh track on the album. It's the LP's only single, reaching #51 on the *Billboard* charts. It spawned a great video as well, featuring a tear breaking a tea glass, tears dropping on a woman's naked chest, and Paul Stanley, who wrote the lyrics, dancing and singing like a hair metal all-star. In the video, KISS looks ridiculous dressed in pink, lavender, and aqua blue, but this song should have been a top-10 hit.

In *KISS: Behind the Mask—The Official Authorized Biography*, Stanley spoke about writing the song: "I was watching MTV and the Eurythmics were doing 'Would I Lie to You?' which reminded me of the beginning of Stevie Wonder's song 'Uptight.' I kind of took my interpretation of that riff and made it the basis of the song. I had also finished a relationship with a girlfriend and the song was pretty much about looking at somebody and knowing that it's over and they're lying."

Tebow, Tim: In 2013, Paul Stanley and Gene Simmons—owners of the Arena Football League team, LA KISS—extended a very public offer to quarterback Tim Tebow, the outspoken Christian football player who was released by the NFL's New England Patriots a few weeks prior. Tebow didn't respond, but Simmons publically defended Tebow, telling Radio.com: "He's got a religious passion, as well he should, we're in America. He's proud to be a Christian, what's wrong with that? And yet, with sports media and pop culture media, they make fun of his religion. Really? In America? If he was wearing a burqa, they wouldn't dare say anything. But if you're a Christian, you get to be picked on? What the hell? The guy's got family values. I never saw the media picking on Michael Vick for torturing dogs. Or this other football player, who's alleged to have killed, committed murder. That's 'cool.' But a guy who's religious and has got family values isn't 'cool?' He's cool to me."

Teeman, Neal: Neal Teeman was the drummer for Paul Stanley's pre–Wicked Lester band, Uncle Joe. A good friend of Stanley, Teeman was at the fateful first meeting between Stanley and Gene Simmons, later acting as second engineer (uncredited) on the double live album *Alive!*

Teenage Lust: Glam rock band Teenage Lust played on the same bill as KISS at the January 31, 1973, show at New York's Academy of Music.

***That '70s Show*:** When the popular sitcom, *That '70s Show*, was launched into syndication in 2002, VH1 aired a celebration special called *That '70s KISS Show*, hosted by Danny Bonaduce (Danny Partridge in *The Partridge Family*) and Susan Olsen (Cindy Brady in *The Brady Bunch*). In the program, teen cast members of *That '70s Show* sneak past security guards to get into a KISS concert (backstage and onstage), which is essentially a new music video for the band's iconic anthem, "Rock and Roll All Nite."

At one point in the program, Dan Weiss, an executive for the music video, says: "When we chose the song, we thought, 'wouldn't it be amazing if we could actually get KISS to perform it with our cast.' From the beginning, KISS understood the natural synergy, and they've been a dream to work with every step of the way." The special also features interviews with the band and the actors, along with appearances by Cher and Cheech Marin.

Gene Simmons, in full makeup and costume, is in the second episode of season three of *That '70s Show*, eating cereal at the family breakfast table and, at the end of the episode, plucking the bass and singing a duet with Charo and Kitty Forman (Debra Jo Rupp).

"That's the Kind of Sugar Papa Likes": A snappy, '50s-meets-'70s tune with a kooky title, female backup singers, and a rocking guitar solo by Toto's Steve Lukather, "That's the Kind of Sugar Papa Likes" is the fifth track on Peter Criss' 1978 KISS solo album. The beginning of the song sounds a little like the intro to Blondie's "Call Me," which was released two years later. Written by Criss and Stan Penridge.

Thayer, Tommy: Born Thomas Cunningham Thayer on November 7, 1960, in Portland, Oregon, Tommy Thayer is the current lead guitar player in KISS. Much to the chagrin of certain longtime KISS fans, he wears Ace Frehley's makeup design and a similar "Space Ace" costume. In fact, Thayer's character is the "Spaceman."

Thayer began playing the guitar when he was 13-years-old. In 1979, when he was in high school, he formed a band with his pal, Jamie St. James, who was then known as James Pond. This band would eventually become Black 'N Blue, a marginally successful metal act that signed with Geffen Records in 1983.

During the Asylum Tour, Black 'N Blue opened for KISS, and Thayer made a good impression on Gene Simmons, who decided to produce two Black 'N Blue records. Around the time Black 'N Blue broke up in 1989, Simmons recruited Thayer to work on *Hot in the Shade*, for which Thayer co-wrote (with Simmons) two songs: "Betrayed" and "The Street Giveth and the Street Taketh Away." Thayer worked on a number of other Simmons-related albums during this era as well, including King Kobra's *King Kobra III* and Doro Pesch's *Doro*.

Thayer played for a number of failed bands during the early 1990s, including All American Man, Harlow, and the Marx Brothers, which included Jaime St. James. In July of 1991, the Marx Brothers made the fateful decision to play an all-KISS show, which led to the group becoming a full-blown KISS cover band called Cold Gin, complete with makeup and costumes. Simmons was so impressed with the act that he hired Cold Gin to play Paul Stanley's birthday party.

In 1993, Simmons and Stanley hired Thayer to work on *KISStory*, the band's massive autobiography. This lead to other work for Thayer in KISS, including a variety of menial tasks. In a 2006 interview published on www.blabbermouth.net, Thayer spoke about his beginnings as a KISS employee. "Working with KISS just started out as a part-time job in 1993–94, working on the *KISStory* book kind of as a photo editor," he said. "I just felt it was something that I was interested in and it was better than when I worked in construction for about a year because I had to make ends meet. I was just happy to have a job. So I started working part-time for Gene and Paul, literally doing anything," including painting Paul's house and cleaning the gutters on Gene's house.

Thayer also managed the World Wide KISS Conventions and the MTV *KISS Unplugged* concert. For the Alive/Worldwide Tour (a.k.a. the

Reunion Tour) of 1996, Thayer helped Ace Frehley and Peter Criss relearn their original guitar and drum parts (respectively) for the classic KISS songs. In addition, Thayer produced and edited such video and film releases as *KISS—The Second Coming*, *Detroit Rock City*, and *The Last KISS*.

Although he said "there was no big goal to be the guitarist in KISS," Thayer was a stand-by in case Ace was a no-show, including at the 2002 Winter Olympics Closing Ceremony in Salt Lake City. Ace showed up, but a month later Thayer filled in as the Spaceman at a private concert in Trelawny, Jamaica, marking his onstage debut with KISS in full costume and makeup. That same year, Thayer appeared with KISS on *Dick Clark's American Bandstand 50th Anniversary* and *That '70s KISS Show*.

On February 28, 2003, KISS, with Thayer on guitar, performed with the Melbourne Symphony Orchestra, a concert recorded for *KISS Symphony: Alive IV* and *KISS Symphony: The DVD*. This date also marks when Thayer officially became a member of KISS.

In March of 2003 in Japan, Thayer began his first extended tour with KISS as their lead guitarist. Later in 2003, many people saw Thayer as the KISS guitarist for the first time live on the World Domination Tour, which the band co-headlined with Aerosmith. More tours followed, including the Rock the Nation World Tour. Thayer produced the accompanying DVD set, *KISS: Rock the Nation Live!*

On June 4, 2006, Thayer married a custom jewelry designer named Amber Peek. In October of 2009, KISS released *Sonic Boom*, their first studio album in 11 years. Thayer co-wrote three songs on the record, including his lead vocal debut for the band, "When Lightning Strikes." That same year, Thayer appeared with KISS on *American Idol*. For KISS's 2012 album, *Monster*, Thayer co-wrote 10 songs and provided lead vocals for "Outta This World."

Despite ridicule and disdain from certain Ace Frehley purists, Thayer continues as a steady, respected, rock solid member of KISS, mimicking Frehley's look, classic solos, smoking guitar, and other Spaceman moves and attributes with (some might say robotic) precision.

Making generous use of his spare time, Thayer participates in a number of charities, including the annual Pacific University Legends Golf Classic.

"Then She Kissed Me": The 10th and final track on *Love Gun*, "Then She Kissed Me" is a tastefully recorded remake of the Crystals' "Then He Kissed Me," a pop hit from 1963 that was written by Phil Spector, Ellie Greenwich, and Jeff Barry. Paul Stanley sings the tale of young love and marriage with a sincerity that is equaled by the instrumentation on the song, including a pretty and refined solo by Ace Frehley. *Love Gun* is a raunchy record, but it ends on a decidedly romantic note.

"Thief in the Night": Written by Gene Simmons and Mitch Weissman, "Thief in the Night," in which a girl breaks into a guy's heart, is the 11th and final track on *Crazy Nights*. It's one of the better Simmons songs from the 1980s, ending the decidedly popish record with a hard rock flourish. Nice harmonizing during the chorus is icing on the proverbial cake. The song was originally written for Wendy O. Williams, who recorded it for her 1984 album, *WOW*.

***Third Watch*:** In the NBC crime drama, *Third Watch* (1999–2005), Gene Simmons played murderous crime lord Donald Mann in three episodes: "Higher Calling," "Monsters," and "More Monsters."

Thompson, Cheryl Anne: During the Peter Criss Imposter incident, Cheryl Anne Thompson claimed to have had an affair with Criss during the early 1980s, when he was newly married to *Playboy* centerfold and Coppertone model Debra Jensen. Criss denied it on *The Phil Donahue Show*.

"Thou Shalt Not": Bruce Kulick shines on guitar in "Thou Shalt Not," an otherwise ordinary rocker written by Gene Simmons and Mark Damon (of Silent Rage), from Simmons' suggestion that they write a song like Humble Pie's "I Don't Need No Doctor." Simmons sings of a man in black who tells him to reconsider the sins of his past, to which the Demon defiantly responds with an invitation for the man to kiss his ass. Simmons got the idea for the title of "Thou Shalt Not," which is the eighth track on *Revenge*, from a girl band of the same name.

***Three Sides of the Coin*:** Hosted by Michael Brandvold, Tommy Sommers, and Mark Cicchini, *Three Sides of the Coin* is an "unofficial and unsanctioned" KISS podcast that was founded in December of 2012. You can find the program at www.ThreeSidesoftheCoin.com.

"Thrills in the Night": Part mysterious metal, part palatable pop, "Thrills in the Night" is a fantastic song filled with after-dark drama, particularly the vibrant vocal work of Paul Stanley. Written by Stanley and Jean Beauvoir, who plays bass on the song, "Thrills in the Night," the seventh track on *Animalize*, also features a terrific intro and solo by Mark St. John. As for the subject matter, it's about a girl who is buttoned-up-tight during the work day and wild and in heat at night. Yeah, it's more than a little sexist, but it rocks.

Tiger Stadium: When the original KISS lineup reunited in 1996, they played their first gig June 28 at Tiger Stadium in Detroit, drawing 39,867 fans. Alice in Chains and Sponge opened the show.

"Time Traveller": The title sounds like something Ace Frehley would write, but "Time Traveller" was penned by Paul Stanley and Desmond Child. It was intended for inclusion on *Crazy Nights*, but didn't make the cut. This is unfortunate because it's more epic in scope and more story-driven than most KISS love songs. Luckily, "Time Traveller" was later included on *The Box Set* as track 8 on disc 4.

Toad the Wet Sprocket: On *Kiss My Ass: Classic KISS Regrooved*, alt rockers Toad the Wet Sprocket, who formed in 1986 in Santa Barbara, California, covered "Rock and Roll All Nite."

Toborg, Dale: Currently the conditioning coordinator for the Chicago White Sox, Dale Toborg is a former professional wrestler who fought in the WCW as The Demon, an officially sanctioned (by KISS) character with Gene Simmons makeup. He wrestled from 1995 to 2002.

The Today Show: On November 4, 2014, Gene, Paul, Tommy Thayer, and Eric Singer appeared in full makeup and costumes on *The Today Show*, talking to Matt Lauer about KISS's induction into the Rock and Roll Hall of Fame. "It was really vindication because the fans have wanted it so long," Stanley said. "It may not have meant as much to us, but it meant a lot to them. We were very happy to be there. We have 40 years of legacy, and it's a proud time for us."

Lauer asked Simmons about the controversy surrounding their induction into the Rock Hall. "There are no solutions, only we get to decide who and what KISS is," Simmons said. "We love Ace and Peter, and they were very gracious yesterday in accepting the award to be a part of the beginning, but we move on. This is a 40-year proud history, and Eric and Tommy make every day on that stage a wonderful, wonderful experience, not just for us, we like being together, bonding on stage, but it's an experience for the fans."

Prior to this appearance, KISS members have been on *The Today Show* for various reasons, including marketing their autobiographies.

Tomarkin, Peggy: Under the pseudonym of Bob Steele, Peggy Tomarkin wrote KISS tour books and fan club newsletters. She also authored *KISS: The Real Story, Unauthorized*.

"Tomorrow": Another unapologetically slick pop number from *Unmasked*, "Tomorrow" is the sixth track on the record. It was written by Vince Poncia and Paul Stanley, who sings the song like he's having a good time and is in his element. During the development phase, it was harder guitar rock, but Poncia, the keyboard-loving producer, made it a lighter tune. Stanley plays bass on the song, which includes handclaps to help give it a fun, party atmosphere.

"Tomorrow and Tonight": A working man's party song, "Tomorrow and Tonight," the fifth track on *Love Gun*, is as upbeat, as energetic, and as much fun to listen to as the band's far more famous anthem, "Rock and Roll All Nite." Paul Stanley, who borrowed elements of Mott the Hoople's "Golden Age of Rock and Roll" when writing the song, begins with a howl and proceeds to sing about rocking all day, rolling all night, and in general having a great time, thumbing his nose at bosses, preachers, and teachers along the way. He even manages to rhyme "cellar" with "fella" as he promises to teach a girl something new (a sex maneuver, no doubt). Lively backup singers during the chorus, including Raymond Simpson, who would later replace the first cop in the Village People, add to the revelry.

The Tomorrow Show: *The Tomorrow Show*, a.k.a. *Tomorrow, Tomorrow with Tom Snyder*, and *Tomorrow Coast to Coast*, aired late nights on NBC from 1973 to 1981. On October 31, 1979, KISS appeared on the program in full costume. While Paul and Gene spoke seriously about the history of the band, a verbose, visibly inebriated Ace Frehley joked around, cackling his trademark laugh. At one point, Paul tells Snyder about excited fans screaming and crying with excitement at a KISS concert, to which Ace replies, laughing: "And crying…. I spent all that money!"

Paul and Gene go along with the jokes to some degree (and tell a few duds of their own), and the interview is very funny (Snyder appears to be having a blast), but the Starchild and the Demon are clearly irritated by the interruptions and how the Spaceman isn't taking much of anything seriously.

In an October 12, 2012, interview with *LA Weekly*, Paul spoke about the appearance: "It wasn't that big of a fun time because you have to respect your position. You have to respect your job. You have to respect the people that you're trying to communicate with. It may seem funny that somebody is drunk … but the fact is that the root of it was, I believe, a contempt and a lack of respect for the audience and the fans. So, sure, can you look at it and chuckle? Yeah. I can, too, but I see deeper. And I look at it and say, what a shame to take this lofty position that somebody gave us and spit in it. Spit in its face. By showing up inebriated or unable to connect a sentence. It may be funny on the surface, but what's below the surface is a lack of appreciation for a gift that you've been given."

Shortly after being dismissed from KISS in 1980, Peter Criss, now infamous for his alcohol and drug abuse, made his first appearance on television sans makeup, on *The Tomorrow Show*. Criss was there to promote his solo album *Out Of Control*, and he talked about being recognized in public and about how he and Ace were the "outlaws" of KISS, that they destroyed hotel rooms out of frustration for not being home for the holidays. Totally straight-faced, he said, "We drank moderately…. KISS was never really into drugs."

The Tonight Show: KISS has performed on *The Tonight Show* a number of times, including with Garth Brooks on July 13, 1994, on *The Tonight Show with Jay Leno*. Backed by KISS, the famed country singer sang "Hard Luck Woman" in support of the tribute album *Kiss My Ass: Classic KISS Regrooved*. On Friday April 11, 2014, on *The Tonight Show Starring Jimmy Fallon*, KISS played "King of the Night Time World" for the television audience, along with four songs fans could watch online: "Deuce," "Hotter Than Hell," "Firehouse," and "Black Diamond."

A talk/variety program, *The Tonight Show* began in 1954 (with Steve Allen as host) and continues to the present day. The show's most iconic host, Johnny Carson, never had KISS as a guest, despite their popularity during the late 1970s.

"Tonight You Belong to Me": The opening track on Paul Stanley's 1978 KISS solo album, "Tonight You Belong to Me" begins in "Black Diamond"-like fashion, with Stanley singing earnestly over beautiful acoustic accompaniment. Then it kicks into gear, giving listeners a romantic rocker that exudes the essence of the Starchild. Listening to the song in retrospect, it evokes future KISS tunes off such albums as *Animalize* and *Crazy Nights*.

"Too Many Mondays": Written by Barry Mann and Cynthia Wiel, "Too Many Mondays" is the first track on Barry Mann's 1971 album, *Lay It All Out*. The song was also recorded for the unreleased Wicked Lester album. Two Wicked Lester versions exist, each with a psychedelic flavor: one sung by Paul Stanley, one sung by Gene Simmons.

Toro, Vinnie: With his partner Louise Heath, Vinnie Toro was the co-winner of "The Great Kiss Off" kissing contest of 1974. The couple smooched for more than 114 hours, with a five-minute break every hour.

"Torpedo Girl": By far the weakest of the three Ace Frehley songs on *Unmasked*, "Torpedo Girl" is the 10th track on the record. It's an odd little number in which Frehley sings about taking a swim and happening upon a submarine that has a pretty girl on the bridge. Written by Frehley and Vini Poncia, "Torpedo Girl" begins with sub sound effects and doesn't get any less silly from there (maybe it was all just a dream). Frehley, who has called it one of the funnier songs he has written, played bass on the track, subbing (so to speak) for Gene Simmons.

"Tossin' and Turnin'": Written by Ritchie Adams and Malou Rene, "Tossin' and Turnin'" was a #1 hit for Bobby Lewis, who recorded the song in 1961. Several musicians have covered the tune over the years, including Peter Criss, who made it the third track on his 1978 KISS solo album. Criss, accompanied by female backup singers, does a fine job, singing with enthusiasm and a sense of fun.

"Tough Love": The third track on *Revenge*, "Tough Love" was written by Paul Stanley, Bruce Kulick, and Bob Ezrin. Sung by Stanley, it is an unremarkable and at times unfocused song with a typical-for-KISS double entendre title. It's a sex song about a girl who says she wants a guy to be good to her, but she really wants him to be bad. Kulick, who has said he does a good Gene Simmons imitation, played bass on the song.

The Tour: Featuring KISS and Mötley Crüe on the same bill in the U.S., Canada, Mexico, and Australia, The Tour took place from July 20, 2012, to October 1, 2012. A band called The Treatment opened all 46 shows. Kelli Skye of *The Orange County Registry* praised the August 14, 2012, performance in Irvine, California thusly: "Very little about their performance disappointed. Simmons once again blew fireballs high into the night sky and spit up blood before launching into 'God of Thunder.' Stanley soared into the audience, landing on a circular platform near the soundboard during 'Love Gun.' Thayer got moments in the spotlight as well, taking lead on the Ace Frehley hit 'Shock Me' and later battling it out with Singer in drum-vs.-guitar solos. Singer also came through strongly on 'Black Diamond.'"

Followed by: Monster World Tour.

Townshend, Pete: The Who guitarist Pete Townshend was a huge influence on Paul Stanley, who copies his guitar-smashing routine, and on Ace Frehley, who, in a March 11, 2010, interview published on www.premierguitar.com, said: "I was really inspired by Keith Richards, but even more so by Pete Townshend. I was such a huge fan when I was a kid, and I used to sit next to the record player and figure out every Who song. What amazed me was the way Townshend did his multiple strums. Playing a lot of Who music really helped develop my right hand, which helped with not only my rhythm technique but my leads, too."

Toy Cars and Trucks: Although there were no 70s-era KISS Hot Wheels or Matchbox cars, several companies have made die-cast KISS vehicles in more recent times, including Action, Johnny Lightning, Racing Champions, and, of course, Mattel, makers of Hot Wheels.

Toy Guitar: Released in two versions—one with a white neck, one with a black neck—the KISS toy guitar, which has six strings, was produced by Carnival Toys in 1977. Two truss rod variations are available as well: an outlined-in-black and a solid black KISS logo. The body of the guitar features a 1976 photo by Barry Levine, along with a red KISS logo. A rare, highly collectible item today, the KISS toy guitar was sold separately and

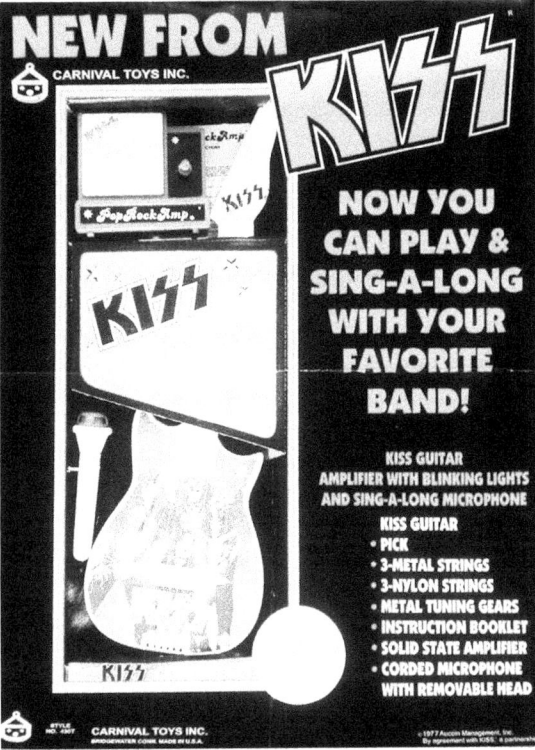

Promo poster for the super rare KISS toy guitar with microphone and amplifier, produced by Carnival Toys in 1977.

as part of a 1978 KISS Concert set that included a wireless microphone and small red and white amplifier.

Toy Hunter: On the April 10, 2013, episode of the Travel Channel's *Toy Hunter* (2012–2014), host Jordan Hembrough locates some KISS collectibles for Gene Simmons, including three flea market finds: a View-Master reel, a *KISS 4K* comic book, and some KISS underwear. Unfortunately, The Demon, a notorious KISS collector, already owns those, so he passes.

Fortunately for Hembrough, he also brings a super rare KISS Radio Control Van, complete in the box, which Simmons wants. Hembrough offers the van for $1,600, but the Demon pays him with a gold *Rock and Roll Over* record instead. After signing the record "To Jordan," Simmons says, "You passed with flying colors. You delivered the goods, that's what I asked for, so you did good. You did good. So I'm gonna give you this, you can put it up in your store."

At the end of the episode, Hembrough says,

"Even though Gene didn't buy any of the KISS stuff that I brought, I have to look at this as a long-term investment. I'm coming out of this trip with a major rock star client, and there's no telling where this relationship will lead somewhere down the line. Plus, I'm coming home with a signed gold record from Gene Simmons, and experiences like this are priceless."

Toy Microphone: According to www.everythingkiss.com, there were two official toy KISS microphones produced during the late 1970s: one by AHI and one by Carnival, the latter of which was sold separately or as part of the Concert Set with the toy guitar and amplifier. The site claims that all others, including the Remco-labeled microphone that shows up on eBay from time to time, are unauthorized fakes. The toy microphones let you speak or, more fittingly, sing through AM radio.

Trading Cards: In 1978, Donruss released a set of KISS bubble gum cards, available in traditional wax packs and sold primarily at convenience stores. Series 1 contained cards 1–66 while the somewhat harder to find series 2 contained cards 67–132. Most of the card backs are puzzle pieces while a few contain bios. According to *The Sport Americana Price Guide to the Non-Sports Cards* (1988, Edgewater Book Company), Donruss reprinted series one in 1980 with new photos on various card fronts (21 in all) and a new puzzle on back. The book mistakenly claims that this was due to the death of Peter Criss, but in reality Criss had simply left the band and was replaced by Eric Carr, who also replaced Peter on the cards. The 1980 set is considered scarce because the cards were only distributed in generic entertainment/sports packs that came in Donruss Fun Bags.

In 1979, Donruss released a set of "Rock Stars" cards featuring four bands: the Babys, Queen, the Village People, and KISS. There were 14 KISS cards in the 66-card set.

Various trading cards from different companies followed in subsequent years, including sets from Cornerstone, Press Pass, Kinetik Arts, Authentic Images, and NECA.

Transformer: Bruce Kulick released his second solo album, *Transformer*, in 2004. It features the following tracks: "Jump the Shark," "I Can't Breathe," "If Love's the Answer," "Crazy," "All That I Need," "Don't Tell Me Something," "Inn of the Mountain Gods," "It's Just My Life," "Do it Right," "Beautiful to Me," "Truth or Dare," and "Against the Grain." *Transformer* is less KISS-like than Kulick's first solo outing, *Audio Dog*.

Trash Can: Released in 1977, the first and only vintage KISS trash can was manufactured by P & K Products. It is a tube-shaped receptacle decorated with several photos of the band, including a large wraparound image on the front (the same photo on the outside cover of the record player) and one on the back. The back photo, taken for the "Evolution of KISS" booklet in the *Alive II* album, is infamous for being reversed on the trash can, making Paul's star appear as though it's on the wrong eye. It's hard to find a KISS trash can in nice condition as most have at least some rust and/or dents.

Treehouse of Horror #10: Published in 2004, Bongo Entertainment's *Treehouse of Horror*

 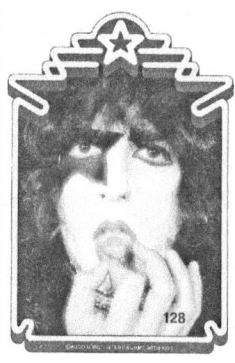  

Donruss trading cards depicting the original KISS band members: Peter Criss, Paul Stanley, Gene Simmons, and Ace Frehley.

#10, a special "Monsters of Rock" issue, includes a story called "Bart Simmons: God of Thunder!," plotted by Gene Simmons, written by Chris Yambar, and drawn by Tone Rodriquez (pencils) and Andrew Pepoy (inks). Bart Simpson, discovering he's the result of a one-night stand between Marge Simpson and Gene Simmons, breathes fire, plays an axe bass, and wears makeup, leather, and studs. The comic book also includes stories starring Alice Cooper, Rob Zombie, and Pat Boone.

"Trial by Fire": Like many KISS songs, "Trial by Fire," the fourth track on *Asylum*, is about believing in oneself, climbing to the top, and in general living life to the fullest, regardless of the circumstances. In this case, the circumstances in question were probably disagreements Gene Simmons had with Paul Stanley during the recording of the album, when Simmons was distracted by Hollywood aspirations and his own record label. Simmons, who wrote the tune with Bruce Kulick, sings rather melodically, helping make for an agreeable (if unexceptional) song. Simmons' original title for the song, prior to some lyrical changes, was "Live Fast, Die Young."

Tribute Bands: There are KISS tribute bands all over the world, wearing the trademark makeup, playing identical instruments, singing the hits (and the album cuts), and, in many cases, using blood, pyrotechnics, flash bombs, and other theatrical effects. Most portray the original lineup of Ace, Gene, Paul, and Peter. Some of the more well-known acts include Strutter, Alive II, Double Platinum, Destroyer, Shock Me, Parasite, and KISS Forever. Especially noteworthy are Mr. Speed, who were awarded in 2012 as the "Greatest KISS Tribute Band in the World," and Almost KISS, who were featured on an episode of *Gene Simmons Family Jewels*.

***A Tribute to the Creatures of the Night*:** Released in 2003 by Nuclear Blast Germany, this German tribute album features music by a variety of acts. Tracks include: "Detroit Rock City" (Hammerfall), "C'mon and Love Me" (Skid Row), "I Stole Your Love" (Helloween), "Hard Luck Woman" (Pretty Maids), "Parasite" (Anthrax), "I Want You" (Galactic Cowboys), "War Machine" (Six Feet Under), "Strange Ways" (Hypocrisy), "Only You" (Doro), "Comin' Home" (Maryslim), "Goin' Blind" (The Melvins), "Creatures of the Night" (Iced Earth), "Deuce" (Overkill), and "Black Diamond" (Bathory).

***A Tribute to…the Hottest Band in the World!*:** Released in 2002 by Nosebleeder Records on 10" vinyl only, this punk rock KISS tribute album includes the following tracks, most by Norwegian bands: "Getaway" (the Carburetors), "Shout It Out Loud" (Kyss), "King of the Night Time World" (Jerryville), "God of Thunder" (Jamesband), "Rock and Roll All Nite" (Electric Ladyland), "I Love It Loud" (Null$katte$nylterne), "Rock Bottom" (Hellride), "I Stole Your Love" (Nuevo Catecismo Catolico), "Beth" (Rickshaw), and "Love Gun" (Destroyer).

***Trick or Treat*:** During much of the 1980s, Paul Stanley was running KISS pretty much by himself as Gene Simmons pursued a side-career in Hollywood, appearing in such films as *Trick or Treat* (1986), which also starred the high priest of heavy metal, Ozzy Osbourne (as the Rev. Aaron Gilstrom, a crusader against rock music).

In the film, which was directed by Charles Martin Smith, devil-worshipping heavy metal star Sammi Curr (Tony Fields) dies in a mysterious hotel fire, much to the dismay of his biggest fan, teenage outcast Eddie Weinbauer (Marc Price of *Family Ties* fame). Curr comes back to life and helps Weinbauer exact vengeance on his high school tormentors. Simmons plays radio DJ "Nuke," a personal friend of Curr who gives Weinbauer Curr's forthcoming unreleased album, *Songs in the Key of Death*, which is to be played in its entirety beginning at midnight on Halloween.

Tropea, John: John Tropea played guitar on Peter Criss's "Easy Thing, "Rock Me, Baby," and "Hooked on Rock 'n' Roll." He's also worked with such acts as Harry Chapin, Dr. John, Eric Clapton, and Paul Simon.

***Trouble Walkin'*:** Released by Megaforce Records October 13, 1989, *Trouble Walkin'* was Ace Frehley's third full-length solo album after leaving KISS. No longer using the band name Frehley's Comet, Frehley produced the record with Eddie Kramer and John Regan. Tracks include: "Shot Full of Rock," "Do Ya" (a cover of the Jeff Lynne tune, which Lynne recorded with the Move and Electric Light Orchestra), "Five Card Stud," "Hide Your Heart," "Lost in Limbo," "Trouble Walkin,'" "2 Young 2 Die," "Back to School,"

"Remember Me," and "Fractured III," which is an instrumental.

Co-written by Paul Stanley, Desmond Child, and Holly Knight, "Hide Your Heart" was first recorded by Bonnie Tyler for her 1988 album of the same name. KISS also recorded the song for *Hot in the Shade*, which was released the same month as *Trouble Walkin.'* Peter Criss sang backup on "Trouble Walkin,'" "2 Young 2 Die," and "Back to School." Skid Row members Sebastian Bach, Rachel Bolan, and Dave Sabo also contributed to the album, which only reached #102 on the *Billboard* 200.

Troyer, Eric: Eric Troyer, a founder of ELO Part II, played piano and sang on Gene Simmons' "Radioactive" and "Living in Sin." Troyer is currently with the Orchestra, a pop rock band founded by former members of the Electric Light Orchestra and ELO Part II.

"True Confessions": Featuring Helen Reddy singing during the terrific, honkytonk piano-laden chorus and a brief appearance by the Citrus College Singers a little over halfway through the song, "True Confessions" is the fifth track on Gene Simmons' 1978 KISS solo album. It's an oddly pleasing, soul-infused pop piece that most anyone can enjoy, KISS fan or not.

Trunk, Eddie: Host of the nationally syndicated radio show, *Eddie Trunk Rocks*, and of VH1 Classic's *That Metal Show*, Eddie Trunk is a huge KISS fan, interviewing various band members over the years. In his review of Paul Stanley's autobiography, Trunk said that Stanley was always his favorite band member, despite their icy relationship.

In an interview with Trunk on *Three Sides of the Coin*, Trunk said this about KISS' induction into the Rock and Roll Hall of Fame: "As KISS fans, we have fought the perception for years that KISS is nothing but a manufactured joke that can't play their instruments or write songs. What's offensive to me is that we're here over 10 years after they first became eligible and still trying to figure out if they should get in. They should have gone in the first time they were eligible."

"Tunnel of Love": Gene Simmons' 1978 KISS solo LP is nothing if not diverse. "Tunnel of Love," the fourth track on the album, is a new wave-influenced pop rock ditty featuring Aerosmith's Joe Perry and Starz' Ritchie Ranno on guitar. Neil Jason, who plays bass on every song on the record, stands out here, providing a funky, yet not-quite-danceable beat. Naturally, coming from the pen of Gene Simmons, the title of the song is a sex organ euphemism, with Simmons wanting to "visit" a girl's tunnel of love.

Turino, Paul: Paul Turino was the keyboardist for Flasher, the band Eric Carr played in before joining KISS. More importantly, Turino told Carr about Peter Criss's departure from KISS, urging him to audition for the band.

"Turn on the Night": Written by Paul Stanley and Grammy Award–winning Diane Warren ("How Do I Live," "Nothing's Gonna Stop Us Now"), "Turn On the Night" is the 10th track on *Crazy Nights* and the third (and final) single from the record. Despite its catchy, celebratory sound, it failed to chart in the U.S, though it did reach #41 in the U.K. An energized Stanley, who wants a particular girl more than any other guy, sounds like he's having a blast singing the keyboard-heavy song, which features strong support by Gene Simmons (chorus) and Bruce Kulick (lead guitar). This is a fine, fist-pumping pop rocker that Warren has said should have been a bigger hit than it was.

Tweed, Shannon: Born in Canada March 10, 1957, Shannon Tweed is an actress and model who was *Playboy*'s Playmate of the Year in 1982. She briefly dated Hugh Hefner around this time and lived at the Playboy Mansion, but she has lived with Gene Simmons since 1983. Simmons, despite stating publicly a number of times that he never wanted to get married, wed the gorgeous blonde October 1, 2011.

Simmons and Tweed have two children, Nick and Sophie, as portrayed in *Gene Simmons Family Jewels*, a reality TV show that aired on A&E from 2006 to 2012. Tweed has appeared in more than 60 films (most of them B-movies and/or erotica), including such pictures as *Hot Dog…The Movie* (1984), *Meatballs III: Summer Job* (1986), and *Detroit Rock City* (1999). On the small screen, Tweed appeared in *The Dukes of Hazzard*, *Days of Our Lives*, *Falcon Crest*, *Frasier*, and *1st and Ten*.

Tweed's autobiography, *KISS and Tell*, includes a foreword by Simmons, where he said he met Tweed at the Playboy Mansion's Midsummer Night's Dream Party, an invitation-only event for 400 guests, in which the men wore pajamas and the women as little as possible. "I had come there with two Playmates and wasn't really looking to flirt with anyone else—I was busy," he wrote. "Then she walked up to me.... I was stunned. I found her instantly desirable and quickly forgot that I had come with two other ladies."

Simmons also described their home life, in which he revealed that he's crazy about everything Tweed does and she is annoyed by him: "She ... couldn't stand the way I chewed my food and left crumbs all over the place. She hates how I rumple the sheets in our bed. She thinks I talk too much. Outside of home, I'm a very important person. At home, I'm usually in the way. And most shocking is that she doesn't feel any reluctance to ask me to take out the garbage. Me! The God of Thunder. The guy with the lasciviously long tongue! The guy who is adored and desired by millions of fans throughout the world."

Gene said he calls her every day while on the road, but she never asks where he's going. She has her own life as well: "She does what she wants when she wants to, and doesn't check with anyone to see if it's okay to do it—me included. I usually ask where she's going and if I can come along. Often, the answer is no. I'm lucky if she lets me tag along to the movies with her. And when we're watching the movie, she will often shush me when I whisper a comment to her."

Getting more serious, Simmons wrote, "She is everything I never knew I wanted. She makes me a better man. She gives me more freedom than I want. I love her more today than I did when we first met."

In the book, Tweed revealed her love for Simmons as well, calling him sober, smart, honorable, and kind-hearted. Regarding Gene's well-known promiscuous nature, Tweed said, "He wants to make the girls swoon, and that's fine with me. After all, who wants a guy no one else wants? But he has never lied to me, and I don't think he cheats. I haven't heard any stories of infidelity, or at least no women have come forward, so speculating is all anyone can do. I choose to believe the best and believe him to be true to me, to our kids, and to our life together."

12 Picks: An Ace Frehley greatest hits album, *12 Picks* was released in 1997 by Megaforce Records to benefit from the 1996 KISS Reunion Tour. It contains six of the more well-known songs from the Spaceman's late-'80s solo albums: "Into the Night," "Words Are Not Enough," "Insane," "Hide Your Heart," "Trouble Walkin,'" and "Rock Soldiers." Plus, it features six KISS songs recorded live by Frehley's Comet at the Hammersmith Odeon in London, England on March 19, 1988: "Rip It Out," "Breakout," "Cold Gin," "Shock Me," "Rocket Ride," and "Deuce." Anton Fig, famous for playing in David Letterman's house band, the CBS Orchestra, plays drums on four of the studio tracks. The Japanese release contains a bonus song, "Calling to You." Produced by John Regan and Ace Frehley.

20th Century Masters—The Best of KISS: The DVD Collection: Released March 30, 2004, this DVD was a disappointment as it only features five music videos: "I Love It Loud," "Lick It Up," "Heaven's On Fire," "Tears Are Falling," and "Crazy Crazy Nights."

20th Century Masters—The Millennium Collection: The Best of KISS: This greatest hits CD, released August 5, 2003, is part of Universal Music's "20th Century Masters—The Millennium Collection" series. It includes the following tracks, each originally released between 1974 and 1979: "Strutter," "Deuce," "Hotter Than Hell," "C'mon and Love Me," "Rock and Roll All Nite" (live), "Detroit Rock City" (remix), "Beth," "Hard Luck Woman," "Calling Dr. Love," "Love Gun," "Christine Sixteen," and "I Was Made for Lovin' You." The collection was later re-released in 2010 as *Icon: KISS*, part of Universal Music's "Icon" series.

20th Century Masters—The Millennium Collection: The Best of KISS, Volume 2: This compilation CD, released by Mercury Universal on June 15, 2004, features songs from the 1980s, but lacks material from *Music from "The Elder"* and *Unmasked*. Tracks include: "Creatures of the Night," "I Love It Loud," "Lick It Up," "All Hell's Breakin' Loose," "Heaven's On Fire," "Thrills in the Night," "Tears Are Falling," "Uh! All Night," "Crazy Crazy Nights," "Reason to Live," "Hide Your Heart," and "Forever."

20th Century Masters—The Millennium Collection: The Best of KISS, Volume 3: This compilation CD, released by Mercury Universal on October 10, 2006, features songs from the 1990s. Tracks include: "God Gave Rock 'N' Roll to You II," "Unholy," "Domino" (from *Alive III*), "Hate," "Childhood's End," "I Will Be There," "Comin' Home" (from *KISS Unplugged*), "Got to Choose" (from *KISS Unplugged*), "Psycho Circus," "Into the Void," "I Pledge Allegiance to the State of Rock and Roll," and "Nothing Can Keep Me from You."

20/20: In 1979, during the *Dynasty* era, an episode of the ABC news program *20/20* included an 11-minute segment on KISS. It shows the band in concert and backstage putting on makeup, and it features interviews with band members, manager Bill Aucoin, business consultant Carl Glickman, and staff member Jared Snyder. During the piece, which focuses primarily on merchandising, money, and concerts that are designed to "titillate, astonish, and revolt the audience," *Rolling Stone* magazine associate editor and KISS detractor Charles M. Young says: "KISS is basically paganism for pubescents. It has very little to do with music ... if you listen to it closely, it's all dissonance, explosions, and moaning, which pretty well sums up the adolescent experience in America."

24 Hours of KISSmas: This marathon of KISS programming, which included music videos, concerts, specials, and the like, aired December 7 and 8 on VH1 Classic. Viewers who ordered the *KISSology—The Ultimate KISS Collection, Vol. 3: 1992–2000* DVD set during the marathon got a bonus disc containing the 1999 feature film, *Detroit Rock City*.

"Two Sides of the Coin": Like "Talk to Me," "Two Sides of the Coin" is a quality Ace Frehley number from *Unmasked*. The seventh track on the record, the song has Frehley singing about needing time to ease his mind and pick a mate (between two women) because he's tired of dating. Interestingly, Frehley plays bass on the song. Includes strong, fast drumming from Anton Fig, who played on the record because Peter Criss, though he appears on the cartoon cover of the album, was out of the band by this time.

"2000 Man": Written by Mick Jagger and Keith Richards, "2000 Man" is a rocked-up cover of a surreal pop song off the Rolling Stones' 1967 experimental psychedelic album, *Their Satanic Majesties Request*. Ace Frehley sings "2000 Man" with a cool, disaffected voice, giving the spacey lyrics the exact flavor they need. The second track on *Dynasty*, this was a great showcase for Space Ace, who has said that it feels like the song was written for him. Anton Fig subs for Peter Criss on drums.

"Two Timer": The second track on *Dressed to Kill*, the slow, but heavy "Two Timer" was written and sung by Gene Simmons, who chastises a fashionable, though unfaithful lover. The theme of the song—cheating—is fairly ironic considering the fact that Simmons had a reputation for having sex with virtually any willing female of age. "Two Timer" notwithstanding, it's hard to imagine a classic KISS-era Simmons giving much thought to monogamy.

***Ugly Betty*:** Gene Simmons portrayed himself in "The Kids Are Alright," the season 2, episode 17 installment of *Ugly Betty*, an ABC television series that ran from 2006 to 2010. While searching for her real father, Amanda Tanen (Becki Newton) discovers that he might be Gene Simmons (she was wrong). She proceeds to perform a song she wrote for him called "The Beer Hole." Hoping to create a reality show with Amanda, Gene lies to her and says he had an affair in 1981 with her mother, Fey Sommers, choosing her over his real-life girlfriend, Cher.

"Uh! All Night": At various points in their career, KISS has shown their humorous side

The Holiday 2009 issue of *Guitar Player* magazine, featuring Gene Simmons, Paul Stanley, and Tommy Thayer on the cover.

(sometimes unintentionally), never more so than in "Uh! All Night," a celebration of having animal-like sex after a long day at work. The 10th and final track on *Asylum*, "Uh! All Night" was written by Paul Stanley (lead vocals), Desmond Child, and Jean Beauvoir, who played bass on the song.

Uhelszki, Jaan: As a journalist for and co-founder of *Creem* magazine, Jaan Uhelszki covered KISS during their formative years. One of the first female rock journalists, she also jammed with KISS onstage in full makeup and regalia for five minutes in 1975 for a *Creem* article entitled "I Dreamed I Was Onstage with KISS in My Maidenform Bra."

"Under the Gun": One of KISS's harder rocking 1980s tunes, "Under the Gun," the sixth track on *Animalize*, evokes Iron Maiden and Judas Priest, but with Paul Stanley's unmistakable voice. Written by Stanley, Eric Carr, and Desmond Child, the song starts off fast and rarely lets up, showcasing Mark St. Johns' blistering fretwork and Carr's pounding drums. That's Jean Beauvoir on bass.

"Under the Rose": "Under the Rose" was Eric Carr's first writing credit with KISS. He penned the song, which is the fifth track on *Music from "The Elder,"* with Gene Simmons, who provides lead vocals. Continuing the epic, mythical tale of a boy hero, the lyrics, sung with a sense of assuredness by Simmons, essentially ask the boy if he's worthy: Will he sacrifice?; Will he take the Oath?; Will he live his life under the rose? Greg Prato of www.allmusic.com called "Under the Rose" "downright embarrassing," probably for its faux medieval/spiritual sound, but it has some nice guitar work and drums.

Undressed: An Unmasked Tribute to KISS: The first and only tribute to KISS's much-maligned 1980 album, *Unmasked*, this CD was released in Germany in April of 2003 by RSR Music. Tracks include: "Is That You?" (Jendza), "Shandi" (Ryan McKay), "Talk to Me" (Shameless), "Naked City" (Nash), "What Makes the World Go Round" (Demon Drive), "Tomorrow" (Pretty Suicide), "Two Sides of the Coin" (the Geminus Sect), "She's So European" (Boot Camp), "Easy as it Seems" (Dressed to Thrill), "Torpedo Girl" (the Torpedo Girls), "You're All That I Want" (Shameless), "Naked City" (Oliver Monroe), "Tomorrow" (Shameless), "Two Sides of the Coin" (Mind Over Me), "Easy as it Seems" (Tykoon), and "Talk to Me" (KISS Forever).

Unfinished Business: The second posthumously released Eric Carr solo album (after *Rockology*), *Unfinished Business* features a cover photo of Carr in his Fox makeup and costume. The disc was released November 8, 2011, by Auto Rock Records and features the following tracks: "Eric Speaks to the Fans" (dialogue); "Just Can't Wait" (a *Rockology* song, but with lyrics sung and written by Ted Poley of Danger Danger); "Troubles Inside You"; "No One's Messin' With You"; "Eric Talks About His Music" (dialogue); "Carr Jam 1981" (performed by Joey Cassata and Benny Doro); "Eric Talks About His Audition" (dialogue); "Shandi" (Eric Carr audition vocal); "All Hell's Breakin' Loose" (performed by ZO2); "Dial L For Love" (instrumental); "Elephant Man"; "Eric Talks About Mark St. John" (dialogue); "Midnite Stranger" (instrumental); "Eyes of Love" (featuring John Humphrey and Benny Doro); "Bill Aucoin Talks About Eric" (dialogue); "Through the Years (Live)" (instrumental); "I Cry At Night" (Eric's first recording with his band the Cellarmen); and "Eric Joking At Rehearsals" (dialogue).

"Unholy": During the 1980s, Gene Simmons was distracted by his Hollywood career and other side projects, and it showed in a number of mediocre songs. Enter the terrific "Unholy," the first track on 1992's *Revenge*, and the first KISS single to feature Simmons on lead vocal since "I Love it Loud," making the top 30 in five countries (including Norway at #2). Jesse Damon provides backup vocals.

A fierce comeback by Simmons, and one of the heaviest and most intelligent songs ever recorded by the band (it was co-written by Vinnie Vincent, who had been fired from KISS eight years earlier), "Unholy" stands alongside "Calling Dr. Love," "God of Thunder," and "I Love It Loud" as one of the definitive heavy metal tunes sung by the Demon, who got the idea for the song from "Unholy Love" (1990), which was written by Adam Mitchell and recorded by Doro Pesch for her *Doro* album.

The video for "Unholy" is a tour de force, featuring a bearded, black-clad, skull-chested Simmons looking cooler and more sinister than he had in more than a decade.

Union: After leaving KISS, Bruce Kulick formed hard rock act Union with John Corabi (lead vocals, guitar), James Hunting (bass), and Brent Fitz (Slash). The band, together from 1997 to 2002 (and in 2005), recorded three albums: *Union* (1998), *Union Live in the Galaxy* (1999), and *The Blue Room* (2000). The Japanese release of *Union* featured "For You" as a bonus song while the 1999 re-issue from Spitfire Records featured "Oh! Darling."

Universal Music Group: KISS released their 2012 album, *Monster*, under the Universal Music Group label.

Universal Presents Gimme KISS: Released in January of 1990 by Mercury/PolyGram, *Universal Presents Gimme KISS* is a promotional cassette tape that was limited to approximately 800 copies. It was not released on CD, helping make the tape a hot commodity for collectors. Tracks include: "Detroit Rock City," "Deuce," "Christine Sixteen," "Calling Dr. Love," "Hide Your Heart," "Forever," "Rise to It," "Love Gun," "Shout It Out Loud," "Strutter," "Rock and Roll All Nite," "Lick It Up," and "Beth."

Unmasked: For reasons that still puzzle many KISS fans, the band decided to abandon their hard rock roots with a disco album in 1979 (*Dynasty*) and an unadulterated pop record the following year, 1980's *Unmasked*. It's not a bad album—in fact, such tunes as "Shandi," the only single from the album released in the U.S., and "Talk to Me," an Ace Frehley gem, are quite good—but the light, airy sound alienated much of the KISS Army. This was evidenced by the record's soft sales: *Unmasked* was the first KISS record since *Dressed to Kill* that failed to reach Gold status in the U.S.

Some argue with good reason that the satirical comic strip cover, illustrated by Victor Stabin from a concept by Mark Samuels and Jose Rivero, hurt sales of the album. It shows a photographer trying and failing to get a shot of KISS sans makeup, and an obnoxious looking kid saying, "I say they still stink." Self-deprecating humor at its worst.

Produced by Vini Poncia for Casablanca Records, *Unmasked*, which was originally packaged with a foldout poster of the final panel of the album cover comic strip, includes the following tracks: "Is That You?," "Shandi," "Talk to Me," "Naked City," "What Makes the World Go 'Round," "Tomorrow," "Two Sides of the Coin," "She's So European," "Easy as it Seems," "Torpedo Girl," and "You're All That I Want." Peter Criss appeared in the music video for "Shandi," but Anton Fig played all the drums on the album.

Unmasked, released on May 20, was a big hit in certain foreign markets, most notably Australia, Norway, Germany, and New Zealand. KISS did not tour in the United States for the album, hurting domestic sales.

In *KISS: Behind the Mask—The Official Authorized Biography*, Stanley complained about the "wimpy" record, but Poncia explained why it has a pop sound. "Those were the kind of songs that Paul was writing," he said. "It wasn't my idea to come in and change anything. They were taking advantage of my pop sensibilities in those areas and I was taking advantage of certain songwriting talents that Paul and Gene had in those areas. Paul and Gene have never done anything that they didn't want to do. They wanted to find out if they could work in that pop area and be effective." Poncia also called the album a "rush job" and said that it "lacked the soulfulness of *Dynasty*."

Unmasked Tour: To support their eighth studio album (not counting the 1978 solo records), KISS played 41 shows from July 25 to December 3, 1980. Because *Unmasked* was more popular overseas than in the U.S., only the first show was played in America: a warm-up gig at The Palladium in New York City. The rest were played in Australia, Europe, and New Zealand. It was Ace Frehley's last tour with KISS until the 1996 Alive/Worldwide Tour, a.k.a. the Reunion Tour.

The Unmasked Tour employed a smaller Dynasty Tour stage and included such props as bombs, a confetti storm, fireworks, fire engine lights, Gene spitting blood, breathing fire, and flying to the rafters, Paul smashing his guitar, a lighted KISS logo, and Ace's lighted, smoking, flying, and rocket-shooting guitars. Band lineup: Paul Stanley, Gene Simmons, Ace Frehley, and Eric Carr, who, replacing Criss on drums, wore Fox makeup. Opening acts: Eyes, Girl, Iron Maiden, the Rockets, and the Techtones.

Followed by: Creatures of the Night Tour.

Unpainted: A Tribute to KISS: This tribute album focuses on the non-makeup era of the band. Tracks include: "Master & Slave" (Dear Victims), "Tears Are Falling" (America To Mars), "Dance All Over Your Face" (Pale Blue Dot, featuring former members of Vandal), "Forever" (KISS Cover Show), "Crazy, Crazy Nights" (Oregon Dream Child), "Who Wants to be Lonely"

(Star 2 K), "Thrills in the Night" (Unmasked), "Lick It Up" (Kisskonfusion), "Heaven's on Fire" (Cyrcle IX), "Thief in the Night" (Kiss Forever Band), "Unholy" (Killaroo), and "Let's Put the X In Sex" (the Pornographs). Released in 2002 by Shark Bite Records.

Uriah Heep: Founded in 1969, Uriah Heep is named after a character from Charles Dickens' classic novel, *David Copperfield*. The band toured with KISS during the mid–late 1970s. In an interview published on heavymag.com.au, Uriah Heep guitarist and co-founder Mick Box said: "We broke KISS in America. They toured with us coast to coast and then when they were huge we went and toured with them. It was one of those things. We broke a number of bands. We broke Foreigner, KISS, ZZ Top outside of Texas, and even Rush. They all got on our tours and then went onto great success from there because of our audiences."

U.S. Postage Stamp: To celebrate Valentine's Day in 2006, and to benefit The Humane Society of the United States, ZazzleStamps partnered with the U.S. Postal Service to release a series of stamps featuring a number of popular celebrities, including Gene Simmons. Each stamp in the series features a lip imprint, the words "Sealed with a Kiss," and the celebrity's autograph.

Valentine, Kevin: Session drummer Kevin Valentine played on "You Love Me to Hate You" and "Take It Off." On *Psycho Circus*, he pounded the skins on every song but "Into the Void." During episode nine of *Three Sides of the Coin*, he talked about his experiences with KISS.

Van Halen: In 1976, Gene Simmons produced an unreleased demo album (known as *Zero*) for Van Halen, who formed in 1972 and whose debut self-titled album hit stores in 1978. Simmons was unable to land Van Halen a record deal and tore up the contract he had with the band. Fortunately for fans, VH hit big anyway, selling close to 100 million albums worldwide.

According to rock expert Mike Ladano (mikeladano.com), "Eddie and Alex Van Halen played on Gene's demos for 'Have Love Will Travel' (aka 'Got Love for Sale'), 'Christine Sixteen,' and 'Tunnel of Love.' These songs were demoed for *Love Gun*, but 'Tunnel of Love' would not be released until Gene's 1978 solo album, in re-recorded form. These songs are considered a Holy Grail for Van Halen and KISS fans alike, and to my knowledge they have never been bootlegged."

During the *Creatures of the Night* era, guitarist Eddie Van Halen wanted to join KISS, but was essentially turned down, as Simmons related in the April 2014 issue of *Guitar World*: "He was so unhappy about how he and [David Lee] Roth were—or weren't—getting along. He couldn't stand him. And drugs were rampant. And so he took me to lunch, to a diner right across the street from the Record Plant. Vinnie Vincent, who was not yet in KISS, tagged along, too. Sneaky guy. And Eddie said, 'I want to join KISS. I don't want to fight anymore with Roth. I'm sick and tired of it.' 'But I told him, 'Eddie, there's not enough room. You need to be in a band where you can direct the music. You're not going to be happy in KISS.' I talked him out of it. It didn't fit."

Variety: Fred Kirby of *Variety* magazine, which was founded in 1905, penned some of the earliest reviews of KISS shows. In the August 22, 1973, issue he wrote: "From the plethora of Gotham glitter-rock acts, comes KISS, who already outshine most of the others in clean, pulsating rock and roll, high in volume and excitement. Facial makeup is more weird than fey. Set momentum is unrelenting and solid. Although all tackle vocals, lead usually falls to bass guitarist Gene Simmons, most ghoulish in appearance. Heavy black makeup around his eyes and white on rest of face is bat-like. His mugging is a theatrical plus, as is his vocal ability. Paul Stanley, who shares lead guitar with Ace Frehley, also usually shares vocals, but all four aid in that department. Drummer Peter Criss even makes screaming fun for the outfit. While Simmons is the most extreme visually, all have some kind of mask effect around their eyes and satiny garb. Simmons removes a black jacket to reveal a black T-shirt with silvery skull and cross-bones. But it's in the music that KISS catches hold and never lets go."

"Venus and Mars/Rock Show": On the tribute album *The Art of McCartney: The Songs of Paul McCartney Sung by the World's Greatest Artists*, KISS covered this two-song medley by Wings.

The Very Best of KISS: Released August 27, 2002, by Mercury Records, *The Very Best of KISS* is a greatest hits album featuring the following tracks: "Strutter," "Deuce," "Got to Choose," "Hotter Than Hell," "C'mon and Love Me," "Rock and

Roll All Nite" (from *Alive!*), "Detroit Rock City" (remix from *Double Platinum*), "Shout It Out Loud," "Beth," "I Want You," "Calling Dr. Love," "Hard Luck Woman," "I Stole Your Love," "Christine Sixteen," "Love Gun," "New York Groove," "I Was Made for Lovin' You," "I Love It Loud," "Lick It Up," "Forever," and "God Gave Rock 'N' Roll to You II." The CD peaked at #52 on the *Billboard* 200.

VH1 Rock Honors: A short-lived annual ceremony that paid homage to influential rock bands, *VH1 Rock Honors* ran from 2006 to 2008. The inaugural event, honoring Queen, Judas Priest, Def Leppard, and KISS, was held at the Mandalay Bay Events Center in Las Vegas, Nevada May 25, 2006. It was hosted by Jaime Pressly and aired on TV May 31. An "all-star super group" comprised of Ace Frehley, Rob Zombie, Slash, Gilby Clarke, Scott Ian, and Tommy Lee played an inspired version of "God of Thunder." KISS themselves closed the show with "Detroit Rock City," "Deuce," "Love Gun," and "Makin' Love."

View-Master: If you grew up during the 1970s, you probably remember View-Master, the stereoscopic viewing device that debuted in 1939 and is still being made today. There were three View-Master products featuring KISS, including the standard three-reel Special Subjects View-Master release from 1979, which shows studio and live stage images from the *Dynasty* era. This is a popular set with collectors, not only because it is compatible with the modern View-Master toy, but also because it features pictures of Gene Simmons with a prototype version of his then-new axe bass guitar.

Less popular, but still collectible is the Double-Vue cartridge, also released in 1979. It is compatible with the Double-Vue Movie Player, a long-out-of-production toy that looks like a small blue movie camera. By plugging in the double-reel KISS cartridge and peering into the device, the viewer could briefly watch (but not listen to—there was no sound) the film clip for the "I Was Made for Lovin' You" music video and concert highlights from 1978.

Unlike the aforementioned items, which show photos, the KISS Show Beam cartridge (1980), which plugs into a flashlight-type device called the Show Beam, depicts the band via 30 cartoon drawings. As the packaging says, you can display the images anywhere (similar to a portable, handheld slide projector), including on the ceiling, on the wall, and on your friends.

The Village Voice: Established in 1955, *The Village Voice* is a free tabloid newspaper. In December of 1972, Paul Stanley placed an ad, which Ace Frehley responded to, that read:
LEAD GUITARIST WANTED
with Flash and Ability. Album Out
Shortly. No time wasters please.
Paul 268-3145

Vincent, Vinnie: Born Vincent John Cusano August 6, 1952, in Bridgeport, Connecticut, Vinnie Vincent had to change his name when he joined KISS to keep his identity secret from the general public, as the band was still wearing makeup. Gene Simmons came up with the name while Paul Stanley proposed Vincent's Egyptian Warrior persona, complete with makeup in the shape of an Ankh spread across his forehead, brow, and bridge of his nose.

Introduced to KISS by songwriter Adam Mitchell, Vincent was a session player (uncredited) and songwriter on *Creatures of the Night*, although Ace Frehley was pictured on the album cover.

Described as a mercurial, egotistical, self-destructive type, Vincent joined KISS after the release of *Creatures of the Night*, replacing Frehley, and he was a key part of *Lick It Up*, the band's first

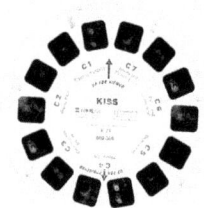

This View-Master release from 1979 shows 3D studio and live stage images from the *Dynasty* era (courtesy KISSmuseum.com).

record sans makeup. Vincent's imprint is heavily stamped on *Lick It Up* as he co-wrote eight of the record's 10 songs and played lead guitar on every track but "Exciter."

Vincent's fast, screechy solos were in marked contrast to Frehley's more laid back style, but *Lick It Up* marked a return for KISS after three commercially disappointing albums, including *Creatures of the Night*, which, despite its hard rock greatness, took years to reach Gold status. Some fans claim Vincent's songwriting and guitar playing saved KISS while others say taking off the makeup drew attention to the band, spurring sales of *Lick It Up*. Whatever the case, Simmons and Stanley fired Vincent for what Simmons has called unethical behavior, not because of lack of talent.

In *Face the Music: A Life Exposed*, Stanley revealed that Vincent simply had to go. "Things with Vinnie were getting worse and worse," the Starchild wrote. "He kept pushing his solos to more and more ridiculously epic lengths, stalling the show. The final straw came at a concert back in the States, in Long Beach, California, in January, 1984. That night he went on for so long that Gene and I just walked back onstage as he was still playing. I went to the mic and said, 'Vinnie Vincent, lead guitar!' When the lights went down after the next song, Vinnie came over to me in the dark and said, 'You bastard, you humiliated me!'... He was done."

After leaving KISS, Vincent formed the Vinnie Vincent Invasion, which recorded two albums: *Vinnie Vincent Invasion* (1986) and *All Systems Go* (1988). In an interview published on www.classicbands.com, Simmons admitted that he wouldn't let Vincent use the KISS name during interviews. "No free rides," the Demon said. "You wanna make it, go and make it. I named Vincent Cusano, Vinnie Vincent. That's the only gift he's allowed. It's interesting that Vinnie hasn't changed his name back to Vinnie Cusano.... I wish him all the best of luck. You're not allowed to use the name KISS. I've worked for 14 years to make that name mean something. Nobody gets a free ride off of me. Now you go and build the Vinnie Vincent Invasion. Good luck, but not with KISS as ammunition."

Despite the fact that he and KISS parted ways under less than ideal conditions, Vincent contributed to 1992's *Revenge*, co-writing "Unholy," "Heart of Chrome," and "I Just Wanna." Vincent recalled the brief reunion in *KISS: Behind the Mask—The Official Authorized Biography*: "I ran into Gene and Paul in A&M studios and we talked about some things. It was good to see them again; I hadn't seen them in a long time. Shortly after, I got a call from Gene asking if I would like to write for the *Revenge* record. I thought it was a great idea."

In 1996, Vincent released a solo EP, featuring Fleischman on vocals. In the album's liner notes, Vincent thanked Paul Stanley, Gene Simmons, and Eric Carr—this despite his tumultuous history with KISS, and despite his suing Stanley and Simmons on various occasions for what he perceived as unpaid songwriting royalties.

Prior to working with KISS, Vincent jammed with such obscure acts as Younger Generation, Warrior, Hunter, Treasure (with Rascals alumnus Felix Cavaliere), Heat, Laura Nyro, and the Hitchhikers. Curiously, he was also a staff songwriter for the TV shows *Happy Days* and *Joanie Loves Chachi*.

At various points during his career, Vincent kept busy working with such acts as Wendy O. Williams, John Waite, Dan Hartman, and the Bangles. He also co-wrote "Tears" on Peter Criss's *Let Me Rock You* album. In 2008, SplitScreen Entertainment released the tribute album *KISS MY ANKH: A Tribute to Vinnie Vincent*.

In an April 8, 2014, article entitled "The Long Kiss Goodbye: The Search for Vinnie Vincent," written by Max Blau for www.rollingstone.com, Bruce Kulick said this about the now-reclusive guitarist: "He's such a mysterious figure. In some ways, he's the Howard Hughes of KISS. Vinnie has laid low for so long that it adds to his legend."

See also: "Cusano, AnnMarie" and "Cusano, Diane."

Vinnie Vincent Invasion: After he left KISS, Vinnie Vincent formed the glam metal band Vinnie Vincent Invasion, active from 1984 to 1989. Band members included Vinnie Vincent (guitar), Robert Fleischman (lead vocals 1984–1986), Mark Slaughter (lead vocals 1986–1989, formed the band Slaughter after he left VVI), Dana Strum (bass guitar, backing vocals), and Bobby Rock (drums). The band recorded two albums: *Vinnie Vincent Invasion* (1986) and *All Systems Go* (1988), the latter of which includes a song—"Love Kills"—that was featured on the soundtrack for *A Nightmare on Elm Street 4: The Dream Master* (1988).

According to music critic Ernest Hilbert, writing for ryeberg.com, the Vinnie Vincent Invasion "broke apart under pressure from the record company, which insisted that Vincent had become megalomaniacal. No one seems to have disagreed."

Vinnie Vincent—Metal Tech: Style, Speed & Phrasing: An instructional VHS video recorded at EQ Sound Studios, *Metal Tech* was released in 1988. Vincent exhibits his unusual approach to soloing.

Vintage KISS Photos: 1974–1981: Published in 2009 by Heavy Metal, *Vintage KISS Photos: 1974–1981* was compiled by "veteran KISS photo archivist" Marc Scallatino. It features 300 black-and-white and color photos, but was pulled from the market due to copyright issues and is now rare and valuable. According to the solicitation for the book, the first 2,000 copies sold included a free 8 × 10 color photo.

Wagner, Dick: Prolific musician Dick Wagner, who worked with such legendary acts as Lou Reed and Billy Joel, played guitar on a number of KISS songs, including "Beth," "Flaming Youth," "Sweet Pain," and "Every Time I Look at You." Perhaps best-known as the co-writer of Alice Cooper's "Only Women Bleed," Wagner has said he wishes he had written "Beth" and that he had fun working with KISS.

"Wall of Sound": Written by Paul Stanley, Gene Simmons, and Tommy Thayer, "Wall of Sound" is the second track on *Monster*. It's a tight and tuneful rocker sung by Simmons, bearing more than a passing resemblance to the Beatles' "Helter Skelter."

Wanted: Dead or Alive: Gene Simmons gets second billing in *Wanted: Dead or Alive* (1987). Directed by Gary Sherman, the film stars Rutger Hauer as Nick Randall, a former CIA operative. Nick Randall, the great-grandson of Josh Randall, the character played by Steve McQueen in the *Wanted: Dead or Alive* television series (1958–1961), is a tech-savvy bounty hunter enlisted to track down terrorist Malak Al Rahim, played by Simmons.

Of Malak Al Rahim, Roger Ebert said: "What would Hollywood do without at least one ethnic group that is fair game for categorical racist stereotyping? I was never quite sure what or whom Al Rahim represented, or what his goals were, apart from the ritualistic destruction of innocent civilians, but who cares? He's an Arab, isn't he? And they all want to blow up everybody, don't they?"

Of Simmons' performance, Ebert said: "Al Rahim is played in the movie by Gene Simmons, of the rock group KISS, who seems to be trying to find a career after music. Since he has few lines and no motivation, this is not the movie that's going to do it for him. But he shouldn't complain, because nobody else in the film does much better."

"War Machine": The "heaviest song on the heaviest KISS album," "War Machine" is "slow, mean, borne on a sinuous riff and heavy with foreboding," wrote Paul Elliott, author of *KISS: Hotter Than Hell*. Collaborating with Bryan Adams (who came up with the title) and Jim Vallance, Gene Simmons wrote the thundering head banger, which is the ninth and final track on *Creatures of the Night*. For the 1985 reissue of the album, producer Dave Wittman remixed "War Machine."

Warman's KISS Collectibles Field Guide: Values and Identification: Published in 2005 by KP Books, this portable volume was written by KISS collector Tom Shannon. It includes listings and pricing for more than 1,500 items (posters, concert programs, action figures, records, magazines, and the like), supplemented by more than 400 color photos. The book also features a history of the band and an interview with Bill Aucoin.

Warner Bros. Records: When Neil Bogart started the Casablanca label in 1973, it was a subsidiary of Warner Bros. Records.

Washburn Guitars: Washburn guitars are Paul Stanley's instrument of choice, and he has appeared in a number of ads for the company, which was founded in Chicago in 1883. In 2008, "Paul Stanley Autographed Edition Guitars" from Washburn were sold in Target stores across Australia.

Wasley, Don: From 1975 to 1980, Don Wasley was the vice president of artist development at Casablanca Records. He helped KISS with marketing during the *Alive!* era.

"Watchin' You": "Watchin' You" is the seventh song on *Hotter Than Hell*. Dave Reynolds, a contributor to the book *KISS: Hotter Than Hell*, called it "A monster metal number that stomps along like Godzilla tearing up everything in his path. Gene spits out the lead vocal with venom. Criss's percussive work and the seemingly never-ending lead play of Ace Frehley prove that, in their day, KISS were beyond compare. It's interesting to note that Simmons admitted to 're-arranging' the guitar lick from Mountain's 'Mississippi Queen' when writing this track."

In *KISS: Behind the Mask—The Official Authorized Biography*, Simmons said "the lyrical notion of 'Watchin' You' came from an Alfred Hitchcock movie called *Rear Window*. The movie is about this guy watching an actual murder going down. James Stewart is in a wheelchair and sees it happening. Also the voyeuristic aspect of watching sexy women get undressed is a common occurrence in New York City because everybody lives in tall buildings and you have windows looking in other people's windows."

"We Are One": An infectious pop number by Gene Simmons, "We Are One" is the fifth track on *Psycho Circus*. It was released as a single, but it failed to chart in the U.S., which is a shame. The Demon "sings with a sensitivity not heard since *Unmasked*," wrote Paul Elliott, author of *KISS: Hotter Than Hell*. "A clever arrangement and sweet harmonies make 'We Are One' one of KISS's very best pop songs." Tommy Thayer plays guitar while Kevin Valentine sits in on drums. When Simmons wrote this Beatles-esque tune, he had "I'd Like to Teach the World to Sing" from the classic Coca-Cola commercial in mind.

"We Want to Shout it Out Loud": Recorded for the unreleased Wicked Lester album, "We Want to Shout It Out Loud," sung by Gene Simmons, was clearly influenced by such bands as the Byrds and the Beatles (the song doesn't sound anything like "Shout it Out Loud"). The song was written by Allan Clarke and Terry Sylvester and was recorded as "I Wanna Shout" by the Hollies, who included it on their 1970 album, *Confessions of the Mind*.

***Welcome to Sweden*:** Gene Simmons guest-starred as himself in "Farthinder"/"Get a Job," which is the April 11, 2014, episode (July 31 in the U.S.) of the Swedish sitcom, *Welcome to Sweden*. Simmons, a previous client, finds out that Bruce has moved to Stockholm.

Welcome to the Spanish Tribute to KISS: This Indie release from Spain features the following tracks: "Tonight You Belong to Me" (United), "Forever" (Mitos), "Love Gun" (Tyr Sound), "Sure Know Something" (4 L), "Naked City" (Johny B. Nasty), "Beth" (Little Rock Star), "Hard Luck Woman" (The Jarluck Band), "Jungle" (KFP), "Shout It Out Loud" (Kiss Fever Band), "100,000 Years" (Lipstick), "Crazy Crazy Nights" (Naxx), "Detroit Rock City" (Paco Stanley), "Hide Your Heart" (Poker), "What's On Your Mind?" (Schizophrenic Spacers), "I Was Made for Lovin' You" (Imagine), and "Strutter" (Kiss Fever Band).

"(What Happens) In the Darkness": An early example of Paul Stanley's prodigious vocal gymnastics (Gene Simmons lends some interesting vocals as well), the very entertaining "(What Happens) In the Darkness" was written by Tamy Lester Smith and recorded for the unreleased Wicked Lester album. The song was also recorded by a soul band called Infinity, who released it as a single in 1972.

"What Makes the World Go Round": An agreeable song with obvious disco and R&B influence, "What Makes the World Go Round" is the fifth track on *Unmasked*. It was written by Vini Poncia and Paul Stanley, who sings about a lovely, head-turning girl he feels deep in his heart.

"What's on Your Mind?": The fifth track on Ace Frehley's 1978 KISS solo album, "What's on Your Mind?" eschews the trippy drug aesthetic of the previous two tracks—"Snow Blind" and "Ozone"—in favor of pure pop. In up-tempo fashion, Frehley expresses his feelings about an uptight girl, how he can't figure her out, and how he'd like to get back together with her. A catchy, likable song.

Whelan, Brian: Brian Whelan played keyboards on "Freak," which is track three on *Monster*. He also played in Dwight Yoakam's band.

***When KISS Ruled the World*:** The seventh installment of VH1's *When __ Ruled the World* pop culture series, *When KISS Ruled the World* (2003) is a candid documentary in which all four original members of the band are interviewed. Gene Simmons and Paul Stanley appear in full makeup, and the show is peppered with lots of vintage photos, concert footage, historical information, and candid admissions. Sample quotes: "I was a 24-hour whore—all I ever thought about was sex" (Simmons); "I smashed up enough furniture to furnish like 10 houses" (Ace Frehley); "There was nobody in this band who wasn't guilty of being full of themselves" (Stanley); "We were drinking a lot, we were partying a lot, because we were unhappy" (Peter Criss).

"When Lightning Strikes": "When Lightning Strikes," the 10th track on *Sonic Boom*, is a fairly generic KISS anthem, but for one thing: the song is sung by lead guitarist Tommy Thayer, who does a yeoman's job on the mic. David Jeffries of www.allmusic.com said "When Lightning Strikes," along with Eric Carr's "All for the Glory," "slow down the proceedings," but it's actually not that bad of a song. In fact, the chorus is kind of catchy.

"When the Bells Ring": Written by Austin Roberts and Christopher Welch, "When the Bells Ring" was recorded by Wicked Lester for the group's unreleased album. Gene Simmons sings the mediocre song, which was also recorded by a band called Newport News, who released it as a single.

"When You Wish Upon a Star": A song also covered by the likes of Billy Joel and Linda Ronstadt, "When You Wish Upon a Star" is Gene Simmons' off-key (if heartfelt) rendition of the all-time classic, which was written by Leigh Harline and Ned Washington for Walt Disney's 1940 animated masterpiece, *Pinocchio*. Backed beautifully by members of the New York and Los Angeles Philharmonic Orchestras, "When You Wish Upon a Star" is the 11th and final track on *Gene Simmons*, the Demon's 1978 KISS solo album. It's a touching tune, but Jiminy Cricket (as voiced by Cliff Edwards) did it better in the film.

In *KISS: Behind the Mask—The Official Authorized Biography*, Simmons revealed why he recorded the song. "All the sights and sounds in America played a very important role in my development as a kid," he said. "When I went to see *Pinocchio* and I heard Jiminy Cricket at the end of the movie singing.... I really thought he was singing to me.... I cried on the recording of the song. It hit me really hard, big lump in the throat." As such, Simmons' voice cracked during the song, but Sean Delaney wouldn't let him re-record the vocal because he thought it captured an emotionally honest moment.

"When Your Walls Come Down": An up-tempo, but generic sounding filler track with cornball lyrics, "When Your Walls Come Down" is the seventh song on *Crazy Nights*. It was written by Paul Stanley (lead vocals), Adam Mitchell, and Bruce Kulick, who, despite the tepid nature of the song overall, provides some tasty licks on lead guitar.

"While the City Sleeps": One of many forgettable Gene Simmons songs of the 1980s, "While the City Sleeps," co-written by Mitch Weissman, is the eighth track on *Animalize*. The film-noirish lyrics aren't particularly well sung by Simmons, and the instrumentation sounds like generic KISS of the era. The Demon got the idea for "While the City Sleeps" from the 1956 Fritz Lang-directed film of the same name.

***White Tiger* (album):** Released in 1986, White Tiger's self-titled album, which was Mark St. John's first published work after leaving KISS, features the following tracks: "Rock Warriors," "Love/Hate," "Bad Time Coming," "Runaway," "Still Standing Strong," "Live to Rock," "Northern Wind," "Stand and Deliver," and "White Hot Desire." In 1999, ECM Records released a CD remaster with an additional version of "Rock Warriors" as the bonus track.

White Tiger (band): After joining KISS, Mark St. John was in a glam metal band called White Tiger, active from 1985 to 1988. Band members included Mark St. John (lead guitar, backing vocals), David Donato (lead vocals), Michael Norton (bass guitar, backing vocals), and Brian James Fox (drums, backing vocals). The group released one album: *White Tiger* (1986).

The Who: Formed in England in 1964, the Who, fronted by Roger Daltrey with songwriter Pete Townshend on lead guitar, were one of the key bands of the British Invasion. Heavily influenced by the Who, KISS has covered the group's "Won't Get Fooled Again" many times in concert. Like KISS, the Who has sold more than 100 million albums worldwide.

***Who Wants to Be a Millionaire*:** In 2000, Gene Simmons appeared on *Who Wants to Be a Millionaire*, playing for the Neil Bogart Foundation (cancer research). His first question was related to music: "At a rock concert, which of the following instruments is plugged into an amplifier?": (A) Triangle (B) Guitar (C) Tambourine (D) Dentist's Drill. Gene got it right, of course, answering "B."

Unfortunately, Simmons missed the $16,000 question: "The word 'pachyderm' is derived from the Greek word for what physical feature?": (A)

Long nose (B) Brushlike tail (C) Three toes (D) Thick skin. Gene answered "A," but the correct answer is "D," which was especially regrettable since Gene hadn't used any of his lifelines.

"Who Wants to Be Lonely": A solid tune written by Paul Stanley, Desmond Child, and Jean Beauvoir, "Who Wants to Be Lonely" is the third track on *Asylum*. Greg Prato, writing for www.allmusic.com, said the song would "benefit from a heavier sound," and that's probably true, but Stanley's vocals are strong as he sings about a girl who is waiting for love, but she should just open up to him (sexually, no doubt).

Beauvoir is a huge fan of the song. In *KISS: Behind the Mask—The Official Authorized Biography*, he said: "Going to see KISS perform a song that I was involved with in front of thousands of people was amazingly gratifying. I felt 'Who Wants to Be Lonely' delivered an emotion that I still feel today when I hear it. It's very honest. It touches on the fear that so many people have about living a life of loneliness."

Wicked Lester: Prior to forming KISS, Paul Stanley was in a band with guitarist Stephen Coronel called Tree, and Gene Simmons played in several bands with Coronel. In 1970, Coronel introduced Paul and Gene, and the trio formed Rainbow with keyboardist Brooke Ostrander and drummer Joe Davidson, who was quickly replaced by Tony Zarrella. In 1971 or 1972 (accounts vary), Rainbow changed its name to Wicked Lester.

Although Wicked Lester was inconsistent stylistically, incorporating rock and roll, pop, psychedelia, and folk rock, they recorded a demo album (produced by Ron Johnsen) for Epic Records, who offered the band a deal, but only if they axed Coronel, which they did. Studio musician Ron Leejack replaced Coronel, who in interviews has said he could have played better.

Managed by Lew Linet, Wicked Lester recorded several demo tapes for Epic, who, according to Dale Sherman's book, *KISS FAQ*, "kept dragging their feet on a release date for the album. As everyone waited, there were problems brewing with the band—suggestions from Simmons that they begin wearing costumes, maybe makeup, play roles onstage were meeting with resistance from Leejack and Zarrella—and Leejack, Ostrander, and Zarrella were all looking to split, while Simmons and Stanley were looking to see if they could get away from the others as well."

Sherman continued: "By this time, Simmons had seen Criss's ad looking for work as a drummer and contacted him about meeting…. Simmons and Stanley would have Criss come up to the Loft and do an audition on Zarrella's drum kit and then try again on his own drum kit at another audition, which got everyone excited about working together. After that date, the Loft was broken into and everyone's equipment was stolen. This was pretty much the last straw for most of the members, and the band broke up by November of 1972 just as Epic announced that they had decided to pass on the album." (Simmons and Stanley have said they walked away from the contract.)

According to *KISS FAQ*, the master tapes of the unreleased Wicked Lester record "sat in the vaults at Epic until 1977 when someone remembered that Simmons and Stanley had played on the album. With the explosive success of KISS ongoing at the time, Epic prepared the album for release. Simmons, Stanley, manager Bill Aucoin, and Casablanca Records owner Neil Bogart all decided that it would not help KISS to have the material appear and managed to work out a deal with Epic to buy back the recordings."

During the late 1980s, fans began discovering Wicked Lester, and in 1987 a small-time outfit called Rockwell & Good released a demo under the name of *Wicked Lester and Progeny Demo Sessions*, which featured nine songs recorded by the band, plus the five-track demo KISS recorded with Eddie Kramer in 1973 and a pair of Ace Frehley demos from 1985: "I Got the Touch" and "Rock Or Be Rocked." The nine songs also appeared on a bootleg called *The Original Wicked Lester Sessions*. Other bootlegs were released as well.

In 2001, KISS included three Wicked Lester songs—"Keep Me Waiting," "She," and "Love Her All I Can"—on *The Box Set*, a five-disc compilation. During a KISS radio interview to support their 2012 album, *Monster*, a caller asked where the name Wicked Lester came from. Paul Stanley said, "I think we were just looking for something cool … it didn't really have a meaning, although we did kind of envision a cartoon-type character."

Wicked Lester and Progeny Demo Sessions: In 1987, around the time many fans were discovering that Paul Stanley and Gene Simmons were in a band called Wicked Lester, Rockwell & Good released this bootleg. It includes nine Wicked Lester songs, the five-song demo KISS recorded in 1973 with Eddie Kramer, and two Ace Frehley demos from 1985.

Wicked Lester tracks include: "Sweet Ophelia," "Keep Me Waiting," "Ladies in Waiting," "She," "Too Many Days," "In the Darkness," "When the Bell Rings," "Some Other Guy," and "(We Want To) Shout It Out Loud." KISS demos include: "Deuce," "Cold Gin," "Strutter," "Watchin' You," and "Black Diamond." Ace Frehley demos include: "I Got the Touch" and "Rock Or Be Rocked."

Williams, Wendy O: After recording three albums as leader of punk rock band the Plasmatics, Wendy O. Williams went solo in 1984 with *WOW*, an LP produced by Gene Simmons. In addition, Simmons played bass on the record under the pseudonym of Reginald Van Helsing. Simmons co-wrote several of the songs on the album, which also features writing credits by Paul Stanley, Eric Carr, and Vinnie Vincent. Further, Ace Frehley plays lead guitar on "Bump and Grind," Stanley plays guitar on "Ready to Rock," and Carr plays the drums on "Legends Never Die." On Williams' 1986 *Kommander of Kaos* album, Simmons, Carr, and Vincent wrote "Ain't None of Your Business." Sadly, Williams died of a self-inflicted gunshot wound in 1998. She was only 48.

Winterland Productions: The first rock and roll merchandising company, Winterland Productions produced numerous KISS products. Currently, Dave and Dell Furano, the brothers who founded Winterland, are partners with Gene and Paul in the Rock & Brews restaurant chain.

"Wiped-Out": Written by Ace Frehley and Anton Fig, "Wiped-Out" is the eighth track on the Spaceman's 1978 KISS solo album. It's a rowdy admission of drunkenness, a "mishmash of fast and slow riffing and cartoonish vocals. Here, more than any other time in his career, Ace Frehley truly sounds like a man on the edge—or a drunken fool having the time of his life" (Paul Elliott, *KISS: Hotter Than Hell*).

Wise, Richie: Richie Wise, who also worked with such acts as Badfinger and Gladys Knight & the Pips, co-produced *KISS* and *Hotter Than Hell* with Kenny Kerner.

Wish You Were Dead: Gene Simmons plays a sadistic beautician in the comedic *Wish You Were Dead* (2002), in which a greedy con woman named Sally Rider (Mary Steenburgen) tricks Mac Wilson (Cary Elwes) into thinking she's having his baby. She then hires Melody 'Jupiter Music' Malloy (Elaine Hendrix) to kill Wilson for insurance purposes. Directed by Valerie McCaffrey, the film also features a sinister Christopher Lloyd and cameos by Billy Ray Cyrus and Robert Englund (as a minister).

"Within": Written and sung by Gene Simmons, "Within" is the second track on *Psycho Circus* and one of the better songs on the album. It's got good soft and hard singing by Simmons, plus some ethereal guitar sounds at the beginning, followed by hardcore riffing. It's a semi-clever song of contradictions as Simmons sings about sleeping without dreaming, feeling without touching. The Demon got the idea for the lyrics from the Beatles' "Within You Without You," which was written and sung by George Harrison for the iconic *Sgt. Pepper's Lonely Hearts Club Band* album (1967).

Wittman, Dave: Dave Wittman was the engineer for the first KISS demo, along with such albums as *Animalize*, *Creatures of the Night*, *Dressed to Kill*, and *Lick It Up*.

Witz, Chaim: Gene Simmons' birth name was Chaim Witz. He changed it to Gene Klein, then Gene Simmons.

Vintage KISS T-shirt featuring an artistic rendering of Gene Simmons, Vinnie Vincent, Eric Carr, and Paul Stanley.

Woloch, Dennis: Art director Dennis Woloch designed the covers for *Alive!, Alive II, Destroyer, Love Gun, The Originals, Rock and Roll Over, Double Platinum, Dynasty, Music from "The Elder," Unmasked, Creatures of the Night, Lick It Up, Animalize, Crazy Nights,* and *Asylum.* In addition, he designed the band's tour books and helped in designing KISS T-shirts and other merchandise.

In an interview published on www.kissfanzine.com, Woloch spoke about his introduction to KISS and his favorite and least favorite album covers: "When I saw one of their very first rehearsals, which was in some little room somewhere, I thought they were very outrageous, kinda scary.... I like *Rock and Roll Over, Destroyer,* and *Creatures of the Night* the best. *Lick It Up* and *Animalize* are my least favorites only because I think I could have done so much more with them. I like my hand lettering for *Animalize,* however. India ink on paper towel."

Wonder, Stevie: On *Kiss My Ass: Classic KISS Regrooved,* Stevie Wonder and Lenny Kravitz covered "Deuce." Born Stevland Hardaway Morris, Wonder is famous for such hits as "Superstition," "You Are the Sunshine of My Life," and "I Just Called to Say I Love You."

World Domination Tour: KISS co-headlined with Aerosmith from August 2 to December 20, 2003, for a total of 59 shows in the U.S., comprising the so-called World Domination Tour. The Aerosmith camp called it the Rocksimus Maximus Tour while it is sometimes informally referred to as the "AeroKISS Tour." KISS introduced a $1,000 platinum ticket that included a seat in the first five rows, a meet-and-greet backstage, and a photo with the band.

This was KISS's first tour performing with lead guitarist Tommy Thayer, who replaced Ace Frehley and wore his Spaceman makeup design. Peter Criss had returned to the band after Eric Singer briefly took his place during the Farewell Tour.

Aerosmith's set was relatively sparse while KISS rolled out their patented explosions, platform boots, themed costumes, and other props and stunts. A fledgling hard rock outfit called Saliva was the opening act. For certain performances, including the December 14 show at the Ford Center in Oklahoma City, Joe Perry joined KISS onstage for a rousing rendition of "Strutter."

Followed by: Rock the Nation World Tour.

A World Without Heroes **(novel):** Written by KISS expert Dale Sherman and published in 2000 by MusiCare Online, this work of fiction is based in part on the KISS concept album, *Music from "The Elder,"* and on the made-for-TV movie, *KISS Meets the Phantom of the Park.*

"A World Without Heroes" (song): The frequently dark Gene Simmons is surprisingly sincere and sympathetic on "A World Without Heroes," in which he sings that a world without heroes is no place for him. The seventh track on *Music from "The Elder,"* the ballad originated from a Paul Stanley song called "Every Little Bit of Your Heart."

"A World Without Heroes" was the only single released from *Music from "The Elder"* in the U.S., reaching a disappointing #56 on the *Billboard* charts. Stanley plays lead guitar on the tune, which the band performed live on the TV show *Fridays,* but never in concert (at least until the KISS Conventions of the mid-'90s and the *KISS Unplugged* performance on MTV). Written by Stanley, Simmons, Bob Ezrin, and Lou Reed, "A World Without Heroes" was the first KISS video played on MTV, and Cher covered the song on her 1991 album, *Love Hurts.*

A World with Heroes—A KISS Tribute for Cancer Care: Released August 27, 2013, to benefit Vaudreuil-Soulanges Palliative Care Residence, a cancer care hospice, this two-disc set features 20 KISS covers by a variety of acts. The Deluxe Edition iTunes release has a re-configured track listing plus 11 bonus songs.

Worldwide KISS Conventions: Beginning in 1995, KISS embarked on a series of Worldwide KISS Conventions (oftentimes called KISS Konventions), in which the band would perform an acoustic set, answer questions from fans, and sign autographs.

On June 17, 1995, in Los Angeles at the first North American KISS Convention, Peter Criss joined KISS onstage to sing "Hard Luck Woman" and "Nothin' to Lose." It was the first time Criss had performed publicly with the band in more than 15 years. KISS Conventions also featured KISS cover bands, memorabilia on display, and vendors selling old and new merchandise.

In a 2006 interview published on www.blabbermouth.net, Tommy Thayer spoke about the KISS Conventions, which he managed: "The whole concept was to do this *Star Trek*–type of fan convention that the band would appear at, and do a Q&A and do an unplugged set—it was all new. We put together a KISS museum that included all the original KISS outfits, and it happened in major city ballrooms, we organized it and did it all ourselves, an in-house thing. I just happened to be there at the right time and they said, here, you go to every city and set up the ballrooms at the Hiltons, and all of a sudden it was more than a full-time job. I was working almost 20 hours a day, but I loved it because it was enjoyable and interesting to me. It wasn't like work; it was just doing KISS stuff."

"Wouldn't You Like to Know Me": A rocker with a catchy, popping chorus, "Wouldn't You Like to Know Me" is the fourth track on the Starchild's 1978 KISS solo album. Paul Stanley loves him some Paul Stanley, and this song shows it. Fans love him as well and would surely like to know him. Despite the narcissistic vibe of the song, Stanley has said it is his homage to the Raspberries, an early 1970s power pop band from Cleveland.

WOW: Released in 1984, *WOW* was Plasmatics singer Wendy O. Williams' debut solo album. Produced by Gene Simmons, the record disappointed many Plasmatics fans because it is more heavy metal than punk. In fact, some call it an unofficial KISS album due to the band's prolific involvement in the record, including bass guitar by Simmons under the pseudonym of Reginald Van Helsing.

Tracks include: "I Love Sex (And Rock and Roll)" (co-written by Simmons), "It's My Life" (written by Simmons and Paul Stanley), "Priestess," "Thief in the Night" (co-written by Simmons), "Opus in Cm7," "Ready to Rock," "Bump and Grind," "Legends Never Die" (co-written by Simmons), and "Ain't None of Your Business" (written by Simmons, Eric Carr, and Vinnie Vincent). Ace Frehley plays lead guitar on "Bump and Grind," Paul Stanley plays guitar on "Ready to Rock," and Eric Carr pounds the skins on "Legends Never Die."

"X-Ray Eyes": Written and sung by Gene Simmons, an avowed horror and science fiction fan, "X-Ray Eyes" possibly pays homage, at least in the title, to the great Roger Corman B-movie, *X: The Man with the X-Ray Eyes* (1963). Instead of being driven mad by the X-ray powers, as happens to Ray Milland in the film, Simmons claims he can see right through a girl's lies and that she'll come crawling back to him. One of the better-sung Simmons songs in terms of range of voice, "X-Ray Eyes" is the eighth track on *Dynasty*. Anton Fig plays drums on the song.

"Yes I Know (Nobody's Perfect)": This Gene Simmons song is tuneful, but fairly standard, with Simmons bragging about being near perfect and that's he's got something a girl can't live without. He also tells a girl to take her clothes off—more than once. Tommy Thayer's guitar solo is tight, but predictable. Laden with innuendo, "Yes I Know (Nobody's Perfect)" is the fourth track on *Sonic Boom*.

Yesterday and Today: Aired August 8, 1983, a little over a month before KISS would remove their makeup live on MTV, *Yesterday and Today* is a USA Cable Network special. It features the "I Love It Loud" video, the promotional film for "Rock and Roll All Nite," clips from *The Young Music Show* and *The Inner Sanctum* specials, and an interview with Paul, Gene, Eric Carr, and Vinnie Vincent.

Ymir: Gene Simmons credits the way he stomps around onstage to the Ymir, a giant creature from the 1957 sci-fi classic, *20 Million Miles to Earth*, featuring monster effects by stop-motion master Ray Harryhausen. "I realized I couldn't copy the movements of Mick Jagger or the Beatles because I didn't have a little boy's body, but I could be a monster," Simmons said in *Nothin' to Lose: The Making of KISS (1972–1975)*.

Yoshiki: *On Kiss My Ass: Classic KISS Regrooved*, Japanese performer Yoshiki covered "Black Diamond."

"You Love Me to Hate You": The 12th track on *Hot in the Shade*, this song is decidedly mediocre, despite some vocal creativity by Paul Stanley (who wrote the song with Desmond Child) during the chorus. It's about a love/hate romantic (and possibly sadomasochistic) relationship.

"(You Make Me) Rock Hard": The second track on the greatest hits package *Smashes, Thrashes and Hits*, "(You Make Me) Rock Hard" is one of two original songs on the album ("Let's Put the X in Sex" is the other). Written by Paul Stanley, Desmond Child, and Diane Warren, the song is, of course, about sex, with Stanley singing that a girl will make him rock hard all night. The double entendre lyrics are typical of a Stanley KISS number of the 1980s, as is the solid (if derivative) pop rock craftsmanship.

"You Matter to Me": The second track and one of two singles on Peter Criss's 1978 KISS solo album, "You Matter to Me" was written by Vini Poncia, Michael Morgan, and John Vastano. It's a listenable, light-as-a-feather pop tune in which Criss croons that his caring for a girl is the only reason he needs to get by.

"You Wanted the Best": Written by Gene Simmons, "You Wanted the Best" is the sixth track on *Psycho Circus* and the fourth single, but it failed to make *Billboard*'s Hot 100 chart. Regardless, it's a rousing reunion song, with Ace, Gene, Paul, and Peter trading vocals—a throwback to the first album by the band. Matthew Wilkening of ultimateclassicrock.com called it "an extremely catchy song that manages to serve as both a historical account of the reunion and a public group therapy/bitch session." "You Wanted the Best" was originally called "Just Give Me Your Love," and the drum opening was cribbed from Chubby Checker's 1961 hit, "Let's Twist Again."

***You Wanted the Best. You Got the Best.*:** As of this writing, this authorized theatrical KISS documentary, directed by Alan G. Parker, is scheduled for release in 2016.

***You Wanted the Best, You Got the Best!!*:** A live hits album released June 25, 1996, to capitalize on the Reunion Tour (*Rolling Stone* called it a "shameless reunion-promotion biscuit"), *You Wanted the Best, You Got the Best!!* is a collection of songs that reached #17 on the *Billboard* charts. Tracks include: "Room Service" (previously unreleased, recorded in Davenport, Iowa, in 1975); "Two Timer" (previously unreleased, recorded in Detroit, Michigan, in May 1975); "Let Me Know" (previously unreleased, recorded in Detroit, Michigan, in May 1975); "Rock Bottom" (from *Alive!*), "Parasite" (*Alive!*); "Firehouse" (*Alive!*); "I Stole Your Love" (*Alive II*); "Calling Dr. Love" (*Alive II*); "Take Me" (previously unreleased, recorded in Los Angeles, California, in 1977); "Shout It Out Loud" (*Alive II*); "Beth" (*Alive II*); and "Rock and Roll All Nite" (*Alive!*). Published by Mercury Records, the album also features Jay Leno interviewing the original KISS lineup. The Japanese release includes "New York Groove."

"Young and Wasted": The fourth track on *Lick It Up*, "Young and Wasted," like "Not for the Innocent," is a hard rocking, but largely unremarkable Gene Simmons tune. Written by Simmons and Vinnie Vincent, the song tells of a youth who is damned if he does, damned if he doesn't—restless, wild, and running out of time. Simmons' singing is energetic, and the song is fast paced, but this is one of the weaker tracks on the record.

In *KISS: Behind the Mask—The Official Authorized Biography*, Simmons said he got the idea for the song from "the title of an article in the *Soho Weekly News* that was all about being young and wasted for the social circle that revolved around art houses and art galleries. I thought the phrase summed up an entire generation so much ... there's certainly a segment of the population that prefers to be wasted than to be alive."

***The Young Music Show*:** This Japanese TV special, which aired on NHK-T during the summer of 1977, features concert footage from two KISS shows filmed at Budokan Hall in Tokyo. Songs include: "Detroit Rock City," "Let Me Go, Rock 'n' Roll," "Firehouse," "Makin' Love," "Cold Gin," "Nothin' to Lose," "God of Thunder, "Rock and Roll All Nite," and "Black Diamond." In August of 1979, the program aired in the U.S. on HBO.

"You're All That I Want": The 11th track on *Unmasked*, "You're All That I Want" is a nondescript pop rock tune, but for one thing: it's an actual monogamous love song by the infamously promiscuous Gene Simmons, who tells a girl that she's all he wants. Co-written by Vini Poncia, the song has a decent guitar riff and some timely cowbell. The demo, which was recorded in 1977 and appears on *The Box Set*, is called "You're All That I Want, You're All That I Need." Simmons has said that he far prefers the demo, comparing it to something recorded by Free.

"You're All That I Want, You're All That I Need": A demo recorded in 1977, "You're All That I Want, You're All That I Need" was shortened to "You're All That I Want," the 11th track on 1980's *Unmasked*. Not only was the title shortened for inclusion on *Unmasked*, the song was reduced in length as well. "You're All That I Want, You're All That I Need" was featured on *The Box Set* as track 12 on disc 3.

"Yume No Ukiyo Ni Saitemina": Composed by Paul Stanley and Greg Collins, with lyrics written by Yuho Iwasato, "Yume No Ukiyo Ni Saitemina" is a collaboration between KISS and the female Japanese pop group, Momoiro Clover Z (commonly abbreviated as Momoclo). Released January 28, 2015, the song was performed by Momoiro Clover Z, with KISS providing background vocals and instruments.

"Yume No Ukiyo Ni Saitemina" was released in two versions: "Momoclo Edition" and "KISS Edition," the latter containing a track called "Samurai Son," which uses "Yume No Ukiyo Ni Saitemina" as its base, but features KISS' vocals more prominently. "Samurai Son" was also featured as the first track on the Japanese compilation, *Best of KISS 40*.

Zappa, Frank: On Gene Simmons' 2004 solo album, *Asshole*, Frank Zappa co-wrote "Black Tongue" with Simmons. Zappa's children, Ahmet, Dweezil, and Moon, and his late wife, Gayle, contributed to the album as well.

Zarrella, Tony: Tony Zarrella played drums for Rainbow/Wicked Lester. He was the replacement for the short-lived original drummer for the band, Joe Davidson. According to *KISS FAQ*, the band members liked him "because of his double-bass drum setup, his adapting to their style easily, and because anyone who looked like Geezer Butler from Black Sabbath had to be good."

Zero: The unreleased Van Halen demo album produced by Gene Simmons in 1976 is known as *Zero*. It includes 10 tracks: "On Fire," "Woman in Love," "House of Pain," "Runnin' With the Devil," "She's the Woman," "Let's Get Rockin,'" "Big Trouble," "Somebody Get Me a Doctor," "Babe, Don't Leave Me Alone," and "Put Out the Lights."

According to rock music expert Mike Ladano (mikeladano.com), "The *Zero* demo is one of those unreleased hard rock cornerstones. Like a fountain it never seems to stop giving. These songs were played live many times by the band before Simmons recorded them, and they are tight. Roth's voice is high, youthful, and powerful. If anything, the band sounded a little generic. It would take Ted Templeman and the debut record for Van Halen to find their own unique sonic niche."

Zildjian: Peter Criss has played and endorsed Zildjian cymbals. In one ad, he was quoted as saying, "Of course I play Zildjians. This is serious music." Eric Singer plays Zildjian cymbals as well, and the company, which was founded in 1623 in Constantinople by Armenian Avedis Zildjian, makes "Eric Singer Artist Series" drumsticks.

Zlozower, Neil: An industry staple for more than 40 years, legendary rock and roll photographer Neil Zlozower has taken iconic photos of some of the most famous bands of all time, including Black Sabbath, Bon Jovi, Mötley Crüe, and Van Halen. He first shot KISS backstage in 1974. "But the first studio shoot I did with them was when Mark St. John got into the band," Zlozower told Dale Sherman, author of *KISS FAQ*. "Then, since he did not last too long, the next one I did with KISS was when Bruce Kulick joined the band."

Zlozower, who still works with KISS, shot the 1985 reissue of the *Creatures of the Night* album cover. He also photographed the covers for Paul Stanley's *Live to Win* and Bruce Kulick's *BK3* albums. Rock music magazine fans have seen the photo he took of Eric Carr for the Ludwig Drums ad.

In *KISS FAQ*, Zlozower revealed that he has a good working relationship with the group: "KISS is one of the biggest rock bands that ever graced this planet, and they have in their mind the right to be a little egotistical and arrogant, but they do not pull that on me. I think they consider me part of the KISS family. I have worked with them long enough, and I have paid my dues with them. I think they appreciate the detail I put into their photos, and I think that they know if their hair or makeup is not right, or if they are posing in an unflattering way that I will open my mouth and give them advice on what to do to make them look better. So when they come to my studio, they do no not seem different to me with the makeup or without the makeup. I treat them the same and they treat me with the respect and courtesy that I think they feel I deserve to be treated with, because I have proven myself time and time again with them."

Bibliography

Books

Abbott, Waring, Gene Simmons and Paul Stanley. *KISS: The Early Years*. New York: Three Rivers, 2002.
Criss, Peter. *Makeup to Breakup: My Life In and Out of KISS*. New York: Scribner, 2012.
Dayton, Chip Rock. *Outtakes*. New York: Studio Chikara, 1999.
Duncan, Robert. *KISS*. New York: Popular Library, 1978.
Elliott, Paul. *KISS: Hotter Than Hell*. New York: Thunder's Mouth, 2002.
Floren, Ingo. *The Official Price Guide to KISS Collectibles*. New York: House of Collectibles, 2004.
Frehley, Ace. *No Regrets*. London: Simon & Schuster, 2011.
Gebert, Gordon G. G., and Bob McAdams. *KISS & Tell*. Fleetwood, NY: Pitbull, 1998.
Gooch, Curt, and Jeff Suhs. *KISS Alive Forever: The Complete Touring History*. New York: Billboard, 2002.
Holm, Anders, and Dave Thomas. *KISS: Still on Fire*. London: Caroline, 1988.
KISS. *KISStory*. Los Angeles: Kisstory, 1994.
KISS. *KISStory II*. Los Angeles: Kisstory, 1995.
Leaf, David, and Ken Sharp. *KISS: Behind the Mask—The Official Authorized Biography*. New York: Warner, 2003.
Lendt, C.K. *KISS and Sell*. New York: Billboard, 1997.
Lesniewski, Karen, and John Lesniewksi. *KISS Collectibles Identification and Price Guide*. New York: Avon, 1993.
Levine, Barry. *The KISS Years*. Westbury, NY: Studio Chikara, 1997.
Prato, Greg. *The Eric Carr Story*. N.p.: Greg Prato, 2011.
Shannon, Tom. *Warman's KISS Collectibles Field Guide: Values and Identification*. Iola, WI: Krause, 2005.
Sharp, Ken. *KISS Army Worldwide! The Ultimate Fanzine Phenomenon*. Beverly Hills, CA: Phoenix, 2009.
Sherman, Dale. *Black Diamond: The Unauthorized Biography of KISS*. Updated ed. Ontario, Canada: Collector's Guide, 2009.
Sherman, Dale. *Black Diamond 2: The Illustrated Collector's Guide to KISS*. Updated ed. Ontario, Canada: Collector's Guide, 1998.
Simmons, Gene. *Kiss and Make-Up*. New York: Three Rivers, 2002.
Simmons, Gene. *Sex Money KISS*. Beverley Hills, CA: Phoenix, 2006.
Stanley, Paul. *Face the Music: A Life Exposed*. New York: HarperOne, 2014.
Swenson, John. *Headliners: KISS*. New York: Tempo Star, 1978.
Tomarkin, Peggy. *KISS: The Real Story*. New York: Delilah, 1980.

Websites

KISS Asylum, www.kissasylum.com.
KISS Online, www.kissonline.com.
The KissFAQ, www.kissfaq.com.

Index

Numbers in **_bold italics_** refer to pages with photographs.

Abbott, Waring 7, 114, 211
Academy of Music 7, 24, 86, 187
Accept 125
AC/DC 12, 52, 55, 58
Ace Frehley (album) 7, 65, 123, 142, 148, 176
Ace Frehley—The Ultimate Fan Scrapbook 7
Ace Vision Volume 1 7
"The Acorn Is Spinning" 167
"Acrobat" 26, 118
action figures 8
Adams, Bryan 9, 55, 93, 159, 202
Aerosmith 9, 64, 76, 91, 115, 147, 149, 153, 155, 188, 194, 207
"Ain't Gonna Die" 23
"Ain't None of Your Business" 206, 208
"Ain't Quite Right" 9, 89, 148
"Ain't That Peculiar" 9, 27
Alice in Chains 12, 30, 85, 87, 133, 167, 189
Alive! 1, 6, 8–11, 16, 19, 25, 26, 40, 42, 51, 52, 55, 59, 67, 85, 94, 97, 105, 114, 116, 120, 138, 141, 146, 156, 158, 160–161, 176, 184, 187, 202, 207, 209
Alive: The Millennium Concert 27, 97, 105
Alive! Tour 10, 19, 28, 56
Alive II 2, 6, 10, **_11_**, 12, 16, 20, 26, 29, 50, 67, 76, 85, 87, 91–92, 97, 105, 114, 120, 122, 155, 162, 177, 192, 207, 209
Alive II Tour 28, 42, 57, 128, 130
Alive III 10, 97, 105, 114, 120–121, 133, 157, 169, 195
Alive/Worldwide Tour 12, 38, 57, 68, 110, 114, 116, 175, 187, 198
"All About You" 125
"All American Boy" 35
"All American Man" 11–12, 28, 91, 103
"All for the Glory" 12, 178

"All for the Love of Rock & Roll" 13, 137
"All Hell's Breakin' Loose" 13, 27, 36, 104, 120, 124, 139, 195, 197
All I Need to Know I Learned from KISS: Life Lessons from the Hottest Band in the Land 12, 50
"All Night Long" 169
"All Right Now" 82
All Systems Go 201
"All the Way" 13, 18, 82, 115
"All We Need" 59
"Almost Human" 13, 69, 83, 86, 91, 117, 120, 127, 154
Along Came a Spider 40, 175
Altyn, John 13
"Always Near You/Nowhere to Hide" 13, 69, 71
American Bandstand 13, 37, 53, 181
American Idol 13, 188
"American Man" 154
American Music Awards 14
American Symphony Orchestra 62
"And I Know" 23
"And on the 8th Day" 14, 124
And Party Every Day: The Inside Story of Casablanca Records **_14_**, 32–33, 77
Anderson, Ken 14
Angel of Babylon 19
"Animal" 15, 157
Animalize 15, 21, 71, 78, 88, 92, 121, 126, 139, 165–166, 189–190, 197, 204, 206, 207
Animalize World Tour 15
Animaniacs 15
Ankh Warrior 15, 43, 130, 200
Anomaly 15–16, 68, 178
Another Ugly EP 138
Anthrax 16, 42, 49, 60, 70, 110, 148, 193
"Any Way You Slice It" 17
"Any Way You Want It" 11, 16, 102–103

"Anything for My Baby" 16, 26, 55, 73, 177
Anything KISS 16
Appice, Carmine 16, 149
Archie Meets KISS **_16_**
Are You Smarter Than a Fifth Grader? 17
Argent 72
The Art of McCartney: The Songs of Paul McCartney Sung by the World's Greatest Artists 133, 199
Die Ärzte 53, 110
"As Time Goes By" 147
Ashley, Phil 17, 42
Asshole (album) 17, 57, 141, 172, 210
"Asshole" (song) 17
Asylum 15, 17, 21, 42, 81, 86, 93, 121, 128, 154, 166–167, 180, 186–187, 193, 197, 205, 207
Asylum Tour 17, 187
At Any Cost 18
Athens High School Choir Original Cast Recording of *The Elder* 18
Atlanta Rhythm Section 11, 56
Atlanta's Best KISSers: An Atlanta Tribute to the Hottest Band in the World 18
Attack of the Killer B's 16
Aucoin, Bill 5, 15, 18–19, 22, 25, 27, 30–31, 37, 39, 50, 54, 56–57, 60, 79, 81–82, 87, 100, 135, 144, 175, 196–197, 202, 205
Aucoin Management 31
Audio Dog 19, 81, 121, 192
Auringer, Charlie 44
Australian Children's Choir 114
Avantasia 19, 175

B-Side Ourselves 176
Babies Go KISS 19
Baby Driver (album) 19
"Baby Driver" (song) 19, 53, 74, 86, 125, 149, 160

Index

Bach, Sebastian 70, 108, 176, 179, 194
Bachman Turner Overdrive 16, 19
"Back on the Streets" 110, 157
"Back to School" 193–194
"Back to the Stone Age" 19, 137
"Bad Attitude" 34
"Bad, Bad Lovin'" 19, 26, 29
"Bad Boys" 124
Bad Boys of KISS Tour 19, 68
"Bad People Burn in Hell" 34
Badlands 20, 174
Baker, Bill 7
Balandas, Eddie 11, 20
Ballard, Russ 20, 68, 72, 88, 142
Balls of Fire 47
Bananas **20**
"Bang Bang You" 20, 42
The Barracudas 45
Batman 20, 175
Baxter, Jeff 20, 28, 167
Beacon Theatre 20, 40, 49
The Beatles 1, 3, 5, 18, 21, 28–30, 51, 64, 66, 69, 90–91, 97, 108, 120, 133, 142, 152–153, 159, 160, 163, 167, 171, 175, 181, 185, 202–203, 208
"Beautiful" 17
Beauvoir, Jean 21, 47, 71, 189, 197, 205
"Beck" 125
Beck, Jeff 22, 28
Beck, Robin 79
Beech, Wes 128
Behind the Player 21
Bell Sound Studios 94, 177
Benjamin, Sid 48
Benvenga, Michael 46, 125
Berg, Ross 69
Berg, Shelley 21
Best of KISS 40 21, 166, 210
Best of Solo Albums 22
"Beth" 7, 11, 13, 18–23, 26, 33–34, 39, 44, 46, 51, 53, 55–56, 58, 60, 64, 73, 75, 77, 83–84, 86, 89, 91, 97, 102–105, 109, 114–116, 125, 142, 148–149, 151, 154, 159, 162, 168, 175–176, 184, 193, 195, 198, 200, 202–203, 209
"Betrayed" 22, 63, 81, 187
"Between the Lines" 23
Bill & Ted's Bogus Journey 72
Billboard 6, 7
Bionic Boogie 32, 125
BK3 23, 121, 210
"Black Diamond" 9, 21, 23, 26, 37, 55, 60, 73, 75, 86–87, 90, 94, 96–97, 99, 103, 110–111, 114, 120, 125, 135, 143, 153, 156, 159, 178, 190–191, 193, 206, 208–209
Black Diamond: The Unauthorized Biography of KISS 23, 98, 211
Black Diamond: The Unauthorized Biography of KISS—10th Anniversary Edition 23

Black Diamond 2: An Illustrated Collector's Guide to KISS 23, 211
"Black Dog" 154
Black Lodge 16
Black 'N Blue (album) 24
Black 'N Blue (band) 18, 23, 54, 61, 187
Black Oak Arkansas 24, 82
Black Sabbath 11, 22, 24, 47, 52, 56, 63, 88, 94, 110, 165, 174, 176, 210
"Black Tongue" 17
Blackjack (album) 24, 121
Blackjack (band) 24, 26, 78, 121
Bleecker Street Loft Party 24, 27
Bloom County 24
"Blue Moon Over Brooklyn" 34
Blue Öyster Cult 11, 18, 24, 52, 115
The Blue Room 198
Bob Seger & the Silver Bullet Band 11, 52, 168
Bodine, Bill 25
Bogart, Joyce 25, 50
Bogart, Neil 14, 18, 25, 32, 54–55, 73, 77, 79, 92, 117, 124, 158, 202, 204, 205
Bolton, Michael 24, 26, 64, 81, 120, 121
Bon Jovi 15, 42, 76, 93, 133, 153, 170, 210
Bonham, John 31, 43, 122, 154
Bono, Sonny 20
Booke, Jane 47
"Boomerang" 26, 81
Born Again 142
Boutwell, Ron 26, 100–101
Bowen, Pamela 26, 182, 185
Bowie, David 26, 51, 58, 120, 138
The Box Set 7, 9, 19, 26–27, 54, 72, 91, 105–106, 123, 128–129, 144, 146, 168, 172, 184, 189, 205, 209
"Boyz Are Gonna Rock" 27, 110
Brandvold, Michael 113
The Brats 24, 27, 38, 81, 151
"Breakout" 7, 27, 56, 68, 75, 126, 195
Brightman, Sarah 85
Britny Fox 158
Brodsky, Joel 27, 94
Brooklyn Boys Choir 27, 74
Brooks, Garth 3, 27, 76, 110, 190
Brotherhood 46
Bruce, Jack 28
Bruce Kulick & Bob Kulick: KISS Forever 28
Brutal Planet 40, 175
Budokan Hall 11–12, 28, 71, 81, 89, 118, 160, 209
Buffet, Jimmy 28
"Bulletproof" 125, 145, 149
Bullfrog Bheer 123, 168, 172
"Bump and Grind" 206, 208
Bumping Into Geniuses: My Life Inside the Rock and Roll Business 28, 73
"Burn" 85
"Burn Bitch Burn" 15, 28

"Burning Up with Fever" 20, 28, 69, 83, 185
Bush, George W. 28, 62
Buslowe, Steve 29
"By Myself" 146

"Cadillac Dreams" 29, 81, 83, 156
Cadillac High School 29, 40, 118, 163
"California Burns" 157
"Calling Dr. Love" 11, 19, 21, 26, 29–30, 33, 54–55, 58, 64, 73, 75, 76–78, 81, 86, 96, 103, 108, 110, 114, 117, 121, 138, 151, 159, 160, 162, 165, 168, 175–176, 178–179, 184, 195, 197–198, 200, 209
"Calling to You" 68, 195
Campise, Mick 30, 147
"Can You Feel It" 162
Capitol Theatre 11
Caravello, Paul Charles 30
Carnahan, Michael 30
"Carnival of Souls" 17
Carnival of Souls: A French Tribute to KISS 30
Carnival of Souls: The Final Sessions 30, 36, 47, 78, 84–85, 87, 88, 90, 121, 133, 155, 167, 175
Carr, Eric 3, 6, 8–9, 13, 15–18, 22–23, 26–27, 30–32, 34, 38, 40–41, 43–44, 46, 49, 59–60, 65, 67–69, 72, 80–81, 84–85, 87–89, 91, 93, 99, 109, 114, 124–125, 129–130, 139–140, 143, 147, 149, 151–153, 157, 159–160, 165, 175–176, 179, 183–184, 194, 197–198, 201, 204, **206**, 208, 210
"Carr Jam 1981" 27, 32, 157, 197
Casablanca Launch Party 32
Casablanca Records 10–11, 22, 25, 32–33, 37, 43–44, 51, 54–55, 57, 77, 79, 87, 92, 94, 127, 137, 140–141, 146, 152, 156, 160, 168, 185, 198, 202, 205
The Casablanca Singles 1974–1982 33
caskets **33**, 34
Castle 34
Castro, Peppy 34, 66, 141
Cat #1 34, 44, 47
Cathedral (Ace's early band) 66
Cathedral (Gene's early band) 40, 172
The Catman 1, 6, 10, 15, 20, 34, 44–47, 51, 53, 81, 84, 86, 95, 103, 104, **105**, 130, 137, 146, 149, 153, 161–162, 168, 174–175
"Celebrate I" 129
"Celebrate II" 129
Celebrity Apprentice 34
The Cellarmen 32, 34, 91, 197
"Ceredigon" 18
Chaney, Lon 34, 69, 131, 150
"Change" 178
"Change Is Coming" 19
"Change the World" 15

"Changes" 22
Chapin, Jim 35
"Charisma" 35, 57, 69, 77–78, 86, 131, 154, 159, 174, 178, 185
Charlie LoBue Guitars 35
Chavarria, Paul 35
Cheap Trick 28, 35, 52, 69, 128, 142
Chelsea (album) **35**
Chelsea (band) 35, 46, 90, 125, 149
Cher 20, 25, 32, 35, 36, 69, 87, 91, 97, 98, 122, 126, 149, 163–164, 172, 182, 187, 196, 207
Chikara 36
Child, Desmond 20, 36, 79, 85–86, 88, 93, 124, 141, 154–155, 169, 189, 194, 197, 205, 208
ChildFund International 36, 173
"Childhood's End" 27, 30, 36, 195
"Children" 18
"Christine Sixteen" 11, 19, 21, 26, 33, 36, 73, 75, 77–78, 86, 91, 105, 108, 110–111, 114, 120, 127–128, 156, 163, 178, 195, 198–200
Christine Sixteen: A High- School Tribute to KISS 36
Christine Sixteen 2: Another High-School Tribute to KISS 36
Christopher, Lyn 37, 58, 90, 144, 172
"Chrome Heart" 78
Cicchini, Mark 10, 54
Circus 2, **37**
Citrus College Singers 13, 194
Clapton, Eric 58, 120, 167, 193
Clark, Dave 16
Clark, Dick 13–14, 37, 53, 181
Clarke, Allan 203
Clarke, Arthur C. 36
Clinton, George 14, 25, 32
Clown White 37
Club Tour 37
"C'mon and Love Me" 9, 19, 26, 33, 38, 55–56, 73–75, 85, 86–89, 91, 103, 105–106, 110, 115, 117, 125, 135, 143, 148, 162, 176, 193, 195, 199
Cobain, Kurt 73
Cobo Hall 9, 15, 38, 99, 118
Cochran, Karl 88, 156
Coffee 172
coins 38
Colan, Gene 83
Cold Gin 6–7, 9, 18–19, 21, 26, 38, 55, 64, 68, 73, 75, 77–78, 83, 86, 88–89, 93–94, 99, 103, 105, 110, 115, 126, 156, 179, 195, 206, 209
Colorforms **38**, 124, 164
Comic Book Men 39
Comics Interview 39
"Comin' Home" 27, 39, 82, 91, 103, 114–117, 193, 195
condoms 39
Contessa, Maria 39
Cooley, Alex 39

Cooper, Alice 22, 32, 39–40, 51, 55, 61, 63, 65, 86, 101, 107, 120, 130, 158, 169, 175, 193, 202
Corbett, Gary 43, 81
Cornyn, Stan 40, 61
Coronel, Stephen 40, 72, 92, 123, 144, 146, 155, 168, 172, 205
Cort Guitars 40
Costello, Fin 9, 40
Countdown 40, 118
The Coventry 41, 48, 118, 155, 185
"Crazy Crazy Nights" 19, 21, 27–28, 86, 103, 105, 137, 176, 195, 198, 203
Crazy Magazine **42**
Crazy Nights 17–18, 20, 42–43, 65, 73, 79, 81, 86, 103, 121, 141, 143, 145, 155, 166, 180, 188, 189–190, 194, 204, 207
Crazy Nights World Tour 18, 42
Creation 32, 125
Creatures of the Night (album) 8, 26, 31, 43, 53, 59–60, 67, 78, 84, 86–87, 89, 93, 107–108, 120, 124, 139–140, 151–152, 159, 165, 199–202, 206–207, 210
"Creatures of the Night" (song) 10, 27, 36, 43, 63, 75, 91, 99, 107, 110, 137, 152, 159, 193, 195
Creatures of the Night Tour 43, 114, 125, 198
Creem 2, 40, 44, 57, 76, 80, 130, 132, 197
The Creeps: Beth/Great Expectations 44
Criscuola, Joey 41, 44
Criscuola, Joseph 45
Criscuola, Loretta 45
Criscuola, Peter 5, 34, 44–45
Criss (band) 44, 47, 146
Criss (EP) 34, 44
Criss, Gigi 44, 47
Criss, Jenilee 44, 47, 150
Criss, Lydia 41, 44, **45**, 46–47, 79, 131, 158, 167
Criss, Peter 1–3, 5–6, 8, 10–13, 16, 18–23, 26, 30, 31, 33–4, **35**, 37–42, 44, **45**, 46, 48, 50–53, 55–59, 61, 63, 67–68, 71, 74–77, **78**, 80, 82–85, 87–90, 93–95, 97–99, 102–104, 106, 108, **109**, 112, 114–120, 122, 124–125, 127–130, 132–133, **134**, 136, 139–140, 142–150, 153, 155, 159–160, 162–163, 165–169, 172, 174–176, 181, 184–185, 188, 190, **192**, 193–194, 196, 198–199, 201–202, 204–205, 207, 209–211
Criss-Penridge Alliance 47
Crown of Thorns 47
CSI: Crime Scene Investigation 47
"Cum on Feel the Noize" 176
Cuomo, Bill 47
Cuomo, Curtis 47, 84–85, 87–88, 90, 133, 153, 155
Curly 47

Cusano, AnnMarie 48
Cusano, Diane 48
Cusano, Vincent 48, 124, 200–201
Custom Chevy Van 48, 124

Daily News 48
The Daisy 7, 48
Daltrey, Roger 11, 101, 204
Damon, Jesse 49, 197
Damon, Mark 188
"Dance All Over Your Face" 49, 124, 198
"Dancin' with Danger" 156, 167
Dancing with the Stars 49
"Danger" 33, 43, 49, 78
"Danger Us" 49, 178
Dangerous Toys 158
"Dark Light" 18, 33, 49, 86, 90, 140, 156
Darrell, Dimebag 3, 15, 34, 49, 156, 179
Dave Clark Five 16, 181
Davidson, Joe 49, 146, 155, 172, 205, 210
Davidson, Lenny 16
Dayton, Chip Rock 49, 147, 211
Deathtongue 24
The Decline of Western Civilization Part II: The Metal Years 49
Deep Purple 85, 94
Def Leppard 42, 105, 128, 155, 186, 200
Delaney, Sean 5, 12, 50, 55, 77, 79, 81, 84, 126, 131, 136, 146, 161–162, 186, 204
DeLeo, Robert 13, 50
Delsener, Ron 51
The Demon 1, 8, 13, 21, 28, 34–35, 47, 51, 62, 69, 72, 79, 81, 86, 95–96, 103, **105**, 107, 112–113, 123, 126, 129–131, 133, 136, 148, 155, 165, 167, 170–171, **173**, 179, 182, 188–191, 197, 201, 203–204, 206
Derringer, Rick 51, 60, 67
"Destiny" 124
Destroyer 1, 6, 8, 10–11, 22, 48, 51–52, 54–55, 58, 61, 63, 74, 85, 90, 92–94, 97, 100, 104, 116, 127, 129, 137, 142, 146, 153, 154–155, 160, 177–178, 207
Destroyer: Resurrected 51
Destroyer Tour 11, 51
Detroit Metal City 52
Detroit Rock City (movie) 52, 68, 118, 188, 194, 196
"Detroit Rock City" (song) 10–11, 18–19, 21–22, 26, 33, 36, 51–53, 55–56, 63, 69, 73, 75–78, 83, 86, 88–89, 91, 93, 96, 99, 103–104, 108, 110, 114–115, 117–118, 124, 128, 135, 148–149, 151, 154, 159, 162, 168–169, 175–176, 178–179, 184, 193, 195, 198, 200, 203, 209
Detroit Rock City: Music from the Motion Picture 27, 105

Index

"Deuce" 9–10, 21, 26, 30, 52, 55, 63–64, 66–67, 69, 73, 75, 77, 85–86, 88–89, 94, 96–97, 103–108, 110, 114, 117, 120, 125, 135, 143, 145, 159, 162, 176, 178–179, 190, 193, 195, 198–199, 200, 206
"The Devil Is Me" 52, 53, 137
Dewey, Warren 63
Dick Clark's American Bandstand 50th Anniversary 13, 53, 188
Dickinson, Christopher 150
DiGerlando, Vincent 100
Diggins, Peter 73
DiMarzio Pickups 53
Dinosaur Jr. 53, 110
"Dirty Girl" 23
"Dirty Livin'" 33, 46, 53, 57, 63, 74, 78, 86, 125, 130, 149, 185
"Disco Duck" 149
Distroya! 53
Dixon, Donna 53, 85, 98, 182
"Do Ya" 126, 193
"Do You Love Me?" 26, 51, 53, 55, 65, 73, 75, 77, 86, 97, 103, 105, 110, 114–116, 149, 178
"Do You Remember Rock 'n' Roll Radio" 54, 103, 114, 155
Dr. Hook & the Medicine Show 160
Dr. John
Dr Pepper Cherry 29, 54
"Doesn't Get Better (Than This)" 145
"Dog" 17
"Dogs of Morrison" 19
Dokken 15
"Dolls" 68
"Domino" 10, 27–28, 54, 60, 91, 103, 106–107, 116, 157, 159, 195
Don Kirshner's Rock Concert 54, 118, 183
Donato, David 47
"Doncha Hesitate" 26, 54
"Don't Ever Wanna Lose Ya" 142
"Don't Let the Blues Surround You" 126
Don't Touch Me There 169
"Don't Touch My Ascot" 54
"Don't You Let Me Down" 19, 22, 26, 33, 55, 73, 86, 125, 149, 150
Doret, Michael 145, 160, 177
Doro 55, 187, 197
Dorsey, Tommy 45
Double Platinum 50, 55, 87, 120, 184, 200, 207
"Down on Your Knees" 9, 55, 89, 93, 105
"Down with the Sun" 34
Dracula **24**, 55
"Dreamin'" 55, 90, 153
Dressed to Kill 1, 6, 16, 38, 40, 55–56, 58, 61, 63, 71, 76, 90, 102, 121, 128, 141, 146, 158, 160, 163, 196, 198, 206
Dressed to Kill: An Independent Tribute to KISS **56**

Dressed to Kill Tour 56, 82, 144
Dressed to Thrill: A Tribute to KISS with Female Vocalists 56
Dudes of Wrath 169
Duncan, Robert 21, 57, 63, 72, 78, 94, 158, 163, 184, 211
Durst, Fred 70
Dylan, Bob 17, 28, 51, 57–58, 76, 84, 89, 184
Dynasty 12, 35, 43, 46, 53–54, 57–58, 63, 67, 77, 85, 87, 92, 101, 124, 130, 139–140, 144, 147, 150, 152, 163, 166, 175, 185, 196, 198, 200, 207–208
Dynasty Tour 12, 57, 87, 198

"Easier Said Than Done" 91
"Easy as It Seems" 57, 197–198
"Easy Thing" 58, 77–78, 86, 149–150, 155, 193
"Eat Your Heart Out" 58, 137
The Ed Sullivan Show 21
Eisen, Eva 58, 180
Eisen, Julia 181
Eisen, Stanley 5, 58, 172, 180
Eisen, William 58, 180
Electric Hellfire Club 58
Electric Lady Studios 9, 11, 17, 37, 46, 55, 58, 90, 92, 127, 129, 172
Electric Light Orchestra 193–194
Ellefson, Dave 70
Elliott, Paul 7, 9, 13, 16, 51, 54–55, 57, 60, 64, 71–73, 87, 90, 106, 122, 129, 136–137, 144–145, 186, 202–203, 206, 211
Ellis, Don 59
Emerald Monkey: Heroes of the Night 59
Empire State Building 59, 116, 124, 163
Engelbert Calling 179
Entertainment Weekly 59, 98, 153
The Envy 59
EP Live+1 68
Epic Records 5, 40, 59, 146, 172, 205
Epting, Chris 13
Erebus Pictures 59
The Eric Carr Story 30, **59**, 211
The Eric Singer Project 47, 60, 127, 175
Ermilio, Brett 73
"Escape from the Island" 18, 60, 93, 103, 140
ESP 60, 175
ESP Live at the Marquee 60
ESP Live in Japan 60, 175
The Eternal Idol 24, 174
Evans, Jay 60, 99, 100, 183
"Every Little Bit of Your Heart" 207
"Every Time I Look at You" 27, 60, 116, 125, 157, 202
"Everybody Knows" 17
"Everybody Needs Somebody" 49
Everything KISS 60

"Everytime I See You Around" 149
"The Evolution of KISS" 11, 192
"Exciter" 51, 60, 86, 88, 124, 201
Expecting Mary 60–61
Exploding: The Highs, Hits, Hype, Heroes, and Hustlers of the Warner Music Group 40, 61
The Exterminators 66
Extract 61
Extreme 61, 110
Extreme Makeover: Home Edition 61
The Eyes of Alice Cooper 40, 175
"Eyes of Love" 162
E-Z-O 61
Ezrin, Bob 22, 49, 51, 52–53, 59–62, 64, 72, 74, 78, 84–85, 90, 140, 144, 148, 157, 160, 169, 186, 191, 207

Face the Music: A Life Exposed 51, 53, 58, 61, 104, 121, 133, 151, 165, 180, 183, 201, 211
"Faces in the Crowd" 145
Fairbairn, Bruce 61, 153
"Fallen Angel" 167
"Falling All Over Again" 145
Fallon, Larry 46
Family Guy 61
Famous Monsters of Filmland **62**
Fandango! 11
"Fanfare" 62, 69, 90, 140, 177
Fangoria 62, 150
Fanzines 39, 62–63, 101, 171
Farris, Steve 43, 63
Faster Pussycat 81, 157
"Fate" 23
"Feel Like Letting Go" 147
"Feels Like Heaven" 124
Fig, Anton 15, 49, 57, 63, 68, 85, 126, 130, 157, 166–168, 185–186, 195–196, 206, 208
Fillmore East Press Launch 63
FINAL EXIT: Tribute to KISS Split EP 63
The Final Frontier 91
"Final Mile" 23
"Fire Brigade" 63, 138
"Firehouse" 9, 26, 37, 55, 63, 73, 87–88, 91, 94, 97, 103, 105, 110, 135, 138, 190, 209
"Firestarter" 17, 141
"First Day in the Rain" 124
First KISS 63
First KISS... Last Licks 63
First KISS: My 40-Year Obsession with the Hottest Band in the World 63
"Fits Like a Glove" 64, 99, 124, 138
"Five Card Stud" 193
Five Finger Death Punch 138
"Flaming Youth" 33, 51, 53, 64, 75, 103, 117, 129, 158, 202
FLAMING YOUTH: A Norwegian Tribute To KISS 64
Flasher 31, 32, 194

Index

Fleetwood Mac 110, 115, 168, 179
Fleischman, Robert 27
Foghat 82
Folgers Coffee 64
Fontana, Richie 64
The Foo Fighters 64, 148
Forbes 64, 122
Ford, Lita 64, 110, 174, 182
Ford, Robben 43, 64, 85, 159
Foreigner 158
"Forever" 10, 17, 19, 22–23, 27–28, 57, 60, 64, 75, 81, 86, 105, 107, 116, 124, 142, 155, 159, 178, 195, 198, 200, 203
Foster, Bruce 65, 143
The Four Roses 66, 68
4th and Loud 65
Fowley, Kim 53, 65
The Fox 30, 65, 130, 149, 197, 198
Fox, Brian James 47
Fox, Rik 65
Fox, Samantha 65, 182
"Fox on the Run" 15
Foxworthy, Jeff 17
"Foxy & Free" 15
"Fractured Mirror" 7, 15, 22, 49, 68, 179, 186
"Fractured Quantum" 15
"Fractured Too" 65, 68, 126
"Fractured III" 126, 194
Frame of Mind 65
"Freak" 66, 137, 203
Free 82, 209
Frehley, Ace 1–3, 5–7, **8**, 10–13, 16–17, 19–22, 26–28, 30, 32–34, 38–44, 46–50, 52, 56–57, 59–61, 63–64, 66–67, 69–70, **71**, 74–77, **78**, 79, 82–83, 85, 87–90, 92–95, 97–99, 102–104, 106–108, **109**, 112, 114–117, 120–124, 126–133, 135–137, 139–140, 142–148, 151–154, 156–157, 159–163, 166–169, 172, 174–179, 181, 184–191, **192**, 193, 195–196, 198–200, 202–203, 205–209, 211
Frehley, Carl 66
Frehley, Charley 68, 146
Frehley, Esther 66
Frehley, Jeanette 67–68, 179
Frehley, Monique 68
Frehley, Paul 5, 46, 66–67
Frehley's Comet (album) 20, 27, 68, 88
Frehley's Comet (band) 65, 68, 98, 126, 157, 161, 167, 193, 195
Frehley's Comet: Live... +4 68
French Kissin': Montreal Salutes the Hottest Band in the Land 68
Fridays 69, 118, 140, 207

Gallup Poll 69
Gass, Craig 69
Gebert, Gordon G.G. 74, 98–99, 211
Gene Simmons (album) 28, 69, 167–168, 172, 204

Gene Simmons: A Rock 'N' Roll Journey in the Shadow of the Holocaust 69
Gene Simmons Dominatrix 70, 170
Gene Simmons Family Jewels 52, 70, 80, 119, 170, 173–174, 193, 194
Gene Simmons House of Horrors 70, 170
Gene Simmons Is a Powerful and Attractive Man: And Other Irrefutable Facts 70
Gene Simmons "Meet and Greet" Bass Experience 70
Gene Simmons Rock Camp 70
Gene Simmons Tongue 70
Gene Simmons Zipper 71, 170
"Genghis Khan" 15
Gerber, Steve 71, 83, 101, 132
Gerstein, Richard 71
"Get All You Can Take" 15, 27, 71
"Get Down" 91
"Getaway" 33, 55, 71, 86, 90, 115, 154, 156, 193
Gibson Guitars **71**, 153
Gill, Julian 72, 146, 159
Gillen, Ray 20, 174
"Gimme a Feelin'" 178
"Gimme More" 72, 75, 124
Gin Blossoms 72, 110
"Give It to Me Anyway" 75, 126
GlamNation 77
Glickman, Carl 72, 131, 196
Glickman/Marks Management 72, 123, 131
"Go All the Way" 52
"Go Now" 72
"God Gave Rock and Roll to You" 20, 72, 117
"God Gave Rock 'N' Roll to You II" 10, 20–21, 27, 31, 72, 75, 86, 105–107, 118, 157, 195, 200
"God of Thunder" 11, 26, 30, 33, 51, 53, 55–56, 72–75, 77, 81, 86, 91, 93, 96–97, 103, 105, 107, 110, 114–115, 136, 154–155, 159, 178–179, 191, 193, 197, 200, 209
Gods of Thunder: A Norwegian Tribute to KISS 72
"Goin' Blind" 26, 40, 53, 60, 72–73, 82, 91, 103, 110, 114, 116–117, 120, 127, 135, 139, 184, 193
Going Platinum: KISS, Donna Summer, and How Neil Bogart Built Casablanca Records 73
Gold 73
Goldberg, Danny 28, 73
"Golden Age of Rock and Roll" 189
Golden Earring 56, 82
Goldmine KISS Collectibles Price Guide 73
Goldmine Magazine 41
Gooch, Curt 14, 33, 41, 97, 211
"Good Company" 35
"Good Girl Gone Bad" 42, 73
Good Morning America 74
"Good Times" 34, 44

"Goodbye" 28, 33, 74, 148–149
Goodman, Benny 45
Gordon, Rachael 66, 74
"Got Love for Sale" 74, 78, 91, 127, 199
"Got to Choose" 9, 27, 73–74, 82, 91, 108, 110, 114–116, 149, 154, 195, 199
Got to Foo: A SAGAFOO.COM Tribute to KISS 74
"Grace" 35
Grammy Awards 12, 40, 74
Grand Funk Railroad 10, 74, 121
The Grateful Dead 3, 132, 159, 166, 181
"Great Expectations" 26–27, 44, 51, 53, 75, 114, 142, 160
The Great Kiss Off 75, 78, 117, 136, 190
Great White 42, 125, 157
Greatest Hits Live 75
Greatest KISS 27, 75
Greco, Joey 45, 46
Greektures of the Night: A Greek Tribute to KISS 75
"The Green Manalishi (with the Two Prong Crown)" 179
Grítalo Fuerte: Tributo a KISS 75
Gruen, Bob 7, 56, 75–76
Guardian of the Gods: An Inside Look at the Dangerous Business of Music 76
Guitar Hero: Warriors of Rock 76
Guitar Player **196**
Guitar World 76, 173, 184, 199
Guitar World Presents KISS 76
Gulliver's Travels 76
Guns N' Roses 158
Gunston, Norman 87
Gypsy Rose 174

Hagar, Sammy 138, 160
Halligan, Bob, Jr. 155, 157
Halloween costumes **76**
Hamersveld, John Van 82
"Hand of the King" 23
Happy Days 201
"Hard Luck Woman" 11, 19, 21, 26–27, 33, 54–55, 57, 73, 75–76, 86, 89, 91, 105, 110, 115–117, 160, 162, 168, 175, 179, 184, 190, 193, 195, 200, 203, 207
Hard Rock Comics 77, 112, 161
"Hard Rock Music" 35
"Hard Times" 33, 57, 69, 86, 91, 185
Hard to Believe: KISS Covers Compilation 53, 77
Harkin, Brendan 77
Harper, Tom 77, 168
Harris, Doyle 77, 157
Harris, Larry 14, 23, 32–33, 37, 44, 77, 79
Hartman, Lisa 78, 182
Haslip, Jimmy 49, 77
"Hate" 30, 78, 195

Index

"Have Love, Will Travel" 78, 127, 199
Hayseed Dixie—Kiss My Grass: A Hillbilly Tribute to KISS 78
"He Hit Me (It Felt Like a Kiss)" 129
Headliners: KISS **78**, 176, 211
Hear 'n Aid 79
Heart 158
"Heart Behind these Hands" 145
"Heart of Chrome" 78, 157, 201
Heat 201
Heath, Louise 75, 78, 136, 190
"Heaven's on Fire" 10, 15, 21, 27, 36, 78–79, 84, 86, 97, 99, 104–105, 107, 114–115, 125, 148, 165, 175–176, 178, 195
"Heavy Metal Baby" 162
Hefner, Hugh 70, 79, 151, 194
Helix 42
"Hell or Hallelujah" 21–22, 74, 79, 105, 108, 137, 151
"Hell or High Water" 27, 42, 79
Hellbox 79
Hello 7
Hendrix, Jimi 58, 67, 87, 102, 110, 120, 179, 181
Henry LeTang School of Dance 25, 50, 77, 79
Hessler, Gordon 109
Heston, Gary 87
Hide Your Heart (album) 79
"Hide Your Heart" (song) 17, 27, 36, 75, 79, 81, 86, 116, 145, 149, 177, 193–195, 198, 203
Hilsen, Jesse 79
Hit 'N Run Mini Tour 80, 158
Hit Parader 2, **80**, 130
Hitchcock, Alfred 84
The Hitchhiker 80, 109
The Hitchhikers 201
"Hold Me, Touch Me (Think of Me When We're Apart)" 22, 33, 80, 91, 105, 128, 148–149
The Hollies 169, 203
Hollywood RockWalk 80, 109
Hollywood Walk of Fame 80, 109
Holmes, Cecil 32
Honey 66
"Hooked on Rock 'n' Roll" 19, 22, 30, 33, 80, 125, 129, 149, 150, 193
"Hooligan" 33, 80, 86, 110, 127, 149
"Hope" 145
"Hot and Cold" 81, 178
Hot in the Shade 9, 17, 22, 26–27, 29, 31, 64, 79, 81, 93, 121, 125, 129, 152, 155–157, 160, 169, 177, 184, 194, 208
Hot in the Shade Tour 43, 81, 157
HOT LICKS—Bruce Kulick of KISS: Rock Guitar Masterclass 81
The Hotel Diplomat 18, 27, 81–82, 144, 151, 184
Hotter Than Hell (album) 1, 6, 9, 13, 39, 63, 71–74, 82, 92, 102, 123, 130, 146, 148, 168, 184, 206

"Hotter Than Hell" (song) 19, 26, 33, 55–56, 69, 75, 82, 85–86, 96, 107, 115, 157, 178, 190, 195, 199
Hotter Than Hell Tour 82, 115
Hotter Than Hotter Than Hell: A Tribute to KISS 82
The Hottest Show on Earth Tour 82, 178
Houdini 73, 135
"Hound Dog" 45
House of Lords 173
How to Rock Fans & Influence People: An Australian Tribute to KISS 83
The Howard Stern Show 69
Howard the Duck 71, **83**, 123
Howarth, Tod 27, 68, 126, 156, 157
Howell, John Shane 83
Humperdinck, Engelbert 179
The Hunchback of Notre Dame 34
Hunter 201

"I" 18, 69, 90, 110, 140, 144, 166, 175, 177
"I Am a Legend Tonight" 75
"I Can't Stop the Rain" 22, 74, 84, 86, 90, 150, 155
"I Can't Take" 19
"I Confess" 30, 84
"I Don't Mind" 19
"I Don't Need No Doctor" 188
"I Don't Think I Love You" 154
"I Finally Found My Way" 21, 84, 86, 153
"I Found Love" 146
"I Got the Touch" 84, 205–206
"I Just Wanna" 10, 84, 107, 110, 116, 157, 201
"I Know Who You Are" 84, 128
"I Love It Loud" 10, 27, 33, 36, 43, 60, 67, 75, 78, 84, 86, 88, 97, 99, 104–108, 110, 118, 124–125, 131, 154, 159, 175–176, 178, 193, 195, 197, 200, 208
"I Love Sex (and Rock and Roll)" 208
"I Pledge Allegiance to the State of Rock & Roll" 27, 84, 119, 153, 195–196
"I Still Love You" 10, 27, 43, 53, 64, 84–85, 88, 99, 110, 116, 148–149, 155
"I Stole Your Love" 11, 26, 73, 75, 85, 103–104, 106, 115, 117, 120, 125, 127, 154, 159, 179, 193, 200, 209
"I Walk Alone" 30, 85
"I Wanna Hold You" 178
"I Wanna Shout" 203
"I Want You" 11, 26, 54–56, 73, 77–78, 85, 90, 103, 115, 117, 149, 159–160, 179, 193, 200
"I Was Made for Lovin' You" 6, 10, 19, 21, 23, 26, 33, 36, 54, 56–57, 64, 69, 73, 75, 83, 85–86, 88–89, 93, 101, 103, 105–106, 114–115,

117, 148, 151, 159, 162, 175–178, 184–185, 195, 200, 203
"I Was There" Button 85
"I Will Be There" 27, 85, 195
"I Will Be with You (Where the Lost Ones Go)" 85
Ian, Scott 16, 70, 179
Icon: KISS 85–86, 195
Icon 2: KISS 86
"I'd Like to Teach the World to Sing" 203
"If I Had a Gun" 17
Iggy & the Stooges 7, 27, 56, 86, 115
IKONS 86
"I'll Fight Hell to Hold You" 42, 86, 103, 137
"I'll Survive" 23
"I'm a Legend Tonight" 21, 73, 86, 90, 93, 103
I'm a Legend Tonight: An Italian Tribute to Eric Carr 86
"I'm Alive" 17, 86–87, 128
"I'm an Animal" 87, 178
"I'm Gonna Love You" 87, 125, 149–150, 161
"I'm in Need of Love" 7, 87, 123
"I'm So Lonely" 34
"I'm the Animal" 23
"Immortal Pleasures" 178
In Concert 37, 54, 87, 117–118
In Deep 72
In Heat 24, 61
"In My Head" 30, 87
"In the Darkness" 206
"In the Mirror" 30, 87
"In Trouble Again" 146
"In Your Face" 153
Incarnate 170, 173
Incubus 181
Infinity 46, 203
The Inner Sanctum 87, 208
"Insane" 68, 126, 167, 195
Inside the Casbah: A History of Casablanca Records and Filmworks 87
Inside the Tale of the Fox: The Eric Carr Story 87
"Inside the Vortex" 178
"Into the Night" 20, 68, 88, 126, 195
"Into the Void" 27, 86, 88, 90, 97, 153, 195, 199
Into the Void… with Ace Frehley 88, 147
Iron Maiden 43, 138, 197, 198
"Is That You?" 77, 83, 88, 134, 197, 198
The Island Years 148
"It Never Goes Away" 30, 88
Italians Kiss Better: An Italian Tribute to KISS 88
"It's a Great Life" 15
"It's Alright" 22, 88, 148
"It's My Life" 27, 93, 208
"It's Not Me" 125

"It's Over Now" 68, 126, 167
"I've Had Enough (Into the Fire)" 15, 88

J. Geils Band 52
The Jackie Gleason Show 45
Jackson, Michael James 43, 59, 89, 93
Jagger, Mick 61, 196, 208
The James Gang 56, 89, 115
Jane 47
Jane's Addiction 17
Japp, Mikel 9, 55, 89, 138, 165, 186
Jason, Neil 69, 89, 194
Jay and Silent Bob 39
"Jealous Guy" 124
Jendel 2, 89, 184
Jensen, Debra 44, 47, 89, 150
The Jewish Mother's Hall of Fame 89
Jigoku No Shosan: KISS Tribute in Japan 89
Jigoku-Retsuden 89
Joanie Loves Chachi 201
Joey Greco and the In Crowd 45
Johnsen, Ron 37, 90, 205
Johnson, Caleb 13
"The Joker" 178
Jones, John Paul 122, 154
Journey 39, 90, 132
"Journey of 1,000 Years" 21, 90, 153
"Jungle" 28, 30, 60, 90–91, 105, 203
"Just a Boy" 18, 62, 90, 140, 145, 177
"Just Can't Wait" 162
Just 4 Fun Tour 7
"Just Like a Woman" 184
"Just Once" 18
"Juvenile Delinquent" 167

Kansas 52
KAOL: A World Without Heroes 90
KAOL: Music from the Folder '99: A Tribute to KISS 90
KAOL: Music from the Folder '99: A Tribute to KISS (Remaster) 91
KAOL 2: Creatures of the Net 91
Katsaros, Doug 91
Kaye, Carol 91
Keel 91, 158
Keel, Ron 124, 159
The Keep 47, 166
"Keep Me Comin'" 43, 91
"Keep Me Waiting" 26, 37, 91, 146, 205, 206
Kelly, Ken 51, 92, 117, 127, 178
Kelly, Larry 92, 157
Kelly, Sue 92, 157
Kerner, Kenny 79, 82, 92, 94, 117, 206
Kerrang! 92
Kids Are People Too 30, 93
"Killer" 43, 93, 110
Killers 55, 67, 86, 89, 93, 119–120, 144, 148

"The Kind of Sugar Papa Likes" 125
King Kobra 18, 93, 187
King Kong (band) 66
"King of Hearts" 81, 93
King of the Hill 93
"King of the Mountain" 17, 81, 86, 93
"King of the Night Time World" 11, 26, 51, 53, 56, 65, 73, 75, 93–94, 110, 114, 117, 148, 154, 179, 190, 193
King's Lounge 94
Kings of the Night Time World, 1972–82 72
The Kinks 181, 184
Kinnaird, Bryan 79
Kirby, Jack 39
Kirshner, Don 54, 87
KISS (album) 1, 52, 63, 65, 92, 94, 102, 106, 117, 123, 141, 146, 176, 183, 206
KISS (book) 21, 57, 63, 72, 78, **94**, 95, 158, 163, 184, 211
KISS (Dark Horse comic book) 95
KISS (IDW comic book) 95
KISS (pinball machine) 95, **96**
The KISS Album Focus, Vol. I: Kings of the Night Time World, 1972–1982 72, 159
The KISS Album Focus, Vol. II: Hell or High Water, 1983–1996 72, 159
The KISS Album Focus, Vol. III: Roar of Grease Paint, 1997–2006 72, 159
The KISS Album Focus, Vol. 4: Never Enough, 2006–2013 72
KISS Alive Forever: The Complete Touring History 41, 97, 211
KISS Alive! 1975–2000 10, 97
KISS Alive! 1998–2008 72
KISS Alive 35 World Tour 97, 105, 118
KISS and Make-Up 67, 97, 136, 139, 171–172, 211
The KISS & Related Recordings Focus: Music! The Songs, the Demos, the Lyrics, and Stories! 72, 159
KISS and Sell: The Making of a Supergroup 72, 98, 123, 131, 211
KISS & Tell (McAdams book) 74, 98–99, 133, 211
KISS and Tell (Tweed book) 79, 194
KISS & Tell More! 99
KISS: Animalize Live Uncensored 15, 38, **99**, 139
KISS Army 3, 6, 55, 60, 72, 92, 96, 99–101, 103–104, 127, 132, 136, 146, 167, 172, 183, 198
KISS Army Brasil: An MP3 Tribute to KISS Vol. 1 101
KISS Army Brasil: An MP3 Tribute to KISS Vol. 2 101

KISS Army Brasil: An MP3 Tribute to KISS Vol. 3 101
KISS Army Norway Magazine 39
KISS Army OnLine 90, 91
KISS Army Worldwide!: The Ultimate Fanzine Phenomenon 101, 211
KISS Asylum 101
KISS: Asylum of Death—Interviews 101
KISS: Behind the Mask—The Official Authorized Biography 10, 13, 22–24, 30, 35–36, 42–46, 52, 71, 81–82, 94, 101, 120–121, 123, 127, 140, 176, 186, 198, 201, 203–205, 209, 211
KISS by Monster Mini Golf 102
KISS: Cat Tales 102
KISS Chronicles: 3 Classic Albums 102
KISS Coffeehouse 102
KISS Collectibles: Identification and Price Guide 102, 211
KISS Conventions 48, 107–108, 187, 207
KISS Cover to Cover 102
KISS Covered in Scandinavia 103
KISS: Crazy Nights 103
KISS Deutschland: A Tribute To KISS 103
KISS Documented Volume One: Great Expectations 1970–1977 103
KISS DVD Board Game **103**
KISS Encyclopedia 104
KISS: Exposed 104
KISS FAQ: All That's Left to Know About the Hottest Band in the Land 10–11, 18, 30, 32, 43, 50, 63, 72, 81, 97, 99, 101, 104, 127, 170, 172, 174, 183, 205, 210
KISS Farewell Tour 68, 92, 104, 175, 207
The KISS 40th Anniversary World Tour 105, 138
KISS 40 105, 156
KISS 4K **105**, 191
KISS Friends Project 106
KISS: Hell's Guardians—Interviews 106
KISS: Hotter Than Hell 7, 9, 13, 16, 23, 51, 54–55, 57, 60, 64, 71, 73, 87, 90, 106, 122, 129, 136–137, 144–145, 186, 202–203, 206, 211
KISS: Immortals 106
KISS in Attack of the Phantoms 107, 118
KISS Instant Live 105, 162
KISS: Interviews 107
KISS—Invasion (A Look at the Lost Egyptian God, Vinnie Vincent) 107
KISS Kids 107
KISS Kollector 40
KISS Kondoms 39
KISS Konfidential 39, 107

Index

KISS—Konfidential & Xtreme Close Up 107, 116
KISS: Krazy Killer 107
KISS Kruise 92
KISS Live! 108
KISS: Live on Letterman 108
KISS Live: The Ultimate Halloween Party 108, 153
KISS Loves You 108
KISS Meets the Phantom 108, **109**
KISS Meets the Phantom of the Park 2, 6, 50, 57, 82, 89, 91, 95, 104, 107–109, 133, 157, 207
KISS "Meets the Press" 109
The KISS Monster World Tour: Live from Europe 138
KISS MY ANKH: A Tribute to Vinnie Vincent **109**, 201
Kiss My Ass: Classic KISS Regrooved 16, 27, 53, 61, 72, 76, 110, 120, 123, 134–135, 139, 168, 189–190, 207, 208
KISS My Ass: The Video 110
KISS My Ass Tour 110, 157
"KISS My Stash" 39
KISS of Death 110
KISS of Death: A SSIK Tribute to KISS 110
KISS of Death—A Tribute to KISS 110
KISS on Tour Game **111**, 124
KISS Online 111
KISS Phono 155, **156**
KISS Pinball **111**
KISS Pre-History 111–112
KISS Psycho Circus (comic book) 95, 106, 112
KISS: Psycho Circus Comic Magazine 112
KISS Psycho Circus: The Nightmare Child 112
KISS: Psycho Circus Tour Magazine 112
KISS Radio 154
KISS Records 112, 177
KISS: Revenge Is Sweet **112**
KISS: Rock the Nation Live! 162, 188
KISS Satan's Music 113
KISS School of Marketing: 11 Lessons I Learned While Working with KISS 113
KISS 7" Vinyl Guide 113
KISS Solo 113
KISS: Still on Fire 113, 211
KISS Symphony: Alive IV 54, 97, 105, 114, 166, 188
KISS Symphony: The DVD 114, 188
KISS, The Auction 114
KISS: The Early Years 7, 114, 211
"Kiss the Girl Goodbye" 114, 150
KISS—The Hottest Band in the Land 114
KISS—The Medley: A Dance Orgasm 114

KISS: The Official Story 115
KISS: The Real Story, Authorized 115, 189, 211
KISS—The Second Coming 115, 188
Kiss This: A Main Man Records Tribute to KISS 115
KISS Tour 38, 115
KISS Trivia Challenge 115
KISS Uncovered 103
KISS Unmasking 5
KISS Unplugged 12, 28, 39, 47, 105, 116, 121, 187, 195, 207
KISS (Virgin Modern Icons) 116
KISS: X-treme Close-Up 107, 116
The KISS Years **116**, 124, 211
KISS Your Face Makeup Kit 117
KISSaholics 50
KISSED BY KISS 117
KISSer **62**
KISSES 117
"Kissin' Time" 33, 91, 94, 102, 117, 168
Kissin' Time: A Tribute to KISS 117
KISSIN' TIME: Canada's Tribute to KISS 117
KISSNation 117
KISSology—The Ultimate KISS Collection, Vol. 1: 1974–1977 29, 118
KISSology—The Ultimate KISS Collection, Vol. 2: 1978–1991 107, 109, 118
KISSology—The Ultimate KISS Collection, Vol. 3: 1992–2000 105, 118, 122, 196
KISS-OPOLY 118
KISSteria 118
KISStory 97, 101, 110, 119, 147, 187, 211
KISStory II: Toys, Games and Girls 119, 211
Kisstory Science Theatre 119
Kitts, Jeff 26, 119
Klein, Flora 69, 89, 97, 170–171
Klein, Gene 66, 119, 172, 206
Knight, Holly 84, 119, 168, 194
Knights in Satan's Service 2, 22, 91, 119, 152
Kobra and the Lotus 174
Kommander of Kaos 206
Korn 12
Kramer, Barry 44, 120
Kramer, Eddie 7, 9, 10–11, 36, 58, 68, 81, 85, 92, 120, 127, 157, 160, 172, 193, 205–206
Krampf, Craig 120
Kravitz, Lenny 3, 14, 101, 110, 120, 207
Krokus 15
KROQ 4th Annual Weenie Roast 12, 118, 120
Krupa, Gene 45, 120
Kulick, Bob 6, 12, 17, 67, 87, 93, 120–121, 138, 141, 149, 162, 179, 188, 210
Kulick, Bruce 3, 6, 10, 15–20, 22–

24, 26, 30–31, 36, 43, 55, 59–60, 64, 73–74, 78–79, 81, 85–88, 90–91, 93, 99, 101, 107, 110, 116, 119, 121, 125–126, 133–134, 139, 143, 149, 152–155, 157, 159–160, 162, 165–166, 169, 175, 177, 182, 190–194, 197, 201, 204

L.A. Guns 156, 158
LA KISS 65, 134, 186
Lacey, Steve 121
"Ladies in Waiting" 26, 55, 121, 206
Ladies of the Night: A Historical and Personal Perspective on the Oldest Profession in the World 121
"Ladies Room" 11, 56, 86, 104, 121, 160
Lambert, Adam 13
Land of Hype and Glory 118, 122
LaPiere, Georganne 122
"Larger Than Life" 11–12, 26, 28, 86, 91, 117, 120, 122
Las Vegas Residency 122
"Last Chance" 122, 137
The Last KISS 64, 105, 118, 122, 188
"Last Night" 145
Late Show with David Letterman 122
Leaf, David 101, 211
Led Zeppelin 7, 58, 69, 73, 79, 87, 91, 120, 122–123, 131, 151, 154, 178, 179
Lee, Christopher **24**
Lee, Jake E. 20, 174
Lee, Stan 39, 101, 117, 123
Lee, Tommy 70, 200
Lee, Will 123
Leejak, Ron 40, 92, 123, 172, 205
"Leeta" 26, 123, 172
LeGaspi, Larry 40
"Legends Never Die" 93, 206, 208
Leialoha, Steve 83
The Lemonheads 110, 123
Lendt, C.K. 98, 123, 211
Lennon, John 58, 69, 76, 124, 155
Leno, Jay 209
Les Paul (guitar) 49, 67, 71, 153, 176
Let It Be 156
"Let It Go" 124
"Let Me Go, Rock 'n' Roll" 9, 26, 33, 55, 73, 82–83, 88, 97, 105, 107–108, 111, 114–115, 117, 123, 153, 154, 209
"Let Me Know" 26, 74, 75, 91, 94, 123, 185, 209
Let Me Rock You (album) 20, 34, 47, 124, 152, 201
"Let Me Rock You" (song) 20, 124
"Let's Call it a Day" 35
"Let's Put the X in Sex" 27, 36, 78, 105, 124–125, 158, 176, 199, 208
Letterman, David 15, 122, 126, 157, 168, 195

Levine, Barry 38, 52, 59, 93, 116, 124, 129, 154, 170, 179, 191, 211
"Liar" 19, 157
Lick It Up (album) 14–15, 40, 43, 49, 60, 64, 72, 88–89, 124, 130, 135–136, 139, 143, 200–201, 206–207, 209
"Lick It Up" (song) 10, 13, 18–19, 21, 27, 36, 77–78, 86, 88, 96–97, 99, 104–105, 107–108, 110, 114, 117, 120, 124, 138, 149, 151, 159, 175–176, 178, 195, 198–200
Lick It Up—A Millennium Tribute to KISS 124
Lick It Up World Tour 44, 125
"Life" 23
"Life in the Woods" 125
"Lift" 125, 149
Lightning 32, 125
Lightning Strikes Twice 79
Lillian Axe 158
Linet, Lew 125, 205
Lips 19, 46, 125, 149
"A Little Below the Angels" 15, 68
"Little Caesar" 9, 81, 95
Little Feat 11
A Live History of Gluttony and Lust 135
Live on Letterman 108
Live+1 68, 126
Live+4 126
Live to Win (album) 125–126, 182, 210
"Live to Win" (song) 125, 145, 148, 149, 178
Live to Win—A Casual Guide to the Music of KISS Frontman Paul Stanley 126
"Living in Sin" 22, 69, 84, 126, 135, 168
Loaded Deck 75, 126
The Loft 13, 59, 66–67, 126, 151, 177, 205
"Lonely Is the Hunter" 15, 121, 126
The Long Island Sounds 40, 172
"Long, Long Road" 126, 146
"Long River" 35
"Long Way Down" 127, 137
Los Angeles Forum 11
Los Angeles Philharmonic Orchestra 204
"Loser in a Fight" 167
Lost and Spaced 60, 127, 175
"Lost in Limbo" 193
Lost in Space Part I 19
Lost in Space Part II 19
The Love Bag 40, 172
"Love 'Em and Leave 'Em" 54, 81, 86, 116, 127, 160, 185
Love Gun (album) 1, 6, 8–9, 11, 13, 21, 36, 38, 48, 67, 74, 80, 85, 87, 90–92, 116, 120, 127–129, 137, 146, 151, 154, 156, 158, 169, 177–178, 188–189, 199, 207
"Love Gun" (song) 11, 14, 26, 33, 36, 55–56, 63–64, 73, 75–78, 83, 86, 88, 91, 93, 96–97, 99, 103, 106, 110, 114, 117, 127–128, 134, 148–149, 151, 154, 159, 162, 176, 178–179, 184, 191, 193, 195, 198, 200, 203
Love Gun: Deluxe Edition 84, 127, 139, 156
Love Gun Tour 85, 128, 160
"Love Her All I Can" 16, 26, 55, 57, 81, 114–115, 128, 146, 154, 156, 205
Love Hurts 207
"Love in Chains" 121, 128, 149
"Love Is Blind" 26
"Love Kills" 110, 201
"Love Me Right" 68
"Love Theme from KISS" 7, 33, 94, 135, 143
"Love Thing" 135
"Love's a Deadly Weapon" 17, 128
"Love's a Slap in the Face" 63, 81, 128
"Loving You Without You Now" 125
Lucenti, Joey 46
Ludwig Drums 129, 149, 210
Lukather, Steve 129, 187
lunch box **129**, 155
Lyn Christopher (album) 129
Lynch, George 21
Lynn, Jeff 193
Lynx 171

Macy's Thanksgiving Day Parade 129
MAD 42, 129
"Mad Dog" 26, 129, 162
Madison Square Garden 12, 19, 39, 94, 118, 129, 160
MADtv 130
Maelen, Jimmy 13
Magic Bullet Theory 130, 166
MAGIC—KISS Kronicles 1973 to 1983 130
The Magic People 66
"Magic Touch" 57, 130, 149, 185
Maher, Bill 70
Makeup to Breakup: My Life In and Out of KISS 34, 44, 46–47, 50, 84, 89, 109, 129, 130, 145, 168, 211
"Makin' Love" 11, 55, 69, 73, 75, 77, 110, 115, 117, 131, 138, 160, 200, 209
Mallet, David 17
"Mama Weer All Crazee Now" 176
"Man of 1,000 Faces" 34, 69, 78, 131
"Mañana" 28
Manfred Mann's Earth Band 115, 131
Mann, Barry 190
The Mansion 7
Mark St. John Project 131, 166

Marks, Howard 35, 72, 100, 126, 131
Mars Attacks KISS **131**
Marsh, Dave 132, 159
Marshall Amps 37, 66, 132
The Marshall Tucker Band 56
"Martya's Prayer" 18
Marvel Comics 42, 50, 71, 109, 123, 132
Marvel Comics Super Special 71, 102, 106, 122–123, 127, **132**, 133, 163
Marzullo, Tom 133
"Master & Slave" 30, 85, 90–91, 133, 198
May, Brian 175
Mazer, Larry 133
McAdams, Bob 41, 66, 99, 133, 211
McCartney, Paul 69, 133, 137, 199
McFarlane, Todd 8, 70
McFarlane Toys **8**
McGhee, Doc 119, 133–134
McGurl, Mike 134
McMahon, Gerard 88, 134
Me, Inc.: Build an Army of One, Unleash Your Inner Rock God, Win in Life and Business 134
Megadeth 42, 134, 184
Mego dolls 8–9, **134**
Melbourne Symphony Orchestra 114, 166, 188
The Melvins 12, 73, 77, 135, 193
"Memories" 145
Mending Kids International 135
Menefee, Pete 40
Mensinger, Eric 135, 174
Mercury Records 10, 15, 17, 28, 32, 42, 51, 63, 73, 75, 86, 135, 152–153, 157, 169, 176, 199, 209
Merlis, Bob 135
Metal Edge 135
Metal Hammer Golden Gods 135
Metalhead to Head 135
Metallica 30
Meyrowitz, Wally 135
Miami Vice 135
The Micro Organism 68
The Midnight Special 2, 118, 135
Mieses, Stan 135
The Mighty Mighty Bosstones 110, 135
The Mike Douglas Show 101, 117–118, 135
"Miles Away, Worlds Apart" 18
Millennium 136
Miller, Alan 136
Miller, Glenn 45
"A Million to One" 90, 110, 124, 136, 145, 148–149
Minnelli, Liza 133, 136
The Missing Links 171
"Mississippi Queen" 203
"Mr. Blackwell" 18, 90, 136, 140, 156
"Mr. Make Believe" 19–22, 69, 107, 136

Index

"Mr. Speed" 26, 33, 91, 106, 136, 160
Mitchell, Adam 42–43, 49, 86, 91, 137, 148, 162, 169, 197, 200, 204
"Modern Day Delilah" 21, 38, 83, 97, 105, 122, 137, 178
Molimo 66, 137
"Molly" 146
Molly Hatchet 44, 79
Momoiro Clover Z 166, 210
Monster (album) 13, 19, 23, 52, 58, 66, 74, 79, 112, 122, 127, 137–138, 147, 169, 175, 186, 188, 198, 202–203, 205
Monster (book) 137
"Monster Island" 19
Monster: The Gene Simmons Boxed Set 138
Monster World Tour 138, 191
Monsters of Rock 42–43, 110
Montrose 11, 52, 56, 138
The Moody Blues 38
Moore, Wendy 88, 147
Morello, Tom 138, 168
Mostyn, Patti 87
Mother Nature/Father Time 32, 125
Mötley Crüe 44, 133, 138, 175, 191, 210
Motörhead 179
Motorpsycho 138
Mott the Hoople 138, 189
Mountain 203
The Move 63, 138, 193
"Move On" 22, 57, 78, 89, 110, 138, 148–149
"Move On Over" 124
MTV 5, 15, 17, 26–28, 31, 39–40, 85, 106, 115–116, 118, 126, 130, 139, 168, 185–187, 207–208
MTV Saturday Night Concerts: KISS Animalize Live 139
MTV Special: KISS Unmasking 40, 118, 130, 139
MTV Unplugged 27, 85, 115–116, 118, 168, 185
MTV Video Music Awards 31, 139
MTV's Most Wanted 139
"Much Too Soon" 127, 139
The Muff Divers 66
Munroe, Rick 139, 147
Munson, Art 139
"Murder in High Heels" 15, 121, 139
Muscular Dystrophy Association 139–140
Music from "The Elder" 6, 13, 18, 27, 30, 36, 43, 49, 55, 60–61, 67, 69, 84, 86, 90–91, 93, 112, 116, 136, 140, 144–145, 152, 156, 177, 185, 195, 197, 207
My Dad the Rock Star 141
My First Mister 141
"My Generation" 84
"My Life" 147
"My Way" 42, 141

"Naked City" 33, 73, 75, 91, 141, 197–198, 203

"Nasty Boys" 162
Nasty Nasty (album) 24
"Nasty Nasty" (song) 54
Nathan, Marc 141
Navarro, Dave 17, 141
Nazareth 25, 56, 115, 141
Neaves, Lee 9, 141, 156
Nebbish, Irving 42
"Need Me" 19
Neff, Jim 29
Nelson, Eric 141
"Never Enough" 141, 178
Never Too Young to Die 142
Nevison, Ron 42, 59
New England 142
The New Guy 142
"New Kind of Lover" 167
New York Dolls 41, 54, 130, 142
"New York Groove" 7, 19, 22, 26, 33, 57, 73, 75, 77, 86, 88, 102, 105, 107, 114, 117, 123, 125–126, 142, 151, 157, 179, 184, 200, 209
New York Philharmonic Orchestra 22, 142, 204
Newman, Randy 142
Nickelback 154
Nielson, Rick 69, 142–143
Night Flight 107
Night of the Fox: The ERIC CARR Tribute Concert 143
Night Ranger 44
"Nightmare" 162
A Nightmare on Elm Street 4: The Dream Master 201
"Ninety-Nine and a Half (Won't Do)" 74
Nirvana 30, 64, 73, 77, 85, 159
A No Balls Records Tribute to KISS 143
"No Friend of Mine" 23
"No, No, No" 42, 143
"No One to Blame" 59
No Regrets: A Rock 'n' Roll Memoir 66, 68, 143, 179, 211
Nolan, Jerry 142
Norton, Mark 143, 165
Norton, Michael 47
"Not for the Innocent" 103, 124, 143, 209
"Nothin' to Lose" 9, 18, 26–27, 33, 37, 60, 65, 67, 72–73, 75, 87, 89–90, 94, 105, 107, 114–116, 143–144, 151, 183, 207, 209
Nothin' to Lose: The Making of KISS (1972–1975) 18, 25, 32, 39, 41, 48, 94, 126, 143, 184–185, 208
"Nothing Can Keep Me from You" 27, 105, 144, 196
"Now That You're Gone" 17
"Nowhere to Run" 27–28, 63, 73, 93, 144
Nugent, Ted 16, 29, 52, 56, 101, 144, 162
"Number One" 93
Nyro, Laura 201

"The Oath" 18, 27, 69, 75, 90, 110, 117–118, 125, 140, 144, 148
Obama, Barack 144, 163
O'Brien, Conan 12
"Odyssey" 90, 140, 144, 166
The Official® Price Guide to KISS Collectibles 145, 211
Oldaker, Jamie 68, 167
Olympic Winter Games 145, 188
One for All (album) 145
"One for All" (song) 145
"100,000 Years" 9, 18, 26, 33, 55, 66, 86, 88, 91, 94, 97, 107, 117, 145, 153, 178, 203
One Life Music—A Tribute to Paul Stanley 145
"One Plus One" 75, 126
"1,000 Dreams" 17
"The One You Run To" 18
"Only Women Bleed" 22, 202
"Only You" 18, 90, 140, 145, 193
"Open My Eyes" 128
"Ophelia" 35
The Oprah Winfrey Show 145
Oreckinto, Peter "Moose" 145, 147
The Original Wicked Lester Sessions 146, 205
The Originals 63, 102, 146, 207
The Originals II 146
Osbourne, Ozzy 16, 20, 42, 50, 101, 174, 193
Ostrander, Brooke 92, 146, 155, 168, 172, 205
The Other Side of the Coin 72, **146**
Out of Control (album) 34, 47, 124, 146, 149, 168, 190
"Out of Control" (song) 147
Out of the Void 88, 147
Out on the Streets—The True Tales of Life on the Road with the Hottest Band in the Land—KISS! 30, 139, 145, 147, 176
"Outer Space" 15
"Outta This World" 137, 147, 188
Outtakes 49, **147**, 211
Oz 147
Ozma 135
"Ozone" 7, 64, 123, 148, 203

Pacific University Legends Golf Classic, Hosted by Tommy Thayer 148, 188
PACO STANLEY: A Tribute to Starchild 148
Page, Jimmy 122, 153–154, 160
"Pain in the Neck" 15
"Pair of Dice" 19
Palisades Free Library 148
Pantera 15, 34, 52
"Paralyzed" 148, 157
"Parasite" 7, 9, 16, 18, 26, 56, 64, 66, 77, 82, 86, 89–91, 103, 110, 114–115, 120, 125, 148, 154, 179, 193, 209
Parenteau, Mark 148

Index

Parliament Funkadelic 14, 25, 32, 87
"Partners in Crime" 63, 93, 148
"Past the Milky Way" 178
The Paul Lynde Halloween Special 6, 118, 148
Paul Stanley (album) 7, 9, 80, 88, 120, 125, 138, 148, 186
Paul Stanley: One Live KISS 149
Pearl Drums 149
Pecorino, Joe 13, 21, 69, 136
Pedulla Guitars 149
Peek, Amber 149, 188
Penridge, Stan 19, 22, 35, 46–47, 53, 55, 58, 80–81, 87, 114, 125, 149, 187
People magazine 25, 36, 45, 149–150
People's Choice Awards 149
Perry, Joe 9, 69, 101, 149, 155, 194, 207
Personality Comics Presents KISS 150
Pesch, Doro 55, 187, 197
Peter Criss (album) 7, 80, 124, 146, 150
Peter Criss Imposter 150, 188
The Phantom of the Opera 34, 65, 150, 182
The Phil Donahue Show 150, 188
Philips, Binky 144, 150–151
Piano Tribute to KISS 151
Pickett, Wilson 74
pinball machine 26, 95–96, 110–111, 118, 151, 163
Pinball Magazine 151
The Planets 27, 38, 81, 144, 150
Plant, Robert 122, 151, 153–154
The Plasmatics 21, 44, 109, 208
"Plaster Caster" 75, 78, 86, 91, 110, 115–116, 123, 127–128, 141, 151
Playboy 44, 79, 95, 98, 174, 194
Plaza Sound Studios 7
"Please Don't Wait" 19
PM Magazine 2, 151–152
Podcast Rock City 152
PodKISSt: The Fanzine for Your Ears 152
Poison 42, 162
"Polly Von" 35
PolyGram 26, 32, 135, 152
Poncia, Vini 29, 53, 57, 80, 85, 93, 124, 129, 141, 150, 152, 168–169, 177, 185, 189–190, 198, 209
Pop, Iggy 32, 86
Popcorn Pub 37, 41, 185
Popeye 152
Porcaro, Mike 43, 152
The Post War Baby Boom 181
Postlethwaite, Fritz 152
Power Play **183**
Powers, Tony 144, 152
Prato, Greg 17, 30, 59, 113, 124, 197, 205, 211
Presley, Elvis 1, 3, 45, 152, 175
"Prisoner of Love" 63, 152

Prodigy 17
"Prologue (Odyssey)" 18
Prophecy: A Tribute to Eric Carr 152
Psycho Circus (album) 8, 12, 21, 47, 61, 68, 84, 88, 90, 92, 106, 115, 135, 199, 203, 206, 209
"Psycho Circus" (song) 21–23, 27, 47, 55, 74–75, 97, 105, 108, 114, 153, 177, 195
Psycho Circus World Tour 12, 38, 104, 108, 112, 153
PUCKER UP: A Canadian Motor-City Tribute to the Hottest Band In the Land 154
Punky 66–67, 154
Pure Prairie League 56
"Put It Back On" 56

Queen 175, 192, 200
Queen 4 A Day 154
Queensrÿche 15, 47
"Question" 38
Quicksilver Messenger Service 82, 115

"Radar for Love" 17, 154
radio **154**
Radio Control Van 154, 191
"Radioactive" 22, 26, 33, 57, 69, 73, 78, 83, 86, 105, 110, 121, 126, 149, 155–156, 168
Rage Against the Machine 12, 138, 168
"Rain" 30, 85, 133, 155
"Rain Keeps Fallin'" 70
Rainbow 40, 49, 146, 155, 172, 181, 205, 210
"Raise Your Glasses" 153, 155
Ramone, Joey 41, 155
Ramone, Tommy 155
The Ramones 41, 54, 142, 155
Randall, Elliot 155
Ranno, Ritchie 155, 194
Rare Earth 56
The Raspberries 52
Rather, Dan 171, 173
Ratt 158, 175
Ravitz, Mark 155
RCA Records 66, 137
"Read My Body" 81, 155
"Ready to Rock" 206, 208
Rear Window 203
"Reason to Live" 27, 42, 103, 105, 155, 195
"Reckless" 178
record player 155, **156**
The Red Hot Chili Peppers 12, 141
Red Surf 156
Reddy, Helen 69, 156, 194
Redoute, Bruce 9, 141, 156
Reed, Lou 49, 61, 64, 120, 136, 156, 202, 207
Regan, John 68, 193, 195
Regan, Pat 156

Reingold, Buck 25, 32, 156
Remedy 156
"Remember Me" 126, 157, 194
REO Speedwagon 11, 56, 82, 156
The Replacements 156
"Reputation" 74, 105, 128, 156
Return of the Comet: A Tribute to Ace Frehley 49, 156
Reunion Tour 3, 6, 12, 57, 68, 71, 76, 81, 110, 112, 126, 175, 182, 188, 195, 198, 209
Revenge 10, 27, 31, 52, 54, 60–61, 72, 78, 84, 101, 107, 121, 133, 148, 157, 160, 175, 182, 186, 188, 190, 197, 201
Revenge Tour 157
Rice, Howard 16
Richards, Keith 191, 196
Rifkin, Adam 52
The Right to Rock 91
"Rip and Destroy" 82, 91, 157
"Rip It Out" 7, 22, 56, 68, 75, 77–78, 86, 92, 103, 115, 120, 126, 143, 154, 156, 176, 179, 195
"Rise to It" 39, 81, 116, 157–158, 198
Rising Sun 172
Rising Sun Tour 158, 162
Roberts, Austin 204
Roberts, Kane 186
Robinson, Richard 146
Rock Against Drugs 109, 158
Rock & Brews 158, 206
"Rock and Roll All Nite" 6, 9–10, 13, 19, 21, 26–27, 33, 36, 49, 52, 55, 57, 64, 67, 73–76, 78, 84–86, 88, 93, 95–97, 99, 103–105, 110, 114, 116–117, 123, 129, 135, 139, 141, 145, 151, 156, 158, 162, 169, 172, 175–176, 178, 184–185, 187, 189, 193, 195, 198–200, 208–209
Rock & Roll All Nite: A Tribute to KISS—1974–2014 158
Rock and Roll All Nite: The Music of KISS 72, 159
Rock 'N' Roll Comics 77, **161**
Rock 'N' Roll Comics Magazine 161
Rock 'n' Roll Fantasy Camp 70, 161
Rock and Roll Hall of Fame 3, 6, 105, 131–132, 138, 159, 163, 189, 194
"Rock and Roll Hell" 9, 43, 64, 86, 90, 159
Rock and Roll Legends: A Conversation with KISS 159
Rock and Roll Over 1, 6, 11, 19, 29, 50, 54–55, 76, 85, 87, 102, 120, 122, 127, 131, 137, 146, 155, 160, 167, 177, 186, 191, 207
Rock and Roll Over Tour 52, 160
"Rock and Roll Party" 51, 160
"Rock and Rolls Royce" 127, 185–186
Rock Band 52
"Rock Bottom" 9, 26, 55, 69, 73,

Index

86, 103, 114, 116, 156, 160, 179, 193, 209
Rock Fantasy 160–161
"Rock Me, Baby" 22, 150, 161, 193
Rock 'N' Roll Sinners—Volume II: Rock Scribes on the Rock Press, Rock Music & Rock Stars 161
"Rock or Be Rocked" 161, 205–206
Rock Scene 80, 130, 161
Rock Soldiers (fan club) 7, 98
"Rock Soldiers" (song) 7, 68, 75, 126, 161, 195
Rock the Nation World Tour 162, 188, 207
Rockabye Baby! Lullaby Renditions of KISS 162
"Rocket Ride" 7, 11, 26, 33, 56, 68, 75, 86, 110, 126, 142, 156, 162, 195
"Rockin' in the USA" 11–12, 91, 120, 162
Rockin' the Corps 162
Rockology 32, 162, 197
Rockpop 118
Rocksimus Maximus Tour 9, 207
Rodgers, Mark 76
Role Models 52, 96, 128, 162
"Rollin' Along" 35
Rolling Stone 5, 7, 9, 11, 22, 31, 46, 51, 56–57, 63, 66, 81–83, 86, 94–95, 105, 127, 132, 150, 163–164, 172, 174, 181, 196, 209
The Rolling Stones 3, 7, 25, 28, 54, 57–58, 120, 159, 163, 166, 168, 196
Romney, Mitt 163
"Room Service" 19, 55, 75, 105, 110, 163, 209
The Rootie Kazootie Club 45
Ross, Carol 163
Ross, Diana 36, 72, 97, 120, 124, 163–164, 172
Roth, David Lee 42, 199
Rothberg, Gerald 164
Rub n' Play Magic Transfer Set **164**
Runaway 15, 109, 151, 164
Rush 11, 56, 82, 100, 115, 164–165, 199
Rush: Beyond the Lighted Stage 164
"Russian Roulette" 165, 178
Rydell, Bobby 117, 168
Ryder, Mitch 13

Sagal, Katey 69, 165, 167
"Saint and Sinner" 43, 89, 93, 165
St. James, Dennis 174
St. James, Jaime 24, 54, 87, 187
St. John, Mark 3, 6, 15, 17, 47, 88, 93, 99, 121, 126, 130–131, 139, 143, 146, 159, 165–166, 189, 197, 204, 210
Salt 'N Pepper 32, 125
Sample This: The Incredible Story of the Incredible Bongo Band 166
"Samurai Son" 21, 166, 210
Sanctuary Records 166

"Sandy" 168
SATIN: A Million to One 166
Saturday Night Concerts 15
"Save Your Love" 57, 75, 86, 120, 159, 166, 179, 185
Savoy Brown 11, 166
"Say Yeah" 97, 166, 178
Scaggs, Boz 11
The Scarecrow 19
Scarlet, Richie 27, 68, 157
Scavullo, Francesco 57
Scher, John 166
Schwartzberg, Allan 84, 144
Scooby-Doo 54, 134, 166–167
Scooby-Doo! and KISS: Rock and Roll Mystery 54, 134, 166
The Scorpions 52
Scott, Neil 25
Sea Tales 167
Sealed with a KISS **45**, 131, 167
Second Sighting 68, 167
"Second to None" 125, 177
"Secretly Cruel" 17, 74, 167
"Seduction of the Innocent" 30, 167
Seduction of the Internet: A Detention Hall Tribute to KISS 167
"See You in Your Dreams" 22, 33, 69, 143, 155, 160, 167
"See You Tonite" 20, 22, 56, 69, 91, 116, 167
Seeff, Norman 82, 168
Seger, Bob 69, 101, 126, 155, 160, 167–168
Segura, Alex 16
"Send in the Clowns" 145
"Separate" 75, 126, 167
Seventh Star 24, 174
Sewitt, George 87, 168
Sex Money KISS 168, 211
Shaffer, Paul 168
Shakur, Tupac 12, 74
Shameless 154
"Shandi" 12, 21, 26, 33, 73, 74, 77, 83, 86, 93, 103, 105, 114, 118, 148, 168, 175, 177, 197–198
Shandi's Addiction 168
Shannon, Tom 73, 168
Sharp, Ken 23, 101, 143–144, 211
Shaw, Tommy 179
"She" 9, 16, 26, 30, 40, 55, 73, 75, 91, 110, 114–115, 120, 125, 135, 146, 168, 178, 205–206
Sherinian, Derek 10, 169
Sherman, Dale 10, 11, 18, 23, 30, 32, 43, 63, 81, 90, 97–99, 127, 170, 172, 174, 183, 205, 207, 210–211
"She's So European" 33, 118, 169, 197–198
"Shock Me" 7, 11, 21, 26, 33, 64, 67–69, 73, 75, 77, 83, 86, 88, 110, 124, 126–128, 142, 169, 179, 191, 195
Shock Rockers: The Story of KISS 169

"Shocker" 169
"Shot Full of Rock" 7, 126, 193
"Shout It Out Loud" 11, 14, 18–19, 21–22, 27, 33, 51, 53, 59, 64, 67, 73, 75, 88–91, 93, 95–97, 103, 105, 108, 110–111, 114, 122, 125, 151, 153, 156, 159, 162, 166, 169, 175–179, 184, 193, 198, 200, 203, 209
Shout It Out Loud: The Story of KISS's Destroyer and the Making of an American Icon 169
"Shout Mercy" 137, 169
"Show Me" 34, 44
Sigerson, Davitt 73
Silent Rage 169, 174
Silver Chair 12
"Silver Lining" 35
"Silver Spoon" 27, 81, 169
Silverhead 170
Simmons, Gene 1–3, 5–7, **8**, 10–22, 24–26, 28–41, **42**, 43–44, 46–49, 51–61, **62**, 63–75, 77, **78**, 79–87, 89–92, 94–99, 101–105, **106**, 107–108, **109**, 110–130, 132–146, 155, 157–172, **173**, 174–187, 189–191, **192**, 193–195, **196**, 197–205, **206**, 207–211
Simmons, Nick 17, 23, 29, 54, 70, 97, 170–171, 173–174, 194
Simmons, Sophie 70, 97, 171, 173–174, 194
Simmons Abramson Marketing 170
Simmons Comics Anthology 170
Simmons Comics Group 70–71, 170
Simmons Records 17, 133, 173
Simon Simonazo 174
"Simple Mind" 37
"Simple Type" 146, 174
Simpson, Raymond 189
Sinatra, Frank 129, 141, 174
"Sincerely" 127
Singer, Eric 3, 6, 10, 12–13, 15, 17, 19–20, 23, 30–31, 34, 47, 53, 60, 64, 77, 79–80, 83, 95, 101, 104, 106–107, 110, 116, 119, 130, 135, 137–138, 145, 149, 151, 154–160, 167, 169, 172, 174, 177–178, 182, 189, 191, 207, 210
The Singles 175
"Sister" 15
16 Magazine 175, **180**
60 Minutes 175
Skid Row 176, 193–194
Skullduggery 170
"Skydome" 19
Slade 11, 176
Slash's Snakepit 158
Slaughter 81, 158, 201
Slaughter, Mark 27, 179, 201
Slayer 110
Slingerland Drums 176
Smalling, J.R. 147, 176
Smashes, Thrashes & Hits 124, 176, 208

Index

The Smashing Pumpkins 108, 153–154
Smith, Joe 176
Smith, Kevin 39
Smith, Michael Buffalo 63
Smith, Tamy Lester 203
Snider, Dee 108, 176, 179
"Snow Blind" 7, 33, 49, 77, 86, 148, 156, 176, 179, 203
So It Goes 118
"So Many Girls, So Little Time" 91
Solan, Eddie 41, 79, 177
Solid Gold 140, 177
A Solo Guitar Tribute to Paul Stanley—The Songwriter 177
"Some Kinda' Hurricane" 124
"Some Other Guy" 206
"Somebody's Waiting" 162
"Something Moved" 68, 126
"Something Tellin' Me" 34
"Somewhere Between Heaven and Hell" 81, 177
songbooks **177**
Sonic Boom 12, 23, 49, 81, 87, 90, 97, 112, 117, 137, 141, 165–166, 175, 177–178, 180, 188, 204, 208
Sonic Boom Over Europe 105
Sonic Boom Over Europe Tour 82, 97, 178
The Soul Lives in Berlin: French Kisses Issue I, Vol. I 178
Soul Station 178
Soundgarden 30
Sounds 11
South Park 178
"Space Ace" 145
"Space Bear" 15
Space Invader (album) 68, 92, 178
"Space Invader" (song) 178
The Spaceman 1, 6, 8, 15, 51, 67–68, 77, 87, 89, 103, 104, **105**, 113–114, 126, 130, 135, 137, 153, 162, 176, 179, 184–188, 195, 206–207
Spacewalk: A Salute to Ace Frehley 49, 179
Speaking in Tongues 179
"Speedin' Back to My Baby" 7, 22, 68, 86, 115, 156, 176, 179
Spin the Bottle: An All-Star Tribute to KISS 179
"Spinning Wheel" 179
Spirit of '76 124, 179
"Spit" 157, 179
SpongeBob SquarePants 180
The Sport Americana Price Guide to the Non-Sports Cards 192
Stabin, Victor 198
"Stand" 178, 180
Stanley, Paul 1–3, 5–6, 8, 10–23, 25–26, 28–35, 37–44, 46, 48–53, 55–69, 71–72, 74–75, 77, **78**, 79, **80**, 81–91, 93–99, 101–108, **109**, 110–134, 136–146, 148–153, 155–163, 165–170, 172, 174–179, **180**, 181–182, **183**, 184–187, 189–191, **192**, 193–194, **196**, 197–205, **206**, 207–211
"Stanley the Parrot" 182–183
"Star Spangled Banner" 10, 107, 179, 183
The Starchild 1, 8–9, 20, 51, 61, 74, 77–80, 84, 86, 88, 96, 103, **105**, 107, 113, 118, 130, 148, 155, 166, 180–182, **183**, 190, 208
Stardust, Ziggy 26
Starkey, Bill 60, 99–101, 104, 136, 183
The Starliters 46
Starr, Ringo 69
"Starship" 178
Stead, Arthur 68
Steele, Bob 115, 183
The Steve Miller Band 178
Stevens, Carrie 183
Stevens, Steve 70
Stewart, Rod 16, 89, 91, 149, 160
Stomp 442 16
Stone, Mike 47, 55
The Stone Temple Pilots 13
"Stop, Look to Listen" 26, 184
"Strange to Me" 19
"Strange Ways" 18, 26, 64, 74, 82, 86, 91, 110, 134, 156, 159, 184, 193
Strange Ways Podcast 184
"Stranger in a Strange Land" 68, 75, 126
"The Street Giveth and the Street Taketh Away" 63, 81, 184, 187
Street Punk 184
"Strike" 34
The String Quartet Tribute to KISS 184
"Strutter" 6, 9, 18–19, 21, 26, 33, 55, 61, 63–64, 73, 75, 85–86, 88, 91, 94, 104, 108, 110–111, 114, 120, 145, 148–149, 154, 162, 176, 179, 183–184, 195, 198–199, 203, 206–207
"Strutter '78" 55, 105, 110, 175, 184
Stuart, Rick 184
Styx 11, 128, 84
Sub, Paul 185
Succession: A 30th Anniversary Tribute to Dynasty 185
Suhs, Jeff 14, 33, 41, 97, 211
Suicidal Tendencies 110
Summer, Donna 25–26, 28, 32, 69, 87, 185
Summer School 15
"Sunday Driver" 123, 185
Super Bowl 185
"Sure Know Something" 19, 26, 33, 54, 56–57, 69, 73–75, 77, 87, 93, 114, 116, 119, 144, 162, 175, 177, 185, 203
"Surrender" 35
Sutton, Erin 182, 185
"Sweet & Dirty Love" 17
"Sweet Ophelia" 146, 185, 206
"Sweet Pain" 33, 51, 53, 91, 127, 185, 202
Swenson, John 78, 211
Swenson, Rod 128
Sylvester, Terry 203
Symphony 85

T. Rex 82, 87, 174
"Take It Off" 10, 107, 157, 186, 199
"Take Me" 33, 86, 110, 160, 186, 209
"Take Me Away (Together as One)" 16, 22, 89, 148, 186
"Take Me Down Below" 137, 186
"Take Me Home" 18
"Take Me to the City" 179
"Talk to Me" 27, 73, 86, 93, 103, 118, 175, 186, 196–198
Tallarico, Carl 186
Tamplin, Ken 84
Taylor, Chip 162
"Tears" 124, 201
"Tears Are Falling" 17, 21, 27, 36, 75, 81, 86, 104–105, 110, 120, 125, 176, 186, 195, 198
Tebow, Tim 186
Teeman, Neal 187
Teenage Lust 187
"Tell Me" 30
That Metal Show 194
That '70s KISS Show 188
That '70s Show 187
"That Time of Year" 110
"That's the Kind of Sugar Papa Likes" 22, 86, 129, 149–150, 187
Thayer, Tommy 3, 6, 15, 19, 22–24, 34, 36, 53–55, 61, 66, 68, 70–71, 79–80, 83, 87, 89, 93, 95, 102, 104, 106, 114–115, 119, 121–122, 127, 135, 137–138, 141, 147–149, 153–154, 157–159, 161–163, 166–167, 169, 172, 174–175, 177–179, 184, 187–189, 191, **196**, 202–204, 207–208
Their Satanic Majesties Request 163, 196
"Then He Kissed Me" 188
"Then She Kissed Me" 102, 114, 127, 175, 188
"There's Nothing Better" 146–147
"Thief in the Night" 42, 188, 199, 208
Thin Lizzy 52, 56, 138
Third Watch 188
38 Special 11, 52
This Is Spinal Tap 6, 158, 179–180
Thompson, Cheryl Anne 150, 188
"Thou Shall Not" 157, 188
Three Sides of the Coin 10, 37, 97, 121, 133, 147, 163, 184, 188, 194, 199
"Thrills in the Night" 15, 27, 36, 99, 106, 189, 195, 199
"Tiara" 162
Tiger Stadium 47, 75, 189
"Time Ain't Runnin' Out" 167

Index

"Time Traveller" 27, 189
Toad the Wet Sprocket 110, 189
Toborg, Dale 189
"Today" 18
The Today Show 189
Tom Petty and the Heartbreakers 160
Tomarkin, Peggy 115, 183, 189, 211
"Tomorrow" 19, 33, 64, 114, 189, 197–198
"Tomorrow and Tonight" 11, 33, 78, 88, 127–128, 169, 189
The Tomorrow Show 6, 147, 118, 189–190
The Tonight Show 27, 190
"Tonight You Belong to Me" 22, 26, 28, 73, 114, 145, 148–149, 190, 203
"Too Cool for School" 162
"Too Many Days" 206
"Too Many Faces" 15
"Too Many Mondays" 146, 190
Toro, Vinnie 75, 78, 136, 190
"Torpedo Girl" 190, 197–198
"Tossin' and Turnin'" 22, 30, 57, 102, 150, 190
"Tough Love" 157, 190
The Tour 191
Townshend, Pete 5, 11, 67, 191, 204
toy guitar **191**
Toy Hunter 154, 191
"Toys" 178
trading cards 26, 124, **192**
Transformer 81, 121, 192
Treasure 201
Tree 40
Treehouse of Horror 192
"Trial By Fire" 17, 193
A Tribute to the Creatures of the Night 193
A Tribute to … the Hottest Band in the World! 193
Trick or Treat 193
Tropea, John 193
Trouble or Nothin' 79
Trouble Walkin' (album) 15, 68, 79, 193–194
"Trouble Walkin'" (song) 193–195
Troyer, Eric 194
"True Confessions" 69, 71, 156, 194
Trunk, Eddie 16, 51, 60, 194
"The Truth" 34
The Tubes 56
"Tunnel of Love" 20, 69, 127, 149, 155, 185, 194, 199
Turgon, Bruce 141
Turino, Paul 31, 194
"Turn on the Night" 42, 103, 177, 194
Tweed, Shannon 17, 70, 79, 97–98, 151, 168, 171, 173–174, 180, 194–195
12 Picks 195
20th Century Masters—The Best of KISS: The DVD Collection 195

20th Century Masters—The Millennium Collection: The Best of KISS 85, 195
20th Century Masters—The Millennium Collection: The Best of KISS, Volume 2 195
20th Century Masters—The Millennium Collection: The Best of KISS, Volume 3 195
24 Hours of KISSmas 118, 196
20 Million Miles to Earth 208
20/20 196
"Two Sides of the Coin" 75, 86, 196–198
"2,000 Man" 57, 86, 97, 102, 114, 116, 163, 185, 196
"Two Timer" 55, 91, 196, 209
"2 Young 2 Die" 193–194
Tyler, Bonnie 79, 194
Tyler, Steven 9

UFO 52, 82
Ugly Betty 196
"Uh! All Night" 17, 27, 36, 81, 86, 104, 195–197
Uhelszki, Jaan 197
The Ultimate KISS Fanzine Phenomenon: 1976–2009 62–63
Uncle Joe 181, 184, 187
"Under the Gun" 15, 86, 99, 197
"Under the Rose" 18, 140, 197
Undressed: An Unmasked Tribute to KISS 197
Unfinished Business 32, 197
"Unholy" 10, 27–28, 39, 53–54, 60, 83, 105, 107, 110, 116, 157, 159, 195, 197, 199, 201
"Unholy Love" 197
Union (album) 198
Union (band) 197
Union Live in the Galaxy 198
U.S. postage stamp 199
Universal Music Group 97, 112, 129, 137, 152, 198
Universal Presents Gimme KISS 198
Unmasked 8, 31, 21, 32, 41, 43, 46, 57, 63, 67, 87–88, 119–120, 124, 134, 140–141, 149–150, 152, 158, 168–169, 186, 189–190, 195–198, 203, 207, 209
Unmasked Tour 15, 31, 38, 57, 198
Unpainted: A Tribute To KISS 198
Uriah Heep 56, 115, 160, 199

Valentine, Kevin 84, 153, 199, 203
Vallance, Jim 159
Van Halen 52, 54, 61, 141, 143, 199, 210
Van Halen, Alex 199
Van Halen, Eddie 165, 199
Van Zen, Scott 167, 179
Variety 199
"Venus and Mars/Rock Show" 133, 199
The Very Best of KISS 199
VH1 18, 194, 200, 203

VH1 Rock Honors 200
Vidal, Bernard 43
View-Master 191, **200**
The Village People 14, 32, 87, 192
The Village Voice 5, 66, 133, 137, 142, 179
Vincent, Vinnie 3, 6, 13, 15, 27, 38, 43–44, 48–49, 60, 67, 72, 78, 88, 107, 109–110, 124–125, 130, 136–137, 139, 143, 151, 158–159, 165, 179, 197, 199–202, **206**, 208–209
Vinnie Vincent Invasion (album) 201
Vinnie Vincent Invasion (band) 15, 27, 128, 158, 201
Vinnie Vincent—Metal Tech: Style, Speed & Phrasing 202
Vintage KISS Photos: 1974–1981 202
Vixen 81
"The Vows" 18

Wagner, Dick 51, 60, 64, 185, 202
"Waiting for the Morning Light" 17, 57
"Wake Up Screaming" 125
"Walk the Line" 34
"Walking in Your Sleep" 18
"Wall of Sound" 137
Walsh, Jan 41
Wanted: Dead or Alive 202
"War Machine" 9, 27, 36, 43, 77, 86, 90–91, 99, 110, 117, 157, 159, 193, 202
Ward, Bill 174–175
Ward, Billy 68
Warman's KISS Collectibles Field Guide: Values and Identification 73, 202, 211
Warner Bros. Records 32, 40, 61, 73, 135, 176, 202
Warren, Diane 144, 194, 208
Warren, Leslie Ann 182
Washburn Guitars 202
Wasley, Don 202
W.A.S.P. 15, 18, 120
"Watchin' You" 9–10, 16, 26, 60, 69, 82, 90, 114, 138, 178, 202–203, 206
Wayne County 24, 27, 38
"We Are One" 153, 203
"We Got Your Rock" 68
"We Want to Shout It Out Loud" 146, 169, 203, 206
"We Want You" 34
"Weapons of Mass Destruction" 17
"Wedding" 129
Weissman, Mitch 13, 21, 69, 71, 136, 139, 157, 188, 204
Welch, Christopher 204
Welcome to Sweden 203
Welcome to the Spanish Tribute to KISS 203
Wenner, Jann 31, 163
We're a Happy Family: A Tribute to the Ramones 54, 155

"What a Difference a Day Makes" 145
"What Every Girl Wants" 178
"What Happens in the Darkness" 146, 203
"What Makes the World Go Round" 197–198, 203
"What U Want Is What You Get" 154
"What You're Doin,'" 44
"Whatever Turns You On" 17
"What's on Your Mind?" 7, 19, 22, 75, 86, 90, 203
Whelan, Brian 203
When KISS Ruled the World 203
"When Lightning Strikes" 178, 188, 204
"When the Bell Rings" 146, 204, 206
"When You Wish Upon a Star" 69, 102, 155, 204
"When Your Walls Come Down" 42, 204
"Where Angels Dare" 125
"Where Will They Run?" 146
"While the City Sleeps" 15, 139, 204
"Whisper" 145
White Lion 42, 158
White Tiger (album) 204
White Tiger (band) 47, 131, 165, 204
Whitesnake 81
The Who 17, 23, 64, 77, 84, 140, 144, 166, 178, 181, 184, 191, 204
"Who Hears the Listener?" 18
Who Wants to Be a Millionaire 204
"Who Wants to Be Lonely" 17, 36, 75, 86, 104, 198, 205
"Whole Lotta Love" 91, 123, 131, 179
Wick, Walter 42
Wicked Lester 5, 26, 37, 40–41, 46, 49, 58, 66–67, 72, 90–91, 94, 112, 119, 123–129, 137, 146, 155, 168–169, 172, 174, 181, 185–186, 203, 205–206, 210
Wicked Lester and Progeny Demo Sessions 84, 161, 205
The Wicked Symphony 19
Williams, Wendy O. 109, 188, 201, 206, 208
Winger 81
Winger, Kip 179
Wings 199
Winter, Edgar 52
Winter, Johnny 52, 56
"Wiped-Out" 7, 123, 206
Wise, Richie 79, 82, 92, 94, 206
Wish You Were Dead 206
"Within" 27, 153
"Within You Without You" 206
Without Love 24
Wittman, Dave 43, 84, 202, 206
Witz, Chaim 5, 61, 69, 119, 170–171, 206
Witz, Feri 170
Wolfman, Marv 39
Woloch, Dennis 92, 145, 207
Wonder, Stevie 120, 207
"Won't Get Fooled Again" 17, 60, 127, 144, 204
"Words" 147
"Words Are Not Enough" 126, 195
World Domination Tour 9, 47, 92, 102, 104–105, 188, 207
A World with Heroes—A KISS Tribute for Cancer Care 207
A World Without Heroes (novel) 90, 207
"A World Without Heroes" (song) 18, 27, 33, 56, 69, 73, 86, 88, 90–91, 105, 116, 118, 140, 156, 177, 207
Worlds Apart 24, 121
"Wouldn't You Like to Know Me" 22, 86, 103, 148–149, 177, 208
WOW 188, 206, 208

"X-Ray Eyes" 57, 91, 185, 208

"Yes I Know (Nobody's Perfect)" 178, 208
Yesterday and Today 208
Ymir 208
Yoshiki 110, 208
"You Better Run" 147
"You Confess" 30
"You Love Me to Hate You" 81, 199, 208
"You Make Me Crazy" 162
"(You Make Me) Rock Hard" 176, 208
"You Matter to Me" 22, 33, 55, 105, 150, 209
"You Wanted the Best" 153, 209
You Wanted the Best. You Got the Best. 209
You Wanted the Best, You Got the Best!! 97, 105, 209
"Young and Wasted" 99, 124, 209
The Young Music Show 208–209
Younger Generation 201
"You're All That I Want" 74, 197–198, 209
"You're All That I Want, You're All That I Need" 26, 209
"You're My Reason for Living" 17, 49, 70
"You're My Woman" 125
"Yume No Ukiyo Ni Saitemina" 209–210

Zappa, Frank 17, 210
Zarrella, Tony 46, 49, 92, 146, 155, 172, 205, 210
Zebra 44
Zen, Scott Van 78, 87
Zero 210
Zildjian 210
Zlozower, Neil 210
ZZ Top 11, 54, 56, 73, 82, 144, 166, 183, 199

www.ingramcontent.com/pod-product-compliance
Ingram Content Group UK Ltd.
Pitfield, Milton Keynes, MK11 3LW, UK
UKHW050530150426
5217IPUK00026B/1880